MW01069490

Criminal Law and Procedure

For Kalief Browder (1993–2015)

"Innocent until proven guilty."

Criminal Law and Procedure

A Courtroom Approach

Stephanie A. Jirard, JD

Shippensburg University

Los Angeles | London | New Delhi
Singapore | Washington DC | Melbourne

FOR INFORMATION:

SAGE Publications, Inc.
2455 Teller Road
Thousand Oaks, California 91320
E-mail: order@sagepub.com

SAGE Publications Ltd.
1 Oliver's Yard
55 City Road
London EC1Y 1SP
United Kingdom

SAGE Publications India Pvt. Ltd.
B 1/I 1 Mohan Cooperative Industrial Area
Mathura Road, New Delhi 110 044
India

SAGE Publications Asia-Pacific Pte. Ltd.
18 Cross Street #10-10/11/12
China Square Central
Singapore 048423

Acquisitions Editor: Jessica Miller
Editorial Assistant: Rebecca Lee
Content Development Editor: Laura Kearns
Production Editor: Jane Martinez
Copy Editor: Colleen Brennan
Typesetter: C&M Digitals (P) Ltd.
Proofreader: Dennis W. Webb
Indexer: Robie Grant
Cover Designer: Gail Buschman
Marketing Manager: Jillian Ragusa

Copyright © 2020 by SAGE Publications, Inc.

All rights reserved. Except as permitted by U.S. copyright law, no part of this work may be reproduced or distributed in any form or by any means, or stored in a database or retrieval system, without permission in writing from the publisher.

All third party trademarks referenced or depicted herein are included solely for the purpose of illustration and are the property of their respective owners. Reference to these trademarks in no way indicates any relationship with, or endorsement by, the trademark owner.

Printed in the United States of America

Library of Congress Cataloging-in-Publication Data

Names: Jirard, Stephanie A., author.

Title: Criminal law and procedure : a courtroom approach / Stephanie A. Jirard, J.D., Shippensburg University.

Description: Thousand Oaks, California : SAGE Publications, Inc., [2019] | Includes bibliographical references and index.

Identifiers: LCCN 2018031038 | ISBN 9781544327501 (pbk. : alk. paper)

Subjects: LCSH: Criminal law—United States. | Criminal procedure—United States. | Criminal justice, Administration of—United States. | Trial practice—United States.

Classification: LCC KF9219 .J575 2019 | DDC 345.73—dc23
LC record available at https://lccn.loc.gov/2018031038

This book is printed on acid-free paper.

Certified Chain of Custody
Promoting Sustainable Forestry
www.sfiprogram.org
SFI-01268

SFI label applies to text stock

19 20 21 22 23 10 9 8 7 6 5 4 3 2 1

BRIEF CONTENTS

DETAILED CONTENTS

PART II • THE CRIMES: CRIMINAL LAW ELEMENTS

PREFACE

The pillars of American democracy depend on the public's trust in government. Our willingness to follow the law is directly linked to our collective belief that justice will prevail. Children learn right from wrong and, as adults, form strong opinions about how best to achieve justice. Justice wins when police officers, court personnel, and corrections officials are highly trained, highly ethical, and highly compassionate. This text seeks to honor those professionals for their selfless service by teaching how the criminal trial process works as the touchstone of civic engagement. Hopefully through this text, students can appreciate the exciting opportunities to have a positive impact in our communities by direct involvement with the justice system.

Prosecuting and defending criminal cases reflect a series of value judgments. What some students find frustrating about the study of law is there seems to be no right answers and the result in one case does not necessarily predict the result in a similar case. But the law is constantly changing. The night sticks of yesteryear have been replaced by the tasers of today; in certain states, the ounce of marijuana that used to net a year in prison may now net $1,000 of profit; a focus on the rehabilitative function of corrections has been replaced with punitive sanctions such as life sentences for juveniles. As of 2018, our prisons are swollen, protests about police conduct are rampant, and many courts try to do more with less. With a solid grounding in the mechanics of the criminal trial process provided in this text, tomorrow will be better. This text is written in an accessible style to invite students to learn the black letter law, think critically about the issues presented, and then apply the law in a way that reflects the principle of fairness that guides the government's behavior from investigation to punishment. The lessons presented in the book have applicability for courses on politics, history, psychology, sociology, economics, social work, counseling, teacher education, and mock trial.

Chapter 1 shows students how the U.S. Constitution is the prism through which all criminal law and procedure operates. To maximize students' potential to succeed in any criminal law course, the following topics are introduced: basic mechanics of how the law works, where law comes from, and how to find it and read it; the role of precedent in shaping future decisions; common terminology such as *due process* and *reasonable man*; the quantum of proof required for certain government interactions with the public; and civil liability for criminal justice professionals and corresponding qualified immunity. In addition, the chapter explores the concept of federalism through a case excerpt from *Murphy v. National Collegiate Athletic Association* (2018).

Chapter 2 is designed to introduce students to the major participants and decisions that the government and criminal suspects and defendants make from arrest to appeal. The trial of the Boston Marathon bomber, Dzhokhar Tsarnaev, forms the backdrop for the concepts under review.

Chapter 3 familiarizes the students with the basic components of criminal liability through *mens rea*, a guilty mind, *actus reus*, a guilty act, and causation analysis. A discussion of inchoate (incomplete) crimes and parties to crimes completes the legal overview.

Chapter 4 is a survey of the major crimes against the person, from assault and battery to terroristic threats, to kidnapping and false imprisonment, to murder, manslaughter and felony murder, to robbery, with a special emphasis on sex crimes. The chapter discusses the 2013 Navy midshipmen rape case to feature the importance of rape shield laws. Computer-based personal crimes such as cyberstalking and cyberbullying are also presented.

Chapter 5 teaches students the traditional, common law definitions of theft crimes now consolidated in present-day theft statutes. Also included is a discussion of financial cybercrime and white-collar crime (including mail and wire fraud), particularly the prosecution of public officials for honest services theft, racketeering, money laundering, and RICO (Racketeer Influenced and Corrupt Organizations) crimes.

Chapter 6 presents crimes against the public that often get ignored as quality-of-life issues, such as drug use, gambling, and panhandling, but also the very damaging crimes of human trafficking, public corruption crimes such as bribery and obstruction of justice, environmental crimes and national security related and terrorism offenses. The chapter uses what has been called the "eBay" of the underground—the Dread Pirate Roberts Silk Road underground website case—to frame the public harm analysis.

Chapter 7 begins the scrutiny of criminal procedure. Topics covered include how the Fourth Amendment controls citizen–police encounters, *Terry* stops, arrests, the amount of force used to effectuate arrests, and it details the Fourth Amendment's specific requirements to secure a warrant. Care is taken to explain the constitutional obligations in executing both arrest and search warrants.

Chapter 8 explores the legal requirements for police action when there is no time to get a warrant or when other circumstances make obtaining a warrant impractical. The chapter gives case excerpts detailing what the U.S. Supreme Court calls the "well-defined" exceptions to the Fourth Amendment's warrant requirement and the legal justification for each exception.

Chapter 9 considers the impact of recent case law and the corresponding obligations of conducting interrogations pursuant to the dictates of *Miranda v. Arizona* (1966), which requires the notification to suspects of their right to remain silent and to have counsel present during questioning. The law now requires defendants affirmatively exercise their right to counsel, and the U.S. Supreme Court considers a long-term prisoner not "in custody" for *Miranda* purposes if he has been returned to his cell block to enjoy his "normal routine."

Chapter 10 explores the requirements of the Sixth Amendment right to counsel and alerts students to the fine details the U.S. Supreme Court requires when conducting an analysis into a defendant's right to represent himself, and his right to control the fundamental conduct of the trial lawyer who can no longer admit the defendant's guilt over his objection (*McCoy v. Louisiana*, 2018).

Chapter 11's examination of the First Amendment underscores the intersectionality of freedom of speech, religion, and assembly when there exists countervailing, compelling state interests. Case excerpts feature laws regulating lying about receiving the Medal of Honor, computer-generated child pornography, cross burning, and killing chickens for religious worship. Although many criminal law and procedure students may question the utility of studying free speech issues, a review of the constitutional issues decided by the U.S. Supreme Court reveals the First Amendment is close to the top of the list of cases decided, well more than the Sixth Amendment, for example, as illustrated in Figure 0.1.

Figure 0.1 "Guns Out, Free Speech In" at the U.S. Supreme Court

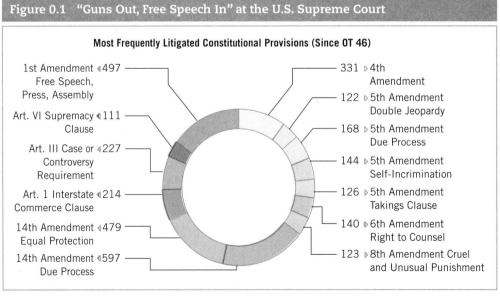

Most Frequently Litigated Constitutional Provisions (Since OT 46)

1st Amendment ◀497 Free Speech, Press, Assembly

Art. VI Supremacy ◀111 Clause

Art. III Case or ◀227 Controversy Requirement

Art. 1 Interstate ◀214 Commerce Clause

14th Amendment ◀479 Equal Protection

14th Amendment ◀597 Due Process

331 ▷4th Amendment

122 ▷5th Amendment Double Jeopardy

168 ▷5th Amendment Due Process

144 ▷5th Amendment Self-Incrimination

126 ▷5th Amendment Takings Clause

140 ▷6th Amendment Right to Counsel

123 ▷8th Amendment Cruel and Unusual Punishment

Source: Reproduced with permission. Jan. 3, 2018. Copyright 2018 by The Bureau of National Affairs, Inc. (800-372-1033) http://www.bna.com

Chapter 12 presents the unique role of recognizing certain defenses in criminal law and procedure. American justice punishes the offender, not the crime, and the chapter informs on the relative culpability of the offender in relation to their *mens rea* state, and defenses based on justification (necessity, self-defense, entrapment, battering and its effects), and excuse (mistakes, infancy, insanity, intoxication, and duress).

Chapter 13 investigates sentencing and the postconviction process, the legality of certain sentences on conviction, and proving "actual innocence" through the writ of *habeas corpus*. Highlights include recent U.S. Supreme Court juvenile justice jurisprudence and death-penalty litigation, with a special emphasis on cases arising out of Florida.

Throughout the text, students are presented with examples of federal and state statutes, and rules of procedure with a courtroom perspective. Although the book strives to incorporate contemporary examples to highlight the applicability of current U.S. Supreme Court decisions to criminal cases, many of the legal issues remain static. Of course, nothing happens in a vacuum, and all users of the text should conduct legal research for updates on all subjects discussed herein. For example, as this text was going to press, the death penalty was abolished in Washington State. I hope this text generates for you as much passion for justice in criminal law and procedure, especially in the courtroom, as it has done for me.

ACKNOWLEDGMENTS

Life is a series of happy events for which I remain grateful, and bringing this book to market is no different. At SAGE Publications, my heartfelt thanks go to Jessica Miller, my editor, for her vision and commitment to excellence that made writing this book a passion project from beginning to end; and to her peerless team of professionals that guided this text from design to marketing, Rebecca Lee, Laura Kearns, Jane Martinez, Gail Buschman, and Jillian Ragusa; to the typesetter C&M Digitals, Ltd., proofreader, and indexer; and to the copy editor, Colleen Brennan, who, with her bottomless pit of patience and good humor, I remain especially indebted. This text could not have been written, however, without my local SAGE sales representative Darlaine Manning, recruiting me to write for the SAGE family. I cannot thank her enough.

I wish to acknowledge the support of my colleagues in the Criminal Justice Department at Shippensburg and my many friends at the university who have been there with me from the beginning. The list includes Alison Dagnes, Jim Griffith, Tom Austin, Sara Grove, Azim Danesh, Cheryl Slattery, Debra Cornelius, Brendan Finucane, Joe Amsler, Sharnine Herbert, Melissa Ricketts, Scott Donald, Mike Yoh, Kara Laskowski, Mary Mowery, Sue Hockenberry, Melodye Wehrung, Cynthia Botteron, Donna Hale, Officer Stephanie Berger, Kim Garris, my cousin Kevin Fitzgerald, and all members of APSCUF, our faculty union. I also value the administrative leadership for their encouragement and inspiration, Dean Nicole Hill, Provost Barbara Lyman, and President Laurie Carter. This text is infused with the classroom insights of my students (undergraduate, graduate, and from the Juvenile Courts Judges' Commission), who give to me more than I can give to them.

Enormous thanks to my loved ones, Lillian Jirard for her devotion, Jackson Jirard for his perceptive insights, Kennedy Jirard for her smarts and wit; to my Fairhurst, Battista, Piso, and Pouliot families; my friends who have remained steadfast in their devotion since 1974, Gina Carter, Sue (Morlino) Ford, and, as always, Mary (Sheeran) Tanner; and to the little kids—B. K. (my favorite), Calypso, Cliff, Joe, Michael, L. G., and Dex—for making me happy every day. A special shout out to the Starbucks™ crew in Carlisle, PA, for their help in getting me to the finish line.

I remain appreciative of the anonymous and named reviewers who took the time to give the drafts a close reading and whose invaluable suggestions improved the manuscript.

Robert M. Clark, PhD
Pennsylvania Highlands Community College

Heather E. Donovan
Lindenwood University

Sarah Jakub, MA, JD
Associate Professor, Criminal Justice and Sociology
Bucks County Community College

Trisha Kipps, MA
John Tyler Community College

Lori S. Kornblum, JD
Milwaukee Area Technical College; Marquette University Law School

Robert B. Lehmann, MS, CHEP
John Tyler Community College

Diane M. Rice, JD
Bucks County Community College

Danyle L. Smith
Cameron University

Lindsey L. Upton, PhD
Tennessee Technological University

Thomas G. Ziesemer
Associate Professor of Criminal Justice
College of Central Florida

Despite my many readings, there will be in the text errors of commission and omission. All mistakes are my own. Please let me know what you think of the book, and like Flat Stanley, feel free to take selfies while working through the material and send to me at sajira@ship.edu or at Shippensburg University, 1871 Old Main Drive, Shippensburg, PA, 17257

Stephanie A. Jirard
Carlisle, Pennsylvania

A Massachusetts native, Stephanie A. Jirard is a professor of criminal justice at Shippensburg University in Pennsylvania. She received her AB in history from Cornell University, her JD from Boston College Law School, and her MA in applied history at Shippensburg. She is a former lieutenant in the U.S. Navy's Judge Advocate General (JAG) Corps, where she defended sailors and Marines at courts-martial across the state of Louisiana. At the Navy's personnel headquarters in Washington, D.C., Jirard provided legal counsel in family and child sexual abuse matters. After leaving the U.S. Navy, Jirard was a trial attorney at the U.S. Department of Justice, Civil Division, Torts Branch, defending the federal government in environmental and human radiation experiment lawsuits. She also served as an assistant U.S. attorney and an assistant federal public defender, both in the District of Massachusetts. Jirard's last litigation post was serving as an assistant state public defender in the Capital Litigation Unit in Columbia, Missouri, representing men in death-penalty cases. Jirard has published on race and politics, the Civil War's U.S. Colored Troops, missing women, cyberbullying, and political sex scandals. This is her second textbook on criminal law and procedure.

PART I

THE BASICS
How the Law Works

1

INTRODUCTION TO THE LAW

First, go to the end of the chapter. Skim the key terms and phrases and read the summary closely. Come back and look at the following news excerpts to focus your reading throughout the chapter as we explore where law comes from, how it is made, the actors in the criminal justice system and their ethical obligations, the reasons for punishing offenders, the public's redress when rights are violated, and the corresponding protection for criminal justice professionals. We also explore case excerpts about legalized gambling on sporting events, marijuana use legal in states but illegal federally, how courts obtain jurisdiction, the conflict between state and federal governments as constrained by the federal Constitution, and how the Supremacy, Equal Protection, and Due Process clauses ensure government fidelity to justice, a theme we return to repeatedly throughout the text.

WHY THIS CHAPTER MATTERS TO YOU	THE LEARNING OBJECTIVES AS REFLECTED IN THE NEWS
After you have read this chapter: **Learning Objective 1:** You will understand the sources of law, where to find the law, and how precedent controls future court decisions.	[Iowa legislators sent the] governor a bill early Wednesday that would ban most abortions once a fetal heartbeat is detected, usually around six weeks of pregnancy . . . That could set up the state for a legal challenge over its constitutionality. Backers of the legislation . . . expressed hope it could challenge *Roe vs. Wade*, the landmark 1973 U.S. Supreme Court ruling that established women have a right to terminate pregnancies until a fetus is viable. (*Chicago Tribune*, May 2, 2018)
Learning Objective 2: You will be able to articulate core legal principles found in criminal law and procedure cases, such as due process and the reasonable person.	Melvina Lewis was so entrenched as a leader of the local Bloods gang, according to court documents and witness testimony, she was known by the nickname "Ma Dukes." She pleaded guilty and received a sentence of more than 13 years. But May 10, she filed a motion seeking to vacate her sentence for violation of her due process rights. She further argues . . . the United States "is not a real person," and the prosecution violated Article III of the U.S. Constitution. (*The Brunswick News* [GA], May 17, 2018)
Learning Objective 3: You will know the actors in the criminal justice system and the purposes of punishment.	The Pennsylvania Superior Court upheld the majority of the sentence levied against former state Supreme Court Justice Joan Orie Melvin, convicted of theft and criminal conspiracy charges, but ruled Thursday that the trial court's condition that she issue apology letters on a photograph of herself wearing handcuffs was unlawful. The three-judge panel largely kept Melvin's sentence intact, including three years of house arrest followed by two years of probation, removal from the Pennsylvania Supreme Court, and fines and restitution. (Law360, August 21, 2014)

WHY THIS CHAPTER MATTERS TO YOU	THE LEARNING OBJECTIVES AS REFLECTED IN THE NEWS
Learning Objective 4: You will understand how federal law protects citizen's rights and immunity for criminal justice professionals.	Former inmate Christopher Bartlett filed the civil rights lawsuit [42 USC §1983] in U.S. District Court in Portland [OR] against Columbia County [jail] and the deputies. He seeks $500,000 in damages. District Attorney Jeff Auxier said the deputies tried to move Bartlett . . . but he refused to put his hands through the cell door's food port to be handcuffed and safely escorted out. He was warned that if he didn't come out of his cell, he would be bitten by the dog that was loudly barking outside the cell. The dog bit the inmate's thigh and left arm, pulled him to the ground and continued to tear at his arm inside a locked cell. (Oregonlive, May 14, 2018)
Learning Objective 5: You will be able to explain the role of federalism in controlling state criminal justice decisions.	On April 19, the Seventh Circuit Court of Appeals (the federal appellate court for much of the Midwest that is based in Chicago) upheld a nationwide injunction against the [executive branch's] efforts to end sanctuary cities, places where the federal government does not find an eager partner in the state or city with respect to immigrant enforcement. The Attorney General sought to cut off federal funding to Chicago if the city did not assist in the recent deportation revival. So Chicago sued [the federal government]. The lesson [of federalism's checks and balances] is humbling. (*The Daily Texan*, May 3, 2018)

SOURCES OF CRIMINAL LAW

Law Is Written to Be Stable but Is Interpreted to Be Flexible

Criminal law is created when the government defines certain acts worthy of punishment. Criminal procedure is a set of laws that guide how a defendant is processed by the justice system, from investigation, to trial, to sentencing. Learning the legal rules of criminal law and procedure is essential because "the language of the law must not be foreign to the ears of those who are to obey it."[1] Societies have certain codes and customs that regulate people's behavior. From early religious pronouncements such as "Thou shall not kill," man has tried to control human behavior by the written word. But words are subject to different interpretations. For instance, imagine you and I are at an art museum gazing at Dutch master Vincent Van Gogh's 1889 self-portrait with a bandage covering what remains of his right ear after an act of self-mutilation.[2] Based on my experience as a criminal trial lawyer, I might see someone recovering from an acute episode of mental illness. You, coming from a visit to Prague, might see someone ahead of his time in today's "medical punk" body modification movement.[3] Our perception is based on our interpretation of what we see. To illustrate further, did you know Van Gogh actually injured his left ear? The injury only appears to be on his right because he painted self-portraits by looking in a mirror. Reading and understanding the law is the same way. Law is nothing more than a string of words whose meaning depends on where we look. The law is written to be stable, but legal interpretation, like our differing interpretations of Van Gogh's art, is contingent on today's realities: The policeman's flashlights of yesteryear are the drones of the present. As you master the legal rules and regulations that guide the government's authority to detain, incarcerate, and even execute its citizens, do not grow frustrated that similar cases have different outcomes. The facts of each case are different, but legal rules typically remain the same. By mastering the rules of law in this text, you will be able to foresee new directions for criminal law and procedure.

Rule of Law: The U.S. Constitution is the only source of power for the federal government.

American Legal History

After declaring independence from Britain in 1776, the colonies adopted state constitutions establishing basic rules of governance for their citizens. The Articles of Confederation (Articles) held the original 13 colonies together much as individual treaties might loosely bind a group of small countries but lacked the basic mechanisms to collect and spend money for the general welfare, to defend against enemies, and to regulate trade and commerce with foreign countries.[4] To fix these and other problems, Congress convened in Philadelphia during the summer of 1787 and drafted a constitution, reprinted in this text, Appendix A. Many delegates were leery of forming a central government that might become a cheap substitute for the British Crown and its abuses of civil liberties. But the proposed form of a tripartite (three-pronged) system of government sharing power between the legislative, executive, and judicial branches consolidated the power in a federal government by dividing it. Our system of government is based on federalism, a political system in which power is shared between one national government and the many states. The separation of powers and the system of checks and balances is illustrated in Table 1.1.

The first three words of the U.S. Constitution, "We the People," guarantee that the federal government is one for the people, by the people. As the first chief justice of the U.S. Supreme Court John Marshall said, "The people made the Constitution and they can unmake it. It is the creature of their will and lives only by their will." Put another way, if the powers granted to Congress are not specifically listed in the constitution, the federal government cannot act. Pursuant to Article I of the Constitution, "All legislative Powers herein granted shall be vested in a Congress of the United States." In part, those powers listed in Article I, Section 8, as matters of exclusive federal regulation are taxes, making and borrowing money, commerce, naturalization, bankruptcy, counterfeiting, patents and copyrights, post offices and roads, crimes on the high seas, raising an army and navy, and declaring war. Article I granted to Congress—which is composed of the House of Representatives, whose members are determined by a state's population, and the Senate, whose members include two from every state—the power to make laws. Both chambers write legislation (laws, statutes), and both chambers must agree on the legislation before ratification by the U.S. president. The U.S. Constitution's Necessary and Proper Clause is the fulcrum on which Congress can leverage its power to make law in areas for which there is no specific grant of constitutional authority.[5] The Constitution is silent on creating a military

Table 1.1 Checks and Balances Chart

Branch	Duties	Checks and Balances
Legislative Makes laws	**Art. 1, Sec. 8,** "The Congress shall have the power to . . . make all laws which shall be necessary and proper"	**Art. II**, The President may veto a federal law, which then needs 2/3 of Congress to override veto **Art. III**, The U.S. Supreme Court can declare federal laws enacted by Congress unconstitutional and invalid
Executive Enforces laws	**Art. II, Sec. 1**, "The executive power shall be vested in a President of the United States of America" President enforces laws passed by Congress	**Art. I**, Congress makes the laws that limit or expand President's power **Art. III**, The U.S. Supreme Court can declare presidential acts unconstitutional and invalid
Judicial Interprets laws	**Art. III, Sec. 1,** "The judicial power of the United States, shall be vested in one supreme court, and in such inferior Courts as the Congress may . . . establish"	**Art. I**, Congress can establish other courts **Art. II**, President appoints federal judges with advice and consent of Senate

draft, but Congress has the "implied power" to "make all laws necessary and proper" to fix the problems of the country and, hence, draft men and women to war.

The U.S. Supreme Court has interpreted Article I to prohibit Congress from sharing its lawmaking power with the executive or judicial branches as a way to keep the three branches of government independent of each other. Congress cannot delegate (give) its law-making power to another governmental branch: This "no sharing of power" rule is known as the **nondelegation doctrine**. Federal agencies that exist and operate under Article II, the executive branch, make rules and **administrative regulations** that have the force of law to "fill in the gaps" when certain laws are silent. The U.S. Supreme Court has recognized that Congress cannot possibly know all the details of the subject matter controlled by the executive or judicial branches, for example, the minutiae of the delivery of nuclear power controlled by the Department of Energy or of all the details that drive federal sentencing guidelines controlled by the U.S. Sentencing Commission. The Court has held Congress can give its power to the co-branches, subject to limitations called an **intelligible principle**. In *Touby v. United States*, a couple was convicted of conspiring to manufacture Euphoria, a designer drug that the Drug Enforcement Agency (DEA) had temporarily classified as a Schedule I controlled substance, a substance that is highly addictive and illegal. The Toubys appealed their convictions, claiming that Congress's authority to enact portions of the federal drug law, the Controlled Substances Act (CSA), could not be delegated to the U.S. attorney general, who is in charge of the Department of Justice, which oversees the DEA. The U.S. Supreme Court upheld the Toubys' convictions, stating that the CSA limited the attorney general's power and discretion to define criminal conduct and such restraint was the intelligible principle that satisfied "the constitutional requirements of the nondelegation doctrine."[6]

Article II of the Constitution granted to the president duly elected by the people to, among other duties, command the armed forces, execute the laws of the United States, and appoint cabinet members with the **advice and consent** of the Senate. The Advice and Consent of Senate Clause in Article II is a legislative check on the executive branch to prevent the president from appointing a mere figurehead to a position of federal power. All presidents appoint to high-ranking federal jobs friends, political supporters, and financial contributors to their election campaigns. To ensure that the executive branch is not overrun with political cronies, the Senate must confirm these presidential appointments. Federal agencies such as the Department of Agriculture and the Department of the Interior enforce administrative rules, even though those who head the federal agencies were not elected by the people.

Article III of the Constitution created one Supreme Court and "such inferior Courts as the Congress may from time to time ordain and establish," which are the lower federal district trial courts and federal courts of appeal. Called "Article III" courts, federal judges are appointed for life and are imbued with the power to interpret laws and presidential acts to ensure they comport with the U.S. Constitution. All federal judges must be confirmed by the Senate, such as the 2018 confirmation of new U.S. Supreme Court Associate Justice Brett Kavanaugh.

Judicial Review

Because the constitution is silent about the scope of judicial power, Congress passed the Judiciary Act in 1789, which attempted to define the high Court's power, including the authority to issue *writs of mandamus* (Latin for "we command") forcing a government official to act. President John Quincy Adams was a federalist who was defeated in his reelection bid by Democratic-Republican Thomas Jefferson. Before he left office, Adams worked with his congressional allies to create and fill with his friends over 200 administrative posts and several judgeships to dilute Jefferson's executive power.

Adams made appointments until midnight on his last day of office, but not all commissions to appoint new justices of the peace in the District of Columbia were delivered on time. Jefferson was furious at Adams's attempt to burden his administration with political rivals and, on taking the presidential oath, ordered Secretary of State James Madison not to deliver the remaining commissions. John Marbury and other justice of the peace hopefuls sued Madison to get the Supreme Court to issue *writs of mandamus* forcing Jefferson to deliver the commissions. When the case reached the **U.S. Supreme Court** in 1803, the Court held that under the Constitution, Congress did not have the authority to enact the Judiciary Act and, therefore, Jefferson did not have to deliver the commissions.

By deciding Marbury's case, the Court defined its own power under Article III and elevated the judicial branch to equal status with the legislative and executive branches. The *Marbury v. Madison* (1803) decision established the doctrine of judicial review, in which only the Supreme Court determines (by interpreting the constitution) if laws made by Congress (the legislative branch) and the acts of the president and the federal agencies (the executive branch) are legal.[7] The Court went on to interpret the U.S. Constitution's Supremacy Clause, Article VI, that says federal law "shall be the supreme Law of the Land," to make its word final when the Court interprets the constitutionality of the laws, rules, and regulations enacted by any government entity. When the U.S. Supreme Court decides an issue—for example, interpreting the Constitution to determine a woman had the right in consultation with her doctor to terminate a pregnancy—that decision cannot be overturned or modified by any state or federal law, only by the U.S. Supreme Court itself.[8]

To ensure the new, national federal government would not abuse its power, the Constitution made clear that the Constitution itself, the document conceived, written and eventually adopted by the states, would be the only source of power for the federal government.

The Bill of Rights

After the U.S. Constitution was ratified, one of the first actions of the new Congress was to amend it. The Bill of Rights are the first ten amendments and protect the public from government abuse of power. The Bill of Rights form a cornerstone of criminal law and criminal procedure because their language is largely negative, mandating that the government "shall not" take certain actions that infringe on people's liberty. The First Amendment says, "Congress shall make no law," and the Fourth Amendment says that the law of search and seizure "shall not be violated." The negative language of the Bill of Rights counterbalances the broad grant of authority that Article I of the Constitution gives to the federal government. In a nutshell, the amendments correspond to the following rights, discussed more fully throughout this text:

Rule of Law: The Bill of Rights protects citizens from the awesome power of the government and is a source of criminal procedure protections.

First: Free speech, religion, press, assembly, petition for redress

Fourth: Free from unreasonable search and seizure

Fifth: Free from compelled self-incrimination

Sixth: Guarantee of a public and speedy jury trial and assistance of counsel

Eighth: Free from cruel and unusual punishment

Tenth: If the federal government does not control the subject matter, states are free to make own laws

The Bill of Rights originally only protected people from abuses by the federal government, but the high Court through the 14th Amendment and the doctrine of incorporation included the Bill of Rights into a state's due process guarantees.[9] Today when you read the Bill of Rights, *Congress* means any government entity—state, town, municipality, school board—that writes policies that impact people's rights.

Interpreting the U.S. Constitution

Criminal law and procedure court decisions interpreting the federal Constitution may be best understood as a snapshot in time. For example, the Civil War Amendments were enacted to protect newly emancipated slaves; the Thirteenth Amendment abolished slavery and involuntary servitude except on conviction of a crime; the Fifteenth Amendment prevented discrimination in the right to vote on account of race, color, or previous condition of servitude; and the Fourteenth Amendment made all people born in the United States citizens and gave everyone rights to due process and what the words above the U.S. Supreme Court say in Washington, D.C.: "Equal Justice Under Law."

Fourteenth Amendment, Section 1

All persons born or naturalized in the United States, and subject to the jurisdiction thereof, are citizens of the United States and of the state wherein they reside. No state shall make or enforce any law which shall abridge the privileges or immunities of citizens of the United States; nor shall any state deprive any person of life, liberty, or property, without due process of law; nor deny to any person within its jurisdiction the *equal protection of the laws* (emphasis added).

The Equal Protection Clause guarantees fairness under the law and has been the legal foundation to racially integrate public schools in *Brown v. Board of Education* (1954), to outlaw anti-miscegenation laws that prevented Blacks and Whites from marrying in *Loving v. Virginia* (1967), to legalizing same-sex marriage in all 50 states in *Obergefell v. Hodges* (2015).[10] The elasticity of the Equal Protection Clause illuminates the tension between two scholarly camps about how the U.S. Constitution should be interpreted.

The "originalist" philosophy that advocates interpreting the Constitution by what the words meant when written "stems from two features of the constitution: (1) that one of its principal purposes is to constrain those who make and enforce laws so as to protect the rights retained by the people, and for this reason, (2) it is put in writing," meaning all law is constrained by the document itself to protect individual rights.[11] Those who say the Constitution was written to be flexible argue present society is more diverse and inclusive than when "We the People" was originally written. Regardless of one's side in the debate, one helpful technique in understanding court cases is to make a snapshot at the intersection of psychology, history, political science, economics, and criminal justice to understand the competing influences on the Court when making its ultimate decision. The following page provides a timeline snapshot of the *Miranda v. Arizona* (1966) decision, where the U.S. Supreme Court interpreted the Fifth and Sixth Amendments to require law enforcement officers to notify suspects of their right to remain silent and to have an attorney present during questioning before a custodial interrogation. The timeline shows that when courts make decisions interpreting the law, the justices are not immune to societal influences, which, at the time of the *Miranda* case, were increased personal freedoms, fear of war, and economic prosperity for the middle class.

> **Rule of Law: Equal protection guarantees equality for everyone under law.**

Springboard for Discussion

Who are "We the People"? Do you agree with Justice John Marshall that the U.S. Constitution is a creature of the people's will and "lives only by their will"? Is the U.S. Constitution meant to be static or a living, breathing document?

The Sources of Law

The colonists brought with them their mother England's common law, which is developed by judges deciding cases based on custom and ritual. Common law remains as a reference for how certain legal principles and doctrines have been interpreted historically. For example, Mr. Keeler in California kicked his pregnant ex-wife in the stomach causing her fetus to be stillborn. He was prosecuted under state law for "the killing of a human being." Researching historical common law determined a human being meant "one born alive," so Mr. Keeler could not be criminally prosecuted for murder.[12] Similarly, case law is law made by judges deciding cases before them. This text uses case law excerpts, almost all of which are appeals from defendants convicted at trial who assert that a legal mistake was made that resulted in their conviction. Once the appellate court makes its decision, courts typically write a decision explaining its ruling.

Offenders are punished after their cases are adjudicated (decided) in court by way of trial or guilty plea. A court's jurisdiction, that is, its power to hear certain cases, is dependent on the original grant of authority that created the court. Both state and federal courts have some separation between minor and felony cases. Many states have trial courts of limited jurisdiction that handle misdemeanor offenses criminally or small claims offenses civilly. In some states, courts of limited jurisdiction are not presided over by a judge or even a trained lawyer. There may be no uniform protocol or rules of law to follow and no court reporter to transcribe the proceedings. Local courts reflect the community that staff them and run off a budget generated by the fines the court

TIMELINE
Snapshot of *Miranda v. Arizona Decision*

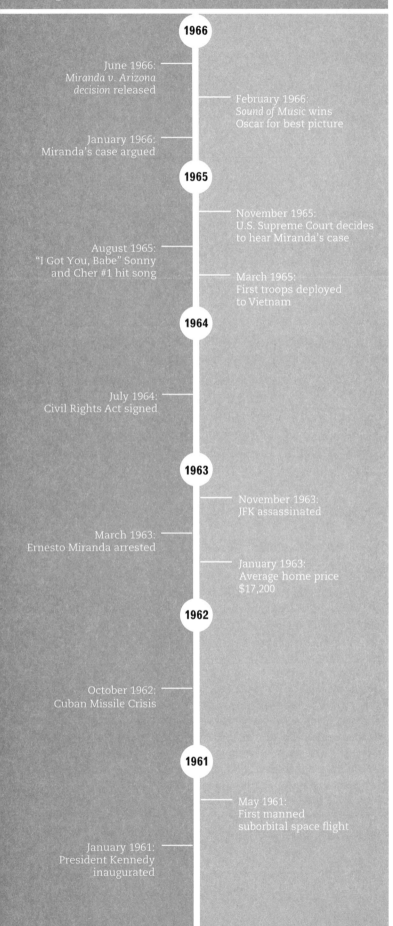

1966

June 1966:
Miranda v. Arizona decision released

February 1966:
Sound of Music wins Oscar for best picture

January 1966:
Miranda's case argued

1965

November 1965:
U.S. Supreme Court decides to hear Miranda's case

August 1965:
"I Got You, Babe" Sonny and Cher #1 hit song

March 1965:
First troops deployed to Vietnam

1964

July 1964:
Civil Rights Act signed

1963

November 1963:
JFK assassinated

March 1963:
Ernesto Miranda arrested

January 1963:
Average home price $17,200

1962

October 1962:
Cuban Missile Crisis

1961

May 1961:
First manned suborbital space flight

January 1961:
President Kennedy inaugurated

assesses and collects. Students are urged to study the type and structure of their respective state's trial and appellate courts. Most of the cases discussed in this text are felony cases that were heard by courts of general jurisdiction that can hear all types of cases, or trial courts with more authority than a limited court.

Statutory law (called "man-made" law) is enacted by legislators and codified in state or federal criminal codes. Statutes define crimes by elements (pieces of the whole), which the prosecutor must prove beyond a reasonable doubt before the defendant can be convicted. Elected officials enact statutes during legislative sessions and often announce the purpose of enacting the law in a preamble so the public is aware of the government's compelling state interest in regulating behavior. For example, the Preamble to the Racketeer Influenced and Corrupt Organization (RICO) Act of 1970 states the law punishing racketeering is required because "organized crime in the United States is a highly sophisticated, diversified, and wide-spread activity that annually drains billions of dollars from America's economy." Most case law involves the application of a statute to a specific offender, for instance, whether the California murder statute applied to Mr. Keeler and his ex-wife's child discussed herein. The **rule of lenity** means judges will interpret criminal statutes in favor of leniency for the defendant. In criminal trials, juries decide whether the statute defines the offender's behavior justifying conviction and punishment. Throughout this text are examples of federal and state statutes as applied to the material under review.

The **Model Penal Code (MPC)** is a concise statement of criminal law adopted by many states in defining their respective state crimes, defenses, and sentencing structure and is referenced in this text as an illustration of generic laws. The MPC was written in the 1960s by the American Law Institute, an organization of law-related professionals. A copy of relevant provisions of the MPC is included in Appendix B of this textbook.

Ordinances are local regulations enacted to protect the health and safety of the community. Common ordinances dictate everything from how often people can put trash on the street curb to how loud they can play their music past a certain hour in the night. City councils or town hall supervisors are often in charge of issuing ordinances for the good of the public order. All regulations imposed on the public by the government, even local government, must comply with state and federal laws, including the U.S. Constitution.

Reading case law is crucial to understanding how criminal law and procedure work to control the criminal justice process.

Understanding case law requires a mastery of the case brief, a synopsis that summarizes the major components of a case. In reading case law, the notation for the judge delivering the opinion might be "J. Smith." This stands for "Judge" or "Justice" Smith; the "J" is not the judge's first initial. A capitalized "Court" refers mostly to the U.S. Supreme Court, unless an appeals court is referring to itself within the opinion. The U.S. Supreme Court is also referred to as the "high Court," a shortcut used throughout this text. Many court opinions will state "the defendant asserts" or "the defendant contends" to reflect the arguments made on behalf of a defendant. To bring a claim against the government, a defendant needs standing, the legal requirement that only a party directly affected by the government action can bring a court claim. The defendant is not advancing arguments in her own name. Her attorney is advancing the arguments on her behalf, and the court simply states that it is the "defendant's" argument. Similarly, all references to the "state" or "government" typically means the prosecutor or state appellate lawyer is making those arguments on the government's behalf. The cases in this text retain most of the original language but have been edited to omit internal quotation marks, string citations to precedent, and include in brackets summaries of omitted material and definitions of technical legal language.

The significance of the court's conclusion—called a holding—and the reasoning the court used to arrive at a specific conclusion suggest how to apply the law in the future to similar cases. Let us use as illustration a case highlighted in Chapter 7, *Riley v. California*, 134 S.Ct. 2473 (2014). The components of a case brief are a case caption, facts, issue, holding, reasoning, and if applicable concurrence, and dissent. Not every case has a concurrence or dissent.

CASE CAPTION: The case name that represents the parties involved. *Riley v. California* indicates David Riley is bringing a legal action against the state of California because the government (prosecutor) introduced enough evidence to convict him. He is claiming on appeal a mistake was made at his trial. The appellant is the one seeking the appeal, and the appellee is the one trying to maintain the conviction. There is also the case citation, 134 S.Ct. 2473, which is where one can find the case in legal books or online, and the year the case was decided (2014).[13] For U.S. Supreme Court case excerpts in this textbook, the name of the justice who wrote the majority opinion and the vote count are provided. There are nine justices on the U.S. Supreme Court, which allows for an uneven vote count and a decisive win for one side of the case. The *Riley* decision was unanimous, 9–0, in favor of Riley that officers should have secured a warrant before searching his cell phone.

FACTS: The actions people took that brought them to court. Riley was a suspected gang member who had been involved in a drive-by shooting. When he was arrested, police officers searched his cell phone. The government used evidence retrieved from Riley's cell phone to convict him at trial.

ISSUE: The legal question the appeals court is being asked to answer. The issue in the *Riley* case was "whether the police may, without a warrant, search digital information on a cell phone seized from an individual who has been arrested?"

HOLDING: A majority of the justices who sit on the appellate court agree on a specific outcome for the case. The holding is also the court's answer to the issue. The holding in Riley's case is yes, police officers generally need a warrant to search someone's cell phone on arrest. The case establishes precedent, which is a rule of law referred to in deciding similar cases.[14] In future cases where police have time to get a warrant for electronic devices, the law requires it, as established by the precedent *Riley v. California*. If exigent circumstances exist, police need not secure a warrant.

REASONING: The reasons the court arrived at its decision, its holding. In the 1960s, the U.S. Supreme Court allowed on arrest of a person the simultaneous search without a warrant of "closed containers" such as purses and backpacks that could hide criminal evidence. The law has had to adapt to technological advances. A cell phone is not a backpack. Chief Justice Roberts wrote in the *Riley* decision,

> Modern cell phones . . . are now such a pervasive and insistent part of daily life, that the proverbial visitor from Mars might conclude they were an important feature of human anatomy.

The high Court reasoned that phones are our "social DNA,"[15] because they are minicomputers that store vast amounts of personal information (e.g., contacts, Internet search history, movies watched, music accessed, text messages, e-mails, and documents, as illustrated in Photo 1.1). Because people use cell phones to organize every aspect of their lives, electronic devices are not a typical "closed container"; therefore, a warrant was required to search the phone's contents.

Throughout the text, we examine cases through a courtroom perspective. People go to court to seek justice. On the scales of criminal justice, one side represents the government's interest and the other side represents an individual's interest. Looking at the *Riley* case from a courtroom perspective is illustrated by Figure 1.2, where the government's interest in seeking evidence to convict David Riley of the drive-by shooting is on one side of the scale, and David Riley's Fourth Amendment privacy interest in the contents of his cell phone are on the other side of the scale. Based on the Court's decision, the scales of justice tipped in Riley's favor.

Students should read a court's reasoning carefully to master learning criminal law and procedure. Typical rules-based reasoning involves a court taking a rule of law and applying it to the facts of the case. The practice of other judges following previous precedents is called *stare decisis*, Latin for "let the decision stand." The judicial system is established on a hierarchy of power among different courts depending on the court's power to hear and decide certain types of cases. A lower court is bound to follow the precedent established by a higher court, and no court is higher than the U.S. Supreme Court.

Figure 1.2 Fourth Amendment Scales of Justice, Riley v. California (2014)

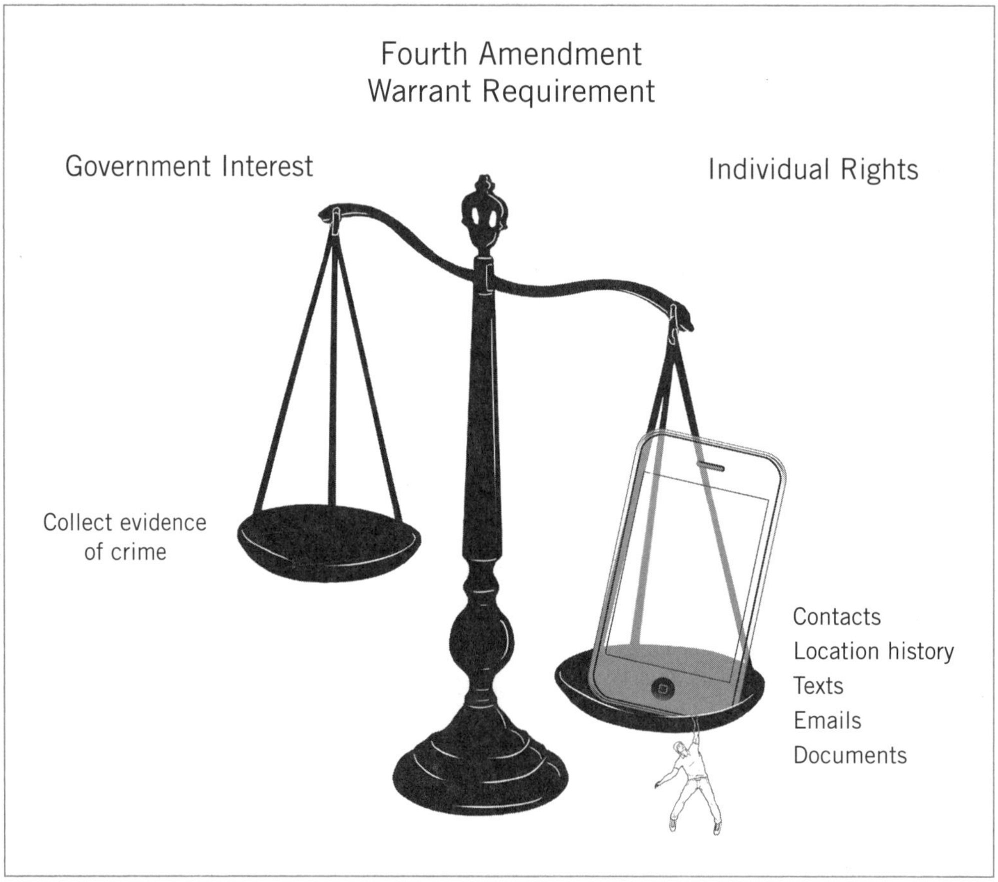

Fourth Amendment
Warrant Requirement

Government Interest

Individual Rights

Collect evidence
of crime

Contacts
Location history
Texts
Emails
Documents

Following precedent gives the public relative predictability in how court cases will be resolved. For instance, police officers searched Samuel Whiteside's car and found a digital camera. Without a warrant, officers looked at all of the photos on the camera and found images of Whiteside holding a gun and used those images against him at trial. The defendant claimed the search of the camera was improper and the court agreed.[16] Using the rule of law from the *Riley* case that a warrant is needed for a cell phone because of its "immense storage capacity," Whiteside's court reasoned officers needed a warrant to search the digital camera. In this textbook, there are opportunities for students to apply the rules of law under consideration to different fact cases, illustrated as follows:

▶ **Photo 1.1**
Do you agree with the court's decision? Do you consider your phone part of your "social DNA"?

© iStock.com/saquizeta

Rule of Law: The *Riley* case precedent says a search warrant is required for cell phones.

New Case Under Review: Whiteside's camera: Need a search warrant for a digital camera?

Answer: Yes, because the rule of law under *Riley* requires that result.

The other common type of reasoning is based on an analogy between the facts of prior cases and the current case. For example, drunk drivers claimed that tests to measure their blood alcohol content (BAC) were searches for which a warrant was required.[17] The *Riley* decision was based, in part, by weighing an individual's privacy rights against the government's police function in catching criminals. Using the factual similarities between the privacy interests in a cell phone and the breath and blood collected by BAC tests, the Court found no warrant was needed for a breathalyzer, but a warrant was required to take someone's blood. Reasoning by analogy looks like this:

Rule of Law: The *Riley* case precedent says search warrant is required for cell phones because, figuratively, cell phones are our "social DNA," in which we have a heightened expectation of privacy.

New Case Under Review: BAC tests: Need a search warrant to take a DUI (driving under the influence of alcohol or drugs) suspect's breath and blood?

Answer: For the government to draw blood: Yes, you need a warrant for blood tests, because, factually, blood really is our DNA and by analogy the *Riley* decision gives lots of protection for private things.

For the government to force you to blow your breath: No, you do not need a warrant for a breathalyzer test because by analogy blowing your breath into a tube does not implicate the same privacy rights as information stored on a cell phone.

As you work through the material in this text, take notice of the court's legal reasoning and then apply your own analysis to criminal law and procedure stories you hear about in the news.

CONCURRENCE: The judges who agree and vote with the majority decision but write a separate opinion to clarify or distinguish their reasoning from the majority.

DISSENT: The judges who disagree with the majority and write a formal rebuke to the majority opinion. Dissents often refer to the court as if it is a foreign body. It is not uncommon for a dissent to proclaim, "I disagree with the court's holding today" even though the judge writing the dissent is a member of the court.

Figure 1.3 illustrates how to read case and statutory citations to find the original source material.

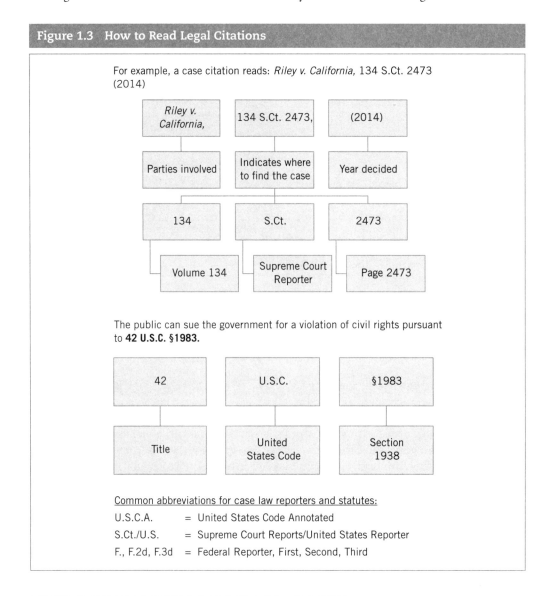

Figure 1.3 How to Read Legal Citations

For example, a case citation reads: *Riley v. California,* 134 S.Ct. 2473 (2014)

Riley v. California,	134 S.Ct. 2473,	(2014)
Parties involved	Indicates where to find the case	Year decided

134	S.Ct.	2473
Volume 134	Supreme Court Reporter	Page 2473

The public can sue the government for a violation of civil rights pursuant to **42 U.S.C. §1983.**

42	U.S.C.	§1983
Title	United States Code	Section 1938

Common abbreviations for case law reporters and statutes:

U.S.C.A.	= United States Code Annotated
S.Ct./U.S.	= Supreme Court Reports/United States Reporter
F., F.2d, F.3d	= Federal Reporter, First, Second, Third

THE GEOGRAPHY OF LEGAL CASES

Think of learning criminal law and procedure as its own culture; the law has its own history, identity, language, and identifiable icons. To understand any culture, it is helpful to learn the language's specific cadence and vocabulary. Throughout this text, there are legal concepts you will encounter repeatedly such as *due process* and *objectively reasonable*, terms used consistently as a shortcut, analogous to using the term *social media* to refer to Facebook, Instagram, Twitter, and Snapchat. Students should become familiar with the geography of legal cases as illustrated in Figure 1.4.

Due Process

The Fifth Amendment, enacted in 1791, provides in part, "No person shall . . . be deprived of life, liberty, or property, without due process of law." The Due Process Clause was repeated in the passing of the Fourteenth Amendment ratified in 1868 to include aliens (immigrants) and former slaves to recognize their rights as new citizens. In a criminal case, due process guarantees the government's fair treatment of the defendant by giving "reasonable notice of a charge against him, and an opportunity to be heard in his defense," which is the right to a fair trial.[18]

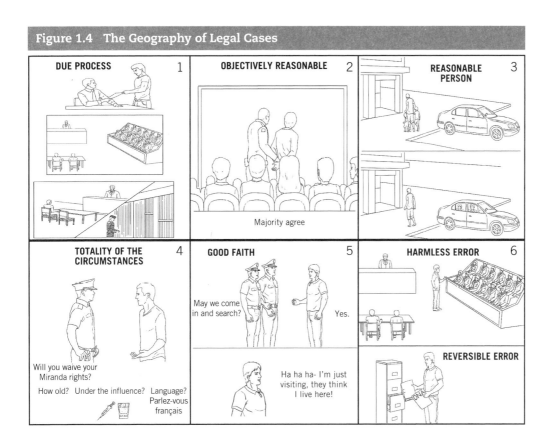

Figure 1.4 The Geography of Legal Cases

In Figure 1.4 box number 1, the defendant receives the charges, deemed "notice" and an opportunity to be heard, which is a trial, before the government may deprive him of liberty by incarcerating him in prison.

Objectively Reasonable

With reference to Figure 1.4 box number 2, imagine everyone watches a movie and the majority of the viewing public agrees the movie is great, as evidenced by ticket sales. One or two people may not like the movie, but the majority do. In criminal law and procedure, the term objectively reasonable means whether members of the public examining the behavior of a suspect or law enforcement officer would agree that their behavior was appropriate under the circumstances. In the illustration, everyone would agree the officer was being objectively reasonable in concluding probable cause exists supporting an arrest.

The Reasonable Man

The reasonable man is one "whose actions display appropriate regard for both his interests and the interests of others," or the "fictional average man or woman that the law uses as a measuring stick to gauge the behavior of others."[19] In Figure 1.4 box number 3, a reasonable person running into the store takes his small children with him. An unreasonable person leaves the children in a running car as he runs into the store. The reasonable person standard is meant to be objective—what most people would do or how they would react in specific circumstances. The law cannot totally ignore, however, the subjective characteristics of the defendant, such as whether the defendant is of average intelligence or particularly vulnerable.[20] The same reasonable standard applies to law enforcement officers in the field in determining whether the officers may be liable (responsible) for violating constitutional protections as courts examine how a "reasonable officer" would react in each situation.

Totality of the Circumstances

In reference to Figure 1.4 box number 4, a court will look not just at one factor but all factors to determine the reasonableness of the criminal justice actor's conclusion about the legality of their conduct in a given situation, called the totality of the circumstances. For example, in concluding a suspect voluntarily, intelligently, and knowingly waived his rights pursuant to *Miranda v. Arizona* (1966), a court will look at the suspect's age, whether he is under the influence of drugs or alcohol, whether English is his native language, as well as other factors influencing the officer's conclusion that the suspect gave up his rights and spoke freely.[21] Other circumstances in criminal procedure that examine the totality of the circumstances are illustrated in Figure 1.5.

Good Faith

In reference to Figure 1.4 number 5, courts often look to see if the law enforcement officers came to the situation in good faith, "with clean hands," with no bad motives or evil intent in its dealings with the public. For example, if officers approached a house and asked for consent to search and the person answering the door said yes, the officers would be acting in good faith if they

Figure 1.5 The Reasonable Man Standard

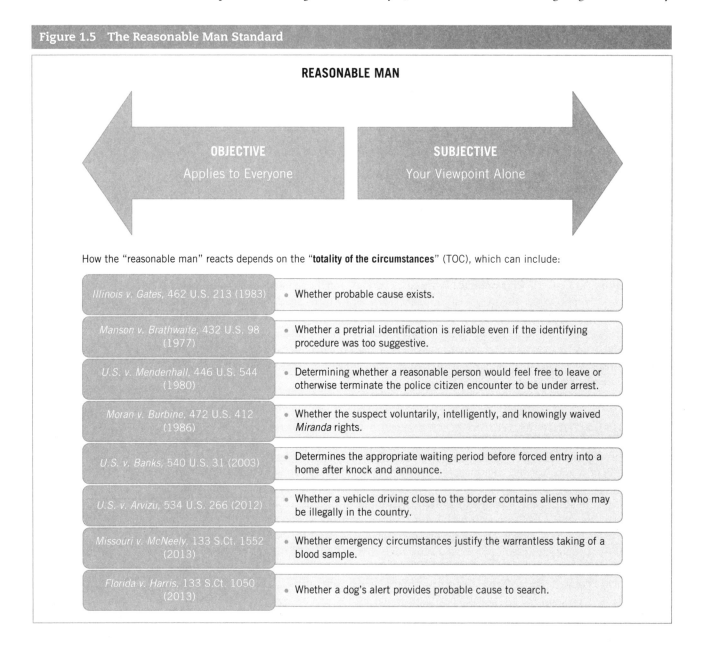

REASONABLE MAN

OBJECTIVE
Applies to Everyone

SUBJECTIVE
Your Viewpoint Alone

How the "reasonable man" reacts depends on the "**totality of the circumstances**" (TOC), which can include:

Illinois v. Gates, 462 U.S. 213 (1983)	• Whether probable cause exists.
Manson v. Brathwaite, 432 U.S. 98 (1977)	• Whether a pretrial identification is reliable even if the identifying procedure was too suggestive.
U.S. v. Mendenhall, 446 U.S. 544 (1980)	• Determining whether a reasonable person would feel free to leave or otherwise terminate the police citizen encounter to be under arrest.
Moran v. Burbine, 472 U.S. 412 (1986)	• Whether the suspect voluntarily, intelligently, and knowingly waived *Miranda* rights.
U.S. v. Banks, 540 U.S. 31 (2003)	• Determines the appropriate waiting period before forced entry into a home after knock and announce.
U.S. v. Arvizu, 534 U.S. 266 (2012)	• Whether a vehicle driving close to the border contains aliens who may be illegally in the country.
Missouri v. McNeely, 133 S.Ct. 1552 (2013)	• Whether emergency circumstances justify the warrantless taking of a blood sample.
Florida v. Harris, 133 S.Ct. 1050 (2013)	• Whether a dog's alert provides probable cause to search.

later discovered the person who answered the door did not have the authority to give consent to search. The person's "apparent ability" to give consent is what the officers relied on in doing their job. "A warrantless entry is valid when based upon the consent of a third party whom the police, at the time of the entry, reasonably believe to possess common authority over the premises, but who in fact does not," and the good faith of the officers means any incriminating evidence seized may be admissible and used at trial against the defendant.[22]

Error

In court cases disposing of criminal law and procedure issues, an appeals court will look to see if mistakes were made, called error, at trial or on initial appeal, as illustrated in Figure 1.4 number 6. If mistakes were made but the mistakes did not affect the outcome of the case, it would be harmless error. For instance, a court mistakenly admits carpet fiber evidence at a murder trial against the defendant. But at trial, five witnesses testified they saw the defendant shoot the victim on the carpet. The mistake admitting the fiber evidence would be harmless error and would not be a basis to overturn the defendant's conviction. If, on the other hand, the government put DNA evidence that exonerated (proved innocent) the defendant in a filing cabinet in a case where there was little evidence linking the defendant to the crime, withholding evidence that would change the outcome of the case would be reversible error, and the defendant's conviction would be set aside and he would get a new trial.

Quantum of Evidence Required at Various Stages of the Trial Process

The following football analogy guides the quantum (amount) of evidence required at various stages of the criminal trial. Imagine a running back on special teams receives a kickoff in his own end zone and seeks to run the ball to the opposite end of the football field, 100 yards, to score a touchdown (Figure 1.6).

The running back runs from his end zone to the 20-yard line. Up to 20 yards, the quantum of proof would be a policeman's "hunch" that something is amiss; perhaps the person does not look like he "belongs" in the neighborhood, but he is not doing anything suspicious, just walking. A hunch is less than mere suspicion and conveys no authority on law enforcement to stop and

Figure 1.6 Quantum of Evidence Required at Various Stages of the Trial Process

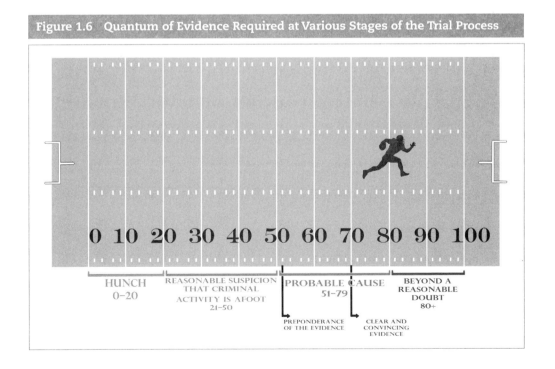

detain people. Based on a "hunch," the police officer can legally do nothing to stop the person from going about his business. From 21 to 50 yards, the running back has established "reasonable suspicion that criminal activity is afoot," the legal basis for a *Terry* stop discussed in Chapter 7. Based on specific and articulable facts that crime is afoot, the officer may briefly stop and talk with a person and, if there exists a reasonable belief the person is armed, pat him down for weapons only as justified for officer safety.

Once the running back crosses midfield and runs from 51 to 79 yards, he has established probable cause, which is the legal basis for an arrest and also the basis for a warrant. Probable cause means it is more likely than not that a specific person has committed a specific crime. With probable cause the police can conduct a full-blown search of the individual and his immediate surrounding area and detain him in jail pending trial. In civil cases, which involve people suing each other for harm and seeking damages (money), 51 yards would establish a preponderance of the evidence standard to find in favor of a plaintiff suing a defendant. At approximately 70 yards, the running back would reach a clear and convincing evidence standard, which is less demanding than beyond a reasonable doubt and used, for example, in a civil commitment proceeding or a sex offender registration classification. At 80 yards, the running back has reached beyond a reasonable doubt required to secure a conviction.[23] The legal standard for a conviction at trial is not beyond all doubt, just a reasonable doubt. If the government gets to the red zone, the running back has made it 80 to 100 yards, and a conviction supports a term of imprisonment or, in a death-penalty case, execution.

THE ACTORS IN
THE CRIMINAL JUSTICE SYSTEM

The pillars of American democracy depend on the public's trust in government institutions. Our willingness to follow the law is directly linked to our collective belief that justice will prevail. Justice wins when professionals in law enforcement, the courts, and the prisons are highly trained, highly ethical, and highly compassionate. Research by justice scholar Tom Tyler shows that people value how they are treated throughout the justice process more highly than the actual outcome of their case, called **procedural justice**.[24] If people perceive the justice system as legitimate and fair, they more willingly follow the law. The essential components of procedural justice are

1. People understand their legal rights and judicial procedures.

2. The judicial process is transparent.

3. People have a voice and an opportunity to be heard.

4. All people are treated with dignity and respect.

Tyler concludes that although people are generally motivated to follow the law because of fear of punishment, procedural justice matters to all those who encounter the criminal justice system.

The Victim

Historically, victims have been a footnote in the criminal justice process. Because the offender is at risk of losing liberty and life because of the government's action, the victim's wishes with respect to the disposition of the offender's case have been less important. According to Harvard history professor Jill Lepore, the turning point in recognizing victims' rights was the 1995 Oklahoma City bombing, "which created thousands of victims beyond those physically wounded and killed." Although the victims had limited "participatory rights" in the defendant Timothy McVeigh's trial, political pressure led federal and state lawmakers to create a victim "Bill of Rights" most patterned on the federal law, reprinted here in part:[25]

18 U.S.C. §3771. Crime victims' rights

a. Rights of Crime Victims.—A crime victim has the following rights:

(1) The right to be reasonably protected from the accused.

(2) The right to reasonable, accurate, and timely notice of any public court proceeding, or any parole proceeding, involving the crime or of any release or escape of the accused.

(3) The right not to be excluded from any such public court proceeding, unless the court, after receiving clear and convincing evidence, determines that testimony
by the victim would be materially altered if the victim heard other testimony at that proceeding.

(4) The right to be reasonably heard at any public proceeding in the district court involving release, plea, sentencing, or any parole proceeding.

(5) The reasonable right to confer with the attorney for the Government in the case.

(6) The right to full and timely restitution as provided in law.

(7) The right to proceedings free from unreasonable delay.

(8) The right to be treated with fairness and with respect for the victim's dignity and privacy.

(9) The right to be informed in a timely manner of any plea bargain or deferred prosecution agreement.

There is often conflict between a defendant's rights to a fair trial and a victim's rights to be heard throughout the trial process. For example, a common tribute to crime victims is the wearing of their photo on T-shirts or buttons. In *Carey v. Musladin* (2006), Mathew Musladin shot and killed Tom Studer. During Musladin's trial, several members of Studer's family sat in the front row of the courtroom wearing buttons with a photo of Studer on them. Musladin's defense counsel objected that the buttons might impermissibly influence the jury to decide the case against Musladin based on emotion rather than the evidence as the law required. Counsel asked the judge to order the family not to wear the buttons, but the judge refused. Musladin was convicted and on appeal, the U.S. Supreme Court found that the buttons were just a normal expression of grief that did not brand Musladin as guilty and upheld his conviction.[26] Courts also allow **victim impact statements** at the defendant's sentencing hearing. Victims can tell the court about the harm caused by the defendant, but they may not ask the jury or judge to impose a specific sentence, as that is in the exclusive province of the fact finder.[27]

The Offender

The school of classical criminology traces back to Cesare Beccaria (1738–1794), who advanced the belief that society's goals are best met by moral law and a limited government to serve the people. Contemporary criminology focuses on offenders and the many reasons they commit crimes. The most notable theories in criminology are listed in Table 1.2.

As society became more industrialized, public shaming, flogging in the town square, and the death penalty as the sole methods of legal punishment gave way to other penological (punishment) goals. Because of the Eighth Amendment's ban on cruel and unusual punishment, we punish the offender, not the crime, for instance, the U.S. Supreme Court has invalidated mandatory death-penalty laws because every sentencing decision must be individualized to the offender.[28]

Incapacitation through **incarceration** as society's punishment of choice has shaped most modern penal policy. **Deterrence** is preventing others from committing a crime

> **Rule of Law: The purpose of criminal law is for an offender to pay back what his crime has taken from society.**

Table 1.2 Notable Theories in Criminology

Social learning theory (Ronald Akers)	People learn from others how to commit crime and keep committing crime depending on reward.
Strain theory (Robert Merton)	When people are unable to achieve socially acceptable goals, they substitute unacceptable goals.
Social control theory (Travis Hirschi)	People who share strong common bonds are less likely to commit crime.
Labeling theory (Edwin Lemert)	Criminal behavior comes from being labeled a deviant by others.
Conflict theory (George Vold & Austin Turk)	The powerful in society control all levers of justice against the powerless lower class.

by imposing a severe sanction on one offender as a warning. Watching an offender receive harsh punishment was meant to deter (prevent) others from committing a crime lest the same pain and public humiliation befall them. Rehabilitation means to restore and offer the offender programs in employment, substance abuse treatment, and social skills to reduce the probability that the offender will commit additional crimes (recidivate) and return to prison.[29] Restitution is making the offender pay the victim and/or society back for the harm caused. Similar to, but different from, the concept of rehabilitation, which focuses on the offender's behavior, restitution focuses on the victim's loss and what the offender can do to make the victim whole again. Retribution is "just deserts" "eye for an eye" punishment, but gratuitous punishments, such as sending selfies in handcuffs to colleagues, imposed to humiliate and embarrass the defendant are unlawful. In *United States v. Brewer* (2013), reprinted in part below, an elderly couple convicted of white-collar fraud for stealing more than 6 million dollars were sentenced to probation rather than incarceration in prison. The prosecution appealed the sentence to the trial court that imposed the sentence. Follow the court's reasoning under the purposes of punishment announced in the federal sentencing law and see if you agree with the court's decision.

UNITED STATES V. BREWER, 978 F.SUPP.2D 710 (W.D. TEX. 2013)

FACTS: Donald Dean Brewer and Sherri Lynn Brewer were indicted by a grand jury of citizens on seventeen counts of conspiracy to defraud, wire fraud, and major fraud against the United States, alleging creation of a sham contracting operation which led to $6,445,370 in ill gotten gains, half of which went to the Brewers, and all of which were stolen from the taxpayers. Following a three week trial, a jury of their peers convicted the Brewers on all counts beyond a reasonable doubt. While the Brewers mounted a vigorous defense, the jury's verdict was supported by overwhelmingly sufficient evidence (some of it being uncontested) of lies, deceit, obfuscation and fiduciary misfeasance, malfeasance and nonfeasance.

The Punishment

The advisory sentencing guidelines called for incarceration of Mr. Brewer for 108 to 135 months [9–11.2 years]

and Mrs. Brewer for 70 to 87 months [5.8–7.2 years]. For the reasons stated in the Court's judgment and those that follow, the Court severely punished the Brewers without imposing a prison sentence, in addition to the punishment inflicted by the Brewers upon themselves and their family. The Brewers have been ordered to disgorge all of their assets except for one vehicle and their personal belongings. After many years of a legitimate $150,000 to $200,000 annual income, they now exist on $2800 per month from Social Security and disability.

The assets to be forfeited included a $930,000 note receivable, the loss of $7,000 per month in so-called "retirement" income, a vehicle, a home, and Mrs. Brewer's ownership interest in a grocery store valued at several hundred thousand dollars. Nonmonetary punishment included being shamed in their lifelong hometown of Clovis, New Mexico, population 39,197, and being ostracized by their professional friends, some of whom testified against defendant Donald Brewer. And for their crime, they will live out their lives as convicted federal felons.

Legal Standard

[Federal Sentencing Guidelines] 18 U.S.C. §3553 . . . calls upon the Court to consider the goals of sentencing. "Retribution, deterrence, incapacitation, and rehabilitation—are the four purposes of sentencing generally, and a court must fashion a sentence 'to achieve the[se] purposes . . . to the extent that they are applicable' in a given case."

Application of Legal Standard

History and Characteristics of the Defendants

[The guidelines] requires the Court to consider "the nature and circumstances of the offense[s] and the history and characteristics of the defendant[s]." Here, the history and characteristics of the defendants weigh heavily on the Court.

Mr. and Mrs. Brewer are both 64 years of age. They wed in January of 1966, have remained married for forty-seven years, and have raised three children together. In August of 2004, Mr. Brewer was involved in an airplane crash. As a consequence of the crash and the related surgeries and procedures, Mr. Brewer has complete paralysis and constant nerve pain in his right leg, partial paralysis in his left leg, severe osteoporosis in his lower extremities, poor circulation, and poor temperature regulation. He has undergone several procedures to remove cysts from his tail bone, repair a broken hip, remove scar tissue near his spinal cord, and treat various leg problems. Mr. Brewer is confined to a wheelchair 99% of the time. His injuries also require him to use a four-inch padded seat to avoid pressure sores, a shower chair and bar for the toilet, leg braces, a walker, a Medtronic Neurostimulation System which is implanted in his waist, and a regimen of half a dozen medications. Mr. Brewer also suffers from depression.

While a guidelines sentence of 108 to 135 months imprisonment for Mr. Brewer may be appropriate for a young or middle aged healthy individual found guilty of these crimes, such a term for a severely infirm 64-year-old man like Mr. Brewer is, as a practical matter, a life sentence. Mr. Brewer deserves to be punished. He does not deserve to die in prison.

Mrs. Brewer's history and characteristics also weigh on the Court. At the sentencing hearing, it was revealed that Mrs. Brewer's resistance to imprisonment stemmed, not from a fear for her own health, happiness, and safety, but for the health, happiness, and safety of her husband. Her defense counsel explained that Mrs. Brewer "lives to take care of Don Brewer." Indeed, while the Bureau of Prisons is equipped to care for prisoners of all levels of need, it would not likely meet the level of care that Mrs. Brewer

has faithfully provided to Mr. Brewer in the years since the airplane crash. Consideration of these issues weigh in favor of a noncustodial sentence.

Retribution

While imprisonment is often necessary for retributive purposes, it is not always the most effective or the most fiscally sound option. The Bureau of Prisons calculated that the "fee to cover the average cost of incarceration for Federal inmates in Fiscal Year 2011 was $28,893.40." In this case, given Mr. Brewer's severe physical limitations and continuing medical issues, his incarceration would cost the government far more than the average federal inmate. In the spirit of sparing dwindling resources by keeping non-violent offenders out of prison, the Court finds that non-custody retribution is appropriate for Mr. and Mrs. Brewer, who have and continue to suffer in other ways.

Deterrence

[The guidelines] requires the Court to impose a sentence "to afford adequate deterrence to criminal conduct." At the sentencing hearing, the Government stated that its "big concern" with regard to sentencing was deterrence, explaining that there are many opportunities to take advantage when dealing with military contracts and citing "a tremendous amount of fraud in the procurement system." While the Court recognizes the importance of deterrence, it is also realistic about its limits, especially in the realm of white collar crime, where the powers of greed and ambition are often stronger than any deterrent effect. The Brewers did not learn from the example of Bernie Madoff, who did not learn from the example of John Rigas, who did not learn from the example of Ivan Boesky. And these criminals did not learn from the horse thieves who came before them, hung in the American West in the name of deterrence.

As journalist H. L. Mencken put it: "Hanging one scoundrel, it appears, does not deter the next." Indeed, despite the use of the cane in Singapore and the blade and stone in Saudi Arabia, Sudan, and Nigeria, crimes continue to be committed around the world. The Court finds that incarceration of the Brewers would not significantly deter future offenders.

Incapacitation

[The guidelines] concerns incapacitation, instructing the Court to impose a sentence "to protect the public from further crimes of the defendant." The Court finds the goal of incapacitation is sufficiently achieved by the conditions of probation in this case. In addition to the applicable mandatory and standard conditions, the Court also prohibited the defendants from becoming employed in any fiduciary position or becoming employed in a position requiring the handling of money or the disbursing of funds without the

(Continued)

(Continued)

prior approval of the Probation Officer. Imprisonment is not necessary to keep the Brewers from committing financial crimes again.

Rehabilitation

[The guidelines] concerns the rehabilitative goals of sentencing. It requires the Court to impose a sentence "to provide the defendant with needed educational or vocational training, medical care, or other correctional treatment in the most effective manner." The Court sentenced the defendants to a term of five years' probation on each count to run consecutively to each other with the intention of keeping defendants on probation for the remainder of their lives. This Court, after having sat through three weeks of trial time and a full day sentencing hearing, is well suited to set aside the one-size-fits-all statutory mandates of the Legislative Branch and instead craft a sentence that fits the facts of this case, the defendants' individual circumstances, and the separate power of the Judicial Branch.

Conclusion

In conclusion, after thoroughly examining the evidence at trial, the defendants' background and circumstances, the guidelines, and the goals of sentencing, the Court finds all factors weigh in favor of a noncustodial sentence for these defendants. Should the appellate court disagree as to Mr. Brewer, separate consideration should be given to Mrs. Brewer for a noncustodial sentence. Significant testimony from several witnesses portrayed Mr. Brewer as authoritarian and controlling in the workplace. This Court reasonably infers that such characteristics were present in the husband-wife relationship, leading Mrs. Brewer to commit the acts required by Mr. Brewer, thus leading to her felony conviction.

Springboard for Discussion

Professor Paul Bator said in 1963:

> We are told that the criminal law's notion of just condemnation and punishment is a cruel hypocrisy visited by a smug society on the psychologically and economically crippled . . . that its reliance on punishment as an educational and deterrent agent is misplaced, particularly in the case of the very members of society most likely to engage in criminal conduct; and that its failure to provide for individualized and humane rehabilitation of offenders is inhuman and wasteful.[30]

Professor Bator seems to agree with the judge in the *Brewer* case that harsh punishment is no deterrent to others from committing crime. Do you agree? Why or why not?

Specialty Courts

Juvenile Courts. Juveniles are minors under the age of 18 years old and are treated differently from adult offenders. For example, no one under the age of 18 who commits homicide is eligible for the death penalty.[31] First established in the 1800s in Cook County, Illinois, juvenile courts separated youthful offenders from the harshest punishments adults may suffer for committing the same crimes, but they also stripped juveniles of full constitutional protections in the criminal trial process. *McKeiver v. Pennsylvania* (1971).[32] In exchange, however, for giving up some basic rights adults enjoy when charged with crimes, juveniles have access to lighter sentences and better access to expungement (elimination) of their criminal records. Juveniles do have due process rights as decided by the U.S. Supreme Court decision *In re Gault* (1967).[33] Gault was a 15-year-old who was on probation for stealing when he was charged with making an obscene telephone call to his neighbor. If he were an adult convicted of making an indecent call, the maximum sentence would have been 2 months in jail and a $50 fine. Gault's hearings before a judge, where he had no counsel, no notice of the charges, no notification to his parents, and no court reporter transcribing the court proceedings, resulted in a 6-year confinement to a youth home.

In overturning Gault's conviction and establishing due process protections for all juveniles facing incarceration, the Court said, "Under our Constitution, the condition of being a boy does not justify a kangaroo court." To give adolescents a chance at a fresh start after juvenile proceedings, court sessions are generally closed to the public and case names for juveniles list only their initials (e.g., *Ohio v. A. J.*), thereby protecting their identity. The basis of juvenile justice is restorative justice, helping the juvenile restore the harm caused to the community. But it is increasingly common for prosecutors to "waive" juvenile offenders into adult court. The special issue of juvenile sentencing, particularly to life without parole is discussed more fully in Chapter 13.

Drug Courts. According to the National Institute of Justice, there are more than 3,000 drug courts operating in the United States that specialize in the criminal disposition of defendants for whom drugs and alcohol have had an adverse impact on their lives, or are members of a population vulnerable to drug abuse, such as juveniles or military veterans. Like most specialty courts devoted to one particular type of offender, drug courts claim success in lowering recidivism rates, lowering the amount of money spent processing each defendant, and lowering the barriers for the judicial system to have a meaningful impact on an offender's long-term rehabilitation.[34]

Defense Counsel

The defense counsel occupies a unique position in the criminal justice system. The major professional association for all attorneys, the American Bar Association (ABA), has ethical rules found in the Model Rules of Professional Conduct and the Model Code of Professional Responsibility, which require the defense lawyer be a zealous advocate for her client, which means she must defend her client fully and with due diligence to test the sufficiency of the government's evidence against the client.

> Client–Lawyer Relationship. ABA Model Rules of Professional Conduct 1.3, comment (1994)
>
> [1] A lawyer should pursue a matter on behalf of a client despite opposition, obstruction or personal inconvenience to the lawyer, and take whatever lawful and ethical measures are required to vindicate a client's cause or endeavor. A lawyer must also act with commitment and dedication to the interests of the client and with zeal in advocacy on the client's behalf.

As the U.S. Supreme Court has said:

> In our system a defense lawyer characteristically opposes the designated representative of the State. The system assumes that adversarial testimony will ultimately advance the public interest in truth and fairness. But it posits that a defense lawyer best serves the public not by acting on behalf of the State or in concert with it but rather by advancing "the undivided interests of his client."

For attorneys to perform their job properly, the attorney–client privilege protects as confidential the communication between the attorney and client. The privilege allows the justice system to function at its best when a client can trust that his lawyer can keep the client's secrets. The U.S. Supreme Court has said the privilege "is to encourage full and frank communication between attorneys and their clients and thereby promote broader public interests in the observance of law and administration of justice."[35] Courts take seriously the attorney's obligation not to disclose the client's confidences. In 1973, Robert F. Garrow, Jr., was charged with murder. In speaking with one of his attorneys, Francis R. Belge, Garrow admitted to three additional murders and told Attorney Belge the location of the victims' bodies. At the time, there were young women who were missing and their families were in anguish over their whereabouts. Based on Garrow's information, Attorney Belge went and examined the deceased victims' bodies but did not alert the authorities. At Garrow's trial and in an effort to establish an insanity defense, Attorney Belge finally revealed Garrow's additional murders. The community was outraged at Belge's conduct. The prosecutor charged Belge with the crime of not reporting the death of someone who had died without medical attention, but the court dismissed the charges in *New York v. Belge* (1975), finding Belge had conducted himself "as an officer of the court with all the zeal [vigorous energy] at his command to protect the constitutional rights of his client" and killer Garrow's disclosure of the bodies' location was private and confidential.[36] As the

Rule of Law: Juvenile court protects minors from the harsh punishments of adult court. In exchange, juvenile offenders do not enjoy the right to a jury trial.

Rule of Law: Defense counsel is ethically bound to be a zealous advocate for her client and to protect all attorney–client communications as confidential.

Springboard for Discussion

Alton Logan from Illinois was convicted of murder for which another man claimed responsibility. The real killer's attorneys knew Logan was innocent but could not disclose their client's secret. Logan spent 26 years in prison before the real killer died, releasing his attorneys to tell the truth. Could you keep a secret that kept an innocent man in jail, even if it meant that you, as an attorney, put your own client in peril of facing capital murder charges?

rules and the code that guide an attorney's conduct provide,[37] even if a client informs his attorney of past crimes or indicates a willingness to commit crime in the future, the attorney does not have to disclose that information to authorities, although he may if he wishes to prevent harm to others.

The Judge

Rule of Law: The judge is to be neutral and detached, which is not to have prior knowledge or preconceived conclusions about the defendant's case.

State trial judges are selected by five different methods: governor's appointment, legislative selection, merit selection, nonpartisan election, and partisan election. Some states use a combination of methods. All federal judges, except federal magistrates, are appointed for life. Magistrates are judges who have considerably less power than a judge selected or elected to the bench. A judge performs many functions: He signs search and arrest warrants, makes bail determinations, makes sure that the defendant understands the charges against him, takes the defendant's plea to the charge, appoints counsel if the defendant cannot afford to hire one, hears pretrial motions, and makes evidentiary rulings during the trial—for example, whether or not certain scientific evidence is admissible. A judge also instructs the jury on the law that applies to the facts of the case. Before and throughout the trial, the judge is to remain neutral and detached, which means the judge is not to take sides during or before trial, nor is the judge to have any personal stake in the outcome of the case, as represented by the statue of justice—a woman wearing a blindfold, with a scale in one hand and a sword in the other.

> Model Code of Judicial Conduct Canon 1
>
> A judge shall uphold and promote the independence, integrity, and impartiality of the judiciary, and shall avoid impropriety and the appearance of impropriety.

The judge should be "blind" to the issues in the case before hearing the facts and evidence, to avoid favoring one party over the other.

In a case where the judge was not neutral and detached, *Lo-Ji Sales, Inc. v. New York* (1979),[38] an investigator for the New York State Police applied to the local judge for a warrant to search the defendant's "adult" bookstore for evidence of state obscenity law violations. Thereafter, the judge, four state police officers, several detectives, and three members of the local prosecutor's office—11 in all—entered the bookstore and engaged in a search that lasted almost six hours. During the search, the judge viewed 23 films, determined that there was probable cause to believe that they were obscene, and then ordered the officers to seize the film, projectors, and 327 magazines, all used as evidence to convict the defendant. On appeal, the U.S. Supreme Court said, the judge "did not manifest the neutrality and detachment of a judicial officer when presented with a warrant application for a search and seizure." He was acting as an adjunct law enforcement officer, which is improper.

If a judge believes he is biased and predisposed to rule in favor of one party over another, he should recuse (remove) himself from hearing the case. Lawyers often file recusal motions asking judges to remove themselves from cases where the litigants believe the judge will play favorites in the case.

APPLYING THE LAW TO THE FACTS

Should the Judge Recuse (Remove) Himself?

The Facts: Ronald Castille was the top prosecutor in Philadelphia. Castille approved capital murder charges against Terrance Williams, who in 1984 received the death penalty. Castille was later elected chief justice of the Pennsylvania Supreme Court overseeing Williams's appeal. Castille voted to uphold Williams's death sentence. Williams complained that Castille had a conflict of interest, as Castille was the one who approved capital punishment in the first place. Cas-

tille responded he could be fair and impartial. Should Judge Castille have recused himself from hearing Williams's appeal?

The Law: Yes, the U.S. Supreme Court held that Castille should not have decided Williams's appeal. Castille had intimate knowledge of Williams's case, and voting on his appeal violated Williams's due process rights to fairness in the criminal process.[39]

The Prosecutor

Prosecutorial discretion, the exclusive power to decide who to charge with a crime and what crimes to charge, makes the prosecutor the most powerful actor in the criminal justice system; the prosecutor's job is to seek justice, not convictions.[40] Although he or she "may strike hard blows, [he or she is] not at liberty to strike foul ones."[41] U.S. Supreme Court Associate Justice Robert Jackson said in 1940:

> The qualities of a good prosecutor are as elusive and as impossible to define as those which mark a gentleman. And those who need to be told would not understand it anyway. A sensitiveness to fair play and sportsmanship is perhaps the best protection against the abuse of power, and the citizen's safety lies in the prosecutor who tempers zeal with human kindness, who seeks truth and not victims, who serves the law and not factional purposes, and who approaches his task with humility.[42]

A prosecutor represents "the people," the public's interests that the criminal has harmed. The reasons prosecutors make certain decisions are as unique and varied as each individual. Some of the factors that a prosecutor weighs in determining what charges to bring against a suspect are the following:

- The nature and seriousness of the crime
- The specific or general deterrent effect of prosecution
- The suspect's role in committing the crime as a principal or accessory
- The suspect's criminal history
- The suspect's willingness to cooperate in the investigation or prosecution of others
- If convicted, the consequences to the suspect and community[43]

Prosecutors as public servants with awesome power have certain ethical obligations to treat everyone fairly. **Selective prosecution** claims are brought by defendants who complain that the prosecutor is maliciously charging them with a crime rather than other criminals whom the prosecutor could also easily pursue.

ABA Rule 3.8 Special Responsibilities of a Prosecutor

The prosecutor in a criminal case shall:

(a) refrain from prosecuting a charge that the prosecutor knows is not supported by probable cause;

(b) make reasonable efforts to assure that the accused has been advised of the right to, and the procedure for obtaining, counsel and has been given reasonable opportunity to obtain counsel;

(c) not seek to obtain from an unrepresented accused a waiver of important pretrial rights, such as the right to a preliminary hearing;

(d) make timely disclosure to the defense of all evidence or information known to the prosecutor that tends to negate the guilt of the accused or mitigates the offense, and, in connection with sentencing, disclose to the defense and to the tribunal all unprivileged mitigating information known to the prosecutor, except when the prosecutor is relieved of this responsibility by a protective order of the tribunal.

> **Rule of Law:**
> Prosecutorial discretion is the power to decide who to charge with a crime and what crimes to charge.

State prosecutors may be called district attorneys, are usually elected, and are responsible for prosecuting state crimes. Lawyers who work under the district attorneys are called assistant district attorneys. Different from district attorneys who prosecute criminals, attorneys general usually prosecute civil and criminal matters on behalf of a state. The U.S. attorney general is the chief law enforcement officer for the country and oversees the U.S. Department of Justice (DOJ). The DOJ is an executive branch agency responsible for a wide range of programs from the national drug interdiction efforts led by the DEA to the federal prison system run by the Bureau of Prisons. Also under the U.S. attorney general are U.S. attorneys, who are appointed by the president as the chief federal prosecutors in every federal district, and his or her subordinates, assistant U.S. attorneys. Federal prosecutors prosecute federal crimes on behalf of the United States.

Law Enforcement

> **Rule of Law: Law enforcement officers serve and protect the community by preventing and investigating crime.**

A prosecutor's success in holding offenders accountable often rests on the relationship with law enforcement. Law enforcement solves crimes by progressing through several, predictable stages of an investigation to identify a suspect. Officers help the prosecutor prepare the case for trial and will often testify under oath about evidence in an effort to prove the defendant guilty. Other law enforcement personnel include sheriffs, deputies, probation and parole officers, and correctional officers who supervise jails and prisons. All law enforcement officers are sworn to serve and protect with malice toward none, as reflected in their code of ethics.

Law Enforcement Code of Ethics

As a law enforcement Officer my fundamental duty is to serve mankind; to safeguard lives and property; to protect the innocent against deception, the weak against oppression or intimidation, and the peaceful against violence or disorder; and to respect the Constitutional rights of all men to liberty, equality, and justice.

I will keep my private life unsullied as an example to all; maintain courageous calm in the face of danger, scorn or ridicule; develop self-restraint; and be constantly mindful of the welfare of others. In thought and deed in both my personal and professional life, I will be exemplary in obeying the laws of the land and the regulations of my department. Whatever I see or hear of a confidential nature or that is confided to me in my official capacity will be kept ever secret unless revelation is necessary in the performance of my duty . . .

I recognize the badge of my office as a symbol of public faith, and I accept it as a public trust to be held so long as I am true to the ethics of the police service. I will constantly strive to achieve those objectives and ideals, dedicating myself before God to my chosen profession . . . law enforcement.

There are times when law enforcement runs afoul of a person's rights and a civil lawsuit follows.

PROTECTING CITIZENS AND CRIMINAL JUSTICE PROFESSIONALS

Government Actions Performed Under the "Color of Law"

The §1983 Claim

Many criminal law and procedure cases involve people suing police officers, correctional officers, and other criminal justice personnel for causing harm or conducting stops, searches, or seizures without legal justification. Under the Civil Rights Act of 1871 as amended, a person may seek redress when a person acting under color of state law deprives a person of constitutional or federal rights pursuant to Title 42 U.S.C. §1983—the so-called §1983 claim. The statute under section 1983 is not a creation of federal rights but a vindication of rights established elsewhere: It allows people to sue in civil court professionals "who act under color of any [state] statute, ordinance, regulation, custom, or usage" in depriving another of "rights, privileges, or immunities secured by the Constitution and laws" of the United States.

> **Rule of Law: Federal law prohibits the deprivation of civil rights as well as provides criminal justice professionals limited protection from civil law suits.**

To establish a typical §1983 claim, the civilian must show that

1. The officer was acting under the color of state law, and

2. The officer's actions deprived the victim of rights protected by the laws or Constitution of the United States.

Courts usually first determine whether the person was acting in a private or professional capacity when the harm occurred, as "under color of state law" means acting in an official capacity.[44] Second, courts then determine if the person's constitutional rights were violated.

Immunity for Criminal Justice Professionals in §1983 Claims

Many criminal justice professionals, typically law enforcement and correctional officers, are entitled to **qualified immunity**, limited protection from civil lawsuits. Certain actors in the criminal justice system, legislators, judges, and prosecutors, enjoy **absolute immunity**, which is complete protection, and they cannot be sued for any harm caused by their acts committed and decisions made in the performance of their professional duties.[45] Pursuant to the U.S. Supreme Court case *Saucier v. Katz* (2001), the test for qualified immunity is, at the time the criminal justice professional (most always a police officer) acted, he

1. Acted reasonably, and

2. When he acted, the constitutional right in question must not have been clearly established.

The test for whether a right is "clearly established" is whether

a. The law prohibits the officer's acts, and

b. The reasonable officer knows his conduct is illegal under existing law.[46]

Let's examine what it means for a constitutional right to not have been "clearly established" for qualified immunity to attach. The Fourth Amendment protects people, not places, and grants someone's home the greatest protection from government intrusion. Afton Callahan sold methamphetamine in Utah, and police officers sent an informant inside Callahan's house to buy drugs. The informant had marked bills to buy the drugs and was wearing a concealed electronic listening device (a wire). When the sale was complete, the informant signaled the officers, who entered Callahan's home without a warrant and seized evidence of drug dealing later used to convict Callahan. Callahan brought a §1983 claim against the officers claiming they illegally entered his home without consent violating the Fourth Amendment.

In 2002 when police officers entered Callahan's home, the Sixth, Seventh, and Ninth federal courts of appeal and the state supreme courts of New Jersey and Wisconsin recognized the legal rule of "consent once removed." If you consent to having a guest in your home, your guest may give consent to others to enter your home; Callahan let the informant in (consent) who then consented to the police entry (once removed). Even though Utah and its federal circuit (Tenth) did not recognize the "consent once removed" rule, the U.S. Supreme Court found the officers were entitled to qualified immunity because the status of the law around the country when they entered Callahan's home was "not clearly established." In sum, if the status of the law under review is variable and shifting, then the professional is entitled to qualified immunity (*Pearson v. Callahan*, 2009).[47]

The case *District of Columbia v. Wesby* (2018), reprinted in part below, is a §1983 civil action against police officers who arrested a number of partygoers in the District of Columbia. The case involves many of the terms discussed in this chapter, for example, whether probable cause to arrest the partiers existed under the totality of the circumstances, what a reasonable officer could conclude or infer from the facts presented on entering the home, and the test for whether a constitutional right is not "clearly established" to cloak the officers with protection from lawsuits (immunity).

DISTRICT OF COLUMBIA V. WESBY, 138 S.CT. 577 (2018)

Supreme Court of the United States

Justice Thomas delivered the opinion of the Court. (9–0)

FACTS: Around 1 a.m. on March 16, 2008, the District's Metropolitan Police Department received a complaint about loud music and illegal activities at a house in Northeast D.C. After the officers knocked on the front door, they saw a man look out the window and then run upstairs. One of the partygoers opened the door, and the officers entered. They immediately observed that the inside of the house "was in disarray" and looked like "a vacant property."

The officers smelled marijuana and saw beer bottles and cups of liquor on the floor. In the living room, the officers found a makeshift strip club. Several women were wearing only bras and thongs, with cash tucked into their garter belts. The women were giving lap dances while other partygoers watched. Most of the onlookers were holding cash and cups of alcohol. After seeing the uniformed officers, many partygoers scattered into other parts of the house.

The officers found more debauchery upstairs. A naked woman and several men were in the bedroom. A bare mattress—the only one in the house—was on the floor, along with some lit candles and multiple open condom wrappers. The officers found one partygoer hiding in an upstairs closet, and another who had shut himself in the bathroom and refused to come out.

The officers found a total of 21 people in the house. After interviewing all 21, the officers did not get a clear or consistent story. Many partygoers said they were there for a bachelor party, but no one could identify the bachelor. Each of the partygoers claimed that someone had invited them to the house, but no one could say who. Two of the women working the party said that a woman named "Peaches" or

"Tasty" was renting the house and had given them permission to be there.

The officers then contacted the owner. He told them that he had been trying to negotiate a lease with Peaches, but they had not reached an agreement. He confirmed that he had not given Peaches (or anyone else) permission to be in the house—let alone permission to use it for a bachelor party. At that point, the officers arrested the 21 partygoers for unlawful entry. See D.C. Code §22-3302 (2008). The police transported the partygoers to the police station, where the lieutenant decided to charge them with disorderly conduct. See §22-1321. The partygoers were released, and the charges were eventually dropped. Respondents, 16 of the 21 partygoers, sued the District and five of the arresting officers. They sued the officers for false arrest under the Fourth Amendment, Rev. Stat. 1979, 42 U.S.C. §1983, and under District law.

ISSUE: [Were the partygoers arrested without probable cause and, if not, could the officers claim qualified immunity?]

HOLDING: [The arrests were supported by probable cause and the officers were entitled to qualified immunity.]

REASONING: To determine whether an officer had probable cause for an arrest, "we examine the events leading up to the arrest, and then decide 'whether these historical facts, viewed from the standpoint of an objectively reasonable police officer, amount to' probable cause." There is no dispute that the partygoers entered the house against the will of the owner. Nonetheless, the partygoers contend that the officers lacked probable cause to arrest them because the officers had no reason to believe that they "knew or should have known" their "entry was unwanted." We disagree. Considering the totality of the circumstances, the officers made an "entirely reasonable inference" that the partygoers were knowingly taking advantage of a vacant house as a venue for their late-night party.

Taken together, the condition of the house and the conduct of the partygoers allowed the officers to make several "common-sense conclusions about human behavior." Most homeowners do not live in near-barren houses. And most homeowners do not invite people over to use their living room as a strip club, to have sex in their bedroom, to smoke marijuana inside, and to leave their floors filthy. The officers could thus infer that the partygoers knew their party was not authorized.

A reasonable officer could infer that the partygoers' scattering and hiding was an indication that they knew they were not supposed to be there. Viewing these circumstances as a whole, a reasonable officer could conclude that there was probable cause to believe the partygoers knew they did not have permission to be in the house.

Under our precedents, officers are entitled to qualified immunity under §1983 unless (1) they violated a federal statutory or constitutional right, and (2) the unlawfulness of their conduct was "clearly established at the time." "Clearly established" means that, at the time of the officer's conduct, the law was "'sufficiently clear' that every 'reasonable official would understand that what he is doing'" is unlawful. In other words, existing law must have placed the constitutionality of the officer's conduct "beyond debate."

To be clearly established, a legal principle must have a sufficiently clear foundation in then-existing precedent. The rule must be "settled law," which means it is dictated by "controlling authority" or "a robust 'consensus of cases of persuasive authority.'" It is not enough that the rule is suggested by then-existing precedent. The precedent must be clear enough that every reasonable official would interpret it to establish the particular rule the plaintiff seeks to apply. Otherwise, the rule is not one that "every reasonable official" would know. This demanding standard protects "all but the plainly incompetent or those who knowingly violate the law."

CONCLUSION: Under these principles, we readily conclude that the officers here were entitled to qualified immunity. Even assuming the officers lacked actual probable cause to arrest the partygoers, the officers are entitled to qualified immunity because they "reasonably but mistakenly concluded that probable cause was present."

Government officials have a legal responsibility to care for those in their custody, whether arrested, detained, and incarcerated. The government has no legal responsibility, and therefore cannot be sued, when one citizen harms another. One case in which a citizen's §1983 claim was unsuccessful involved serial killer Jeffrey Dahmer. On May 27, 1991, two Milwaukee, Wisconsin, police officers, John Balcerzak and Joseph Gabrish, responded to a 9-1-1 call about an injured, bleeding "butt naked young boy."[48] Jeffrey Dahmer, the now-notorious serial killer, greeted police in the alley and told them that the injured boy was "John Hmong." He said that "Hmong" was his 19-year-old boyfriend who had wandered naked in the street while Dahmer went to get more beer. Dahmer invited police to his apartment to verify his story. Two teenage cousins who were on the street and had called emergency services tried to convince police that Dahmer was lying because they had seen the boy playing with earthworms in the rain. In the apartment, Dahmer showed police photographs of the boy, who, because of his disorientation was speaking only Lao. Officer Gabrish later recounted that Dahmer "appeared to be a normal individual" and they were convinced "all was well." The boy his neighbors tried to save was 14-year-old Konerak Sinthasomphone.[49] When the officers returned Sinthasomphone to Dahmer's care, Dahmer drilled holes in Konerak's head and then strangled him to death. Sinthasomphone's estate brought a §1983 claim against the officers and the city of Milwaukee for depriving Konerak's federal civil rights to due process and equal protection.[50] The federal court dismissed the Sinthasomphone family's claim because the police officers who encountered Konerak did not harm him, Dahmer did.

FEDERALISM AND STATES' RIGHTS

Federal Preemption of State Law

One aspect of the federal Constitution's Supremacy Clause is the federal preemption doctrine. The federal preemption doctrine establishes federal law will trump a state law that

Rule of Law: Federal
law preempts state law
when both governments
have laws controlling
the same issue.

Springboard for Discussion

The U.S. Supreme Court held in *Trump v. Hawaii* (2018) that the president has the authority to prevent people from designated countries from entering America. Do you think the executive or the legislative branch should have the power to define the conditions of entry to the United States?[54]

is *not* aligned with a federal objective. The increased enforcement of the nation's immigration laws has put the preemption doctrine in the national spotlight. The U.S. Constitution grants exclusive jurisdiction to the federal government to control the borders as a matter of national security. In 2010, the state of Arizona enacted Senate Bill 1070, which gave state and local law enforcement officers the authority to enforce federal immigration laws, made it a crime for people in the country illegally to not carry appropriate legal documents, and penalized those businesses that hired or otherwise profited from illegal immigration. The U.S. Department of Justice on behalf of the federal government sued Arizona for superseding (overruling) federal authority because if the federal government has made laws to control a matter (e.g., immigration), any inferior state laws on the same subject must fail. In deciding the case *Arizona v. United States* (2012), the U.S. Supreme Court struck down the sections of SB 1070 that required legal papers to travel within the state of Arizona and prosecuting people for obtaining employment in the state.[51] Left intact was law enforcement's ability, in the context of a routine criminal investigation, to try and determine suspects' immigration status. The high Court reminded Arizona that it is not ordinarily an arrestable offense to be in the country without authority and the proper remedy is a civil removal proceeding.

MAKING THE COURTROOM CONNECTION

When local and state police officers respond to a call they secure the crime scene, seek medical help, and possibly take care of children who are present. If a suspect is later found to be in the country illegally, U.S. Immigration and Customs Enforcement (ICE) is typically notified. Federal agents may or may not pick up the offender when agents make rounds to pick up federal suspects in local jails—it depends on the crime charged. A person not in the country legally but who is the victim of a crime may appeal to the police for a report to attach to form I-918, Petition for U Nonimmigrant Status, which provides "temporary immigration benefits to foreign nationals who are victims of qualifying criminal activity, and to their qualifying family members, as appropriate." Some jurisdictions (e.g., Seattle and Boston) refuse to assist federal immigration authorities because local victims may fear the police as proxy federal deportation authorities and not report crime to the police.[52] Such refusal has lead the executive branch to try and withhold federal community aid funds from the so-called "sanctuary cities" for their non-cooperation, but courts have ruled against the federal government.[53]

The Tenth Amendment and States' Rights

Springboard for Discussion

The U.S. Supreme Court has said in *Boyd v. United States* in 1886, "Illegitimate and unconstitutional practices get their first footing . . . by silent approaches and slight deviations from legal modes of procedure."[60] Do you think the *Murphy v. NCAA* (2018) case is an example of the principle announced in *Boyd*?

Can the federal government enforce state laws, and can the state enforce federal laws? The Constitution gives specific powers to the federal government, and the Tenth Amendment provides that "the powers not delegated to the United States by the Constitution, nor prohibited by it to the States, are reserved to the states respectively, or to the people." As Alexander Hamilton wrote in the *Federalist Papers*, which were written and published to enlist support from the colonies to ratify the U.S. Constitution, "The Constitution leaves in the possession of each State 'certain exclusive and very important portions of sovereign power.' Foremost among the prerogatives of sovereignty is the power to create and enforce a criminal code."[55] Most criminal law is state law. Each state government is said to have general "police power," which means enacting laws for the general health, safety, and welfare of its citizens, such as fixing roads, improving schools, or regulating conduct.[56]

In the wake of John W. Hinckley, Jr.'s 1981 assassination attempt on the life of President Ronald Reagan, a shooting that also grievously wounded Press Secretary James Brady, President Bill Clinton signed into the law the Brady Handgun Violence Prevention Act,[57] requiring gun dealers to conduct background checks on potential firearm purchasers. Because conducting background checks involve state actors spending time and money, sheriffs in Montana and Arizona challenged the federal law, in the *Printz v. United States* (1997) case.[58] The U.S. Supreme Court found in the states' favor holding that the federal government's attempted "commandeering" (officially take control) of state resources violated the Tenth Amendment.

In 2018 the high Court used the *Printz* precedent in deciding federal law could not stop states from betting on sport events. In striking down the federal Professional and Amateur Sports Protection Act (PASPA) which, with limited exceptions, outlawed sports betting across the country,[59] the high Court accepted New Jersey State's arguments that PASPA violated the "anticommandeering" principle by preventing New Jersey from enacting or repealing state laws authorizing legal gambling. In the case excerpt provided below, the Court traces the separation of powers on which our government is founded in striking down federal law as an intrusion on the states' power under the Tenth Amendment.

> **Rule of Law:** A Commerce Clause nexus is required for federal jurisdiction over crimes not uniquely federal.

MURPHY V. NATIONAL COLLEGIATE ATHLETIC ASSOCIATION, 584 U.S. ___ (2018)

Supreme Court of the United States

Justice Alito delivered the opinion of the Court. (7–2)

REASONING: The anticommandeering doctrine may sound arcane, but it is simply the expression of a fundamental structural decision incorporated into the Constitution, i.e., the decision to withhold from Congress the power to issue orders directly to the States. When the original States declared their independence, they claimed the powers inherent in sovereignty—in the words of the Declaration of Independence, the authority "to do all . . . Acts and Things which Independent States may of right do."

The legislative powers granted to Congress are sizable, but they are not unlimited. The Constitution confers on Congress not plenary legislative power but only certain enumerated powers. Therefore, all other legislative power is reserved for the States, as the Tenth Amendment confirms. And conspicuously absent from the list of powers given to Congress is the power to issue direct orders to the governments of the States. The anticommandeering doctrine simply represents the recognition of this limit on congressional authority.

Justice O'Connor's opinion for the Court [in *New York v. U.S.*, 505 U.S. 144 (1992)] traced [the anticommandeering] rule to the basic structure of government established under the Constitution. The Constitution, she noted, "confers upon Congress the power to regulate individuals, not States." The Constitutional Convention considered plans that would have preserved this basic structure, but it rejected them in favor of a plan under which "Congress would exercise its legislative authority directly over individuals rather than over States." As to what this structure means with regard to Congress's authority to control state legislatures, New York was clear and emphatic. The opinion recalled that "no Member of the Court ha[d] ever suggested" that even "a particularly strong federal interest" "would enable Congress to command a state government to enact state regulation."

[T]he rule serves as "one of the Constitution's structural protections of liberty" . . . the Constitution divides authority between federal and state governments for the protection of individuals." "'[A] healthy balance of power between the States and the Federal Government [reduces] the risk of tyranny and abuse from either front.'" Second, the anticommandeering rule promotes political accountability. When Congress itself regulates, the responsibility for the benefits and burdens of the regulation is apparent. Voters who like or dislike the effects of the regulation know who to credit or blame. By contrast, if a State imposes regulations only because it has been commanded to do so by Congress, responsibility is blurred.

[T]he anticommandeering principle prevents Congress from shifting the costs of regulation to the States. If Congress enacts a law and requires enforcement by the Executive Branch, it must appropriate the funds needed to administer the program. It is pressured to weigh the expected benefits of the program against its costs. But if Congress can compel the States to enact and enforce its program, Congress need not engage in any such analysis.

(Continued)

(Continued)

The PASPA provision at issue here—prohibiting state authorization of sports gambling—violates the anticommandeering rule. That provision unequivocally dictates what a state legislature may and may not do. And this is true under either our interpretation or that advocated by respondents and the United States. In either event, state legislatures are put under the direct control of Congress. It is as if federal officers were installed in state legislative chambers and were armed with the authority to stop legislators from voting on any offending proposals. A more direct affront to state sovereignty is not easy to imagine.

The legalization of sports gambling is a controversial subject. Supporters argue that legalization will produce revenue for the States and critically weaken illegal sports betting operations, which are often run by organized crime. Opponents contend that legalizing sports gambling will hook the young on gambling, encourage people of modest means to squander their savings and earnings, and corrupt professional and college sports. The legalization of sports gambling requires an important policy choice, but the choice is not ours to make. Congress can regulate sports gambling directly, but if it elects not to do so, each State is free to act on its own. Our job is to interpret the law Congress has enacted and decide whether it is consistent with the Constitution. PASPA is not. PASPA "regulate[s] state governments' regulation" of their citizens. The Constitution gives Congress no such power.

The judgment of the Third Circuit is reversed. It is so ordered.

Federal Jurisdiction and the Commerce Clause

Congressional power to create and define criminal law is restricted by the specific language of the Constitution. The **Commerce Clause** grants Congress the power to, among other things, "regulate commerce with foreign nations and among the several states, and with the Indian Tribes."[61] The Supreme Court has held that if a certain interstate (between states) activity or intrastate (within the state) activity affects interstate commerce, which is the buying and selling of goods and services, the federal government may obtain jurisdiction to regulate the activity.[62] The U.S. Supreme Court has found a Commerce Clause nexus to support federal jurisdiction to enforce civil rights laws outlawing racial discrimination at hotels that accept out-of-state travelers, or at restaurants whose supplies cross state lines, or regulating coal mining or wheat production that occurred within a state but affected national markets.[63]

As an example of a federal law struck down in part for failing the required Commerce Clause nexus involves the case of Alfonso Lopez. Lopez was 18 years old and in the 12th grade when he carried a concealed handgun and bullets to school in San Antonio, Texas, in violation of the federal Gun Free School Zones Act of 1990. Lopez was convicted in federal court and, on appeal, argued the federal government had no jurisdiction to enact the "School Zones" law because carrying a gun in a public school has no arguable connection to interstate commerce and, therefore, the law was illegal. The U.S. Supreme Court agreed with Lopez. To determine whether federal jurisdiction exists via the Commerce Clause, federal courts examine whether the state criminal activity

1. Uses channels of interstate commerce (planes, trains, and automobiles)

2. Uses instrumentalities of interstate commerce (wire transfer, telephones), and

3. Is an activity that, in the aggregate, "substantially affect[s] interstate commerce."

The Court declared the law did not implicate using interstate channels or instrumentalities and, if the "School Zones" law was to be a legal law under the Constitution, Lopez's gun possession at school would have to have a "substantial affect" on interstate commerce. Finding no such effect, the Court said to find in the government's favor would "convert congressional authority under the Commerce Clause to a general police power of the sort retained by the States," which the Court refused to do because the "lines between national and local power to prosecute crime would be forever blurred."[64] Similarly, in striking down portions of the federal Violence Against

Women Act for failing a Commerce Clause nexus with campus sexual assaults and retaining police power for the states, the Court stated:

> The regulation and punishment of intrastate violence that is not directed at instrumentalities, channels, or goods involved in interstate commerce has always been the province of the States. . . . Indeed, we can think of no better example of the police power, which the Founders denied the National Government and reposed in the States, than the suppression of violent crime and vindication of its victims.[65]

How does Commerce Clause jurisdiction interact with states' rights protected by the Tenth Amendment? In 2002, federal drug agents seized Angel Raich and Diane Monson's marijuana plants even after deciding that their possession was legal under California's medicinal marijuana law. The women sued the federal government for having no jurisdiction over state drug laws, and the federal government won in *Gonzales v. Raich* (2005). Below shows an excerpt of the case.

GONZALES V. RAICH, 125 S.CT. 2195 (2005)

United States Supreme Court

Justice Stevens delivered the opinion of the Court. (5–4)

FACTS: Respondents Angel Raich and Diane Monson are California residents who suffer from a variety of serious medical conditions and have used on a daily basis medical marijuana pursuant to [California law which allows the legal use of marijuana for medicinal use].

On August 15, 2002, county deputy sheriffs and agents from the federal DEA came to Monson's home. After a thorough investigation, the county officials concluded that her use of marijuana was entirely lawful as a matter of California law. Nevertheless, after a 3-hour standoff, the federal agents seized and destroyed all six of her cannabis plants. [Raich and Monson] thereafter brought this action against the Attorney General of the United States and the head of the DEA . . . prohibiting the enforcement of the federal Controlled Substances Act to the extent it prevents them from possessing, obtaining, or manufacturing cannabis for their personal medical use.

ISSUE: [Does Congress' power to regulate interstate markets for medicinal substances encompass those markets that are supplied with drugs produced and consumed locally?]

HOLDING: [Yes, the federal government has the power under the Commerce Clause to prohibit the local cultivation and use of marijuana grown and used legally under California law.]

REASONING: Shortly after taking office in 1969, President Nixon declared a national "war on drugs." As the first campaign of that war, Congress set out to enact legislation that would consolidate various drug laws on the books into a comprehensive statute, provide meaningful regulation over legitimate sources of drugs to prevent diversion into illegal channels, and strengthen law enforcement tools against the traffic in illicit drugs. That effort culminated in the passage of the Comprehensive Drug Abuse Prevention and Control Act of 1970 [CSA]. The main objectives of the CSA were to conquer drug abuse and to control the legitimate and illegitimate traffic in controlled substances.

[Raich and Monson] argue that the CSA's categorical prohibition of the manufacture and possession of marijuana as applied to the intrastate [within one state] manufacture and possession of marijuana for medical purposes pursuant to California law exceeds Congress' authority under the Commerce Clause. Our decision in [*Wickard v. Filburn* (1942)] is of particular relevance.

In *Wickard*, we upheld the application of regulations promulgated under the Agriculture Adjustment Act of 1938, which were designed to control the volume of wheat moving in interstate and foreign commerce in order to avoid surpluses and consequent abnormally low prices. Filburn [sowed 23 acres of wheat rather than the federal limit of 11 acres] intending to use the excess by consuming it on his own farm. Filburn argued that [Congress had no authority to regulate crop production not intended for any commerce. In rejecting Filburn's argument, the Court

(Continued)

(Continued)

wrote] the effect of the statute before us is to restrict the amount which may be produced for market. That Filburn's own contribution to the demand for wheat may be trivial by itself is not enough to remove him from the scope of federal regulation . . .

Wickard thus establishes that Congress can regulate purely intrastate activity that is not itself "commercial" if it concludes that failure to regulate that class of activity would undercut the regulation of the interstate market in that commodity. The similarities between this case and *Wickard* are striking. The diversion of homegrown marijuana tends to frustrate the federal interest in eliminating commercial transactions in the interstate market in their entirety. In both cases, the regulation is squarely within Congress' commerce power because production of the commodity meant for home consumption, be it wheat or marijuana, has a substantial effect on supply and demand in the national market for that commodity.

CONCLUSION: [By operation of the Commerce Clause, the federal government can regulate intrastate cultivation and use of the controlled substance marijuana.]

The Court's rationale in *Raich* accepted the proposition that locally grown marijuana does *not* involve any interstate commerce. That is, if all the dirt, water, and sunlight used to grow the marijuana seed into the plant were local to California, assuming the seed is a few plants removed from the original plant imported from another country, there is no effect on interstate commerce. By relying on the Supreme Court precedent regulating homegrown wheat in *Wickard*, the Court reasoned by analogy that illegal drugs grown and consumed locally (intrastate) may affect the supply and demand of illegal drugs in other states. Congress has the authority under the Commerce Clause to make marijuana possession and use illegal, even if legal under state law. Limited enforcement resources explain why the federal government does not shut down dispensaries in Colorado, California, and other states where the sale and use of marijuana is legal.

SUMMARY

1. You will understand the sources of law, where to find the law, and how precedent controls future court decisions. Federal and state constitutions, judge-made common law, and statutes enacted by legislatures, are subject to interpretation by courts. The nondelegation doctrine says Congress can share its power subject to an "intelligible principle" to limit the discretion of an administrative agency's regulations, which often have the force of law. Article I of the U.S. Constitution established the legislative branch, which makes laws; Article II established the executive branch and entrusts to the president and the federal government the responsibility for enforcing the laws; and Article III established the Supreme Court, which granted for itself through the case *Marbury v. Madison* (1803), the authority of judicial review to invalidate the acts of the other two branches. The Bill of Rights is a set of amendments to the Constitution designed to protect citizens from government abuses.

    The three branches of government ensure a separation of powers within the government, and each branch can check the unrestrained power of the coordinate branches. Equal protection is the concept of treating everyone equally under the law. There are two schools of thought on interpreting the constitution: by the original intent and meaning of the words when enacted versus a flexible perspective yielding to today's sociopolitical realities.

2. You will be able to articulate core legal principles found in criminal law and procedure cases, such as due process and the reasonable person. Procedural justice is about treating people fairly and giving them a voice in the judicial process. All lawyers, judges, and law enforcement are bound by a code of ethics that guide their behavior in criminal cases. Cases have a common core of principles such as (a) due process, which guarantees a fair trial; (b) the reasonable person, whose behavior is judged by prudent conduct that must be (c) objectively reasonable, as if everyone watching a movie would agree the conduct is acceptable under the (d) totality of the circumstances, which is looking at all the circumstances under which the person made his decision and whether or not he acted in (e) good

faith, which means he came to the situation with "clean hands" and not an evil motive, which may lead to a (f) harmless error in a court case (a mistake that would not have changed the outcome), or a (g) reversible error, which would have changed the trial's outcome.

3. You will know the actors in the criminal justice system and the purposes of punishment. Although the offender is facing deprivation of life and liberty at the conclusion of a criminal trial, victims have a similar Bill of Rights to participate in the criminal trial process that is controlled by the prosecutor who has discretion in deciding who to charge and for what crime, which is largely dependent on a thorough criminal investigation conducted by law enforcement. Notable theories in criminology include (a) the social learning theory, indicating crime is learned; (b) the strain theory, which holds if people cannot legally achieve goals, they turn to unacceptable ones; (c) social control theory, which says a community that cares for one another can prevent crime; (d) labeling theory, which infers if you call someone a bad actor that person will become one; and (e) conflict theory, wherein the strong control justice for the weak.

The types of punishment are (a) incarceration in prison; (b) deterrence in using the defendant as an example to prevent others from committing crimes; (c) restitution to pay back society; (d) restorative justice, which is the community working with the offender to make the victim whole; and (e) rehabilitation, which is teaching the offender life skills to reenter society. The purposes of punishment were explored in sentencing the elderly clients to probation in *United States v. Brewer* (2013). Defense counsel is bound to represent their clients with all zeal and fidelity, helped by the law protecting attorney–client conversations as confidential. The judge is to be neutral and detached in hearing cases. A court's jurisdiction (power to hear cases) determines the type of cases a judge will hear. Specialty courts, such as juvenile and drug courts, treat offenders identified by certain traits to lower recidivism.

4. You will understand how federal law protects citizen rights and the corresponding immunity for criminal justice professionals (police officers, correctional officers). If criminal justice professionals deprive a person of a constitutional right as explained in the case *District of Columbia v. Wesby* (2018), they may bring a civil lawsuit pursuant to 42 U.S.C. §1983. To obtain qualified immunity, the professional must have acted reasonably and have violated a right that was not clearly established by court precedent, prior court decisions controlling future cases through the doctrine of *stare decisis*.

5. You will be able to explain the role of federalism in controlling state criminal justice decisions. Federalism is the dual sharing of power between the federal and state governments. Federal law is superior to and preempts state law, such as in the area of immigration. Most criminal law is state law even though the Supremacy Clause says when the Supreme Court interprets the Constitution, it is the final word. The federal government derives its power only from the Constitution, and those powers not delegated to the federal government are left to the states and the people pursuant to the Tenth Amendment. The case *Murphy v. NCAA* (2018) reaffirmed the police power of the states to regulate the health and safety of its own citizens against federal overreach. In this case the U.S. Supreme Court, through the "anticommandeering principle," held invalid federal laws outlawing state gambling. The federal government obtains jurisdiction over state criminal matters by operation of the Commerce Clause illustrated by the *Gonzales v. Raich* (2005) case establishing federal supremacy over state laws legalizing marijuana use.

Go back to the beginning of the chapter and reread the news excerpts associated with the learning objectives. Test yourself to determine if you can understand the material covered in the text in the context of the news.

KEY TERMS AND PHRASES

absolute immunity 25
administrative regulations 5
advice and consent 5
appellant 9
appellee 9
Article I of the Constitution 4
Article II of the Constitution 5
Article III of the Constitution 5
attorney–client privilege 21
Bill of Rights 6

case brief 9
case law 7
Commerce Clause 30
common law 7
conflict theory 18
criminal law 3
criminal procedure 3
deterrence 17
due process 12
equal protection 7

federal preemption 27
federalism 4
Fourteenth Amendment 6
good faith 14
harmless error 15
holding 9
incarceration 17
incorporation 6
intelligible principle 5
judicial review 6

PROBLEM-SOLVING EXERCISES

1. The law of U.S. citizenship for babies born to American citizens overseas requires the married American citizen parent to establish physical presence in America for at least 5 years prior to the overseas birth. The physical presence rule was extended from married couples to unwed U.S. citizen fathers. For unwed U.S. citizen mothers, however, the 5-year requirement was reduced to 1 year. Luis Ramón Morales-Santana was born in the Dominican Republic and his unwed U.S. citizen father was 20 days short of the 5-year physical presence rule for Luis to claim U.S. citizenship rights. When immigration officials sought to remove Luis from the United States as a noncitizen because his father's citizenship status did not transmit to Luis because of the failure to meet the time requirements, Luis sued because the law treated men and women differently. Which side will win? (**ROL: Equal Protection Clause**)

2. Law enforcement was called to the scene of a domestic disturbance in Denver, Colorado, where it is legal to possess one ounce of marijuana for personal use. On arrival, the officer learned that the source of the dispute was Brad smoking marijuana in front of the couple's children. Brad willingly showed the officer the bag of marijuana he was smoking. The officer knew that the amount of marijuana contained in the bag was legal to possess for personal use, but not by much.

   The officer has now entered the prosecutor's office to discuss whether (a) Brad should be prosecuted for having too much marijuana under state law, and (b) Brad should be turned over to the federal DEA, which can prosecute Brad in federal court for having any amount of marijuana for personal use. How should the case be resolved? (**ROL: Prosecutorial discretion, Tenth Amendment, Supremacy and Commerce clauses**)

3. Police were investigating three people suspected of committing a string of residential burglaries. Police intercepted one suspect, Claire, who admitted that Richard drove Claire and her friend Rachel around neighborhoods looking for houses to burglarize. Richard drove an Infiniti with Texas plates. Police saw Richard driving around, stopping and letting Rachel out in a neighborhood. Richard parked on a corner and was using the Internet on his handheld tablet when police approached and arrested him on suspicion of burglary. Richard is now suing the officers in a §1983 action, and the officers in turn have claimed qualified immunity. How should the case be resolved? (**ROL: §1983 claim, qualified immunity, objectively reasonable, *Wesby* precedent**)

2

THE CRIMINAL TRIAL PROCESS

Go to the end of the chapter. Skim the key terms and phrases and read the summary closely. Come back and look at the following news excerpts to focus your reading throughout the chapter to follow a criminal defendant from pretrial investigation to sentencing by examining the case of Dzhokhar Tsarnaev, convicted of a 2013 terrorist bombing near the Boston Marathon finish line. Tsarnaev's case is used to illustrate the pretrial identification process, the formal bringing of charges against a suspect, the constitutional mandates of evidence disclosure and sharing (called discovery), jury selection, the order of a criminal trial, and presentation of evidence, with a unique focus on a death-penalty case. The chapter also gives the courtroom perspective of plea bargaining in exchange for testimony or the government's recommendation for a lenient sentence.

WHY THIS CHAPTER MATTERS TO YOU	THE LEARNING OBJECTIVES AS REFLECTED IN THE NEWS
After you have read this chapter: **Learning Objective 1:** You will understand the requirements and pitfalls of the pretrial identification process.	A man who spent 21 years behind bars for murder was set free Wednesday after prosecutors abandoned his conviction, saying their office improperly withheld information and allowed a mistaken impression that a wounded eyewitness implicated him. The eyewitness, who'd been shot in the robbery, identified Washington in a 1996 lineup as one of the men involved. But before testifying at the grand jury, the witness clarified to a prosecutor that she just recognized Washington as a neighbor, not as one of the robbers, the prosecutor's office said. (Associated Press, July 12, 2017)
Learning Objective 2: You will be able to articulate the legal requirements of discovery and the definition of exculpatory evidence.	The leader of a Massachusetts crime lab that certifies the reliability of drunken-driving breath tests has been fired after a report found the office routinely withheld exculpatory evidence from defense lawyers since 2011. Melissa O'Meara, who was technical leader of the Office of Alcohol Testing, was fired on Monday. The investigation was prompted by lawyers representing about 750 defendants who complained in a lawsuit that the office was withholding documents about the maintenance and calibration of the breath test machines . . . the office withheld worksheets and documents that sometimes showed a device had failed to calibrate at some point during certification, or that showed how many times the device had been repaired . . . the office's discovery responses "appeared to have been designed to minimize disclosure." (*American Bar Association Journal*, October 17, 2017)

(Continued)

(Continued)

WHY THIS CHAPTER MATTERS TO YOU	THE LEARNING OBJECTIVES AS REFLECTED IN THE NEWS
Learning Objective 3: You can distinguish the various steps taken before the trial, including the plea bargaining process.	A Virginia man has pleaded guilty in a 2017 drunken driving crash that killed an 18-year-old Chesapeake high school student and critically injured her friend. The *Virginian-Pilot* reports that Jerode Demetrius Johnson entered conditional guilty pleas Tuesday to aggravated DUI manslaughter, DUI maiming, felony hit and run, possession of cocaine and driving on a suspended license. The conditional plea allows him the right to appeal certain issues. (CBS19 News [VA], May 2, 2018)
Learning Objective 4: You will be able to explain the mechanics of a criminal trial and the different types of evidence.	The "Golden State Killer" was meticulous at his crime scenes over the course of a decade and in several cities, leaving scant evidence for police. There were no fingerprints. Few saw his face. And what he did leave—his DNA—was, at the time, not useful to police. Four decades later, with far better DNA technology and widespread use of it, that genetic material became critical to possibly solving one of the most vexing serial murder cases in U.S. history. Authorities said they were able to link a suspect to the string of crimes by using a genealogy service to trace the genetic material to one man they believe killed at least a dozen people: Joseph James DeAngelo. (*Washington Post*, April 27, 2018)
Learning Objective 5: You will identify how a criminal case gets to the U.S. Supreme Court.	Lost in the hoopla surrounding Bill Cosby's criminal conviction is an interesting defamation suit brought by one of his accusers. Earlier this week, that accuser, Katherine McKee, asked the United States Supreme Court to consider her appeal. The question is whether Ms. McKee made herself a "public figure" by accusing Cosby of sexual assault . . . The Supreme Court doesn't have to hear every case brought before it. In fact, it declines to hear the overwhelming majority and grants "*certiorari*" only a fraction of the time. In her petition she notes she has not become a prominent advocate in any public controversy . . . and has consistently maintained her privacy other than to say, as many other women have said, "me too." (Cincinnati.com, May 2, 2018)

Chapter-Opening Case Study: *United States v. Dzhokhar Tsarnaev*

From all accounts, in his spare time at the University of Massachusetts, Dartmouth campus, 19-year-old Dzhokhar Tsarnaev liked to smoke marijuana and listen to music.[1] Dzhokhar grew up in the former Soviet Republic of Kyrgyzstan and came to America when he was 8 years old, the same age as Martin Richards when, on April 15, 2013, Dzhokhar killed Richards by detonating a pressure cooker bomb on Boylston Street during the final stretch of the 117th running of the Boston Marathon. The bomb that killed Martin was the second bomb to explode that day. Five minutes earlier, Dzhokhar's older brother, Tamerlan, had detonated a similar device located close to the marathon finish line. In what now seems a prophetic gesture, the brothers Dzhokhar and Tamerlan took the oath to become naturalized citizens in 2012 on September 11.

Tamerlan's bomb killed Krystle Campbell and Lingzi Lu, both in their 20s. In addition to the three deaths, 260 people were grievously injured. Dzhokhar's college friends, Kazakhstan natives Azamat Tazhayakov and Dias Kadyrbayev and Massachusetts native Robel Phillipos, saw police-broadcast photos of Dzhokhar, who they called "Jahar," and then emptied his dorm room. On the run, the brothers shot and killed Massachusetts Institute of Technology (MIT) police officer Sean Collier and, after a shootout with law enforcement, Dzhokhar got into an SUV to escape and ran over Tamerlan, killing him. Dzhokhar hid in a covered boat parked in a driveway. When Dzhokhar was captured one day later, law enforcement took a piece of the boat in which he had scribbled, "Know you are fighting men who look into the barrel of your gun and see heaven, now how can you compete with that." **(Rule of Law [ROL]: The defendant's hearsay statements are admitted at trial as party-opponent statements.)**

When the trio of Dzhokhar's friends were later caught and charged with obstruction of justice, friend Kadyrbayev pleaded guilty pursuant to a plea agreement. This agreement included the requirement that Kadyrbayev would testify against Dzhokhar at Dzhokhar's trial. Dzhokhar was charged with 30 federal crimes, 17 of which carried the possibility of a death sentence, namely, conspiracy to use a weapon of mass destruction resulting in death and bombing a public place resulting in death. **(ROL: First-degree murder + aggravating circumstances = death eligibility.)**

Jury selection took 2 months. **(ROL: *Voir dire* is the questioning of potential jurors to assess if they can be fair and impartial in deciding the defendant's case.)** Massachusetts does not have the death penalty, but the federal government does, and the United States prosecuted Dzhokhar in federal court. During Dzhokhar's trial, the prosecution introduced testimonial, demonstrative, expert and physical evidence, including Dzhokhar's message in the boat. Dzhokhar was convicted of all 30 counts. On June 24, 2015, Dzhokhar was sentenced to death.

PRETRIAL IDENTIFICATION PROCEDURES

There are many ways a defendant may be identified as the perpetrator of a crime before trial. Identifying suspects is a three-step process: perceiving, remembering, and reporting.[2] Because some methods of pretrial identification are unduly suggestive and may impermissibly convince a witness that the suspect is the one who committed the crime even though he may be innocent, there are legal protections and technical considerations that protect a suspect from being misidentified as the perpetrator.

Eyewitness Identification

An eyewitness is a person who saw a crime being committed. Eyewitness identification is the process by which the eyewitness identifies the suspect or the defendant as the actual perpetrator of the crime. Eyewitness identification is very potent evidence in court; when an eyewitness takes the witness stand, points to the defendant, and says, "That's the person who did it!" it has a strong impact on the jury. In recent years, though, many experts and psychological studies have indicated that eyewitness testimony may be unreliable and the results of a mistaken identification damaging. Early in the Boston Marathon bombing investigation, the *New York Post* published a photograph of two men wearing backpacks with the heading "Feds seek this duo pictured at the Boston Marathon." The two men later identified as Salaheddin Barhoum and Yassine Zaimi sued the *Post* for the harm suffered by the misidentification.[3] Out of the first 100 people exonerated and found not guilty due to DNA analysis, 98 had been convicted after being identified by an eyewitness as the one who committed the crime. Research shows that, at trial, the confidence an eyewitness expresses in making the identification is the single most important factor of whether or not the jury believes the eyewitness's identification of the defendant. The primary criticism of eyewitness confidence at trial is that "accuracy of description is a rather poor predictor of accuracy of identification. Even more problematic is that biased line-up procedures can actually lead eyewitnesses to overestimate how good of a view they had of the perpetrator as well as lead them to develop false confidence."[4]

> Rule of Law: If the pretrial identification procedure is too suggestive, the identification may not be introduced against the defendant at trial.

The evolution of the legal standard relating to the admissibility of an eyewitness identification of a suspect was clarified by two important decisions that remain the legal standard today, *Neil v. Biggers* (1972) and *Manson v. Braithwaite* (1977).[5] In *Biggers*, the victim was grabbed from behind in her home and screamed. When she screamed her daughter came running. The assailant warned her to "tell her [daughter] to shut up, or I'll kill you both." The intruder then took the victim two blocks away and raped her. The police apprehended Biggers as a suspect. The victim could not identify the rapist from photographs or a line-up but identified Biggers as her attacker after police told him to say "shut up or I'll kill you." The high Court determined that even if an identification was unduly suggestive, it would be admissible if, under the totality of the circumstances, the identification was reliable.

How does a court determine whether the police essentially delivered the suspect to the witness to get the witness to identify the suspect creating an unduly suggestive identification that may be excluded at trial or whether the witness did, indeed, identify the suspect as the perpetrator without any outside influence? The U.S. Supreme Court addressed this issue in *Foster v. California* (1969), where the Court found the authorities essentially spoon-fed the witness during the identification process that Foster was the man who had robbed a Western Union office. The witness was an office manager, and officers arranged the following opportunities for the manager to identify the culprit:

1. Put Foster in a line-up in which Foster was 6 inches taller than everyone else.

2. In the line-up, Foster was wearing the clothes the manager said the robber had worn.

3. Still unsure Foster was the robber, officers brought Foster in to speak with the manager.

4. When the manager was still unsure Foster was "the man," officers conducted another line-up where Foster was the only person from the original line-up.

The manager identified Foster in court as the robber, and Foster was convicted. Overturning his conviction on appeal, the high Court found that under the totality of the circumstances, the repeated and suggestive nature of the identification procedure made it all but inevitable that the witness would identify Foster as "the man," which violated Foster's due process rights.[6]

Even if an identification is suggestive, it may still be admissible if reliable.[7] Courts use a five-part test called the *Biggers* test to determine whether the eyewitness identification is reliable and, therefore, admissible against the defendant in court.

1. The opportunity of the eyewitness to view the offender at the time of the crime

2. The witness's degree of attention (during the crime)

3. The accuracy of the witness's prior description of the offender

4. The level of certainty displayed by the witness at the identification procedure

5. The length of time between the crime and the identification procedure

In *Braithwaite*, the U.S. Supreme Court established an additional test to determine eyewitness reliability. The *Braithwaite* test has two prongs. First, the Court looked at whether the identification procedure itself was unduly suggestive. If the identification was unduly suggestive, the Court moved to the second prong, which evaluated for reliability the circumstances under which the eyewitness made the initial identification. The facts of *Braithwaite* are illustrative. A police officer made a positive out-of-court photo identification of Braithwaite 2 days after the officer had conducted an undercover purchase of drugs from Braithwaite. The prosecution and defense both agreed that the identification was improperly suggestive, but the Supreme Court held that under the totality of the circumstances, the identification was reliable. The *Braithwaite* decision reaffirmed the *Biggers* case holding and confirmed that "reliability is the linchpin in determining the admissibility of identification testimony. . . . The factors to be considered are set out in *Biggers*."

Photo Arrays, Line-Ups, and Show-Ups

The photo array, also called the photospread, is a collection of at least six photographs of similar-looking people that is shown to the eyewitness in an effort to identify the offender. If the witness does identify the suspect from the photospread, the officer is to keep the entire spread and initial, date, and tag it as evidence for use at a later possible trial. In a line-up, at least six similar-looking people are brought into a room where the witness can view those in the line-up but those in the line-up cannot see the witness. In a show-up, the suspect is the only person brought before the eyewitness to answer the question, "Is this the guy who did it or not?" Most people believe that only guilty people are arrested and, therefore, that if a suspect is in handcuffs, he must be the one who committed the crime. One of the main problems with false identifications, according to research, is that eyewitnesses identify people in a line-up or a photo array who look most like the offender relative to the other people in the spread. For example, if a photo array contains six White men with long moustaches, and the real perpetrator was a White male with a long mustache, the eyewitness is going to pick out from the photo array the one who looks most like the offender, relative to (in relation to) the other five men. This process of making a relative judgment where the person in the photo array looks most like the offender, but may not actually be the offender, means that the victim may feel confident about his or her choice even if the person they chose is innocent. According to eyewitness identification researcher Gary Wells, the primary antidote to the relative judgment process is to show the witness sequential photos (one after the other)—so that the eyewitness views only one photo at a time and makes an absolute decision that the person in the photo is, or is not, the suspect before viewing another person's photo. The sequential showing of photographs is an inexpensive and relatively easy way to, according to Wells, reduce mistaken identification by 50%.[8] Photo 2.1 illustrates the difference between the simultaneous identification method and the more reliable sequential identification method, by using mug shots of famous men. If singer Johnny Cash were the culprit and the traditional six-person photo array were used, a witness might choose singer Jerry Lee Lewis as the suspect, because Lewis looks like Cash relative to the other five men, singers Frank Sinatra, Jim Morrison, David Crosby, Sid Vicious, and Elvis Presley. The better way to conduct the photo array is to show the witness the photos sequentially, first Elvis, then Crosby, and so forth, and after each viewing ask the witness to make an absolute decision—is this the guy?

The Department of Justice issued a January 6, 2017, memorandum to all federal law enforcement officers on how to conduct photo arrays, and students should study the federal standards for applicability in the field. The legal remedy when an identification made pretrial is too suggestive is the exclusion of that identification from trial. The eyewitness can still identify the defendant in court as the person who committed the crime but only if this identification has an independent source other than the suggestive identification procedure.

The Line-Up and Right to Counsel

If the right to counsel attaches because formal adversarial proceedings have begun against a suspect, usually once a

Springboard for Discussion

Facial recognition technology is a computer algorithm that captures an image of a person's face and matches the person with a stored image in a database. Facebook's identity recognition technology is powerful because their algorithm is constantly improving every time one of the social media giant's 1.65 billion users uploads or tags a selfie or photos of friends. Facebook claims their technology can accurately identify someone 98% of the time. Do you think Facebook should lend its facial recognition expertise to law enforcement to identify suspects and solve cases, particularly when witnesses are reluctant to come forward and testify?

Rule of Law: Once the right to counsel attaches, the suspect has a right to counsel at the line-up.

▶ Photo 2.1

Top (left to right): Frank Sinatra, Jim Morrison, David Crosby. Middle: Sid Vicious, Jerry Lee Lewis, Elvis Presley. Bottom: Johnny Cash.

In the case *Perry v. New Hampshire* (2012),[9] the defendant claimed that, given the inherent unreliability of the pretrial identification process, it was a violation of his due process rights not to have the judge act as a gatekeeper to first determine if the officers "got the right guy." The high Court disagreed and held the jury is the proper body to conclude whether the witness made the correct identification. Which side of the issue do you agree with and why?

suspect is formally charged, the suspect is entitled to have her lawyer notified, and present, before the suspect is placed in a line-up. If the right to counsel is violated, the line-up identification of the defendant cannot be used at trial, as held in *United States v. Wade* (1967).[10] Students should note where in the criminal trial process the pretrial identification occurs. Most suspect identifications are conducted before charges are filed when no right to a lawyer has attached to protect the suspect.

THE ADVERSARY SYSTEM

America's adversarial system of justice is designed to discover the truth where two sides, the prosecution and defense, go against each other with the judge as referee. There are inherent advantages to the government prosecuting citizens for crimes and corresponding protections for defendants from abuses by the government. Table 2.1 summarizes these powers and protections.[11]

Prosecutorial Discretion and the Death-Penalty Decision

As discussed in Chapter 1, the prosecutor is "the single most powerful figure in the administration of criminal justice," for only the prosecution decides whether to make a first-degree murder charge a capital case in death-penalty jurisdictions.[12] Every first-degree murder case could, ostensibly, be a death-penalty case. Death cases are first-degree murder plus special circumstances, or aggravating circumstances, which justify a longer or harsher sentence for the defendant. Also included in death-penalty statutes is a list of mitigating circumstances that are introduced by the defendant at trial. Mitigating circumstances explain, but rarely excuse, the crime and may justify a less harsh sentence for the offender. In a death-penalty case, mitigators may convince a jury to decide that a life without parole sentence is more appropriate for the defendant. In the chapter-opening case study, defense counsel argued to the jury the mitigating circumstance that Dzhokhar Tsarnaev was under the dominion and control of his older brother, Tamerlan, who enticed the easy-going college student into the life of a radical jihadist. The argument was successful in a similar case of terrorism committed by 42-year-old John Muhammad and 18-year-old Lee Boyd Malvo, known as the D.C. Snipers, convicted of random killings in Maryland, Virginia, and Washington, D.C., in October 2002. Both were tried for capital murder. Muhammad was sentenced to death and eventually executed in 2009, whereas Malvo received a life without parole sentence based on the mitigating circumstance that, as a teenager, he had been under the dominion and control of the father-figure Muhammad for years. In Tsarnaev's case, however, the same argument in mitigation did not sway the jury, and they sentenced Tsarnaev to death.

Rule of Law: The formula for the death penalty is first-degree murder + aggravating circumstances = the offender is "death eligible."

Table 2.1 Prosecution Powers and Corresponding Defense Protections

Prosecution Powers	Defense Protections
Decides who to charge and what to charge	Cannot be tried for the same crime twice by the same sovereign (government body)
In a death-penalty case, can exclude all jurors who are opposed to capital punishment	Is protected against the state removing jurors based on race or gender
Can generate testimony for trial through the offer of plea bargains	Can compel the testimony of witnesses for the defense through the court's subpoena power
Gets first and last bite of the apple at trial in opening and closing statements	Need do nothing at trial because the burden of proving guilt rests solely with the government

A death-penalty trial is bifurcated into two minitrials, one to determine guilt of first-degree murder and another (the sentencing phase), with the same jury, to determine if the defendant receives death or life without parole. A guilty finding in a death-penalty case ensures the defendant will die in prison; it is simply a matter of how and when. Life without parole means dying in prison, whereas the death penalty means dying in the execution chamber.

The significance of the government seeking the death penalty is in the jurors who will self-select for jury duty. To sit in judgment in a death-penalty case, a potential juror must commit, before hearing one shred of evidence, to giving serious consideration to both a death sentence and a life without parole sentence. Those who will never impose a death sentence and those who will always impose a death sentence are unsuitable to be fair and impartial in weighing the evidence and assessing the appropriate sentence for the defendant. Research has shown that the process of choosing a jury to hear a death-penalty case, called death qualification, results in a jury predisposed to finding the defendant guilty. That is, if the primary question on the jurors' minds is whether the defendant should live or die, then jurors are not focused on whether or not the defendant is actually innocent; they already presume guilt and focus solely on sentencing.[13] One notable example of the decision not to seek the death penalty and therefore sitting a jury with diverse views on punishment (a jury that would consider an innocent verdict) is Los Angeles District Attorney Gil Garcetti's decision to not seek the death penalty in the 1994 case against former professional football player Orenthal James (O. J.) Simpson. Former prosecutor Vincent Bugliosi believed that Garcetti's decision was the major factor in the jury returning a not guilty verdict in the double homicide case dubbed the "Trial of the Century."[14] Had Garcetti sought the death penalty, potential jurors opposed to executing Simpson would have been removed from the jury pool. Only jurors willing to impose capital punishment on O. J. would have judged the murder charges, and a death-qualified jury returns a guilty verdict on murder charges more often than not. In our chapter-opening case study on Dzhokar Tsarnaev, the U.S. attorney general must approve the local U.S. attorney's decision to seek the death penalty.

Discovery

Discovery is the legal process by which the parties share with the opposing side the evidence it intends to introduce at trial.[15] Because prosecutors have an advantage in controlling the information that will be used against the defendant at trial, the prosecutor's first duty to the defendant is to turn over discovery, which is defined under federal, state, and local statutes and rules. The high Court held in *Brady v. Maryland* (1963)[16] that the prosecutor must give to the defense all exculpatory evidence (i.e., evidence that tends to prove the defendant innocent) in the government's possession, even if the prosecutor does not physically possess the evidence but another government actor such as the police or jail personnel have the information in their files.[17] In the *Brady* case, the defendant John Leo Brady was found guilty of murder and sentenced to death. At trial, Brady admitted to participating in the murder but claimed that his partner, Donald Boblit, who was tried separately, did the actual shooting. Before trial, Brady's lawyer specifically asked to see the statements made by Boblit to the police. The prosecutor gave Brady's lawyer copies of many statements Boblit made but withheld the one statement in which Boblit admitted to the killing for which Brady was on trial. Boblit's admission that he committed the killing is exculpatory to Brady because Boblit's confession "tends to prove" Brady's innocence. The Court held that withholding exculpatory evidence violated Brady's due process rights under the Fourteenth Amendment and ordered a new trial. "Due process also requires disclosure of any evidence that provides grounds for the defense to attack the reliability, thoroughness, and good faith of the police investigation, to impeach [show bias] the credibility of the state's witnesses, or to bolster the defense against prosecutorial attacks" (*Kyles v. Whitley*, 1995).[18]

The import of informing the defense of impeachment information about government witnesses lies in the Sixth Amendment's Confrontation Clause requirement, discussed in Chapter 10. Defense counsel cross-examines government witnesses to expose any biases the witness may have in testifying for the prosecution, and if the jury learns the witness is obtaining

> Rule of Law: Discovery rules of law require both sides share information prior to trial, but the government has an affirmative duty to disclose to the defense exculpatory evidence.

a "get-out-of-jail-free" card by testifying favorably for the government, the jury may not believe the witness when the witness says the defendant is guilty of the crime charged (*United States v. Bagley*, 1985; *Giglio v. United States*, 1972).[19] According to Ira Mickenberg, some examples of *Brady* material include the following:

1. If one or more government witnesses change their stories about the crime or description of the defendant, if their "memories" improve or their descriptions of the defendant become more "accurate" after meeting with police or prosecutors or testifying at a hearing;

2. If the informant working the case against the defendant is under investigation, has pending charges, made inconsistent statements about the defendant's case, or matches the description of the actual assailant; or

3. If police had other investigative leads they failed to follow that could have implicated someone other than the defendant.

Who decides whether evidence in the prosecutor's files is exculpatory to the accused and must, therefore, be turned over to the defense? The answer: only the prosecutor. There is no judicial oversight over exculpatory information in the prosecutor's possession.

APPLYING THE LAW TO THE FACTS

Is It a *Brady* Violation?

The Facts: John was charged with armed robbery and capital murder in two separate cases. He was convicted of both crimes and spent 18 years in prison, many of those years on death row. In the armed robbery case, the suspect had bled on one victim's pants leg and the police took the pants as evidence. John was then charged with murder and the armed robbery conviction was used as an aggravating circumstance justifying the death penalty. The jury convicted John and sentenced him to death. Three weeks before John's scheduled execution, a private investigator working on his behalf, Elisa Abolafia, discovered the prosecutor's office had signed out of the evidence room the bloody pants from the armed robbery case and never returned them. In the evidence locker were the laboratory results confirming the blood type of the assailant was B+. John's blood type was O+. The prosecution kept the lab results from John and his defense team.[20] Did the prosecutor's office commit a *Brady* violation?

The Law: Yes. According to the precedent of the *Brady* case, when the government keeps exculpatory evidence from the defendant and if the evidence had been turned over it would have changed the outcome of the case, the defendant should get a new trial.

The Arrest and Charging Process

There are two types of "charging documents" that transform a suspect into a defendant. An **information** is a written accusation of charges by a prosecutor without the grand jury or a judge binding (holding) the defendant over after a preliminary hearing. Unlike a trial jury that determines the defendant's innocence or guilt, a grand jury decides only whether there is enough evidence to bring felony charges by way of returning an **indictment**, a formal charge. Prosecutors often use grand juries in complex cases, such as international drug or money laundering conspiracies, or in politically sensitive cases, such as whether charges should be brought against police officers involved in fatal citizen encounters.[21]

The Grand Jury

A **grand jury** is a collection of citizens called to hear evidence presented by prosecutors to determine whether there is sufficient evidence to charge someone or a corporate entity with a crime.

A federal grand jury is composed of 16 to 23 members. The size of the state grand jury depends on the jurisdiction but often mirrors the federal system. [22]

Grand jury proceedings are conducted in secret, and only the prosecutor, investigators, grand jurors, and witnesses are allowed inside the grand jury room. Unlike a criminal trial, there is no defense counsel present to ask witnesses questions or otherwise defend the target of the investigation, and there is no judge present. If most of the grand jurors believe there is probable cause that a crime has been committed, which means that it is more likely than not that a crime has been committed and a specific person or corporation has committed it, they vote to "return" the indictment. The foreperson swears to the judge that the "**true bill**" (indictment) is correct. If most of the grand jurors are not convinced that probable cause exists that a crime has been committed, they return a "no bill," and no criminal charges are filed.

Bail and the Preliminary Hearing

After **arrest**, which is the initiation of the suspect's deprivation of liberty, the suspect is booked. At **booking**, a suspect's identifying information, circumstances of arrest, and possible charges are logged at a police station. If the suspect is going to be detained in lockup for a period of time, he is searched, and his personal belongings are inventoried and stored. The detainee must be brought before a magistrate, typically the next available business day or within 72 hours. This **initial appearance** is when the judge must determine whether there is enough probable cause to believe that the suspect is more likely than not the person who committed the crime. Once in front of the judge, the suspect is informed of the charges against him, of his right to remain silent, his right to have counsel appointed if he cannot afford one, and, if the charge is serious, his right to a jury trial. Once a defendant secures counsel, the judge holds an **arraignment** where the defendant formally enters a plea to the charges, often "not guilty." If the defendant refuses to enter a plea, the judge enters a "not guilty" plea on his behalf.

Bail. **Bail** is set of conditions often involving a pledge of an amount of money or collateral—a house, boat, or something of value—that the court requires to ensure the defendant appears at court hearings and trial. The Eighth Amendment says bail shall not be excessive. The U.S. Supreme Court has said that setting bail "at a figure higher than an amount reasonably calculated [to ensure the defendant's presence at trial] is excessive" (*Stack v. Boyle*, 1951).[23] The options for the court in determining the pretrial release of defendants are

1. Release on own recognizance, which does not require the defendant to pledge security while requiring the defendant to meet certain conditions, such as drug testing or looking for work; or

2. Detain the defendant in jail pending trial or judicial disposition of the charges.

The decision to release or detain the defendant is within the judge's discretion, depending on the alleged crime committed. Idaho's bail statute provides that persons charged with noncapital (no death penalty) crimes must be released on bail, whereas persons facing capital punishment may be released on bail.

> **Rule of Law: The Eighth Amendment states bail shall not be excessive.**

Idaho Criminal Rule 46. Bail or Release on Own Recognizance (2017)

(a) Bail or Release in Non-Capital Cases. A defendant who is charged with a crime that is not punishable by death must be admitted to bail or released on the defendant's own recognizance at any time before a guilty plea or verdict of guilt. In the discretion of the court, bail or release on the defendant's own recognizance may be allowed in the following cases:

(Continued)

(Continued)

(1) after the defendant pleads guilty or is found guilty and before sentencing;

(2) while an appeal is pending from a judgment of conviction, an order withholding judgment, or an order imposing sentence, except that a court must not allow bail when the defendant has been sentenced to death or life imprisonment;

(3) on a charge of a violation of the terms of probation; or

(4) on a finding of a violation of the conditions of release . . .

(b) Bail Where Offense Is Punishable by Death. A person arrested for an offense punishable by death may be admitted to bail by any magistrate or district court authorized by law to set bail in accordance with the standard set forth in Article I, Section 6 of the Idaho Constitution.

In determining if to grant bail within the bounds of the law, courts examine several factors, such as[24]

a. The nature and circumstances of the offense charged

b. The weight of the evidence against the suspect indicating guilt

c. Whether the defendant is a flight risk for fleeing the jurisdiction to avoid the charges

d. The history and characteristics of the person, including the following:

- The defendant's character
- Physical and mental condition
- Family ties
- Employment
- Financial resources
- Length of residence in the community
- Community ties
- History of drug or alcohol abuse
- Criminal history and record of past arrests and convictions
- Record of appearance at prior court appearances
- Whether at the time of the current offense, the defendant was already on judicial release or facing charges elsewhere
- The nature and seriousness of the danger to any person or the community that would be posed by the defendant's release

A bail bondsman or bonding agent collects a percentage of the bail, which he keeps even if the defendant shows up for court. If the defendant fails to show up for court, the bondsman is responsible to the court for the entire amount of bail. Current trends in bail reform reflect social justice initiatives to remove the financial conditions of bail. Social commentators reflect the current bail system is a modern-day "debtor's prison," where those without financial resources remain incarcerated for months to years awaiting their day in court.[25] In our chapter-opening case study, bombing defendant Dzhokhar Tsarnaev's three friends were charged in federal court with conspiracy to obstruct justice by not notifying the authorities of Tsarnaev's identity when his photo was broadcast and for cleaning his dorm room of incriminating evidence. Arrested on April 20, 2013, Kazakhstan natives Azamat Tazhayakov and Dias Kadyrbayev had family in the States willing to post bond, but both were denied bail, presumably because as noncitizens they posed a flight risk, but Massachusetts native Robel Phillipos was released on bail both pending trial and after conviction while awaiting sentencing.

Preliminary Hearing. The purpose of the **preliminary hearing**, which is a minitrial before trial, is to test the sufficiency of the charges by introducing evidence that tends to show there is enough probable cause to bind the defendant over for trial. The preliminary hearing is like a grand jury proceeding, except that the hearing is held in public, there is a defense counsel present, and a judge rather than a collection of citizens makes the probable cause determination. Witnesses are called to testify, and the defense often gets a first-hand glimpse of the strength and quality of the prosecution's case. Usually the rules of evidence are relaxed, and hearsay, which is an out-of-court statement offered for its truth, is admissible. The defendant typically does not testify at the hearing because if he chooses to testify at trial and his story changes from the one given at the preliminary hearing, his previous testimony can be used against him.

Speedy Trial

Federal and state laws demand criminal defendants get a "speedy trial." The federal law, Speedy Trial Act of 1974, states an information or indictment must be filed 30 days after an arrest, and trial must begin 70 days from the filing of the charging document or from the day the defendant first appeared before a judge, whichever date is later.[26] Consent by the defendant to stop the clock, usually to get more time to prepare for trial, and other pretrial delays, such as the disposition of **pretrial motions**, tolls (stops) the counting of the clock. If the government fails to bring the defendant to trial and the clock expires, the defendant must be released, and the process must start over.

---

18 U.S.C. § 3161. Time limits and exclusions

(a) In any case involving a defendant charged with an offense, the appropriate judicial officer, at the earliest practicable time, shall, after consultation with the counsel for the defendant and the attorney for the Government, set the case for trial on a day certain, or list it for trial on a weekly or other short-term trial calendar at a place within the judicial district, so as to assure a speedy trial.

In *Barker v. Wingo* (1972), the high Court listed four questions to assess the reasonableness of the speedy trial delay:

1. The length of the delay
2. The reason for the delay
3. Whether the defendant contributed to the delay in requesting continuances
4. Did the delay harm the defendant's due process rights to a fair trial?[27]

As in most situations concerning criminal procedure, the U.S. Supreme Court refuses to draw "bright line rules" and instead gives criminal justice professionals wide latitude to make decisions within the bounds of the law such as what constitutes a "reasonable delay" for speedy trial purposes.

Pretrial Motions

A **motion** is an application for a court order where lawyers are asking the court to do something for the side they represent, defendant or government. Pretrial motions (applications for court order made before trial) are heard in front of the judge only, no jury. The reason the judge alone makes decisions on pretrial matters such as what evidence will be admitted or excluded at trial is that those decisions could affect the outcome of the jury's verdict. Sometimes, when a defendant is claiming, for example, that police conducted an illegal search or made an illegal arrest, the judge holds an evidentiary hearing and takes testimony from witnesses, such as the police officers involved in the search or seizure, and even the defendant himself. The judge then renders a decision. Some typical motions brought by criminal defendants before or during trial are listed here.

- A motion to suppress seeks to keep out incriminating evidence at trial usually on the grounds that the government seized evidence illegally.

- A motion *in limine* seeks to limit the introduction at trial of irrelevant evidence.

- A motion to dismiss is when the defendant asks the court to dismiss all or some of the charges against him because of legal defects in the investigation or charging process.

- A motion to sever is when the defendant has one or more codefendants; he can ask for separate trials because his defense may conflict with that of his codefendants.

- A motion to change venue is when the defendant asks to have his case tried in a place that is outside the prosecuting jurisdiction because extensive pretrial publicity may prevent a fair trial.

An abbreviated version of a pretrial motion to suppress in the Boston Marathon case is reproduced below. Note the legal format of a motion is to connect the particular facts of the case with the applicable law.

UNITED STATES OF AMERICA V. DZHOKHAR TSARNAEV, NO. 13-CR-10200-GAO

United States District Court District Of Massachusetts

Motion to Suppress Fruits of Searches at Norfolk Street and University of Massachusetts

Defendant, by and through counsel, moves this Court to suppress any physical evidence seized, observed, or photographed, or any fruits of such evidence, that was unlawfully obtained during searches of the defendant's home on Norfolk Street in Cambridge and of his dorm room and property at the University of Massachusetts ("U-Mass") at Dartmouth.

As grounds for this motion, undersigned counsel state that the searches violated Mr. Tsarnaev's rights under the Fourth Amendment to the U.S. Constitution because:

1) The lists of items to be searched for and seized were overly broad and lacking in particularity;

2) Law enforcement agents observed, seized, and photographed items that fell outside the scope of the warrants;

3) The warrantless inspection of Mr. Tsarnaev's dorm room and personal property at the University of Massachusetts at Dartmouth was not justified by any recognized exception to the warrant requirement; and

4) The July search warrant for the dorm room did not have an independent source.

Background

On April 15, 2013, two bombs exploded at the Boston Marathon, killing three spectators and injuring many others. The suspects remained unidentified until the evening of April 18, when Tamerlan Tsarnaev was killed in a shootout with law enforcement agents in Watertown. Tamerlan's younger brother, Dzhokhar, fled the scene of the gun battle. A lengthy manhunt ensued.

On April 19, after Tamerlan was identified through fingerprints and while law enforcement agents sought Dzhokhar, the FBI applied for and received a search warrant for 410 Norfolk Street, Apartment 3, where Tamerlan and Dzhokhar lived. The search warrant for the Norfolk Street apartment issued at 11:50 a.m. The search began an hour later and lasted for nearly 12 hours, according to discovery. At about 9 p.m. on April 19, Mr. Tsarnaev was arrested and rushed to Beth Israel Hospital, in critical condition. On the evening of April 20, through the morning of April 21, members of the FBI's High Value Interrogation Team questioned him.

Just after midnight on the morning of April 21, the FBI obtained a search warrant for Mr. Tsarnaev's dormitory room at U-Mass Dartmouth. The search began at 2:43 a.m. and lasted approximately 6½ hours. On May 3, the FBI obtained a second search warrant for the Norfolk Street apartment, which was executed on May 5. On June 27, FBI agents entered Mr. Tsarnaev's dorm room a second time, without a warrant, and observed and photographed various items while U-Mass police collected Mr. Tsarnaev's property and removed it. The university police also took a swab of a "reddish-brown powder" seen on a window sill. On July 24, the government obtained a second search warrant for Mr. Tsarnaev's dorm room and for property that had been removed by university officials from the room. The search was executed on July 26 . . .

The April 19 and 21 Search Warrants

The lists of items to be seized under the April search warrants for the apartment and the dorm room are substantially similar. The April warrant for the apartment specified the following:

All evidence inside the premises and curtilage located at the Target Residence, related to violations of 18 U.S.C. §§ 2332(a) (Using and Conspiring to Use a Weapon of Mass Destruction), 844(i) (Malicious Destruction of Property by Means of an Explosive Device Resulting in Death), 2119 (Carjacking), 1951 (Interference with Commerce by Violence), 924(c) (Use of a Weapon During a Crime of Violence) and 371 (Conspiracy to Commit Offenses), including but not limited to:

1. Property, records, items, or other information, related to violations of the aforementioned statutes, including but not limited to, bomb making material and equipment, ammunition, weapons, explosive material, components of bomb delivery devices;

2. Property, records, or other information related to the ordering, purchasing, manufacturing, storage, and transportation of explosives;

3. Property, records, or other information related to the ordering, purchasing, manufacturing, storage, and transportation of firearms;

4. Property, records, or other information related to the ordering and purchasing of pressure cooker devices, BBs, nails, and other small metallic objects;

5. Property, records, or information related to the Boston Marathon;

6. Property, records, or information related to any plans to initiate or carry out any other attacks inside or outside the United States, or any records or information related to any past attacks;

7. Property, records, or information related to the state of mind and/or motive of Tamerian [sic] and Dzhokhar to undertake the Boston Marathon bombings;

8. Property, records, or other information related to the identity of Tamerian and Dzhokhar . . .

The attachment goes on to define "digital evidence" and to provide a protocol for seizure and search of digital evidence.

The list of the items to be seized in the April 21 warrant for the dorm room was identical except for the omission of "[p]roperty, records, or other information related to the ordering, purchasing, manufacturing, storage, and transportation of firearms[.]"

Argument

The Search Warrants Were Lacking in Particularity

We begin with the basic proposition that the Warrant Clause of the Fourth Amendment prohibits the issuance of a warrant, except one "particularly describing the place to be searched, and the persons or things to be seized." U.S. Const. amend. IV. A search "intruding upon [an individual's] privacy interest . . . must satisfy the particularity requirement, which limits the scope and intensity of the search."

"General warrants, of course, are prohibited by the Fourth Amendment." *Andresen v. Maryland*, 427 U.S. 463, 480 (1976). General warrants are impermissible because they permit "a general, exploratory rummaging in a person's belongings." To avoid this problem, the Fourth Amendment requires "a 'particular description' of the things to be seized." "As to what is to be taken, nothing is left to the discretion of the officer executing the warrant." "The *Marron* standard finds its derivation in Colonial America's aversion to writs of assistance and general warrants which placed broad discretionary authority with British Custom officials to search anywhere for smuggled goods and seize anything they pleased."

The list of items to be seized includes "property, records, or information related to . . . the state of mind and/or motive of Tamerlan and Dzhokhar to undertake the Boston Marathon bombings" . . . These categories do not provide sufficient limitations on what the agents could search for and seize. The "state of mind and/or motive" could have been construed to allow the agents to examine or seize every item in the apartment in the hope that it might shed light on the religious, political, or other beliefs of the Tsarnaev brothers, as well as anything that might provide the slightest insight into their psychological makeup. No temporal limitation is provided. The same is true of "any bank records, checks . . . and other financial records." This provision is not limited by a time frame, the identity of an individual, or the nature of the transactions reflected in these records. Among the items seized from the Norfolk Street apartment was a paystub for Tamerlan from a 2010 job at a pizza restaurant. Agents seized a pizza box from Mr. Tsarnaev's dorm room.

(Continued)

(Continued)

The Entry Into the Dorm Room by the FBI and Campus Police on June 27, 2013 Was an Impermissible Warrantless Search

On June 27, two months after the April 21 search of Mr. Tsarnaev's dorm room with a search warrant, an FBI agent accompanied campus police into the dorm room to observe as they collected his personal property. According to an FBI report on this event, the agent entered "at the invitation and with the consent of the University of Massachusetts Dartmouth Police Department." Defendant submits that this entry was an unconstitutional warrantless search and that its fruits—which include photographs taken by the FBI, a videotape made by U-Mass police, the powder sampled by the campus police, and the items seized during the execution of a second search warrant a month later—must be suppressed. "The right to be free from unreasonable searches and seizures as guaranteed by the Fourth Amendment to the United States Constitution applies when the police search a dormitory room in a public college."

Conclusion

For the foregoing reasons, the defendant requests that this Court suppress items of physical evidence seized as a result of searches of 410 Norfolk, Cambridge, Massachusetts and Mr. Tsarnaev's dorm room at U-Mass Dartmouth.

Request for Evidentiary Hearing

Defendant requests an evidentiary hearing to determine whether items were seized outside the scope of the warrants, the circumstances of the warrantless June 27 entry, and the role that the June 27 entry played in the agents' decision to seek a second search warrant in July for the dorm room and its contents.

DZHOKHAR TSARNAEV

by his attorneys. . . .

The way motions work throughout a criminal trial and appeal is illustrated by the hypothetical court case in Figure 2.1.

Per number 1, the defendant Smith through his lawyer claims that the police collected the evidence illegally—here the knife and the defendant's confession, "I did it"—because the constitutional mandates of the Fourth and Fifth Amendments were ignored. Per number 2, the motion to suppress, to keep the evidence out, is made to the judge before trial so there is no jury present. Per number 3, if the judge denies the suppression motion, the evidence is admissible at trial and used against the defendant to secure a conviction. Per number 4, once convicted, the defendant appeals to overturn his conviction, typically, by claiming the trial judge made a mistake of law not to suppress the evidence and the prosecutor fights to maintain the conviction arguing the trial was fair. A sports analogy works best in describing what an appeals court does.

Let's imagine a professional football game. The quarterback threw a pass to his receiver running along the sideline to get a first down. There is a rule that both receiver's feet must be inbounds for the catch to count as a completed pass. Let's imagine that the referee signaled a completed pass and a first down. Let us also imagine the defense decided to challenge the call disputing the receiver's feet were inbounds. If this were a court case, the offense would be the prosecution and the defense counsel would be the defense. The referee making a ruling on the field as a completed pass would be the trial judge.

To take our sports analogy one step further, instead of the trial judge reviewing instant replay to see if the receiver's feet were inbounds, there would be an appeal to a higher authority in a booth high in the stadium who would review the call. If the higher authority reviewing officials were an appeals court, they would *not* be looking at instant replay to see if the player's feet were inbounds but rather at whether the referee made the right call according to the rules book. That is, when a case is appealed, the appeals court is typically not able to second-guess the facts introduced at trial (i.e., feet inbounds or not); rather, the court is reviewing the play to assess if the judge or lawyers followed the rules of law at trial; whether the ruling on the field stands. There are times when appellate courts do look at the sufficiency of the evidence to sustain the charges (analogous to the instant replay), but their primary job is reviewing a case to ensure all complied with the law. Once an appeals court makes its decision, its opinion is case law, such as the case excerpts in this text. Sometimes the defendant's conviction is upheld or overturned based on whether the appeals court agrees that legal mistakes were made at the trial court level.

Figure 2.1   A Motion Travels Through the Court System

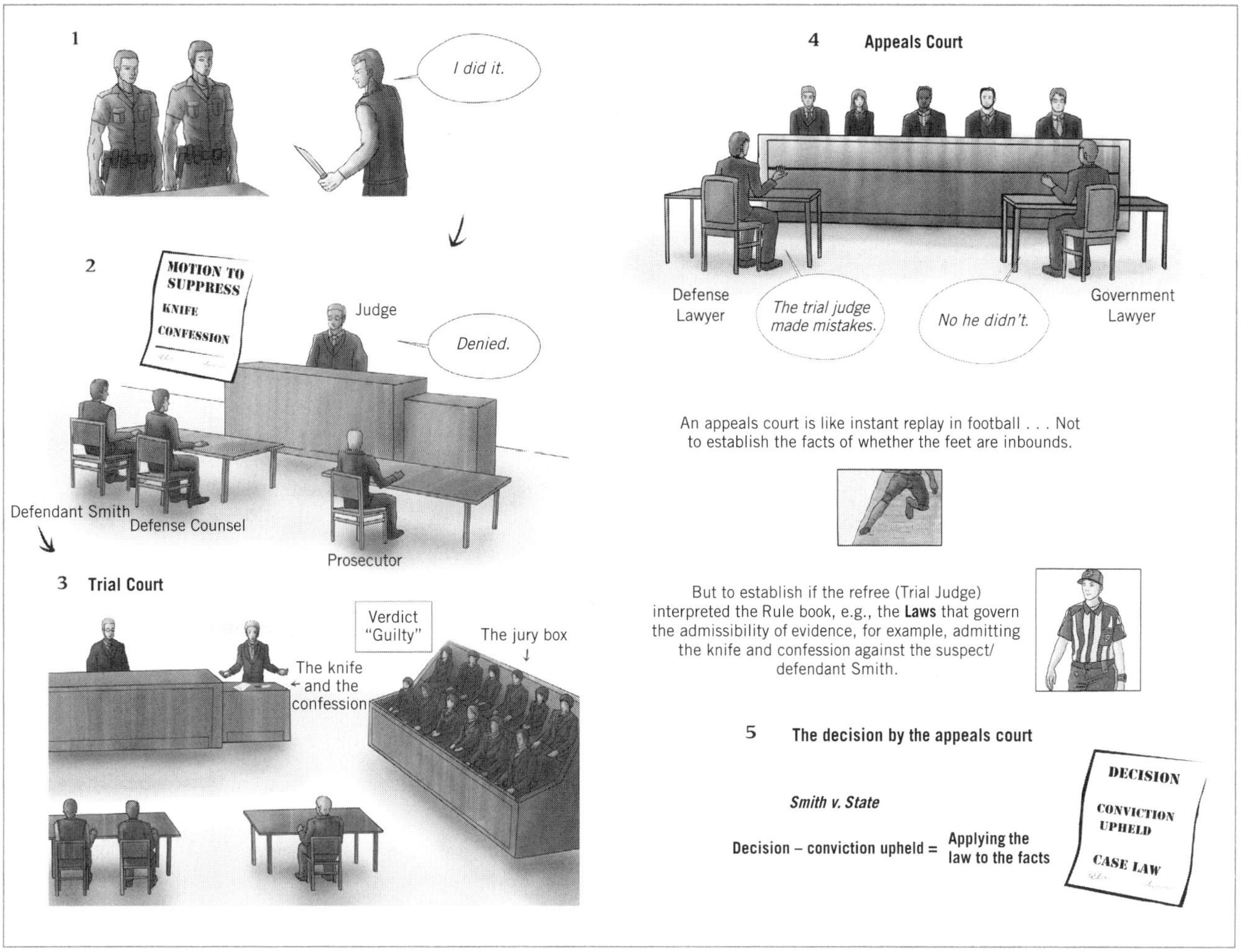

Venue

The Sixth Amendment to the U.S. Constitution and many state constitutions provide that a criminal trial shall be held in the state, district, or county where the crime occurred, called venue, discussed more fully in Chapter 10. Venue in the district where the crime occurred ensures both that the people most affected in the community have a chance to see justice served and that the defendant has access to witnesses and evidence that are geographically close. In high-profile cases, defendants often make motions for change of venue because extensive publicity may have tainted the potential jury pool. Potential jurors may ignore the defendant's presumption of innocence because of the "facts" of the case they have learned through the newspapers and television coverage. In the chapter-opening case study, Tsarnaev's lawyers conducted research that showed most people in Massachusetts had an opinion about his guilt and either attended the Boston Marathon or knew someone who did. The defense filed a motion to change venue, but the judge was confident the court could seat an open-minded jury and denied the motion. The defense objected to the judge's ruling preserving the issue for appeal. The trial was held in downtown Boston.

> **Rule of Law: The Sixth Amendment provides that the trial venue is in the district where the crime took place.**

Plea Bargaining

Plea bargaining is a mutual exchange between the prosecutor and the defendant for mutual benefit and gain where the prosecutor gets a conviction and win, and the defendant usually gets

> **Rule of Law: The defendant must willingly plead guilty under oath in open court to all elements of the offense and cannot withdraw the guilty plea once sentenced.**

charges dropped and a lesser sentence than she would if had she elected to go to trial. The reduced sentence is the payment for saving the government time and money that would otherwise be spent on jury selection, expert testimony, overtime for court personnel, and similar court-related expenses of proving the accused guilty. Plea bargains occur in 90% of criminal cases and are a necessary and vital tool to keep court dockets (judge schedules) flowing quickly. The plea agreement is a legally enforceable contract, as the high Court has said, "When a plea rests in any significant degree on a promise or agreement of the prosecutor, so that it can be said to be part of the inducement or consideration, such promises must be fulfilled" (*Santobello v. New York*, 1971).[28]

Types of Pleas

A guilty plea is when the defendant admits to all elements of the offense, agrees to waive (give up) most constitutional rights that protect him, and agrees to submit to the government's authority to sentence him for the crime. There are many types of guilty pleas, but they involve two basic formats:

1. Defendant pleads guilty in exchange for the prosecutor's agreement to drop charges or refuse to stack additional charges that the evidence will support.

2. Defendant pleads guilty in exchange for the prosecutor's promised recommendation to the judge for a specific sentence or a willingness not to oppose defense counsel's sentence recommendation to the judge.

Even if the government and defendant enter into a plea agreement, and the defendant pleads guilty fully expecting to get the benefit of his bargain, the judge need not accept the plea agreement. Judges rarely reject plea agreements because it would slow their docket, but the court does retain the authority to accept or reject the plea and the defendant is made aware of the judge's authority prior to pleading guilty.

> **Rule of Law: The judge does not have to accept the plea pursuant to a negotiated plea agreement for a specific, agreed-to sentence by the prosecution and defense.**

An *Alford* plea is where the defendant denies committing the crime yet concedes the government has enough evidence to convict him. Courts allow *Alford* pleas because "reasons other than the fact that [the defendant] is guilty may induce a defendant to so plead . . . [and] he must be permitted to judge for himself in this respect."[29] An *Alford* plea is similar to a *nolo contendere*, or "no contest," plea where the defendant does not plead guilty but simply refuses to contest the charges against him. Both the *Alford* and no contest pleas operate as guilty pleas, and states may treat each plea differently for determining three-strikes sentencing eligibility, discussed in Chapter 13.

A conditional plea is taken when the defendant wishes to challenge a judge's ruling on the admissibility of evidence despite his guilty plea. Often, defendants file motions to suppress certain evidence before trial. If the judge admits the evidence, the defendant may plead guilty *on the condition* that he still be allowed to appeal the judge's ruling on the admissibility of the incriminating evidence. There is a risk that the defendant will plead guilty and be sentenced to prison, and then the appellate court will rule in the defendant's favor. Since the defendant has already been incarcerated, it would be small solace that the trial judge was mistaken in admitting the incriminating evidence against him.

The most common type of plea bargain is the plea pursuant to a negotiated agreement, which is a contract between the prosecutor and the defendant that spells out the details of the mutual bargain. There is a risk in the negotiated plea. Let's say the plea calls for the defendant, Bob, to plead guilty to money laundering, which carries a maximum sentence of 50 years. Bob has a plea agreement with the prosecutor where, in exchange for Bob's guilty plea, the prosecutor will recommend to the judge that Bob only serve 10 years. Bob first must plead guilty and face the maximum sentence before the judge will consider accepting the prosecutor's recommendation. That is, under the law the judge does *not* have to accept Bob's negotiated plea deal. After Bob pleads guilty, the judge could sentence Bob to 50 years imprisonment. The judge tells all of this to Bob before he pleads guilty. But most defendants know that 90% of all criminal cases in

America are resolved by guilty plea and remain confident that the judge will honor the terms of the agreement and plead guilty anyway.

The Plea Colloquy

A defendant's plea of guilty to the crimes charged is a substitute for a trial. To take a defendant's guilty plea, the judge must conduct a **plea colloquy**, which is a conversation conducted in open court in which the defendant under oath admits all the elements of the offense as charged. The colloquy also is conducted to ensure that the defendant is of sound mind, not under the influence of drugs or alcohol, and pleading guilty willingly because he truly is guilty. A sample transcript of a plea colloquy in federal court is provided in this text in Appendix C. Under the rules of criminal procedure enacted by the federal and most state governments, a defendant may withdraw his guilty plea before the court accepts the plea or after the court accepts the guilty plea but before sentencing. After the court sentences the defendant, he may not withdraw his guilty plea. Many jurisdictions include as part of the negotiated plea agreement the defendant's affirmative waiver of his right to appeal his sentence.

MAKING THE COURTROOM CONNECTION

As detailed in Table 2.1, defining the corresponding powers of the prosecutor and the defense in the adversary system of criminal justice, the government can generate testimony by using the plea bargain as leverage to obtain favorable testimony for the prosecution. In a criminal trial the government has all the power: It runs the state laboratories to test evidence, it has subpoena power to retrieve phone records and other documents, and it is the only party that can offer a plea bargain.

Let's look at how testimony is generated, in part, with transcripts in a real case, *California v. Wozniak*, Case No. 12ZF0137, out of Orange County. Prosecutors are not witnesses to crimes, they are not present when the murder occurs, so the government does not know, for a fact, what actually happened. Prosecutors can meet their burden of proof at trial by finding witnesses to testify they saw the suspect commit, or heard them confess to, the crime. Studies show confessions are powerful evidence at trial because if someone says, "I did it, I'm guilty," he or she is probably not innocent.[30] The District Attorney's Office (prosecutor), Central Court Santa Ana, California, received a letter from an inmate from the Orange County jail that said:

> To whom it may concern. My name is Daniel Elias and I'm housed in jail next to Quong Quan. He has told me very personal information about himself and reguarding [sic] his case . . . I'm here in jail for drug and gun charges and am facing a max of 8 years, 8 months. I'm willing to testify in exchange for time off my sentence [underline in original]. Please feel free to contact me here at the jail. My

case is out of Harbor Court . . . I deserve a chance and will help you if you help me.[31]

Quong Quan was a suspect in a triple murder. Elias wrote to the prosecutor that the price of his "helping" the government secure a conviction against Quan was "time off on my sentence" "in exchange" for testifying at Quan's trial that Quan had confessed to Elias, something that cannot be independently verified.[32]

Let's imagine in a hypothetical that a suspect, Brian, has been charged but not convicted and is awaiting trial in the same jail as Quan. Let us also imagine Brian has contacted prosecutors and offered to testify that Brian heard Quan confess in exchange for the prosecutor dropping some of the charges Brain is facing. The typical timeline in such a case is as follows:

1. Brian and the prosecutor agree that in exchange for the government dropping some of Brian's charges and making a recommendation for a reduced sentenced, Brian will testify at Quan's trial that Quan confessed. There is no legal requirement that the prosecutor or Brian prove Quan confessed; Brian simply has to testify under oath on the witness stand that he heard Quan confess.

2. Before Brian testifies at Quan's trial, the prosecutor will bring Brian before a judge to plead guilty to the charges and face the maximum sentence for those charges. Brian will not be sentenced immediately and will still have a lengthy prison sentence hanging over his head.

(Continued)

(Continued)

3. At Quan's trial, the prosecutor will put Brian on the witness stand to testify Quan confessed. The prosecutor will declare that Brian is testifying because of his "good conscience" and, because he took an oath to tell the truth in the courtroom, Brian is testifying "truthfully" that Quan confessed. Quan typically cannot take the witness stand and testify that he never confessed, because there are certain risks if defendants take the witness stand.

4. Once the jury believes Brian and convicts Quan of committing murder, in part because Brian said Quan confessed, the prosecutor will then schedule a sentencing hearing for Brian.

5. At Brian's sentencing hearing, the prosecutor will recommend a light sentence based on Brian's "cooperation" with the authorities.

The allegorical "Sword of Damocles" refers to a fourth century B.C. court figure in a royal house in Sicily and represents the peril of having something hanging "over your head," represented in Richard Westall's painting (Photo 2.2). The power in the sword over your head (testify the defendant is guilty) is not that it falls but that it hangs (Our hypothetical Brian and the real Elias only get the reduced sentence after they testify at Quan's trial that Quan confessed).

▶ **Photo 2.2**
The Sword of Damocles

In a typical scenario of a criminal agreeing to testify against a defendant in exchange for a lighter sentence the prosecutor will have the criminal plead guilty to crimes with stiff sentences but will not actually recommend a sentence until *after* they testify against the prosecutor's target. The prosecutor's anticipated good recommendation for a light sentence is the sword hanging over head. The reason prosecutors do *not* sentence testifying criminals *before* they testify against the target defendant is because the government then loses all control over what they might say at trial. Once someone is sentenced, the case is closed, and the double jeopardy doctrine prevents resentencing of a convict.

If the testifying criminal was sentenced (so the sword no longer hangs) before testifying against the target, they could get on the witness stand and say, "I want to tell you the truth, the defendant said nothing incriminating and he is innocent." But if the testifying criminal said the defendant was innocent before he was sentenced, then the sword of Damocles would fall, the plea bargain for the shorter sentence would disappear, and the informant would be sentenced to the maximum allowable years of imprisonment to which he already pleaded guilty.[33]

TRIAL

The Presumption of Innocence and the Burden of Proof

At trial, the prosecution maintains the burden of proof to convince a jury beyond a reasonable doubt that the defendant is guilty of the crime charged. **Beyond a reasonable doubt** means the jury is convinced and confident the defendant committed the crime, but beyond a reasonable doubt does not mean beyond all doubt. At trial, the defendant enjoys a presumption of innocence—an assumption that he is innocent until the government proves him guilty. A presumption is an assumption; the law requires that the jury assume that the defendant is innocent, even when the defendant's guilt seems obvious to all, until the government proves him guilty. U.S. Supreme Court Justice John Marshall Harlan II famously wrote about reasonable doubt in 1970, "It is *far worse to convict an innocent man than to let a guilty man go free*" (emphasis added).[34] The Court explained that the reasonable doubt standard

Rule of Law: The prosecutor must prove the defendant guilty beyond a reasonable doubt.

plays a vital role in the American scheme of criminal procedure. It is a prime instrument for reducing the risk of convictions resulting from factual error. Accordingly, a society that values the good name and freedom of every individual should not condemn a man for commission of a crime when there is reasonable doubt about his guilt.

Conversely, a defendant need not prove anything at trial. He may, if he chooses, provide a defense with relevant evidence, cross-examine witnesses, or testify on his own behalf, but he need not do anything, as illustrated by Maryland jury instruction §1.05.

---

1 Maryland Criminal Jury Instructions and Commentary §1.05 Beyond a Reasonable Doubt

The State has the burden of proving the guilt of the defendant beyond a reasonable doubt. This burden remains on the State throughout the trial. The defendant is not required to prove [his] [her] innocence. However, the State is not required to prove guilt beyond all possible doubt or to a mathematical certainty. Nor is the State required to negate every conceivable circumstance of innocence.

A reasonable doubt is a doubt founded upon reason. Proof beyond a reasonable doubt requires such proof as would convince you of the truth of a fact to the extent that you would be willing to act upon such belief without reservation in an important matter in your own business or personal affairs. However, if you are not satisfied of the defendant's guilt to that extent, then reasonable doubt exists and the defendant must be found not guilty.

The Criminal Trial Sequence

During the trial, each side—the prosecution and the defense—tries to establish the strength of its own case while exposing the other side's weaknesses. The party with the burden of proof—the prosecution—presents its "case in chief" first, and when it "rests" (stops), the defendant presents his case. In short, the order of a trial proceeds as follows:

Springboard for Discussion

Do you agree with U.S. Supreme Court Associate Justice Harlan about proving the defendant guilty beyond a reasonable doubt that "it is far worse to convict an innocent man than to let a guilty man go free"?[35] Why or why not?

1. Preliminary jury instructions by the judge (Keep an open mind; don't talk about the case with anyone until deliberations)

2. Opening statements, first by prosecutor (they have the burden of proof), then defense

3. Prosecutor presents case in chief by introducing evidence tending to prove defendant guilty

   a. Prosecutor conducts direct examination of witnesses

   b. Defense conducts cross-examination of prosecution's witnesses

4. Prosecutor rests[36]

5. Defense presents its case in chief by introducing evidence tending to show that the government has failed to meet its burden of proof

   a. Defense conducts direct examination of witnesses

   b. Prosecution conducts cross-examination of defense witnesses

6. Defense rests

7. Charge conference out of presence of jury

8. Closing arguments, first by prosecutor, then defense, then prosecutor again to get the final word

9. Judge gives jury instructions defining the law the jury *must* follow concerning the evidence

10. Jury deliberations

11. Jury renders a verdict

Jury Selection

Voir Dire

Many issues must be discussed with the **venire**, the potential jury pool before selection and during jury selection to ensure that the defendant is tried in front of a group of people who can fairly and impartially judge the facts and evidence. The questioning of the venire is called *voir dire*, French for "to speak the truth." The Sixth Amendment guarantees the defendant a speedy and public trial in front of a fair and impartial jury. The requirement that a defendant be tried by a "jury of [his or her] peers" does *not* necessarily mean that the defendant must be tried before a panel of people who share his socioeconomic background. It does mean that the government cannot systematically exclude people based on race or gender from the jury simply because the state thinks it has a better chance at convicting the defendant if the jury is homogenous (all the same).

> **Rule of Law: The questioning to determine if potential jurors can be fair and impartial in deciding the defendant's case is called** *voir dire.*

From a courtroom perspective, prosecutors want homogenous juries because it is easier to get a unanimous verdict if all jurors have the same cultural background and think alike; it helps the government secure convictions if their jurors resemble eggs in a carton. Conversely, the defense only needs one juror to think differently and vote not guilty and heterogeneous juries comprised of diverse viewpoints is ideal. When jurors fail to all agree, the outcome is a hung jury, the trial ends, and the government must repeat the entire trial. Sometimes when there is a hung jury, the prosecutor will offer the defendant a plea bargain and exchange a lenient sentence in exchange for admitting guilt and avoiding another trial.

There are two types of challenges to remove potential jurors during jury selection. **Challenges for cause** are made when a lawyer believes the potential juror cannot be fair and impartial in deciding the case; perhaps a **venireman** who suffered a childhood filled with trauma might be biased against a defendant charged with familial abuse. Such a juror, however, may be a suitable candidate to sit in judgment in a medical malpractice case. This is not to say someone who has personal experience with the subject matter of a trial cannot be fair, but the venireman must answer truthfully questions in court about his or her personal feelings and ability to listen to all the evidence fairly. Each side has an unlimited number of challenges for cause. The judge makes the final decision to allow or reject all challenges.

> **Rule of Law: In criminal prosecutions, the government cannot eliminate potential jurors based solely on their race or gender.**

The second type of challenge to remove potential jurors during jury selection is a **peremptory challenge**, which allows a lawyer for either side to strike (remove) potential jurors for no reason at all. The number of peremptory challenges is limited and depends on the nature of the case and the jurisdiction of the court. The lawyer does not have to explain to the court why he is exercising a peremptory challenge. But the U.S. Supreme Court has imposed on the government the obligation to explain peremptory challenges if the government exercises the challenge in what appears to be a racially discriminatory manner. In *Batson v. Kentucky* (1986),[37] James Batson, an African American man, was convicted of second-degree murder by an all-White jury after the prosecutor during jury selection used four out of six peremptory strikes to dismiss African Americans. On appeal, the high Court found the prosecutor's peremptory challenges in Batson's case violated his Fourteenth Amendment's right to equal protection, treating everyone the same under the law. White defendants may also make *Batson* claims of discrimination through the state's exercise of peremptory challenges because discrimination practiced by the state interferes with *any* defendant's right to be tried by a fair and impartial jury.[38] *Batson*, the Court has said in *Snyder v. Louisiana* (2008),[39] "is a rule about purposeful discrimination, about intent. And so, it doesn't really matter that there might have been a bunch of valid reasons out there [to use a peremptory strike to get rid of a juror], if it was clear that the prosecutor was thinking about race," then the challenge was illegal.[40] Parties also may not use peremptory challenges to eliminate potential jurors on the basis of gender. Once all challenges have been ruled on by the judge, 12 jurors and typically 2 alternates are chosen to decide the case. The jurors designated as alternates are not notified of their status until the close of the case and deliberations are about to begin. Alternate jurors do not deliberate unless a regular juror is excused.[41]

APPLYING THE LAW TO THE FACTS

Improper Use of Peremptory Challenges?

The Facts: In a capital murder trial where an African American defendant was charged with killing an elderly White woman, the prosecutor had highlighted all Black prospective jurors' names on the venire sheets, where the jurors had indicated their race. The African American veniremen were the first five out of seven the prosecutor struck by use of peremptory challenge. The prosecutor gave "race-neutral" explanations for striking each Black venireman, such as they were too busy to pay attention during trial. The all-White jury then convicted the defendant and sentenced him to death. Is noting the race of veniremen and then using peremptory strikes to eliminate them illegal?[42]

The Law: Yes. Under the precedent of *Batson v. Kentucky* (1986), the U.S. Supreme Court stated "two peremptory strikes on the basis of race are two more than the Constitution allows" (*Foster v. Chatman*, 2016).[43]

Opening Statements

Opening statements are brief summaries of what the attorneys expect the evidence to show during the trial. Such statements are not arguments, and what the attorneys say during opening statements is not evidence. The defense counsel can present an opening statement immediately after the government or wait until it is their time to present a defense. In the chapter-opening case study, the federal prosecutor said of Dzhokhar Tsarnaev in opening that he was a "holy warrior" and his motive on April 15, 2013, in planting the pressure cooker bomb "was to kill as many people as possible." Given the overwhelming physical evidence proving guilt, Tsarnaev's defense counsel said in her opening statement, "It was him," but attributed his actions to the influence and dominion of his older brother, Tamerlan, to convince the jury to vote for a life without parole sentence rather than the death penalty.[44]

The Presentation of Evidence

After opening statements, the prosecution calls its witnesses. Witnesses may be the officers who first responded to the crime scene, the family members or friends who last spoke to the victim, or witnesses who encountered the defendant or victim and could testify about their statements or demeanor. When a lawyer calls a witness to the stand, the examination is called **direct examination**. The questions are open-ended, meaning that there is no suggested answer and the questions are designed to allow the witness to do all of the talking. Most direct examination questions begin with *who, what, where, how, why, when,* and *where* because the goal is to let the witness tell what happened. After direct examination, the opposing counsel gets an opportunity to conduct cross-examination.

The goal of **cross-examination** is very different from that of direct examination and often involves attacking a witness's credibility as one way to reach the truth.[45] In cross-examination, lawyers try to highlight any inconsistencies in the witness's testimony, and to expose any bias the witness may have in testifying. The cross-examination question is a close-ended question, one that suggests the answer and invites the witness to simply answer yes or no. For example, if Tsarnaev took the witness stand in the Boston Marathon trial, the prosecutor might ask the following cross-examination questions:

You went to the Marathon? (Yes)

You were carrying a backpack? (Yes)

You placed that backpack down near the finish line? (Yes)

Direct and Circumstantial Evidence

Typical jury instructions distinguish between direct and circumstantial evidence as follows: Direct evidence is evidence that directly proves a fact. It is evidence which by itself, if found to be true, establishes that fact. An example is eyewitness testimony from Sondrea that she watched the snow fall last night. Circumstantial evidence is evidence that, if found to be true, proves a fact from which an inference of the existence of another fact may be drawn. A factual inference is a deduction that may logically and reasonably be drawn from one or more facts established by the evidence. For instance, if Sondrea wakes up in the morning and sees the snow-covered ground but she did not see it snow last night, she can draw an inference that it snowed last night. Facts at trial can be proved by both direct and circumstantial evidence, and both have equal weight as acceptable means of proof.[46]

Physical Evidence

Evidence Collection. Evidence technicians are called to the crime scene to collect and catalogue where evidence was found. A chain of custody is a paper trail that links the evidence, similar to chain links, from initial discovery to the defendant's trial. To ensure that evidence has not been altered, substituted, or tampered with, the chain of custody records every person who has touched the evidence from initial retrieval to trial.

Testimonial Evidence

Witnesses at trial give testimonial evidence when they speak under oath from the witness stand and give information to the court. There are two types of witnesses at trial: the lay witness, who is a regular person describing the facts and events relating to the trial, and the expert witness, hired by either side to give technical or specialized testimony about the issues in dispute at trial.

Lay Witnesses. A lay witness is an average person who has experiences common to most adults and who can testify in court about facts such as the speed a car was traveling, if someone was intoxicated, and if someone the lay witness knew very well was insane. Before a witness can testify at trial, the witness must be personally familiar with the subject he or she is talking about. A fisherman may know something about the steak he eats but would probably be poorly qualified to testify to what a butcher does daily. Before evidence can be admitted to the jury, there are specialized rudiments and procedures to make evidence admissible, and the opponent can make objections to try and keep the evidence out. Only the judge decides if evidence is admissible or not, and the jury can reach a verdict only on the evidence admitted during trial.

Expert Witnesses and Scientific Evidence. In certain trials, the jury needs detailed scientific or technical knowledge to help make their decision about guilt or innocence, controlled by the applicable federal or state Rules of Evidence dependent on the jurisdiction.[47] The prosecution or defense hires an expert witness who is paid to evaluate the evidence and render an opinion about the case in court. There are two legal standards governing the admissibility of expert testimony. One, still viable in states such as New York, is the standard enunciated in *Frye v. United States* (1923),[48] where lie detector results were inadmissible because they are unreliable and the results produced are not the product of rigorously tested and well recognized scientific methods.

Although polygraphs are often used as an investigation technique, the results generally remain inadmissible at trial.[49] The court in *Frye* adopted the "general acceptance" standard: If the science or technique had achieved general acceptance in the relevant scientific community that used it, it would be admissible in court.

Federal courts announced a new standard in 1993 in the case *Daubert v. Merrill Dow Pharmaceuticals* (1993).[50] In *Daubert*, petitioners were minor children born with serious birth defects who brought a lawsuit alleging that the defects had been caused by the mothers' ingestion of Bendectin, a prescription drug to combat nausea. At trial, the judge excluded the petitioners' scientific evidence because it failed the general acceptance test. On appeal, the U.S. Supreme Court held that the "general acceptance test" was too narrow and enunciated five factors, now known as the *Daubert* test, that a judge should look at in determining whether expert testimony would be admissible at trial:

1. Has the theory the expert will testify about been tested?

2. Has it been subject to peer review?

3. What is the known rate of error?

4. Do standards and controls to test the theory or instrument exist?

5. Is the theory/instrument generally accepted within the relevant scientific community?

The trial judge, deemed the "gatekeeper" of all admissible evidence, determines whether the expert's proposed testimony sufficiently meets the *Daubert* criterion that has been held to apply to all expert testimony, not just "scientific" testimony.[51]

APPLYING THE LAW TO THE FACTS

Does Terrorist Radicalization Expert Testimony Meet the *Daubert* Standard?

The Facts: The following expert testimony was offered at the Boston Marathon bombing trial to explain the "radicalization" process that inspires someone to commit terrorist acts.

Mr. Chakravarty (prosecutor): And how does radicalization take place?

Matthew Levitt (expert witness): There is no one model for how radicalization takes place. Every single one of us is an individual. Our experiences are different. . . . And you'll be able to find cases that are similar to one another . . . but at the end of the day it's the combination of these two baskets: grievances, local and international; and some type of ideology. Now, mind you, of course, it doesn't have to be a deviation of Islam. It doesn't have to be radical Islamist ideology, right? We've seen a rise of white supremacist activity in this country since we elected an African-American president, right? But that combination of grievance and ideology. . . .

[N]ow in the age of social media and digital media, someone doesn't have to be in person, but someone has to be able to kind of hold your hand and pull you across that dividing line to the point where you mobilize and actually do, operationalize, these ideas.

Prosecutor: Is there a way to measure how radicalized somebody is?

Expert witness: Lots of people have tried. The simple answer is: Until someone actually acts, there's complete room for debate, all right? There's no quantifiable, this is a 3.2 radicalization . . .

Mr. Bruck (defense counsel): Your Honor, if you'd please, I'm going to object to any further testimony along this line without a showing of any scientific basis for measuring how radical someone is whether they have acted or not. This is a *Daubert* issue . . .[52]

Question: Is the expert's testimony grounded in sufficient scientific fact under the *Daubert* criteria to be admissible against Dzhokhar Tsarnaev at trial?

The Law: Yes. Under the *Daubert* precedent, the judge allowed Mr. Levitt to testify that material found on Tsarnaev's computer indicated that Tsarnaev was radicalized and motivated to commit terrorist acts.

Expert testimony often introduces scientific evidence, which links the methods used to commit the crime—for instance, firearm and tool marks, fire debris from arson and explosives, or digital evidence from electronic devices and transmissions—to the offender, who may have left impressions and prints from fingers, hands, feet, shoes, or tires as well as biological or serological evidence of blood or other bodily fluids. Only reliable scientific evidence is admissible in court. There have been notable examples of systemic failures in state and federal laboratories that have resulted in the exonerations of men and women wrongfully convicted on the basis of faulty or fraudulent scientific methods.[53]

Demonstrative Evidence

Springboard for Discussion

The Federal Bureau of Investigation (FBI) revealed that their expert examiners conducting hair analysis had given testimony unsupported by reliable scientific methods.[54] What do you believe is the proper acceptable rate of error for scientific evidence in criminal trials?

Demonstrative evidence is anything that can help a jury, or a judge in a case where the defendant chooses a bench trial, understand the issues in the case. Where oral testimony may describe a crime scene, a photograph of the crime scene will be much more helpful to the jury and is something they can take back into the deliberation room as they consider the evidence in the case. Common types of demonstrative evidence introduced at trial are photographs, maps, illustrations, and models that show a particular place or scene. At the Boston Marathon trial, the government introduced replica pressure-cooker bombs lined with pellets and stuffed with fireworks in black backpacks as the types used by the bombers to illustrate for the jurors how the defendant committed the crime. The prosecution also showed the jury the boat where Tsarnaev was found hiding and where he scrawled his justification for his criminal acts.

Hearsay and the Defendant's Confession

The technical definition of hearsay is a written or spoken statement made outside of court and offered in court to prove the truth of the matter at issue. The common definition of hearsay is "he said, she said" evidence. For example, Sue is a witness at Graham's bank robbery trial and testifies that "Michael told me that Graham robbed the bank." Sue's statement about what Michael said is hearsay. Hearsay is generally excluded from trial because the individual making the out-of-court statement (Michael) or providing the written document cannot be challenged, which deprives the defendant of his right to confrontation. Allowing hearsay evidence at trial also prevents the jury from examining the demeanor and credibility of the person making the statement because that person is typically not in court. The U.S. Supreme Court has said about hearsay:

> Out-of-court statements are traditionally excluded [in court] because they lack the conventional indicia of reliability: they are usually not made under oath or other circumstances that impress the speaker with the solemnity of his statements; the declarant's word is not subject to cross examination; and he is not available in order that his demeanor and credibility may be assessed by the jury.[55]

A defendant's statements or confession made during the investigation are made "out of court" and offered for their truth—that the defendant *is*, indeed, guilty. When two parties are on opposite sides of the "*v*" in a legal proceeding, the participants can introduce statements made by their opponent, called a party opponent. *U.S. v. Tsarnaev*, for example, permits the prosecution to introduce Tsarnaev's statements (opposite side of the *v*.) and Tsarnaev can introduce statements made on behalf of the U.S. government (on the other side of the *v*.). Tsarnaev's written statement made in the boat where he was captured was admissible against him at trial as a party opponent admission. When informants testify for the government that the defendant confessed, that testimony is also admissible as a party opponent admission.

Closing Arguments

The closing argument is the opportunity for attorneys to summarize the evidence for the jury and advocate for the conclusions they wish the jury to draw from the evidence before the jury retires to deliberate and return a verdict. Prosecutorial ethics demand that government actors ensure that justice is served in each and every case, but also constrain prosecutorial activities during trial. Many prosecutors during their closing arguments invite the jury to "do their duty" and convict the defendant or "speak for the victim" and convict. The Supreme Court of Georgia found error (a mistake) when a prosecutor cited the Bible as justification for a jury to award a death sentence. The prosecutor talked to the jury and said:

Rule of Law: Closing arguments are not evidence, but in arguing to the jury lawyers must follow evidence law.

> Now, ladies and gentlemen, let me talk to you a moment about some biblical references that help us in this case. Deterrence is very important, and the Bible suggests to us why deterrence is appropriate. Romans tells us that every person is subject to the governing authority, every person is subject. And in Matthew it tells us, who sheddeth man's blood by man shall his blood be shed for in the image of God made [he] man.[56] For all they who take the sword shall die by the sword, and this is a message that is very clear, that society must deter criminals.

In overturning the defendant's death sentence, the court held that any actions designed to improperly inflame the jury's passion and to invite the jurors to decide cases on the basis of emotions rather than facts and evidence violated the defendant's due process right to a fair trial.[57]

In Dzhokhar Tsarnaev's case, the prosecution at closing argument urged the jury to find Dzhokhar guilty and said, "The defendant brought terrorism to backyards and main streets . . . [and] chose a day when the eyes of the world would be on Boston. He chose a day when there would be civilians on the sidewalks." In contrast, even though defense counsel admitted Tsarnaev's guilt in opening statements, counsel argued in closing, "We are not asking you to excuse the conduct, but let's look at the varying roles . . . We don't deny that Dzhokhar fully participated in the events, but if it were not for Tamerlan, it would not have happened."[58]

The Jury

Charge Conference

Before closing arguments, the judge meets with the lawyers for a charge conference during which the lawyers submit proposed jury instructions that each side wants the judge to give to the jury. If the judge does not give an instruction, the jury cannot consider the charge. The judge decides what instructions to give based on the evidence introduced at trial. If no evidence was introduced to support the charge or defense, the judge will not give the jury instruction.

Jury Instructions

After both sides make closing arguments, the judge instructs the jury on the law to apply to the facts. Jury instructions are technical definitions that define the elements of the crimes charged, that give the applicable defenses, if any, and that define burdens of proof and presumptions. A standard jury instruction, for instance, in a criminal case where the defendant did not take the stand in his defense, is that the jury can draw no adverse inference from the defendant's exercising his right to remain silent.

Deliberations and the Verdict

After the end of the presentation of evidence and closing arguments by counsel, the jury retires to deliberate, which is to discuss and evaluate the evidence to come to a conclusion about the case to render a verdict. During deliberations, all the jurors assess the credibility of witnesses and weigh the evidence admitted at trial to render a verdict. It is the jury's first opportunity to discuss the case. Even if the trial lasted for weeks and the jury was together taking breaks and eating lunch together and, in the case of a sequestered jury, sleeping in the same hotel together, the judge has admonished them not to talk about the facts of the case because all of the evidence has yet to be introduced. Typically, jury deliberations are secret, but if a juror engages in discriminatory conduct during deliberations, such violations of the defendant's due process rights to a fair trial can be made public. In *Pena-Rodriguez v. Colorado*, (2017),[59] a juror made inflammatory remarks about Hispanic men to conclude that the defendant was guilty of sexual assault. On appeal, the high Court reversed Pena-Rodriguez's conviction saying that the Sixth Amendment guarantee of a fair trial requires the jury arrive at a verdict *not* based on ethnic stereotypes.

In all states except Oregon and Louisiana, a unanimous verdict of all 12 jurors is required to convict. If deliberations come to a standstill and the jury seems deadlocked (unable to decide), then the judge will often give an *Allen* charge that says, "Keep going until a decision is made."[60] In the June 2017 sexual assault trial of comedian Bill Cosby, the jury deliberated for 6 days and received *Allen* charges from the judge to keep going before declaring the jury deadlocked and a **mistrial**, where the court decides that the trial fatally flawed, and the government must start the prosecution anew. At retrial in 2018, Cosby was convicted. Typically in a death-penalty case, if the verdict to impose the death penalty is not unanimous, most states require the imposition of a life without parole sentence.

Verdict Form. Before the jury retires for deliberations, the Clerk of Court will hand the bailiff the verdict forms, which are to be filled out and signed by the jury foreperson. The **verdict form** will reflect the charges and defenses that were the substance of the jury instructions given by the judge. Once the jury begins its deliberations, they typically elect a jury foreperson who will then be tasked with tallying votes on the charges and, when a verdict is reached, fills out the verdict form and signs it as a true conclusion of the jury. A mistake made on the presentation of the charges on the verdict form may be a mistake on appeal that results in the defendant being granted a new trial.

HOW A CASE GETS TO THE U.S. SUPREME COURT

Federal or Federal Constitutional Issue Required

The United States has a two-tiered court system called a **dual court system.** The two courts run parallel to each other like two sets of train tracks that may eventually meet at the same big train station, the U.S. Supreme Court. On one track are the state systems that may vary how a case works through the trial and appellate courts, and on the other train track is the federal system, as illustrated in Figure 2.2. Both state and federal court systems have trial courts where cases are initially heard and appellate courts where the losing party at trial often complains about the outcome at trial. In criminal law, typically the losing party is a convicted criminal defendant. In the chapter-opening case study, Dzhokhar Tsarnaev's case is eligible for review at the U.S. Supreme Court because all death-penalty cases involve an assessment of the Eighth Amendment's ban on cruel and unusual punishment, a federal issue.

Appellate courts are typically composed of three to six judges, and the U.S. Supreme Court has nine judges, an uneven number to ensure one party will win a decisive vote, by 5–4 for example. In the federal circuit, after the initial denial of the motion for a new trial, the appeal travels to the Circuit Court of Appeals for the federal circuit in which the federal trial court sits. Once the appellate court makes its decision, it can **affirm** (uphold), the lower court's decision or **reverse** (overturn) the lower court's decision, which means to nullify the jury's verdict and **remand** the case (send the case back) to the trial court with the admonishment to take the appellate court's decision into account in retrying the case.

The U.S. Supreme Court today operates as the country's highest appellate court. The U.S. Supreme Court receives thousands of petitions to hear cases. For those it wishes to hear, the court grants a *writ of certiorari*, which roughly translates to a request to bring the case record

Figure 2.2   Dual Court System

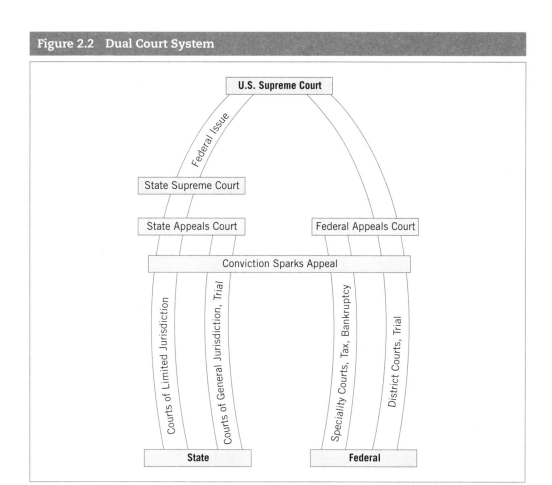

U.S. Supreme Court

Federal Issue

State Supreme Court

State Appeals Court

Federal Appeals Court

Conviction Sparks Appeal

Courts of Limited Jurisdiction

Courts of General Jurisdiction, Trial

Speciality Courts, Tax, Bankruptcy

District Courts, Trial

State

Federal

forward. One of the factors the court uses to decide which cases to hear is the national import of the Court's decision. By operation of the Constitution's Supremacy Clause, once the Supreme Court speaks, it is the final word. So, rather than take one case that may affect a small segment of the population, the high Court usually takes a case that affects everyone.

Rule of Law: All cases decided by the U.S. Supreme Court involve a federal issue.

SUMMARY

1. You will understand the requirements and pitfalls of the pretrial identification process. Pretrial identification procedures include the line-up, in which several people are placed behind a two-way mirror and the "fillers" are chosen for their similarity in appearance to the suspect; the photo array, in which one suspect is shown with at least five other fillers who are not suspects but may look similar to the suspect; and the most suggestive pretrial identification procedure, the show-up, in which the suspect, alone, is paraded past or in front of the eyewitness. One way to

    reduce mistakes is showing the witness sequential photos, one after the other, to force him to make an absolute, rather than a relative, decision in identifying a suspect. The pretrial identification procedure must be reliable, or it will be excluded at trial as determined by the five-part *Biggers* test.

2. You will be able to articulate the legal requirements of discovery and the definition of exculpatory evidence. Exculpatory evidence is any evidence tending to prove the defendant is innocent. The U.S. Supreme Court requires the

government under *Brady v. Maryland* (1963), to disclose to the defendant any exculpatory information learned during the investigation. Under the ancillary cases of *Giglio v. United States* (1972), *United States v. Bagley* (1985), and *Kyles v. Whitley* (1995), the government must also tell the defense impeachment information if witnesses change their stories about the crime or defendant, if their "memories" improve, all details about informants working the case, inconsistent statements, and if police had other suspects they failed to investigate.

3. You can distinguish the various steps taken before the trial, including the plea bargaining process. After a suspect is arrested, he is booked. The suspect's personal information is processed into the system, and the suspect must be brought before a judge within a reasonable time, usually 48 hours, for an initial appearance. The defendant enters a formal plea at an arraignment. A bail determination is made, and the suspect is released into the community to await trial if he is not a danger to others or does not pose a flight risk. A defendant may file many pretrial motions, or applications for court orders, before trial. The defendant may file a motion to suppress (i.e., ask the court to exclude specific evidence, usually due to government misconduct in procuring the evidence), a motion *in limine* (i.e., ask the court to rule on the admissibility of evidence before trial), a motion to dismiss the case or certain charges for insufficient evidence, a motion to sever from her codefendants to ensure her right to a fair trial, or a motion to change venue (the place where the trial will be held) because of extensive pretrial publicity or other factors that may reduce her chance of receiving a fair hearing. Plea agreements benefit both prosecutors and defendants. In exchange for eliminating some charges or for promising to argue for leniency in sentencing in front of the judge, the prosecutor gets a sure conviction and the defendant gets a known and certain jail time. There are many types of pleas (*Alford*, no contest, and pursuant to a plea agreement), but all defendants must successfully survive the plea colloquy in which the judge ensures that the defendant is making a voluntary, intelligent, and knowing waiver of all his trial rights by pleading guilty.

4. You will be able to explain the mechanics of a criminal trial and the different types of evidence. The prosecution carries the burden of proof (i.e., to prove the defendant guilty beyond a reasonable doubt) and presents evidence first. The U.S. Supreme Court has interpreted the Sixth Amendment's requirement of a fair trial to mean that a defendant can be tried by a jury of his peers taken from a representative cross-section of the community. The fair cross-section of the community requirement does not mean that a defendant has a right to be tried in front of a panel of people who are similar to him in race, age, or socioeconomic background. In jury selection, called *voir dire*, lawyers can remove jurors for cause or by peremptory strike. The government cannot use its peremptory challenges to eliminate potential jurors on the basis of their race under *Batson v. Kentucky* (1986), or gender under *J.E.B. v. Alabama ex rel. T.B.* (1994). Both sides make an opening statement that tells the jury what the evidence will show during trial. The primary types of evidence at trial are direct evidence (e.g., a gun, witness testimony about who saw the events in question, or test results), circumstantial, testimonial, demonstrative, expert, and scientific evidence. After the prosecution presents its case, the defendant can present his case, although, legally, the defense does not have to put forth a case. Before closing arguments, the attorneys meet with the judge for a charge conference and discuss what instructions to submit to the jury. After closing arguments, in which both counsel summarize the evidence and argue why the jury should find the defendant not guilty or guilty, the judge gives jury instructions that tell the jury the law to follow to render their verdict. Then the jury deliberates and decides whether to acquit or convict the defendant. The jury fills out a verdict form that announces its verdict.

5. You will identify the process by which a criminal case gets to the U.S. Supreme Court. America has a dual court system with trial and appellate courts at both the state and the federal level. Once a defendant loses at trial and is convicted, he or she often complains to an appellate court about legal errors that were made during trial. If a state case involves a federal or federal constitutional issue, the defendant can appeal to a federal appellate court. The highest federal appellate court is the U.S. Supreme Court, which decides what cases it wants to hear when it grants *writs of certiorari*.

Go back to the beginning of the chapter and reread the news excerpts associated with the learning objectives. Test yourself to determine if you can understand the material covered in the text in the context of the news.

KEY TERMS AND PHRASES

absolute decision 39

adversarial system 40

affirm 60

aggravating circumstances 40

Alford plea 50

appellate court 60

arraignment 43

arrest 43

bail 43

beyond a reasonable doubt 52

booking 43

burden of proof 52

chain of custody 56

challenge for cause 54

charge conference 59

circumstantial evidence 56

closing argument 59

conditional plea 50

PROBLEM-SOLVING EXERCISES

Problems 1 through 3 are based on the following adapted case:

A man with no criminal history, Davy Blue, went to his wife's place of employment and killed her and seven others with an assault rifle. Blue was placed in the Orange County (CA) jail and assigned a public defender to represent him. The jail had a medical unit named L-20 that housed "jail-house snitches," who were well known to the authorities for their success in obtaining incriminating information from unsuspecting detainees awaiting trial. Blue was placed in a cell next to L-20 and, over several months, simultaneously worked on his defense with his lawyer and made friends with Daniel Bond. Daniel Bond wrote a letter to Blue's prosecuting attorney, Marvin Havel, which said:

"I know your [sic] prosecuting the high-profile murder case. The shooter has confessed to me and I am willing to testify about his admission of guilt at his trial if you will help me in my current case."

Bond told Havel that Blue confessed that he was very angry with his wife about the pending divorce and wanted to kill her. Havel offered Bond a plea bargain in exchange for his testimony. Bond pleaded guilty to all his charges and was facing 25 years imprisonment, but his sentencing was continued until a later date. Bond then testified against Blue, told the court Blue confessed, and Blue was found guilty and sentenced to death. Blue then appealed his conviction.

You are a clerk to a California appellate court who asks you to read this chapter and answer the following questions:

1. Subsequent investigation determined that the jail's handling of the informant unit was tracked by an internal computer program that traced known informants and placed them in or near cells of pretrial detainees to obtain incriminating information. Blue had filed a general discovery motion before trial, but the government did not disclose the L-20 informant unit TRED. Blue claims he had a right to the jail's computer file. Did Blue have a right to the jail's computer file? (**ROL: Exculpatory evidence**)

2. Blue denies saying anything to Bond and says he never confessed or admitted any details of the crimes. Blue claims that admitting Bond's testimony was a violation of the hearsay rule, which does not allow for "he said, she said" information in a court of law. Was admitting the defendant's confession a violation of the hearsay rule that keeps evidence out at trial? (**ROL: Hearsay, defendant's confession as party opponent admission**)

3. At Blue's trial, Prosecutor Havel introduced Dr. Sacramento as a witness to testify that Blue fit the profile of a life-long criminal and, because of his mindset to kill lots of people, the death penalty would be an appropriate sentence. The defense objected based on the *Daubert* standard of admissibility of expert testimony. Does the expert's testimony about Blue's profile as a "life-long" criminal meet the *Daubert* admissibility standard? (**ROL: *Daubert* test, death-penalty eligibility**)

3

CRIMINAL LAW BASICS

First, go to the end of the chapter. Skim the key terms and phrases and read the summary closely. Come back and look at the following news excerpts to focus your reading throughout the chapter to understand the law that gives authority to the government for putting people in jail for committing crimes; the mental states that govern how harshly an offender may be punished; how to determine whether an offender actually causes harm to, or the death of, another; and the legal requirements to hold offenders responsible for incomplete crimes. This chapter examines the basics of criminal law concepts that remain the same regardless of jurisdiction; these concepts include *mens rea*, *actus reus*, intent, criminal causation, and parties to crimes. It also discusses how society punishes the crimes of attempt, solicitation, and conspiracy. We open the chapter with a hypothetical (not real) case study loosely based on a series of events related to hurricanes hitting the American Gulf Coast. The case study illustrates the concepts under review in the chapter and the associated rules of law (ROLs) that apply in similar situations. As you read through the chapter, look for the references to the case study to help understand how the law is applied in specific fact situations.

WHY THIS CHAPTER MATTERS TO YOU	THE LEARNING OBJECTIVES AS REFLECTED IN THE NEWS
After you have read this chapter: **Learning Objective 1:** You will understand the four *mens rea* states to establish the defendant's "guilty mind."	Gaul's friends reported him after he fired two bullets at Walker's house from a position outside. One bullet became stuck in the wall. The other entered the wall and struck Walker in the head, killing her instantly. At trial, the defense admitted Gaul was the triggerman, but disputed his intent. Prosecutors said he committed premeditated, intentional murder. Gaul already admitted to a reckless conduct charge for firing into the occupied Walker house. (*Law & Crime*, May 4, 2018)
Learning Objective 2: You will be able to explain the legal basis for volitional *actus reus*, the "guilty act."	Seven Supreme Court of Canada judges have agreed with the legal team of a former Alberta couple, Collet and David Stephan, that the original trial judge erred in instructions to the 2016 jury who convicted the couple in the death of their toddler son. The two elements the judges believe were combined by the trial judge are *actus reus* and *mens rea*. *Actus reus*, Latin for guilty act, raises the question of whether the Stephans failed to provide their son with the medical attention that was necessary in the circumstances . . . in this case meaning not taking a child displaying symptoms of meningitis to the hospital. (CBC News, May 15, 2018)

WHY THIS CHAPTER MATTERS TO YOU	THE LEARNING OBJECTIVES AS REFLECTED IN THE NEWS
Learning Objective 3: You will competently discuss the elements of "causation" to assign criminal responsibility.	Kalo Doyle, 25, is charged with racing on a roadway causing serious bodily injury or death. He and Gilbert Burton, 52, both of Texarkana Texas, were said to be racing at a high rate of speed on the afternoon of March 20 [2018]. Police say Doyle's Mustang struck the side of LaQuania Hopkins' Toyota Avalon. She later died at the scene . . . [the crime of] 'Racing on Roadway Causing Serious Bodily Injury or Death' is a second-degree felony. (KSLA News [TX], April 27, 2018)
Learning Objective 4: You will know the common law differences between principals and accessories.	Sierras Cobb, 42, was on trial on a charge of accessory after the fact to second-degree murder. Forsyth County prosecutors accused Cobb of driving Anthony Abran away after Abran fatally shot Delmorio Blockson, 26, just after 3 a.m. May 27, 2015. When Abran got into Cobb's car, Cobb asked, "Bro, are you alright?" Then Cobb asked, "What can I do?" [The prosecutor] said those questions indicate that Cobb knew Abran had killed a man and Cobb wanted to see what he could do to help Abran get away from the crime scene. (*Winston-Salem Journal* [NC], April 20, 2018)
Learning Objective 5: You will understand the elements of inchoate crimes, such as solicitation, conspiracy, and attempt.	Last week, [the Vermont Legislature] was far less united in its response to the case of Jack Sawyer, the 18-year-old Poultney man police said had plans to kill as many people as he could at Fair Haven Union High School before the plot was foiled. The justices said merely planning a crime under state law does not rise to an attempt. As a result, prosecutors have since dismissed the most severe charges against the Poultney teen, including three counts of attempted murder. In its ruling, the high court invited the Legislature to make changes to the state's attempt law to avoid a similar situation from occurring again. (VTDigger, May 2, 2018)

Chapter-Opening Case Study: Hurricane Michael, October 2018

In Mexico Beach, Florida, on October 8, 2018, a few days before Hurricane Michael hit Florida's Panhandle, officials asked the owners of a local nursing home, Gerald Smith, 65, and his wife Mary, 62, whether they wanted to move the 71 residents to a safe shelter. The Smiths said no. They had been caring for the elderly at their nursing home for more than 10 years and had a spotless record. Gerald assured officials that they would evacuate if necessary. When Michael made landfall, 200,000 homes and businesses lost power. At the nursing home, 10 seniors died when the air conditioners, breathing machines, and dialysis machines failed. **(Rule of Law [ROL]: Reckless means you are aware of the risk of harm your behavior creates and you ignore it.)** A prosecutor charged the Smiths with 10 counts of homicide under the statute:

Whoever purposely, knowingly, recklessly, or negligently causes the death of another, shall be guilty of homicide.

The Smiths were charged with manslaughter, but asserted in their defense that they had no duty to save the residents **(ROL: Duty by contract = the document defines affirmative obligations; duty by statute = the law creates affirmative obligations)** from a natural disaster and that they did not *cause* their deaths. **(ROL: Factual cause: "but for"; proximate**

cause: whether the harm was foreseeable; intervening cause: any events that broke the causal chain from the offender to the ultimate harm?)

The Smiths were not the only people in court after the hurricane. People who could not evacuate crammed into a local sports venue. Ken, who was pushed to the basketball court in a wheelchair and who was attached to a blood purification machine that required electricity to run, was placed next to an outlet powered by a generator, but no one knew the generator was not working. One man, Billy Bob **(ROL: Principal is the main actor in committing the crime)**, approached Charles **(ROL: Accessory is a helper, before, during, or after the crime)** and asked if Charles wanted to make some easy money by robbing all the old people in the venue. **(ROL: Solicitation is asking someone to commit a crime)** Charles agreed to rob the seniors. **(ROL: Conspiracy is an agreement to commit a crime.)** Carrying out their plan, Billy Bob and Charles approached vulnerable seniors. Billy Bob saw Ken near the outlet and hit Ken over the head, intending to kill him before robbing him. Unbeknownst to Billy Bob, at the time of the robbery Ken was already dead from the lack of electricity to run his life-saving machine. **(ROL: Attempt is specific intent + unsuccessful *actus reus*; ROL: impossibility is a defense based on the physical impossibility of completing the crime.)**

Billy Bob was charged with solicitation and, along with Charles, was charged with conspiracy and the attempted murder of Ken. How will the cases against Billy Bob, Charles, and the Smiths be resolved?

MENS REA: THE GUILTY MIND

Rule of Law: One can only be in one *mens rea* state at a time.

In criminal law, the defendant's state of mind when she committed a crime, or *mens rea*, is critical for judges and juries to assign the proper level of responsibility for the crime. A contract killer who kills his victim after loading a pistol, pointing it, and shooting at the victim's vital organs is more responsible, blameworthy, and culpable than a driver who is obeying the speed limit in a residential neighborhood who hits a child who unexpectedly runs into the street. The *mens rea* is the springboard for the criminal act, called the *actus reus*. The *mens rea* for an intentional killing is purposely, whereas the *mens rea* for the accidental killing would be negligently.

Based on the state of mind of the offender, the law defines crimes and grades offenses, such as the difference between murder and manslaughter in the previous example. Some regulatory crimes designed to protect public safety, such as food inspections at restaurants and traffic offenses, require no *mens rea* for the offender to be found guilty. Such crimes are called strict liability crimes, discussed later in this chapter. One is guilty under strict liability by the simple act of committing the prohibited conduct, regardless of intent.

Today's criminal law can trace its roots to early church doctrine that defined acts that harmed society in terms of moral purity.[1] Early definitions of *mens rea* were described as acting "wantonly," "heedlessly," "maliciously," with a "depraved heart," "evil," and with "knowledge aforethought." Today, crimes are defined by legislatures enacting statutes defining forbidden conduct and the required mental state necessary for conviction. The words used to describe the various *mens rea* states can be a confusing and jumbled mess, as scholar Geraldine Moohr writes,

> By one count, federal criminal laws use seventy-eight different *mens rea* terms. These terms often have numerous and conflicting meanings. For example, in bribery and obstruction statutes, Congress uses the *mens rea* term "corruptly," which has no intrinsic meaning, and then guarantees indeterminacy by failing to define it. Courts must construe the term as best they can, depending on the circumstances of the case and a reading of congressional intent. Understandably, interpretations of identical terms have come to vary significantly.[2]

Students are advised to research their respective state jurisdictions and criminal codes to learn the state's crime definitions. A typical law assigning criminal responsibility by requiring concurrence of *mens rea* and *actus reus* is illustrated in the Ohio statute reprinted, in part, on the following page.

To be found guilty in Ohio, an offender needs a culpable mental state (called *culpability* in the statute), a voluntary act, and the absence of a defense, such as intoxication that might interfere with the formation of the requisite *mens rea*.[3] Remember from Chapter 1 the common law rule of lenity applies where courts will resolve any ambiguity in criminal statutes in the defendant's favor to lessen, rather than increase, the punishment.[4]

Ohio Revised Code Annotated 2901.21 (2015)

Requirements for Criminal Liability

(A) Except as provided in division (B) of this section, a person is not guilty of an offense unless both of the following apply:

    (1) The person's liability is based on conduct that includes either a voluntary act, or an omission to perform an act or duty that the person is capable of performing;

    (2) The person has the requisite degree of culpability for each element as to which a culpable mental state is specified by the language defining the offense.

(B) When the language defining an offense does not specify any degree of culpability, and plainly indicates a purpose to impose strict criminal liability for the conduct described in the section, then culpability is not required for a person to be guilty of the offense.

(C)

    (1) When language defining an element of an offense that is related to knowledge or intent or to which *mens rea* could fairly be applied neither specifies culpability nor plainly indicates a purpose to impose strict liability, the element of the offense is established only if a person acts recklessly . . . .

(D) Omitted . . .

(E) Voluntary intoxication may not be taken into consideration in determining the existence of a mental state that is an element of a criminal offense. Voluntary intoxication does not relieve a person of a duty to act if failure to act constitutes a criminal offense. Evidence that a person was voluntarily intoxicated may be admissible to show whether or not the person was physically capable of performing the act with which the person is charged.

(F) As used in this section:

    (1) Possession is a voluntary act if the possessor knowingly procured or received the thing possessed, or was aware of the possessor's control of the thing possessed for a sufficient time to have ended possession.

    (2) Reflexes, convulsions, body movements during unconsciousness or sleep, and body movements that are not otherwise a product of the actor's volition, are involuntary acts.

    (3) "Culpability" means purpose, knowledge, recklessness, or negligence, as defined in section 2901.22 of the Revised Code.

    (4) "Intoxication" includes, but is not limited to, intoxication resulting from the ingestion of alcohol, a drug, or alcohol and a drug.

Mens Rea and the Model Penal Code

To streamline the various definitions of mental states used to assign criminal responsibility for an offender's actions, the Model Penal Code (MPC) offers four standard definitions of *mens rea* states. The *mens rea* states listed in order of culpability (blame) from most to less serious are purposely, knowingly, recklessly, and negligently. Figure 3.1 illustrates how the *mens rea* states resemble the food chain in the sea where big fish eats little fish. The bigger the fish is, the higher the state of moral culpability will be and the more severe the punishment for the offense committed. The *mens rea* states are also exclusive—that is, one cannot possess more than one mental state at a time. One cannot both intentionally and negligently shoot someone even if a statute lists all four mental states, which is common, for example, defining homicide as the "purposeful, knowing, reckless, or negligent killing of another." The public policy reasons behind separating *mens rea* states are similar to the reasons we recognize certain defenses. Society does not hold the person who kills another on purpose to the same level of culpability as the careless smoker who falls asleep with a lit cigarette, setting a house on fire and killing people trapped inside. The average sentences for such crimes differ based on the *mens rea* of bringing about the result where people are harmed. The MPC also addresses attendant circumstances, which are external facts surrounding the criminal act required for conviction for certain crimes. In a sexual assault case, if the victim was under the influence of drugs and alcohol, was a child, or was intellectually or physically disabled, those attendant circumstances of victim vulnerability justifies elevating the assault to aggravated status eligible for harsher sentencing.

Rule of Law: Purposely is taking a specific act to bring about a specific result.

Purposely

The MPC §2.02 defines *Purposely* in the following way:
A person acts purposely with respect to a material element of an offense when

(i) if the element involves the nature of his conduct or a result thereof, it is his conscious object to engage in conduct of that nature or to cause such a result; and

(ii) if the element involves the attendant circumstances, he is aware of the existence of such circumstances or he believes or hopes that they exist.

Acting purposely is taking a specific act to bring about a specific result. If an offender takes a crow bar and creeps about at night with the intent to force open a window in an empty house with the specific intent to rob the house, he has acted purposefully to bring about a specific result, to steal things of value from the home. Purposely is the most culpable *mens rea* state, which would, for example, sustain a first-degree murder conviction, for which the death penalty may be imposed.

Figure 3.1   *Mens Rea* Food Chain

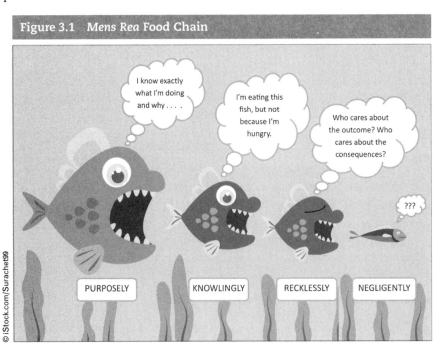

Knowingly

The MPC §2.02 defines *Knowingly* in the following way:
A person acts knowingly with respect to a material element of an offense when

(i) if the element involves the nature of his conduct or the attendant circumstances, he is aware that his conduct is of that nature or that such circumstances exist; and

(ii) if the element involves a result of his conduct, he is aware that it is practically certain that his conduct will cause such a result.

> **Rule of Law: Knowingly means the offender was substantially certain that his conduct would bring about a specific result.**

Acting knowingly is acting not to bring about a specific result but knowing that such a result is practically certain to occur from one's actions. If a suspect running from the police is caught and flails his arms to free himself, he can be convicted of battery because he knew that his actions of resisting arrest would cause injury to an officer, even though the reason or purpose he flailed his arms was to escape. But the knowing requirement does not mean that the defendant knew a specific injury would result from his conduct, and the prosecutor need not prove that the defendant knew his acts would cause injury.

For instance, Morris burglarized a second-floor apartment and held a knife to the home's occupants, Truman and Harper, and demanded money. When Morris's back was turned, Truman jumped off the balcony. Harper, confused and not wanting to be in the apartment alone with Morris, also jumped off the balcony and sustained serious injuries. Morris was convicted of causing Harper's injuries because escape is a natural reaction to being held hostage. Because Harper's injuries were sustained as she tried to escape from Morris, Morris *knowingly* caused her serious physical harm.[5]

Recklessly

The MPC §2.02 defines *Recklessly* in the following way:
A person acts recklessly with respect to a material element of an offense when he consciously disregards a substantial and unjustifiable risk that the material element exists or will result from his conduct. The risk must be of such a nature and degree that, considering the nature and purpose of the actor's conduct and the circumstances known to him, its disregard involves a gross deviation from the standard of conduct that a law-abiding person would observe in the actor's situation.

> **Rule of Law: Recklessly means the offender was aware of the risk of harm to others that his actions created, and he ignored the risk.**

An example of reckless conduct would be drag racing on a crowded street at rush hour. The racers are aware of but ignore the risk of injury to others that their behavior (driving too fast) creates. Similarly, two friends arguing on the street each pull out a handgun with the intent to scare the other; both guns go off, but a stray bullet enters an adjacent house injuring a man standing in his kitchen. The friends were aware of the risk of harm their behavior (shooting guns to scare each other) created, yet they both ignored the risk and acted anyway. Referring back to the chapter-opening case study, Florida has suffered through many storms, and the Smiths were reckless in not evacuating the residents because power failure is a known risk of hurricanes; they ignored the risk that medically infirm nursing home residents could suffer and perish.

Negligently

The MPC §2.02 defines *Negligently* in the following way:
A person acts negligently with respect to a material element of an offense when he should be aware of a substantial and unjustifiable risk that the material element exists or will result from his conduct. The risk must be of such a nature and degree that the actor's failure to perceive [the risk] considering the nature and purpose of his conduct and the circumstances known to him, involves a *gross deviation from the standard of care that a reasonable person* would observe in the actor's situation (emphasis added).

> **Rule of Law: Negligently means the offender is unaware of the risk of harm his behavior creates, but he should be aware.**

Negligent acts are often defined as accidents. Negligence is the smallest of the *mens rea* fish in Figure 3.1, and negligent offenders are the least culpable and suffer less severe punishment than more culpable offenders. The negligence mental state is often used to hold people responsible for accidents or harm caused by ignorance.

Laws That Criminalize Behavior and Identify More Than One *Mens Rea* State

If someone is convicted of a "misdemeanor crime of domestic violence," federal law prohibits them from possessing a firearm.[6] In 2004, Stephen Voisine pleaded guilty to assaulting his girlfriend, a misdemeanor under Maine law that makes it a crime to "intentionally, knowingly or recklessly cause[ ] bodily injury or offensive physical contact to another person."[7] Years later when Voisine killed a bald eagle and authorities found that Voisine owned a rifle, he was charged with violating the federal gun law prohibiting his possession. Voisine was convicted and argued on appeal that he was only "reckless" in assaulting his girlfriend, and his behavior was not the intentional and knowing use of force contemplated by the federal law when Congress decided who should, and who should not, possess a firearm. The U.S. Supreme Court disagreed with Voisine. In relying on the MPC's definitions of the *mens rea* states, the Court made some of the following distinctions and gave the following boyfriend/girlfriend examples about an offender's state of mind when taking actions to hurt people.[8] The examples of each *mens rea* state described by the Court are reflected in Figure 3.2.

Intentionally/Purposely = Act with a state of mind to take actions to hurt someone with the resulting harm the "conscious object" of taking the action. Boyfriend knows his girlfriend is trailing closely behind him and opens the door, turns around as she is about to walk through, and slams the door in her face to cause her harm.

Knowingly = Taking action with the state of mind that you are aware that harm is practically certain to result from your conduct/action. Boyfriend knows his girlfriend is trailing closely behind him and opens the door. If he slams the door shut with his girlfriend following close behind, then he has done so—regardless of whether he thinks it absolutely sure or only quite likely—knowing that he will catch her fingers in the jamb.

Recklessly = Act with a state of mind that a substantial risk of harm to another will result from your actions, but you ignore that risk of harm your behavior creates. Boyfriend throws a plate in anger against the wall near where his girlfriend is standing. The boyfriend was reckless even if he did not know for certain (or have as his state of mind the conscious object of his actions), but only "recognized a substantial risk, that a shard from the plate would ricochet and injure his girlfriend."

Negligently = An accident: Boyfriend "with soapy hands loses his grip on a plate, which then shatters and cuts his" girlfriend, the resulting harm unintentional.

The *Voisine* case is an example of how the high Court interprets criminal law statutes, discusses the antiquated role of common law in defining present-day criminal conduct, and relies on common sense and everyday appreciation for what the phrase "use of force" means in sustaining domestic violence convictions based on reckless conduct.

Springboard for Discussion

Give the definitions of the *mens rea* states of purposely, knowingly, recklessly, and negligently, and give a brief example of each from your own life experiences sufficient to show your understanding of the differences and similarities among the four mental states.

Intent

Specific and General Intent

Mens rea incorporates the concept of intent, and the terms may be used interchangeably. Some crimes require specific intent, which is similar to purposely taking a specific act for a specific

Figure 3.2 *Mens Rea* States

Purposely (specific intent)	Purposely (specific intent) Act with a state of mind to take actions to hurt someone with the resulting harm the "conscious object" of taking the action.	
Knowing (general intent)	Taking action with the state of mind that you are aware that harm is practically certain to result from your conduct/action.	
Reckless	Act with a state of mind that a substantial risk of harm to another will result from your actions, but you ignore that risk of harm your behavior creates.	
Negligent	An accident, you are unaware of the risk of harm your behavior creates.	

result, for example, punching someone in the nose to bring about the desired result—a broken nose. **General intent** crimes occur when the offender takes a specific action without necessarily desiring a specific result.[9] Today the distinctions between specific and general intent are less common but remain viable to determine if the offender can avail himself of certain defenses. For example, intoxication may be a defense to the charge that the offender had the specific intent to commit a crime such as first-degree murder, but intoxication may not be a defense to general intent crimes such as arson.

In *Linehan v. Florida* (1983),[10] the defendant set fire to his girlfriend's apartment, and a squatter who lived in a storage room died as a result. Linehan was drunk at the time but was convicted of arson (a felony) and felony murder (death occurring as a result of a felony). Linehan appealed his conviction and argued his voluntary intoxication was a defense to the general intent crime of arson. But the Florida

Rule of Law: Specific intent = purposely; general intent = knowingly.

appeals court disagreed and articulated a formula, illustrated by Figure 3.3, to distinguish specific intent from general intent crimes even when both statutes use specific intent language, such as committing a crime "willfully" or "intentionally."

Under the law it is presumed that a man intends the natural and foreseeable results of his actions. But a specific intent crime has an added, or plus, factor that satisfies something unique to the offender that motivates him to commit the crime. Something that is personal to the offender is called subjective, a common legal term of art that is best described by imagining a person is looking in a mirror and seeing his own reflection. The *Linehan* court said the crimes of arson, burglary, and kidnapping all require the offender "willfully" and "intentionally" take some action to bring about a desired result such as the burning of a building, the breaking and entering into a structure, the holding someone hostage. The crime of arson is general intent because by starting the fire, the natural consequence of damaging a building will ensue, pursuant to number 1 in Figure 3.3.

MAKING THE COURTROOM CONNECTION

You may find while watching trials, the government may have difficulty in proving a defendant's *mens rea* as defined in the statute under which the defendant has been charged. For instance, at a congressional hearing to confirm the U.S. attorney general in January 2017, a 61-year-old woman who was part of a self-described "Code Pink" activist group laughed out loud in response to a statement that the candidate "treated people equally." She was arrested and charged with "disorderly and disruptive conduct" intending "to impede, disrupt, and disturb the orderly conduct" of the hearing. She was convicted on counts related to the laugh, but a judge threw out her conviction and ordered a retrial because the government could not prove that the laugh fit the required *mens rea* state in the law to disturb the congressional hearing. Judges must apply the law as written.

But burglary and kidnapping are specific intent crimes because of the added plus factor of the offender getting something more out of the crime. The offender is breaking and entering, but it makes it burglary (imagine the offender looking in the mirror to get something more, to determine his subjective intent/reason for committing the crime) because he is going to commit a felony once inside the structure, pursuant to number 2 in Figure 3.3. Similarly, the offender is holding someone against their will by force, but it makes it kidnapping (imagine offender looking in the mirror to get something more, to determine his subjective intent/ reason for committing the crime) because he is going to get ransom money in exchange for his hostage, pursuant to number 3 in Figure 3.3. When you read statutes that define crimes, examine whether there is just a general harm that the law proscribes (e.g., general intent in burning a building causing damage), or a more significant harm caused by the offender's personal motivation in committing the crime (e.g., specific intent in burning a building to commit insurance fraud and make money).

Specific Intent Required for Criminal Responsibility for Internet Threats. What happens in criminal law when, in a person's mind, he is just expressing fantasy wishes but other people become afraid and, in their minds, come to believe the fantasies are actual threats? The case excerpt *Elonis v. United States* (2015) concerns a Pennsylvania man who was charged and convicted under a 1939 federal law criminalizing threatening speech affecting interstate commerce. Elonis claimed his Internet postings were a form of online therapy, an activity protected by the First Amendment. In overturning Elonis's conviction, Chief Justice Roberts wrote that "wrongdoing must be conscious to be criminal." As you read the case excerpt on page 74, imagine you are a prosecutor. What type of proof would you introduce to convince a jury that Elonis intended to harm each of the targets named in his "rap"-like poetry?

Linehan v. Florida, 442 So.2d 244 (1983)

The words "willfully" and "intentionally" are often used **NOT** to characterize specific intent, but to separate the volitional act from the accident.

1. **GENERAL INTENT ARSON**   **Fla. §806.01**

"Any person who willfully and unlawfully by fire or explosion, damages or causes to be damaged any dwelling"

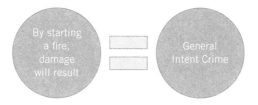

2. **SPECIFIC INTENT BURGLARY**   **Fla. §810.02**

"Entering a dwelling, a structure, or a conveyance with the intent to commit an offense therein."

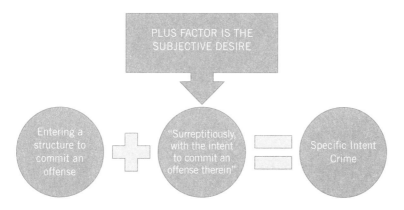

3. **SPECIFIC INTENT KIDNAPPING**   **Fla. §787.01**

"Forcibly, secretly, or by threat confining, abducting, or imprisoning another person against her or his will and without lawful authority"

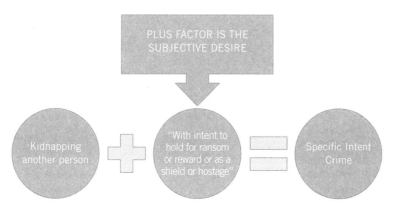

ELONIS V. UNITED STATES, 135 S.CT. 2001 (2015)

Supreme Court of the United States

Chief Justice Roberts delivered the opinion of the Court. (7–2)

FACTS: Anthony Douglas Elonis was an active user of the social networking Web site Facebook. Users of that Web site may post items on their Facebook page that are accessible to other users, including Facebook "friends" who are notified when new content is posted. In May 2010, Elonis's wife of nearly seven years left him, taking with her their two young children. Elonis began "listening to more violent music" and posting self-styled "rap" lyrics inspired by the music. Eventually, Elonis changed the user name on his Facebook page from his actual name to a rap-style nom de plume, "Tone Dougie," to distinguish himself from his "on-line persona." The lyrics Elonis posted as "Tone Dougie" included graphically violent language and imagery. This material was often interspersed with disclaimers that the lyrics were "fictitious," with no intentional "resemblance to real persons." Elonis posted an explanation to another Facebook user that "I'm doing this for me. My writing is therapeutic."

Elonis's co-workers and friends viewed the posts in a different light. Around Halloween of 2010, Elonis posted a photograph of himself and a co-worker at a "Halloween Haunt" event at the amusement park where they worked. In the photograph, Elonis was holding a toy knife against his co-worker's neck, and in the caption Elonis wrote, "I wish." Elonis was not Facebook friends with the co-worker and did not "tag" her, a Facebook feature that would have alerted her to the posting. But the chief of park security was a Facebook "friend" of Elonis, saw the photograph, and fired him.

In response, Elonis posted a new entry on his Facebook page:

> Moles! Didn't I tell y'all I had several? Y'all sayin' I had access to keys for all the f***in' gates. That I have sinister plans for all my friends and must have taken home a couple. Y'all think it's too dark and foggy to secure your facility from a man as mad as me? You see, even without a paycheck, I'm still the main attraction. Whoever thought the Halloween Haunt could be so f***in' scary?

This post became the basis for Count One of Elonis's subsequent indictment, threatening park patrons and employees. Elonis's posts frequently included crude, degrading, and violent material about his soon-to-be ex-wife. Shortly after he was fired, Elonis posted an adaptation of a satirical sketch that he and his wife had watched together. In the actual sketch, called "It's Illegal to Say . . .," a comedian explains that it is illegal for a person to say he wishes to kill the President, but not illegal to explain that it is illegal for him to say that. When Elonis posted the script of the sketch, however, he substituted his wife for the President. The posting was part of the basis for Count Two of the indictment, threatening his wife:

> Hi, I'm Tone Elonis.
>
> Did you know that it's illegal for me to say I want to kill my wife? . . .
>
> It's one of the only sentences that I'm not allowed to say. . . .
>
> Now it was okay for me to say it right then because I was just telling you that it's illegal for me to say I want to kill my wife. . . .
>
> Um, but what's interesting is that it's very illegal to say I really, really think someone out there should kill my wife. . . .
>
> But not illegal to say with a mortar launcher.
>
> Because that's its own sentence. . . .

After viewing some of Elonis's posts, his wife felt "extremely afraid for [her] life." A state court granted her a three-year protection-from-abuse order against Elonis (essentially, a restraining order). Elonis referred to the order in another post on his "Tone Dougie" page, also included in Count Two of the indictment:

> Fold up your [protection-from-abuse order] and put it in your pocket
>
> Is it thick enough to stop a bullet?
>
> Try to enforce an Order
>
> that was improperly granted in the first place
>
> Me thinks the Judge needs an education
>
> on true threat jurisprudence
>
> And prison time will add zeros to my settlement ...
>
> And if worse comes to worse
>
> I've got enough explosives
>
> to take care of the State Police and the Sheriff's Department.

At the bottom of this post was a link to the Wikipedia article on "Freedom of speech." Elonis's reference to the police was the basis for Count Three of his indictment, threatening law enforcement officers.

[At trial] the jury instructions [read:]

A statement is a true threat when a defendant intentionally makes a statement in a context or under such circumstances wherein a reasonable person would foresee that the statement would be interpreted by those to whom the maker communicates the statement as a serious expression of an intention to inflict bodily injury or take the life of an individual.

The Government's closing argument emphasized that it was irrelevant whether Elonis intended the postings to be threats—[the prosecutor said] "it doesn't matter what he thinks."

[Elonis was convicted and sentenced to three years.]

ISSUE: [Even though the federal threat statute makes no mention of *mens rea*, is the specific intent *mens rea* to make a threat required for a conviction, or is it enough that the people hearing the defendant's words feel threatened?]

HOLDING: The Third Circuit's [jury] instruction, requiring only negligence with respect to the communication of a threat, is *not sufficient to support a conviction* under Section 875(c) (emphasis added).

REASONING: An individual who "transmits in interstate or foreign commerce any communication containing any threat to kidnap any person or any threat to injure the person of another" is guilty of a felony and faces up to five years' imprisonment. 18 U.S.C. §875(c). This statute requires that a communication be transmitted and that the communication contain a threat. It does not specify that the defendant must have any mental state with respect to these elements. In particular, it does not indicate whether the defendant must intend that his communication contain[s] a threat.

The fact that the statute does not specify any required mental state, however, does not mean that none exists. We

have repeatedly held that "mere omission from a criminal enactment of any mention of criminal intent" should not be read "as dispensing with it." This rule of construction reflects the basic principle that "wrongdoing must be conscious to be criminal." As Justice Jackson explained, this principle is "as universal and persistent in mature systems of law as belief in freedom of the human will and a consequent ability and duty of the normal individual to choose between good and evil."

The "central thought" is that a defendant must be "blameworthy in mind" before he can be found guilty, a concept courts have expressed over time through various terms such as *mens rea*, scienter, malice aforethought, guilty knowledge, and the like. Although there are exceptions, the "general rule" is that a guilty mind is "a necessary element in the indictment and proof of every crime." We therefore generally "interpret criminal statutes to include broadly applicable scienter requirements, even where the statute by its terms does not contain them."

This is not to say that a defendant must know that his conduct is illegal before he may be found guilty. The familiar maxim "ignorance of the law is no excuse" typically holds true. Instead, our cases have explained that a defendant generally must "know the facts that make his conduct fit the definition of the offense," even if he does not know that those facts give rise to a crime. The "presumption in favor of a *scienter requirement* should apply to each of the statutory elements that criminalize otherwise innocent conduct" (emphasis added). The mental state requirement must therefore apply to the fact that the communication contains a threat.

Elonis's conviction, however, was premised solely on how his posts would be understood by a reasonable person. Such a "reasonable person" standard is a familiar feature of civil liability in tort law, but is inconsistent with "the conventional requirement for criminal conduct—awareness of some wrongdoing." In light of the foregoing, Elonis's conviction cannot stand. The jury was instructed that the Government need prove only that a reasonable person would regard Elonis's communications as threats, and that was error.

CONCLUSION: The judgment of the United States Court of Appeals for the Third Circuit [upholding Elonis's conviction at trial] is reversed, and the case is remanded for further proceedings consistent with this opinion.

The high Court's reasoning in the *Elonis* case was based on the precedent that to be guilty of a crime that required intent, the government must prove the defendant's intent beyond a reasonable doubt. You recall from the discussion about jury instructions in Chapter 2 that the jury is only allowed to follow the law the judge defines. In *Elonis*, "The jury was instructed that the Government need prove only that a reasonable person would regard Elonis's communications as threats," and that was a mistake because the government had to prove Elonis *intended* to threaten his wife and others. The reasonable person standard from a victim's perspective is not a substitute for the government proving a defendant's specific intent *mens rea*.

The Scienter Requirement

Scienter is a legal term for knowledge of wrongdoing that some statutes require before a defendant may be found criminally responsible, such as receiving stolen property where the law requires the defendant have scienter that the property is, in fact, stolen. As noted in the *Elonis* case excerpt, the "presumption in favor of a scienter requirement should apply to each of the statutory elements that criminalize otherwise innocent conduct," which means the law requires the government prove the defendant knew the conduct she was engaging in was criminal. For instance, to be charged with assaulting a police officer, an offender would typically have to know that the victim was a police officer.

> **Rule of Law: Scienter is knowledge of wrongdoing.**

In federal law, there is no scienter requirement to be found guilty of assaulting an officer.[11] In *United States v. Feola* (1975),[12] undercover federal law enforcement agents agreed to purchase heroin from Feola and others. Feola and his confederates planned to deliver fake heroin to their prospective buyers (the undercover officers) or, alternatively, to rob them. The U.S. Supreme Court upheld Feola's conviction for attacking the officers, despite his claim he had no scienter (i.e., no knowledge) that the victims were federal officers, because the law required only an intent to assault, not necessarily the intent to assault a federal officer. The Court declared that to hold otherwise—that Feola and friends could go home despite their criminal acts—would give no protection to undercover officers and society could not abide by such a result.

Strict Liability

> **Rule of Law: Under strict liability, an offender is guilty for the act alone; no mental state is required.**

Under early common law, crimes were often defined or separated based on their perceived evil or damage to society. Regulatory crimes are typically strict liability, which means the offender may be found guilty simply by performing the prohibited act, no *mens rea* required. Strict liability crimes typically prohibit or constrain the sale of liquor, food, drugs, motor vehicle violations, and other safety regulations passed for the well-being of the general public. The Supreme Court described the genesis of strict liability crimes in *Morissette v. United States* (1952):

> Congestion of cities and crowding of quarters called for health and welfare regulations undreamed of in simpler times. Wide distribution of goods became an instrument of wide distribution of harm when those who dispersed food, drink, drugs, and even securities, did not comply with reasonable standards of quality, integrity, disclosure and care. Such dangers have engendered increasingly numerous and detailed regulations which heighten the duties of those in control of particular industries, trades, properties or activities that affect public health, safety or welfare.[13]

Thus, a manager at a gas station where they sell hot dogs that roll under hot lights overnight might receive a citation from the city health inspector for serving tainted food products, regardless of whether the station manager "intended" or "knew" (had the requisite *mens rea*) that the food sat out for far too long. Punishing the manager solely because of the act of leaving food out to spoil, and not his subjective intent to harm the public with contaminated hot dogs, sends a message to all establishments serving food that they had better pay attention to the quality of the food they sell or suffer the consequences. Traveling above the speed limit is often a strict liability crime. If people know they will receive an expensive fine if caught speeding regardless of their excuse or *mens rea* while driving fast, they will generally obey the speed limit, which, in turn, protects the public from unnecessary car accidents caused by reckless driving. The typical punishment for violating a strict liability statute is a fine and not jail.

Transferred Intent

Rule of Law: Intent
to harm someone
transfers to an
unintended target.

Transferred intent is specific intent in which the offender intends to cause harm but hurts or damages the wrong target; the intent to harm transfers to the unintended target and the offender will be held responsible for the mistake. We see the doctrine of transferred intent most often in homicide cases where the defendant has bad aim and kills an innocent victim. Surely, no one wants to let the offender go free simply because he made a mistake and claims, "But I did not mean to kill Sally; I was aiming at Laval." The offender is responsible for the specific intent first-degree murder because the intent for the intended victim transferred to the bystander.

An offender has the same defenses under the doctrine of transferred intent as he would have in an ordinary case. For instance, Sam does not mean to kill Leslie, only hurt her. When Sam moves to hit Leslie, but Leslie ducks and Sam kills Bill instead, Sam still has a defense that he only meant to cause serious bodily harm to Leslie, not death. Likewise, if a police officer were executing a lawful arrest and unintentionally caused injury to a bystander, the officer's defense of simply doing her job would extend to the bystander.

Element Analysis

Elements are like spokes on a wheel, without which the wheel could not turn; each element of a crime is an integral part of the crime that the prosecutor must prove beyond a reasonable doubt to convict the defendant. The elements of a criminal definition typically include a *mens rea* state (purposefulness, knowingness, recklessness, or negligence) and the prohibited conduct the law seeks to prevent or punish, as illustrated in Figure 3.4. For example, the basic elements of robbery are, while committing a theft, the offender purposely (*mens rea*) puts the victim in fear of immediate serious bodily injury (SBI), inflicts SBI, or commits or threatens immediately to commit any first- or second-degree felony (the *actus reus*). If the prosecutor fails to prove any element of the crime, the law requires that the defendant *must* be found not guilty of the charge. Learning the elements of crimes is a great aid in understanding what type of proof the prosecutor is required to introduce to convince a jury of the defendant's guilt.

Rule of Law: To find a
defendant guilty, the
prosecution must prove
every element (piece)
of a crime beyond a
reasonable doubt.

Sometimes elements of charged crimes overlap. The same elements that might support a charge of assault and battery will also be included in the more serious charge of attempted murder.

Figure 3.4 Elements of Robbery Wheel

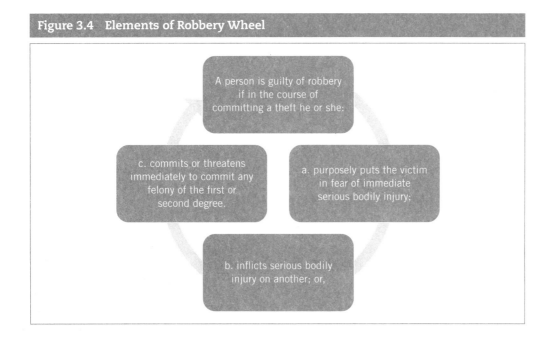

A person is guilty of robbery if in the course of committing a theft he or she:

a. purposely puts the victim in fear of immediate serious bodily injury;

b. inflicts serious bodily injury on another; or,

c. commits or threatens immediately to commit any felony of the first or second degree.

Assault and battery are charges lesser in severity than attempted murder; called lesser included offenses, they are the less serious crimes that are naturally part of the more serious crime. The doctrine of merger holds that if the defendant is convicted of the more serious offense, the lesser included offenses merge (get absorbed); for example, the crimes of assault and battery will merge on the defendant's conviction for murder. Often prosecutors charge a defendant with many different serious crimes and their lesser included offenses to ensure that the defendant is convicted of at least one crime. Notice that motive, the reason an offender may commit the crime, is not an element the prosecution must prove at trial.

Principle of Legality

Society needs to clearly define criminal conduct to inform people which acts are criminal. The principle of legality requires that the law notify what conduct will be punished. Giving citizens fair warning of what conduct will be punished fosters respect for the law. Many states have written criminal codes based on the MPC's elements of crimes that establish liability on the part of the offender. To criminalize specific conduct, the government must state with specificity what behavior, if engaged in, will or will not be a crime.

An example of the principle of legality is the case *Commonwealth v. Twitchell* (1993),[14] in which the Christian Scientist Church of Boston, Massachusetts, asked the state's top legal authority, the state attorney general, if the adherents could choose prayer instead of seeking medical treatment. The state's answer was "yes," but when the Twitchell's 2-year-old son, Robyn, died of an easily curable bowel obstruction, the parents were prosecuted for allowing their son to die. The Twitchell's appeal was based on the principle of legality arguing that because the attorney general gave permission for the Church to choose prayer instead of medicine, how were the Twitchells to know they were breaking the law? The state argued in response that everyone should know a sick child requires a doctor's care and failure to seek care leads to criminal responsibility for the child's death. The appellate court found the principle of legality was violated because the law governing faith-based healing and the state's legal response to the church's practice were nonspecific; the Twitchells' conviction was overturned. The state declined to prosecute the Twitchells again, but the couple remained under court order to provide medical care for their other children until they reached adulthood. From a courtroom perspective, the *Twitchell* case demonstrates the balance of justice is in favor of the government's compelling state interest protecting the health and safety of children, which outweighs the family's First Amendment right to choose prayer over modern medicine, as illustrated by the scales of justice in Figure 3.5.

An example of the intersection of the law's requirement that the government prove the defendant guilty beyond a reasonable doubt of each and every element of the crime and the principle of legality's requirement that the law define what conduct will be punished is the federal law, the Armed Career Criminal Act (ACCA), initially passed into law to increase the severity of punishment for those repeat offenders who use firearms in the commission of their crimes (18 U.S.C. §924, 1984). The ACCA provides that if an offender has three or more previous convictions for a "violent felony" or a "serious drug offense," and she was convicted of a crime involving the use of a firearm, she would serve no less than 15 years in prison and up to a maximum life sentence. In defining the predicate (triggering) offenses for the ACCA sentencing enhancement, the law defined a "violent felony" as "otherwise involves conduct that presents a serious potential risk of physical injury to another," known as the residual clause. Samuel Johnson was convicted and sentenced under the ACCA's residual cause because one of his prior violent felonies was possession of a sawed-off shotgun. His appeal made it to the U.S. Supreme Court, which ultimately struck down the ACCA's residual clause as too "vague" in *Johnson v. United States* (2015).[15] Because people had to guess what "otherwise involves conduct" meant, the public did not know what acts were criminal, and the evidence was too imprecise to meet the burden of proof for that ACCA element violating the Constitution's guarantee of due process, the high Court said.

Lawmakers must ensure that the public is aware that the conduct sought to be punished is specifically described to put them on notice of the potential criminal liability of their actions.

Figure 3.5 The Scales of Justice Illustrating the *Twitchell* Case

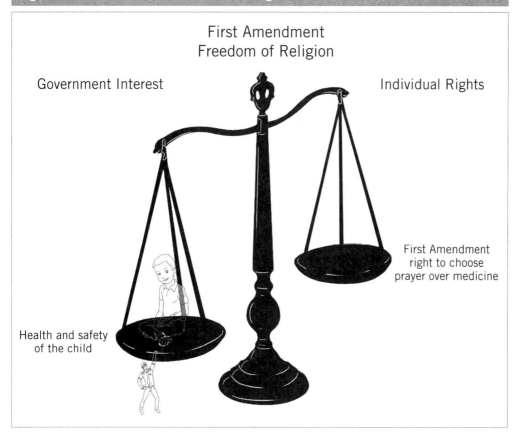

First Amendment
Freedom of Religion

Government Interest

Individual Rights

First Amendment
right to choose
prayer over medicine

Health and safety
of the child

ACTUS REUS: THE GUILTY ACT

Actus Reus Must Be Voluntary

Under the traditional common law, a person could not be charged with a crime for having criminal thoughts alone. Typically, individuals are free to think of committing criminal acts, and if they do not act on those desires, they will not be prosecuted.[16] The term *actus reus* means "guilty act"—a voluntary act that gives rise to criminal liability. Criminal acts must be voluntary. The MPC §2.01 has expressly excluded the following acts from those making one criminally responsible:

> **Rule of Law:** To be criminal, a person's acts must be voluntary.

1. A reflex or convulsion;

2. A bodily movement during unconsciousness or sleep;

3. Conduct during hypnosis or resulting from hypnotic suggestion;

4. A bodily movement that otherwise is not a product of the effort or determination of the actor, either conscious or habitual.

In the "Making the Courtroom Connection" feature earlier in this chapter, the woman prosecuted for laughing and disrupting a congressional hearing has the defense that her laugh was involuntary and, therefore, not criminal.

The *mens rea* must launch the offender into taking the *actus reus*, as the high Court has said, "an evil meaning mind with an evil doing hand."[17] Concurrence is the marriage of *mens rea* and *actus reus* at the time the crime is committed making the offender criminally responsible. If Joe

**Rule of Law:
Concurrence is the
marriage of *mens rea*
and *actus reus* at the
time of committing
the crime.**

wants his neighbor dead and thinks about it all day and, while at the supermarket, backs out of his parking space without looking and strikes a pedestrian, later discovered to be his hated neighbor Frank, Joe will not be responsible for intentionally killing Frank. Joe's murderous thoughts about Frank did not form the springboard of the act of running Frank over. The concurrence requirement saves the criminal justice system from pursuing fruitless prosecutions for acts unconnected to any specific intent, even though those acts may be punished under a theory of negligence.

The Duty to Act and Liability for Acts by Omission

To determine whether someone has a duty to act under the law, the omission of which would lead to criminal liability, the first question to ask is to whom does a person owe a duty of reasonable care? In the seminal civil tort (injury) case *Palsgraf v. Long Island Railroad* (1928),[18] a woman was waiting on a train platform to go to Rockaway Beach, New York, when an outbound train stopped at the station. As the train was moving away from the station, a man carrying a package of fireworks jumped onto the train while one guard grabbed his arm and another pushed him from behind to get him onto the train. The package of fireworks fell from the man's arms onto the rails, exploded, and knocked over a set of scales next to Mrs. Palsgraf, who was injured. She sued the train company for her injuries, claiming that the employees' actions of pulling and pushing the man caused the fireworks to fall and explode, but her lawsuit failed. The court said, "Proof of negligence in the air, so to speak, will not do . . . negligence is the absence of care, according to the circumstances." The court said the railroad owed Mrs. Palsgraf *no* duty of care; rather, the railroad owed a duty of care directly to the man pushed and pulled before he boarded the train. A person owes a duty of care *only* to those whom he might injure by his actions.

Under the law today, we still punish those who have a certain duty of care to others and who breach (break) that duty by some act of commission or omission (failure to act). Different types of duty are recognized by the law. There is a **duty by contract**, which is a document creating affirmative legal obligations for the parties who sign the contract: for example, after a tenant signs a lease with a landlord, the landlord has a duty to provide a decent place to live and the tenant has a duty to pay rent. Similarly, there is a **duty by statute**, which are affirmative obligations stated in the law, such as the law that requires people involved in car accidents to remain at the scene and, in some instances, to render aid to known victims. In our chapter-opening case study, the Smiths had a duty by contract and by statute to care for the residents entrusted to them. The resident signed a contract agreeing to pay fees in exchange for care, and state law imposes responsibilities on those running assisted living facilities. In a **duty by relationship**, a parent, spouse, or other responsible family member has a legal obligation to provide medical, dental, and educational services to a dependent family member. The failure to do so could be considered a criminal act.

There is also an **assumption of the duty**, which is help freely given to others with no attendant legal obligation. People may help others in peril, and this creates no legal obligation between the parties. An individual who is an expert swimmer is not required by law to try and rescue a floundering swimmer in distress. But if someone undertakes the duty to rescue, then it is incumbent on the would-be rescuer to finish the job. That is, if a person on a crowded beach sees a swimmer floundering and says to the crowd of onlookers, "I'll save him; everybody stay here," and then halfway to the drowning victim, the rescuer changes his mind and turns back to shore, his actions prevented others from undertaking a rescue attempt and he may be criminally responsible for thwarting a successful rescue attempt if the swimmer does, indeed, drown and die.

Good Samaritan Laws. **Good Samaritan laws** protect from personal injury lawsuits those who rescue those in peril. Bad Samaritan laws punish people for failing to help victims in need.[19] All U.S. jurisdictions have a Good Samaritan statute whereby people who help others in distress are immune from liability (cannot be sued) for the help they give. Although each state's laws are different—for instance, in some states only those who are certified and trained as first-aid responders are protected from a lawsuit, and in other states all helpers are legally protected—there are some general features common to most Good Samaritan laws:

1. There is no duty to act unless a duty by relationship exists.

2. The help provided cannot be in exchange for money or financial reward.

3. The person giving aid need not put himself in any danger by providing services, but if there is no threat of harm and the giving of aid has begun, usually the first one to give aid should stay until help arrives.

Typically, there is no affirmative duty to report a crime and many states do not have laws imposing an obligation on people to help one another. But after gut-wrenching stories of people witnessing brutal sexual assaults, particularly against children, and doing nothing, many states enacted laws imposing a duty, in certain circumstances, on the bystander to attempt a rescue of a stranger in peril or to contact the authorities for help. If someone knows of the actual commission of a federal crime and does not alert authorities, the person may be guilty of the crime Misprision of a Felony, which carries on conviction the punishment of fines and imprisonment (18 U.S.C. §4).

Springboard for Discussion

In 2017, teenagers taunted 32-year-old James Dunn, who appeared to be drowning in a Cocoa, Florida, pond. The teens swore at the man and laughed as they filmed his last breath on a cell phone. One of the teens can be heard saying, "Oh, he just died." Florida's Good Samaritan laws do not require bystanders to help those in peril, so the teens did not face any criminal liability for their actions. Do you agree that the law should not force people to help others in need? How would the prosecutor prove the bystander's *mens rea* to hold them responsible?

Possession as an Act

In strict legal terms, possession of drugs, possession of contraband (items that are illegal to possess), and possession of illegal weapons are not acts, but under the law, possession is treated as *actus reus* for criminal responsibility. There are two types of possession generally recognized in the law, actual and constructive. **Actual possession** is physically possessing contraband—vials of crack cocaine in a pants pocket, for instance. **Constructive possession** is a legal fiction (false reality) that arises from inferences from facts that lead a jury to assume a logical conclusion. For example, three roommates share an apartment and share common living areas, the bathroom, kitchen, and living room. All roommates are deemed to have control over the common spaces. If the roommates are aware that there are bricks of marijuana hidden in the freezer and do nothing to terminate the possession (e.g., throw the marijuana away), then when the police come to execute a search warrant, all roommates can be arrested for drug possession. The prosecutor will have to prove that all the roommates knew or should have known that the drugs were in the freezer even though when seized, technically, none of the roommates "possessed" the drugs. The MPC, section 2.01, expressly provides that one is criminally responsible for possession if

Springboard for Discussion

What goals in society do possession laws help achieve? What type of evidence would sustain a constructive possession conviction?

1. The possessor knowingly procured or received the thing possessed.

2. The possessor was aware of his control thereof for a sufficient period to have been able to terminate his possession.

Status as an Act

One's **personal status** as an alcoholic, drug addict, or pedophile is not a crime because of the lack of a guilty act. Even though one's personal status as a drug addict may lead to criminal activity, such as stealing to support one's habit, the mere act of being a drug addict is not criminal. In *Robinson v. California* (1962), the U.S. Supreme Court overturned a California statute that criminalized status as an addict.[20] The Court invalidated the statute, and any others like it across the country, because "a law which made a criminal offense of such a disease would doubtless be universally thought of to be an infliction of cruel and unusual punishment in violation of the Eighth and Fourteenth Amendments." Lower courts in subsequent cases have discussed whether alcoholism is a disease.[21] If alcoholism were a disease, and many medical experts agree that it is, alcoholics would be exempt from crimes committed while

> **Rule of Law: Personal status is not inherently criminal because there is no *actus reus*.**

under the influence, because the alcoholic would have no control over his status. But the court went on to distinguish the status of being an alcoholic from the physical act of drinking and stated, "Alcoholics should be held responsible for their conduct; they should not be penalized for their condition."

Rule of Law: The offender must be the factual and legal cause of the victim's harm/death to be held criminally responsible.

CAUSATION

Causation Analysis

The concept of criminal causation serves to assign the appropriate level of blame in accordance with the offender's *mens rea* state and the ultimate harm or death the offender caused by his acts. For a defendant to be held responsible for a victim's harm or death, she must be *both* the factual and legal cause of the ultimate harm *without* an intervening cause severing the offender's original acts from the ultimate injury or death. The causation formula is

1. Factual cause = "but for" the offender's conduct, would the victim have been harmed?

2. Proximate cause = is the ultimate harm foreseeable from the offender's conduct?

3. Intervening cause = is there something external to the offender's conduct breaking the causal chain from the offender to the ultimate harm?

The factual cause is established by asking the question, "but for the defendant's acts, would the ultimate harm have happened?" or "but for X, would Y have happened?" If the answer is NO, the victim's harm would not have happened if the offender did not first act, then the offender is the factual cause of the victim's harm.[22] In the chapter-opening case study, "but for" the Smiths' decision not to move the residents before Hurricane Michael made landfall, would the residents have died? If the answer is "no," then the Smiths are the factual cause of the 10 resident deaths.

The next question in the causation analysis is whether the ultimate harm was foreseeable or predictable from the offender's first act. Proximate cause is the naturally foreseeable last event from the offender's action that caused the victim's harm. The law seeks to punish people for the natural consequences of their acts, not freakish random acts, even if their initial conduct started the chain of events that ended in harm. If one friend chases another into a swollen creek where he drowns, the drowning is a natural, foreseeable consequence of the initial chasing act. But if one friend chases another into a swollen creek where she is picked up by a band of pirates and forced to walk the plank to her death, this event is not a foreseeable consequence from the initial act of chasing. The chaser is the factual cause of the death: "But for" the chase into the creek, no death would have occurred. However, the harm suffered must be reasonably foreseeable as a natural consequence of the defendant's actions, which the pirate abduction is not. In our chapter-opening case study, the Smiths are the proximate cause of the residents' deaths because it is predictable that people will die in severe and violent storms and deciding not to evacuate increases the risk of harm.

Even if the ultimate harm was foreseeable, there may be an intervening cause that breaks the causal chain between the offender's act and the victim's harm. An intervening cause is external to the offender's conduct. But the existence of an intervening cause may not totally relieve the defendant from liability, as some jurisdictions find that if the defendant's initial conduct created intervening events they "do not operate to exempt a defendant from liability if the intervening event was put into operation by the defendant's" actions.[23]

For example, the state of New Jersey allows patients to make end-of-life decisions and terminate their life support and die peaceably. In a drunk-driving case, *New Jersey v. Pelham*, excerpted on the following page, the victim decided to die by shutting off his life support. The question for the court is whether the victim's suicide is an intervening cause breaking the causal chain between the drunk driver's responsibility for the accident and injury and the ultimate death of his victim. Read the case excerpt and question whether you agree with the court's reasoning under the traditional causation analysis.

NEW JERSEY V. PELHAM, 824 A.2D 1082 (N.J. 2003)

Supreme Court of New Jersey

FACTS: The facts of the horrific car accident in which [the] defendant, Sonney Pelham, was involved are summarized from the trial record. On the evening of December 29, 1995, William Patrick, a sixty-six-year-old lawyer, was driving his Chrysler LeBaron . . . At approximately 11:42 p.m., a 1993 Toyota Camry driven by [the] defendant struck the LeBaron from behind. The LeBaron sailed over the curb and slid along the guardrail, crashing into a utility pole before it ultimately came to rest 152 feet from the site of impact. The Camry traveled over a curb and came to rest in a grassy area on the side of the highway. Patrick was making "gurgling" and "wheezing" sounds, and appeared to have difficulty breathing. His passenger, Jocelyn Bobin, was semiconscious. Emergency crews extricated the two using the "jaws of life" and transported them to Robert Wood Johnson University Hospital. Bobin was treated and later released.

At the accident scene, Officer Heistand smelled an odor of alcohol on [the] defendant's breath, and noted that he was swaying from side to side and front to back. Three field sobriety tests were conducted. Defendant failed all three. Two separately administered tests indicated that [the] defendant's blood alcohol content (BAC) at that time was .18 to .19. Experts assessed his BAC between .19 and .22 at the time of the accident.

On March 13, 1996, Patrick was transferred to the Kessler Institute for Rehabilitation (Kessler), because it specialized in the care of patients with spinal cord injuries. When he arrived, Patrick was unable to breathe on his own, and was suffering from multi-organ system failure. Medication was required to stabilize his heart rhythm. He was extremely weak, with blood-protein levels that placed him at high risk of death. He was unable to clear secretions in his airways, and thus his oxygen levels would drop requiring medical personnel repeatedly to clear the secretions. Complications from the ventilator caused pneumonia to recur due to his inability to cough or to protect himself from bacteria. Bowel and urinary tract infections continued.

While at Kessler, Patrick also was monitored by psychiatric staff. He presented as depressed, confused, uncooperative, and not engaged psychologically. At times, he was "hallucinating," even "psychotic." The staff determined that he was "significantly" brain injured. Nonetheless, Patrick was aware of his physical and cognitive disabilities. During lucid moments, he expressed his unhappiness with his situation, and, on occasion, tried to remove his ventilator. Patrick improved somewhat during the month of April, but then his condition rapidly regressed. By early May, severe infections returned, as well as pneumonia.

It was undisputed at trial that Patrick had expressed to his family a preference not to be kept alive on life support. Because of his brain damage, his lack of improvement, and his severe infections, Patrick's family decided to act in accordance with his wishes and remove the ventilator. He was transferred to Saint Barnabas Medical Center and within two hours of the ventilator's removal on May 30, 1996, he was pronounced dead. The Deputy Middlesex County Medical Examiner determined that the cause of death was sepsis and bronchopneumonia resulting from multiple injuries from the motor vehicle accident.

ISSUE: Whether a jury may be instructed that, as a matter of law, a victim's determination to be removed from life support is a foreseeable event that does not remove or lessen criminal responsibility for death.

HOLDING: We hold that there was no error in instructing the jury that a victim's decision to invoke his right to terminate life support may not, as a matter of law, be considered an independent intervening cause capable of breaking the chain of causation triggered by defendant's wrongful actions.

REASONING: New Jersey has been in the forefront of recognizing an individual's right to refuse medical treatment. It is now well settled that competent persons have the right to refuse life-sustaining treatment. Even incompetent persons have the right to refuse life-sustaining treatment through a surrogate decision maker. We turn then to examine the effect to be given to a victim's exercise of that right in the context of a homicide trial.

Defendant was charged with aggravated manslaughter, which, according to the New Jersey Code of Criminal Justice (Code), occurs when one "recklessly causes death under circumstances manifesting extreme indifference to human life." The trial court charged the jury on aggravated manslaughter and the lesser-included offense of second-degree vehicular homicide, defined as "[c]riminal homicide . . . caused by driving a vehicle or vessel recklessly." Causation is an essential element of those homicide charges.

The Code defines "causation" as follows:

> . . . Conduct is the cause of a result when: (1) It is an antecedent but for which the result in question would not have occurred; and (2) The relationship between the conduct and result satisfies any additional causal requirements imposed by the code or by the law defining the offense. . . .

(Continued)

(Continued)

When the offense requires that the defendant recklessly or criminally negligently cause a particular result, the actual result must be within the risk of which the actor is aware or, in the case of criminal negligence, of which he should be aware, or, if not, the actual result must involve the same kind of injury or harm as the probable result and must not be too remote, accidental in its occurrence, or dependent on another's volitional act to have a just bearing on the actor's liability or on the gravity of his offense.

The causation requirement of our Code contains two parts, a "but-for" test under which the defendant's conduct is "deemed a cause of the event if the event would not have occurred without that conduct" and, when applicable, a culpability assessment. Under the culpability assessment, [w]hen the actual result is of the same character, but occurred in a different manner from that designed or contemplated [or risked], it is for the jury to determine whether intervening causes or unforeseen conditions lead to the conclusion that it is unjust to find that the defendant's conduct is the cause of the actual result. Although the jury may find that the defendant's conduct was a "but-for" cause of the victim's death, it may nevertheless conclude that the death differed in kind from that designed or contemplated [or risked] or that the death was too remote, accidental in its occurrence, or dependent on another's volitional act to justify a murder conviction.

Our Code [New Jersey law], like the Model Penal Code (MPC), does not identify what may be an intervening cause. "Intervening cause" is defined as "[a]n event that comes between the initial event in a sequence and the end result, thereby altering the natural course of events that might have connected a wrongful act to an injury" *Black's Law Dictionary* (7th ed., 1999).

Generally, to avoid breaking the chain of causation for criminal liability, a variation between the result intended or risked and the actual result of defendant's conduct must not be so out of the ordinary that it is unfair to hold defendant responsible for that result. A defendant may be relieved of criminal liability for a victim's death if an "independent" intervening cause has occurred, meaning "an act of an independent person or entity that destroys the causal connection between the defendant's act and the victim's injury and, thereby becomes the cause of the victim's injury." Removal of life sustaining treatment is a victim's right. Because the exercise of the right does not break unexpectedly or in any extraordinary way, the chain of causation that a defendant initiated and that led to the need for life support, it is not an intervening cause that may be advanced by the defendant.

CONCLUSION: [Pelham's conviction is upheld.]

Springboard for Discussion

An offender led police on a high-speed chase. When the officer chasing him killed an innocent bystander, such a result was the natural, predictable consequence of the high-speed chase and the offender was held responsible for the bystander's death. But had the offender led the police on a high-speed chase and, as he was driving, the side of a building randomly and unpredictably collapsed on a bystander killing him, the result would be "so extraordinary or surprising" that the offender could not, under the law, be responsible for the bystander's death. Should people be responsible for all the harm caused when they set events in motion whether foreseeable or not? (*State v. Lovelace,* 1999).

In *Pelham,* state law allowed people to end life support, so the victim's decision to die was a naturally foreseeable result of the defendant's drunk driving. Because the victim's suicide was not an intervening cause, breaking the causal chain between the drunk driving and the victim's death, Pelham remained responsible for Patrick's death. Another example of the causation doctrine is a man who smokes a cigarette while pumping gas in a high-performance vehicle, causing an explosion, as illustrated in Figure 3.6. The subsequent explosion rocks the gas station and an ambulance driving nearby, causing a needle intended to be placed in the patient's arm to jerk and pierce the victim's neck, killing her. Is the smoking man criminally responsible for the ambulance patient's death? But for the smoking man, would the gas pumps have exploded? The answer is no, so the man is the factual cause. Is an explosion a foreseeable predictable event from smoking while pumping gas into a specialty car? The answer is yes, so the man is the proximate cause of the patient's death. The last question to ask is whether there is any intervening causes breaking the causal chain between the offender and the victim. The answer is yes; the emergency medical technician's slip of the intravenous needle, severing the patient's carotid artery while in the ambulance breaks the causal chain between the smoking man and the patient's death. The intervening cause is external to the smoker, and the patient's death was caused by the technician. The smoker will be responsible for harm flowing from the explosion but not the patient's death, because death by a needle in the neck is not a natural consequence of smoking at a gas station. In our chapter-opening case study, there was no intervening cause breaking the chain from the Smiths and the residents' deaths because loss of power is a natural consequence of a hurricane.

Figure 3.6 Causation Analysis Illustration

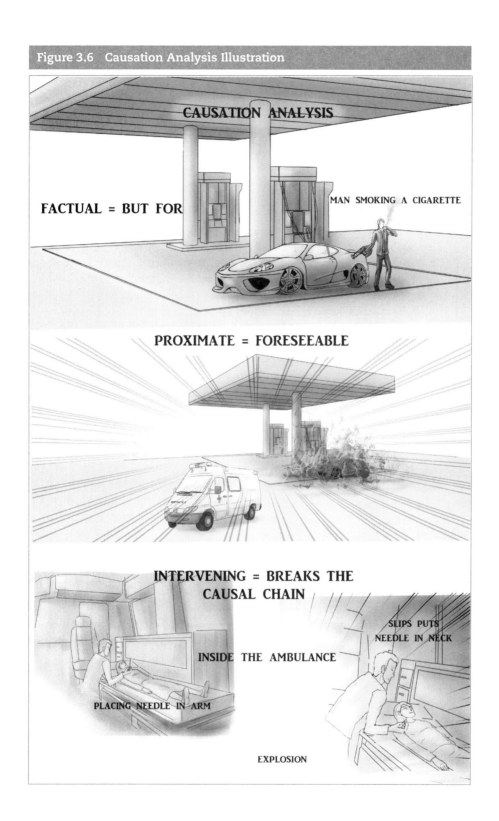

PARTIES TO CRIME

In common law, parties to crimes were defined either as principals, who committed the crime, or as accessories, those who helped the principals commit the crime or escape afterward. The common law distinction between principals and accessories went further and separated such parties

> **Rule of Law: An offender aids and abets a crime when, in addition to taking a step toward committing the crime, he intends to facilitate that offense's commission.**

> **Rule of Law: Common law distinguished between principals and accessories to determine grades of punishment; under today's modern statutes, they are typically punished equally.**

by degree, or an accessory before or after the fact—distinctions based on the level of participation and involvement of each actor.

Principals and Accessories

A principal to the crime is the primary perpetrator. Under common law, principals were divided into first and second degrees. A principal in the first degree is one who committed the crime, and one in the second degree (an aider or abettor) was one who aided, counseled, and assisted the commission of the crime and was present during the crime. An accessory is one who was absent during the commission of the crime but who participated as a contriver, instigator, or advisor. If the accessory gives help to the criminal principal before the crime, she is called an accessory before the fact. If she helps the criminal principal escape from the crime scene or hide from authorities, she is called an accessory after the fact. The common law distinction between principals and accessories was important for sentencing such offenders; society wanted to punish more harshly those who had committed the crime than those who merely helped. Today under many state statutes, the distinctions between principals and accessories are blurred and they are punished equally. The philosophy behind punishing them equally is that the crime could not be committed without both accessories and principals playing primary roles. The Michigan Compiled Laws §767.39 (2015), titled "Abolition of distinction between accessory and principal" is such an example and provides

Every person concerned in the commission of an offense, whether he directly commits the act constituting the offense or procedures, counsels, aids, and abets in its commission may hereafter be prosecuted, indicted, tried and on conviction shall be punished as if he had directly committed such offense.[24]

In the chapter-opening case study, Billy Bob was the principal in organizing the crime and Charles was his accessory, but under present-day law, they would face similar penalties for their acts.

INCHOATE CRIMES

Inchoate crimes are preparatory or incomplete. Society punishes unsuccessful criminals who are unable to complete their criminal acts because their repeated attempts to achieve their criminal goals may pose more of a danger to society than the successful criminals.

Solicitation

Solicitation is defined by the MPC §5.02 as "asking, encouraging or demanding another commit a crime or an attempt to commit a crime." The crime is often associated with prostitution, where the sex worker will ask people to pay money in exchange for sexual favors. To be convicted of solicitation, an offender must demonstrate specific intent to engage someone else in the commission of the crime: the act of asking is the crime. Early solicitation statutes divided the crime into degrees, but most states have enacted comprehensive statutes that stipulate that once one person invites another to commit a crime, the harm has been done.

> **Rule of Law: Solicitation is asking, encouraging, or demanding someone commit a crime.**

It is a defense to the crime of solicitation if the offender voluntarily renounces (abandons) the plan; that is, once you have asked someone to commit a crime, you may change your mind and withdraw by telling the person you solicited that you no longer wish to commit the crime, or if the criminal activity continues, by notifying the authorities that they should attempt to prevent the crime. Pennsylvania's statute is illustrative of how to renounce:

It is a defense that the actor, after soliciting another person to commit a crime, persuaded him not to do so or otherwise prevented the commission of the crime, under circumstances manifesting a complete and voluntary renunciation of his criminal intent. (18 Pa. Code §902)

It is not a defense for the one who asked another to commit a crime that the person so solicited could not have committed a crime, called factual impossibility. For example, if a businessman solicits murder by hiring a hit man to kill his partner, and the hitman turns out to be an undercover police officer, the businessman remains criminally responsible. The businessman will still be guilty of solicitation because the facts as he believed them to be, if true (hiring a hitman, not an undercover officer), would have led to the commission of the crime. Solicitation is not prosecuted as an attempt crime because the solicitous acts are preparatory and attempts require *actus reus* that goes beyond mere preparation.

Conspiracy

Conspiracy is a common charge in criminal cases because the elements are easy to prove when more than one person agrees to commit a crime. The basic element of a criminal **conspiracy** is an agreement to commit a crime and, in many jurisdictions, committing an overt act toward completing the object of the conspiracy. An example of a state statute of conspiracy is in the Texas Penal Code.

Texas Penal Code, Title 4 Inchoate Offenses, Chapter 15 Preparatory Offenses §15.02 (2015)

§15.02. Criminal Conspiracy

(a) A person commits criminal conspiracy if, with intent that a felony be committed:

  (1) he agrees with one or more persons that they or one or more of them engage in conduct that would constitute the offense; and

  (2) he or one or more of them performs an overt act in pursuance of the agreement.

(b) An agreement constituting a conspiracy may be inferred from acts of the parties.

(c) It is no defense to prosecution for criminal conspiracy that:

  (1) one or more of the co-conspirators is not criminally responsible for the object offense;

  (2) one or more of the co-conspirators has been acquitted, so long as two or more co-conspirators have not been acquitted;

  (3) one or more of the co-conspirators has not been prosecuted or convicted, has been convicted of a different offense, or is immune from prosecution;

  (4) the actor belongs to a class of persons that by definition of the object offense is legally incapable of committing the object offense in an individual capacity; or

  (5) the object offense was actually committed.

The U.S. Supreme Court has stated the fundamental characteristic of a conspiracy is two or more people agree to an "endeavor which, if completed, would satisfy all of the elements" of the crime the conspirators want to achieve.[25] Under the law of conspiracy, all conspirators are responsible for the aggregate (combined) results of the crime. In a drug smuggling ring with 10 people, if a low-level drug dealer sells 2 ounces of cocaine, but the entire conspiracy is responsible for selling 2,000 ounces of cocaine, the low-level dealer will be sentenced for the weight of 2,000 ounces rather

Rule of Law: Conspiracy is an agreement to commit a crime usually accompanied by an overt act toward completing the conspiracy.

than the 2 ounces she is directly responsible for selling. In many cases, the harsh sentencing for the entire "weight" of the drug conspiracy is often used as leverage to obtain guilty pleas and cooperating witness testimony from the low-level dealers in exchange for a reduced sentence that reflects their own, individual criminal involvement. The agreement to commit a crime does not have to be written; usually it is oral. Prosecutors can obtain a conviction for conspiracy even if the conspirators failed to achieve the conspiracy's goals and their criminal objective failed. For example, Tom and Kate get together and agree to rob the bank. If they take an overt act toward the completion of their planned act, such as buying guns and masks, they will be guilty of conspiracy even if they never accomplish the robbery. In our chapter-opening case study, Billy Bob and Charles entered into a conspiracy when they agreed to rob seniors in the sports venue and started to approach seniors looking for vulnerable targets.

Limitations on Parties to Conspiracy

The law establishes some limitations on parties to the crime of conspiracy even though not all jurisdictions recognize these limitations. One limitation on the extent of a conspiracy is Wharton's Rule, which provides offenders not be prosecuted for conspiracy to commit crimes that, by definition, require more than one person to commit. For example, the crime of adultery can only be accomplished by two people; therefore, the offenders cannot commit conspiracy to commit adultery. Similarly, the definition of conspiracy precludes one person from conspiring alone, courts have taken different positions on what happens if, for example, one of two alleged conspirators is acquitted. Technically, if there are only two alleged conspirators and one is acquitted, the other may not be convicted, as there would be only one party to the conspiracy. Some courts have taken this position, whereas others look to the reason why a second alleged co-conspirator was not convicted. For example, if one defendant was granted immunity (protection from being charged) in exchange for testifying against the second co-conspirator, a conspiracy conviction may be upheld on the defendant without immunity.

Springboard for Discussion

Do you believe all conspirators should be responsible for the entire extent of the criminal enterprise, or just their individual contribution? Why or why not?

Defenses to a conspiracy charge are similar to a solicitation charge and include renunciation (removing oneself from the agreement to commit a crime) by communicating to other co-conspirators that one wants out. Renunciation is difficult to prove, but the defense is often provided by law as illustrated by the Pennsylvania statute, which provides the following:

> It is a defense . . . that the actor, after conspiring to commit a crime, thwarted the success of the conspiracy, under circumstances manifesting a complete and voluntary renunciation of his criminal intent.[26]

If an original conspirator successfully presents a renunciation defense, he may be acquitted on the original conspiracy charges. In the chapter-opening case study, if Charles, after he had agreed, told Billy Bob he had changed his mind and then never participated in achieving their joint criminal goals, he could still be convicted of conspiracy. Renunciation requires an affirmative act.

Attempt

Rule of Law: Attempt = specific intent *mens rea* to commit a crime + unsuccessful *actus reus*.

Attempt is a crime when one takes steps toward the commission of a crime and has a specific intent to commit that crime but, for some reason, is unable to complete the crime. Although in early English common law the attempt to commit a crime by itself was not a crime, it soon became a separate and distinct crime, and today most states criminalize the conduct of the unsuccessful criminal. Many jurisdictions have one statute that covers all attempt crimes, whereas some include a separate statute for each crime, for example, attempted rape, attempted robbery. An illustration of a comprehensive attempt statute can be found in the Texas Criminal Code.

Texas Penal Code, Title 4 Inchoate Offenses, Chapter 15 Preparatory Offenses §15.01 (2015)

§15.01. Attempt

(a) A person commits an offense if, with specific intent to commit an offense, he does an act amounting to more than mere preparation that tends but fails to effect the commission of the offense intended.

(b) If a person attempts an offense that may be aggravated, his conduct constitutes an attempt to commit the aggravated offense if an element that aggravates the offense accompanies the attempt.

(c) It is no defense to prosecution for criminal attempt that the offense attempted was actually committed.

(d) (omitted)

The crime of attempt has two elements:

1. Specific intent *mens rea* to commit a crime

2. Unsuccessful *actus reus*

The intent to commit an attempt crime is the intent to commit a crime that, for some reason, the defendant is unable to complete. Usually courts require that the defendant went beyond merely preparing for the crime and moved toward committing the crime. Preparing to commit a crime may be drawing a map of the bank to rob, whereas attempting to commit a crime involves taking direct steps to rob the bank, such as conducting surveillance and assembling the burglar tools. A nonexhaustive list of steps taken toward the commission of the crime, which may lead to criminal liability for attempt, may be found in the MPC's "substantial step" test. If the defendant takes one of these "substantial steps" toward completing the crime, he may be guilty of attempt.

Model Penal Code §5.01 Criminal Attempt

(2) Conduct Which May Be Held Substantial Step . . .

(a) lying in wait, searching for or following the contemplated victim of the crime;

(b) enticing or seeking to entice the contemplated victim of the crime to go to the place contemplated for its commission;

(c) reconnoitering the place contemplated for the commission of the crime;

(d) unlawful entry of a structure, vehicle or enclosure in which it is contemplated that the crime will be committed;

(e) possession of materials to be employed in the commission of the crime, which are specially designed for such unlawful use or which can serve no lawful purpose of the actor under the circumstances;

(f) possession, collection or fabrication of materials to be employed in the commission, at or near the place contemplated for its commission, where such possession, collection or fabrication serves no lawful purpose of the actor under the circumstances;

(g) soliciting an innocent agent to engage in conduct constituting an element of the crime.

APPLYING THE LAW TO THE FACTS

Is It Preparation or Criminal Attempt?

The Facts: Paul lived in Georgia and his daughter, Ann, lived in Florida with Paul's ex-wife and her boyfriend, Vic. Paul believed that Vic threatened to abuse Ann. In a plan to kill Vic, Paul called a contact in Florida to obtain two firearms. However, Paul's contact was also a confidential informant who told police of this communication. After Paul traveled to Florida and acquired the firearms, he was arrested and charged with attempted murder. Paul asserts in his defense that his actions were merely preparatory and did not constitute the legal definition of attempt. Is Paul correct?

The Law: No. Paul took the substantial step of obtaining the firearms to effectuate his plan to kill Vic, so he is guilty of attempted murder.[27]

In the *Indiana v. Haines* case reprinted in part below, the trial judge granted defendant Haines's motion to vacate his conviction of attempted murder charges. Even though Haines took actions he believed would infect first responders to human immunodeficiency virus (HIV), the judge found HIV transmission through biting and scratching was impossible and, therefore, Haines could not be convicted. In a rare appeal by the state to reinstate the conviction, the appellate court found in favor of the state and overturned the trial judge's decision because Haines had the specific intent and unsuccessful *actus reus* to meet the elements of an attempt crime. As you read the case, keep in mind the snapshot of time the case was pending and decided in the late 1980s.

INDIANA V. HAINES, 545 N.E.2D 834 (1989)

Court of Appeals of Indiana, Second District

PROCEDURAL HISTORY: [T]he State of Indiana (the State), appeals from the trial court's grant of . . . Donald J. Haines' (Haines) motion for judgment on the evidence, claiming that the trial judge erred in vacating the jury's verdicts of three counts of attempted murder . . .

FACTS: On August 6, 1987, Lafayette, Indiana, police officers John R. Dennis (Dennis) and Brad Hayworth drove to Haines' apartment in response to a radio call of a possible suicide. Haines was unconscious when they arrived and was lying face down in a pool of blood. Dennis attempted to revive Haines and noticed that Haines' wrists were slashed and bleeding. When Haines heard the paramedics arriving, he stood up, ran toward Dennis, and screamed that he should be left to die because he had AIDS [acquired immune deficiency syndrome]. Dennis told Haines they were there to help him, but he continued yelling and stated he wanted to f*** Dennis and "give it to him." Haines told Dennis that he would "use his wounds" and began jerking his arms at Dennis, causing blood to spray into Dennis' mouth and eyes. Throughout the incident, as the officers attempted to subdue him, Haines repeatedly yelled that he had AIDS, that he

could not deal with it and that he was going to make Dennis deal with it.

Haines also struggled with emergency medical technicians Dan Garvey (Garvey) and Diane Robinson threatening to infect them with AIDS and began spitting at them. When Dennis grabbed Haines, Haines scratched, bit, and spit at him. At one point, Haines grabbed a blood-soaked wig and struck Dennis in the face with it. This caused blood again to splatter onto Dennis' eyes, mouth, and skin. When Dennis finally handcuffed Haines, Dennis was covered with blood. He also had scrapes and scratches on his arms and a cut on his finger that was bleeding. When Haines arrived at the hospital, he was still kicking, screaming, throwing blood, and spitting at Dennis, Garvey, and another paramedic, Rodney Jewell. Haines again announced that he had AIDS and that he was going to show everyone else what it was like to have the disease and die. At one point, Haines bit Garvey on the upper arm, breaking the skin.

Roger Conn, Haines' homosexual lover and former roommate, recalled that Dr. Kenneth Pennington (Pennington) informed Haines that he had the AIDS virus. Haines told Conn that he knew AIDS was a fatal disease. Haines

---

was charged with three counts of attempted murder. At trial, medical experts testified that the virus could be transmitted through blood, tears, and saliva. They also observed that policemen, firemen, and other emergency personnel are generally at risk when they are exposed to body products. One medical expert observed that Dennis was definitely exposed to the HIV virus and others acknowledged that exposure of infected blood to the eyes and the mouth is dangerous, and that it is easier for the virus to enter the blood stream if there is a cut in the skin. Following a trial by jury, Haines was convicted of three counts of attempted murder on January 14, 1988. On February 18, 1988, Haines moved for judgment on the evidence as to the three counts of attempted murder, which the trial court granted.

ISSUE: [Did Haines commit attempted murder with the HIV virus?]

HOLDING: [Yes.]

REASONING: When the trial judge sentenced Haines on February 2, 1988, he made this statement:

> I believe my decision in this case was made easier by the State's decision to not introduce any medical expert scientific evidence. The State believed that the disease known as AIDS was irrelevant to its burden of proof; that only the intent or state of mind of the defendant was relevant. I disagree with that. All of us know that the conduct of spitting, throwing blood and biting cannot under normal circumstances constitute a step, substantial or otherwise, in causing the death of another person, regardless of the intent of the defendant. More has to be shown, more has to be proven, in my judgment. And the more in this case was that the conduct had to be coupled with a disease, a disease which by definition is inextricably based in science and medicine.

There was no medical expert evidence that the person with ARC [AIDS-related complex] or AIDS can kill another by transmitting bodily fluids as alleged in this case. And there was no medical evidence from any of the evidence that the defendant had reason to believe that he could transmit his condition to others by transmitting bodily fluids as are alleged in this case. The verdicts of the jury as to attempted murder will be set aside and judgment of conviction of battery on a police officer resulting in bodily injury as a Class D felony will be entered on each of the three counts. A sentence of two years will be ordered on each of the three counts. Those sentences will run

consecutively because I find aggravating circumstances and I will set those out at this time.

The trial judge's failure to consider all of the evidence and his comment at the February 2, 1988, sentencing hearing that he weighed the evidence in deciding whether to grant judgment on the evidence constituted error. Haines misconstrues the logic and effect of our attempt statute. While he maintains that the State failed to meet its burden insofar as it did not present sufficient evidence regarding Haines' conduct which constituted a substantial step toward murder, subsection (b) of [Indiana Code, section] 35-41-5-1 provides: "It is no defense that, because of a misapprehension of the circumstances, it would have been impossible for the accused person to commit the crime attempt."

In *Zickefoose v. State* (1979), our supreme court observed: "It is clear that section (b) of our statute rejects the defense of impossibility. It is not necessary that there be a present ability to complete the crime, nor is it necessary that the crime be factually possible. When the defendant has done all that he believes necessary to cause the particular result, regardless of what is actually possible under existing circumstances, he has committed an attempt. The liability of the defendant turns on his purpose as manifested through his conduct. If the defendant's conduct in light of all the relevant facts involved, constitutes a substantial step toward the commission of the crime and is done with the necessary specific intent, then the defendant has committed an attempt."

In accordance with [Indiana's attempt statute] the State was not required to prove that Haines' conduct could actually have killed. It was only necessary for the State to show that Haines did all that he believed necessary to bring about an intended result, regardless of what was actually possible. While we have found no Indiana case directly on point, the evidence presented at trial renders any defense of inherent impossibility inapplicable in this case. See *King v. State* (1984) (a defendant's intent and conduct is a more reliable indication of culpability than the hazy distinction between factual and legal impossibility). In addition to Haines' belief that he could infect others there was testimony by physicians that the virus may be transmitted through the exchange of bodily fluids. It was apparent that the victims were exposed to the AIDS virus as a result of Haines' conduct.

CONCLUSION: From the evidence in the record before us we can only conclude that Haines had knowledge of his disease and that he unrelentingly and unequivocally sought to kill the persons helping him by infecting them with AIDS, and that he took a substantial step towards killing them by his conduct believing that he could do so, all of which was more than a mere tenuous, theoretical, or speculative "chance" of transmitting the disease. [Haines's conviction for attempted murder reinstated.]

The unusual facts of the Haines case bear analysis. First, it is unusual when the prosecutor gets to appeal a favorable result for the defendant. Because Haines was incarcerated on other charges, the state could appeal without risking unlawful deprivation of Haines's liberty. Secondly, the state of knowledge of HIV transmission in 1989 was just becoming cemented into public consciousness. In the early to mid-1980s, many people believed one could get HIV from kissing, bathroom seats, and doorknobs. Contributing to the HIV hysteria was the belief that HIV was almost always fatal. The judge was bold to rule that it was impossible for Haines to kill the emergency medical technicians and officers in the way he tried, with scratches and bites. The federal Center for Disease Control has medical facts about HIV transmission. In August 1990, Haines was sentenced to 30 years for his attempt crime and died in prison the following year.

> **Rule of Law: Impossibility is the defense that the offender cannot meet the elements of the offense as charged.**

The Defense of Impossibility

Should the defense of impossibility—that it was physically impossible to commit the crime—relieve the offender of criminal responsibility? There are two types of impossibility: factual and legal. Factual impossibility is when the offender takes all the steps necessary to complete the crime, but certain facts make the crime impossible to achieve, for example, trying to steal someone's wallet when the person's pocket is empty. The facts as the pickpocket believed as true—there was a wallet to steal from the person's pocket—were not true, and therefore it was impossible to pick an empty pocket. Such factual impossibility will generally *not* be a defense to attempt crimes because the pickpocket had the specific intent to steal and the unsuccessful *actus reus* of stealing the wallet. The justification for not recognizing factual mistakes as a defense is because the offender took all the necessary steps to complete the crime and she should escape criminal liability because the facts turned out differently than she planned.

Legal impossibility is when the offender takes all steps necessary to complete what he believes to be a crime, but the acts do not meet the legal definition of a crime. For example, John, who is 19 years old, engages in sexual intercourse with his girlfriend, Wanda, whom John believes is 15 years old, which, if true, would be a crime of statutory rape (consensual intercourse with a minor who is at least 4 years younger). In reality, Wanda is 18 years old and under the law it is impossible for John to commit the crime of statutory rape, even if his *mens rea* is criminal. The law recognizes legal impossibility based on the principle of legality, which requires the government inform the public what acts are criminal. If a statute defines a crime and the offender's behavior does not fall within the statute's definition, there can be no crime.

APPLYING THE LAW TO THE FACTS

Guilty of Attempted Murder?

The Facts: Ralph Damms forgot to put bullets in the gun when he aimed at his wife's head and pulled the trigger more than once. He was convicted of attempted murder. Damms appealed on the grounds that it was impossible to kill his wife with an unloaded gun. Is Damms correct?

The Law: No. Damms conviction is upheld because if Damms's gun had had bullets in it, his wife would be dead. The factual impossibility defense will not work.[28]

In our chapter-opening case study, Billy Bob could be charged with the attempted murder of Ken because he took specific acts and his *actus reus* was unsuccessful. Charles, as a co-conspirator, would be equally guilty of the attempt charge because once a conspirator enters into the agreement to commit the crime, he is responsible for its consequences. The men could raise the defense that it is factually impossible to kill a man who is already dead, but they will likely be unsuccessful.

1. You will understand the four *mens rea* states to establish the defendant's "guilty mind." The law seeks to assign an appropriate level of punishment based on the defendant's *mens rea*, or guilty state of mind, at the time the crime was committed. The *mens rea* states are *purposely*, which is specific intent where the actor desires his conduct to cause a specific result; *knowingly*, which is a general intent crime where the actor undertakes an action but not necessarily to bring about a specific result; *recklessly*, where the actor ignores the risk of harm his behavior creates; and *negligently*, where the actor is unaware of the risk of harm his behavior creates, but he should be aware. Some crimes are strict liability crimes, which require no *mens rea*, and the actor will be guilty simply by performing the illegal act. Other crimes require scienter, which is knowledge of wrongdoing, such as knowing the property is stolen to be convicted of receiving stolen property. The public must be informed what behavior the law will punish; this is referred to as the principle of legality. The government must prove each and every element of the crime, such as the concurrence of the *mens rea* and *actus reus*, beyond a reasonable doubt; otherwise, the defendant must be found not guilty. The doctrine of merger operates to absorb the lesser included offenses on conviction of a more serious offense; for example, battery merges into murder.

2. You will be able to explain the legal basis for volitional *actus reus*, the guilty act. *Actus reus* is a voluntary act that leads to criminal liability. Some crimes that are defined as acts, such as possession of drugs, can be proven by surrounding circumstances such as constructive possession. Other so-called acts, such as personal status as a drug addict, may not be punished, but status as a pedophile may lead to legal restrictions. The law imposes a legal requirement to care for people in certain relationships recognized in law, for example, duty by relationship, such as parent–child; duty by contract, such as landlord–tenant; and duty by statute, such as police officer–citizen. There are also acts of kindness freely given, assumptions of the duty that, if undertaken, may impose legal liability if these acts create more danger. Many states have Good Samaritan laws that protect people in certain professions (e.g., emergency medical technicians) and others who try and help people in emergency situations from criminal and civil liability, but many states do not.

3. You will competently discuss the elements of "causation" to assign criminal responsibility. A causation analysis of the facts examines whether a person should be held responsible for committing certain acts. First, is the actor the factual cause of the harm? That is, "but for" the actor's initial conduct, would the harm have happened? Next, is the actor the proximate cause of the harm? Was the ultimate harm foreseeable by the actor's initial conduct? Last, were there any intervening causes that broke the causal chain from the actor's initial conduct to the ultimate harm? If the actor is both the factual and legal cause and there are no intervening causes, she will be liable for the harm caused.

4. You will know the common law differences between principals and accessories. Under common law, individuals who helped criminals, but did not directly participate in a crime, were punished less severely than those who actually participated in the crime. Today the modern trend in state statutes is to treat principals to crime (i.e., the offenders) the same as accessories (i.e., those who are there or who are close by when the crime is being committed and who assist the principals). An accessory before the fact helps the principal get ready to commit the crime by giving aid, instruction, or materials, whereas an accessory after the fact might, for example, give shelter to the fugitive.

5. You will understand the elements of inchoate crimes, such as solicitation, conspiracy, and attempt. The law seeks to punish those who try to commit crimes and fail or try to commit crimes that are otherwise incomplete. Solicitation is asking someone else to commit a crime, conspiracy is an agreement to commit a crime, and attempt is having the *mens rea* and taking a substantial step toward completing the crime but for some reason not being able to complete it. Factual impossibility—the fact that it would be impossible to complete the crime—is often no defense for people who attempt crimes, because society seeks to punish the intent and criminal effort to complete the act, even if it was unsuccessful. Legal impossibility is a defense because the law, as applied, does not define the defendant's conduct as a crime.

Go back to the beginning of the chapter and reread the news excerpts associated with the learning objectives. Test yourself to determine if you can understand the material covered in the text in the context of the news.

accessory after the fact 86
accessory before the fact 86
actual possession 81
actus reus 79

assumption of the duty 80
attempt 88
attendant circumstances 68
causation 82

concurrence 79
conspiracy 87
constructive possession 81
duty by contract 80

PROBLEM-SOLVING EXERCISES

1. "Bid night" at the local fraternity is a big party where new pledges make their formal decision to join the brotherhood. In preparation, older brothers purchased $2,000 worth of alcohol. One drinking game for new pledges is to drink as much alcohol as possible in 2 minutes. Ron drank hard liquor and immediately became disoriented. Ron tried walking around, fell down, and passed out on the floor. Partygoers simply assumed Ron was drunk and "sleeping it off." While Ron was seemingly unconscious, fraternity brothers searched the Web for "alcohol poisoning remedies." By the time the brothers called 9-1-1, it was too late. Autopsy results indicated Ron's blood alcohol level (BAC) was "life-threatening." The frat brothers who purchased the alcohol and those who had walked by Ron without helping him were all charged under the following statute:

   Anyone who purposely, knowingly, recklessly, or negligently causes the death of another shall be guilty of a felony.

   All brothers facing charges claim they are not the cause of Ron's death and had no duty to help him. The brothers who walked by Ron when he was passed out claim they had no *mens rea* to harm Ron and are, therefore, not responsible for his death. Who will win at trial, the prosecution or defense? (**ROL: Purposely, knowingly, recklessly, negligently; causation; duty to act**)

2. A prisoner at the local jail, Kent Cool, was awaiting trial on the charge of conspiracy to commit tax fraud when he learned that one of his codefendants, who was also in jail, Miles Friend, was going to become a state's witness and testify against Cool. Cool saw Friend at lunch and told him to "keep his mouth shut." At Cool's pretrial hearing, Cool put two fellow prisoners, Blank and Macaw, on his witness list even though the two men did not testify. On return to prison, Blank and Macaw beat up Miles Friend. The government then charged Cool with conspiracy to retaliate against a witness. Does the government have enough evidence to sustain a conviction? (**ROL: Conspiracy**)

3. Betsy bought some jewelry thinking it was stolen, but it was not; it was just cheap. The jewelry was legally owned. Betsy was charged with receiving stolen property. She raised the defense of impossibility. Will she win her case? (**ROL: Scienter, impossibility**)

PART II

THE CRIMES
Criminal Law Elements

4

CRIMES AGAINST THE PERSON

Go to the end of the chapter. Skim the key terms and phrases and read the summary closely. Come back and look at the following news excerpts to focus your reading throughout the chapter to help understand the law punishing offenders when they hurt people mentally, physically, or sexually or cause their death. This chapter examines the most common crimes against the person, such as assault and battery; the *mens rea* distinctions that separate one type of homicide from another; sex offenses, including laws to combat juvenile "sexting" and "revenge porn"; stalking crimes, both in person and online; hate crimes; and robbery. The chapter begins with a hypothetical case study of Ben, Jerry, and Kathy on a crime spree. Follow the trio as they encounter the rules of law presented throughout the chapter, and connect their criminal activities with the relevant section of text.

WHY THIS CHAPTER MATTERS TO YOU	THE LEARNING OBJECTIVES AS REFLECTED IN THE NEWS
After you have read this chapter: **Learning Objective 1:** You can discuss the differences among the many crimes against the person.	Teachers are to be issued new guidance this week to help children cope with the "unimaginable" pressures of the modern digital age, including cyberbullying, sexting and "revenge porn." [United Kingdom, England] Education Secretary Nicky Morgan said last night that Personal, Social and Health (PSHE) lessons needed to be improved—and placed at the heart of the curriculum—to give young people the tools to cope with these growing demands. Children will also be taught about consensual sex to help vulnerable girls "spot, report and tackle abuse." (*The Daily Mail* [UK], March 10, 2015)
Learning Objective 2: You will be able to distinguish kidnapping from false imprisonment.	A 38-year-old transient accused of trying to "snatch" a 15-year-old girl in Canyon Country last summer pleaded no contest Tuesday to false imprisonment by violence and misdemeanor child molesting. Santos Martinez, who was charged with kidnapping, appeared Tuesday in San Fernando Superior Court where he entered his plea. A female, 15, was standing in a parking lot when she was approached by a Hispanic male. He tried to strike up a conversation with her. Then he asked, "Can I kiss you?" She said, "I don't know you, get away from me." She . . . began screaming for help. The victim was moved a short distance against her will. (*The Signal* [CA], February 20, 2018)
Learning Objective 3: You will understand the elements of sex-related offenses and rape shield laws.	Samuel Shaffer, a self-proclaimed doomsday prophet, will serve 26 years in the Utah state prison for a child rape case. Last week, he was sentenced 25 years to life for child rape and one to 15 years for child abuse. Back in February, the leader of the Knights of the Crystal Blade admitted to committing a sexual act with an 8-year-old, the daughter of a member of the cult. The court documents state that he inspected the girl to find out if she was a virgin. (Uinterview, May 28, 2018)

WHY THIS CHAPTER MATTERS TO YOU	THE LEARNING OBJECTIVES AS REFLECTED IN THE NEWS
Learning Objective 4: You will be able to distinguish the various degrees of homicide.	A jury found Tex McIver guilty on four counts, one including felony murder, for the shooting death of his wife Diane McIver. The difference between felony murder and murder is the absence of intent to kill. What is required for felony murder is for the victim's death to occur during the commission of a felony. . . Tex intended aggravated assault with his weapon against Diane but did not intend to kill her. The felony comes because he was found guilty of aggravated assault and Diane died. (13WMAZ [GA], April 23, 2016)
Learning Objective 5: You will understand the elements of robbery.	A 70-year-old woman was robbed as she was leaving bible study by a thief who allegedly drove up next to her in his silver Dodge 1500 pickup truck and asked her if she knew where any nearby shelters were located . . . The two talk for several seconds before the driver is seen appearing to snatch her purse from her left arm. The woman maintains her grip on the handbag until the suspect drives away. The force sends her to the ground face-first, and several contents of her purse are seen flying out. (CBS News [TN], May 4, 2018)

Chapter-Opening Case Study: Ben, Jerry, and Kathy Go on a Crime Spree

Ben, Jerry, and Kathy were desperate for money. Kathy said her stepmother, who lived nearby, owned some very expensive diamond jewelry and they should take it tonight. Kathy went to her stepmother's house, and later that night Ben and Jerry knocked on the door. The stepmother answered the door, and once inside, Jerry said to the stepmother, "Don't scream or I'll punch your lights out!" **(Rule of Law [ROL]: Assault is placing someone in fear of an imminent battery.)** They took the stepmother to her bedroom and tied her up. When the stepmother got loose, Ben and Jerry blocked the bedroom door, so she could not get out. **(ROL: False imprisonment interferes with the victim's liberty of movement.)** Ben then punched the stepmother in the face and knocked her out. **(ROL: Aggravated battery is done in the commission of another crime.)** Ben pulled down the stepmother's pants and tried to insert his penis into her vagina, but he was only able to penetrate her a little. **(ROL: Rape is unconsented to, forcible sex.)** Frustrated, Ben and Jerry lifted the stepmother, put her in the trunk of their car, and drove off with Kathy. **(ROL: Kidnapping is asportation of victim by force or threat of force.)** While they were driving, Kathy was in the back seat of the car lifting her shirt and bra and taking selfies. Kathy then sent her semi-nude selfies to five of her girlfriends who were still in high school and asking for similar photos in return. **(ROL: "Sexting" is using electronic devices to transmit sexual material.)**

The teenagers stopped at a convenience store, and Kathy said that the Korean American grocer who owned the store gave her a funny look. Ben said, "Welcome to America, macaca," as Ben hit the grocer over the head with a beer bottle cutting off his ear lobe **(ROL: Mayhem is permanent disfigurement)** and causing severe lacerations on his face **(ROL: Hate crime victim of physical violence is chosen based on perceived personal characteristic).** Outside of the store a woman was walking toward the front door when Ben, still carrying the broken beer bottle, put the broken glass in the woman's face and said, "Give me all your money or I'll cut you" The victim gave Ben $100. **(ROL: Robbery is assault or battery plus stealing).** The trio drove for 20 miles before state troopers pulled them over for speeding; the stepmother was found in the trunk of the car dead of asphyxiation. **(ROL: Felony murder is when murder is committed in the commission of a felony [here, a kidnapping] and a death results.)** What crimes have the three friends committed?

Rule of Law: The threat of harm, assault, and the actual physical harm, battery, were two different crimes under common law, although in modern statutes assault is synonymous with battery.

CRIMES AGAINST THE PERSON

Assault and Battery

Traditionally assault and battery were two distinct crimes, but today under most modern statutes the terms are used interchangeably to mean hitting someone. In common law, assault was the crime of placing someone in fear of a hurtful touch, and battery was the actual hurtful or offensive touching. Someone might say, "John assaulted Leiko when he punched him in the face," describing the punch as the assault when, technically under the common law, the assault happened when Leiko was put in fear of John's incoming punch, not when he was punched. The Model Penal Code §211.1 definition of assault reflects both the common law and the modern statutory approach of defining assault. One commits assault when one

1. Attempts or does cause bodily injury to another, or

2. Negligently causes injury to another with a deadly weapon, or

3. Puts another in fear of imminent bodily injury.

The threat of physical injury in an assault must be imminent. It is not the words, alone, that constitutes an assault, but the words coupled with the apparent ability to carry out the threat of physical harm immediately. A threat to beat someone to a pulp an hour later is not an assault because, even though the offender may have the apparent ability to carry out the threat, the threat of physical harm may never materialize, as there may be many intervening events separating the threat from the threatened physical harm. The assault need not be committed with hands. If a person points an unloaded gun at someone who does not know that the gun has no bullets in it, such an act constitutes an assault under the definitions provided here.[1]

> Georgia Code Annotated §16-5-20 Simple Assault
>
> (a) A person commits the offense of simple assault when he or she either:
>
> (1) Attempts to commit a violent injury to the person of another; or
>
> (2) Commits an act which places another in reasonable apprehension of immediately receiving a violent injury.

Under common law, battery is the

1. Intentional

2. Unconsented to

3. Touching of another

4. That is harmful or offensive.

The touching is unlawful if the person being touched has not consented. A female waitress at a bar may get pinched on the buttocks as a matter of routine during her employment, but it does not mean she has consented to such unwanted touching just because she chose to be a waitress. The pinch constitutes battery. The offensiveness of the touching is often defined by the circumstances surrounding the touching; spitting in someone's face could be construed as a battery, as is forcibly grabbing a plate out of someone's hand, for example.

Rule of Law: Aggravated status often depends on the victim's vulnerability, or the assault or battery is done in the commission of another crime.

Aggravated Assault and Battery

The significance of elevating a crime to "aggravated" status means that on conviction, the defendant's sentence may be harsher, and the prison sentence, if any, may be longer.

In aggravated assault cases, the crime is often defined by the status of the victim or by the presence of a weapon. If an assault is committed on a prison guard, police officer, young child, or one who suffers from a mental or physical disability, then the assault may be elevated to "aggravated" status. A simple assault is typically a misdemeanor, but an aggravated assault is usually a felony. Similarly, battery is elevated to aggravated status when the amount of force used is excessive or committed with the intent to cause serious bodily harm to the victim, as illustrated in New Mexico's aggravated battery statute, reprinted in part here. Both assault and battery may be aggravated if they are done in the commission of another crime. For instance, assault or battery committed during a rape, or assault or battery committed during a robbery with a dangerous weapon, would constitute the higher degree of the crime. If a man hit, groped, and squeezed a woman to rape her but did not commit the rape, his actions would be considered aggravated battery (in addition to attempted rape), because he harmed the victim with the intent to sexually assault her.

New Mexico Statute Annotated §30-3-5 (2017) Aggravated Battery

    a. Aggravated battery consists of the unlawful touching or application of force to the person of another with intent to injure that person or another.

    b. Whoever commits aggravated battery, inflicting an injury to the person which is not likely to cause death or great bodily harm, but does cause painful temporary disfigurement or temporary loss or impairment of the functions of any member or organ of the body, is guilty of a misdemeanor.

    c. Whoever commits aggravated battery inflicting great bodily harm or does so with a deadly weapon or does so in any manner whereby great bodily harm or death can be inflicted is guilty of a third-degree felony.

Another form of aggravated battery is the common law crime of mayhem, which is the malicious and permanent disfigurement of another. The elements of mayhem are the

1. Specific intent

2. To commit a battery, with

3. The result of permanent disfigurement, such as cutting off a nose, putting out an eye, or rendering an appendage such as an arm, hand, or ear useless.

A very public incident of mayhem occurred during a 1997 heavyweight boxing match between Mike Tyson and Evander Holyfield when, in a clutch and hold pose between the boxers, Tyson bit the top of Holyfield's ear off, leaving a ragged gash in place of cartilage. Under present-day statutes, mayhem has been redefined as aggravated battery.

In the chapter-opening case study, Jerry assaulted the stepmother by placing her in fear of an imminent battery when he told her, "Don't scream or I'll punch your lights out." Jerry had the apparent ability to carry out the battery immediately. Ben then battered the woman when he punched her in the face and knocked her out. Both the assault and the battery were aggravated because the offenders were engaged in the commission of another crime, burglary, when the assault and battery took place. Ben committed mayhem when he cut off the grocer's ear lobe.

Terroristic Threats

A crime similar to the assault of placing one in fear of imminent physical harm is the making of terroristic threats. The crime is different from the crimes of terrorism, menacing, or harassment. Terroristic threats are made when the offender

1. Threatens to commit violence

Springboard for Discussion

Young people often say hurtful things to others that may communicate threats of bodily injury, such as "I'm going to kill you" or "I wish you were dead." Should teenagers be charged with terroristic threatening when they voice common expressions of violence?

2. With the purpose of terrorizing another, or

3. With the purpose of causing the evacuation of a public venue, such as making a bomb threat to cause people to flee an airport, school, or other inhabited building.

The *mens rea* for threat crimes is a reckless disregard of the risk of harm to the intended victim who believes the threat and fears serious bodily injury with the *actus reus* of making (but not carrying out) the threat. A common example of a state statute defining terrorist threats is Delaware's statute, excerpted here.

Title 11 Delaware Code §621

Terroristic Threatening

(a) A person is guilty of terroristic threatening when that person commits any of the following:

(1) The person threatens to commit any crime likely to result in death or in serious injury to person or property;

(2) The person makes a false statement or statements:

a. Knowing that the statement or statements are likely to cause evacuation of a building, place of assembly, or facility of public transportation;

b. Knowing that the statement or statements are likely to cause serious inconvenience; or

c. In reckless disregard of the risk of causing terror or serious inconvenience; or

(3) The person commits an act with intent of causing an individual to believe that the individual has been exposed to a substance that will cause the individual death or serious injury.

Note that terroristic threatening is a different crime than terrorism, menacing, or harassment.

The primary difference between a terroristic threat and an assault placing someone in fear of imminent battery is the threat of physical violence and injury need not be immediate.

Kidnapping and False Imprisonment

Under common law, false imprisonment meant interfering with a person's physical liberty by unlawful confinement, whereas kidnapping was the forcible taking of a person from one place to another. Such a distinction in the amount of movement—called *asportation*—is the focal point in defining the crimes in modern statutes today. Kidnapping became a federal crime as a result of the Lindbergh baby kidnapping. Aviator Charles A. Lindbergh became a national hero in 1927 when he made the first transcontinental solo flight in his plane, the *Spirit of St. Louis*, from New York to France. Wealthy, telegenic, and famous, the Lindbergh family was an attractive target for extortion attempts. In 1932, Lindbergh's first-born son, Charles A. Lindbergh, Jr., was kidnapped for ransom from his crib. The marriage of celebrity and crime caused a media frenzy "for kidnapping-related news, and the few television [stations] in existence kept vigil night and day with a continuous beam of the baby's photograph."[2] The media frenzy about kidnapping resulted in a substantially longer prison sentence on conviction than one for false imprisonment.[3]

Rule of Law: The primary difference between kidnapping and false imprisonment is the degree, not necessarily the distance, of asportation (i.e., the movement of the victim).

Common statutory elements define **kidnapping** as the

1. Unlawful

2. Asportation [movement]

3. Of another, by

4. Force or threat of force.

In contrast to kidnapping, the crime of **false imprisonment** is the restraint of another's liberty by force or threat of force. If the movement of the victim is incidental to another crime—for example, moving a rape victim from a park bench to behind a nearby bush to conceal the act of rape from public view—such movement will not be considered the separate crime of kidnapping. The analysis is not necessarily based on the distance the offender moves the victim, but whether the *mens rea* for the movement is to effectuate the initial crime or is the separate crime of kidnapping for which the prosecution can meet the *mens rea* requirement and sustain the burden of proof. Other factors that indicate an offender has committed kidnapping as opposed to false imprisonment is whether the movement of the victim did any of the following:

1. Increased the risk of physical or psychological harm to the victim,

2. Decreased the likelihood of detection of the offender holding the victim,

3. Increased the danger to the victim of a foreseeable escape attempt, or

4. Gave the offender a greater opportunity to commit additional crimes against the victim.[4]

Most jurisdictions today classify kidnapping as a serious felony and describe a series of conditions that define kidnapping. These conditions, which include holding an individual for ransom money or to perpetrate another crime, are illustrated by Hawaii's kidnapping statute.

Springboard for Discussion

Imagine the court had decided in defendant Lussier's favor that because he did not physically keep the victims in the crawl space, they were free to leave anytime. Analyzing the elements of false imprisonment and kidnapping, make a compelling argument defending the court's decision to find Lussier not guilty.

Hawaii Revised Statutes §707-720 (2017) Kidnapping

(1) A person commits the offense of kidnapping if the person intentionally or knowingly restrains another person with intent to:

(a) Hold that person for ransom or reward;

(b) Use that person as a shield or hostage;

(c) Facilitate the commission of a felony or flight thereafter;

(d) Inflict bodily injury upon that person or subject that person to a sexual offense;

(e) Terrorize that person or a third person;

(f) Interfere with the performance of any governmental or political function; or

(g) Unlawfully obtain the labor or services of that person, regardless of whether related to the collection of a debt.

(2) Except as provided in subsection (3), kidnapping is a class A felony.

(3) In a prosecution for kidnapping, it is a defense which reduces the offense to a class B felony that the defendant voluntarily released the victim, alive and not suffering from serious or substantial bodily injury, in a safe place prior to trial.

APPLYING THE LAW TO THE FACTS

Is It Kidnapping or False Imprisonment?

The Facts: In a racially charged incident at a state university involving a football player and a coach in 1968, students demanded a meeting with the athletic department administrators. Twenty students met with three administrators in the athletic building. The meeting grew contentious and students demanded the administrators speak directly with the university president. The group of students "escorted" the administrators approximately 700 yards from the athletic building to the president's office. Along the way, students jostled the administrators, made disparaging comments, threatened to "stick" the administrators, and, when the administrators stopped or tried to leave the escort, students prevented their freedom of movement. Did the students kidnap the administrators, or was the movement between the two buildings merely incidental to the crime of false imprisonment?

The Law: The students kidnapped the administrators. The analysis is not the actual distance of the asportation, but the intimidation, fear, threats, and increased danger posed to the administrators as they were, essentially, held against their will (*People v. Apo*, 1972).[5]

Hawaii's kidnapping statute includes the caveat that if the victim is safely released prior to trial, the seriousness of the grading of the offense will be reduced.

In the chapter-opening-case study, when Ben and Jerry blocked the door of the stepmother's bedroom preventing her from leaving, they committed the crime of false imprisonment. When Ben, Jerry, and Kathy placed the stepmother in the trunk of the car and drove away for miles, they kidnapped her. In analyzing the distinction between kidnapping and false imprisonment, read the case excerpt *United States v. Lussier* (2017) below, in which the defendant was convicted of second-degree kidnapping because the court found that he had specific intent *mens rea* to confine the victims above and beyond the incidental movement in the commission of another offense.

UNITED STATES V. LUSSIER, 844 F.3D 1019 (8TH CIR. 2017)

Eighth Circuit Court of Appeals

FACTS: On or about February 7, 2015, David Roy and Gregory Maxwell were drinking alcohol together at Maxwell's house. When Maxwell left to buy more alcohol, he instructed Roy not to let Darrell Lussier and Lussier's girlfriend Cristy Sumner into the house. [Lussier and Sumner lived with Maxwell for approximately one month.] When Maxwell returned home a few hours later, David Roy, his sister Nancy Roy, Lussier, and Sumner were present at his house. Lussier proceeded to beat Maxwell, David Roy, and Nancy Roy. According to Maxwell, Lussier hit him, jumped on his stomach and side, wrapped a bootlace around his throat, and dragged him by the bootlace, choking him. When Maxwell tried to leave, Sumner blocked the door, and Lussier told him: "Tonight is the night. Tonight is the night. You gonna die tonight. You got one hour to live." David Roy and Nancy Roy were also badly beaten by Lussier. Lussier and Sumner threw Maxwell, David Roy, and Nancy Roy through a trap door into the crawl space underneath the house. They then shut the trap door to the crawl space, which was cold and poorly lit. Maxwell and Nancy Roy attempted to find the trap door and push it open but were unable to do so. The three remained in the crawl space until Maxwell's nephew, Lawrence Kingbird, discovered them on the morning of February 9, 2015. [Maxwell, David Roy, and Nancy Roy all sustained severe physical injuries.]

ISSUE: [Is the act of placing victims into an unlocked crawl space and leaving the residence sufficient to sustain a conviction for the crime of kidnapping?]

HOLDING: [Yes.]

REASONING: Lussier contends that the evidence was insufficient to convict him of kidnapping. We draw all reasonable inferences in the government's favor and reverse only if no reasonable jury could have found the defendant guilty beyond a reasonable doubt. Under 18 U.S.C. §1201(a), a defendant is guilty of a crime if the defendant "unlawfully seizes, confines, inveigles, decoys, kidnaps, abducts, or carries away and holds for ransom or reward or otherwise any person." Kidnapping under §1201(a) thus has two elements: that of seizing, confining, inveigling, decoying, kidnapping, abducting, or carrying away; and holding for ransom or reward or otherwise. As to the second element, "[t]he act of holding a kidnapped person for a proscribed purpose necessarily implies an unlawful physical or mental restraint for an appreciable period against the person's will and with a willful intent so to confine the victim."

Lussier argues that the evidence was insufficient because it did not show that he "held" the victims. The district court instructed the jury that Lussier was charged with holding each victim "for the purpose of preventing him or her from contacting law enforcement and preventing the discovery of Defendant's crime." Lussier contends that the evidence does not show he held or had the intention to hold the victims because the trap door to the crawl space was not locked or obstructed, and there is no evidence that Lussier remained at Maxwell's house to prevent the victims from escaping.

CONCLUSION: We conclude that the evidence was sufficient to convict Lussier of kidnapping. A jury could reasonably infer from these facts that Lussier intended to confine the injured, incapacitated victims and prevent them from reporting the assault notwithstanding his failure to lock or obstruct the trap door or personally stand guard to prevent them from escaping.

Parental Kidnapping

As the ease with which couples could obtain a divorce increased over the past decades, so, too, did the number of custody disputes involving minor children with attendant custody decrees issued by courts. Some custody disputes end with one parent kidnapping his or her own children to prevent the other parent from having a relationship with the children. If a parent kidnaps his or her own child and crosses state lines, the Federal Parental Kidnapping Act becomes relevant.[6] This law was enacted to "deter interstate abductions and other unilateral removal of children undertaken to obtain custody and visitation awards." The *mens rea* of parental kidnapping is the specific intent to keep the child or children away from one parent, and the *actus reus* is the actual asportation of the child or children away from the other parent's dominion and control.

AMBER Alert

The America's Missing Broadcast Emergency Response (AMBER) alert system is a nationwide electronic notification system that distributes important information about abducted children and the offender, such as vehicle description, license plate numbers, direction traveling, and last location seen. The information appears on electronic billboards and television stations in hopes that the kidnapping victim will be found, and it is responsible for finding many victims in the critical first few hours after abduction. The information distribution system was named after 9-year-old Amber Hagerman, a kidnap victim from Texas.[7] As with any kidnapping, studies show that time is of the essence in trying to recover the victim.

Stalking

Stalking is a compulsive act usually performed by an offender who most likely suffers from a mental illness and who continually harasses and threatens the object/victim of his or her obsession. Of course, having a mental illness is not a crime. Stalkers usually exhibit the same type of behavior that revolves around the delusion (false fixed belief) that they must be in contact with their target, either for a love reason or to hurt, harm, or kill the object of their attentions. Actress Rebecca Schaeffer, from the 1990s television show "My Sister Sam," was 21 years old when she was shot and killed by an obsessive fan who had stalked her for 2 years. The killer had paid a private detective to retrieve Schaeffer's home address from driver's license records. Her murder led to legislative changes to create the crime of stalking and also to protect people's personal information contained in public records. Other notable cases of celebrity stalking victims include the singer Madonna; the

Rule of Law: The *mens rea* for stalking is that the offender should have known his repetitive harassment caused distress for the victim.

actor Alec Baldwin, repeatedly contacted by Genevieve Sabourin, who insisted they were involved romantically; and Ivanka Trump, who was stalked by Justin Massler beginning in 2009 when he wrote love letters, sent a photo staged to look as if he was covered in blood, condemned her for her wealth, and threatened her then-fiancé whom, Massler had written, "had stolen everything from me, leaving me with nothing, no sun in the sky, no stars in the wind and no moon in the trees."[8] Massler was charged in 2012 with aggravated harassment and ordered to stay away from Ms. Trump but was arrested on November 29, 2016, near Trump Tower trying to reinitiate contact.

Stalking behavior may have its origins in a disruption of the neurobiological function (nervous system physiology). Common psychosocial traits of the disorder reveal, regardless of gender, that people who stalk tend to be isolated and lonely, socially incompetent, and narcissistic. Research about stalking reveals the following information:[9]

1. Stalking is likely precipitated by a current personal loss that agitates or reconfirms earlier childhood trauma surrounding a severed attachment to a caregiver.

2. Stalking victims tend to be females and their stalkers tend to be men with whom they were previously sexually intimate.

3. Men who stalk have a history of mental, drug, and criminal problems.

4. Stalkers suffering from psychosis (break from reality) represent a small number of cases and typify the type of offender whose "object of pursuit" is a stranger.

5. One in three stalking cases involves physical violence toward the victim the stalker obsesses about, which in the case of a former boyfriend is, according to researcher J. Reid Meloy, "probably an impulsive response to the emotional upheaval that accompanies a severe attachment disruption where actual intimacy previously existed."

6. Stalking victims are truly harmed by the severe personal and professional disruption in their lives caused by the stalking and suffer severe psychological distress even long after the stalking has ended. In a subcategory of stalking victims, one third of psychologists who had been stalked seriously considered leaving the profession as a result of their victimization.

7. At least half of stalkers explicitly threaten their victims, and even though most threats are not carried out, the risk of violence likely increases when there is an articulated threat.

An example of an antistalking law is illustrated by the following Louisiana law.

Louisiana Revised Statutes §14:40.2 Stalking

A. Stalking is the intentional and repeated following or harassing of another person that would cause a reasonable person to feel alarmed or to suffer emotional distress. Stalking shall include but not be limited to:

- the intentional and repeated uninvited presence of the perpetrator at another person's home, workplace, school, or any place which would cause a reasonable person to be alarmed,

- or to suffer emotional distress as a result of verbal, written, or behaviorally implied threats of death, bodily injury, sexual assault, kidnapping, or any other statutory criminal act to himself or any member of his family or any person with whom he is acquainted.

According to Meloy, there are four recommendations for stalking victims: Do not talk yourself out of the belief that you are being stalked; contact authorities; keep a log of all contact, no matter how distasteful; and, most importantly, do not initiate contact with the offender for any reason, because personal attention from the stalker's "object of pursuit" only reinforces the stalking behavior.

Cyberstalking and Cyberbullying

The federal government makes stalking that crosses state lines a crime, and states have enacted laws designed to prevent "cyberstalking" and its cousin "cyberbullying," defined as the "willful and repeated harm inflicted through the use of computers, cell phones, and other electronic devices."[10] The difficulty of prosecuting cyber aggression is that the perpetrator can remain anonymous behind internet service provider (ISP) addresses. While most cyber aggression research is focused on children, adolescents, and young people, adults, too, are victims and all report feeling, among other emotions, "anxiety, depression, sadness, frustration, anger, and embarrassment."[11] Despite the anguish many victims experience, many do not press charges because they believe that "nothing can be done" and no punishment will actually befall the perpetrator.[12] An example of the difficulty of prosecuting harmful behavior committed online is presented in an excerpt from *People v. Marquan M.* (2014) below. In this case the New York court found the law under which a juvenile was punished for cyberbullying was too broad because it made criminal speech and expression people could post legally, a subject we address more fully in Chapter 11 on the First Amendment.

PEOPLE V. MARQUAN M., 19 N.E.3D 480 (N.Y. 2014)

FACTS: Bullying by children in schools has long been a prevalent problem but its psychological effects were not studied in earnest until the 1970s. Since then, "[b]ullying among school-aged youth" has "increasingly been recognized as an important problem affecting well-being and social functioning," as well as "a potentially more serious threat to healthy youth development." At its core, bullying represents an imbalance of power between the aggressor and victim that often manifests in behaviors that are "verbal (e.g., name-calling, threats), physical (e.g., hitting), or psychological (e.g., rumors, shunning/exclusion)." Based on the recognized harmful effects of bullying, many schools and communities now sponsor anti-bullying campaigns in order to reduce incidents of such damaging behaviors. Unlike traditional bullying, victims of cyberbullying can be "relentlessly and anonymously attacked twenty-four hours a day for the whole world to witness. There is simply no escape."

In 2010, the Albany County Legislature adopted a new crime—the offense of cyberbullying—which was defined as:

"any act of communicating or causing a communication to be sent by mechanical or electronic means, including posting statements on the internet or through a computer or email network, disseminating embarrassing or sexually explicit photographs; disseminating private, personal, false or sexual information, or sending hate mail, with no legitimate private, personal, or public purpose, with the intent to harass, annoy, threaten, abuse, taunt, intimidate, torment, humiliate, or otherwise inflict significant emotional harm on another person."

A month later, defendant Marquan M., a student attending Cohoes High School in Albany County, used the social networking website "Facebook" to create a page bearing the pseudonym "Cohoes Flame." He anonymously posted photographs of high-school classmates and other adolescents, with detailed descriptions of their alleged sexual practices and predilections, sexual partners and other types of personal information. The descriptive captions, which were vulgar and offensive, prompted responsive electronic messages that threatened the creator of the website with physical harm.

A police investigation revealed that defendant was the author of the Cohoes Flame postings. He admitted his involvement and was charged with cyberbullying under Albany County's local law. Defendant moved to dismiss, arguing that the statute violated his right to free speech under the First Amendment . . . because it is *overbroad*

(Continued)

(Continued)

in that it includes a wide array of protected expression, and is *unlawfully vague* since it does not give fair notice to the public of the proscribed conduct (emphasis added).

Under the Free Speech Clause of the First Amendment, the government generally "has no power to restrict expression because of its message, its ideas, its subject matter, or its content." Consequently, it is well established that prohibitions of pure speech must be limited to communications that qualify as fighting words, true threats, incitement, obscenity, child pornography, fraud, defamation or statements integral to criminal conduct. Outside of such recognized categories, speech is presumptively protected and generally cannot be curtailed by the government. Yet, the government unquestionably has a compelling interest in protecting children from harmful publications or materials. Cyberbullying is not conceptually immune from government regulation, so we may assume, for the purposes of this case that the First Amendment permits the prohibition of cyberbullying directed at children, depending on how that activity is defined. Our task therefore is to determine whether the specific statutory language of the Albany County legislative enactment can comfortably coexist with the right to free speech.

Based on the text of the statute at issue, it is evident that Albany County "create[d] a criminal prohibition of alarming breadth." The language of the local law embraces a wide array of applications that prohibit types of protected speech far beyond the cyberbullying of children. As written, the Albany County law in its broadest sense criminalizes "any act of communicating . . . by mechanical or electronic means . . . with no legitimate . . . personal . . . purpose, with the intent to harass [or] annoy . . . another person." On its face, the law covers communications aimed at adults, and fictitious or corporate entities, even though the county legislature justified passage of the provision based on the detrimental effects that cyberbullying has on school-aged children. The county law also lists particular examples of covered communications, such as "posting statements on the internet or through a computer or email network, disseminating embarrassing or sexually explicit photographs; disseminating private, personal, false or sexual information, or sending hate mail." But such methods of expression are not limited to instances of cyberbullying—the law includes every conceivable form of electronic communication, such as telephone conversations, a ham radio transmission or even a telegram.

In addition, the provision pertains to electronic communications that are meant to "harass, annoy . . . taunt . . . [or] humiliate" any person or entity, not just those that are intended to "threaten, abuse . . . intimidate, torment . . . or otherwise inflict significant emotional harm on" a child. In considering the facial implications [looking at the law "on its face"], it appears that the provision would criminalize a broad spectrum of speech outside the popular understanding of cyberbullying, including, for example: an email disclosing private information about a corporation or a telephone conversation meant to annoy an adult.

It is undisputed that the Albany County statute was motivated by the laudable public purpose of shielding children from cyberbullying. The text of the cyberbullying law, however, does not adequately reflect an intent to restrict its reach to the three discrete types of electronic bullying of a sexual nature designed to cause emotional harm to children.

There is undoubtedly general consensus that defendant's Facebook communications were repulsive and harmful to the subjects of his rants, and potentially created a risk of physical or emotional injury based on the private nature of the comments. Although the First Amendment may not give defendant the right to engage in these activities, the text of Albany County's law envelops far more than acts of cyberbullying against children by criminalizing a variety of constitutionally protected modes of expression.

We therefore hold that Albany County's Local Law No. 11 of 2010—as drafted—is overbroad and facially invalid under the Free Speech Clause of the First Amendment. Accordingly, the order of County Court should be reversed and the accusatory instrument dismissed.

DISSENT BY: SMITH

Albany County has conceded that certain provisions of its Cyber-Bullying Law are invalid. It seems to me that those provisions can be readily severed from the rest of the legislation and that what remains can, without any strain on its language, be interpreted in a way that renders it constitutionally valid.

Laws Against "Revenge Porn"

Many states have enacted laws to punish what is known as "revenge porn," which is distributing sexually explicit images of another without their consent and typically after the victim initially willingly shared the intimate photos. The term is derived from the offender seeking to punish a former partner by publishing photos shared during the partnership. The laws to punish such behavior suffer from the same free speech challenges as cyberbullying laws do because people have a right to share information online. Title 13, Vermont Statutes Annotated, 2606(b)(1) (2015), prohibits "knowingly disclosing a visual image of an identifiable person who was nude or was engaged in a sexual conduct, without his or her consent." In one case interpreting the statute, a woman took partially nude photos of herself and sent them to Anthony Coon's Facebook account.

Coon was romantically involved with Rebekah Van Buren. Van Buren accessed Coon's account and posted the photographs on a public Facebook account "to get back" at the woman for getting involved with Mr. Coon.[13] Van Buren was criminally charged; she moved to dismiss the criminal complaint, and the court agreed. Finding that so-called revenge porn did not meet the definition of obscenity, that Coon legally possessed the photographs because the victim consented to the initial disclosure, and that the circumstances did not fit the type of behavior the law was meant to capture (here, Van Buren posted the photographs, not Coon), the case was dismissed.[14]

Hate Crimes

This country has many freedoms, and one freedom is to hate someone because of a person's identity and to express that hatred in a hurtful way. But once those permissible thoughts go beyond speech into hurtful acts, then the individual who acted may be punished or have his or her punishment enhanced because of targeting someone for who they are, which is a hate crime. Such sentence enhancements have withstood challenges by convicted defendants who claim such enhancements violate their freedom to hate under the First Amendment (*Wisconsin v. Mitchell*, 1993).[15] The justification for harsh punishment is that hate crimes are "at once discriminatory and terroristic" and "are a qualitatively unique category of offenses. Compared to non-bias motivated crimes these crimes are more likely to involve violence, injury, hospitalization, psychological trauma and a greater risk of retaliatory attacks."[16] Targeting people because of their immutable characteristics, such as race, or because of their perceived characteristics, such as gender identity or religion, has a long terrible history from World War II's Holocaust to the 2018 ethnic cleansing in Myanmar. Because the consequences flowing from hate crimes are so severe, public policy justifies punishing hate crime offenders more severely.

> **Rule of Law: It is legal in America to hate others, but it is illegal to hurt others based on that hate.**

Springboard for Discussion

Before the *Brown v. Board of Education* decision in 1954 declaring racial segregation in public schools unconstitutional, Blacks and Whites, especially in the South, rarely interacted socially or politically, which is not the case today. Which came first, the chicken or the egg? Does the law change people's behavior and beliefs, or do beliefs and behavior change the law?

It is sometimes difficult to prove that the offender was motivated by hate. In early 2017, two cases brought within one week of each other illustrate the type of evidence of hate that may motivate an offender to act. On January 3, 2017, a 14-year-old freshman at Saucon Valley High School, Pennsylvania, was charged with ethnic intimidation and cyber harassment for posting a video on Snapchat of a 16-year-old African American male student eating chicken at lunch. The student taping can be heard saying, "Look at that f****** n*****, you know he's on welfare. He can't even buy any chicken." The video was discovered after the Black student, in response to the video, battered the White freshman at a football game. Civil libertarians argued that the White student's speech, although offensive, was legal, which is quite different from actual, physical assaults motivated by hate. On January 5, 2017, four African American teenagers were charged in Chicago after 37 minutes of a 4- to 5-hour attack of an intellectually disabled teenager was posted on Facebook Live. The offenders bound and gagged the victim and can be seen punching, slapping, and stomping on his head and can be heard saying "F*** White people." Without such explicit statements connecting the victim's personal characteristic with the physical violence, prosecutors may have difficulty proving the offender's *mens rea* for the attack. The Illinois hate crime statute used to charge the four teenagers includes disability as a protected class, reprinted in part here.

Hate Crime 720 Illinois Compiled Statutes §5/12-7.1 (2016)

(a) A person commits hate crime when, by reason of the actual or perceived race, color, creed, religion, ancestry, gender, sexual orientation, physical or mental disability, or national origin of another individual or group of individuals, regardless of the existence of any other motivating factor or factors, he commits assault, battery, aggravated assault, misdemeanor theft, criminal trespass to residence, misdemeanor criminal damage to property, criminal trespass to vehicle, criminal trespass to real property, mob action, disorderly conduct, harassment by telephone, or harassment through electronic communications as these crimes are defined [by applicable law].

The four Illinois teenagers were also charged with aggravated kidnapping, aggravated battery, and aggravated unlawful restraint. Those with physical or mental challenges are often targets for violence because of their obvious vulnerabilities and, as discussed earlier in this chapter, a victim's status may increase the criminal charge to an aggravated status. In the chapter-opening case study, because Ben said to the Korean American grocer, "Welcome to America, macaca," before committing mayhem, his act qualifies as a hate crime because the aggravated battery was motivated by racial animus.

SEX OFFENSES

Various crimes are defined under the rubric of sex offenses, including rape, sexual assault, sodomy, incest, deviant sexual intercourse, and statutory rape. Typically, in sex offenses, sex is used to dominate and control the victim whether or not such acts are sexually gratifying. A penis or object is used to defile a bodily orifice, such as the mouth, vagina, or anus of another, and that penis or object is a weapon used to commit the offense much like a handgun is a weapon used to commit armed robbery. Traditional beliefs that people engage in sexual activity with people to whom they are attracted make it difficult to understand how a popular and attractive young man could rape his elderly neighbor. Sex-related offenses are crimes of violence, not sex. For instance, rape in a men's prison rarely occurs because of a lack of female companionship; prison rape is an act of dominance in a confined setting with a defined hierarchy of power.[17] Such an awareness of the power dynamic in sex offenses is critical to understanding the *mens rea* of such crimes.

Rape

> **Rule of Law: Rape is a sex act committed with force or threat of force against the victim's will and without the victim's consent.**

Under common law, rape was defined as "carnal knowledge of a woman against her will." Rather than focus on the offender's actions during a rape, the law turned its attention to the victim's state of mind regarding consent to decide whether or not the sexual intercourse constituted rape. Early development of rape law was a disastrous mine field for female victims. A woman's claim of rape was not to be believed if she could not show physical injury proving that she resisted "to the utmost" and if she had not reported the crime immediately to the police. Wives could not refuse their husband's demands for sex because "the husband cannot be guilty of a rape committed by himself upon his lawful wife, for by their mutual matrimonial consent and contract, the wife hath given up herself in this kind unto her husband, which she cannot retract."[18] Judges instructed juries that an alleged victim's testimony about rape was inherently untrustworthy because "women lie about their lack of consent [to engage in sexual relations] for various reasons: to blackmail men, to explain the discovery of a consensual affair, or because of psychological illness."[19] Moreover, to be admissible in court, a victim's testimony that she had been raped required independent corroboration (verification) by other evidence.

Laws criminalizing rape changed rapidly in the late 1960s and early 1970s as leading feminist scholars changed the legal discourse on rape by defining it as an extension of patriarchal dominance, which coincided with legal control over family planning, when birth control for unmarried women was legalized in *Griswold v. Connecticut* (1965), and a woman's right to decide in consultation with her physician to terminate a pregnancy was legalized in *Roe v. Wade* (1973).[20] As Susan Brownmiller wrote in her seminal work on rape, *Against Our Will* (1975), "Man's discovery that his genitalia could serve as a weapon to generate fear must rank as one of the most important discoveries of prehistoric times, along with his use of fire and the first crude stone axe. From prehistoric times to the present, I believe, rape has played a critical function. It is nothing more or less than a conscious process of intimidation by which *all* men keep *all* women in a state of fear" (emphasis in original).[21] By defining rape as a tool to oppress female victims, the law began to give female victims more legal protections. The most dramatic legal development of this era was the passage of rape shield laws to prevent victim character assassination through cross-examination, which implied that the victim was, at best, of loose moral character and, at worst, "asking" to be raped by the way she moved, dressed, or behaved.

The common law definition of rape is

1. Penile penetration, however slight, emission not required, by

2. Force or threat

3. Against a victim's will and without that person's consent.

Today the definition of rape is dependent on state jurisdiction, but most rape statutes are gender-neutral. . Students are urged to check their respective state definitions for acts of sexual violence and abuse. For example, many state statutes define rape "per os" (mouth) or "per anus" and have special categories for the rape of children or other vulnerable people (e.g., those with physical or intellectual limitations) as "deviate sexual intercourse." In the chapter-opening case study, Ben raped the stepmother when he placed his penis inside her vagina only a little while she was unconscious and, therefore, unable to consent. Most rape statutes do not include a required *mens rea* state, because, to be guilty of rape, one must necessarily engage in forcible conduct. As some legal scholars have said,

> Although the *actus reus* of rape has two critical components—force and absence of consent—issues of *mens rea* have revolved almost exclusively around the element of nonconsent, that is, the defendant's state of mind with respect to the victim's consent. Very little attention has been paid to the *mens rea* applicable to the element of force, that is, the defendant's state of mind with respect to the presence of force. For example, in discussing the types of *mens rea* issues that arise in rape cases, one commentary noted that "the mistake-of-fact defense in a rape prosecution is almost always that the actor thought the victim had consented" and then dropped a footnote to make the point that "it is highly unlikely that a defendant would be mistaken about whether he is having intercourse"— thus completely ignoring the question of *mens rea* as applied to the element of force.[22]

With respect to the amount of force necessary to prove a charge of rape, it may be enough for the offender to have threatened the victim to the extent where he or she believed resistance would be futile.

Sexual Assault and College Campus Disciplinary Proceedings

The problem of sexual assaults on college campuses has received nationwide media attention with emphasis on what is commonly known as Title IX (Title 9), which guarantees equal treatment of students, as it provides:

> No person in the United States shall, on the basis of sex, be excluded from participation in, be denied the benefits of, or be subjected to discrimination under any education program or activity receiving Federal financial assistance.

Originally enacted in 1972, Title 9 is credited with elevating collegiate women's sports teams because the law prohibits discrimination on the basis of sex in federally funded education programs.[23] Because most colleges receive federal financial aid and other federal support, women gained equal access to men's sports' team funding. The term *sex discrimination* includes harassing behavior that is "so severe, pervasive, and objectively offensive that it effectively bars the victim's access to an educational opportunity or benefit," and college students who are sexually molested by fellow students, faculty, or staff can file Title 9 discrimination complaints. In one notable civil lawsuit, *Doe v. Brown University* (2016), the federal trial court, in refusing to dismiss a male student's lawsuit against the university, said, "This case is one of a number of recent [cases] in which a male student has sued a university that found him responsible for committing sexual assault after an allegedly flawed and deficient disciplinary proceeding."[24] At issue is the standard of evidence at honor board hearings, either a preponderance standard (51%) or the more stringent "clear and convincing" standard, which implicated the student's claim that the university process was biased against male students charged with sexual misconduct.

Rape Shield Laws

To encourage rape victims to come forward and report the crime and to prevent emotional harassment at trial of those victims who do come forward, the federal government and many states have enacted rape shield laws, which limit the type of questions defense counsel representing the offender on trial for rape can ask the victim, while at the same time preserving the defendant's constitutional right to confront witnesses against him by trying to show that the victim could be lying. Federal Rule of Evidence (FRE) Rule 412 is like many state statutes that control the type of questioning that is permissible of a sex victim about his or her sexual past.

FRE 412 Sex Offense Cases; Relevance of Alleged Victim's Past Sexual Behavior or Alleged Sexual Predisposition

(a) <u>Evidence generally inadmissible</u>. The following evidence is not admissible in any civil or criminal proceeding involving alleged sexual misconduct except as provided in subdivisions (b) and (c):

(1) Evidence offered to prove that any alleged victim engaged in other sexual behavior.

(2) Evidence offered to prove any alleged victim's sexual predisposition.

(b) <u>Exceptions:</u>

(1) In a criminal case, the following evidence is admissible, if otherwise admissible under these rules:

(A) Evidence of specific instances of sexual behavior of the alleged victim offered to prove that a person other than the accused was the source of semen, injury or other physical evidence;

(B) Evidence of specific instances of sexual behavior by the alleged victim with respect to the person accused of the sexual misconduct offered by the accused to prove consent or by the prosecution; and

(C) Evidence the exclusion of which would violate the constitutional rights of the defendant.

The significance of the rape shield laws is that a defendant cannot introduce as evidence the alleged victim's reputation of loose sexual morality or promiscuity because such factors are irrelevant to whether, on this occasion with this defendant, the victim consented and whether the victim was forced to submit to unwanted sex. But the defendant does have a right to introduce evidence of a victim's past sexual behavior with him or her, because the victim's willingness to consent to sex with the defendant in the past may have affected the defendant's *mens rea* about whether or not the victim was consenting on the night of the alleged rape. Also, allowable under rape shield laws is evidence of a victim's past sexual conduct to prove that some other person is the source of injury or semen. The defense in criminal law circles is that "Some Other Dude Did It" (S.O.D.D.I.), and the defendant has a constitutional right under the Sixth Amendment's Confrontation Clause to cross-examine the victim to prove that another person may have been the perpetrator. This is the exception in FRE 412 rape shield law that allows "Evidence the exclusion of which would violate the constitutional rights of the defendant."

The operation of rape shield laws can be understood by examining the way rape allegations are handled in the military under the Uniform Code of Military Justice (UCMJ), which is federal law that applies solely to the conduct, crimes, and procedures of military justice. In September 2013 at a public hearing conducted pursuant to Article 32 of the UCMJ, the military counterpart to a civilian preliminary hearing a female complainant was cross-examined for 30 hours over 4 days and asked questions technically to elicit whether or not she consented to having sex with three Naval Academy midshipmen at an off campus party in 2012. The questions were perceived by the complainant's counsel as attempts to harass the sophomore in an effort to get her to drop the charges. The UCMJ does not have a rape shield provision at a preliminary hearing. Defense counsel Andrew Weinstein asked the putative victim whether she wore a bra or underwear to the party and if she "felt like a 'ho'" afterward. In addition, the victim was asked whether she carried condoms in her purse. Lieutenant Commander Angela Tang, another defense counsel, asked how wide the woman opened her mouth when she performed oral sex on the theory that the woman's oral sex practices may indicate "active participation," which would also indicate consent to sexual relations.[25] The ensuing outcry that the questions were out of bounds and that the military should adopt rape shield protections at Article 32 hearings died in Congress. The woman admitted that on the night of the party she had so much to drink that her memory was partly blank and she only learned the full extent of the alleged sexual assault when she saw certain tweets and heard rumors that the three football players used her for intercourse. Charges against two of the midshipmen were dropped, and the third midshipman was acquitted at a judge-only trial, all in 2014.

Statutory Rape

Different from forcible rape is statutory rape to which criminal liability attaches because of the age difference between the victim and offender, even though the victim may have "consented" to the sexual activity. Today most statutory rape laws define the crime as sex between a teenager and a person who is at least 4 years older than that teenager. For example, it qualifies as statutory rape for a 20-year-old to have sex with a 15-year-old, but not for a 17-year-old to have sex with a 15-year-old.

The early public policy supporting the enactment of statutory rape laws was that a woman below a certain age was incapable of consenting to sexual acts even if she were naked on a bed and shouting, "Come get me!" The crime developed in early common law to protect the chastity "of vulnerable, virtuous young women, treating them as 'special property in need of special protection'" and to prevent teenage pregnancy—a legitimate government interest recognized by the U.S. Supreme Court in *Michael M. v. Sonoma County Superior Court* (1981), because children born to teenagers most often need government financial support until they reach adulthood.[26] Statutory rape laws today recognize the reality that boys and young men are also victims.[27]

> **Rule of Law:** Statutory rape is typically defined as consensual sex between partners who are 4 or more years apart in age, when one of the partners is under the age of consent.

Mistake of Age as a Defense to a Charge of Statutory Rape. What happens when the defendant claims "an honest and reasonable mistake of fact regarding the victim's age?" Can a defendant's mistake of fact that the child was the age of consent be a defense? The age of consent to engage in sex acts varies, based on jurisdiction, from 16 to 18 years old. Early statutory rape statutes were strict liability: If the sex act was committed, regardless of *mens rea* or intent, the defendant was guilty. But as the penalty for rape increased to long prison sentences, some legislatures amended their statutory rape laws to require *mens rea* and, on the flip side, to allow certain defenses, most often that the offender thought the victim was of age. North Dakota recognizes such a defense: "When criminality depends on the victim being a minor, it is an affirmative defense, that the actor reasonably believed the victim to be an adult."[28] But New Jersey does not: "It shall be no defense to a [statutory rape] prosecution that the actor believed the victim to be above the age stated for the offense, even if such a mistaken belief was reasonable."[29]

In *State v. Guest* (1978),[30] two defendants were charged with the statutory rape of a 15-year-old girl. The issue in the case was whether the statute was strict liability, for it failed to list an applicable *mens rea* state. The Supreme Court of Alaska held that when a statute was not of the regulatory, health, and welfare type commonly associated with strict liability crimes (e.g., speeding or health inspection), then "either a requirement of criminal intent must be read into the statute or it must be found unconstitutional." Thus, the Alaska high court held with respect to its statutory rape law, if the statute required an intent/*mens rea* element, then the law would also permit the affirmative defense of mistake, which the defendants in *Guest* were allowed to raise.

Child Sex Abuse

Children cannot consent to sexual relations; they are presumed under the law to not have the mental capacity to agree to sexual activity. Studies show the adults who pose the greatest risk of harm for sexual exploitation of children are those adults in a position of trust over the child, for example, a family member, teacher, or beloved coach. As Federal Bureau of Investigation (FBI) child sex abuse expert Kenneth V. Lanning writes,

> People seem more willing to accept a sinister, unknown individual or "stranger" from a different location or father/stepfather from a different socioeconomic background as a child molester than a clergy member, next-door neighbor, law-enforcement officer,

pediatrician, teacher, coach, or volunteer. Acquaintance molesters often gain access to children through youth-serving organizations. The acquaintance molester, by definition, is one of us. He is not simply an anonymous, external threat. He cannot be identified by physical description and, often, not even by "bad" character traits.

There are typically two types of child molesters, the one who has sex with children because the child is available, called a situational child molester, and the person commonly thought of as a "pedophile," who prefers children over all else for sexual gratification.[31] The situational offender may molest children related to his or her basic sexual needs (e.g., the child is there), or, in the traditional concept of rape, the sex is related to a need for dominance and control. The FBI's behavioral analysis finds the situational offender less educated, more likely to commit a variety of crimes, and, in general, "morally indiscriminate." The preferential pedophile is someone whose sex with children is highly ritualistic, a result of turning fantasy into reality, and marked by "specific victim preferences," as in the case of convicted serial molester and former Penn State football coach, Jerry Sandusky. Agent Lanning says that men who are sexually attracted exclusively to adolescent boys are the "most persistent and prolific" abusers. The preferential molester comes from a higher socioeconomic background, and because their molestation is largely rooted in fantasy, "they tend to 'audition' their potential victims, selecting them primarily based on their similarity to and consistency with that script. There can be a lengthy 'rehearsal' or grooming process leading up to the victimization."[32] Both types of child molesters may have overlapping behavior, as indicated in Figure 4.1.

Figure 4.1   Child Molesters' Motivation Continuum

Motivation Continuum	
Biological/Physiological Sexual Needs	Psychosexual/Deviant
Power/Anger Nonsexual Needs	Sexual Needs
(Not one or the other, but a continuum)	
Situational Sex Offender: (>More Likely)	Preferential Sex Offender: (>More Likely)
Less Intelligent	More Intelligent
Lower Socioeconomic Status	Higher Socioeconomic Status
Personality Disorders	Paraphilias
• Antisocial/Psychopathy	• Pedophilia
• Narcissistic	• Voyeurism
• Schizoid	• Sadism
Varied Criminal Behavior	Focused Criminal Behavior
Violent Pornography	Theme Pornography
Impulsive	Compulsive
Considers Risk	Considers Need
Sloppy Mistakes	Needy Mistakes
Thought Driven	Fantasy Driven
Spontaneous or Planned	Scripted
• Availability	• Audition
• Opportunity	• Rehearsal
• Tools	• Props
• Learning	• Critique
Method of Operation (MO) Patterns of Behavior	Ritual Patterns of Behavior
• Works	• Need
• Dynamic	• Static

Source: Reprinted with permission, National Center for Missing and Exploited Children.

Law enforcement personnel should take advantage of any specialized training opportunity to learn the unique aspects of sex crimes and, specifically, how to treat and interview both offenders and victims. For victims, feelings of shame, discomfort, and embarrassment can be made worse by insensitive or repetitive questioning. For offenders, learning to overcome their many excuses justifying their actions ("I was just showing love. The victim wanted me") is important to uncover the truth. Time and effort are required to learn interrogation techniques to lead sex offenders to confess their crimes. Moreover, courses in how to download information from electronic devices is paramount because evidence in the form of text messages, pornography collections, and chat room discussions can be used to help prove a defendant's *mens rea* in a court of law. The government has at its disposal, though, a wide range of criminal laws to prosecute sex crimes as many statutes overlap in criminalizing a variety of sexual behavior. On the other hand, defense counsel's job is to defend the client zealously, which, in sex abuse cases, often means testing the credibility of the complaining witness. Care must be taken to treat victims with respect, but it is counsel's job to investigate all possible explanations of events that might bear on the client's *mens rea* providing a defense to the charges.

Incest. **Incest** is sexual relations between nonspousal family members, regardless of how they are related by blood, adoption, or marriage. It is an important legal distinction to ask whether childhood victims of sexual abuse can, once they reach adulthood, eventually "consent" to sexual relations with their abusers. Delbert Roy Douglas fathered two children with his daughter, whom he raped when she was a minor and continued into her adulthood. Douglas challenged his convictions for both incest and sexual assault because he argued his incest was consensual and, by legal definition, rape is not. In rejecting Douglas's arguments, the Supreme Court of Nevada stated, "It would seem a strange rule of law that a man indicted for incest might escape conviction and secure an acquittal, by satisfying the jury that he overcame the woman by force and violence."[33] Incest presumes nonconsensual sexual activity. "The goals incorporated within traditional incest statutes include: the orderly regulation of marriage, the prevention of biologically harmful inbreeding . . . and the setting out of punishment for sexual behavior perceived as deviant or exploitative."[34] A perspective that incest, under the law, is somewhat less egregious a sex crime because it is viewed as a crime against "the family," is embodied in statutes that can vitiate (make null and void) the crime of incest by the act of marriage in states such as Indiana, Louisiana, Maine, Michigan, Ohio, and South Dakota.

> **Rule of Law: Incest is sexual relations among nonspousal family members.**

Deviate Sexual Conduct

The history of sexual crimes includes acts called deviate sexual intercourse, such as sodomy, which consists of penile and oral or penile and anal contact. The U.S. Supreme Court struck down laws criminalizing sodomy between consenting heterosexual and homosexual adults in *Lawrence v. Texas* (2003), but many state statutes still outlaw certain types of sodomy, defined generally as oral/genital, oral/anal, or genital/anal contact, especially those acts involving unwilling partners, children, and other vulnerable victims.

Juveniles and "Sexting" Offenses

Finding a juvenile "delinquent" is not a criminal conviction but rather placing the juvenile in a special status. If a juvenile is delinquent, punishment is focused on treatment and restorative justice rather than incarceration. Many juvenile "sexting" cases involve delinquency adjudications. The National Center for Missing and Exploited Children explains that "'Sexting' refers to youth sending sexually explicit messages or sexually explicit photos of themselves or others to their peers. Teens are using cell phones, computers, web cams, digital cameras, and even video game systems to take and distribute sexually explicit photographs of themselves or others." There are many issues involved in juvenile sexting, including determining who is the offender and who is the victim in the "traditional" sex abuse case. As discussed in examining the Fourth

Amendment and technology in Chapter 7, the law takes time to catch up to changing technologies and social norms. When the law is unclear, results for the same type of conduct tend to be unpredictable. An example is Ohio law.

Ohio Revised Code Annotated §2907.31 Disseminating matter harmful to juveniles.

(A) No person, with knowledge of its character or content, shall recklessly do any of the following:

(1) Directly sell, deliver, furnish, disseminate, provide, exhibit, rent, or present to a juvenile, a group of juveniles, a law enforcement officer posing as a juvenile, or a group of law enforcement officers posing as juveniles any material or performance that is obscene or harmful to juveniles . . .

At first blush, Ohio's law is seemingly designed to prohibit adults from sending harmful material to children, but on closer reading, the law does not exempt juveniles from sending "matter harmful to juveniles" to one another. In the case, *In re L.Z.* (2016),[35] a 12-year-old girl sent via text message a selfie of her face and bare breasts to L.Z., a 12-year-old boy (initials are used to protect the children's identity). The girl said L.Z. threatened to "sexually assault" her if she did not send the photo. L.Z. then texted and showed the girl's selfie to five other juveniles. L.Z. was found guilty under the Ohio law of five counts of delinquency for distributing "matter harmful to juveniles." L.Z. argued the girl's selfie was not harmful or obscene and he was, therefore, not guilty. The appeals court disagreed, finding that in some contexts, the girl's photo could be considered pornography and L.Z.'s "perverse disregard" for how he showed the photos to his friends supported the court's finding of delinquency. Many laws to specifically redress "sexting" crimes place burdens on schools, which, as institutions, do not have much control over the off-campus behavior of students. In the chapter-opening case study, Kathy could be charged with "sexting" sexually provocative photos of herself via text message on her cellphone to her five girlfriends.

HOMICIDE

Rule of Law: Homicide is the killing of one human being by another.

In the 1797 *Institutes of the Laws of England*, Sir Edward Coke defined murder as "when a man of sound memory, and of the age of discretion, unlawfully killeth within any country of the realm any reasonable creature *in rerum natura* [in the natural world] under the King's peace, with malice aforethought, either expressed by the party or implied by law, so as the party wounded, or hurt, etc. die of the wound or hurt, etc. within a year and a day after the same."

Sir James Stephen in his 1887 *Digest of the Criminal Law* defined malice aforethought as the predetermination (premeditation) to commit an unlawful act, especially murder, and defined murder as

One or more of the following states of mind preceding or co-existing with the act or omission by which death is caused, and it may exist where that act is premeditated.

(a) An intention to cause the death of, or grevious [sic] bodily harm to, any person, whether such person is the person actually killed or not;

(b) knowledge that the act which causes death will not probably cause the death of, or grevious [sic] bodily harm to, some person, whether such person is the person actually killed or not, although such knowledge is accompanied by indifference whether death or grevious [sic] bodily harm is caused or not, or by a wish that it may not be caused;

(c) an intent to commit any felony whatever;

(d) an intent to oppose by force any officer of justice on his way to, in, or returning from the execution of the duty of arresting, keeping in custody, or imprison, or the duty of keeping the peace or dispensing an unlawful assembly, provided that the offender has notice that the person killed is such an officer so employed.[36]

Over time, state statutes defining murder embodied Sir Coke and Sir Stephen's conceptualization of homicide and recognized the different methods of killing with the attendant *mens rea*. Recall from our discussion in Chapter 3 on *mens rea* when big fish eats little fish. It may be helpful to remember that first-degree murder is the biggest fish deserving of the most punitive punishment, whereas involuntary manslaughter is the littlest fish deserving of the least harsh punishment.

First- and Second-Degree Murder

In general, the elements of first-degree murder are

1. The willful, deliberate, and premeditated

2. Killing

3. Of another.

The term *willful* means specific intent to bring about the victim's death; *deliberate* means the offender had a cool mind, was able to think rationally, and was not acting under any rage, fear, or prejudice; and *premeditated* means that the offender at least planned the killing in some way, either by lying in wait or by bringing a weapon to the place of the crime. In many state jury instructions, deliberate and premeditated can mean as little as picking up a loaded gun, pointing it, and pulling the trigger, but historically the terms meant to punish those most harshly who clearly gave the killing some thought in cool reflection before they intentionally killed their victim. Only first-degree murder is punishable by the death penalty.

Usually the jury has to infer the offender's intent to kill from the circumstances surrounding the killing, such as the use of a deadly weapon, which is the use of any object in a manner designed to cause serious bodily injury or death. The deadly weapon doctrine allows the jury to infer the specific intent to kill to support a guilty verdict for first-degree murder. For instance, a pencil may be intended for writing, but when it is used to poke out someone's eyeballs or is sharpened to a fine point and plunged in a victim's jugular vein, that pencil is a deadly weapon, and if the person dies, the jury can infer that the defendant meant to kill, not merely to injure.

When is someone dead for purposes of a homicide prosecution? If a victim suffers serious harm and is put on life support, is he still alive? Many state jurisdictions define brain death as "dead" for murder statutes, and if the family cuts off life support, the offender may still be prosecuted for murder even though he is not the immediate cause of death. The concept discussed by Sir Edward Coke is the year-and-a-day rule, which still retains vitality in federal courts. Essentially, if the victim died within one year and one day after suffering harm at the offender's hands, the offender would legally be responsible for the death. With the advances of medical technology and more awareness as to the causes of death, the rule has limited applicability, but in most situations where there might be present-day confusion about the interpretation of statutes, the common law fills in the gaps.

The elements of second-degree murder are

1. The willful and intentional intent to commit serious bodily harm

2. That results in the death

3. Of another.

Second-degree murder is defined as missing one of the elements of first-degree murder (the willfulness, the premeditation, or the deliberateness). A murder that results from an offender's desire to commit serious bodily harm but not necessarily death is considered to be in the second degree. For example, if Tommy strikes Joey's nose with a book intending to cause serious bodily harm in breaking his nose, but instead the cartilage in his nose pierces his brain, causing death, the murder will be in the second degree. Typically, a book is not a deadly weapon. Note the differences from and similarities to the North Carolina Statute provided herein and the 17th-century definitions of murder.

North Carolina General Statute §14-17. Murder in the First and Second Degree defined, Punishment

(a) A murder which shall be perpetrated by means of a nuclear, biological, or chemical weapon of mass destruction, poison, lying in wait, imprisonment, starving, torture, or by any other kind of willful, deliberate, and premeditated killing, or which shall be committed in the perpetration or attempted perpetration of any arson, rape or a sex offense, robbery, kidnapping, burglary, or other felony committed or attempted with the use of a deadly weapon shall be deemed to be murder in the first degree, a Class A felony, and any person who commits such murder shall be punished with death or imprisonment in the State's prison for life without parole as the court shall determine

(1) If a murder was perpetrated with malice as described in subdivision (1) of subsection (b) of this section, and committed against a spouse, former spouse, a person with whom the defendant lives or has lived as if married, a person with whom the defendant is or has been in a dating relationship, or a person with whom the defendant shares a child in common, there shall be a rebuttable presumption that the murder is a "willful, deliberate, and premeditated killing" under subsection (a) of this section and shall be deemed to be murder in the first degree . . .

(b) A murder other than described in subsection (a) or (a1) of this section shall be deemed second degree murder.

(1) The malice necessary to prove second degree murder is based on an inherently dangerous act or omission, done in such a reckless and wanton manner as to manifest a mind utterly without regard for human life and social duty and deliberately bent on mischief.

(2) The murder is one that was proximately caused by the unlawful distribution of any opium, opiate, or opioid; any synthetic or natural salt, compound, derivative, or preparation of opium, or opiate, or opioid; cocaine; methamphetamine; or a depressant, and the ingestion of such substance caused the death of the user.

(c) For the purposes of this section, it shall constitute murder where a child is born alive but dies as a result of injuries inflicted prior to the child being born alive . . .

States have wide latitude to define and categorize the types of homicide, for example, punishing drug dealers whose buyers end up dead by charging the drug dealers with murder, or punishing more harshly intimate partner violence that leads to death. In your research of your state's laws, notice the interchangeability of language used to describe the requisite *mens rea*, such as "wanton" and "reckless" to denote a manifest indifference to the value of life that is commonly used to describe murder in many homicide statutes.

**Rule of Law:
Manslaughter is an intentional killing done in the heat of passion or an unintended killing that is an accident.**

Manslaughter

Manslaughter may be voluntary or involuntary. Voluntary manslaughter is when the person willingly takes the act that results in death. Involuntary manslaughter is a death caused by an offender who engages in reckless or negligent conduct and typically causes an accident. Historically, common law distinctions of homicide focused on the level of risk created by the offender sufficient to sustain a conviction. The California statute is an example of the common distinctions of manslaughter:

California Penal Code §192 (2018)

Manslaughter is the unlawful killing of a human being without malice. It is of three kinds:

(a) Voluntary – upon a sudden quarrel or heat of passion.

(b) Involuntary – in the commission of an unlawful act, not amounting to a felony; or in the commission of a lawful act which might produce death, in an unlawful manner, or without due caution and circumspection.

(c) Vehicular-
. . . (2) . . . driving a vehicle in the commission of a lawful act which might produce death, in an unlawful manner, but with gross negligence . . .

Notice in the California law, involuntary manslaughter is described as taking a lawful act that might produce death. For example, an adult who takes a hyperactive child who needs constant supervision out for walk on a busy highway, and then leaves the child, may be charged with involuntary manslaughter if the child gets hit by a car and dies. The adult took a lawful act, taking a child on a walk, that ended in an unlawful death caused by a failure to take due caution. Similarly, it is also involuntary manslaughter to cause a car accident while driving under the influence. The person drinking is intending to drive home, not to kill someone. The fact that he causes an accident as a result of his drunken state is unintentional, even if he should know better than to drink and drive.

Heat of Passion

In a murder case that arises out of the "heat of passion," the element of cool deliberation of first-degree murder is missing and typically the resulting charge is voluntary manslaughter. If someone has a hot, enraged mind, one cannot "think straight" and properly reflect on the consequences of one's actions.

For an offender to avail himself of a "heat of passion" defense after he kills someone, courts will examine the act that enraged the killer (e.g., the offender was provoked by acts that would make a reasonable man in the offender's shoes react violently). The provoking act must be so severe that people in a similar situation would react equally as violently. In June 2012 near Houston, Texas, a 24-year-old father was looking for his 5-year-old daughter and walked in on 47-year-old Jesus Flores raping the young girl. The father beat Flores to death. We should judge the provoking act based on how a reasonable parent would react to witnessing the abuse to conclude the killing was done in the "heat of passion."

Words alone are not enough to justify killing someone. That is, if someone says, "Jeez, you are the nastiest person I have ever known," the response to kill will not be justified or excused merely because such words made the offender's blood boil. Some courts have held, however, that words that describe "an act" that would cause a reasonable person in the offender's shoes to kill may be deemed adequate provocation. In the *People v. Viramontes* (2014) case, reprinted in part on the following pages, analyze whether the words conveyed via text messages indicating a claim of infidelity should suffice as sufficient provocation to justify reducing the first-degree murder charge to a lesser offense, or whether the text messages were an excuse to commit murder.

Whether or not a "heat of passion" defense reduces the charges to second-degree murder or manslaughter depends on the jurisdiction.

Springboard for Discussion

Is it a myth or reality that people "snap"? Do people lose control or gain control over others by using violence? In the *Viramontes* case, Illinois law recognizes four situations of serious provocation, including "illegal arrest," "mutual combat," and "adultery with the offender's spouse." Are Illinois's provoking acts sufficiently gender neutral to apply to all people?[37]

PEOPLE V. VIRAMONTES, 20 N.E.3D 25 (2014)

Appellate Court of Illinois, First District, Third Division

FACTS: A newlywed, defendant Luis Viramontes, discovered his wife's infidelity by reading text messages and seeing naked pictures she exchanged with her lover. Married for only a few months after a 16-year relationship and two children, Luis confronted her and she admitted to the liaisons. He then brutally beat her as she struggled to defend herself. She later died from her injuries. At trial, Luis admitted he caused the injuries that led to the death, but claimed he was seriously provoked by her infidelity and that she willingly engaged in aggression against him. A jury convicted Luis of first-degree murder.

On January 9, 2010, Luis and his wife Sandra were still newlyweds, having married a few months earlier. Their relationship as a couple, though, went back 16 years, and for the last 8 years, they had lived together and had two young children. The couple went out for dinner and drinks with family and friends to celebrate Luis's birthday. Sandra's mother watched their children overnight. The party ended around 11 p.m. Luis testified that on the drive home, he noticed Sandra received a text message, which he thought was strange. Sandra fell asleep in the car, so when they arrived home, Luis carried her inside and put her to bed. When he returned to the car for their belongings, he checked Sandra's phone and saw a sexually explicit text message exchange between Sandra and "Denise."

Luis testified that, concealed to him at the time, Sandra was having an extramarital affair with Andres (Andy) Ochoa, a former coworker. Sandra and Andy met in 2004 and their relationship became sexual in 2007. Sandra saved Andy's phone number in her cell phone as "Denise." On January 9, Sandra and Andy exchanged 18 text messages. Their conversation mentioned meeting up and a request from Andy for suggestive photographs. In reply, Sandra sent four or five naked pictures of herself.

Luis testified that when he saw the messages and photographs, he "felt like [his] whole life was turned upside down." He tried calling Denise's number to discover who Sandra had been texting, but no one answered. Luis testified that when he saw the text from Denise stating "you're making me hard," he knew it was from a man and that Sandra was having an affair.

Luis testified he was "angry" and "devastated." He hit Sandra in the face with an open hand. Sandra ran into the bedroom and locked the door. Luis continued to yell at Sandra, calling her vulgar names and reading the text messages aloud. Luis then spray painted the living room and hallway walls and their wedding pictures with explicit words related to the affair. He sat at the kitchen table, put his head down and cried. Sandra came out of the bedroom and when she saw the spray-painted walls, ran toward Luis screaming and swinging at him. She began to hit him in the

chest, so he grabbed Sandra's shoulders, "threw her against the door, and then tossed her over the table." Luis told Sandra he was leaving her. She got up and ran at him again. Luis grabbed her by the shoulders and threw her against the refrigerator and then onto the kitchen floor, telling her "Get off me. Leave me. I'm leaving you. I'm not going to be with you no more." He then walked toward the back door.

Sandra got up from the floor, threw her wedding rings at Luis and said she did not want to be married. Luis testified Sandra then told him that when he had driven her to a doctor's appointment for a cancer scare, she had misled him and was really having an abortion. Sandra told him, "I don't want to have no more kids with you, that's why I killed your baby. I had an abortion and killed your baby." Luis testified that after Sandra told him about the abortion, he "felt like [he] was part of what she had did." He testified he "lost it" and "couldn't control [himself] after that." He then threw her onto the floor, where she hit her head again. On the floor in the fetal position, Sandra tried to cover herself as Luis hit her in the face with his hands four or five times. Luis testified that although he hit and threw Sandra, he was not trying to kill her. He said he was close to potential weapons, including knives, but did not use any because, as he put it, "I wasn't trying to kill her."

In the emergency room, Sandra was unable to communicate. Photographs were taken of her injuries and extensive bruising. She had no fractures or injuries to her internal organs, other than her brain. Toxicology reports were positive for cocaine. Sandra was put on life support. Sandra remained in a coma until her family had her ventilator removed when they were informed she would not recover. Sandra died on January 31, 2010. Dr. Michael Humilier performed Sandra's autopsy. He testified that Sandra was 30 years old and weighed 91 pounds (the parties stipulated she weighed 104 pounds when she entered the hospital). Dr. Humilier noted 27 external evidences of injury and extensive bruising covering almost every body surface. He ruled the death a homicide. He also testified a drug overdose did not contribute to or cause Sandra's death.

At the jury instruction conference, the defense tendered 18 jury instructions, including a lesser-included instruction for second-degree murder based on provocation. The defense argued sufficient evidence existed for provocation based on adultery and mutual combat. The State responded that the case did not fit into any of the four categories meriting a second-degree instruction. The court agreed. The defense also sought instructions on involuntary manslaughter, domestic battery and aggravated battery. The court denied these as well. The jury found Luis guilty of first-degree murder. The trial court sentenced Luis to 25 years in prison.

ISSUE: [Did the defendant who beat his wife to death introduce sufficient evidence of provocation at trial to warrant a jury instruction to reduce the first-degree murder charge?]

HOLDING: [No. Given the victim's injuries sustained at the hands of her husband, the trial judge was correct in denying a second-degree murder or manslaughter jury instruction.]

REASONING: Jury instructions guide the jury toward a proper verdict by defining the law that the jury must follow in coming to its decision. As a reviewing court, we determine whether the instructions fully and fairly set out the law applicable to the theories of the State and the defense. First-degree murder may be reduced to second-degree murder when, at the time of the killing, the defendant "is acting under a sudden and intense passion resulting from serious provocation by the individual killed or another whom the offender endeavors to kill, but he or she negligently or accidentally causes the death of the individual killed." Serious provocation is "conduct sufficient to excite an intense passion in a reasonable person."

Illinois courts recognize four categories of serious provocation:

(1) substantial physical injury or assault;

(2) mutual quarrel or combat;

(3) illegal arrest; and

(4) adultery with the offender's spouse.

The trier of fact [jury or, when there is no jury, judge] determines the sufficiency of the provocation to cause intense passion. Luis claims a second-degree murder instruction because, if believed by the jury, the evidence demonstrated that when Luis beat Sandra, he acted under a sudden and intense passion stemming from serious provocation.

Luis's discovery of Sandra's infidelity through sexual text messages and exchanged naked photographs does not, as a matter of law, constitute adultery under the specified bases for provocation in *People v. Chevalier* (1989), and its progeny [cases following the stated precedent]. In each of the consolidated cases in *Chevalier*, the defendant shot and killed his wife and was convicted of murder. In each case, the defendant suspected his wife of infidelity. And, just before the killing, the defendant and his wife argued, during which she admitted having an affair and either disparaged her spouse's sexual abilities or flaunted that she had slept with her lover in the marital bed. The victims were shot during the arguments. The common issue in both appeals was whether the provocation of the victim sufficed to reduce the killing from murder to voluntary manslaughter . . . [No.] The provocation claimed was legally insufficient to constitute the serious provocation necessary to reduce the homicide from murder to voluntary manslaughter.

The court stated that in Illinois, a spouse's adultery as provocation is limited to situations in which "the parties are discovered in the act of adultery or immediately before or after such an act, and the killing immediately follows such discovery." Addressing the legal requirements for provocation, our supreme court noted the appellate court correctly stated "Passion on the part of the slayer, no matter how violent, will *not* relieve him from liability for murder unless it is engendered by a serious provocation which the law recognizes as being reasonably adequate. If the provocation is inadequate, the crime is murder." Words, no matter how aggravated, abusive or indecent, are not enough.

Luis did not come upon his wife and her lover engaged in an act of adultery; all of the evidence established that Luis learned of the adultery from Sandra's cell phone and through her later admission when confronted. A confession of adultery by a spouse is not legally adequate provocation. ("The rule that mere words are insufficient provocation applies no matter how aggravated, abusive, opprobrious or indecent the language.")

CONCLUSION: Luis received a fair trial. The trial judge properly instructed the jury and followed the law.

Felony Murder

Felony murder is a widely criticized method of attaching accomplice liability for murder, as all co-felons are responsible for the death that occurs as a result of a felony. The felony murder doctrine provides that if one is engaged in the commission of a felony (e.g., burglary, rape, arson, felonious escape, mayhem, robbery, or kidnapping) and someone dies, everyone involved in the felony is responsible for the death. The theory behind the felony murder doctrine is that certain enumerated felonies are so inherently dangerous to human life that everyone who commits one is liable for any death that ensues. Critics of the doctrine find fault with holding people responsible for the death when they had no intent to kill and they did not kill. Many jurisdictions have repudiated the doctrine, but it is still a valid basis for the death penalty in some states and under the federal jurisdiction. The elements of felony murder are

> **Rule of Law: An offender will be responsible for felony murder if, during the commission or attempted commission of a felony, a death results and there is a nexus between the felony and the death.**

1. In the commission or attempted commission of a felony

2. A death occurs, and

3. There is a nexus (connection) between the felony and the death.

The causation analysis, introduced in Chapter 3, establishes the nexus between the felony and the death:

a. Factual cause: But for the commission or attempted commission of the felony, the death would not have occurred.

b. Proximate cause: In felony murder, death is always foreseeable because felonies are inherently dangerous.

c. There are no intervening causes breaking the causal chain between the felony and the death.

The analysis focuses on the point at which the liability of the accomplice stops. In *Auman v. People* (2005), the Colorado Supreme Court held Lisl Auman, who had been arrested and placed in the back of a police cruiser, liable for the death of a police officer who was killed by her accomplice Mattaeus Jaehnig after Auman had been arrested.[38] On November 12, 1997, Auman and a group of friends that included Jaehnig broke into Auman's ex-boyfriend's apartment to retrieve her belongings, but they also stole some items that did not belong to her. The police pursued Auman and Jaehnig in a stolen Trans-Am in a high-speed chase that included Auman holding the steering wheel while Jaehnig shot at officers. The two parked at Jaehnig's apartment complex and ran into the woods. Auman turned herself in and was arrested. Minutes later, Jaehnig shot and killed Officer VanderJagt and then killed himself with VanderJagt's weapon.

The jury was instructed that Auman could be found guilty if they "found beyond a reasonable doubt that . . . [the] death was caused by anyone 'in the course of or in the furtherance of [a felony], or in the immediate flight therefrom.'" Auman argued that not only was she not in immediate flight from the burglary but that Jaehnig's drug use (he was allegedly high on methamphetamines) was an intervening cause severing the causal chain from Auman's initial actions in participating in the burglary to the officer's ultimate death. Auman was convicted of felony murder and sentenced to life without parole. Based on the public protest that Auman's sentence was unjust, Auman was eventually paroled after serving 8 years in prison.

Even in those death-penalty states that have reduced felony murder to second-degree murder, certain felonies are aggravating circumstances that make the offender eligible for capital punishment. In general, to receive the death penalty for felony murder, co-conspirators must intend the death. In *Enmund v. Florida* (1982),[39] Earl Enmund sat in the car while his two co-felons rang the doorbell of an elderly couple, the Kerseys, intending to rob them. Shots rang out and the Kerseys were killed. Enmund still received the death penalty. As the getaway driver, Enmund did not have the specific intent to kill the victims and his sentence was overturned as excessive in violation of the Eighth Amendment's ban on cruel and unusual punishment. Similarly, in *Tison v. Arizona* (1987),[40] two sons in their 20s helped their father and his cellmate escape from an Arizona prison. Their getaway car broke down and the father, Gary Tison, flagged down an unsuspecting family, killing all four, before stealing their car. Gary Tison subsequently died in the desert. The sons were tried for capital murder and sentenced to death. On appeal, the sons' sentences were overturned because they did not have the specific intent to kill the family as they were hiding behind a rock during the shooting. The Court held that felony murder in a death-penalty context requires more stringent analysis of the offender's intent to kill during the felony. In the chapter-opening case study, Ben and Jerry will be directly responsible for the felony murder of the stepmother as a result of the kidnapping. If the death penalty were sought as a punishment, Kathy may have a defense that she did not intend her stepmother's death as a result of the initial burglary and she was simply a passenger in the get-away car.

Rule of Law: Robbery is larceny plus assault and battery.	## ROBBERY

Robbery is the taking of personal property of another by force or threat of force; the crime is represented by the formula stealing + assault + battery. The distinguishing feature of robbery is that there is an immediate threat of bodily harm to, or the actual use of force on, the victim in order to take something of value. So, a victim of pickpocketing who never feels their wallet disappearing from their back pocket is not a victim of robbery, but of larceny. But a person walking down the street whose backpack is snatched from their shoulder is the victim of a robbery because of the use of force. The common law elements of robbery that are largely retained in statutes today are

1. A trespassory taking (without consent), and

2. Asportation

3. Of personal property, with

4. Force or threat of force

5. From the person or in the presence of another.

How are the elements of robbery used to support a conviction of bank robbery or robbery of a jewelry store, for example, when the elements define robbery as the taking of "personal property"? As discussed in Chapter 3, under the doctrine of constructive possession, a bank teller is presumed to have dominion and control over the money and is therefore deemed under the legal fiction the "owner" of the property for robbery purposes. This element distinguishes robbery from larceny in that it involves the aggravating factor of risk of harm to another by forcibly taking property from the person or in the person's presence. But the threat of force will do as well. In the chapter-opening case study, Ben committed robbery when he waved broken glass in the woman's face and threatened to cut her if she did not hand over all her money. Similar to the crime of assault, in which threats of a battery are made, the threat must be capable of being carried out immediately. If the threat of harm to get the money or thing of value is in the future, the crime is extortion, not robbery.

As in most theft crimes, the *mens rea* of the defendant is to permanently deprive the owner of possession. In *State v. Williams* (2014), reprinted in part below, the issue before the court is whether the defendant's conviction for armed robbery can stand given that he used an inhaler rather than a real gun. These cases often arise when the robber does not have a weapon but simulates having one (e.g., putting his hand in his jacket to make the victim believe he is armed) or when the robber uses a toy gun. In many jurisdictions, the defendant can still be charged with armed robbery.

In our chapter-opening case study, Ben committed robbery when he took the victim's $100 by threatening force when he said, Give me all your money or I'll cut you."

Springboard for Discussion

Recall the Internet threat case discussed in Chapter 3, *Elonis v. United States* (2015),[41] where Elonis had communicated threats on Facebook. Elonis was convicted on the basis that his intended targets felt threatened. On appeal, the U.S. Supreme Court overturned his conviction because under the federal threat statute, the government had to prove Elonis intended to threaten people and not just that his purported targets felt afraid. Does the court in the *State v. Williams* (2014) case make the same argument rejected in *Elonis*, that what the victim believes or feels is enough to justify a conviction? In your opinion, which is the better approach to convict a defendant, proving intent or the victim's reaction?

STATE V. WILLIAMS, 95 A.3D 721 (2014)

Supreme Court of New Jersey

FACTS: On the morning of October 8, 2008, defendant Kelvin Williams, wearing bright orange pants, an oversized white t-shirt, and a camouflage hooded sweatshirt with the hood pulled over his head, entered the Sun National Bank in Somerdale, New Jersey. Defendant leaned on the counter and told head bank teller Cheryl Duncan "that he had a bomb and to give him seven million dollars." Duncan did not see a bomb but testified that defendant was wearing a big hooded sweatshirt and his body and hands were not visible. Although Duncan initially did not believe that defendant had a bomb, she ultimately reconsidered, thinking he might be "crazy enough" to blow himself up. Refusing to take any chances, she handed defendant $552 from her teller's drawer. Defendant left the bank and got in a cab, and Duncan called 9-1-1. Defendant was arrested at a nearby mall, and Duncan identified him as the robber. No evidence was recovered suggesting defendant was armed with a bomb.

(Continued)

(Continued)

At trial, defendant moved for a judgment of acquittal on the first-degree robbery charge, arguing that, where a robber is not actually armed with a weapon, the State must show a threat and demand for money, as well as an accompanying gesture giving the impression of a weapon. Defendant submitted that only uttering the words, "I have a bomb" and "Give me the money" was insufficient to support a finding of guilt on the first-degree robbery charge.

ISSUE: [If the defendant was unarmed, but the bank teller believed the defendant possessed a weapon, is the teller's belief alone sufficient to sustain a conviction for armed robbery?]

HELD: [Yes. Conviction reinstated.]

REASONING: To find a defendant guilty of first-degree robbery in a simulated deadly-weapon case, the victim must have an actual and reasonable belief that the defendant threatened the immediate use of such a weapon, which factfinders must ascertain through application of a totality-of-the-circumstances standard, which includes consideration of the nature of any verbal threat, the defendant's conduct, his dress, and any other relevant factors.

CONCLUSION: Applying that standard here, defendant's words, conduct, and clothing provided sufficient evidence for a reasonable jury to convict defendant of first-degree robbery.

SUMMARY

1. You can discuss the differences among the many crimes against the person. Under common law, assault and battery were two distinct crimes. Assault is placing someone in fear of an imminent battery, which is defined as the intentional, unconsented to touching of another that is harmful or offensive. Today most state statutes refer to crimes that combine traditional battery elements as assault. Both assault and battery can be aggravated, which will result in stiffer sentences on conviction. Such a determination often is based on whether the victim was a child, police officer, or prison guard. Making terroristic threats is threatening bodily harm or causing the evacuation of a public venue. Stalking is a type of obsessive–compulsive behavior usually exhibited by mentally ill defendants who simply cannot divert their attention from the victim. Acts that constitute stalking include surveillance, monitoring, letter writing, believing that the victim will reciprocate love to the offender, and the constant sending of electronic mail and telephone messages, which could be cyberstalking, similar to cyberbullying, which is using computer devices to continually harass the target victim or "revenge porn," which is posting without consent a victim's intimate photos. Laws designed to punish online harassment, discussed in *People v. Marquan M.* (2014), must balance free speech rights, and this is not always done successfully. A hate crime is an act against a victim based on the victim's race, ethnicity, gender, religion, or sexual orientation or identity. Although everyone has the freedom to hate in this country, no one is free to hurt people based on that hate. Offenders may receive enhanced penalties in sentencing if it is determined by the jury that the defendant's actions were motivated by hate.

2. You will be able to distinguish kidnapping from false imprisonment. *Kidnapping* is the unlawful confinement and taking (*asportation*) of a person by force or threat of force, while *false imprisonment* is restraining a person's liberty of movement. In *U.S. v. Lussier* (2017), the defendant was convicted of kidnapping by putting the victims in a crawl space beneath a house, even though he did not block their exit, because his *mens rea* was to increase the victims' risk of harm.

3. You will understand the elements of sex-related offenses and rape shield laws. Typically, sex offenses are abuses of power and are committed by inserting a penis or other object into a body orifice (mouth, vagina, or anus) of another. The common law elements of rape were sexual penetration against a woman's will and without her consent. Some type of forcible compulsion is required in addition to the victim's nonconsent to the act. If the victim is intellectually disabled or under the influence of drugs or alcohol or is passed out or if the consent is procured by fraud, trickery, and deceit, it is rape. Rape shield laws are designed to protect the victim from abuse on the witness stand at trial. Statutory rape is typically consensual intercourse with a teenager and a partner with at least a 4-year age gap. The history of statutory rape is from a strict liability to a *mens rea*–based defense, which allows mistake of age as a valid defense. Child sex abuse is often committed by offenders in a position of known trust with direct access to children. Children cannot consent to sexual activity, and the abuser often has different types of motivation in using children sexually. Incest is sexual relations between nonspousal family members regardless of whether they are related by blood, marriage, or adoption. Deviate sexual intercourse often includes crimes against children or sodomy, which is defined as oral–genital contact or anal penetration. Sodomy is legal between consenting adults. "Sexting" is a crime often

committed by juveniles sending sexually explicit photos via text messages on cell phones.

4. You will be able to distinguish the various degrees of homicide. Homicide is the killing of another. First-degree murder is willful, premeditated, and deliberate, which means that the offender carried out the act with specific intent and with a cool mind and planned or thought about it prior to the act of the killing. Some homicides are justified, such as those that occur in self-defense. Second-degree murder occurs when the offender intends to commit serious bodily harm and a death results. Involuntary manslaughter is typically an unintentional killing as a result of reckless or negligent conduct, and voluntary manslaughter is an intentional killing that is somewhat justified, such as in a "heat of passion" killing,

reducing the charge of first-degree murder, a strategy that did not work in the *People v. Viramontes* (2014) case. The deadly weapon doctrine is a type of first-degree murder that allows the jury to infer specific intent to kill by the offender's use of a deadly weapon that is any object used in a manner designed to cause serious bodily injury or death. The anachronistic year-and-a-day rule is the common law causation requirement that if the victim died more than one year and one day after the offender caused harm, the offender would not be considered the legal cause of death.

5. You will understand the elements of robbery. Robbery is assault and battery plus larceny. The *State v. Williams* (2014) case ruled that simulating that you have a weapon is enough to sustain an armed robbery conviction.

KEY TERMS AND PHRASES

aggravated assault and battery 98
AMBER alert stem 103
alert system 103
assault 98
battery 98
child sex abuse 111
cyberbullying 105
cyberstalking 105
deadly weapon 115
deadly weapon doctrine 115
deviate sexual intercourse 113
false imprisonment 101

felony murder 119
first-degree murder 115
hate crime 107
heat of passion 117
homicide 115
incest 113
kidnapping 100
malice aforethought 114
manslaughter 116
mayhem 99
premeditation 115
provoking act 117

rape 108
rape shield laws 110
"revenge porn" 106
robbery 120
second-degree murder 115
sexting 113
sodomy 113
stalking 103
statutory rape 111
terroristic threats 99
Title IX 109
year-and-a-day rule 115

PROBLEM-SOLVING EXERCISES

1. Tim and Tom were roommates and best friends, but their relationship soured when Tim lost his job and stopped paying the bills. After 4 months of Tim's freeloading, Tom ordered Tim to leave the apartment, but Tim refused. Tom approached Tim and said, "I'm going to kill you," and then squeezed Tim's arm really hard. Tim moved out. When Tom learned where Tim was living, Tom parked in front of Tim's apartment and followed him to work every day for 6 months. Tim has reported Tom's behavior to the police. What crimes, if any, has Tom committed, and what defenses may he raise? **(ROL: Assault, battery, stalking, terroristic threats)**

2. Ken and Fred hated each other. They were next-door neighbors who often exchanged unkind words. One day the two were cutting the hedges that spread along the boundary of their property. As Ken was at one end of the hedges, Fred began to taunt Ken. Fred said to Ken, "I hear your wife was at the local tavern looking to score some real action," at which point Ken took his hedge trimmers, which looked like large scissors, and stuck them in Fred's leg. As Fred screamed in pain and tried to crawl back into his house, Ken walked away. Fred

later died. When police came to arrest Ken, he confessed that he only meant to hurt Fred, not to kill him. What crimes against Ken can be charged? **(ROL: First-degree murder with a deadly weapon, second-degree murder, heat of passion manslaughter)**

3. Erin left her dormitory room to visit a male friend in another dorm. When she knocked on the door, there was no answer, but the door was unlocked, so Erin went inside. Her friend was not there, but his roommate, Marty, was sleeping in the nearby bed. Marty asked Erin to stay and she agreed. Marty asked for a back rub, but Erin declined and sat on the floor. Marty got out of bed and sat on the floor beside Erin. Marty lifted Erin's shirt and massaged her chest. They both stood up and Marty locked the door. He then placed Erin on the bed, removed her undergarments and penetrated her vagina with his penis. After withdrawing, Marty said, "I guess we got carried away," to which Erin replied, "No, we didn't get carried away; *you* got carried away." Police have charged Marty with raping Erin under the traditional, common law definition of rape. Does Marty have a defense? **(ROL: Rape)**

5

CRIMES AGAINST PROPERTY

Go to the end of the chapter. Skim the key terms and phrases and read the summary closely. Come back and look at the following news excerpts to focus your reading throughout the chapter to understand the development of the legal recognition of property rights, the various methods an offender can use to deprive the owner of his possessory interest in property (crimes that have as their common denominator the specific intent to take someone else's property and to permanently deprive the owner of possession; or to make money by devising a scheme committed through the mail or wires, telephone, or computer; or a criminal racketeering conspiracy; or simply to destroy property, usually for financial gain. The chapter begins with a hypothetical case study of the Family Toy Company. Follow the company as they encounter the rules of law presented throughout the chapter, and connect the company's criminal activity with the relevant section of text.

WHY THIS CHAPTER MATTERS TO YOU	THE LEARNING OBJECTIVES AS REFLECTED IN THE NEWS
After you have read this chapter: **Learning Objective 1:** You will be able to discuss the legal foundation for possessory rights in property.	A Chester man who pleaded guilty last year in a scheme to gain ownership over government- and bank-owned properties in Delaware County was sentenced last week to more than eight years in a federal prison. The defendants filed bogus deed documents in the Delaware County Recorder of Deeds office between Feb. 2010 and March 2013 labeled with some variation of "Revised Full Reconveyance of Living Trust Deed Claims" or "Revised Full Reconveyance of Trust Deed of Release." The defendants would use the fictitious deeds to either live in the homes, or rent or sell them to unsuspecting third parties, according to prosecutors. Hameed was sentenced to 97 months in a federal prison on charges of bank fraud, conspiracy, corrupt interference with Internal Revenue laws, conversion of government property and creating fictitious obligations. (*Delaware County Daily Times* [PA], February 21, 2017)
Learning Objective 2: You can analyze the legal basis for common law differentiation in property crimes.	We're learning more details after Michigan State Police arrested a former public safety officer accused of stealing money from her department. The Wexford County Prosecutor, who has taken the case, says former lieutenant, Cindy Finkbeiner, is accused of three counts of getting paid between $1,000 and $20,000 under false pretenses. She's also charged with stealing more than $50 as a public official and common law fraud. (9 & 10 News [MI], April 13, 2017)

WHY THIS CHAPTER MATTERS TO YOU	THE LEARNING OBJECTIVES AS REFLECTED IN THE NEWS
Learning Objective 3: You will be able to evaluate the wide-ranging scope of mail and wire fraud crimes.	According to admissions made as part of his plea agreement, [Nicholas A. Borgesano Jr., 45, of New Port Richey, Florida] owned and operated numerous pharmacies and shell companies that he and his co-conspirators used to execute a fraud scheme involving prescription compounded medications. The scheme generated over $100 million in fraud proceeds, he admitted. Borgesano . . . admitted using these pharmacies to cause the submission of false and fraudulent reimbursement claims for prescription compounded medications. (U.S. Department of Justice, November 6, 2017)
Learning Objective 4: You will articulate the interrelationship between financially based crimes such as computer fraud, racketeering, and money laundering.	The indictment alleges that MS-13 is an international criminal enterprise that is active throughout the United States. In the Washington, D.C. metropolitan area, including in Prince George's County, Maryland, MS-13 generates income from various sources, including the extortion of sums of money from persons who engage in activities such as controlled substances sales, illegal brothels, and unlicensed stores where items such as food, alcoholic beverages, and cigarettes are sold, as well as legitimate businesses including food and beverage sales or distributors. The indictment further alleges that members of the gang often refer to these extortion payments as rent. (U.S. Department of Justice, April 26, 2018)
Learning Objective 5: You will understand burglary and arson crimes.	A man who entered his former girlfriend's home and put a tea towel in the oven to burn has failed in his appeal against conviction. Michael John Malone was convicted of assault, trespass, burglary and attempted arson. It was reasonable to infer that Mr. Malone intended for the fire to cause the damage that would normally be expected from something that was left to burn in a confined space, either as a result of fire damage to the oven itself or through smoke damage to the room the oven was in. Nor did he find the sentencing judge had made any errors over the burglary conviction as Malone had entered the home with the intention of taking property from it. (*National* [CN], May 29, 2018)

Chapter-Opening Case Study: The Family Toy Company

When the first check came into the Family Toy Company as payment pursuant to a government contract to make toys for underprivileged kids, Kelly, an employee, signed the company president's name without his knowledge and permission and deposited the check in the corporate bank account **(Rule of Law [ROL]: Forgery is altering a document for financial gain)** keeping $40,000 for herself to satisfy a personal gambling debt **(ROL: Embezzlement is obtaining money lawfully before converting it to your own use).** Back at her desk, Kelly was surfing the Internet, and in the comment section of a news article, she clicked on a posting that began, "I am making $3,500 a week working at home on the Web. Ask me how!" The ad required Kelly to input her name, address, and credit card information to learn the "secret" formula for getting rich quick. Kelly reached over and got a purse belonging to her friend, DeShawn, and entered DeShawn's personal and financial information. **(ROL: Identity theft is stealing information for financial gain.)** Little did Kelly know, but the person who placed the "get rich quick" ad was an older woman, Rachel, who lived in Hawaii and offered nothing in return in exchange for the deposit of money from the credit card charges the public sent to her. **(ROL: Wire fraud is using computers/phones to commit a scheme to defraud.)**

To ensure her illegal gains would not be detected, Rachel took the money she stole from the credit card transactions and invested in a new restaurant. Rachel used the stolen money to purchase equipment and supplies for the restaurant, and Rachel's criminal fruits from her fraudulent Internet "get rich quick" scheme were therefore "cleansed." **(ROL: Money laundering is placing illegally gained money into legitimate commerce.)** When Rachel's sister, Bernadette (Bernie), learned of Rachel's fraud, Bernie threatened to report Rachel to the police unless Rachel paid Bernie $500 per week for her silence. **(ROL: Extortion is threatening to ruin someone's reputation unless the victim gives the offender something of value.)** In retaliation, Rachel wanted to burn Bernie's house down. Rachel didn't have a gas can, so she went to the local store and put it in her backpack and walked out. **(ROL: Simple larceny is taking the personal property of another without the other's consent and with the intent to permanently deprive the owner of possession.)** Rachel filled the can with gas, went to Bernie's house, and smashed a window to get inside. **(ROL: Burglary is breaking and entering with the intent to commit a felony [here, arson] once inside.)** Rachel then spread the gas, lit a match, and watched from the street corner as Bernie's house burned to the ground. **(ROL: Arson is intentional and unlawful burning.)** Will prosecutors have enough evidence to successfully prosecute the various crimes against property that Kelly, Rachel, and Bernie committed?

THEFT CRIMES

Larceny

> **Rule of Law: Larceny is taking the personal property of another without the other's consent and with the intent to permanently deprive the owner of possession.**

To be a thief, one must have the specific intent to steal. Larceny as defined in early English law was *trespass de bonis asportatis* (trespass for goods carried away), but not all interference with an owner's possessory rights in his property qualified as larceny. To be guilty of larceny, the person taking the property need not have damaged, converted, or disposed of the property; he only needed to take it without the owner's consent. Conversion is the legal term for acquiring someone's property and transforming it for personal use and benefit. Therefore, if the owner gave the property willingly, but then its value was destroyed, there was no larceny. If a would-be thief only borrowed an item with the intent to return it, there was no larceny. If people acquired property lawfully and then converted it to their own use, there was no larceny. The common law responded by defining various theft situations by the way the property was taken, and the crimes of larceny by trick, embezzlement, and false pretenses were created, distinctions that are confusing and arbitrary, but which we use in this chapter to illustrate the development of the criminal law of property. Thus, the basic elements of larceny are

1. Trespassory taking (without the owner's consent)

2. Of another's property

3. By carrying away or secreting (hiding and then taking)

4. With the intent to permanently deprive the owner of possession.

Personal property is moveable, such as laptops and money, distinguished from real property, which is immoveable land and other fixtures attached to the property, such as barns and buildings. Other terms for property are chattel or personalty. Modern-day statutes, illustrated by the Massachusetts statute reprinted in part here, use one comprehensive definition of property as money and paper representing ownership of things of value:

Mass. General Law - Chapter 266: §30. Larceny; general provisions

(2) The term "property," as used in the section, shall include money, personal chattels, a bank note, bond, promissory note, bill of exchange or other bill, order or certificate, a book of accounts for or concerning money or goods due or to become due or to be delivered, a deed or writing containing a conveyance of land, any valuable contract in force, a receipt, release or defeasance, a writ, process, certificate of title, a public record, anything which is of the realty or is annexed thereto, a security deposit, electronically processed or stored data, either tangible or intangible, data while in transit, telecommunications services, and any domesticated animal, including dogs, or a beast or bird which is ordinarily kept in confinement.

The intent to permanently deprive the owner of the property or its value must be present at the time of the taking of the property. The return of the property to the owner does not negate the initial intent to steal. But the intent to permanently deprive the owner of the value of the property may form after the owner has willingly let another "borrow" the property. If a neighbor borrows a lawn mower and returns the mower an unusable, worthless molten mass of steel, should the neighbor not offer to repair the mower or replace the fair market value, the neighbor has committed larceny because he has deprived the owner of the property's value.

Today grading of the offense of larceny as either a misdemeanor or felony depends on the value of the property stolen. The crimes are simple larceny when the property's value is below a certain dollar amount or grand larceny for more valuable property. An example is South Carolina's law that distinguishes between petit (misdemeanor) and grand (felony) larceny based on whether the stolen goods are valued more or less than $2,000.

South Carolina Code Annotated, §16-13-30. Petit larceny; grand larceny

(A) Simple larceny of any article of goods, choses in action [right to sue], bank bills, bills receivable, chattels, or other article of personalty of which by law larceny may be committed, or of any fixture, part, or product of the soil severed from the soil by an unlawful act, or has a value of two thousand dollars or less, is petit larceny, a misdemeanor, triable in the magistrates court or municipal court . . . Upon conviction, the person must be fined not more than one thousand dollars, or imprisoned not more than thirty days.

(B) larceny of goods, chattels, instruments, or other personalty valued in excess of two thousand dollars is grand larceny. Upon conviction, the person is guilty of a felony and must be fined in the discretion of the court or imprisoned not more than:

(1) five years if the value of the personalty is more than two thousand dollars but less than ten thousand dollars;

(2) ten years if the value of the personalty is ten thousand dollars or more.

Any interference with an owner's use and enjoyment of her property is considered a crime of theft, as illustrated in *New York v. Alamo* (1974), reprinted in part on the following page, where the court holds breaking into a car, but not driving the car away, qualifies as larceny. Do you agree with the court's reasoning?

Unlike the *Harrison* and *Alamo* cases where there is no asportation but completed larceny, in the chapter-opening case study, Rachel committed simple larceny when she stole a gas can from the local store.

NEW YORK V. ALAMO, 315 N.E.2D 446 (1974)

Court of Appeals of New York

FACTS: [The officers testified] "[A]s we approached the intersection of Hillside Avenue and Virginia Road, we noticed a vehicle to our right parked facing north with the engine running with the lights on just starting to pull out of a parking space." There was additional evidence that the side vent window of the car had been forced.

The Judge instructed the jury on the larceny count reading to them subdivision 1 of section 155.05 of the Penal Law, i.e., that larceny consists of the wrongful taking, obtaining or withholding of property. He also told them that if they found that defendant Alamo had forced the window, removed the ignition switch, started the automobile and exercised control over the automobile by any act, then they could find him guilty of larceny. After some deliberation the jury returned for further instruction on the meaning of control and whether movement of the vehicle was required to effectuate control. The Judge answered as follows:

> Control would be a proprietary act, any act which constituted appropriating the automobile to the defendant's own use, exercising some degree of jurisdiction over the automobile, taking an affirmative act. In this case, the entering of the car, the closing of the door, turning the lights on, and starting the vehicle may be considered acts of control. You have asked further the question: "Does control require movement of the vehicle?" I would say to you that control in the sense as [proving] larceny . . . would not require movement of the vehicle.

ISSUE: [Should the judge have given a jury instruction on attempted larceny rather than larceny because the car Alamo broke into did not move?]

HOLDING: [No. The crime of larceny is complete once the offender exercises dominion and control over property he does not own.]

REASONING: It is woven into the fabric of the common law that asportation [movement] is an element of a completed larceny. The authoritative case in this jurisdiction on the essential elements of larceny is *Harrison v. People* (1872).[1] There a pickpocket grasped the victim's wallet and lifted it no more than several inches and not all the way out of the pocket when the victim, having become aware, grabbed at the wallet and thrust it back down to the bottom of the pocket. The court held that a completed larceny had been committed. The temporary possession by the thief, even though for a moment, was sufficient as was the slight movement accompanying the possession.

While it is to be conceded that the element of movement was a consideration in the [*Harrison*] court's reasoning, critical analysis of that reasoning discloses that the elements of possession and control were the paramount elements sought and that the fact of movement merely tended to support the idea of control. Thus, it was stated: "To constitute the offence of larceny, there must be a taking or severance of the goods from the possession of the owner. * * * But possession, so far as this offense is concerned, is the having or holding or detention of property in one's power or command."

There ensued discussion concerning instances where the object of the theft was connected to the owner by a string or chain and where, therefore, there could be no completed larceny because of the continued connection to the owner even though there was limited asportation. It was then stated concerning the wallet: "It was in his possession. He directed, and, for the instant of time, controlled its movements."

. . . A wallet, or a diamond ring, or a safe are totally inert objects susceptible of movement only by physical lifting or shoving by the thief. An automobile, however, is itself an instrument of transportation and when activated comes within the total possession and control of the operator. In this situation movement or motion is not essential to control. Absent any evidence that the vehicle is somehow fastened or immovable because of a mechanical defect, the thief has taken command of the object of the larceny. He has, in the words of [the law], wrongfully "taken" the property from its owner surely as much so as had the [wallet] thief in *Harrison*.

CONCLUSION: To require that the vehicle be moved by the operator is to slavishly adhere to the auxiliary common-law element of asportation which is simply not necessary to the finding of the primary elements of dominion and control where an activated automobile is concerned.

Before we get to court: Imagine Shannon has been charged with grand theft larceny of a big screen television that she tried to move, but because the TV was too heavy, she managed just to drag it a few feet. Shannon has filed a pretrial motion to dismiss the charges.

1. You are the prosecutor. Argue that Shannon has committed larceny.

2. You are a defense counsel. Argue that Shannon has not interfered with the owner's possessory rights.

False Pretenses

In a traditional business exchange, there is no law that requires total disclosure of all information during a transaction. For instance, the government sells at auction seized property "as is," with no warranty or guarantee. There is an opportunity before the sale to inspect the goods, but the buyer is put on notice that if he or she buys something and it does not work, it is not the seller's responsibility; the concept of *caveat emptor* (buyer beware) applies. The common law definition of false pretenses, lying to induce another to turn over his or her property, is still salient today. For the prosecutor to prove false pretenses, she has to "prove that the defendant obtained title or possession of money or personal property of another by means of an intentional false statement concerning a material fact upon which the victim relied in parting with the property."[2] The elements of **false pretenses** are[3]

> **Rule of Law: False pretenses is the crime of lying to obtain a thing of value.**

1. Obtaining property

2. By a false representation (a lie)

3. Of a material past or present fact

4. That the defendant knew to be false

5. To induce the owner to transfer a thing of value to the thief.

The false representation made to persuade the property owner to give the property to the thief may be written or oral. The thief must know that the misrepresentation is untrue at the time of the making, and the lie must directly convince the owner to confer title to the property or possession of the property if it is money. The offender must know he is lying to obtain another's property to satisfy the *mens rea* element of false pretenses.

To qualify as a false representation, the misrepresentation must be about a material present or past fact, not an expectation, hope, or promise of things to come true in the future. The statement, "Buy my car and I'm sure you are going to get at least another 100,000 miles out of it," is not actionable when the car engine explodes 5 miles down the road even though the representation of expectation of how long the car would last is what enticed you to buy the car in the first place.

Conversely, if the seller states that the car has 20,000 miles on it and it actually has 200,000 miles on it, the discrepancy in mileage is a material fact. If the seller says that the car was recently cleaned and, in fact, it has not been, this discrepancy is not a material fact; old Cheerios stuffed in the back seat have less bearing on the decision to buy a car than excessive mileage does. A good rule of thumb to determine whether a fact is material is to ask if it would change the outcome of the transaction.

It is a defense to a charge of false pretenses that the buyer knew of the lie but bought anyway. If the buyer inspects under the hood and knows full well that the engine has 200,000 miles on it and buys it despite the claim of 20,000 miles, he cannot successfully press a claim that he was deceived, because the lie did not induce the purchase. It is important to note that the crime of false pretenses requires that title to the property pass to the offender as a result of the lie. Under common law, if mere possession passed to the offender as a result of a lie, that crime was larceny by trick.

APPLYING THE LAW TO THE FACTS

Voluntary Transfer of Money or False Pretenses?

The Facts: Ernest put an advertisement on a dating site stating he was an eligible bachelor looking for "a good woman, possibility of matrimony (marriage)." Aileen replied, and Ernest told her that he had a sure business deal that, if successful, would allow him to finance their wedding. Aileen loaned Ernest $5,000 for his deal. Aileen then received an e-mail from Ernest saying the deal had gone bad and he would be in touch soon to return her cash. Aileen never heard from Ernest again and later learned the business deal was a lie. Is Ernest guilty of false pretenses, or is Aileen simply gullible?

The Law: Ernest has committed false pretenses. He lied about a past or present material fact (a nonexistent business deal), which induced Aileen to hand over her money even though the marriage proposal was a mere future expectancy.[4]

Rule of Law: Embezzlement is the conversion of property belonging to another that was acquired lawfully.

Embezzlement

Sometimes the temptation of having access to other people's money is too much to resist for certain people, and they resort to stealing when they have a fiduciary duty to protect the assets of others. The one factor that distinguishes embezzlement from other theft crimes is that the thief acquires the property lawfully before converting it to his own use. As one South Carolina court opinion discussed the history of the development of the law of embezzlement:

> In other states, the crime, as known to us, is called by different names, such as "larceny after trust," "larceny by a bailee," "larceny by false pretenses," and very commonly as "embezzlement" . . . acts which were formerly not deemed to be larceny at common law, because possession of property had been obtained through the consent of the owner.[5]

The typical people who embezzle are those who have lawful access to money, such as trustees, attorneys, accountants, and those who act in a relationship of trust over money within an organization, such as an executive officer or treasurer. The elements of embezzlement are

1. The lawful acquisition and conversion of

2. Personal property

3. Of another

4. With the intent to permanently deprive the owner of possession.

The concept of "personal property of another" is a legal fiction for embezzlement purposes. For example, a bank employee might embezzle money from the bank, which is not a person. The property does not "technically" belong to the bank; rather, it belongs to depositors, and the bank uses it in various ways for the depositors' benefit, such as giving the money out as loans and paying the depositors interest. But the teller has a fiduciary duty to safeguard the money. A fiduciary duty is a protective status to safeguard the interests of another.

The prosecution must prove that the embezzler took and converted the money to his own use, not merely took and possessed the property. Even if the owner had no knowledge that the property was missing, the embezzler is guilty for substantially interfering with the owner's possessory rights in the property. Because of the embezzler's actions, the owner could not have used his own money even had he wanted to.

Interviews with convicted embezzlers led criminalist Donald Cressy to compile a sociological profile of those who abused positions of financial trust. Cressy discovered that certain events triggered typically honest people to steal from their employers. Many embezzlers whom Cressy interviewed in jail said, "I had no idea I was going to do this until the day it happened," or "For two years I have been trying to understand why I did this after being honest all my life," or "I thought this looked like a pretty good score so I took it."[6] Although the typical embezzler seemingly took an opportunity that presented itself unexpectedly, Cressy discovered a common set of life situations among embezzlers at the time they started to steal. The common denominators among embezzlers are the following:

1. A personal problem arises that the potential embezzler feels he cannot share with others.

2. The problem appears solvable by money.

3. The embezzler develops technical skills that allow him or her to steal the money without detection.

4. The embezzler adopts a mind-set that deceives him or her into thinking that the theft is temporary. The thief has every intention of returning the money but never does.

Other research indicates that embezzlers are people who have high levels of debt, change jobs frequently, and have lower incomes than employees in similar positions with other companies. People who embezzle the most often are contractors working on commission, that is, where salary is determined by how much product they sell. A way to detect an embezzler is to watch for an employee's rising spike in disposable income. Studies show that, as a rule, "persons who embezzle do not hide the money in a secret account; they tend to spend the money as soon as they embezzle it."[7] Embezzlers sometimes steal other items of value over which the company has loose oversight, such as the company's stock of products and supplies, including electronics, jewelry, or other small items. They also may pad expense accounts and submit false reimbursement claims for money never spent. Business behavior that might, initially, appear benign—when examined from a law enforcement perspective—may identify embezzlers. Typical behavior by those who embezzle indicate they are people who

1. Do not take vacations, turn down promotions, and regularly work overtime;

2. Prevent others from having access to records;

3. Work on company records excessively because, in their words, the records must be "checked" or rewritten for neatness;

4. Are defensive regarding questions about their routine work activities;

5. Have creditors calling at work;

6. Explain a rapid increase in income as an inheritance or winning the lottery; and

7. Have a new and improved standard of living.[8]

There are certain defenses to embezzlement, as there are for most specific intent crimes. If one converted property by negligence, there's no embezzlement. Mistake of both law and fact are other defenses if they negate the specific intent *mens rea*, as discussed in Chapter 12, Defenses. For example, if Trudy the lawyer was under the mistaken impression of fact or law that she could keep a client's money as payment for attorney's fees, there's no embezzlement because Trudy had no intent to steal. In the chapter-opening case study, Kelly embezzled corporate funds when she skimmed $40,000 and converted it with the specific intent to satisfy her personal financial obligations.

Springboard for Discussion

If you were a company's loss prevention specialist, what procedures would you design or implement to detect or prevent employee embezzlement?

Forgery and Passing Bad Checks

Many theft crimes do not involve the passing of money, but commercial paper which is a legal instrument representing ownership of property, such as a check represents money in a checking account. Uttering is typically writing checks when the person knows there are insufficient funds in the account to cover the purchase, sometimes called a "rubber check" that "bounces." To successfully prosecute uttering, the prosecution must prove that the defendant knew at the time of presenting the check as payment that there was not enough money in the bank account to pay the vendor. If, for example, the person had an automatic debit card in a joint account and wrote a check at the grocery store while his partner was buying a new computer depleting the account, there would be insufficient *mens rea* to defraud the grocery store because he had a good faith belief there were sufficient funds in the account.

> **Rule of Law: Forgery and uttering are stealing by trickery with commercial paper.**

Forgery is altering a written document or instrument with the intent to obtain the property of another. The traditional elements of forgery are

1. A material alteration of

2. An existing document

3. With the intent to deprive the owner of a thing of value permanently.

For criminal liability to attach to the crime of forgery, the document or instrument, if genuine and real, must create a legal right or legal obligation of significance. If someone forges *Vampire Diaries* actor Paul Wesley's signature on a poster to impress a date, there is no forgery because the fraudulent signature neither created a legal right or obligation nor induced a transfer of something of value. If someone forged Wesley's signature and sold it as an authentic autograph in exchange for money, then the crime would be forgery. The Kansas forgery statute is a model.

Kansas Statutes Annotated 2016 §21-5823(a)

Forgery

(a) Forgery is, with intent to defraud:

  (1) Making, altering or endorsing any written instrument in such manner that it purports to have been made, altered or endorsed by another person, either real or fictitious, and if a real person without the authority of such person; or altering any written instrument in such manner that it purports to have been made at another time or with different provisions without the authority of the maker thereof; or making, altering or endorsing any written instrument in such manner that it purports to have been made, altered or endorsed with the authority of one who did not give such authority.

  (2) issuing or distributing such written instrument knowing it to have been thus made, altered or endorsed; or

  (3) possessing, with intent to issue or distribute, any such written instrument knowing it to have been thus made, altered or endorsed. Forgery can also occur by interposing or adding numbers to checks, making $10,000 into $100,000, for instance.

In the chapter-opening case study, Kelly committed forgery when she signed the company president's name without his knowledge and consent in endorsing the government check and taking a portion of the money.

Counterfeiting

Forgery is different from, but similar to, the federal crime of counterfeiting, which is making fake stuff or fake money and passing it off as something of value. The federal Constitution, specifically the Patent and Copyright Clause, Article I, Section 8, Clause 5, grants exclusive power to Congress to "coin money, regulate the value thereof, and to foreign coin, and to fix the Standard of weights and measures." A high school student who made fake $20 bills on his color copier at home, purchased fast food items for a nominal fee, and received real money back in change was convicted under the federal counterfeiting statute 18 U.S.C. §471, that provides

> Whoever, with intent to defraud, falsely makes, forges, counterfeits, or alters any obligation or other security of the United States, shall be fined or imprisoned not more than 20 years, or both.

Counterfeiting money is not the only crime. "While luxury brand items are commonly associated with counterfeits, any manufactured good can be counterfeited, including aircraft and automobile parts, artwork, batteries, agricultural products, chemicals and pesticides, clothing, collectables, electronics, food and drinks, healthcare products, household products, jewelry, tobacco, and toys."[9] Estimates about the economic loss from counterfeiting, which includes theft of intellectual property generally defined as copyrights, patents, and trademarks, is approximately 461 to 650 billion dollars a year. Although federal law guides counterfeiting, all 50 states have similar anti-counterfeiting laws allowing for civil relief or criminal prosecution. Students are encouraged to research their respective state jurisdictions to determine what, if any, criminal sanction attaches to mimicking as real someone else's goods, thoughts, or ideas.

Receiving Stolen Property

For many theft crimes to be profitable, the thief not only has to steal another's property but, in some cases, needs someone else to buy it. The people who routinely give money for stolen goods they later turn around and sell to others are called "fences," as a fence is between two parties. The crime of receiving stolen property is the *actus reus* of obtaining another's property with the scienter of knowing that it is stolen with the *mens rea* intent to permanently deprive the rightful owner of the property. The elements of the crime of receiving stolen property are

1. Receipt of property

2. Knowing that the property was stolen

3. With the intent to deprive the owner of possession permanently.

The *mens rea* can be proved through actual knowledge, as when the original thief informs the recipient of its stolen nature, or by constructive knowledge that receiving property at such a reduced rate indicates that the item must have been stolen. For instance, if Calypso were approached by a thief who wanted to sell for $200 an authentic Rolex watch that retails for approximately $1,500, the prosecutor could argue that Calypso's willful ignorance about the origin of the watch was constructive knowledge that he knew it was stolen. No one can legitimately buy a genuine Rolex watch for $200. The last element of the crime is that the defendant must intend to keep the property from the owner, whether by keeping it, selling it to another, giving it away, or destroying it. Receiving stolen property that travels in interstate commerce is a federal crime.

Springboard for Discussion

In New York City, street merchants who deal out of black plastic bags sell passersby knock-off Gucci, Louis Vuitton, and Dooney & Bourke handbags, all of which look genuine but are, in fact, fake counterfeits. Are people who know the goods are fake and buy them anyway also guilty of a crime? Should those buyers be prosecuted for participating in a counterfeit conspiracy causing harm to the American economy? Why or why not?

Rule of Law: To be convicted of receiving stolen property, the defendant has to know that the property is stolen.

Rule of Law: Extortion is blackmail—threatening someone into performing certain acts or paying money to keep the defendant from ruining the victim's business, reputation, or relationships.

Extortion

Often called blackmail, extortion is the acquisition of the property of another by threatening to injure the victim's person, relationships, reputation, or financial status to force the victim to surrender something of value. For example, if a judge learns that an attorney has embezzled money from a client and threatens to expose the lawyer to the authorities, then the judge's threat is legal. But if the judge offers to stay silent if the lawyer pays him $10,000, the judge has committed extortion by threatening to expose the lawyer's secret for financial gain. The Model Penal Code (MPC) defines extortion.

§223.4 Theft by Extortion

A person is guilty of theft if he purposely obtains property of another by threatening to:

(1) inflict bodily injury on anyone or commit any other criminal offense; or

(2) accuse anyone of a criminal offense; or

(3) expose any secret tending to subject any person to hatred, contempt or ridicule, or to impair his credit or business repute; or

(4) take or withhold action as an official, or cause an official to take or withhold action; or

(5) bring about or continue a strike, boycott or other collective unofficial action, if the property is not demanded or received for the benefit of the group in whose interest the actor purports to act; or

(6) testify or provide information or withhold testimony or information with respect to another's legal claim or defense; or

(7) inflict any other harm which would not benefit the actor.

It is an affirmative defense to prosecution that the property obtained by threat of accusation, exposure, lawsuit, or other invocation of official action was honestly claimed as restitution or indemnification for harm done. Remember, to be a thief one has to have the specific intent to steal. If the person makes threats to obtain what she believes is legally owed to her, then she may have a defense.

APPLYING THE LAW TO THE FACTS

Is It Extortion?

The Facts: Jake and Marianne were having an affair. Marianne was married to another man. She ended the affair and argued with Jake over money she had lent him. Jake threatened to reveal their affair unless Marianne continued to have sexual relations with him, which she did. Jake also planned to reveal their affair to Marianne's husband if she pestered him about the money he owed to her.[10] Has Jake blackmailed Marianne?

The Law: Yes, extortion statutes generally condemn forcing people to perform certain acts or to transfer things of value under compulsion and intimidation based on an "embarrassing truth."

In the chapter-opening case study, Bernie blackmailed Rachel when she threatened to disclose Rachel's criminal scheme to the police unless Rachel paid Bernie $500 per week for her silence.

Financial Cybercrime

One trait successful cybercriminals seem to have in common is a unique talent to understand, and exploit, computer code. There are as varied motivations to commit crime as there are people. According to Federal Bureau of Investigation (FBI) statistics, property crimes are the majority of crimes committed. Many thieves are impulsive and simply take advantage of an opportunity to enrich themselves; other thieves are professionals. Those who steal by computer are consummate professional thieves who, if they trained their skills in legitimate business, could rival any chief executive officer of a major, multinational organization. One such criminal is Albert Gonzalez.[11]

Albert had a natural affinity for computers and taught himself enough code to hack into National Aeronautics and Space Administration (NASA) computers at age 14, causing the FBI to visit him at home in Miami, Florida. A college dropout, Albert learned to hack financial networks and was caught by an observant police officer who watched Albert in New York City drain an automatic teller machine (ATM) with one fake bank card after another. Wanting to save himself from prosecution, Albert became an informant for the Secret Service. One Secret Service agent said of Albert's skill in committing **financial cybercrime**, "We in law enforcement had never encountered anything like [him]." The agent continued, "We had to learn the language, we had to learn the characters, their goals, their techniques. Albert taught us all of that."[12]

But after helping the federal government catch and prosecute others, the thrill was gone for Albert. Along with co-conspirators in America and abroad, he stole millions of credit and debit card numbers, resold the numbers to others, and cleared millions of dollars in profit for themselves. According to at least one indictment returned by a New Jersey grand jury on August 17, 2009, the hackers used **malware** (computer programs that can corrupt connected computers) and found the "sweet spot" of time to steal customers' financial information between the customer swiping their credit or debit card in a terminal attached to a cash register and the card's bank approval. The indictment read as follows:

Methods of Hacking Utilized by Defendants

a.   Structured Query Language ("SQL") was a computer programming language designed to retrieve and manage data on computer databases.

b.   "SQL Injection Attacks" were methods of hacking into and gaining unauthorized access to computers connected to the Internet.

c.   "SQL Injection Strings" were a series of instructions to computers used by hackers in furtherance of SQL Injection Attacks.

d.   "Malware" was malicious computer software programmed to, among other things, identify, store, and export information on computers that were hacked, including information such as credit and debit card numbers and corresponding personal identification information of cardholders ("Card Data"), as well as to evade detection by anti-virus programs running on those computers.

From approximately 2006 to 2009, the defendants retrieved over 130 million credit card numbers from people shopping at companies such as Forever 21, the 7-Eleven convenience store, and Heartland Payment Systems, Inc., which is one of world's largest credit and debit card payment processing companies. When caught, again, Albert talked and pleaded guilty to federal conspiracy (18 U.S.C. §1371) and conspiracy to commit wire fraud (18 U.S.C. §1349). He received a 20-year prison sentence in a series of consolidated cases in New Jersey and Massachusetts, one of the longest sentences in the country for a computer-based crime not involving drugs or violence.[13]

The Dark Web, Cryptocurrency, and the Market for Illicit Goods

They say, "imitation is the most sincerest form of flattery," meaning if someone is copying you, they admire you; so, too, in the ways to commit crime where offenders have imitated the success of online retail and auction sites such as Craigslist, eBay, and Amazon and have proliferated on the Dark Web as sites such as the now defunct Silk Road or AlphaBay and BTH-Overdose, which traffic in illegal sales of goods and services outside the reach of traditional law enforcement.

American intelligence agencies created Dark Web technology, which is a way to communicate anonymously on the Internet. Many users access the Web via "Tor" (which stand for "The Onion Router"), "a network of encrypted, virtual tunnels that allows people to use the internet anonymously, hiding their identity and network traffic. Using Tor's hidden service protocol, people can also host websites anonymously that are only accessible by those on the Tor network."[14]

As discussed in Chapter 6, Ross Ulbricht called himself "Dread Pirates Roberts" and managed the Silk Road website, a marketplace for illegal goods and services. Silk Road consumers conducted their business by Bitcoin, an anonymous shared peer-to-peer digital cryptocurrency that is money represented by electronic code and purchased from exchanges. While the identity of Bitcoin users remains anonymous, the currency is traceable by publicly stored transactions on the "Blockchain," which prevents users from respending the same Bitcoin. The hiding of the identity of those making Bitcoin purchases (transactions are broadcast in electronic addresses) generated for Silk Road over $1.2 billion in sales. But Blockchain can also help law enforcement catch criminals if investigators are able to connect criminal activity to an electronic address and then monitor in which account the exact amount reappears. To catch and identify Ulbricht, Congress expanded the federal money laundering statute to include digital currency.

Recent law enforcement partnerships with analytic firms such as Chainalysis, which can monitor the market for virtual currency making it harder for offenders to convert Bitcoin into cash, has made "other cryptocurrencies such as monero, etherum and Zcash [increase in] popularity within the digital underworld. . . . [M]onero . . . encrypts the recipient's address on its blockchain and generates fake addresses to obscure the real sender [and] the amount of the transaction"[15] Law enforcement must work closely with researchers and software developers for the labor-intensive work of tracing cryptocurrency and catch offenders who commit financial cybercrimes.

Identity Theft

Identity theft is stealing unique identifying characteristics of someone such as a name, address, e-mail address, date of birth, social security number, bank account number, or credit card numbers to acquire something of value. Identity theft has a long history. Before computers could be used as instruments to commit wide-scale fraud, "people were pickpockets, dove into dumpsters for discarded financial records, stole preapproved credit card applications from mailboxes, completed change-of-address forms to divert victims' mail, and accepted low-level employment to gain and steal consumers' social security numbers to parlay into financial gain."[16] Some common methods of committing identity theft are listed here:

1. Opening a new credit card account in the victim's name

2. Forging checks from the victim's bank accounts

3. Opening a bank account in the victim's name and writing checks

4. Using the victim's birth date or social security number for personal gain

Rule of Law: Identity theft is posing as someone else to obtain something of value.

In 2014 the Federal Trade Commission (FTC), the federal agency responsible for watching the goods and services in the marketplace, cited that the Bureau of Justice Statistics found in 2012 the financial losses from identity theft totaled nearly $25 billion, in comparison to the $14 billion total loss from traditional property crimes. In 2013 the FBI announced nearly 519 million financial records were stolen from banks, retailers, and other businesses as a result of identity theft. Sandwiched between the 2013 data breach by the retailer Target Corporation and the 2017 breach of 148 million consumers' social security numbers, addresses, and dates of birth from the credit reporting company Equifax, an October 2014 Gallup Poll that surveyed American households on a variety of issues and concerns reported[17]

• 62% of Americans worry about computer and smartphone hacking, and

• One-quarter report credit card information was hacked through a store.

The FTC has said, "Identity theft is really 'the crime' of our interconnected technological world . . . [and] unlike a stolen wallet, can lead to years of financial loss and remediation." The criminal justice response has been proactive in securing compliance from companies doing business online to protect consumer privacy. For instance, the FTC brought a complaint against PayPal, which runs the peer-to-peer payment site Venmo, for misrepresenting to users the extent to which they could control their privacy. This was in violation of the federal Gramm–Leach–Bliley Act enacted in 1999 to regulate, in part, the financial services industry.[18] The FTC approved a settlement with Venmo on May 25, 2018, to ensure strict compliance with Title V of the Act regulating privacy of consumer financial information.

Title V- Privacy

Sec. 501. Protection of Nonpublic Personal Information.

(a) Privacy Obligation Policy.—It is the policy of the Congress that each financial institution has an affirmative and continuing obligation to respect the privacy of its customers and to protect the security and confidentiality of those customers' nonpublic personal information.

(b) Financial Institutions Safeguards.—In furtherance of the policy in subsection (a), each agency or authority described in section 505(a) shall establish appropriate standards for the financial institutions subject to their jurisdiction relating to administrative, technical, and physical safeguards—

(1) to insure the security and confidentiality of customer records and information;

(2) to protect against any anticipated threats or hazards to the security or integrity of such records; and

(3) to protect against unauthorized access to or use of such records or information which could result in substantial harm or inconvenience to any customer.

At the federal level, laws against credit card fraud, wire fraud, bank fraud, and identity theft can be used against identity thieves. Almost every state has its own criminal and consumer protection laws that deal with identity theft, such as the Virginia statute reprinted in part here.

Virginia Code Annotated §18.2-186.3

Identity theft; penalty; restitution; victim assistance

A. It shall be unlawful for any person, without the authorization or permission of the person or persons who are the subjects of the identifying information, with the intent to defraud, for his own use or the use of a third person, to: . . .

B. . . . use identification documents or identifying information of another person, whether that person is dead or alive, or of a false or fictitious person, to avoid summons, arrest, prosecution, or to impede a criminal investigation.

C. As used in this section, "identifying information" shall include but not be limited to: (i) name; (ii) date of birth; (iii) social security number; (iv) driver's license number; (v) bank account numbers; (vi) credit or debit card numbers; (vii) personal identification numbers (PIN); (viii) electronic identification codes; (ix) automated or electronic signatures; (x) biometric data; (xi) fingerprints; (xii) passwords; or (xiii) any other numbers or information that can be used to access a person's financial resources, obtain identification, act as identification, or obtain money, credit, loans, goods, or services.

Identity theft cases typically involve many theft-related crimes, such as forgery, bank fraud, and receiving stolen property. For instance, Alan Scott was a paralegal at a Boston law firm. The law firm often received insurance settlements to be paid to clients. Scott took the checks and forged the clients' names on the backs of the checks, endorsing them for deposit into his personal bank account. Scott then filed income tax returns in the names of 12 fictitious people and had the "refund" money also deposited into his account. He also applied for and received automobile loans for cars in the names of other people.[19] Often, fraud cases involve expert testimony to match the defendant's handwriting to forged financial documents and an accountant's expertise to trace funds from the source into accounts the defendant ultimately controls. In the chapter-opening case study, Kelly committed identity theft when she stole DeShawn's personal information to purchase the "get rich quick" work at home Internet scheme.

APPLYING THE LAW TO THE FACTS

Is It Identity Theft?

The Facts: A school principal was informed of a derogatory webpage on Myspace.com that was purportedly created by the principal, but in fact it was not. On the site were profanity-laced tirades attributable to the principal.[20] The student who created the page was found delinquent and appealed on the grounds that there was no identity theft. Is the student correct?

The Law: Yes, using personal information for no financial gain is not identity theft. The finding of delinquency was overturned.

Phishing. "Dear PayPal, valued member, it has come to our attention that your account information needs to be updated due to inactive members, frauds, and spoof reports. If you could please take 5 to 10 minutes out of your online experience and renew your records, you will not run into any future problems. However, failure to update your records will result in account suspension. Please follow the link below to log in to your account and renew your account information."

Phishing is the fraudulent use of e-mail and websites to obtain something of value, notably a victim's credit card information. The offender typically sends e-mails as bait to catch "fish" to eat by having the victim log into what appears to be a legitimate financial institution or Internet service provider (ISP). The real danger of being a victim of a phishing attack is that victims may not find out about the theft until long after it has occurred. Phishing e-mails elude fraud and spam filters. Like most Internet criminals, phishers are hard to catch because they use multiple ISPs, redirect services, and post fraudulent sites usually for no more than 24 hours and disappear before law enforcement officials have working information on how to shut them down. The FBI reports that as of January 2017, there has been a substantial increase in phishing scams purportedly from the Internal Revenue Service (IRS) seeking information and payment to resolve nonexistent tax disputes. **Whaling** is a sophisticated phishing scam that targets businesses and executives with access to millions of dollars. One type of a whaling attack is a business e-mail compromise scam, which infiltrates legitimate e-mail accounts of companies with international business accounts posing as a high-ranking executive requesting a transfer of a large sum of money.

The multidimensional criminal enterprise of a phisher simply sitting at home with a computer is illustrated in a brief excerpt from the case *EarthLink, Inc. v. Carmack* (2003) on the following page, in which ISP EarthLink sued Howard Carmack for harm suffered from Carmack's multiple fraudulent phishing schemes.

EARTHLINK, INC. V. CARMACK, 2003 U.S. DIST. LEXIS 9963 (N.D. GA. MAY 7, 2003)

For the past two years, Carmack has used stolen and/or bogus credit card numbers and bank account numbers to fraudulently purchase (i.e., to steal) hundreds of dial-up Internet accounts from EarthLink. Carmack has in turn used the stolen EarthLink accounts in furtherance of his campaigns of unsolicited commercial e-mail ("spamming" and "spoofing") which are illegal in and of themselves. Moreover, Carmack has assumed the identities of other Carmack family members and of innocent third-parties to disguise his own involvement in these illegal activities. The egregious nature of Carmack's acts is further compounded by (1) the fraudulent and illegal products advertised in his e-mails; and (2) the knowledge that Carmack necessarily had and has regarding the gravity of his offenses, especially in light of his prior imprisonment for similar offenses.

Credit Card and Bank Fraud

Carmack used hundreds of bogus and/or stolen credit card numbers and bank account numbers to "purchase" at least 343 EarthLink dial-up Internet accounts. Carmack used the illegally-obtained accounts for, among other purposes, the sending of unsolicited commercial e-mails promoting both his own schemes and products and those of third-parties who hired Carmack to spam for them. Each fraudulently-obtained EarthLink account remained active until Earth-Link terminated it after discovering the underlying financial fraud or the improper spam-related use.

Identity Theft

In October 2002, Carmack assumed the identity of an unsuspecting North Dakota man to obtain an extra phone line at Carmack's residence, the home base of his and his cohorts' spamming operations. Carmack also stole telephone resources from an unrelated second floor tenant at 341 Parkridge Ave., again seeking to hide his identity and continue his offenses with impunity. Finally, Carmack likewise stole the identity of his mentally-disabled brother.

Spamming and Spoofing

Carmack uses the stolen EarthLink accounts to carry out massive spamming campaigns. By EarthLink's best estimates, since March 2001, Carmack sent at least 857.5 million illegal e-mails using computer resources stolen from EarthLink. Compounding the illegality of his other violations, the content of his e-mails is often illegal or, at best, dubious. Carmack's e-mails have included advertisements for such items as (1) viral scriptbased code (i.e., a computer virus) that, when included in a "blank" e-mail, purports to give the sender control over any computer at which the e-mail is received and opened; (2) numerous work-at-home and "get rich quick" schemes; (3) bulk e-mail software and e-mail lists to be used by other spammers; and (4) cable descramblers that allow the interception of scrambled cable and pay-per-view transmissions without payment to the cable company or distributor.

Consolidated Theft Statutes

Because of the confusion created by many different types of theft, many state legislators have moved to consolidate all theft crimes into one statute.[21] The primary change in law enforcement of theft crimes under a consolidated theft statute is that prosecutors no longer need to charge the specific crime that has occurred. At trial, if the jury decides that a defendant has committed a larceny and not an embezzlement, they can still convict under the consolidated statute. Under common law, if the defendant was charged with embezzlement, not larceny, the jury would be forced to acquit if they determined that the defendant committed larceny rather than embezzlement.

Consolidation usually includes only misappropriations of property that do not involve personal violence. Robbery is usually not included in consolidated theft statutes because it carries a significant threat of harm or personal injury to the victim. The crimes that are included in consolidation statutes are not always punished equally. It is common to grade such offenses based on the value of property appropriated, the nature of the theft, and the type of property stolen.

The MPC consolidates theft offenses in a way that is similar to state laws that define theft under one, comprehensive statute. Provided that a defendant is not prejudiced by doing so, the specification of one theft crime by the prosecution does not prohibit a conviction for another. The MPC recognizes the following forms of theft:

1. Theft by taking (exercising control over another's property)

2. Theft by deception (lies about a material fact to the transaction)

3. Theft by extortion (taking by threat)

4. Theft of property known to be mislaid, misdelivered, or lost by one who does not make any reasonable attempt to find the rightful owner (keeping what is not yours)

5. Receipt of stolen property (knowing the property is stolen and keeping it)

6. Theft of professional services by deception or threat (not paying people who perform a service)

7. Conversion of entrusted funds (embezzlement)

8. Unauthorized use of another's automobile (not receiving permission to drive someone else's car)

The MPC declares that thefts are felonies of the third degree if the amount stolen exceeds $500 or if the property stolen is a firearm, automobile, airplane, motorcycle, motorboat, or other vehicle. In cases of receipt of stolen property, if the receiver of the property is a fence or middleman, then it is a felony of the third degree regardless of the value of the property.

WHITE-COLLAR CRIME

White collars describe the white shirts office workers wear, and blue collar represents those who wear blue work shirts while working a trade. White-collar crime is the term used to describe the series of theft offenses a person commits when, in a position of trust, the person uses his or her influence and power, usually in an office setting, to steal from the public. Most white-collar crime happens in the corporate world. Corporations and businesses are typically owned by shareholders, or people who invest their money in the company by buying stock. Let us assume that to start the Microsoft Corporation, cofounder Bill Gates asked people to invest money in his company. If an investor gave Bill $1,000, she would receive in return stock that represented part ownership of Microsoft. If the company did well and prospered, the investor could sell her stock and get her money back; she would also receive any profit from the increased value of the company, called the rate of return. People usually invest their money in corporations on a promised rate of return on their initial investment. Corporate executives answer to the shareholders to act in the best interests of the company; they protect the shareholders' initial investments, take actions that benefit the corporation, and take actions that do not harm the company.

The Securities and Exchange Commission (SEC) is the federal administrative agency tasked with investigating fraud in business and corporations that issue stock (securities). The SEC is an investigative body that turns to the Department of Justice or the Economic Crime Division of the local U.S. attorney's office for criminal prosecution. Those who suffer economic losses due to securities fraud can also seek remedy in civil court, as can the SEC on behalf of defrauded shareholders.[22] Most white-collar crime is prosecuted federally because of the number of crimes that cross state lines and because the required specialized training to conduct complex investigations often exceed local law enforcement resources. A very common crime charged in the white-collar context is fraud, committed by mail or wire.

Mail and Wire Fraud

Mail fraud and wire fraud are very similar crimes, and the statutes preventing such crimes are often used in conjunction with one another. The mail fraud statute punishes the use of the mail and private delivery carriers to commit a scheme to defraud, whereas **wire fraud** punishes the use of wire-based systems such as telephones, fax machines, modems, and the Internet to commit a scheme to defraud. The statutes are used today to prosecute a variety of schemes designed to cheat the public and institutions such as banks, insurance companies, and businesses. Former U.S. Supreme Court Chief Justice Warren Burger said the mail fraud statute was the traditional first line of defense to catch new fraudulent schemes that take legislators time to define and criminalize.[23]

The mail fraud statute 18 U.S.C. §1341 provides in part

Whoever, having devised or intending to devise any scheme or artifice to defraud, or for obtaining money or property by means of false or fraudulent pretenses, representations, or promises, or to sell, dispose of, loan, exchange, alter, give away, distribute, supply, or furnish or procure for unlawful use any counterfeit or spurious coin . . . for the purpose of executing such scheme . . . places in any post office or authorized depository for mail matter . . .

The wire fraud statute, 18 U.S.C. §1343, provides in part

Whoever, having devised or intending to devise any scheme or artifice to defraud, or for obtaining money or property by means of false or fraudulent pretenses, representations, or promises, transmits or causes to be transmitted by means of wire, radio, or television communication in interstate or foreign commerce, any writings, signs, signals, pictures, or sounds for the purpose of executing such scheme or artifice . . .

The elements of the mail fraud and wire fraud crimes are very similar, although the crimes can be, and often are, charged independent of one another. Mail fraud and wire fraud share the common elements:[24]

1. A scheme to defraud that includes a material deception

2. With the intent to defraud, and

3. Use of the mail (U.S. Postal Service), private commercial carriers (such as United Parcel Service [UPS] or Federal Express), or wires in furtherance of that scheme

4. That results in the loss of something of value, money, or honest public services.

The first common element in both mail and wire fraud statutes is a scheme to defraud, which is to take something of value from another by a trick, lie, or deceitful practice. Similar to the crime of false pretenses, the deceit in a mail or wire fraud scheme must be something material to the transaction—something important and not merely collateral or ancillary.[25] Unlike the crime of false pretenses, mail or wire fraud crime need not cause the victim of the deception to turn over anything of value—the scheme to defraud need not be successful. The defendant merely has to instigate the scheme to defraud to be criminally responsible.

The second element common to both the mail and wire fraud statutes is that the defendant must have possessed the intent to defraud the victim. Sometimes advertisers puff up descriptions of their product's effectiveness to induce buyers to try the product. Again, as in a false pretenses type of crime, one who merely expresses an opinion about something cannot be charged with intent to defraud. In an intent-to-defraud situation, the seller knows the information is false and represents the fact as true with the intent to obtain something of value, usually money, from the victim. The seller may make specific claims such as "This weight loss supplement is totally safe and guaranteed to help you lose 10 pounds in 48 hours" when no supplement can safely do this or "This land has clear title" when a lien indicating that the property was used as security for payment was attached to the property many years ago.

The third common element is using the mails or the wires or knowing that the mails and wires would be used even if the defendant himself did not use them. In *Pereira v. United States* (1954),[26] the high Court said that when someone acts "with knowledge that the use of mails will follow in the ordinary course of business, or where such use can reasonably be foreseen, even though not actually intended, then he 'causes' the mails to be used." The same criteria apply to wire transmissions. If a person went to the bank to effectuate a wire transfer or knew that checks deposited would cause funds to be electronically transferred from one account to another, the element of using the wires has been met. Note that the intent element in mail or wire fraud is for the fraud itself, not necessarily the use of the mails or wires. That is, the *mens rea* applies to the trick or deceit to get something of value, and it becomes mail or wire fraud because of the way the fraud is carried out (i.e., by using mail or wire).

The last common element is causing the loss of something of value (money or property) or honest public services. In *United States v. Weaver*, reprinted in part below, the defendant was convicted of mail and wire fraud when selling candy machines to investors, promising $800 per day profit with the knowledge that selling 25-cent gumballs yields little to no cash flow. The defendant appealed on the grounds that the customers suffered no harm. As you read the court's decision, note that a victim's harm is not an element of the crime. The intent to promote a scheme to defraud and using the mails or wires is sufficient to sustain the conviction.

In the chapter-opening case study, Rachel committed wire fraud with her false advertisement for her "get rich quick" scheme to defraud people through the Internet.

UNITED STATES V. WEAVER, 860 F.3D 90 (2017)

United States Court of Appeals for the Second Circuit

FACTS: From 2004 to 2010, Edward Weaver was the CEO [chief executive officer] of Vendstar, a corporation that sold candy-vending machines to approximately 7,000 customers who spent a total of about $62 million on the investments. Vendstar purported to offer customers the ability to "build a successful home-based vending business" that would earn them profits of as much as $800 a day. The company sold small vending machines that included three clear canisters and dispensed loose handfuls of candy for twenty-five cents.

Although Vendstar's promotional materials and salespeople represented that the investment opportunities would be lucrative, for the most part the vending machines would earn Vendstar's customers almost no money. Customer complaints became so frequent that Weaver assigned a Vendstar employee to respond to those complaints full time. In the end, many customers lost virtually all of their investments in Vendstar. The size of the investments varied, and the most common transaction involved the victim paying $10,000 for a package that included 30 candy-vending machines and an initial supply of candy, although some customers spent significantly more than that.

In general, the Vendstar scheme operated as follows. Potential customers would respond to Internet or newspaper advertisements, approved by Weaver, for the vending machine investments. After potential customers inquired about the opportunity, Vendstar would mail them a brochure, order form, and certain disclosure documents. The brochure, which Weaver also approved, included claims that the salespeople were "Vendstar vendors themselves" and promised that the investments had "little risk." Vendstar salespeople would then follow up with customers over the phone. During those phone conversations, salespeople routinely lied to customers, promising them utterly unrealistic earnings and claiming that the investments were sound. Salespeople also falsely stated that they owned their own Vendstar machines, a misrepresentation that encouraged customers to trust them and buy the machines. At trial, victims of the scam testified that those lies influenced their decision to purchase the machines. After customers agreed to purchase the machines, they were required to sign a contract setting forth the terms of those purchases. The contracts included disclaimers in capital letters, providing in relevant part that:

Purchaser understands that seller has no affiliation or financial relationship with professional locating companies and that seller has no involvement whatsoever in securing retail locations. . . .

Purchaser and seller agree that this purchase order contains the entire understanding of the agreement between the parties and there is no reliance upon any verbal representation whatsoever. Seller has not guaranteed any minimum or maximum earnings. . . .

It is further acknowledged that no statements, promises[,] or agreements influenced this purchase or are expected other than anything contained in this purchase order. . . .

When customers expressed concern about these disclaimers, salespeople misleadingly dismissed the provisions as unimportant "legalese" or "mumbo-jumbo."

In 2013, a grand jury returned a superseding indictment charging Weaver with mail and wire fraud, conspiracy to commit mail and wire fraud, [and] making false statements to government officials. The government alleged that Weaver, along with many of his employees, sought to defraud Vendstar's customers by promising profits that they knew would not materialize. Weaver was convicted on all counts after a six-week jury trial. The district court later sentenced Weaver principally to 60 months' imprisonment. Weaver timely appealed.

ISSUE: [Was the evidence sufficient to convict Weaver of the charges at trial?]

HOLDING: [Yes. Conviction on all counts affirmed.]

REASONING: The essential elements of [mail and wire fraud] are (1) a scheme to defraud, (2) money or property as the object of the scheme, and (3) use of the mails or wires to further the scheme. Because the mail fraud and the wire fraud statutes use the same relevant language, we analyze them the same way. The gravamen [basis of complaint] of the offense is the scheme to defraud. *In order to prove the existence of a scheme to defraud, the government must also prove that the misrepresentations were material, and that the defendant acted with fraudulent intent* (emphasis added).

A *statement is material* if the misinformation or omission would naturally tend to lead or is capable of leading a reasonable [person] to change [his] conduct. In other words, a lie can support a fraud conviction only if it is material if it would affect a reasonable person's evaluation of a proposal. A false statement is material if it has a natural tendency to influence, or is capable of influencing, the decision of the [decision maker] to which it was addressed. Recently, the Supreme Court explained that, under any understanding of the concept, materiality looks to the effect on the likely or actual behavior of the recipient of the alleged misrepresentation.

We have noted the connection between the materiality element and the additional requirement that the government prove fraudulent intent. The role of the ordinary prudence and comprehension standard [in the materiality element] is to assure that the defendant's conduct was calculated to deceive, not to grant permission to take advantage of the stupid or careless . . . [T]he government need not prove that the victims of the fraud were actually injured, but only that defendants contemplated some actual harm or injury to their victims.

Weaver has not otherwise contested the materiality of the oral misrepresentations, and we independently conclude that they had the natural tendency to influence the decisionmakers to whom they were addressed—potential Vendstar customers.

[W]here the government criminally prosecutes defendants for participating in a *scheme or artifice to defraud*, 18 USC §§1341, 1343, [f]raudsters may not escape criminal liability for lies told to induce gullible victims to make worthless investments by inducing them to sign a contract containing disclaimers of reliance (emphasis added). Finally, [Weaver] apparently assumes that Vendstar employees could not have been charged with mail or wire fraud until customers signed the agreement and paid Vendstar for the machines. That is, he assumes that the fraud would need to be successful in order for Weaver to be criminally liable for it.

But under the plain language of [the mail and wire fraud statutes], the crimes were complete when, with fraudulent intent, Vendstar employees used the wires or mail in furtherance of a scheme to extract money from their victims via material misrepresentations. No customers had to be tricked into purchasing the doomed vending-machine business opportunities in order for Weaver and his team to be charged criminally because the government is not required to prove that an intended victim was actually defrauded to establish guilt of mail or wire fraud.

Indeed, the only significance in a fraud case of proof of actual harm befalling the victim as a result of the scheme is that it may serve as circumstantial evidence from which a jury could infer the defendant's intent to cause harm.

CONCLUSION: For the foregoing reasons, and for the reasons stated in the accompanying summary order, we affirm the judgment of conviction and sentence in all respects.

What if the court in the *Weaver* case had found in favor of the defendant and had overturned his conviction? Is it the job of the courts to ensure that all investors do their homework and research the companies with which they do business? What would happen in society if there were little to no criminal prosecution for fraudulent schemes based on a twist on *caveat emptor* (let the buyer beware) to "let the investor beware"?

Title 18 U.S.C. §1346 says, "For the purposes of this chapter [mail and wire fraud], the term *scheme or artifice to defraud* includes a scheme or artifice to deprive another of the intangible right of honest services." History is replete with people in positions of public trust abusing that power for personal gain. Fraud crimes dilute the integrity of institutions on which we all depend to be free from undue or unlawful influence. The public official is a caretaker of the public trust. If the official is not faithful to the elected office, he or she is prosecuted federally. A jury found C. Ray Nagin guilty through a bribery and kickback scheme of defrauding the people of New Orleans of his honest services, when he traded the benefit of his office as mayor of New Orleans for personal profit. In February 2014, trial evidence showed Nagin had taken bribes when, in exchange for access to lucrative city contracts, he took from businessmen free trips and free granite for his son's countertop business. Often called "pay to play," the official wants something of value in exchange for government dealings that he can control. What in Latin is called *quid pro quo*, this is an exchange of benefits. To convict of theft of honest services fraud, the federal prosecutor had to prove Ray Nagin used "wire communication in interstate commerce" to commit a "scheme or artifice to defraud," by depriving another of "the intangible right of honest services." So long as Nagin used the wires to personally profit from bribes "in return for being influenced in his performance of an official act," the government met its burden that Nagin stole from the public the right to his faithful service as mayor to act in the best interests of New Orleans, and not himself.[27] Nagin was sentenced in 2016 to serve 10 years in prison.

Money Laundering

Money laundering is the crime of taking the proceeds derived from criminal activity and "laundering" it, that is, making it clean through investing the criminal fruit in a legitimate business enterprise, to conceal the criminal origin of the profits. The federal money laundering statute states, in part:

---

18 U.S.C. §1956 Laundering of Monetary Instruments

(1) Whoever, knowing that the property involved in a financial transaction represents the proceeds of some form of unlawful activity, conducts or attempts to conduct such a financial transaction . . .

    (B) knowing that the transaction is designed in whole or in part—

        (i) to conceal or disguise the nature, the location, the source, the ownership, or the control of the proceeds of specified unlawful activity . . .[28]

shall be sentenced to a fine of not more than $500,000 or twice the value of the property involved in the transaction, whichever is greater, or imprisonment for not more than twenty years, or both.

Money laundering operations are depicted in Figure 5.1. Criminals make money from their illicit activity and then (1) place it in a bank; (2) layer it through a variety of financial institutions to obscure the original criminal origin of the money; and (3) integrate it into legitimate businesses and ventures, thereby "cleansing" it, as investigators will have difficulty separating illegal money from the profits made from the legitimate business. In the chapter-opening case study, Rachel committed money laundering when she took her illegally derived financial gains and used the money to purchase equipment and supplies for a legitimate business venture, the new restaurant.

Figure 5.1   Money Laundering Operations

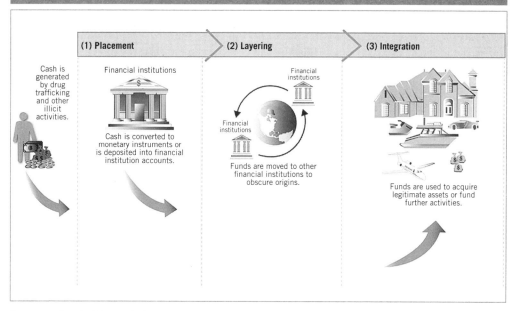

Source: Reprinted with permission, Financial Crimes Enforcement Network.

Racketeer Influenced and Corrupt Organizations (RICO) Act

The Statute

The Racketeer Influenced and Corrupt Organizations (RICO) Act was enacted by Congress in the 1970s to increase federal prosecutorial power to combat organized crime and seize criminals' substantial financial assets. Prior to enacting laws, legislative bodies often make findings of fact, with or without public hearings and testimony, explaining the reasons the new law is needed. Congress enacted RICO for the following reasons as stated in the findings of fact supporting enacting the law:

Racketeer Influenced and Corrupt Organizations (RICO); Statement of Findings and Purpose; Organized Crime Control Act of 1970, 84 Stat. 922-923

The Congress finds that:

(1)   organized crime in the United States is a highly sophisticated, diversified, and widespread activity that annually drains billions of dollars from America's economy by unlawful conduct and the illegal use of force, fraud, and corruption;

(2)   organized crime derives a major portion of its power through money obtained from such illegal endeavors as syndicated gambling, loan sharking, the theft and fencing of property, the importation and distribution of narcotics and other dangerous drugs, and other forms of social exploitation;

(3)   this money and power are increasingly used to infiltrate and corrupt our democratic processes;

(4)   organized crime activities in the United States weaken the stability of the nation's economic system, harm innocent investors and competing organizations, interfere with free competition, seriously burden interstate and foreign commerce, threaten domestic security, and undermine the general welfare of the Nation and its citizens . . . 18 U.S.C. §§1961-1962

RICO was conceived as a weapon for prosecution of organized crime, but it has become the basis of prosecution against white-collar criminals as well. There need not be a financial motive to bring a RICO claim. For example, health care providers brought a civil RICO action against antiabortion protesters, alleging a nationwide effort to close clinics based on extortionate activity. While the ultimate issue was not decided by the U.S. Supreme Court, the justices did find economic motive for racketeering activity is not required to find an offender liable under the RICO statute (*NOW v. Scheidler*, 1994).[29]

The elements of RICO are

1. The defendants committed two or more predicate acts,

2. Two predicate acts which occurred within 10 years of each other formed a pattern of racketeering activity,

3. The money gained was reinvested in the enterprise, and

4. The enterprise affects interstate commerce.

To be charged with a RICO offense, the defendants must first commit two or more predicate acts. The predicate acts include a variety of state and federal offenses such as violent crimes (e.g., murder or terrorist activities), extortion, bribery, dealing in obscene matter, human trafficking, drug dealing, all types of fraud (e.g., bankruptcy, securities, welfare), money laundering, sexual exploitation of children, illegal gambling, embezzlement, counterfeiting and immigration offenses.[30] To be considered a pattern of racketeering activity, the criminal activity must pose a threat to continue, and not just be isolated, sporadic criminal acts that the government tries to lump together.[31]

RICO prosecutions are often the umbrella for a wide variety of financial crimes. For example, Scott Tucker of Overland, Kansas, made a fortune from "payday" lending schemes where consumers who needed short-term, immediate loans for relatively small sums of cash agreed to repay the loans on their next payday by allowing the lender to make automatic withdrawals from their bank accounts. Consumers do not often read the fine print on the contracts they sign, and those who borrowed from Scott Tucker's payday fraud were unaware that borrowing $500 meant repaying $1,925. The loan paperwork falsely stated the finance charge on $500 would be $150, but the scheme to defraud increased the charges to $1,425 based on a series of undisclosed, triggering events. Moreover, Tucker and his lawyer and codefendant Timothy Muir induced Native American Tribes to sign on as unwitting partners in the fraud to take advantage of the Tribes' sovereignty in governing their own affairs. By using the Tribes' legal autonomy, Tucker and Muir willingly evaded American consumer protection laws to effectuate their fraud. The federal prosecutor for the Southern District of New York where Tucker operated charged the predicate crimes and, in a press release, defined Tucker and Muir's activities as RICO crimes:[32]

> From at least 1997 until 2013, TUCKER engaged in the business of making small, short-term, high-interest, unsecured loans, commonly referred to as "payday loans," through the Internet. TUCKER's lending enterprise, which had up to 1,500 employees based in Overland Park, Kansas, did business as Ameriloan, Cash Advance; OneClickCash, Preferred Cash Loans; United Cash Loans; US FastCash; 500 FastCash; Advantage Cash Services; and Star Cash Processing (the Tucker Payday Lenders). TUCKER, working with MUIR, the general counsel for TUCKER's payday lending businesses since 2006, routinely charged interest rates of 600 percent or 700 percent, and sometimes higher than 1,000 percent. These loans were issued to more than 4.5 million working people in all 50 states, including more than 250,000 people in New York, many of whom were struggling to pay basic living expenses. Many of these loans were issued in states, including New York, with laws that expressly forbid lending at the exorbitant interest rates TUCKER charged. Evidence at trial established that TUCKER and MUIR were

fully aware of the illegal nature of the loans charged and, in fact, prepared scripts to be used by call center employees to deal with complaints by customers that their loans were illegal.

The elements of RICO to prosecute Tucker and Muir were the following:

1. The two or more predicate acts were the charging exorbitant interest, "600 percent or 700 percent, and sometimes higher than 1,000 percent," in violation of the law;

2. The predicate acts formed a pattern of racketeering activity which, because it went on for 15 years, had a threat of continuing;

3. Tucker and Muir used the money gained to reinvest in the enterprise ("TUCKER's lending enterprise, which had up to 1,500 employees");

4. That affected interstate commerce ("These loans were issued to more than 4.5 million working people in all 50 states").

Overall, Ticker and Muir's payday loan scam resulted in a loss to consumers valued at $3.5 billion. On January 5, 2018, Tucker was sentenced to 16 years and Muir sentenced to 7 years in federal prison.

BURGLARY

Under common law, burglary was a crime against habitation, the place where one lives, and the elements were that the offender broke into and entered a dwelling during the nighttime. In popular culture, a burglar is a cartoon figure wearing a striped shirt carrying a bag of contraband. Such a portrayal has led the public to conclude that burglary is stealing, but it is so much more than that. Modern statutes have eliminated the nighttime requirement, and a dwelling can be any type of building, not necessarily a residence. The elements of burglary as represented in modern statutes today are

> **Rule of Law: Burglary is not stealing; it is breaking and entering a structure with the intent to commit a felony once inside.**

1. The unlawful breaking and entering (which can be achieved through fraud and deceit)

2. Into any structure (four walls and a roof)

3. With the intent to commit a felony or felonious theft

4. Once inside.

The breaking and entering requirement means the changing or altering of a structure to enter with the intent, formed before one does the breaking, to commit a felony, such as rape, arson, or felonious larceny, once inside. Walking into an open door is trespassing, not breaking. But slipping a credit card to open a lock on a dorm room satisfies the breaking element; and if, at the door, one formed the intent to commit a felony, such as rape, once inside, then the crime is burglary. One can burglarize one's own home. For instance, if a husband who has received a court order to stay away from his home to prevent abuse comes to the door of his own home with the intent to harm his wife but tells her that he just "wants to talk" so that she will let him inside, he has committed a burglary.

The breaking element of burglary can be accomplished through fraud and deceit. If an art thief realizes that a socialite has a Renoir painting on her wall and poses as a vacuum salesperson to get inside the house to steal the Renoir, it is burglary. But if the thief did not know that the Renoir or anything of value was inside the house until after he entered the socialite's home, it is not burglary because the intent to commit felonious theft was not formed until after the offender was inside the home. To be guilty of burglary, the offender need not complete the intended felony once inside; an attempt of the intended felony is sufficient.

At common law, burglary only applied to dwellings and could be committed only during the night. The primary difference between burglary and other crimes is that burglary poses more risk of danger to the dwelling's inhabitants and, therefore, carries a more severe penalty than simple breaking and entering where there is no intent to commit a felony once inside the dwelling. In *Murphy v. State* (2012), the case excerpt below, the question for the court was whether a man who carried a weapon at a health care clinic could be convicted of second-degree burglary because he intended to commit a felony once inside (firing shots in an effort to get mental health help). The answer was yes.

MURPHY V. STATE, 108 SO.3D 531 (2012)

Court of Criminal Appeals of Alabama

FACTS: The evidence presented at trial established the following pertinent facts. On Thursday, February 1, 2007, Murphy, who was then living in Auburn, was in Dothan visiting his mother, Sharon Murphy. Murphy was congested, had a stuffy nose, and was coughing periodically. Murphy's mother, a registered nurse, took Murphy to PrimeCare in Dothan, where he was examined by Dr. Steve Sherrer. After an examination, Dr. Sherrer prescribed Avelox (an antibiotic), Tessalon Perles (cough medicine), and Sudex (to relieve congestion). Dr. Sherrer also provided Murphy with an injection of Kenalog (a steroid for inflammation). Murphy took the Avelox and the Sudex that evening, but was awake for most of the night because of a severe headache. At this time, Murphy experienced no problems with his memory and was not confused in any manner.

The following morning Murphy called PrimeCare to complain about his headache, and Dr. Sherrer prescribed Darvocet (pain medication), a drug to which Murphy may have been allergic. Later that day Murphy went back to PrimeCare, where he was examined by Dr. Michael Williams. Dr. Williams diagnosed Murphy with an ear infection, muscle-tension headaches, and neck strain. Dr. Williams was notified that Murphy, who was a member of the United States National Guard at the time, had a physical-fitness test with the National Guard the following day. Dr. Williams wrote a doctor's excuse for Murphy, recommending that Murphy not participate in rigorous physical activity.

The next day Murphy had to wake at 6:30 a.m. to attend drill with the National Guard. Murphy was also confused and disoriented for most of the evening. Murphy again slept very little, talking with his mother until around 5:00 a.m., even though he had to attend National Guard drill the following day. At drill the next day Murphy ignored Dr. Williams's warnings and attempted to take the physical-fitness test. During the test, Murphy experienced chest pains, vomited, and passed out. The following morning Murphy and his mother went to see Dr. Warren Rollins,

an ear, nose, and throat specialist. Dr. Rollins examined Murphy and diagnosed him with a sore throat. Dr. Rollins recommended Murphy undergo a chest X-ray and an EKG and that Murphy discontinue the use of Avelox because it could cause heart damage.

Murphy and his mother left Dr. Rollins's office at approximately 9:00 a.m., and returned home so they could make an appointment with PrimeCare for the chest X-ray and EKG. While Mrs. Murphy was out, Murphy left his mother's home and drove to PrimeCare at approximately 9:45 a.m. Murphy entered PrimeCare agitated and angry, holding numerous bottles of medicine in his hands. Murphy approached the receptionist, Robin Dunn, and screamed, "You gave me too much medicine, you are trying to make me have a heart attack." Christie McLean, the office manager, heard Murphy screaming and took him from the lobby to an examination room.

Murphy was then examined by Dr. Joseph Sewell, who noted Murphy's blood pressure and heart rate were a bit higher than normal, but not dangerously high. Dr. Sewell ordered the chest X-ray and found no abnormalities. Dr. Sewell prescribed Mobic (an anti-inflammatory) and Albuterol (an inhaler) for Murphy; he directed Murphy to continue taking the antibiotics as he had been prescribed. As Murphy left PrimeCare, he looked at Dunn, smiled and calmly stated, "I'm going to the bank. I'm coming back to see you."

Not long thereafter, Michael Wright, an Iraq war veteran who had come to PrimeCare for a job-related physical, looked outside the waiting-room window and saw Murphy marching in "parade formation," wearing a camouflage helmet and carrying a M14 rifle on his shoulder. Wright stepped outside of PrimeCare and telephoned the police. Dunn, whose reception desk faced PrimeCare's glass front doors, also saw Murphy's return. Murphy walked in the building and started firing his weapon. He shattered the glass windows that lined the front of the building and shot out the glass walls that separated the reception area from the waiting room. Dunn ducked as the shooting started, then ran and hid in an examination room with a few patients, believing that each shot fired was likely killing someone. As patients fled from the lobby and staff members scrambled to get out of the line of fire, Murphy began yelling, "I'm not here to hurt y'all. Get out, get out. I'm not mad with y'all . . . I'm mad with the army." Murphy was "upset" because of the difficulty he was having in getting a medical clearance from the National Guard for deployment to Iraq.

Jennifer Herring, human-resources director at Prime-Care, was in an examination room when she heard loud screaming. When Herring realized other employees were still in the facility, she returned to the building with McLean to try and help as many people escape as possible. Herring was in the doorway of an exam room looking for patients when she heard another shot. Murphy had shot blindly through a closed door at the end of a hallway; the bullet passed by Herring and struck the lead wall of the X-ray room, causing the bullet to fragment. A fragment of the bullet grazed Herring, tearing her blouse and drawing a small amount of blood. This was the last shot fired by Murphy.

At trial, Murphy based his defense on a theory of temporary, drug-induced psychosis. The circuit court ordered Dr. Doug McKeown, a clinical and forensic psychologist, to determine Murphy's mental state at the time he attacked the PrimeCare facility and to determine whether Murphy was competent to stand trial. Murphy was determined to be competent to stand trial.

LAW: Murphy contends that the State failed to prove a *prima facie* [without more] case of second-degree burglary because, he argues, the State failed to prove that he unlawfully entered PrimeCare or that he unlawfully remained at PrimeCare with the intent to commit theft or a felony.

[The law of burglary states] . . .

(a) A person commits the crime of burglary in the second degree if he or she knowingly enters or remains unlawfully in a building with intent to commit theft or a felony therein and, if in effecting entry or while in the building or in immediate flight therefrom, the person or another participant in the crime:

(1) Is armed with explosives; or

(2) Causes physical injury to any person who is not a participant in the crime; or

(3) In effecting entry, is armed with a deadly weapon or dangerous instrument or, while in the building or in immediate flight from the building, uses or threatens the immediate use of a deadly weapon or dangerous instrument against another person."

§13A-7-6(a), Ala. Code 1975.

Alabama's burglary statute further provides that:

[a] person "enters or remains unlawfully" in or upon premises when he is not licensed, invited or privileged to do so. §13A-7-1(4), Ala. Code 1975.

An unlawful entry or unlawful remaining constitutes the trespassory element of burglary, which element, when coupled with the intent to commit a crime inside, forms the nucleus of the burglary.

Our review of the record indicates that the State presented sufficient evidence from which the jury could have concluded that Murphy remained unlawfully on the premises of PrimeCare. After [the decision in] *Davis v. State* (1990), "the State is no longer required to prove that the defendant broke and entered the premises. Instead, the strictures of that element have been replaced with the general requirement of a trespass on premises through an unlawful entry or an unlawful remaining."[33]

In the instant case, Murphy entered the publicly accessible areas of the PrimeCare facility with an M14 automatic rifle, a significant amount of ammunition, and a military helmet. Murphy then shot out the windows in the front of the building, shot out the glass in the reception area, and shot other items in the building . . . The record also indicates that the State presented sufficient evidence to support a conclusion by the jury that Murphy had the requisite intent to commit a felony when he entered PrimeCare. In a prosecution for second-degree burglary the intent of the defendant "must be inferred by the jury from a due consideration of all of the material evidence." While inside PrimeCare, Murphy committed two felonies. Murphy destroyed property worth at least $2,500 during his occupation of PrimeCare, constituting the felony of *criminal mischief*, a violation of §13A-7-21.

Murphy also terrorized PrimeCare's employees and patients, constituting the felony of making terrorist threats, in violation of §13A-10-15. Because the *jury is allowed to infer intent* "from a due consideration of all of the material evidence," and because the material evidence indicated that Murphy entered PrimeCare with guns and live ammunition, then used the guns and live ammunition to commit two felonies, the logical inference is that Murphy intended to commit those felonies when he entered PrimeCare (emphasis added).

CONCLUSION: Although conflicts in the evidence existed, the State's evidence, when considered as a whole, could have permitted the jury to reasonably conclude that Murphy intended to commit the felonious crimes that formed the basis for his second-degree burglary conviction. [Conviction affirmed.]

The Facts: One night, Kyle was visiting his brother at a warehouse where the brother was a security guard. Kyle looked around the warehouse and broke open a door where he thought expensive stereos were stored. He was charged with burglary and raised the defense that he did not steal anything. Did Kyle commit burglary?

The Law: Yes. Actual stealing is not an element of burglary. "When it is shown that one accused of burglary broke and entered . . . it is presumed he did so with the intent to steal [a felony]."[34]

In the chapter-opening case study, Rachel committed burglary when she went to Bernie's house with the intent to commit a felony, arson, once inside and broke and entered by smashing a window to achieve her criminal intent.

ARSON

Under common law, arson was the malicious burning of another's home. As with the other property crimes, the initial definition did not include much behavior that was criminal, but not covered by the law. For example, it did not count as arson if a homeowner burned his or her own house or burned his business contained in a warehouse, because the definition was restricted to dwellings where people live. Today arson is defined by statute, and the basic elements are

1. The intentional and unlawful
2. Burning
3. Of any structure.

Arson is often separated by degrees, so a burning committed recklessly or negligently is often punished less harshly that a first-degree arson. There is also a federal Anti-Arson Act for those crimes that have an interstate commerce nexus.[35] Moreover, many modern statutes include the burning of other property, such as automobiles and personal property, in the criminal definition of arson. Such separation of arson into degrees is best illustrated by the Iowa arson statute, reprinted here.

> Iowa Code §712.1 (2007) Arson defined.
>
> 1. Causing a fire or explosion, or placing any burning or combustible material, or any incendiary or explosive device or material, in or near any property with the intent to destroy or damage such property, or with the knowledge that such property will probably be destroyed or damaged, is arson, whether or not any such property is actually destroyed or damaged.

Arson is typically a general intent crime. That is, the offender needs only to start the fire to burn a structure and does not need to undertake the burning for the specific result of the structure burning to the ground. In the chapter-opening case study, Rachel committed arson when she willfully spread gasoline, lit a match, and burned down Bernie's house.

Criminal Mischief

A common ancillary property crime is criminal mischief, defined as the willful defacing and destruction of property, such as defacing cemetery headstones during Halloween, not to be confused with the Hate Crime of choosing headstones of a particular religion to deface. A common statute is represented by Nebraska law:

Nebraska Statutes 28-519. Criminal Mischief

(1) A person commits criminal mischief if he or she:

(a) Damages property of another intentionally or recklessly; or

(b) Intentionally tampers with property of another so as to endanger person or property; or

(c) Intentionally or maliciously causes another to suffer pecuniary loss by deception or threat.

In the *Murphy* case, when the defendant's bullets destroyed property worth at least $2,500, he committed criminal mischief in violation of Alabama law.

SUMMARY

1. You will be able to discuss the legal foundation for possessory rights in property. Larceny is the specific intent to steal the personal property of another with the intent to permanently deprive the owner of possession. Even if the thief intends to "borrow" property belonging to another, if he takes it, exercises dominion and control over it, or otherwise interferes with the owner's use and enjoyment of the property, the thief has "stolen" the property, as in *New York v. Alamo* (1974). False pretenses is making a false statement to another (lying) to induce another to turn over title representing ownership of property or to turn over money. Conversion is taking someone else's property and making it your own.

2. You can analyze the legal basis for common law differentiation in property crimes. Scholars condemn many of the technical distinctions of common law crimes, and the modern trend has been to consolidate theft crimes in one statute that keeps the basic elements of larceny and then defines the distinctions on the basis of how another's property is acquired, whether lawfully in embezzlement or by threat in extortion. To be found guilty of receiving stolen property, the defendant must have knowledge (scienter) that the property is stolen when he takes possession of it. Uttering is passing checks with insufficient funds, and forgery is signing someone else's signature to create a legal obligation, often financial, in order to steal something of value. Counterfeit violations are defined as crimes against the property value of the item illegally copied and sold as if genuine. The true value of the property is the public's perception that the item is genuine.

3. You will be able to evaluate the wide-ranging scope of mail and wire fraud crimes. White-collar crime is usually business-related crime committed by a variety of fraudulent schemes by people in positions of power. Mail fraud is using the mail service and private carriers to commit a scheme to defraud, whereas wire fraud uses telephones and computers for the same purpose. *United States v. Weaver* (2017) details a scheme to defraud investors in promising "too good to be true" returns on candy-vending machines. The mail and wire fraud statutes may be used to prosecute the theft of honest services when public officials trade the influence of their elected office for personal gain, such as a *quid pro quo* exchange of benefits. Mail and wire fraud and a host of violent crimes are predicate offenses for criminal liability under the Racketeer Influenced and Corrupt Organizations Act (RICO).

4. RICO was enacted by Congress in 1970 to combat organized crime by enacting a comprehensive criminal statute under which defendants can be convicted if they commit two or more predicate acts, be they state and/or federal crimes, to form a pattern of racketeering and if money obtained from such enterprise is reinvested in the enterprise and affects interstate commerce.

You will articulate the interrelationship between financially based crimes such as computer fraud, racketeering, and money laundering. Financial cybercrimes use computers to steal from people and financial institutions. There are many types of malware that enables criminals to commit crimes via technology, including the Dark Web where illicit goods are bought and sold, often with the use of cryptocurrency such as Bitcoin. Identity theft is stealing one's personal identifying information to obtain things of value. Identity thieves are very prolific, as evidenced in the case *EarthLink v. Carmack* (2003). Phishing is setting up a realistic-looking fraudulent website that appears to accept legitimate payment for goods and services on the Internet, and whaling is attacking large corporate targets. Money laundering is taking the financial gains from committing crimes and comingling the funds with legitimate businesses to "cleanse" the money and hide its criminal origins.

5. You will understand burglary and arson crimes. Burglary is breaking into and entering a structure with the intent to commit a felony once inside. To constitute burglary, the intent to commit the felony must be formed before the offender enters the structure. In *Murphy v. State* (2012),

a man with a gun went to a clinic to get health care and fired shots inside. He was convicted of, among other crimes, burglary. Arson is the malicious burning of a structure, and criminal mischief is the damaging of property, either through acts of vandalism or through the specific intent to deface the property. The property need not be destroyed; it is enough if the integrity of the structure is defaced, such as painting a public statue.

Go back to the beginning of the chapter and reread the news excerpts associated with the learning objectives. Test yourself to determine if you can understand the material covered in the text in the context of the news.

KEY TERMS AND PHRASES

affirmative defense 134
arson 150
Bitcoin 136
breaking and entering 147
burglary 147
consolidated theft statutes 139
conversion 126
counterfeit 133
criminal mischief 150
cryptocurrency 136
Dark Web 136
embezzlement 130

extortion 134
false pretenses 129
financial cybercrime 135
forgery 132
identity theft 136
larceny 126
larceny by trick 130
mail fraud 140
malware 135
money laundering 144
pattern of racketeering activity 146
personal property 126

phishing 138
predicate acts 146
quid pro quo 144
Racketeer Influenced and Corrupt
    Organizations (RICO) Act 145
real property 126
receiving stolen property 133
theft of honest services 144
uttering 132
whaling 138
white-collar crimes 140
wire fraud 141

PROBLEM-SOLVING EXERCISES

1. The Drake Hair Braiding Company sold plastic braiding tools that made it appear easy to arrange long hair into complicated French braids. The company sold the braiding tools through sales agents and direct mailings that showed consumers how the sophisticated braids could be made in three easy steps. In reality, the Drake Company knew that the average consumer could not operate the tools correctly and easily. Can the Drake Company be prosecuted under the mail fraud statute for making faulty claims, or is Drake involved in mere puffery about the braiding tools, which is not criminally actionable? **(ROL: Mail fraud)**

2. SAFECO was a road construction firm whose employees belonged to the local union. Mike, the union treasurer, collected members' dues and deposited the money in the union's bank account. Mike's wife needed an urgent liver transplant, and Mike had to come up with the $10,000 insurance deductible immediately. Mike told the doctor, "I know where I can borrow the money," and he went to the bank and withdrew $10,000 of the union's money. On the way into the hospital to visit his wife after her surgery, Mike saw 3 dozen roses on a secretary's desk and took them to

give to his wife. The roses then died. What theft crimes, if any, has Mike committed? **(ROL: Embezzlement, larceny)**

3. A group of friends got together and decided to sell marijuana and cocaine to make money. Penny maintained a Facebook page through which she would send private messages to other friends in other states letting them know of the drugs available for sale. Penny and Asia also confirmed the financial arrangement of how all the friends would pay dues for the purchase of firearms or to pay bribes to local officials so their drug sales would run uninterrupted. When a local gang moved into the friends' neighborhood as rival drug sellers, two members of the group texted that the gang leader would be "faded straight up." The gang leader's body was found floating in the river 2 weeks later. The friends made so much drug money that they purchased and invested their money in local laundromats surrounding their neighborhood. One bank manager became suspicious of the large wads of cash the friends placed for deposit and alerted authorities. What would federal authorities have to show to bring a criminal RICO action against the group of drug-dealing friends? **(ROL: Money laundering, RICO)**

6

CRIMES AGAINST THE PUBLIC

Go to the end of the chapter. Skim the key terms and phrases and read the summary closely. Come back and look at the following news excerpts to focus your reading throughout the chapter to understand how crimes against the public are typically defined in relation to the religious moralism that has formed the backbone of American law since the country's infancy. One should not lie, cheat, steal, or take advantage of people or the public trust. Moral crimes are typically *mala prohibita*, behavior made criminal by statute, such as gambling, prostitution, and the use of illicit drugs. *Mala in se* crimes are perceived to be inherently evil, such as murder and rape, and are discussed in Chapter 4. This chapter begins with a hypothetical case study of Don looking for an easy way out. Follow Don as he encounters the rules of law presented throughout the chapter, and connect Don's criminal acts with the relevant section of text.

WHY THIS CHAPTER MATTERS TO YOU	THE LEARNING OBJECTIVES AS REFLECTED IN THE NEWS
After you have read this chapter: **Learning Objective 1:** You will be able to articulate the laws combatting crimes tied to addiction.	Na Chu, 37; Yeyou Chu, 36; Cuiying Liu, 62; and Keping Zhang, 62, all Chinese nationals, were charged . . . with international money laundering conspiracy . . . The charges come as part of Operation Denial, an Organized Crime and Drug Enforcement Task Force (OCDETF) investigation into the international trafficking of fentanyl and other lethal drugs, and was significantly aided by the national and international coordination led by the multi-agency Special Operations Division (S.O.D.) near Washington D.C. as part of Operation Deadly Merchant. (*News Service*, April 30, 2018)
Learning Objective 2: You will know the difference between riot and peaceful protest.	Federal prosecutors Thursday dropped their cases against seven people charged with rioting during President Trump's inauguration after a D.C. judge determined that the government intentionally misrepresented information and withheld evidence from the defense. A week before the case was to go to trial, Assistant U.S. Attorney Ahmed Baset said prosecutors would withdraw charges, with the option of reinstating them. He did not offer an explanation. Over Baset's objection, Morin dismissed the conspiracy to riot cases with prejudice, meaning the charges cannot be reinstated. (*Washington Post*, May 31, 2018)

(Continued)

(Continued)

WHY THIS CHAPTER MATTERS TO YOU	THE LEARNING OBJECTIVES AS REFLECTED IN THE NEWS
Learning Objective 3: You will understand crimes that interfere with government services.	A former Texas Alcoholic Beverage Commission (TABC) employee is suing the agency for improperly firing him, claiming he was told to stop investigating violations at a bar the lawsuit says a state senator partly owned. The lawsuit claims Stokke was fired after reporting Sen. Joan Huffman's "public corruption and obstruction of justice," as well as TABC employees' "obstruction of justice and falsification of government documents" to a federal prosecutor, an FBI agent and a TABC investigator. The lawsuit states that TABC employees told Stokke "to dismiss, and delete from the commission's records . . . digital or paper documentation of the suspected violations [which included] multiple aggravated breaches of the peace." "These claims are false and have no merit, and are not deserving of any further comment," Huffman said in a prepared statement. (*Dallas News*, May 8, 2018)
Learning Objective 4: You will understand cybercrimes and attendant public harm.	Georgia has made cybersecurity headlines twice in recent months for two isolated cases, each questioning how organizations should respond in the aftermath of a cyberattack. Not long after Atlanta disclosed a citywide ransomware attack, the state government proposed a cybercrimes bill that was met with security industry criticism . . . Proposers of Georgia's vetoed "hack back" bill thought it would ultimately benefit the cybersecurity community. Hack back bills are founded on the same grounds as any other law designed for self-preservation . . . the bill would have legalized an organization's right to hack a perceived attacker's systems in retaliation. Experts widely agree bills legalizing hacking back are simply "a desire primarily born out of frustration." (*CIO Dive*, May 29, 2018)
Learning Objective 5: You will know the relevant statutes to prosecute terrorism.	A federal grand jury in January indicted Everitt Aaron Jameson on a charge of attempting to provide material support and resources to a designated foreign terrorist organization and distributing information related to destructive devices . . . Jameson offered his military training with the M-16 and AK-47 assault weapons, at least $400 a month in support of "The Cause" and a deadly plan to use explosives and gunfire to kill people on Christmas Day in San Francisco. (*Modesto Bee* [CA], April 24, 2018)

Chapter-Opening Case Study: Don Is Looking for an Easy Way Out

Don was looking for a lazy man's way to make money. He had downloaded the Tor application on his computer that concealed his identity as he surfed the Web. While clicking, he found "Backpage," a website that had photos of people offering to exchange sex for money. **(Rule of Law [ROL]: Prostitution is exchanging sexual services for something of value.)** He also found the "NarcoBoss" site, which was offering for sale "2 grams China white synthetic heroin fentanyl mix." **(ROL: Computer crimes are those in which computers are used to facilitate criminal activity.)** While Web surfing, Don came across a website showing photographs of young people who spoke about the glory of fighting against those who oppress the weak. The speeches implored,

"It is better to die fighting for a noble cause than to live on our knees," and the speakers asked for financial support to overthrow the local government. **(ROL: Terrorism is using illegal means to achieve illegitimate political objectives.)** Don donated $1,000 to the online group. Don's online activity attracted the attention of federal law enforcement agents. When agents traced Don's Internet service provider (ISP) address to his home, they arrived and interrogated Don. Don was afraid of going to jail and took $1,000 out of his pocket and said to agent Wolf, "If you just walk out of here now and don't arrest me, this money is yours." Agent Wolf took the money and walked away. **(ROL: Bribery is exchanging something of public value for personal gain; obstruction of justice is the willful interference with judicial, administrative, or legislative functions.)** Agent Banks, however, did arrest Don and placed him in the local jail. When they heard about Don's illegal activities, Don's neighbors gathered downtown at the jail and clapped loudly while they sang fight songs in an effort to bring Don to justice. An officer ordered the crowd to disperse, and they refused. **(ROL: Breach of the peace is disorderly conduct and a refusal to obey a lawful order.)** What will happen to Don's case?

CRIMES AGAINST THE PUBLIC

Gambling

Gambling is placing money, bets, and wagers that a certain outcome in a game of chance or sporting event will occur. The federal and state governments make gambling illegal because of its association with organized crime and, to a lesser extent, to try and prevent addictive behavior among those who can least afford to gamble. In the past, bookmaking operations and sports betting were neighborhood affairs. States have legalized certain types of gambling, such as participating in multistate lotteries and betting on animal races. State governments garner public support for their gambling activities by linking proceeds from gambling to activities that benefit the public, such as education (in Missouri) or programs for senior citizens (in Pennsylvania). Native American Tribes have their own sovereign law and operate gambling casinos and entertainment resorts on their land, in Connecticut, Arizona, and other states.

Gambling on the Internet is very lucrative, and like most Internet-based activities, it is very difficult to control through law enforcement activities. On October 14, 2006, President George W. Bush signed the Unlawful Internet Gambling Enforcement Act, which makes it illegal for American banks to transfer money to online gambling sites.[1] The law prohibits "businesses from accepting credit cards, checks, or other bank instruments from gamblers who illegally bet over the Internet." Many online gambling sites operate internationally and skirt the law by having American banks transfer funds to foreign banks, which then distribute the money to the gambling sites. According to scholar Ronald J. Rychlak, enacting laws to regulate online gambling stems from several threats:[2]

> **Rule of Law:** *Mala prohibita* crimes are crimes only because lawmakers define the activity as criminal.

1. Underage gamblers can easily access Internet sites.

2. Internet casinos can engage in fraud by not paying their customers.

3. An increase in isolated (from one's own home) video gambling ("whose addictive nature has been compared to crack cocaine") is possible.

4. There may be a drain on tax revenue paid by state casinos.

As discussed in Chapter 1, the State of New Jersey successfully sued the federal government in overturning the Professional and Amateur Sports Protection Act of 2006,[3] the law prohibiting sports betting in all states except Nevada, on the grounds that the U.S. Constitution's Tenth Amendment forbids the federal government from compelling states to enforce federal law in *Murphy v. National Collegiate Athletic Association* (2018).[4] Sports gambling has traditionally been illegal because of the threat that wagering on games might infect the integrity of the contest.

Famous baseball player Pete Rose was banned from the game for life for betting on games while he managed the Cincinnati Reds. But many National Football League (NFL) teams have sponsorship deals with casinos or state lotteries. On the day that the U.S. Supreme Court announced its ruling in the *Murphy* case, Rich Muny, president of the Poker Players Alliance, said:

> Today marks an important date for the future of gaming in the United States . . .
> The future of sports betting will continue to rely on internet and mobile technologies, and this is also true for all gaming. Now more than ever, states should take control of unregulated internet poker and sports betting and create systems that protect adult consumers and provide governments with new streams of revenue.[5]

Typical law enforcement activities will remain concentrated on local illegal games of chance while federal law enforcement will focus on the money laundering associated with illegal international gaming.

Prostitution

Often called "the world's oldest profession," prostitution is typically defined as "the market exchange of sex for money." Scholars Balos and Fellows write, "We use the term 'money' for simplicity but intend it to encompass both money and money's worth so as not to exclude bartering situations in which sex is exchanged for shelter, drugs, or other goods or services."[6] The term *john* was invented by women in the business to convey the notion that men who purchase sex are ubiquitous and indistinguishable from one another. Prostitution continues to survive "because it offers a commodity that cannot be readily found in other sexual arenas. That commodity involves the marketplace exchange of money for the unemotional provision of sexual gratification with no strings attached."[7] It is also a crime to live off the earnings of a prostitute.

Prostitution is erroneously called a victimless crime because it appears that the two parties are engaging in consensual sexual conduct, but studies show that sex workers are a vulnerable population. Most sex workers have a history of childhood physical and sexual abuse, many were recruited into the trade at age 12 or 13 years old, and they have an extraordinarily high rate of homelessness, drug use, and victimization by physical and sexual assaults.[8] Sex workers can be either male or female, but their customers are overwhelmingly male. Examine a typical law criminalizing sex work and note the list of common behaviors of sex workers who must attract customers off the street, to be criminal.

> **Rule of Law: Prostitution is exchanging sexual services for a thing of value.**

California Penal Code -§653.20: Loitering with the Intent to Commit Prostitution

For purposes of this chapter, the following definitions apply:

(a) "Commit prostitution" means to engage in sexual conduct for money or other consideration, but does not include sexual conduct engaged in as a part of any stage performance, play, or other entertainment open to the public . . .

   (a) (1) Except as specified in paragraph (2), it is unlawful for any person to loiter in any public place with the intent to commit prostitution. This intent is evidenced by acting in a manner and under circumstances that openly demonstrate the purpose of inducing, enticing, or soliciting prostitution, or procuring another to commit prostitution.

   (2) Notwithstanding paragraph (1), this subdivision does *not* apply to a child under 18 years of age who is alleged to have engaged in conduct that would, if committed by an adult, violate this subdivision.

Notice California's prostitution law excludes minors from criminal punishment; there has been a paradigm shift in criminal justice to recognize children in the sex trade as exploited victims rather than willing actors. California's law outlawing loitering, and many like it, is becoming obsolete as the negotiating and arranging of commercial sex acts routinely happens online. Because prostitution is viewed as a public nuisance, most people arrested for such crimes spend little to no time in jail and are often released with minimal bail. If convicted, they usually serve light sentences. In Las Vegas, Nevada, prostitution is legal and heavily regulated.

Human Trafficking

Human trafficking is a term often used interchangeably with the sex trafficking of children, but the United Nations describes the practice as forcing a person to work either as free labor or in the trade for commercial sex by the threat or use of force, coercion, abduction, by fraud, deception, or the abuse of power.[9] The enactment of the Victims of Trafficking and Violence Protection Act of 2000 (TVPA) focused on immigrants brought into the United States for mistreatment as sex workers or cheap labor.[10] The federal law makes it a crime to recruit, entice, harbor, transport, provide, or obtain a minor to engage in commercial sex acts or to financially benefit from the victims. Shortly after TVPA was enacted, all 50 states passed laws criminalizing human trafficking with exclusive focus on the victims of the child sex trade but not forced labor.[11] Forced labor as human trafficking is often overlooked as a 2011 Department of Justice (DOJ) report of 2,500 federal cases of trafficking revealed 82% of the prosecutions were for sex-related crimes, and half of the victims were minors. Given that choices must be made where to spend criminal justice resources, catching and punishing those who traffic in minors for sex receive the highest priority.

Drug and Alcohol Offenses

Illegal Drugs

The history of criminalizing illegal drug possession and use has been a hodgepodge effort of legal reform. In the early 20th century, opiates and cocaine were legal medicine. To limit opiate ingestion and the addiction often associated with opium use, Congress passed the Pure Food and Drug Act of 1906,[12] which was

> a direct effort to place some federal controls on patent medicines that contained opiates, cocaine, and other drugs. By requiring manufacturers of over-the-counter patent medicines to label their products and to disclose the amount of drugs contained in them, the government hoped to greatly reduce the use of such medicines.[13]

The next federal effort at drug control was the Harrison Act in 1914, which allowed certain opiates to be used as medicine while also criminalizing their sale and possession. The Marijuana Tax Act, passed in 1937, criminalized the sale of marijuana, a drug associated with criminal activity. There was little, if any, scientific data or research to support any definitive conclusions about the effects of recreational drug use, other than the addictive nature of such use, but illegal drug use was soon commonplace in American society. From the 1940s to the 1970s, avant-garde artists, musicians, and filmmakers began to explore and advertise the liberating effects of drugs. College students not only smoked marijuana freely but also experimented with lysergic acid diethylamide (LSD) and other mind-altering substances. Many military veterans came back from Vietnam and Laos with heroin addictions.

When the American middle class was affected with drug use and addiction—problems formerly believed to be the exclusive province of the inner-city poor—President Nixon advanced an aggressive law enforcement and drug treatment approach as a way to reduce drug-related crime. In 1970, Congress passed the Comprehensive Drug Abuse and Controlled Substances Act (Controlled Substances Act), which

Springboard for Discussion

The Court said in *Cleveland v. United States*, 329 U.S. 14 (1946), "Whether an act is immoral within the meaning of the statute is not to be determined by the accused's concepts of morality. Congress has provided the standard." Do you agree with the Court? Which segment of society has the power to define morality?

Rule of Law: Human trafficking is the coercing of people to work in the sex trade or as forced labor.

Rule of Law: Drug and alcohol offenses are crimes associated with the manufacture, possession, or distribution of illegal drugs or alcohol consumption.

consolidated the numerous federal drug laws then in existence. President Nixon also created the Drug Enforcement Administration (DEA) to oversee federal enforcement of federal drug laws. The new effort to combat illegal drugs was a multipronged approach that attacked the importation of drugs from foreign countries, incapacitated the distribution chain from supplier to street dealer, and provided prevention and treatment programs for the buyers and addicts.

Federal drug policy shifted dramatically in the 1980s and 1990s with the enactment of mandatory minimum prison sentences for drug offenses. The shift away from a comprehensive approach of education and drug prevention programs to harsher sentences and punitive sanctions led to an explosion in the prison population, especially among the poor. The new sentencing schemes had the most impact on the powder cocaine/crack trade, which, for many years, had a 100:1 ratio under the federal sentencing guidelines; that is, for every 100 grams of powder cocaine, an offender who possessed crack (cocaine diluted with additives) would receive the same 5-year minimum prison sentence per 1 gram. In 2010, the Fair Sentencing Act reduced the sentencing disparity between the two forms of the drug, and many defendants who had been imprisoned for nonviolent crack possession were released from prison. Figure 6.1 is the federal sentencing guidelines statistics for drug offenders for the fiscal year 2016.

Figure 6.1 Federal Sentencing Guidelines Statistics for Drug Trafficking Offenses, Fiscal Year 2016

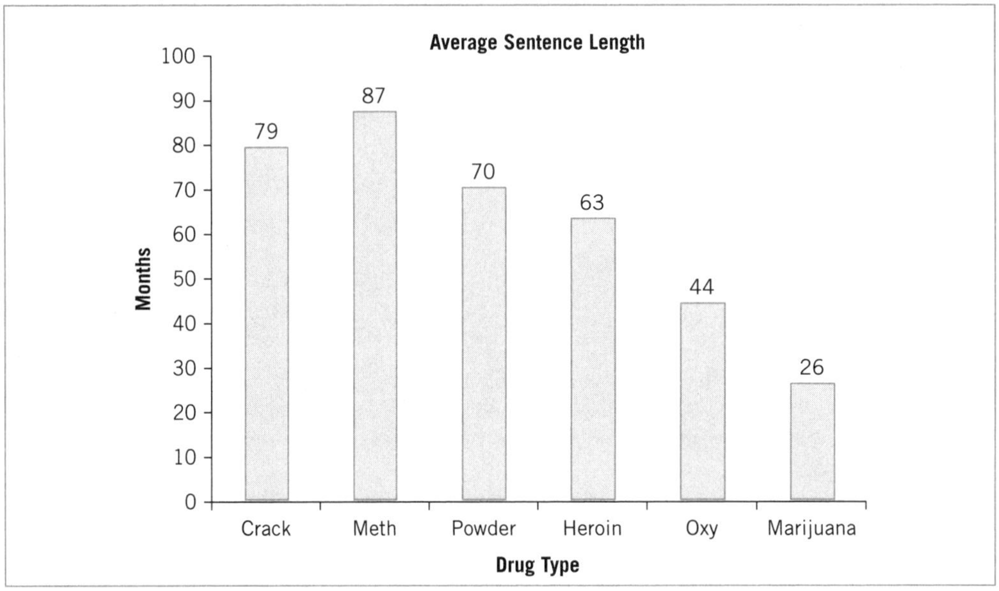

Source: U.S. Sentencing Commission.

MAKING THE COURTROOM CONNECTION

According to the U.S. Sentencing Commission, in 2016 85% of drug offenders were male and almost half of the drug trafficking defendants had little or no prior criminal history. Of particular note, 45.5% of offenders were facing mandatory minimum sentences which, depending on type and weight of drug, can be 5, 10, or 20 years. That is, the defendant will serve no less than the mandatory minimum term of years. But defense attorneys will often negotiate plea bargains with prosecutors. Under the federal sentencing guidelines, only the prosecutor can make what is commonly known as a "5k.1 Motion," referencing the guideline provision that allows the government to recommend an escape from the mandatory minimum, most often because the offender has "provided substantial assistance in the investigation or prosecution of other offenders," which in a typical multiparty, drug conspiracy means one defendant agrees to testify against his co-conspirators. According to the 2016 statistics, from the 45.5% facing mandatory minimums, 21.66% of them helped the government, thereby escaping the minimum sentence they were facing.

Today's drug epidemic is addiction to heroin, prescription painkillers, and synthetic opioid known as fentanyl. From 2000 to 2015, according to the federal Centers for Disease Control and Prevention (CDC), "More than half a million people died from drug overdoses [and] 91 Americans die every day from an opioid overdose." The burden on combatting rampant addiction and overdoses falls most heavily on the states. For example, from 2011 to 2015 there were 4 billion opioid pills prescribed across Ohio despite no appreciable increase in the amount of pain patients reported experiencing. Law enforcement efforts to control the flow of illicit fentanyl has been hampered by the proliferation of dealers on the Dark Web, an encrypted Web browser that allows anonymous commercial transactions, often for illegal items. Most illegal synthetic opioids are produced in Asia. On the site AlphaBay, drug dealer BenzoChems revealed that "routing packages through Hong Kong, and then through the United States Postal Service, was the most efficient method of transit."[14]

Ross Ulbricht, the founder of Silk Road, one of the first Dark Web exchanges for illegal goods and services, was sentenced in federal court to life in prison for the quantity of illegal drugs sold on his site. Ulbricht went by the alias Dred Pirate Roberts, after a book and movie character in *The Princess Bride*. When Ulbricht argued that his sentence was too severe, in part, because selling drugs online reduced the risk of street crime often associated with the drug trade, the court summarily dismissed his argument noting that Ulbricht facilitated the sale of over $183 million dollars' worth of drugs and was willing to commit murder to protect his enterprise. By focusing on the general deterrent (preventing crime by making an example of others) effects of a life sentence, the court upheld Ulbricht's conviction. Read the case excerpt below and see if you agree with the court.

UNITED STATES V. ULBRICHT, 858 F.3D 71 (2D CIR. 2017)

REASONING: . . . Reasonable people may and do disagree about the social utility of harsh sentences for the distribution of controlled substances, or even of criminal prohibition of their sale and use at all. It is very possible that, at some future point, we will come to regard these policies as tragic mistakes and adopt less punitive and more effective methods of reducing the incidence and costs of drug use. At this point in our history, however, the democratically-elected representatives of the people have opted for a policy of prohibition, backed by severe punishment. That policy results in the routine incarceration of many traffickers for extended periods of time. This case involves a defendant who stood at one remove from the trade, who did not for the most part dirty his hands with the actual possession and sale of drugs and other contraband that his site offered. But he did take a cut of the proceeds, in exchange for making it easier for such drugs to be purchased and sold, in a way that may well have expanded the market by allowing more people access to drugs in greater quantities than might otherwise have been available to them. In the routine instances of sentencing drug sellers, the dangerous aspects of the trade are close to the surface and require little emphasis. In this case, a reminder of the consequences of facilitating such transactions was perhaps more necessary, particularly because Ulbricht claimed that his site made the drug trade safer, and he appeared to contest the legitimacy of the laws he violated.

The court described the crime as a "planned, comprehensive, and deliberate scheme . . . which posed serious danger to public health and to our communities." Silk Road was a "worldwide criminal drug enterprise with a massive geographic scope." The fact that Ulbricht operated the site from behind a computer, rather than in person like a more prototypical drug kingpin, does not make his crime less serious or less dangerous. Moreover, Silk Road uniquely expanded the drug market by providing an easy avenue for people to become first-time drug users and dealers. Because drugs were shipped to customers in the mail, Silk Road brought "drugs to communities that previously may have had no access to such drugs . . . in such quantities."

The quantity and nature of the drugs sold on Silk Road are staggering. According to [Ulbricht's presentence report], from 2011 through 2013, Silk Road customers transacted in approximately $183 million worth of illegal drugs. At the time the government shut down Silk Road on October 2, 2013, there were approximately 13,802 listings for controlled substances on the website. Of those listings, there were 643 listings for cocaine-based products, 305 for LSD products, and 261 for methamphetamine products. The drugs were sold mostly for individual, personal use, but some drugs such as heroin and cocaine were also available in "multi-kilogram quantities." The available drugs were not limited to heroin, narcotics, synthetic marijuana, and

(Continued)

(Continued)

other dangerous but recreational substances. For example, after being told that cyanide was "the most well known assassination suicide [sic] poison out there," Ulbricht allowed vendors to sell it on Silk Road despite its singular, deadly purpose. As the district court noted, despite earlier protestations that Silk Road would not allow the sale of products that could be used to inflict deliberate harm on others, it took Ulbricht all of six minutes to decide "that it is okay to sell cyanide," in exchange for the customary cut of the proceeds.

Accordingly, while a life sentence for selling drugs alone would give pause, we would be hard put to find such a sentence beyond the bounds of reason for drug crimes of this magnitude.[15] But the facts of this case involve much more than simply facilitating the sale of narcotics.

The district court found by a preponderance of the evidence that Ulbricht commissioned at least five murders in the course of protecting Silk Road's anonymity, a finding that Ulbricht does not challenge in this appeal. Ulbricht discussed those anticipated murders callously and casually in his journal and in his communications with the purported assassin Redandwhite. For example, in connection with the first hit, he wrote to Redandwhite that "FriendlyChemist is a liability and I wouldn't mind if he was executed." In the course of negotiating the price for the killing, DPR [Dread Pirate Roberts] claimed that "[n]ot long ago, I had a clean hit done for $80k," but that he had "only ever commissioned the one other hit, so I'm still learning this market." He then paid $150,000 in Bitcoins for the murder, and he received what purported to be photographic documentation of its completion. Ulbricht then wrote in his journal that he "got word that the blackmailer was executed," before returning quickly to other tasks associated with running the site.

Both the sentencing *amici* [friends of the court briefs, usually submitted by parties with a special interest in the outcome of a particular case, even though they are not a party to the case] and Ulbricht further contend that the district court placed too much weight on the notion of general deterrence in meting out the life sentence. . . . Ulbricht identifies several lucrative dark markets that have emerged since Silk Road's demise in 2013. In his view, the existence of multiple copycat Tor-based illegal marketplaces proves that general deterrence is illusory and that the district court placed too much weight on that factor.

Although those arguments have some support among scholars and researchers, the ability of a sentence to "afford adequate deterrence to criminal conduct" is a factor that district courts are required by Congress to consider in arriving at the appropriate [federal] sentence. Congress, moreover, has not concluded that the persistence of narcotics crimes is a reason to abandon the efforts to deter them by lengthy sentences.

CONCLUSION: [Life sentence affirmed.]

Springboard for Discussion

In February 2016, the federal government sued Apple Corporation to disclose its encryption code to bypass security on an iPhone 5c used in the December 2015 terror attack in San Bernardino, California. Apple refused because the code was their intellectual property. Do you agree that encryption services that hide their users' identity or security features on electronic devices should be immune from government intrusion for law enforcement purposes? Why or why not?

In the chapter-opening case study, Don used a computer to facilitate his illegal access to the "Backpage" Web prostitution service and to purchase illegal drugs.

Alcohol Offenses

The public harm associated with illegal drugs apply in equal force to alcohol offenses, which include driving under the influence and the attendant social costs of alcohol addiction. Alcohol offenses cover a wide range of behaviors from being intoxicated in public to supplying minors with alcohol. All states have laws that punish adults who corrupt minors by providing drugs or alcohol. Massachusetts law provides that "whoever furnishes . . . alcohol for a person under 21-years of age shall be punished by a fine of not more than $2,000 or by imprisonment for not more than one year or both."[16] In 2004, Mr. and Mrs. Moulton of Danvers, Massachusetts, allowed their teenage daughter and her friends to drink Jack Daniels whiskey, beer, rum, and other intoxicants at a party at their house to celebrate after their high school prom.[17] The Moultons took all of the kids' car keys, and Mr. Moulton even joined the kids' celebration. For their efforts in trying, in their view, to protect the kids from drinking and driving, the parents were convicted of illegally supplying alcohol to minors and received probation for 18 months, were fined $500, and were ordered to complete 40 hours of community service. Many states have laws that make it a crime for an adult to furnish liquor to individuals who are not yet 21 years old. Such laws can be difficult to enforce, considering that 18-year-olds are legal adults.

Drinking and Driving. In the mid-1980s, the federal government responded to the great number of drunk-driving fatalities by enacting the National Minimum Drinking Age Act (NMDA),[18] which tied federal funding for state transportation needs to the state raising its minimum drinking age to 21 years old. **Driving under the influence** (DUI) laws generally punish people for operating a motor vehicle (e.g., car, truck, or boat) while under the influence of alcohol. Often, to be convicted of being legally impaired, the driver's blood alcohol content (BAC) must typically be at least 0.08, as determined by a breathalyzer test administered on the scene or by a blood test taken at a hospital. Some state statutes, such as Arizona's DUI law, which follows, use the concept of "controlling" the vehicle as opposed to "driving" the vehicle.

> **Rule of Law:** An offender's blood alcohol content sufficient to sustain a conviction for driving under the influence is dependent on state law.

Arizona Revised Statutes §28-1381.

Driving or actual physical control while under the influence

It is unlawful for a person to drive or be in actual physical control of a vehicle in this state under any of the following circumstances:

1. While under the influence of intoxicating liquor, any drug, a vapor-releasing substance containing a toxic substance or any combination of liquor, drugs or vapor-releasing substances if the person is impaired to the slightest degree.

2. If the person has an alcohol concentration of 0.10 or more within two hours of driving or being in actual physical control of the vehicle and the alcohol concentration results from alcohol consumed either before or while driving or being in actual physical control of the vehicle.

3. While there is any drug defined in section 13-3401 or its metabolite in the person's body.

States have a range of punishments that escalate in range of severity with either (a) the amount of alcohol in the driver's system, or (b) the number of DUI offenses committed. As discussed in Chapter 8 about warrantless searches, a warrant is required to take blood from someone suspected of drunk driving, but a warrant is not required to give a breathalyzer test. In many states, a driver suspected of driving under the influence who refuses a breathalyzer test automatically forfeits his or her license to drive for a certain period.

People who drink and drive and kill innocent people are almost never charged with murder because they lack the specific intent to kill. If there is a death that results from a drunk-driving accident, the driver is typically charged with negligent homicide or involuntary manslaughter because of the paradox (opposed to common sense) that, by consuming an abundance of alcohol, the person's *mens rea* is impaired, which negates the specific intent to cause harm.

Firearm Offenses

Citizens have a constitutional right protected by the Second Amendment to own and possess firearms subject to a number of state and federal regulations. The Gun Control Act of 1968 is the federal law that regulates gun ownership and, like every federal law, is dependent on an interstate commerce nexus.[19] The federal gun law prohibits the interstate transfer of firearms and limits

Rule of Law: The Second Amendment grants citizens the right to possess firearms, subject to federal and state regulations.

the transfer and sale of weapons to licensed firearm dealers. The Brady Handgun Violence Prevention Act[20] was named after President Reagan's press secretary, James Brady, who in March 1981 was critically wounded by a handgun during the assassination attempt on Reagan's life. "The Brady Bill" mandated a waiting period before people could purchase a handgun in any state, a requirement no longer in effect now that states can run National Instant Criminal Background Check System (commonly known as NICS) to get background information quickly. Gun ownership is a highly regulated and licensed activity, and some people are categorically prohibited from legally owning firearms; these people include convicted felons, people addicted to drugs or any controlled substance, service members who received dishonorable discharges, fugitives from justice, and the mentally ill.[21] Despite the many federal laws that regulate weapons, state and local law enforcement are responsible for the majority of firearm licensing and registration requirements.

The legal history of the "right to bear arms" was dominated until 2010 by the U.S. Supreme Court's refusal to recognize a constitutional right for an individual to own firearms. The language of the Second Amendment says, "A well regulated Militia being necessary to the security of a free State, the right of the people to keep and bear Arms shall not be infringed."

The District of Columbia (D.C.) is a federal enclave, not a state, which sits on 68 square miles carved out of land ceded by Maryland and Virginia and is the seat of our national government. In 1975 the District government prohibited its residents from legally possessing firearms in their homes. If they did own firearms, for example as part of their job, the law required the weapons remain nonfunctional at all times by disassembly or by placement of a trigger lock.[22] Dick Heller was a special police officer working at the Thurgood Marshall federal judiciary building and a D.C. resident. Heller applied to register his firearm for lawful use in his home for self-defense. When D.C. denied Heller's request, Heller sued, claiming a violation of his Second Amendment right. When the U.S. Supreme Court decided the case in Heller's favor, for the first time in history, the Court recognized an individual's right to bear arms (*District of Columbia v. Heller*, 2008).[23]

By examining, in part, the debate surrounding the writing of the Second Amendment and comparable state constitutions, the high Court held the D.C. restrictions made it impossible for Heller to exercise his right to self-defense in his home. The Court found the Second Amendment's first militia-related clause was prefatory (an introduction), but the second clause about individual rights was operational. Thus, the Court said the first clause announced the purpose of the amendment was to maintain a militia, but an individual could bear arms without connection to militia activity. Because D.C. laws restricted rights that other people in the country enjoyed, the D.C. gun prohibition law could not withstand constitutional scrutiny.

The *Heller* decision left open the question whether the Court's precedent would apply to the states, as D.C. is controlled exclusively by federal law. In *McDonald v. City of Chicago* (2010),[24] the high Court said yes, a ruling the Court also extended to stun guns.[25] But every state's gun laws are different, and students would be wise to research their relevant jurisdiction. As of this writing, a bill to make conceal and carry laws universal across state lines has passed the House of Representatives, but its final fate is yet uncertain.

APPLYING THE LAW TO THE FACTS

Does the Second Amendment Trump Federal or State Gun Regulations?

The Facts: Freddy was a police officer in Indianapolis who was convicted of misdemeanor domestic violence. State and federal laws prevent those convicted of intimate partner violence from possessing firearms. Freddy sued saying his right to earn a living as an officer trumped licensing laws on gun possession and that the Constitution's Second Amendment is a greater force of law than state and federal regulations. Will Freddy win his case?

The Law: No. Freddy can be legally disqualified from possessing a firearm even though his job requires it as a condition of employment.[26]

Breach of the Peace

Vagrancy and Panhandling

It is not a crime to depend on the generosity and kindness of strangers. Those who **panhandle** and ask people for money on the street are protected by the First Amendment's free speech rights.[27] Similarly, **vagrancy** is the crime of wandering aimlessly with no visible means of support. For example, Mississippi law states:

Mississippi Code Annotated §97-35-29. Tramps, Definition

> Any male person over sixteen years of age, and not blind, who shall go about from place to place begging and asking subsistence by charity, and all who stroll over the country without lawful occasion, and can give no account of their conduct consistent with good citizenship, shall be held to be tramps.

Most state laws outlawing vagrancy and panhandling are broad and intended to punish a wide variety of undesirable behaviors. Whereas anyone can ask someone for money on the street and they may refuse and walk away, one cannot stalk an automatic teller machine (ATM) or otherwise trap would-be donors because harassing behavior is threatening and can be punished.

> **Rule of Law: The First Amendment grants the right to ask people for money and to peaceably assemble, but no such gathering may advance criminal objectives such as gang activity.**

Disorderly Conduct and Riot

People have a First Amendment right to assemble in a peaceful manner. There are times when crowds become unruly, and there are various laws to punish people for their behavior when they are in a group. These laws are often lumped under the definition of disorderly conduct. The crime of **disorderly conduct** is committed when people get together and **disturb the peace** but do not necessarily intend to incite violence. Such conduct may include **breach of the peace**, in which a party or some other gathering produces too much noise, or if one or more people refuse to follow a police officer's lawful command. A representative breach of peace statute (reprinted in part here) is Mississippi's law criminalizing conduct or language that may be "insulting or profane."

Mississippi Code Annotated §97-35-15. Disturbance of the public peace or the peace of others:

> Any person who disturbs the public peace, or the peace of others, by violent, or loud, or insulting, or profane, or indecent, or offensive, or boisterous conduct or language, or by intimidation, or seeking to intimidate any other person or persons, or by conduct either calculated to provoke a breach of the peace, or by conduct which may lead to a breach of the peace, or by any other act, shall be guilty of a misdemeanor.

Noting the difference between lawful assembly and protest and illegal breaches of the peace and riots is important to prevent unlawful arrests. Riots are different from unruly crowds because the collective *mens rea* of the group is to terrorize the community or to commit criminal mischief (i.e., the destruction of personal or public property). Riots are dangerous because both the act of rioting and the law enforcement response to suppress the riot may result in personal injury or death. The basic elements of **riot** under common law are

1. At least three people

2. Sharing a common purpose

3. To commit violence or to terrify others.[28]

Riot is commonly charged as a catch-all offense in connection with other criminal acts such as assault, battery, and even murder. For instance, in 1959 in North Carolina, striking mill workers threw rocks and bottles at replacement workers crossing the picket line. Because the strikers unlawfully assembled with the intention to commit acts of violence, their convictions for riot and prison sentences were upheld as lawful in *State v. Moseley* (1959).[29] In the chapter-opening case study, Don's neighbors committed a breach of the peace, but not a riot, when they clapped loudly marching down the street and refused to disperse after they were lawfully commanded to do so.

Gangs

In criminologist Albert Cohen's book *Delinquent Boys: The Culture of the Gang* (1955), Cohen presented the theory that young, lower-class males, unable to assimilate into the middle class, turned their frustrations outward to defy conventional norms. As they bonded together, young men turned to property, economic, and vice crimes (prostitution and drugs) not only to elevate their status within the group but to have a steady stream of income.[30] Much of the early work in trying to curb delinquent behavior led to federal policies aimed at creating education and work opportunities for youth, embodied in the Juvenile Delinquency Prevention and Control Act of 1968.[31] The proliferation of drugs and guns during the 1980s brought stopping gangs and gang violence to the forefront of law enforcement efforts. Most gangs form along ethnic and geographic boundaries, such as California's African American "Crips" and "Bloods," El Salvadorian "MS 13," Chicago's "Latin Kings," to the South's White nationalist "Simon City Royals," of which one former member, Benny Ivey, said, "A lot of us were raised in the pits, and that's where almost all gang life begins."[32] Despite no single definition, the U.S. DOJ says a gang is a group of three or more people who adopt a group identity through identifiable clothing, hand signs, graffiti, and nicknames, which they use to create fear or intimidation.

To curb gang activity, many states formed anti-gang units in local law enforcement or passed anti-loitering statutes that prohibited young people from congregating on street corners. The laws must be narrowly tailored to survive a challenge to the right to peaceably assemble. The high Court invalidated an anti-gang statute in *City of Chicago v. Morales* (1999), because the law was too vague in determining who was a "gang" member, thereby giving law enforcement officers too much discretion to criminalize behavior protected by the First Amendment.[33] Gang behavior as monitored by the National Gang Center is often prosecuted under racketeering statutes to punish the variety of crimes commonly committed by street gangs, drug dealing, prostitution, robbery, burglary, and murder.[34] A common statute is illustrated by Maryland's definition of a gang.

Maryland Code Annotated §9-801, Definitions

(c) Criminal gang means a group or association of three or more persons whose members:

   (1) individually or collectively engage in a pattern of criminal gang activity;

   (2) have as one of their primary objectives or activities the commission of one or more underlying crimes, including acts by juveniles that would be underlying crimes if committed by adults; and

   (3) have in common an overt or covert organizational or command structure.

. . .

(e) Pattern of criminal gang activity—means the commission of, attempted commission of, conspiracy to commit, or solicitation of two or more underlying crimes or acts by a juvenile that would be an underlying crime if committed by an adult, provided the crimes or acts were not part of the same incident.

Many anti-gang activities involve local law enforcement partnering with former gang members and community leaders to intervene in many turf disputes or to diffuse retaliatory violence to reduce gang-related homicides. The gang program model, with some success in Boston and Chicago, is to balance law enforcement suppression activities with providing social services to help young people escape the social pressures that make gang membership a rite of passage.

CRIMES THAT INTERFERE WITH GOVERNMENT SERVICES

Bribery

As discussed in Chapter 5, public corruption is often prosecuted under the wire fraud statute as a theft of "honest public services." One of the most common forms of government corruption is bribery.

> **Rule of Law:** Bribery is exchanging something of public value for personal gain.

The federal statute provides the following elements of bribery in 18 U.S.C. §201:

1. A public official must be involved: who is a "person [who] occupies a position of public trust with official federal responsibilities;"[35]

2. The defendant must have offered to give or receive a "thing of value": interpreted by the defendant's subjective view of what is valuable. What one offender deems valuable, another might not think so. If public official behavior is influenced by the thing of value, it satisfies this element.

3. The act must involve something official: if the official acted in a way that was legally permissible within her scope of employment, even if the act she took was not part of her defined duties, she could be held criminally responsible if the government proves she took the official act in exchange for a thing of value.

To determine whether bribery has been committed, courts examine the party's *mens rea* and intent in giving the thing of value to the official, which distinguishes the act from merely presenting a gift. Bribery requires the specific intent to influence a public official's actions and is different from an illegal gratuity, which is payment for a public act that may or may not happen.

Whereas "theft of honest services" prosecutions included a wide range of fraudulent conduct, the high Court limited the "theft" of intangible honest services in wire fraud prosecutions of corrupt public officials to bribery or receiving kickbacks only in deciding the appeal of Jeffrey Skilling. Skilling was the chief financial officer of the Enron Corporation, once the seventh largest company in the country. Initially Enron provided energy, gas, and electricity; later, it branched out into broadband Internet and other ventures designed to infiltrate the global economy. When regulators gave Enron permission to use mark-to-market accounting, a practice that allows companies to count ideas as profits, Enron began "cooking" the books (i.e., posting fraudulent numbers on ledger sheets to deceive the public about the financial health of the company) and recording anticipated earnings as real profit. When the company could no longer service its debt because the anticipated earnings never materialized, it had to file for bankruptcy and collapsed entirely within 7 months. The chief executives, Kenneth Lay, Jeffery Skilling, and Andrew Fastow, were charged with knowingly projecting false information that kept the stock prices high, which all three men and many more senior executives cashed in on, when in fact the shares were nearly valueless. Fastow became a government informant and testified against Skilling and Lay, who were both convicted on a number of fraud counts in May 2006. Lay died unexpectedly on July 5, 2006, and his death rendered his conviction null and void. Skilling was sentenced to 24 years and 4 months in prison, but parts of his case were overturned on appeal by the U.S. Supreme Court.[36] Because

Skilling had not bribed anyone and had not received a kickback in the Enron scheme to defraud, some of his charges were overturned on appeal; this was also the case for many others who had been similarly convicted.[37] A kickback is awarding a contract and getting a percentage in return (a "kick" back of some money to the one who helped procure the contract).

The federal bribery statute was at the heart of the defense for former Virginia governor Robert "Bob" McDonnell, who, while in office, accepted from businessman Jonnie Williams an opportunity to drive Williams's Ferrari, thousands of dollars to help pay for the catering at McDonnell's daughter's wedding, free rounds of golf at exclusive clubs, thousands of dollars in loans McDonnell failed to report, and a $6,500 Rolex inscribed with "71st Governor of Virginia." Williams was seeking favorable promotion by the state for his company Star Scientific's product Anatabloc. After a trial on fraud, bribery, and corruption charges, Governor McDonnell and his wife Maureen were convicted.

On appeal, the U.S. Supreme Court overturned the convictions, holding that an *official act* meant the exercise of some government function on a "question, matter, cause, suit, proceeding or controversy . . . pending or may by law be brought" before the public official.[38] Any acts McDonnell took on behalf of Williams's company Star Scientific, for example, "setting up a meeting, talking to another official, or organizing an event—without more—does not fit that definition of official act."[39] As the unanimous U.S. Supreme Court said in overturning former Virginia governor McDonnell's conviction, "There is no doubt that this case is distasteful; it may be worse than that. But our concern is not with tawdry tales of Ferraris, Rolexes, and ball gowns. It is instead with the broader legal implications of the Government's boundless interpretation of the federal bribery statute." In the chapter-opening case study, Don and Agent Wolf committed bribery when Don offered Agent Wolf $1,000 not to arrest him, both things of value to Don, and the agent accepted the money in exchange for a public service only he could provide, which is not to arrest Don (but Don was arrested anyway by Agent Banks).

APPLYING THE LAW TO THE FACTS

Is It Bribery?

The Facts: By the election of then Illinois senator Barack Obama to the presidency, the governor of Illinois, Rod Blagojevich, was legally entitled to appoint Obama's successor. Blagojevich sought to auction off the Senate position to the highest bidder, seeking $1.5 million in campaign contributions. With no takers, Blagojevich proposed to a friend that he would appoint to the Senate one of president-elect Obama's close associates, Valerie Jarrett (unbeknown to her), in exchange for a federal Cabinet position for himself.

Blagojevich was convicted on many counts related to public corruption. On appeal, the court examined if Blagojevich had committed bribery with his bid for a federal Cabinet position. Did Blagojevich commit bribery?

The Law: The appeals court said Blagojevich had not committed bribery for the Senate appointment because a "proposal to trade one public act for another, a form of logrolling, is fundamentally unlike the swap of an official act for a private payment."[40]

Obstruction of Justice, Perjury, and False Statements

Rule of Law: Obstruction of justice is the willful interference with judicial, administrative, or legislative functions.

Acts that interfere with the "administration of justice" interfere with the integrity of the criminal justice system, and the resulting distrust harms the public. Interrelated crimes that fall under the rubric of obstruction of justice include any act that interferes with judicial, administrative, or legislative proceeding by, for instance, destroying or altering physical evidence, procuring false testimony, or threatening witnesses, jurors, and others involved in official proceedings. Utah law, for example, defines obstruction of justice as any act taken with the "intent to hinder, delay, or prevent the investigation, apprehension, prosecution, conviction, or punishment of any person regarding conduct that constitutes a criminal offense."[41]

Perjury is willfully lying under oath in a judicial, administrative, or legislative proceeding. Some state laws, such as in Nebraska illustrated here, also punish affirming previous statements as true, knowing the previous statement was a lie.

> A person is guilty of perjury if, in any (a) official proceeding he or she makes a false statement under oath or equivalent affirmation, *or swears or affirms the truth of a statement previously made*, when the statement is material and he or she does not believe it to be true (emphasis added).[42]

The *mens rea* for perjury is specific intent to lie about a material fact, and the punishment is generally a felony. A related crime is the subornation of perjury, which is getting someone else to lie under oath to benefit the offender. The crime of making a false statement is to knowingly and willfully lie to a federal agent pursuant to 18 U.S.C. §1001. On December 1, 2017, the former national security adviser and retired army lieutenant general Michael Flynn pleaded guilty in federal court to one count of "willfully and knowingly" making "false, fictitious and fraudulent" statements when he lied to federal agents investigating General Flynn's foreign contacts during the presidential campaign of 2016.[43] Taken together, any act committed with the willful intent to derail an investigation, for example, by lying, misleading, or hiding people or facts from investigators to subvert the course of justice, is a crime.

Environmental Crimes

Criminal law and procedure students should have some familiarity with environmental laws and the criminal or civil liability that may attach to government actors or private entities that harm the public through pollution. Environmental crimes harm the public by polluting our common air and water supply. The Environmental Protection Agency (EPA) is the executive branch agency responsible for criminal and civil enforcement of environmental laws, but often criminal prosecutions are handled by the DOJ's Environmental Resource and Natural Division. The Clean Air Act (1970) requires at a minimum that "for a discrete set of pollutants and based on published air quality criteria that reflect the latest scientific knowledge, the EPA must establish uniform national standards at a level that is requisite to protect public health from the adverse effects of the pollutant in the ambient air."[44] As the name implies, the Clean Water Act (1972) is designed to protect people's welfare, health, and the environment by controlling how much pollution can legally be discharged in different waterways and navigable systems in the United States.[45] The criminal provisions are "public welfare legislation" because the Clean Water Act "is designed to protect the public from potentially harmful or injurious items," and it criminalizes "a type of conduct that a reasonable person should know is subject to stringent public regulation and may seriously threaten the community's health and safety."

In 2017, the Michigan attorney general charged at least six public health administrators for the City of Flint with involuntary manslaughter related to an outbreak of Legionnaires' disease believed to have killed as many as 12 people.[46] The city, in conjunction with state officials, in an effort to save money, switched their water supply to a source that flowed through contaminated pipes. After citizen complaints "that the water was cloudy and discolored in appearance and foul in taste and odor," city and state officials failed to take corrective action and failed to notify the public of the health hazards associated with water contamination, such as lead poisoning, which can cause irreversible brain damage in children. In addition to the criminal charges, residents sued the city in civil court as well.[47]

> **Rule of Law: Crimes that harm the environment can be committed by government actors or private entities.**

COMPUTER CRIMES

Computer Fraud Crimes

The federal government gives computer crime a broad definition. Computer crimes are "any violations of criminal law that involve a knowledge of computer technology for their perpetration, investigation, or prosecution."[48] Computer crimes cover a wide variety of activities, the nature and sophistication of which make them difficult to prosecute. "People may encrypt data so that even if law enforcement seizes or intercepts the data, they will be unable to understand its contents or use it as evidence. The nature of the Internet allows people to engage in criminal conduct online with virtual anonymity." Whereas there is no concrete definition of computer crime, there are three general areas of computer protection that criminal law statutes are designed to combat or protect.

1. Protection of privacy

2. Prosecution of economic crimes

3. Protection of intellectual property

Similar to federal statutes, many state statutes divide computer crimes into three categories: crimes in which a computer is the target, crimes in which a computer is a tool of the crime, and crimes for which a computer is incidental. First, a computer may be the object of a crime when computer hardware or software is stolen. Second, a computer may be the subject of the crime when it is the target of attack—for example, when spam, worms, viruses, and Trojan horses infect computer hard drives and software, rendering the computer inoperable. Such subject-type crimes are often committed by disgruntled business employees who want to cause maximum damage to their employer's ability to conduct business. Professional hackers and juveniles who may want to prove their intellectual superiority are also the types of offenders likely to commit subject-type computer offenses. Third, computers may be an instrument used to commit traditional crimes such as identity theft, child pornography, copyright infringement, and mail and wire fraud. Computers enable criminals to commit the same types of property, theft, or pornography crimes but in the different forum of the World Wide Web. The federal computer fraud statute is the typical prototype for state statutes and is reprinted in part here.

Rule of Law: Computer crimes are those in which a computer is used to commit the crime or in which a computer's integrity is violated.

---

18 U.S.C. §1030 Fraud and related activity in connection with computers

(a) Whoever—

   (1) having knowingly accessed a computer without authorization or exceeding authorized access . . .

   (2) intentionally accesses a computer without authorization or exceeds authorized access, and thereby obtains—

      (A) information contained in a financial record of a financial institution, or of a card issuer;

      (B) information from any department or agency of the United States; or

      (C) information from any protected computer;

   . . .

   (4) knowingly and with intent to defraud, accesses a protected computer without authorization, or exceeds authorized access, and by means of such conduct furthers the intended fraud and obtains anything of value . . .

   (5) (A) knowingly causes the transmission of a program, information, code, or command, and as a result of such conduct, intentionally causes damage without authorization, to a protected computer . . .

(B) intentionally accesses a protected computer without authorization, and as a result of such conduct, recklessly causes damage; or

(C) intentionally accesses a protected computer without authorization, and as a result of such conduct, causes damage and loss . . .

(6) knowingly and with intent to defraud traffics in any password or similar information through which a computer may be accessed without authorization, if

(A) such trafficking affects interstate or foreign commerce; or

(B) such computer is used by or for the Government of the United States; [or]

(7) with intent to extort from any person any money or other thing of value, transmits in interstate or foreign commerce any communication containing any—

(A) threat to cause damage to a protected computer;

(B) threat to obtain information from a protected computer without authorization or in excess of authorization or to impair the confidentiality of information obtained from a protected computer without authorization or by exceeding authorized access; or

(C) demand or request for money or other thing of value in relation to damage to a protected computer, where such damage was caused to facilitate the extortion;

. . . shall be punished . . . [10 years or 20 years depending upon crime of conviction, and a fine]

(e) As used in this section—

(1) the term "computer" means an electronic, magnetic, optical, electrochemical, or other high speed data processing device performing logical, arithmetic, or storage functions, and includes any data storage facility or communications facility directly related to or operating in conjunction with such device, but such term does not include an automated typewriter or typesetter, a portable hand held calculator, or other similar device.

Notice, as discussed in Chapter 1, the hook for federal jurisdiction is the Commerce Clause requirement that crimes cross state lines and affect interstate commerce, which is easy to prove if the offender uses wires (e.g., the Internet) to commit her crime. The type of harm that can be caused by a computer breach (hack), to be punishable as a felony under the federal statute §1030, can be summarized by an excerpt from law professor Orin S. Kerr's book, *Computer Crime Law* (2018), detailing the Senate Report where in 1983:

> A group of adolescents known as the "414 Gang" broke into the computer system at Memorial Sloan Kettering Cancer Center in New York. In doing so, they gained access to the radiation treatment records of 6,000 past and present cancer patients and had at their fingertips the ability to alter the radiation treatment levels that each patient received . . . Convictions are attainable [under §1030] without a showing that the victim was actually given an incorrect or harmful treatment . . . That his examination, diagnosis, treatment, or care was potentially changed or impaired is sufficient to warrant prosecution.[49]

The all-encompassing federal law is designed to capture and punish those who pose threats to public health and safety by means of the Internet.

APPLYING THE LAW TO THE FACTS

Is a Cell Phone a "Computer" as Defined by Federal Law?

The Facts: Defendant pleaded guilty to transporting a minor in interstate commerce with the intent to engage in criminal sexual activity. Defendant acknowledged that he used his cellular telephone to make calls and send text messages to the victim. The court concluded that under the federal law defining a computer, 18 U.S.C. §1030(e)(1), the phone was a "computer," and the court enhanced the defendant's sentence for using a computer to commit a sex crime. Is a cell phone a "computer" under the federal statute?

The Law: Yes. "If a device is an electronic or other high-speed data processing device performing logical, arithmetic, or storage functions, it is a computer. This definition captures any device that makes use of an electronic data processor, examples of which are legion. Just think of the common household items that include microchips and electronic storage devices, and thus will satisfy the statutory definition of computer. That category can include coffeemakers, microwave ovens, watches, telephones, children's toys, MP3 players, refrigerators, heating and air-conditioning units, radios, alarm clocks, televisions, and DVD players, in addition to more traditional computers like laptops or desktop computers. Additionally, each time an electronic processor performs any task—from powering on, to receiving keypad input, to displaying information—it performs logical, arithmetic, or storage functions. These functions are the essence of its operation."[50]

Nonfinancial Cybercrime

> **Rule of Law: The general criminal law statutes that protect access to computer information are used to prosecute cybercrime.**

In general, cybercrime is defined as any act or intrusion that "jeopardizes the integrity, confidentiality, or availability of computers, information or communications systems or networks."[51] Those who use the Internet to manipulate the computers, hardware, software, and network connections of others can generate public harm on a vast scale with minimal effort. Law enforcement officers and lawmakers are seemingly always in the position of playing "catch-up" and trying to catch and punish hackers who are experts at leaving virtually no trace of their identity. According to the Federal Bureau of Investigation (FBI)'s Cyber Division, the perpetrators have different motivations. The FBI asks,

> Who is behind such attacks? It runs the gamut—from computer geeks looking for bragging rights . . . to businesses trying to gain an upper hand in the marketplace by hacking competitor websites, from rings of criminals wanting to steal your personal information and sell it on black markets . . . to spies and terrorists looking to rob our nation of vital information or launch cyber strikes.[52]

There are many divisions in federal law enforcement agencies dedicated to fighting cybercrime, but a comprehensive, coordinated response remains elusive.[53] Some of the most notable hacks for which no one has been caught or prosecuted involved breaches of private companies, such as the credit data reporting company Equifax, the private driver company Uber, or Facebook, which resulted in the disclosure of personal, identifying information of millions of Americans. One scholar says of the difficulty in preventing cybercrime,

> Less detection means less prosecution and less deterrence. When a potential criminal weighs the benefits to be gleaned from hacking . . . against the minimal risk of being caught and jailed for a maximum of two years for hacking a device that cannot encrypt its data or even register the breach in most cases, the choice is obvious: hacking is worth the risk.[54]

Three common targets of cybercrimes are financial networks, personal victims, and distribution chains for public services. Financial cybercrime is discussed in Chapter 5.

Social Media and Personal Victimization

Social media platforms such as Facebook, Twitter, Instagram, and MySpace have been used as conduits (artificial channels) for criminal activity. In response, federal and state laws have been expanded to catch the catfishers, the swatters, and the trolls. An Internet troll purposely disrupts an online community by posting inflammatory comments meant to provoke respondents' anger, for example, posting contrary and negative opinions on political websites dedicated to one, particular point of view. **Catfishing** is impersonating someone else online, and **swatting** is calling in false reports of a crisis to get emergency special weapons and tactical (SWAT) teams to respond to an unsuspecting victim's house.

Swatting can have fatal results, as evidenced by the December 29, 2017, shooting of Andrew Finch in Wichita, Kansas. An online gamer in a dispute over a $1.50 wager called Tyler Barriss. The gamer wanted Barriss to swat the rival gamer. Unknown to Barriss, the rival gamer used innocent Andrew Finch's address as his own. Barriss called 9-1-1 directing a tactical team to Finch's address. Posing as a resident of the home, Barriss falsely claimed he had killed someone, was holding family members hostage, and intended to burn the house down. When Finch came out of the house to see why the police were surrounding his home, after a brief encounter, an officer shot Finch dead. As of this writing, Barriss was charged with involuntary manslaughter, but prosecutors may have difficulty proving that Barriss "caused" Finch's death when an innocent person being shot by a response team is not a naturally foreseeable result of a telephone prank, and his *mens rea* was to harass the rival gamer, not kill Finch.

Another personal harm that occurs online is repeated harassment, which may be prosecuted under the Federal Interstate Stalking Punishment and Prevention Act (FISPPA).[55] Law professor Thaddeus Hoffmeister[56] has diagrammed the elements of FISPPA as[57]

Use of:

    a. The mail,

    b. Any interactive computer service, or

    c. Any facility of interstate or foreign commerce

To engage in a course of conduct, defined as a pattern of conduct composed of 2 or more acts, evidencing a continuity of purpose;

That causes:

    d. Substantial emotional distress, or

    e. Reasonable fear of death or serious bodily injury, to a person in another state or tribal jurisdiction or within the special maritime and territorial jurisdiction; and

Intent by the defendant to:

    f. Kill

    g. Injure

    h. Harass

    i. Place under surveillance with intent to kill, injure, harass, or intimidate, or

    j. Cause substantial emotional distress to that person.

Because online communications cross state lines, federal jurisdiction can prosecute most crimes as wire fraud violations if prosecution under computer harassment statutes fail. Note the similar provision in FISPPA to the RICO anti-racketeering statute discussed in Chapter 5, as both laws require two or more predicate acts indicating a pattern of continuing activity.

Malware and Disruption of Public Services

Some cyberhacks are aimed at disrupting public services and government functions. For instance, in April 2017, the City of Dallas's emergency system was hacked and all 156 sirens went off for a full 90 minutes before city administrators were able to manually override the system. Russian hackers infiltrated 21 states' electronic voting systems; the Department of Homeland Security's undersecretary Jeanette Manfra said the infiltration was "intended or used to undermine public confidence in electoral processes." A hospital in Hollywood, California, was the victim of a ransomware attack (a software virus that blocks computer access until a sum of money is paid) and had to pay ransom in Bitcoin to obtain a decryption key to get their servers back online after a week of blackout access to their computers. The hospital president Allen Stefanek released the following statement:

> The reports of the hospital paying 9000 Bitcoins or $3.4 million are false. The amount of ransom requested was 40 Bitcoins, equivalent to approximately $17,000. The malware locks systems by encrypting files and demanding ransom to obtain the decryption key. The quickest and most efficient way to restore our systems and administrative functions was to pay the ransom and obtain the decryption key. In the best interest of restoring normal operations, we did this.[58]

Law enforcement reports that the Monero cryptocurrency is growing in popularity over Bitcoin. Those who deploy malware and demand a ransom in exchange for the decryption code to unlock data on a computer system are increasingly demanding Monero as payment. If and when malware offenders are caught, they may be prosecuted under the computer fraud statute.

TERRORISM

Terrorism is generally understood as people committing acts involving threats, murder, and mayhem to achieve illegitimate political goals. The psychological makeup of people who commit terrorist acts have certain personality traits in common, according to University of Maryland professor Arie Kruglanski. People, typically young men, attracted to terrorist organizations see the world in black and white and join organizations—particularly fundamentalist religious groups that give clear guidelines on how to live, think, and act—to become an important part of a whole. Making a significant contribution to a cause larger than themselves fulfills a sense of identity they often lack.[59] Psychologists say would-be terrorists have a strong "need for cognitive closure," defined as living a life of structure, order, and an overwhelming desire for certainty. As Kruglanski says "If you go through the world needing closure, it predisposes you to seek out the ideologies and belief system that most provide it,"[60] and when such a person decides to kill innocent people in the name of the cause, such acts show their devotion and commitment to the group.

> **Rule of Law: Terrorism is using illegal means to achieve illegitimate political objectives.**

The USA PATRIOT Act

The September 11, 2001 (9/11), airline hijackings led to the death of nearly 3,000 people, injured scores of others, destroyed the World Trade Center Towers in New York City, damaged the Pentagon in Washington, D.C., and caused the crash of United Airlines flight 93 in Shanksville, Pennsylvania. On October 26, 2001, Congress responded by enacting the Uniting and Strengthening America by Providing Appropriate Tools Required to Intercept and Obstruct Terrorism Act of 2001, otherwise known as the USA PATRIOT Act,[61] which consolidates law enforcement resources to investigate threats to national security with the aim of preventing another such terrorist attack on the United States.

Supporters of the USA PATRIOT Act praise its authority to gather and share investigative information between law enforcement agencies, whereas its critics point to the dismantling of citizens' civil liberties, especially in the search and seizure context, to fight an amorphous "war on terror."

The PATRIOT Act at Work

In 1972, the U.S. Supreme Court reviewed a case of electronic wiretapping to determine whether the government had to adhere to the Fourth Amendment's warrant requirement in investigating matters of domestic security. Holding that the Fourth Amendment did apply to the government in such circumstances, the Court said,

> Given these potential distinctions between Title III criminal surveillances and those involving the domestic security, Congress may wish to consider protective standards for the latter which differ from those already prescribed for specified crimes in Title III. Different standards may be compatible with the Fourth Amendment if they are reasonable both in relation to the legitimate need of Government for intelligence information and the protected rights of our citizens.[62]

In 1978, Congress responded to the Court's 1972 decision by enacting the Foreign Intelligence Surveillance Act (FISA)[63] to broaden the government's authority to gather intelligence via wiretapping in the name of national security. Unlike a typical Fourth Amendment probable cause determination that the person or place is connected to criminal activity, the FISA probable cause determination focuses on whether the target of American surveillance is an agent of a foreign power. The Office of Intelligence Policy and Review of the DOJ prepares and submits FISA applications, which are reviewed by the Foreign Intelligence Surveillance Court (FISC) that operates in secrecy behind steel walls in a secure location within the DOJ.

To achieve the dual goals of protecting both national security and individual civil liberties with respect to the government's surveillance activities, Congress created a legal wall between the activity of eavesdropping to learn about foreign threats and the criminal prosecutions that result from information learned by the eavesdropping. The intelligence–prosecution wall created problems for investigators and prosecutors in using FISA, and many federal agents blame the "FISA wall" in hampering investigative efforts that may have alerted authorities to the impending attacks on September 11, 2001.

The USA PATRIOT Act amended parts of FISA to eliminate the wall and permit information sharing between domestic law enforcement and foreign intelligence agencies as well as permitting electronic surveillance where obtaining foreign surveillance is necessary and may lead to other surveillance in the name of national security. Another salient feature of the PATRIOT Act that has expanded law enforcement surveillance functions has been more authority for the "trap and trace" devices that record telephone devices dialing in to a particular location. The devices may be used "to obtain foreign intelligence information not concerning a United States person or to protect against international terrorism or clandestine intelligence activities."[64] The PATRIOT Act also amended Title III to allow any investigative or law enforcement officer or prosecutor to obtain foreign intelligence information that will help the United States protect itself from terrorism; permit wiretap orders for terrorism investigations, chemical weapons investigations, and computer fraud and abuse investigations; and permit wiretaps of voicemail messaging systems.

The act also allows federal law enforcement to delay giving notice that a search warrant is about to be served until after it has been served. If authorities have reasonable cause to believe that giving notice of the warrant would have an "adverse effect" on an investigation, it may be delayed until after the warrant has been served. The "delayed action" warrants have been described as "sneak and peek" warrants allowing agents to go into a home or business to "conduct covert searches, notifying the occupant weeks or months after the search." One commentator notes, "These warrants also sometimes authorize covert seizures—a 'sneak and steal' search—in which investigators seize evidence, often staging the scene to look like a burglary."[65]

On March 2, 2006, Congress reauthorized the PATRIOT Act and made certain provisions permanent that were temporary measures when the law was first enacted.[66]

1. The FISA wall has been dismantled.

2. The crimes for which wiretaps could be sought under Title III have been expanded to include, for example, chemical weapons offenses, weapons of mass destruction threats, nuclear threats, and computer espionage.

3. Internet service providers (ISPs) can disclose customer records voluntarily in emergency situations to save lives.

4. Computer trespass (hacking) victims are permitted to request law enforcement assistance to apprehend offenders.

The FISA Amendments Act of 2008 amended Section 702 to allow intelligence officers to monitor electronically non-U.S. citizens outside of the United States and, under federal authority, private telecommunications companies such as Facebook and Google must help the National Security Agency (NSA) by turning over customers' messages, e-mails, and video posts. The FBI may also conduct warrantless searches of the NSA database. In 2013, Edward Snowden, a former Central Intelligence Agency (CIA) employee and government contractor, leaked without authority details of the NSA surveillance programs. The DOJ charged Snowden with violating the Espionage Act of 1917[67] and to avoid prosecution, Snowden moved to Russia. In January 2018, Congress reauthorized Section 702 for 6 years.

Aiding and Abetting the Islamic State of Iraq and the Levant (ISIL)

The federal law often used to prosecute people for terrorist activities is a law against providing support to illegal organizations (most notably, al-Qaeda and ISIL [also known as Islamic State of Iraq and Syria (ISIS) or the Islamic State]), reprinted in part here.

---

18 U.S.C. §2339B Providing material support or resources to designated foreign terrorist organizations

Prohibited Activities. —

Unlawful conduct. —

Whoever knowingly provides material support or resources to a foreign terrorist organization, or attempts or conspires to do so, shall be fined under this title or imprisoned not more than 20 years, or both, and, if the death of any person results, shall be imprisoned for any term of years or for life.

To violate this paragraph, a person must have knowledge that the organization is a designated terrorist organization that the organization has engaged or engages in terrorist activity or that the organization has engaged or engages in terrorism.

Researchers at George Washington University have studied extremists and particularly the demographics of those attracted to committing acts of terror. Figure 6.2 shows statistics of the general demographics of those convicted of terrorist acts.

Figure 6.2   GW Extremism Tracker: The Islamic State in America

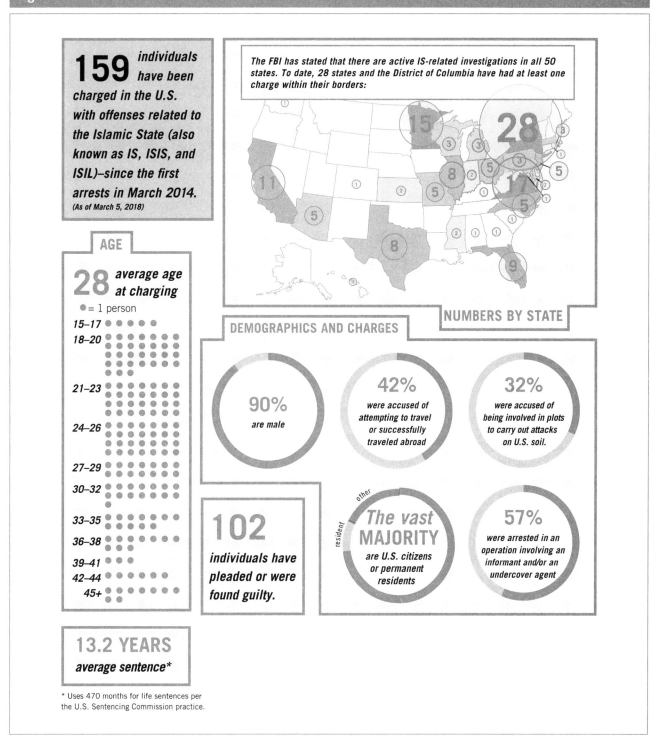

159 individuals have been charged in the U.S. with offenses related to the Islamic State (also known as IS, ISIS, and ISIL)—since the first arrests in March 2014. (As of March 5, 2018)

The FBI has stated that there are active IS-related investigations in all 50 states. To date, 28 states and the District of Columbia have had at least one charge within their borders:

NUMBERS BY STATE

AGE

28 average age at charging

● = 1 person

15–17
18–20
21–23
24–26
27–29
30–32
33–35
36–38
39–41
42–44
45+

DEMOGRAPHICS AND CHARGES

90% are male

42% were accused of attempting to travel or successfully traveled abroad

32% were accused of being involved in plots to carry out attacks on U.S. soil.

102 individuals have pleaded or were found guilty.

The vast MAJORITY are U.S. citizens or permanent residents

57% were arrested in an operation involving an informant and/or an undercover agent

13.2 YEARS average sentence*

* Uses 470 months for life sentences per the U.S. Sentencing Commission practice.

Source: Reprinted with permission, George Washington University Extremism Tracker.

Terrorism suspects are prosecuted federally because their criminal goals threaten national security. At sentencing, federal sentencing guideline calculations allow lengthening the sentence of a person convicted of terrorist-related activity. Read the case excerpt on the following page where American-born Bell went for training in Yemen to carry out attacks on American soil. Examine the judge's dilemma in fashioning an appropriate sentence.

UNITED STATES V. BELL, 81 F.SUPP.3D 1301 (M.D. FL 2015)

[Shelton Thomas] Bell stands convicted of one count of conspiracy to provide material support to terrorists and one count of attempt to provide material support to terrorists, both in violation of 18 U.S.C. §2339A(a). Each count carries a statutory maximum imprisonment of "not more than 15 years," for a maximum imprisonment in Bell's case of thirty years. There is no mandatory minimum sentence.

Factual Background

. . . The investigation into these offenses began in June 2012 with a tip from the leaders at the Islamic Center of Northeast Florida in Jacksonville, Florida. The leaders notified the FBI that an individual attending the Center had been speaking about "jihad," that the individual had gathered some young people to him with his message, and that the leaders were concerned about his influence. The leaders identified the individual as Shelton Thomas Bell. Leaders at the Center had tried to intervene and discuss the issue with Bell, but he was defiant.

Bell had first begun giving voice to his desire to travel overseas to engage in violent jihad in May 2012. A recent convert to Islam in 2011 when he was seventeen years old, Bell had thrown himself headfirst into studying the religion. He first found a role model in the faith in a local, American-born imam. But Bell also looked for other sources of information, including online. His online search eventually led him to the radical preaching of Anwar al-Awlaki, once the most important spokesman for the terrorist group first known as al-Qai'da in the Arabian Peninsula and later rebranded as Ansar al-Shari'a. Al-Awlaki, a dual citizen of Yemen and the United States, was killed in 2011 in Yemen by an American drone strike. Before then, he was the most significant recruiter for Ansar al-Shari'a and had published many hours of propaganda online that are still effective recruitment tools for extremists, particularly among English-speakers. Al-Awlaki preached a violent strain of jihad that espoused that Islam is under attack and that it is the duty of every Muslim to defend Islam by either conducting their own attacks wherever they live or traveling to wherever the jihadists are fighting, like Yemen, and joining the fight.

By his own admission, Bell found al-Awlaki "captivating" and believed everything he preached. All told, Bell accumulated and consumed hundreds of hours of al-Awlaki's speeches and propaganda. By listening to al-Awlaki, Bell came to accept al-Awlaki's mission as his own, specifically to forcibly establish a severe reading of Islamic law, or "Sharia," throughout the world. Following al-Awlaki's posthumous call, Bell decided that his small group of young people should go to Yemen and join al-Awlaki's group, Ansar al-Shari'a.

To prepare themselves mentally and physically, Bell and his group began to train with firearms that Bell supplied, to continue consuming extremist media, and to record their own videos that Bell, as the group's "commander," directed another member of the group to post online (though the videos never were uploaded). (In the early morning hours of July 4, 2012, Bell and another group member recorded themselves carrying out a "mission" Bell had conceived of to destroy two statues of Jesus at the Chapel Hill Cemetery in the Arlington neighborhood of Jacksonville. One of the videos depicts Bell supplying the equipment for the mission, including black masks and gloves and black tape for their shoes, and a handgun Bell describes as having "full mags, fully loaded, ready to go, in case any kuffar [unbeliever, infidel] wants to cause some trouble." The other individual later explained that Bell intended to use the gun to shoot anyone who tried to stop the mission, including the police.) Other videos of the mission include Bell explaining the plan to the other individual lecturing him about how destroying these "idols" fits with his plan for jihad. In one video made during the drive to the cemetery, Bell says that Muslim scholars in America would see their actions and say, "'You're a terrorist,'" that he and the individual would be demonized as terrorists, "just as they do the Taliban, just as they do the brothers in Somalia, just as they do the brothers everywhere across the globe." The two were ultimately unable to completely destroy the statues, but did succeed in knocking off their heads with sledgehammers, causing $17,000 in damage.

In September 2012, Bell and a juvenile member of his group began to prepare for their trip to Yemen. Their cover story for their families was that they were going to the Middle East to "make Hajj," a yearly pilgrimage to Mecca in Saudi Arabia. So the day before they left, Bell obtained a certificate of his conversion to Islam from the Islamic Center to make the story seem believable. Because the juvenile could not obtain a student visa to travel directly to Yemen, the trip now included a stop in Israel before the two would travel to Yemen to join Ansar al-Shari'a. Bell ordered an expedited passport and purchased one-way tickets to Tel-Aviv for himself and the juvenile.

On September 25, 2012, Bell and the juvenile departed Jacksonville on their way to Tel-Aviv via New York and Poland. Bell and the juvenile were detained and interrogated by authorities in Tel-Aviv, however, and sent back to Poland on September 27, 2012. At the juvenile's suggestion, they then bought one-way tickets to Amman, Jordan, where the juvenile had relatives. Bell and the juvenile stayed for a time with the juvenile's aunt until she asked Bell to leave. They then went to a local mosque, but Bell was eventually kicked out for being vocal about wanting to wage jihad.

Upon his return, Bell made a number of intercepted telephone calls to his associates in which he said he had some "substantial stuff" planned for Jacksonville and that he intended to build a "masjid," or mosque, of his own in the woods by his father's house so that he could continue to speak with other young people about jihad. However, Bell's plans were interrupted on January 29, 2013, when he was arrested by the Jacksonville Sheriff's Office on state criminal charges. Based on a brief exchange with a Muslim sheriff's detective after a custodial interview, even after his arrest, Bell evidently still persisted in his radicalization, calling the detective "Taghut," or disbeliever, telling the detective that he represented the "wrong law," and pointedly telling the detective that he had gone overseas to be a soldier.

Base Offense Level

Terrorism Enhancement

Section 3A1.4(a) provides that "[i]f the offense is a felony that involved, or was intended to promote, a federal crime of terrorism, increase by 12 levels" the base offense level. The term 'federal crime of terrorism' has the meaning given that term in 18 U.S.C. §2332b(g)(5)." That statute defines a federal crime of terrorism as "an offense that is calculated to influence or affect the conduct of government by intimidation or coercion, or to retaliate against government conduct; and is a violation of" one of a list of specified federal statutes. The first part of the definition of federal crime of terrorism focuses on the intended outcome of the defendants' unlawful acts—i.e., what the activity was calculated to accomplish, not what the defendants' claimed motivation behind it was.

As for whether Bell's offenses were "calculated to influence, or affect the conduct of government by intimidation or coercion, or to retaliate against government conduct," the evidence shows that they were. "It is the defendant's purpose that is relevant, and if that purpose is to promote a terrorism crime, the enhancement is triggered." The many images found on Bell's computer indicate that his goal was to play a role in the overthrow of secular governments and their replacement with governments rooted in Sharia, as symbolized by the removal of the flag of the secular government—the flag of Taghut—and the raising of the black flag of Tawheed—adopted by the jihadist movement—over every continent. Bell expressed that precise sentiment himself before, during, and after his trip to Jordan on his mission to join Ansar al-Shari'a in Yemen. "It's quite saddening to

see the flag of Taghut instead of the flag of Tawheed. . . . Wouldn't you be much happier? Wouldn't it put a smile on your face to see a black flag declaring Shahadah [there is no god but Allah, and Muhammed is his prophet] above the city? Inshallah, one day.")***

Acceptance of Responsibility

Bell is entitled to the full three-level decrease to his offense level permitted in USSG §3E1.1 [for pleading guilty].

Criminal History

The next step in identifying Bell's advisory guideline range is to determine his criminal history category. The presentence report reveals one adult criminal conviction for trespass committed after the offense in this case, for which adjudication was withheld. This offense does not score towards Bell's criminal history. USSG §4A1.2(c). Bell committed the instant offenses while he was on probation until age nineteen for violating a temporary injunction while he was a minor. His violation of the temporary injunction scores as one criminal history point under §4A1.1(c). Then, two additional points are added because Bell "committed the instant offenses while under any criminal justice sentence, including probation . . ." A total criminal history score of three would place Bell in criminal history category II. However, the terrorism enhancement in §3A1.4, in addition to adding twelve levels to a defendant's offense level, provides that "the defendant's criminal history category . . . shall [automatically] be Category VI," the highest criminal history category. . . .

Deterrence and Protection of the Public

According to the Government, "Bell poses a likelihood of recidivism, no meaningful chance of rehabilitation, and due to his virtual tutelage by al-Awlaki, a heightened risk of dangerousness." . . . "Terrorists [even those] with no prior criminal behavior are unique among criminals in the likelihood of recidivism, the difficulty of rehabilitation, and the need for incapacitation." The Government contends the Court should therefore impose a long sentence out of concern for the danger Bell and those like him pose to the public and to deter youths in the local community who have not yet started down the path towards radicalization.

Bell counters that, if the Government is right that terrorists cannot be deterred or rehabilitated, then a long sentence only serves to encourage terrorists to succeed in their plans and evade capture. As it has from the start, the Court struggles to discern the true level of future threat Bell would pose to the public were he given anything other than the

(Continued)

thirty-year statutory maximum imprisonment. He certainly was a serious and growing threat as he sought to carry out his plan and before his apprehension by law enforcement. The testimony of Braniff suggests that there is little reason to believe such a threat could ever be extinguished short of permanent incapacitation.

On the other hand, Bell's seemingly sincere expressions of remorse and Dr. Cohen's testimony provide some hope that a counseling component to Bell's incarceration could have a positive effect. This is concerning and sad because it demonstrates that, in the age of the internet, a disaffected young American can be so easily indoctrinated into terrorism. That Bell so readily bought into al-Awlaki's

call to hate and violence means others will as well, as confirmed by terrorism expert Braniff. Thus, the Court agrees that general deterrence of others from taking the first step along the path to radicalization is an important component of Bell's sentence.

A substantial sentence is likely necessary to have any deterrent effect. But the Court is not convinced that only the statutory maximum will work, while anything less would embolden would-be terrorists. ***

The Court finds that a sentence of twenty years (240 months), followed by a lifetime period of supervised release will be, in the words of the law, "sufficient but not greater than necessary. . . ." 18 U.S.C. § 3553(a).

Springboard for Discussion

What harm, if any, to the United States' interests can come by depriving those suspected of aiding al-Qaeda or the Taliban the full rights and protections that American citizens, or even those not in the United States legally, enjoy, such as the right to appointed counsel and to a fair jury trial?

Criminal law and procedure are best illustrated by sentencing decisions, as the case excerpts featured in this chapter against Ross Ulbricht and Shelton Bell show. Courts must always balance the defendant's characteristics against the larger goal of punishment and retribution. In the chapter-opening case study, Don provided material assistance to a purported terrorist group when he sent $1,000 in response to their financial appeal.

Detention of Terror Suspects

A component of the government's effort to investigate crime is the ability to detain and interrogate witnesses or suspects who may or may not have information that relates to a criminal investigation. Beginning in 2002, American forces seized suspects who are believed to be linked to terrorist organizations such as al-Qaeda and the Taliban and have held approximately 500 of them at the naval base in Guantánamo Bay, Cuba, labeling the suspects "enemy combatants." Calling the detainees enemy combatants allows the executive branch to hold and treat them differently from prisoners of war or other criminal suspects. For example, as of September 2018, Khalid Sheikh Mohammad, a suspect in planning the 9/11 attacks, was still awaiting trial at Guantánamo since 2006.

But detainees' rights and access to the American justice system have been vigorously litigated on American soil. The primary cases heard by the U.S. Supreme Court are *Rasul v. Bush* (2004) and *Hamdi v. Rumsfeld* (2004).[68] In *Rasul*, the Court held that American courts have jurisdiction over foreign nationals held at Guantánamo Bay but did not address the issue of the legality of the detainees' imprisonment. In *Hamdi*, decided the same day as *Rasul*, the Court considered whether an American citizen (Hamdi, an American who fought for the Taliban) could be classified as an enemy combatant and denied due process through the normal criminal trial process.[69] The high Court held that Hamdi's detention was lawful under the express congressional authority to the president under the Authorization for Use of Military Force statute that allowed captured U.S. citizens to be classified as enemy combatants who could be tried before military tribunals rather than U.S. criminal courts. In response to the Court's decisions, Congress passed the Detainee Treatment Act of 2005, which specifically denied the right to file *habeas corpus* petitions (writs/motions filed to challenge the legality of a prisoner's detention) for noncitizens held as enemy combatants at Guantánamo Bay, effectively overruling the high Court's decision in *Rasul*.[70]

The next case to address detainee court access via the military tribunal system that the executive branch established to bring the detainees to trial was *Hamdan v. Rumsfeld* (2006). In this case, the Supreme Court held that using the procedural safeguards afforded by the Uniform Code of Military Justice could be a proper avenue for trying the suspects, rather than the unconstitutional military commissions proposed by the president.[71]

Rule of Law: Terror suspects have the right to access American courts through the writ of *habeas corpus.*

Largely in response to the U.S. Supreme Court's ruling in *Hamdan*, Congress hammered out the Military Commissions Act of 2006 (MCA). President George W. Bush signed this act into law on October 17, 2006, calling it "a way to deliver justice to the terrorists we have captured." The enactment of the MCA illustrates how the three branches of government work (as explored in Chapter 1). The MCA gave the legislative branch endorsement to the executive branch's exercise of power concerning detainees that the judicial branch found excessive in its *Hamdan* decision.[72] The MCA authorizes the president to issue an executive order clarifying the rules for questioning high-level detainees. The MCA also sets up a separate system of justice for anyone the administration classifies as an "unlawful enemy combatant," defined as those who fight against the United States and also those who have "purposefully and materially supported hostilities against the United States," thereby including in the prosecutorial net those who provide financial or material support to terrorists.

MAKING THE COURTROOM CONNECTION

One growing area of concern for correctional officers is the active recruitment of inmates for terrorist activity after release from prison. Authors Gene Atherton and Andjela Jurisic recommend five steps to manage terrorists in prison: (1) good administrative management that distinguishes between freedom of religion and speech and discussion intending to recruit inmates to extremist viewpoints; (2) staff training to conduct risk assessment of prisoners who may be susceptible to terrorist "grooming" (preparing); (3) wise use of religious imams and other clergy to foster respect for religious converts, which is not the same as radicalization; (4) emphasis on staff training to treat everyone equally, as discriminatory views toward one person or group can breed resentment and attract a radicalized response; and (5) isolating and segregating prisoners who may be involved in radicalizing new prisoners to dilute their potential impact.[73]

TREASON

The only crime mentioned in the Constitution is treason. Article III, Section 3 states the following:

Clause 1: Treason against the United States shall consist only in levying War against them, or in adhering to their Enemies, giving them Aid and Comfort. No person shall be convicted of Treason unless on the testimony of Two Witnesses to the same overt Act, or on Confession in open Court.

Clause 2: The Congress shall have Power to declare the Punishment of Treason, but no Attainder of Treason shall work Corruption of Blood, or Forfeiture except during the Life of the Person attained.

Treason is levying war against the United States from within the country. To sustain a treason charge requires the testimony of two witnesses to the alleged treasonous acts. The last treason conviction to withstand U.S. Supreme Court review was the case of Tomoya Kawakita, convicted in 1952 of helping the Japanese war effort. Two other convictions that were overturned on appeal were the 1943 conviction of Hans Haupt, the father of a German saboteur, and Anthony Cramer, convicted of aiding a German saboteur in 1945. The elements of treason are

1. A person who owes allegiance to the United States

2. Levies war or adheres to an enemy of the United States and

3. Commits an overt act, and

4. Possesses treasonable intent

5. With two attesting witnesses.

Treason prosecutions are rare. According to an interview with the *New York Times*, Peter S. Margulies, an expert on national security issues said, "You need witnesses who are actually familiar with the terms of cooperation of the person charged—whether they were coerced, whether they were paid," which contributes to the difficulty of treason prosecutions.[74]

Sedition

Sedition has been recognized as a crime since the first days of the Constitution. The Alien and Sedition Acts of the late 18th century defined **sedition** as the crime of writing false, scandalous, or malicious stories about the government; lengthened the residency period to become a citizen; and amplified the president's authority to deport dangerous aliens. The sedition laws were controversial because of their effect on the free speech right to criticize the government, and many prominent Americans opposed the laws, including Thomas Jefferson and James Madison. **Espionage** is spying and giving away government secrets to benefit a foreign power. Today, the Logan Act[75] prohibits individuals from corresponding with foreign governments in relation to disputes such governments may have with the United States, and prohibits the recruitment of United States service members to act against the United States.[76] Many forms of espionage and subversive activities are federal crimes and share the common *mens rea* element of the intent to harm the security interests of the United States and the performance of overt acts in furtherance of that objective.

SUMMARY

1. You will be able to articulate the laws combatting crimes tied to addiction. Crimes against morality are largely defined by behavior deemed "immoral" or against the consensus of mainstream society and are referred to as either *mala in se* (inherently evil) or *mala prohibita* (that which society generally condemns). One such crime is prostitution (receiving payment or other things of value in exchange for sexual favors). Some laws exclude minors from being prosecuted as criminal sex workers. The nature of the prostitute relationship is usually exploitive, and the profession is filled with violence and drugs and is closely associated with human trafficking, which is forcing people (mainly children) into sex work or forced labor. Gambling is wagering on events such as sports or card games for money. International Internet gambling is illegal, and the *Murphy v. National Collegiate Athletic Association* (2018) case makes sports betting in states legal. Illegal drugs and alcohol can lead to addiction for which the proper remedy is rehabilitation and treatment, but because those who use illegal substances often are involved in crime such as driving under the influence or violent crime, the criminal justice system must respond appropriately with punishment as well as rehabilitation.

2. You will know the difference between riot and peaceful protest. Society punishes behaviors that disturb or interfere with the order found in a peaceful society. Some of these behaviors come under the rubric of disorderly conduct, for example, breach of the peace, which is loud behavior that disrupts others or not following a lawful order; and riot, which is at least three or more people getting together to commit violence, which sometimes involves a gang defined as a group identifiable by distinctive clothing and hand signals. Vagrancy is being homeless and loitering in public areas, and panhandling is begging from passersby in public. Firearm offenses have the potential to cause great bodily harm and even death. There is a constitutional right to own a gun, and there are many federal and state laws that regulate gun possession.

3. You will understand crimes that interfere with government services. Many crimes constitute public corruption, but the most common are bribery, in which the public official accepts something of value to affect his or her official action; perjury, which is lying under oath, usually to cover up and conceal an initial illegal action;

subornation of perjury, which is inducing another to lie under oath for the benefit of the offender; and making false statements to federal officials with the intent to deceive. All those acts can constitute obstruction of justice, which is deliberately interfering with the administration of justice in a judicial, legislative, or administrative proceeding. Wire fraud convictions for "theft of honest services" are limited to bribery and kickbacks as predicate acts. A kickback is the government awarding a contract with a percentage in return for the facilitating elected official. Environmental statutes are designed to protect the public by attaching civil and criminal liability for violations of the Clean Air Act and the Clean Water Act.

4. You will understand cybercrimes and attendant public harm. People who commit nonfinancial cybercrimes use computers to cause personal harm, such as catfishing (impersonating someone else online), or to disrupt public services, such as swatting (fraudulently calling for emergency services). There are many types of malware that enable criminals to commit crimes via technology. Law enforcement officers must work to stay current on changes in modern technology. The *United States v.*

Ulbricht (2017) case describes the multimillion-dollar Dark Web marketplace for drugs and murder-for-hire.

5. You will know the relevant statutes to prosecute terrorism. Terrorism is understood as acts of threats, murder, and mayhem perpetrated to achieve illegitimate political goals, prosecuted under the PATRIOT Act and under statutes criminalizing aiding terrorists. Enemy combatants are held in Cuba and have successfully petitioned for American courts to hear their writs of *habeas corpus*, which is a way to be brought before a tribunal. The case *United States v. Bell* (2015) illustrates the mechanics of giving support to terrorist organizations. Crimes against the national security of the United States have traditionally been punished under laws that deal with espionage (spying), sedition (plotting to harm the interests of the United States), and treason (waging war against the United States).

Go back to the beginning of the chapter and reread the news excerpts associated with the learning objectives. Test yourself to determine if you can understand the material covered in the text in the context of the news.

KEY TERMS AND PHRASES

breach of the peace 163
bribery 165
catfishing 171
Clean Air Act (CAA) 167
Clean Water Act (CWA) 167
computer crime 167
crimes against the public 155
disorderly conduct 163
disturbing the peace 163
driving under the influence 161
drug and alcohol offenses 157
environmental crimes 167
espionage 180

false statements 166
firearm offenses 161
gambling 155
gang 164
habeas corpus 178
human trafficking 157
kickback 166
mala in se 153
mala prohibita 153
nonfinancial cybercrime 170
obstruction of justice 166
panhandling 163

perjury 167
prostitution 156
public corruption 154
riot 163
Second Amendment 161
sedition 180
subornation of perjury 167
swatting 171
terrorism 172
treason 179
USA PATRIOT Act 172
vagrancy 163

PROBLEM-SOLVING EXERCISES

1. Officer Ryan was friends with Bill, who owned an auto body shop. While Ryan and Bill were fishing, Ryan told Bill that he heard at the police station that all auto body shops were going to be investigated as "chop shops," where stolen cars were dismantled and sold for parts. When the chief of police found out Ryan had told Bill about the investigation, the chief asked the prosecutor to charge Ryan with obstruction of justice. Does Ryan have a defense? **(ROL: Obstruction of justice)**

2. At the end of a racially tense criminal case, several people gathered on the street corner outside and began to chant, "No justice, no peace." When the verdict of acquittal was announced to the public, the chant changed to "Let's burn this courthouse down!" Several protesters were arrested and charged with inciting a riot; the protesters say they were merely exercising their First Amendment freedom of speech rights to criticize the verdict. Who will win, the government or

the protesters? **(ROL: Disorderly conduct, breach of the peace, riot)**

3. Six suspects in the war on terror were taken from their homeland in Afghanistan and placed in the American prison in Guantánamo Bay, Cuba. After 10 years, they still had no idea when or whether they would be brought before a judge or tribunal. All proclaimed their innocence and filed *habeas corpus* petitions in federal court for the District of Columbia naming the U.S. Secretary of Defense as the defendant. Given the rulings in *Hamdi* and *Hamdan* and the Military Commissions Act of 2006, what is the likely outcome of the detainees' challenges to their confinement? **(ROL: *Habeas corpus* for enemy combatant detainees)**

PART III

THE PROCEDURE
The Bill of Rights

7

THE FOURTH AMENDMENT AND WARRANTS

Go to the end of the chapter. Skim the key terms and phrases and read the summary closely. Come back and look at the following news excerpts to focus your reading throughout the chapter to understand the law guiding citizen–police encounters, including when officers (a) stop people on the street to talk and ask questions, (b) place their hands on people to pat down for weapons, (c) arrest people and use force to effectuate an arrest, and (d) secure and execute warrants to search and seize. The chapter begins with a hypothetical case study of Charlie the spy. Follow Charlie as he encounters the rules of law presented throughout the chapter, and connect Charlie's exploits with the relevant section of text.

WHY THIS CHAPTER MATTERS TO YOU	LEARNING OBJECTIVES AS REFLECTED IN THE NEWS
After you have read this chapter: **Learning Objective 1:** You will be able to analyze Fourth Amendment problems.	One of the tools in the federal government's immigration enforcement kit is the detainer—a written request by Immigration and Customs Enforcement agents to a state prison or local jail to hold a person suspected of being in the country illegally for up to 48 hours beyond his or her scheduled release to give immigration agents time to go get the person for possible deportation. But, as a federal judge recently told the federal government—again—holding someone without charge or a court order violates the 4th Amendment protection against unreasonable seizure. (*Los Angeles Times*, February 14, 2018)
Learning Objective 2: You will appreciate how Fourth Amendment analysis has changed with advancing technology.	As I write these words, there are more than 30 Oakland Police Department patrol cars roaming the city with license plate readers, specialized cameras that can scan and record up to 60 license plates per second. Meanwhile, the Alameda County Sheriff's Office maintains a fleet of six drones to monitor crime scenes when it sees fit. The Alameda County district attorney's office owns a StingRay, a device that acts as a fake cell tower and forces phones to give up their location. And that's just in one little corner of California. (*Los Angeles Times*, May 2, 2018)
Learning Objective 3: You will understand the role race may play in the intersection of the citizen–police encounter in assessing reasonable suspicion that criminal activity is afoot.	Philadelphia's mayor's office and Police Department have begun separate investigations into the arrest of two African American men waiting to meet an acquaintance at a Center City Starbucks after a video of the incident was widely shared on social media. In the clip, the two men can be seen being escorted from a table at the cafe in handcuffs while a white man, who has been identified as Philadelphia real estate investor Andrew Yaffe, asks why officers were called. "What did they get called for, because there were two black guys sitting here, meeting me?" [The police chief responded,] "The police did not just happen upon this event—they did not just walk into Starbucks to get a coffee . . . They were called there, for a service, and that service had to do with quelling a disturbance, a disturbance that had to do with trespassing. These officers did absolutely nothing wrong." (www.philly.com, April 14, 2018)

WHY THIS CHAPTER MATTERS TO YOU	LEARNING OBJECTIVES AS REFLECTED IN THE NEWS
Learning Objective 4: You will be able to distinguish the legal basis for a *Terry* stop, arrests, and claims of excessive force.	A man who was shot and killed by a Kansas City, Kansas, police officer Wednesday had previously won a $300,000 excessive force settlement from police across the state line in Kansas City [MO]. Manuel G. Palacio, 27, was the man fatally shot by the police officer. Years earlier, Palacio had sued Kansas City police, alleging that officers used excessive force even though he complied with their commands during a 2014 arrest that was captured on dashcam video. At the time, Palacio was a suspect in a robbery. None of the three officers are still with the Police Department. (*Kansas City Star*, May 3, 2018)
Learning Objective 5: You will be able to articulate the sources of probable cause and the procedure for obtaining and serving a warrant.	A Merced County Sheriff's detective testified Thursday in the Ethan Morse's federal civil rights trial he had probable cause to arrest District Attorney Larry Morse's son in July 2014 in connection with a triple murder because he was suspected of being the driver in a drive-by shooting. But detective Erick Macias also admitted that he omitted key evidence from Morse's arrest warrant that would have shown he was innocent. That's important because Morse's lawyers contend an arrest warrant requires a detective to state incriminating evidence—as well as any evidence that exonerates a suspect—so a judge can make an independent decision whether to sign the warrant. (*The Fresno Bee*, April 26, 2018)

Chapter-Opening Case Study: Charlie the Spy

Charlie worked for the Central Intelligence Agency (CIA) and lived in Brooklyn, New York. His coworkers called Charlie "Gollum" behind his back because he resembled the small, troll-like creature from the *Lord of the Rings* movie series. One of his coworkers, Beth, believed Charlie was a spy and she reported Charlie to the Federal Bureau of Investigation (FBI). **(Rule of Law [ROL]: Members of the public are deemed reliable informants.)** The FBI placed Charlie under surveillance by attaching a global positioning system (GPS) tracker under the bumper of Charlie's car. **(ROL: A warrant is needed to attach a device to a suspect's car even though electronic monitoring on public streets is not a search.)** One night, agents watched as Charlie met two suspicious individuals, Elaine and Jamal, in front of an electronics store. The three friends walked up and down the street in an obvious agitated manner, constantly looking around, and pacing back and forth in front of the store. Thinking the trio was about to commit a crime, Agent Wick approached and began to ask routine questions about what the three were doing in the area. **(ROL: The *Terry* stop is a brief encounter between police and the public to confirm or dispel the reasonable suspicion that criminal activity is afoot.)** Because Agent Wick saw a weapon protruding from Elaine's pocket, he immediately put his hands on Elaine and took the gun out of her pocket. **(ROL: If, during a *Terry* stop, an officer has a reasonable belief that the suspect is armed, the officer can legally disarm the suspect.)** Because Elaine did not have a permit to carry a concealed weapon, she was placed under arrest. As she was taken into custody, she blurted out that Charlie was a spy for North Korea. Agents prepared an affidavit of probable cause to attach to the search warrant for Charlie's house. **(ROL: Probable cause means it is more likely than not that a specific person has or will commit a specific crime or specific evidence will be found in a specific place.)** On the face of the warrant in the space where the list of things to be seized was to be typed, the agents mistakenly typed Charlie's home address in Brooklyn. **(ROL: If the warrant is so facially defective that no reasonable officer would serve it, the officer who executes the warrant may be personally liable.)**

At Charlie's house, agents directed Charlie to sit on the couch while they searched and discovered evidence related to spying. At an open laptop, an agent started clicking on files and opened one labeled "private," where encryption codes for offshore bank accounts were discovered. **(ROL: Warrant is to search for only those items listed; a computer search generally requires a separate warrant.)** While the agents were focused on the computer contents, Charlie got up and ran out the door. One agent yelled, "Stop!" but when Charlie kept running, the agent shot Charlie, killing him. **(ROL: The amount of force used to effectuate an arrest is subject to the Fourth Amendment's reasonableness clause.)** Were the agents' actions lawful?

THE FOURTH AMENDMENT

How did the law evolve in America to protect people suspected of committing a crime? We turn to history to understand what life was like before we had a Bill of Rights. The genesis of the Fourth Amendment was the Crown of England's abuse of criminal and civil process. Early American colonists witnessed the king abuse both writs of assistance, which were papers authorizing the seizure of property to help pay the king's debtors, who would in turn pay dues to the king, and general warrants that were issued by King George III to seize and arrest in the Colonies authors, publishers, and printers of "seditious libels," pamphlets advocating for government reform.

When America became a country, adopted the Constitution, and enacted the Bill of Rights in 1791, the Fourth Amendment established the minimum requirements for the government to search and seize people and personal property.[1] The late Honorable Charles E. Moylan, Jr., offered the following schematic device to conceptualize the exact language of the Fourth Amendment as it protects people from government abuse of power. The Fourth Amendment provides that

The right of the people to be secure in their

(1) persons,

(2) houses,

(3) papers, and

(4) effects

against unreasonable searches and seizures, shall not be violated, and no warrants shall issue, [except]

(1) upon probable cause,

(2) supported by oath or affirmation, and

(3) particularly describing

(a) the place to be searched, and

(b) the persons or things to be seized.[2]

The two prongs of the Fourth Amendment are generally known as the "reasonableness clause" and the "warrant clause." The Fourth Amendment does not prevent all searches and seizures, only unreasonable ones. For instance, a suspect can be arrested on a public street without a warrant because there is no invasion of privacy, but on the other hand, "a man's home is his castle," and a warrant is required to search such an intimate space. Searches and seizures are two distinct actions. A search is looking for evidence to use against a suspect in a criminal prosecution. A seizure denotes taking the evidence found, or taking or arresting a suspect.

How to Analyze the Fourth Amendment

A method of analysis, represented in Figure 7.1, determines whether the Fourth Amendment's protections apply, whether the government has violated those protections, and, if it has, what the appropriate legal remedy should be.

Figure 7.1 How to Analyze Fourth Amendment Problems

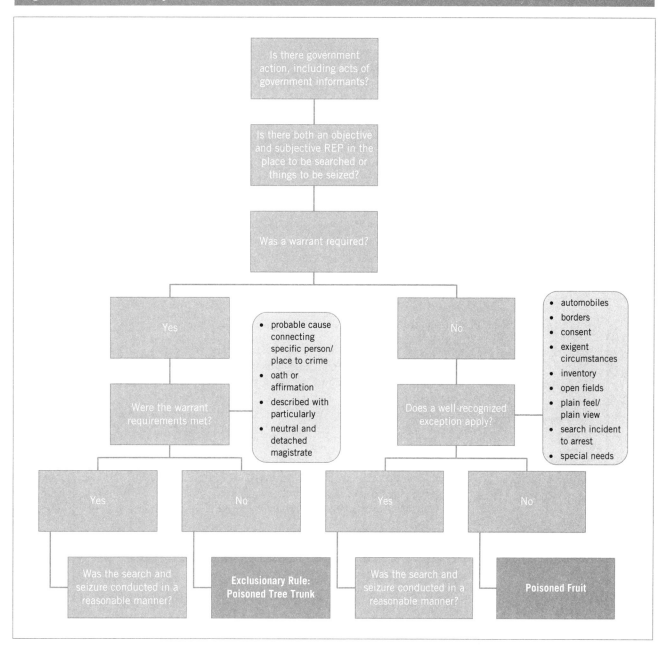

The first step in analyzing whether the Fourth Amendment protects a person's right against unreasonable search and seizure is to determine whether a government actor is involved. If a neighbor trespassed into her drug-dealing neighbor's house and took a kilogram of cocaine to turn over to the police, the Fourth Amendment is not implicated because the government was not involved in invading the drug dealer's privacy. If the neighbor, however, was acting under the direction and control of the police as an informant, then the Fourth Amendment applies.

The second step is to determine whether there exists an expectation of privacy in the place to be searched or the thing to be seized. The reasonable expectation of privacy must be subjectively and objectively reasonable as determined in *Katz v. United States* (1967), reprinted in part on the following page.

The third step is to determine whether the police action in conducting the search and seizure was "reasonable." For example, choking a suspect to get the bag of drugs the suspect just swallowed is reasonable if done to save the suspect's life but unreasonable if done to get the drugs to use as evidence against the suspect.

The fourth step is to determine whether sufficient probable cause exists to support the warrant or arrest. The U.S. Supreme Court has stated probable cause exists if "[under] the totality of the circumstances, as viewed by a reasonable and prudent police officer in light of his training and experience, would lead that police officer to believe that a criminal offense has been or is being committed."[3]

What may suffice as probable cause in one case may not in a similar case. The probable cause standard is flexible, but it must be based on more than a "hunch" or "reasonable suspicion" that someone is engaged in criminal activity.[4]

The fifth step is to determine whether, in the case of a Fourth Amendment violation, the evidence seized will be excluded or admitted. The exclusionary rule is designed to punish the police for not following the law by preventing the government from using illegally seized evidence against the defendant and any derivative evidence (something based on another source) found as a result of the illegal search and seizure. Trees get nourished by drinking water from their trunks. If the tree trunk is poisoned by the illegal search, then the leaves and fruit are going to be poisoned as well. Hence, the phrase "fruit of the poisonous tree" describes inadmissible evidence derived from the initial illegality committed in seizing the evidence without legal authorization. The good faith exception may allow such evidence to be used at trial because the officers were simply doing their job and made innocent mistakes. Both concepts are discussed more fully in Chapter 8.

The Expectation of Privacy

> **Rule of Law: The Fourth Amendment protects a reasonable expectation of privacy, which must be both subjective (personal) and objective (relative to everyone else).**

People do not forfeit their Fourth Amendment right to be free from unreasonable search and seizure by engaging in criminal activity. In *Katz v. United States* (1967), the defendant had been convicted for wagering illegal bets across state lines using the telephone, a federal crime. The evidence against him was obtained when federal agents put listening devices on the exterior panels of the public telephone booth where Katz conducted his gambling business. The U.S. Supreme Court found in favor of Katz because Katz subjectively expected his conversations inside the booth would be private, and everyone else passing by the telephone booth had an objective belief that Katz expected to have a private conversation in the telephone booth. As you read the case excerpt below, note how the Court formulated the legal definition for a reasonable expectation of privacy that the Fourth Amendment would protect.

KATZ V. UNITED STATES, 389 U.S. 347 (1967)

Supreme Court of the United States

Justice Stewart delivered the opinion of the Court. (8–1)

FACTS: The petitioner was convicted in the District Court for the Southern District of California under an eight-count indictment charging him with transmitting wagering information by telephone from Los Angeles to Miami and Boston, in violation of a federal statute.[5] At trial the Government was permitted, over [Katz's] objection, to introduce evidence of [his] end of telephone conversations, overheard by FBI agents who had attached an electronic listening and recording device to the outside of the public telephone booth from which he had placed his calls. In affirming his conviction, the Court of Appeals rejected the contention that the recordings had been obtained in violation of the Fourth Amendment, because "[t]here was no physical entrance into the area occupied by [Katz]."

ISSUE: [Katz] has phrased those questions as follows:

A. Whether a public telephone booth is a constitutionally protected area so that evidence obtained by attaching an electronic listening and recording device to the top of such booth is obtained in violation of the right to privacy of the user of the booth.

B.	Whether physical penetration of a constitutionally protected area is necessary before a search and seizure can be said to violate the Fourth Amendment to the United States Constitution.

We decline to adopt this formulation of the issues. In the first place, the correct solution to Fourth Amendment problems is not necessarily promoted by incantation of the phrase "constitutionally protected area." Secondly, the Fourth Amendment cannot be translated into a general constitutional "right to privacy." That Amendment protects individual privacy against certain kinds of governmental intrusion, but its protections go further, and often have nothing to do with privacy at all . . .

HOLDING: The Government's activities in electronically listening to and recording the petitioner's words violated the privacy upon which he justifiably relied while using the telephone booth and thus constituted a "search and seizure" within the meaning of the Fourth Amendment. The fact that the electronic device employed to achieve that end did not happen to penetrate the wall of the booth can have no constitutional significance.

REASONING: [Katz] has strenuously argued that the booth was a "constitutionally protected area." The Government has maintained with equal vigor that it was not. But this effort to decide whether or not a given "area," viewed in the abstract, is "constitutionally protected" deflects attention from the problem presented in this case.[6] *For the Fourth Amendment protects people, not places* (emphasis added). . . .

The Government urges that, because its agents relied upon [prior case law and] did no more here than they might properly have done with prior judicial sanction, we should retroactively validate their conduct. That we cannot do. It is apparent that the agents in this case acted with restraint. Yet the inescapable fact is that this restraint was imposed by the agents themselves, not by a judicial officer. They were not required, before commencing the search, to present their estimate of probable cause for detached scrutiny by a neutral magistrate. They were not compelled, during the conduct of the search itself, to observe precise limits established in advance by a specific court order. Nor were they directed, after the search had been completed, to notify the authorizing magistrate in detail of all that had been seized.

In the absence of such safeguards, this Court has never sustained a search upon the sole ground that officers reasonably expected to find evidence of a particular crime and voluntarily confined their activities to the least intrusive means consistent with that end. "Over and again this Court has emphasized that the mandate of the [Fourth] Amendment requires adherence to judicial processes," and that searches conducted outside the judicial process, without prior approval by a judge or magistrate, are *per se* [on its face] unreasonable under the Fourth Amendment—subject only to a few specifically established and well-delineated exceptions. And bypassing a neutral predetermination of the scope of a search leaves individuals secure from Fourth Amendment violations "only in the discretion of the police."

These considerations do not vanish when the search in question is transferred from the setting of a home, an office, or a hotel room to that of a telephone booth. Wherever a man may be, he is entitled to know that he will remain free from unreasonable searches and seizures. The government agents here ignored "the procedure of antecedent [prior] justification that is central to the Fourth Amendment," a procedure that we hold to be a constitutional precondition [a legal requirement that must be met in order to satisfy the Constitution] to the kind of electronic surveillance involved in this case.

CONCLUSION: Because the surveillance here failed to meet that condition, and because it led to the petitioner's conviction, the judgment must be reversed. It is so ordered.

In the *Katz* decision, the high Court said the Fourth Amendment protects "people, not places." What about people who come visit you at your house? Should they, too, have a reasonable expectation of privacy in the guest room and should their belongings be protected against unreasonable search and seizure even though you own the house? In *Minnesota v. Olson* (1990), the high Court held houseguests enjoy the same expectation of privacy as the homeowner or apartment dweller, because visiting one's friends and relatives is a long-standing social custom.[7] On the other hand, if houseguests are using the home for purely commercial transactions, such as the weighing and packaging of illegal drugs as happened in *Minnesota v. Carter* (1998), the guests do not enjoy the same privacy rights as social guests because selling drugs is not a social custom or norm.[8]

What happens if you borrow a friend's rented car to deliver drugs? Terrence Byrd's girlfriend rented a car but did not list Byrd as an authorized driver. Byrd was pulled over and police asked for consent to search the car. Byrd refused consent, but when officers discover Byrd was not on the car rental agreement, they decide he had no expectation of privacy and proceeded to search the car.

In the trunk, officers discovered 49 bricks of heroin and body armor, which, as a felon, Byrd was not allowed to possess. Officers arrested Byrd, and he moved to suppress the evidence based on the lawfulness of the stop and search. The contraband was not suppressed and Byrd was found guilty. But on appeal to the U.S. Supreme Court, Byrd won. The Court found that Byrd, as the driver with dominion and control over the car and the right to exclude others from the car whether or not he was listed on the rental agreement, indicated Byrd had a right of privacy in the car that law enforcement was obligated to respect. *Byrd v. United States*, 2018.[9]

The Fourth Amendment and Modern Technology

One of the many hallmarks of American democracy is the U.S. Constitution's bedrock of law that guides government conduct. Although the Constitution lists many rights, it does not explicitly describe those rights, leaving the community to define its own rights and liberties. Community values change over time as do the public's perception of constitutional rights. For instance, before drugs and guns in middle and high schools became a focus of student discipline, students had a right of privacy in their school locker. Once the community demanded more proactive school surveillance, schools changed their policies to reflect the school "owned" the locker which the student merely "borrowed," eliminating students' legal claim to a right of privacy in their lockers. Nowhere has the definition of the right of privacy seen more evolution in the past 20 years than the Fourth Amendment's applicability to technology and new definitions of what government behavior constitutes a search and a seizure.

Searching and Seizing an Electronic Device. Modern technology has advanced to such a degree that commonly understood Fourth Amendment privacy analysis is constantly changing. For example, when officers have probable cause to arrest someone, they may also, without a warrant, search the area within the arrestee's immediate control and accessible "closed containers," such as briefcases and purses. For a long time, cell phones were considered "closed containers," and on arresting suspects, officers would often scroll through the suspect's phone contents searching for incriminating information. Read the case excerpt of *Riley v. California* reprinted in part below, initially discussed in Chapter 1, and focus on the Court's reasoning that cell phones have now become such an indispensable part of everyday life that officers should now make a probable cause showing before a judge to obtain a warrant before searching a cell phone for evidence of a crime.

> **Rule of Law: Electronic devices such as cell phones that store a person's "social DNA" require a warrant to search.**

RILEY V. CALIFORNIA, 134 S. CT. 2473 (2014)

Supreme Court of the United States

Chief Justice Roberts delivered the opinion of the Court. (9–0)

FACTS: [P]etitioner David Riley was stopped by a police officer for driving with expired registration tags. In the course of the stop, the officer also learned that Riley's license had been suspended. The officer impounded Riley's car, pursuant to department policy, and another officer conducted an inventory search of the car. Riley was arrested for possession of concealed and loaded firearms when that search turned up two handguns under the car's hood.

An officer searched Riley incident to the arrest and found items associated with the "Bloods" street gang. He also seized a cell phone from Riley's pants pocket. According to Riley's uncontradicted assertion, the phone was a "smart phone," a cell phone with a broad range of other functions based on advanced computing capability, large storage capacity, and Internet connectivity. The officer accessed information on the phone and noticed that some words (presumably in text messages or a contacts list) were preceded by the letters "CK"—a label that, he believed, stood for "Crip Killers," a slang term for members of the Bloods gang.

At the police station about two hours after the arrest, a detective specializing in gangs further examined the contents of the phone. The detective testified that he "went through" Riley's phone "looking for evidence, because . . . gang members will often video themselves with guns or take pictures of themselves with the guns." Although there was "a lot of stuff" on the phone, particular files that "caught [the detective's] eye" included videos of young men sparring while someone yelled encouragement using the moniker "Blood." The police also found photographs of Riley standing in front of a car they suspected had been involved in a shooting a few weeks earlier.

ISSUE: [Is the search of a cell phone seized without a warrant and searched incident to arrest lawful?]

HOLDING: [No. Police are not allowed, without warrant, to search digital information on a cell phone seized from an individual who has been arrested.]

REASONING: As the text [of The Fourth Amendment] makes clear, "the ultimate touchstone of the Fourth Amendment is 'reasonableness.'" Our cases have determined that "[w]here a search is undertaken by law enforcement officials to discover evidence of criminal wrongdoing . . . reasonableness generally requires the obtaining of a judicial warrant."[10] Such a warrant ensures that the inferences to support a search are "drawn by a neutral and detached magistrate instead of being judged by the officer engaged in the often competitive enterprise of ferreting out crime." In the absence of a warrant, a search is reasonable only if it falls within a specific exception to the warrant requirement.

Cell phones differ in both a quantitative and a qualitative sense from other objects that might be kept on an arrestee's person. The term "cell phone" is itself misleading shorthand; many of these devices are in fact minicomputers that also happen to have the capacity to be used as a telephone. They could just as easily be called cameras, video players, rolodexes, calendars, tape recorders, libraries, diaries, albums, televisions, maps, or newspapers. The storage capacity of cell phones has several interrelated consequences for privacy. First, a cell phone collects in one place many distinct types of information—an address, a note, a prescription, a bank statement, a video—that reveal much more in combination than any isolated record. Second, a cell phone's capacity allows even just one type of information to convey far more than previously possible. The sum of an individual's private life can be reconstructed through a thousand photographs labeled with dates, locations, and descriptions; the same cannot be said of a photograph or two of loved ones tucked into a wallet. Third, the data on a phone can date back to the purchase of the phone, or even earlier. A person might carry in his pocket a slip of paper reminding him to call Mr. Jones; he would not carry a record of all his communications with Mr. Jones for the past several months, as would routinely be kept on a phone.

Modern cell phones are not just another technological convenience. With all they contain and all they may reveal, they hold for many Americans "the privacies of life." The fact that technology now allows an individual to carry such information in his hand does not make the information any less worthy of the protection for which the Founders fought.

CONCLUSION: Our answer to the question of what police must do before searching a cell phone seized incident to an arrest is accordingly simple—get a warrant.

If the government, generally, needs a warrant to search cell phones, what is legally required to capture information gathered from an electronic device's output? As stated in the *Katz* decision, the "Fourth Amendment does not protect what one knowingly exposes to the public," and the U.S. Supreme Court has said personal information we share with the public, so-called third parties, is not expected to be private and, therefore, not protected by the Fourth Amendment.

Searching and Seizing the Output of an Electronic Device. Pursuant to the **third-party doctrine**, if you voluntarily share private information with a nonconfidential third party (a bank, a telephone company, even a friend in whom you confide your secrets), you have no control over what the third party does with your information and there is no reasonable expectation of privacy. The third-party doctrine was articulated in *Smith v. Maryland* (1979), where a woman was robbed by a man she later identified drove a Monte Carlo.[11] After the robbery, the suspect would call the victim on the telephone. On one occasion, the robber told her to come outside and she recognized the Monte Carlo, which police traced to defendant Smith. Without securing court approval, police asked the telephone company for a list of all telephone numbers used by the subscriber's telephone, called a **pen register**. When phone company records showed Smith's phone had called the victim's house, he was arrested, tried, and convicted. On appeal, Smith claimed a privacy right

> **Rule of Law:** Once a person shares his or her personal information with a "third party," such as a bank or phone company, there is a diminished reasonable expectation of privacy.

in his phone's dialing activity, but the high Court disagreed. The Court said society was not willing to respect a privacy interest in automated, routine, business activities.[12]

The same rationale of the third-party doctrine can be applied when law enforcement uses a device to track a suspect in a public location. Without a warrant but with the consent of the store's owner, federal agents placed a beeper in a container of chloroform in a store, suspecting people were buying the chemical to produce methamphetamine. Someone bought the chloroform, and agents followed the beeper to a cabin. The officers then obtained a search warrant for the cabin and arrested the occupants, who claimed the search violated the Fourth Amendment. The high Court found in *United States v. Knotts* (1983), because the beeper signal had only a limited range, its signal was followed only on public roads, so there was no expectation of privacy the Fourth Amendment was bound to protect.[13] Conversely, in *United States v. Karo* (1984), the Court held a beeper to track a suspect's movements inside a house was too invasive, and the Court held a warrant was required to protect privacy interests inside a home.[14]

Based on the *Knotts* holding that there is no warrant required for outside, public activity, agents used a thermal imaging device to capture heat coming off a roof. Growing marijuana inside requires strong lamps to give the plants the light they need for full development. When agents used the thermal images of heat emanating from Danny Kyllo's roof to get a warrant to search his house and, indeed, found marijuana plants inside, the Supreme Court held in *Kyllo v. United States* (2001) that when "the Government uses a device that is not in general public use, to explore details of the home that would previously have been unknowable without physical intrusion, the surveillance is a 'search' and is presumptively unreasonable without a warrant."[15] The Court was saying if the government uses equipment not generally available to the public to expose private activity, a search without a warrant is unreasonable.

APPLYING THE LAW TO THE FACTS

Reasonable Expectation of Privacy in a Car's Black Box?

The Facts: On October 6, 2013, Charles Worsham, Jr., was the driver in a crash in which his passenger, Amanda Patterson, was killed. His vehicle was seized and impounded by police. Twelve days later, police in Palm Beach County, Florida, accessed the data in the car's black box without first obtaining a warrant. The information retrieved from the black box indicated Worsham was speeding at the time of the crash. Worsham was convicted of vehicular manslaughter and challenged the lawfulness of the warrantless search of the car's black box. The police maintained the black box was full of third-party records such as data on speed, braking, and steering, data that required no warrant or consent from the vehicle's owner. Moreover,

black boxes are in vehicles so car companies can comply with national safety standards, not for everyday use by the individuals who drive the car. Which side will win, and why?

The Law: A divided appellate court decided that the police should have obtained a warrant for the black box. Stating that retrieving information from a black box is not like putting a car on a lift and inspecting the tires, the court said, "Modern technology facilitates the storage of large quantities of information on small portable devices. The emerging trend is to require a warrant to search these devices" (*Florida v. Worsham*, 2017).[16]

Searching and Seizing the Output of an Electronic Device to Pinpoint Location. Using the *Kyllo* precedent that the government needs a warrant to use enhanced technology, but tracking movements on public streets with a beeper is legal under the *Knotts* precedent, which legal standard is applicable when the government uses a GPS on a vehicle's undercarriage to track the car's movements on public streets? In 2012, federal agents suspected Antoine Jones of drug dealing. Officers, without a warrant, placed a GPS on Jones's Jeep and tracked his movements for 28 days. Like a beeper, GPS is an attachment-based technology and has limited range because satellite signals can be lost. Evidence retrieved from the GPS showed Jones traveling to and from drug deals and, based on the evidence, he was convicted at trial. On appeal, Jones argued that his Fourth Amendment rights were violated by the warrantless GPS tracking. The U.S. Supreme Court agreed, based on the historical doctrine of trespass (unlawful interference with property), that officers physically placing a GPS on

Jones's Jeep was a trespass without legal justification. Jones won his appeal in *United States v. Jones* (2012).[17] In the chapter-opening case study, officers probably needed a warrant to place the GPS tracker on Charlie's car for long-term surveillance, because even though a beeper on public streets is not a search, it is an act of trespass for the warrantless placement of a tracking device on a person's personal property.

The way law enforcement is currently using advanced technology "not in use by the general public," as stated in the *Kyllo* case, to track and catch suspects is illustrated in Figure 7.2.[18]

Referring to Figure 7.2, let's say that (1) there is a suspect who is in a crowd using a cell phone, and law enforcement—without being detected—would like to track the suspect's movements. (2) Officers can use mobile technology called a **StingRay** (manufactured by Harris Corporation), which is a briefcase-size international mobile subscriber identity (IMSI) catcher that acts as a roving cell phone tower and intercepts the suspect's cell phone signal by temporarily disconnecting the phone from its contracted wireless provider. Cell phones are designed to automatically connect to the strongest cell tower signal, whether or not the phone is turned on. If police have a StingRay in a car or van, the StingRay sucks up all the cell phone signals from nearby phones and can be downloaded directly to law enforcement computers using mapping software. IMSI catchers can capture and download information, even behind walls, from voice communication, texts, websites requested, and other data and apps stored on all phones within a certain distance from the catcher.[19]

Another form of direct government surveillance is the **dirtbox** (made by Digital Receiver Technology, Inc.), which also mimics cell phone towers and (as shown in Figure 7.2 [3]) attached to the underside of low-flying aircraft, allowing law enforcement to sweep large areas to intercept

Figure 7.2 Government Surveillance With StingRays and Dirtboxes

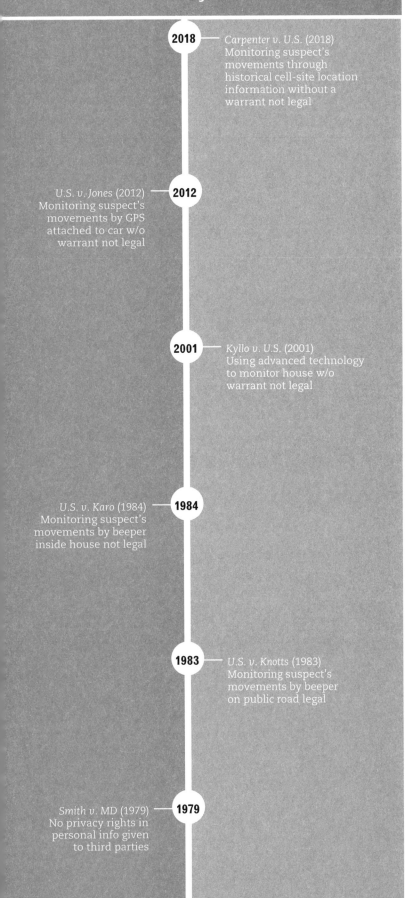

TIMELINE
Precedent Hierarchy From Third-Party Doctrine

2018 — *Carpenter v. U.S.* (2018) Monitoring suspect's movements through historical cell-site location information without a warrant not legal

U.S. v. Jones (2012) Monitoring suspect's movements by GPS attached to car w/o warrant not legal — **2012**

2001 — *Kyllo v. U.S.* (2001) Using advanced technology to monitor house w/o warrant not legal

U.S. v. Karo (1984) Monitoring suspect's movements by beeper inside house not legal — **1984**

1983 — *U.S. v. Knotts* (1983) Monitoring suspect's movements by beeper on public road legal

Smith v. MD (1979) No privacy rights in personal info given to third parties — **1979**

the suspect's cell phone location. Reporters reveal that the U.S. Marshals, responsible for catching suspects, fly planes with dirtboxes attached scanning tens of thousands of cell phones at a time in the hunt for fugitives.[20] (4) Sometimes, the Sting-Ray has to keep moving to be able to triangulate the suspect's location via his cell phone signal. (5) The data collected from both cell-site simulators can be transmitted and analyzed by law enforcement either on laptops or back at the police station, and used to locate and apprehend the suspect. Dirtboxes are effective for finding contraband, such as cell phones behind prison walls.

The timeline to the left represents the hierarchy of case precedent of the third-party doctrine, starting with *Smith v. Maryland* (1979), that says people lose privacy rights in the information they share with third parties (such as banks) and follows up the steps through case decisions controlling the use of electronic monitoring devices such as GPS attached to cars without a warrant (*United States v. Jones*, 2012). The next step in the analysis is tracking location through cell phone signals.

In 2011, the FBI, investigating cell phone robberies, obtained from Timothy Carpenter's cell phone carrier his historical cell-site location information (CSLI) data over a 127-day period. According to the American Civil Liberties Union, which is representing Carpenter, this information "revealed 12,898 separate points of location data—an average of 101 each day over the course of four months." The FBI did not obtain a warrant but relied on the Stored Communications Act, 18 U.S.C. §2703, which does not require probable cause for a court order to issue a warrant, but only "specific and articulable facts showing reasonable grounds to believe are relevant and material to an ongoing criminal investigation." Carpenter was convicted of the robberies based on the evidence of his location culled from his cell phone signal. He appealed, and the U.S. Supreme Court found in Carpenter's favor that the "seismic shift in digital technology" means that the government can access "deeply revealing" information about people the Fourth Amendment was designed to protect (*Carpenter v. United States*, 2018).[21] Therefore, officers should have established probable cause and secured a warrant for the information leading to Carpenter's location as transmitted by his cell phone.

SEIZURES OF THE PERSON

America, as our national anthem the "Star-Spangled Banner" proclaims, is the "land of the free and home of the brave."[22] People can go about their daily business free from government interference. When the police stop members of the public, whether it is to ask questions or to arrest and take to jail, there is a corresponding legal basis for police action. If the minimum legal requirement is not met for the citizen–police encounter, the detention, however brief, is unlawful.

The *Terry* Stop

Police officers can approach and ask anyone questions, and the person approached can consent to answer or not. The brief investigatory detention, also called the *Terry* stop, is a temporary restraint of a citizen based on reasonable suspicion that criminal activity is afoot. The detention is brief and designed to allow officers the freedom to ask questions to confirm or dispel their suspicion that a crime has been or will be committed. How can the public distinguish between a detention and an arrest?

In *Terry v. Ohio* (1968),[23] Detective Martin McFadden was on duty one night when he noticed three men behaving suspiciously. Two of them were walking up and down the same street to look into a store window. They made 24 trips back and forth, while a third man stood watch. McFadden approached the two men, Terry and Chilton, and asked their names. When the men mumbled a response, McFadden turned them to face one another, patted Terry down, and removed a gun from his coat pocket. Terry was convicted for carrying a concealed weapon. On appeal, the Supreme Court found that the officer's patdown, even without probable cause, was legal. The *Terry* Court stated,

> where a police officer observes unusual conduct which leads him reasonably to conclude in light of his experience that criminal activity may be afoot and that the persons with whom he is dealing may be armed and presently dangerous . . . and nothing . . . serves to dispel his reasonable fear for his own or others' safety, he is entitled for the protection of himself and others in the area to conduct a carefully limited search of the outer clothing of such persons in an attempt to discover weapons which might be used to assault him.

The **reasonable suspicion** standard states that if police have specific and articulable facts that a crime was about to happen or did just happen—that criminal activity was afoot—then the police could briefly detain the suspect and ask questions. **Specific and articulable facts** means that at the time of the seizure, the officer "must be able to articulate [speak to] something more than an 'inchoate and unparticularized suspicion or hunch.' From a courtroom perspective, when judging the legality of a *Terry* stop, criminal justice professionals should always envision themselves in a courtroom, testifying under oath to the specific facts that justified their behavior. The Fourth Amendment requires 'some minimal level of objective justification' for making the stop."[24] Some circumstances that contribute to the "reasonable suspicion" determination are the following:[25]

- The person approached: Does the officer know this person? Does the person fit a description of the suspect in a reported crime? Does the person appear cooperative? Is the person dressed appropriately given the weather and circumstances?

- The initial encounter: Is the area typically populated with people at this time of day? Is the area known by law enforcement as a "hot spot" for repeated criminal activity?

- Specific and articulable facts: What evidence supports the suspicion that a person is, has, or will commit a crime? Is the person known to law enforcement? Has there been a police report; if so, for what type of crime?

Furthermore, if the officers had a **reasonable belief** that the person is armed, police could lawfully conduct a patdown (frisking) for weapons by placing hands on the suspect's outer

> Rule of Law: Every citizen–police encounter, from briefly stopping a person to ask questions to the government securing a conviction, has a specific legal basis.

> Rule of Law: The *Terry* stop is a brief encounter between police and the public to confirm or dispel the reasonable suspicion that criminal activity is afoot.

clothing. The patdown is to ensure the safety of both the officers and the public and is not a full-blown search; probable cause is required to search.

Figure 7.4 illustrates the *Terry* stop, the patdown, and the full-blown arrest.

In the chapter-opening case study, Agent Wick was within the law to stop and talk to Charlie, Elaine, and Jamal because of the reasonable suspicion that criminal activity was afoot by the late-night rendezvous and "casing" the electronics store for a possible robbery. Wick could also pat Elaine down for weapons because he had a reasonable belief she was armed when he saw the weapon protruding from her pocket.

Duration of a *Terry* stop

A *Terry* stop is to last only as long as to either confirm or dispel the officer's reasonable suspicion that criminal activity is afoot. The *Terry* reasonable suspicion legal standard does not provide officers with authority to take a suspect to the police station to take mug shots or fingerprints or to put the suspect in a line-up without his or her consent or a warrant authorizing such behavior.[27] If a *Terry* stop lasts too long, the person is not free to leave and is, therefore, under arrest without legal authority. Any evidence retrieved from the suspect unlawfully detained may be suppressed by operation of the exclusionary rule.

There is no concrete defining moment when a *Terry* stop becomes an unlawful arrest. The U.S. Supreme Court declared, "Much as a 'bright line' rule would be desirable in evaluating whether an investigative detention is unreasonable, common sense and ordinary human experience must govern over rigid criteria."[28] Courts examine the totality of the circumstances in making the determination whether the *Terry* stop was proper and whether the detention lasted too long. For example, after an officer observed a vehicle swerve from the highway onto the shoulder and back again, he pulled the vehicle over. A traffic stop is a *Terry* stop based on the reasonable suspicion the driver has committed a traffic violation. The driver, Dennys Rodriguez, explained that he had swerved to avoid a pothole. After checking Rodriguez's driver's license, registration, and insurance, the officer asked Rodriguez a number of questions regarding his travels. When the officer returned the documents and issued a warning for improper driving, the officer asked for permission for the officer's K-9 dog to walk around Rodriguez's vehicle, and he lawfully refused. The officer then ordered Rodriguez out of the car and called for a second officer to arrive at the scene. When the second officer arrived, the first officer walked the police dog around the vehicle. The dog alerted to the presence of drugs and a subsequent search revealed a big bag of methamphetamine. Did the *Terry* stop last too long, transforming the stop into an illegal arrest? Yes, the stop lasted too long. In *Rodriguez v. United States* (2015), the high Court held the stop went beyond the "time reasonably required to complete" the stop making the stop "unlawful." Rodriguez's case was remanded back to the trial court for further disposition.[29]

Springboard for Discussion

Two women were speaking Spanish in a gas station in Montana. A federal Border Patrol agent approached the women, asked for identification, and detained the women for 30 minutes on the basis that Montana is a "predominately English speaking state" and the women were "pretty far north."[26] Was the agent's stop lawful? What's the difference between a hunch and "specific articulable facts" that criminal activity is afoot?

> **Rule of Law:** If a *Terry* stop lasts too long to either confirm or deny the reasonable suspicion that criminal activity is afoot, it transforms to an arrest unsupported by probable cause, which is an unlawful arrest.

Requests for Identification

> **Rule of Law:** Requests for personal identification can be made only in the context of a *Terry* stop and, without consent, should be supported by state law.

Are individuals legally required to identify themselves to police officers or run the risk of being arrested? In Nevada, police received a report of an assault and saw Larry Hiibel and a woman parked by a side of the road. Officers asked Hiibel for his name and identification. Hiibel, who appeared to be intoxicated, refused 11 times to identify himself and was arrested under Nevada's "stop and identify" statute. Hiibel challenged his arrest under the Fourth Amendment as an unreasonable seizure. The Supreme Court found in favor of the officers in *Hiibel v. Nevada* (2004), holding that the statute requiring identification serves the "purpose, rationale, and practical demands of a *Terry* stop" and was a limited intrusion when weighed against the government's interest in identifying a suspect's criminal record or mental disorder, or in clearing the suspect as

Figure 7.4 The Three Steps From Talking to Arrest

Terry Stop

Terry Patdown

Arrest

| Reasonable suspicion that criminal activity is afoot | Reasonable belief person is armed | Probable cause to arrest |
| Brief investigatory detention: Stop and ask questions | Pat down outer clothing for weapons only | Full search of the person and the area within his immediate control |

the object of the investigation.[30] The Court limited its holding to asking for identification within the context of the *Terry* stop only; authority to demand identification does not extend to anyone for any reason. As always, police may ask for identification and the person may agree and consent, but refusal to comply without a supporting state law does not confer authority to arrest.

Terry Stops of Automobiles

What happens when, during a roadside encounter, officers have a reasonable suspicion that criminal activity is afoot on the basis of the actions and statements of a driver and passengers in a vehicle? What does the law allow the officer to do? According to the decision made in *Delaware v. Prouse* (1979), if officers have reasonable suspicion that the motorists are engaged in criminal activity, then the officers can detain motorists in their vehicles.[31] Once the car is seized, passengers are also seized and have a Fourth Amendment claim as well, as held in *Brendlin v. California* (2007).[32] To balance the safety concerns of the officer with the need to minimize intrusion on the privacy of the motorists, the officers not only can detain the motorists but also order both the driver, *Pennsylvania v. Mimms* (1977), and the passengers, *Maryland v. Wilson* (1997), out of the car until the officer completes the traffic stop.[33]

> **Rule of Law: The same legal standard that guides *Terry* stops of people applies with equal force to automobiles.**

But if, during the stop, the driver and passengers make the officer fear for her safety, and if she believes that the motorists may be armed or that the passenger compartment (where everyone sits) contains weapons, the officer may order everyone out of the car and search for and remove those weapons. In *Arizona v. Johnson* (2009), officers were part of a gang task force when they stopped a vehicle with a suspended registration.[34] While speaking to the driver and passengers, officers noted Johnson was wearing a blue bandana consistent with Crips gang membership, there was a police scanner in the car, and Johnson volunteered he was from Eloy, Arizona, home to a Crips gang. Officer Trevizo ordered Johnson out of the car and patted him down for her safety and discovered a gun in his waistband. The U.S. Supreme Court upheld the legality of the officer's actions because she had a reasonable suspicion Johnson was armed.

The Intersection of the *Terry* Stop and the Suspect's Race

When the *Terry* case was decided in 1968, U.S. Supreme Court Chief Justice Earl Warren's opinion cautioned against the potential abuse of power that might come from a relaxation of the rules controlling law enforcement's relationship with the public. Warren wrote for the majority,

> Proper adjudication of cases in which the exclusionary rule is invoked demands a constant awareness of these limitations. The wholesale harassment by certain elements of the police community, of which minority groups, particularly Negroes, frequently complain, will not be stopped by the exclusion of any evidence from any criminal trial. Under our decision, courts still retain their traditional responsibility to guard against police conduct which is overbearing or harassing, or which trenches upon personal security without the objective evidentiary justification which the Constitution requires.

Chief Justice Warren was saying that the rule that excludes evidence from being used against a defendant because it was seized unlawfully will not cure the "wholesale harassment by certain elements of the police community" that people of color often report. Although law enforcement has a duty to investigate and prevent crime, men of color frequently complain that race was a motivating factor in their being stopped. But if the stop was based on what Justice Warren said was "an objective evidentiary justification," what the officer subjectively had in his mind about the suspect's race does not matter (*Whren v. United States*, 1996).[35] However, the statistical racial disparities in analyzing *Terry* stops either on foot (which led a federal judge to stop New York City's aggressive stop and frisk policy because of unconstitutional racial profiling[36]) or in a car (e.g., a federal judge reduced a man's sentence because his criminal history was for traffic violations that, on closer inspection, amounted to little more than "driving while Black"[37]) raise questions whether all of the *Terry* stops in minority communities have been "objectively reasonable." In *Utah v. Strieff* (2016), the U.S. Supreme Court held that drug evidence could be used against a defendant because officers discovered an outstanding arrest warrant while conducting a *Terry* stop. The problem in the case was there was no legal authority for the *Terry* stop. All citizen–police encounters are analyzed from the beginning of the encounter, not what happens later, which means since there was no legal authority to stop Strieff, all evidence seized from him should have been suppressed. In a notable dissent, Justice Sotomayor disagreed with the *Strieff* majority's holding. She wrote that not requiring officers to follow the law in the initial stop would have far-reaching consequences, particularly for minorities:

> The white defendant in this case shows that anyone's dignity can be violated in this manner. But it is no secret that people of color are disproportionate victims of this type of scrutiny. For generations, black and brown parents have given their children "the talk"—instructing them never to run down the street; always keep your hands where they can be seen; do not even think of talking back to a stranger—all out of fear of how an officer with a gun will react to them.[38]

If people of color are stopped without legal authority, such police conduct may breed "cynicism and distrust" of the police in minority communities. In *Illinois v. Wardlow* (2000), the U.S. Supreme Court held that a suspect who, on sight, runs from the police may indicate that the person is involved in criminal activity. Justice Stevens, however, noted in his dissent that minority communities may believe "that contact with the police may be dangerous, even for innocent people."[39] In 2016, the Massachusetts Supreme Court found the Boston City Police Department had a longstanding problem with racially profiling African Americans. When Jimmy Warren ran from the police, who wanted to question him about a recent breaking and entering, officers used his flight to justify stopping him, eventually using the illegal handgun found on the ground next to Warren against him. In suppressing the gun on the basis that the officers did not have reasonable suspicion to stop Warren, the state court noted the Boston Police's own Field Interrogation and Observation (FIO) data indicated that

> Black men in the city of Boston were more likely to be targeted for police-civilian encounters such as stops, frisks, searches, observations, and interrogations. . . . We do not eliminate flight as a factor in the reasonable suspicion analysis whenever a black

male is the subject of an investigatory stop. Such an individual, when approached by the police, might just as easily be motivated by the desire to avoid the recurring indignity of being racially profiled as by the desire to hide criminal activity.

The Massachusetts court concluded judges should use the FIO conclusions that Black men might flee simply to protect themselves in considering whether a suspect's unprovoked flight from the police indicated reasonable suspicion that the man running was involved in criminal activity.[40]

The Arrest

The Arrest as a Fourth Amendment Seizure

As the U.S. Supreme Court has said, officers "do not violate the Fourth Amendment by merely approaching an individual on the street or other public place, by asking him if he is willing to answer some questions, by putting questions to him if the person is willing to listen, or by offering in evidence in a criminal prosecution his voluntary answers to such questions."[41] Consent to abide by police wishes must be voluntary and must not be the product of unlawful coercion, such as by the threat or show of force or authority. Courts examine the totality of the circumstances surrounding the restraint to determine whether a reasonable person would have believed he was not free to leave.[42] An arrest is a seizure; a formal arrest with handcuffs is not required. "If a reasonable person would feel free to terminate the encounter, then he or she has not been seized,[43] and courts consider the following factors:[44]

> **Springboard for Discussion**
>
> Is it reasonable for African Americans to perceive a *Terry* stop differently from other members of the public? If so, should courts take a community's experience with local law enforcement into account when judging the reasonableness of the citizen–police encounter, or should the law be color blind?

1. Whether the person was approached by more than one police officer in a show of force and the officers' demeanor (friendly, hostile, professional)

2. The basis for the police encounter

3. The duration of the police encounter

4. Whether an officer told the person he was under investigation

5. Whether an officer told the person she was not free to leave

6. Whether an officer blocked the person's path or blocked his progress when he tried to leave

7. Whether an officer displayed a weapon or police dogs were present

8. Whether the encounter was in a public or private location

> **Rule of Law:** A person is under arrest if he or she does not feel free to leave or otherwise terminate the police encounter.

The significance of a person being "under arrest" is that certain constitutional protections attach, such as whether or not the so-called *Miranda* warnings are required before an interrogation or whether the person has a right to a lawyer.

For a seizure to occur, the suspect must actually submit to police authority. The high Court held in *California v. Hodari D.* (1991) that even though the police yelled "Stop!" at a suspect who was running away, that suspect was not seized until he actually stopped.[45] The issue was important because if Hodari D. was "under arrest" when he was running and throwing away his drugs, he might have had a sufficient legal challenge to the police seizure of the drugs. But by throwing his drugs away, Hodari D. also threw away his reasonable expectation of privacy and the drugs became abandoned property that could be seized without violating the Fourth Amendment.

Reasonable Force. Because an arrest involves the restraint of a person and, sometimes, the use of force, the Fourth Amendment is the touchstone for determining if the amount of force used was reasonable. The seminal case is *Tennessee v. Garner* (1985).[46] Police responded to a call about a

Rule of Law: The
amount of force used
to effectuate an
arrest is subject to the
Fourth Amendment's
reasonableness clause.

prowler, saw Garner run away, and ordered him to stop. Garner was a 15-year-old boy who was 5'4" and weighed between 100 and 110 pounds. When Garner kept running away, an officer shot him once in the back of the head, killing him. Garner's family sued the officer for violating Garner's rights under 42 U.S.C. §1983 (discussed in Chapter 1), but the officer acted lawfully as the Tennessee statute said police could use "all the necessary means to effect the arrest" of a fleeing suspect. After reviewing the case, the high Court decided that deadly force had to be limited to dangerous situations.

The use of deadly force to prevent the escape of all felony suspects, whatever the circumstances, is constitutionally unreasonable. It is not better that all felony suspects die than that they escape. Where the suspect poses no immediate threat to the officer and no threat to others, the harm resulting from failing to apprehend him does not justify the use of deadly force to do so.

Today's statutes give officers wide latitude in using their discretion on how much force is "reasonable" and recognizes the split-second decision officers must make under pressure, as the Court stated in *Graham v. Connor* (1989): "The 'reasonableness' of a particular use of force must be judged from the perspective of a reasonable officer on the scene, rather than with the 20/20 vision of hindsight."[47] Legal scholars surveyed how the *Garner* decision prompted states to change their laws defining when officers could use deadly force.[48] Reasonable force laws cover a wide range of activities, as illustrated by the Chippewa Cree Tribe statute as compared to California's Code, reprinted in part here.

Chippewa-Cree Tribal Law and Order Code Title IV, §1.6 Use of Reasonable Force by Police Officers

A police officer must not use unnecessary or unreasonable force in carrying out the apprehension, arrest, search, summons, interrogation, traffic supervision, and other procedures the police force is authorized or obligated to perform.

California Code Annotated §835a Reasonable force to effect arrest; Resistance

- Any peace officer who has reasonable cause to believe that the person to be arrested has committed a public offense may use reasonable force to effect the arrest, to prevent escape or to overcome resistance.

- A peace officer who makes or attempts to make an arrest need not retreat or desist from his efforts by reason of the resistance or threatened resistance of the person being arrested; nor shall such officer be deemed an aggressor or lose his right to self-defense by the use of reasonable force to effect the arrest or to prevent escape or to overcome resistance.

If the suspect is posing a danger, police officers can use deadly force to protect the public, including during high-speed chases. In one case where a suspect was driving in excess of 100 miles per hour for many miles while fleeing police, officers used what is called a "pit maneuver" (i.e., applying the police cruiser's push bumper to the rear of the fleeing vehicle), causing the car to crash and rendering the driver a quadriplegic. The high Court found the officer's action was not an unreasonable seizure because the officer protected innocent bystanders from injury.[49]

Thus, if police use excessive force in effectuating arrests, they have violated the Fourth Amendment's reasonableness clause, but the legal analysis is whether the use of such force is objectively (to everyone's perspective) reasonable, which may be determined by reference to the "use of force" model that shows the behavior of the suspect and the corresponding appropriate level of force used by an officer. For example, if a suspect is compliant, using a baton to subdue the suspect would be inappropriate. In the chapter-opening case study, officers would be unreasonable to shoot Charlie, a fleeing suspect not known to be armed or dangerous. Figure 7.5 illustrates the use of force continuum.

Figure 7.5 Use of Force Model

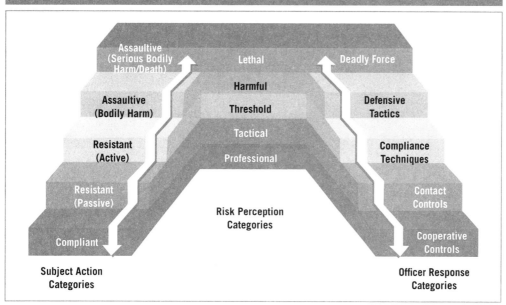

Risk Perception Categories

Subject Action Categories

Officer Response Categories

Source: University of Illinois Police Training Institute. All rights reserved. Reprinted with permission.

Arrest Warrants

An arrest warrant is a piece of paper signed by a judge allowing for the legal seizure of a person and is generally not required if the person has committed a felony and is found on a public street or if the officer witnessed the commission of a crime. Prior to the 1980s, if a person was suspected of committing a felony, state laws allowed police to enter private homes without a warrant to arrest the suspects, but the high Court interpreted the Fourth Amendment to require more protection for the sanctity of the home. In *Payton v. New York* (1980), state law allowed for warrantless entry into private homes to make felony arrests.[50] In finding police merely entering a home without a warrant "the chief evil against which the wording of the Fourth Amendment is directed," the high Court required arrest warrants for the home and also recognized that such warrants carried the authority to enter the home "in which the suspect lives when there is reason to believe the suspect is within," a phrase that has generated much litigation. Officers challenged on entering homes in which it is later determined a suspect does not live are frequently asked in court (a) how they determined a suspect was using the dwelling as a primary residence and (b) how they determined the suspect was inside the home at the time they entered.

> **Rule of Law:** State and federal laws guide when arrest warrants shall issue, but absent exigent circumstances, a warrant is required to enter a personal residence to effectuate an arrest.

Moreover, a warrant to enter to arrest does not grant the authority to enter someone else's home. The high Court said the Fourth Amendment right that "protected—that of presumptively innocent people to be secure in their homes from unjustified, forcible intrusions by the Government—is weighty," and officers generally have to ask for consent to enter the third-party's home or wait for the suspect to come out.[51]

THE WARRANT REQUIREMENT

The Procedure to Obtain a Warrant

A warrant is the legal document that notifies the person the cause for his arrest or notifies the person whose property is to be searched of the legal authority for, and the limits of, the proposed search. An arrest warrant and a search warrant protect two, separate interests. An arrest warrant protects a person from an unreasonable seizure, and a search warrant protects a person's privacy interests from unreasonable government intrusions. The procedure to obtain a warrant justifying the search or seizure is as follows, as illustrated by Figure 7.6:

1. Officers investigate to establish probable cause to search or seize.

2. The officer, or in complex cases an assistant district attorney (ADA, prosecutor), writes an affidavit in support of probable cause tracking the elements of the crime the suspect has alleged to have committed.

   a. The officer or ADA typically has a list of things to seize based on similar cases.

   b. The officer or ADA types the relevant information on the face of the warrant, incorporating by reference the attached affidavit of probable cause.

   c. When completed, a copy of the warrant and affidavit is typically given to the magistrate (judge) to examine before the officer appears to swear the facts contained in the affidavit are true to the best of his knowledge and belief.

   d. The officer, often accompanied by the ADA, makes an appointment with the magistrate's clerk.

Figure 7.6   Officer Obtaining, Executing, and Returning a Warrant

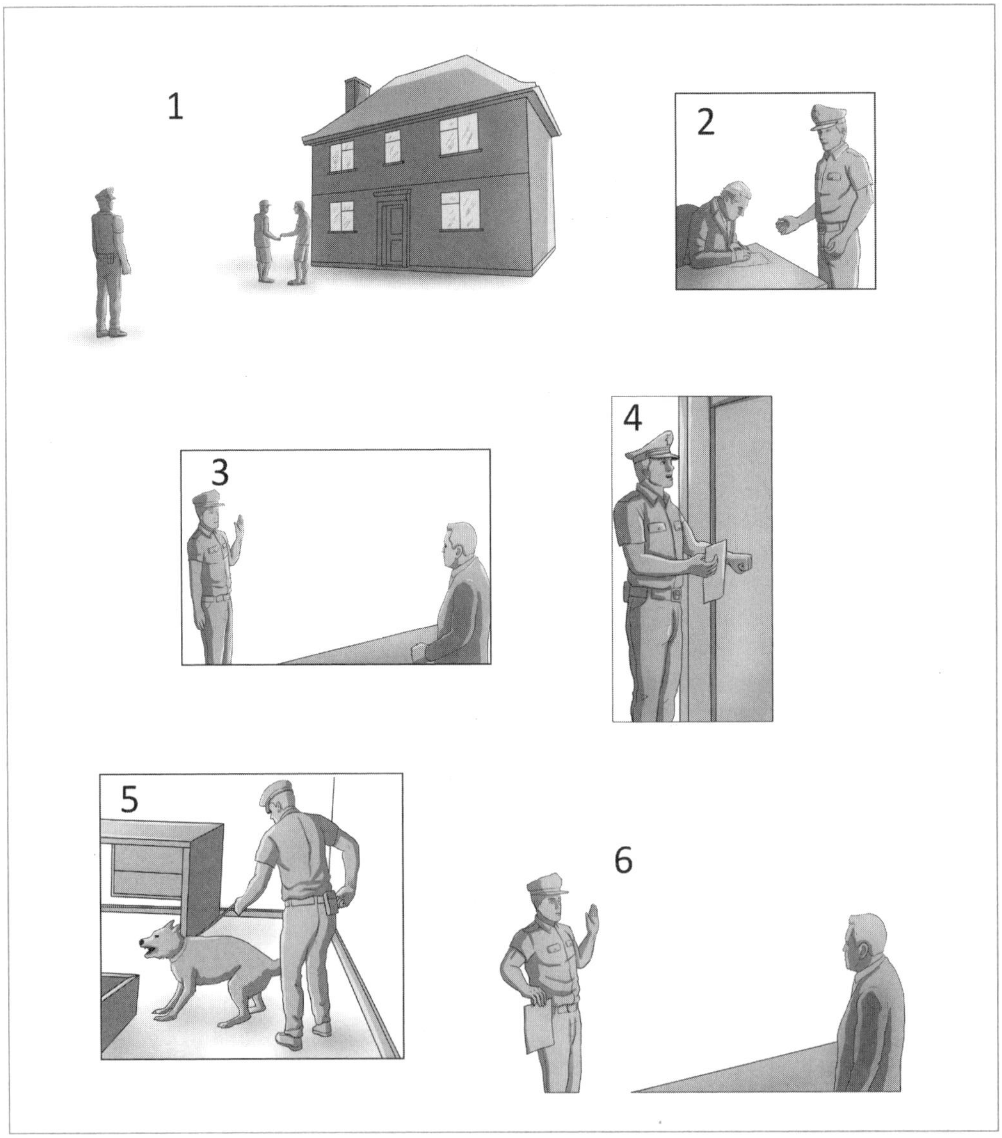

3. The officer appears before the magistrate, raises his right hand, and swears that the information contained in the affidavit attached to the warrant and on the warrant is true.

   a. The magistrate may ask questions to ensure sufficient probable cause exists.

4. If there are special circumstances in the service of the warrant (e.g., serving in the middle of the night and eliminating the "knock and announce" requirement because of a fear for officer safety), the magistrate will modify the conditions on the face of the warrant. Typically warrants must be executed within 10 days of being signed and during the hours of 6:00 a.m. and 10:00 p.m.

5. Once the warrant has been executed, officers leave a copy at the place searched or with the person arrested.

6. Once an inventory of the things taken are listed on the back of the warrant, the officer comes back before the magistrate and swears the list of evidence seized is true.

If there is not enough time to go to the courthouse and personally appear before a magistrate, the federal rules governing search and seizure provide for methods of securing a warrant, including by telephone.

Federal Rule of Criminal Procedure 41

(d) Obtaining a Warrant.

   (1) *In General.* After receiving an affidavit or other information, a magistrate judge—or if authorized by Rule 41(b), a judge of a state court of record—must issue the warrant if there is probable cause to search for and seize a person or property or to install and use a tracking device. . . .

   (3) *Requesting a Warrant by Telephonic or Other Means.* In accordance with Rule 4.1 [Complaint, Warrant or Summons by Phone], a magistrate judge may issue a warrant based on information communicated by telephone or other reliable electronic means.

An example of a federal warrant can be found on the student study site at edge.sagepub .com/jirard.

Probable Cause

The probable cause determination is a flexible calculation based on an objective analysis that a specific person is committing, has committed, or will commit a crime or specific evidence of criminal activity is going to be found at a specific place.[52] There are many sources of probable cause.

> **Rule of Law: The Fourth Amendment demands probable cause to search and seize.**

Sources of Probable Cause

Officer's Perceptions. The law does not expect police officers to shut their eyes, cover their ears, and perform their jobs in a sensory vacuum. All officers have been trained at professional academies and typically gain some experience early in their careers investigating crimes and interviewing witnesses, victims, and suspects. Officers can rely on their training and experience to determine whether probable cause exists to search and seize. A person's acts cannot merely suggest that a crime is being committed but must specifically indicate criminal activity.

Collective Knowledge. A common source establishing probable cause is the **collective knowledge** of all the information gathered by law enforcement agents during an investigation. One police officer trying to establish probable cause to arrest or search can rely on what other officers tell him and on information learned from other investigations, including those in different jurisdictions. An officer in Indiana who has received an all-points bulletin (APB) or a "be on the lookout" (BOLO) notice from neighboring Ohio describing a car last seen at a crime scene has probable cause to arrest a suspect driving that car based on the collective knowledge of all the officers. Also, second-hand hearsay (e.g., "Bill told me that Suzy said Mary sold drugs") is considered reliable in a preliminary investigation because of the nature of police work.

Presence in a "High-Crime" Area. Just because people live in a densely packed urban area known for illegal drug activity does not give rise to probable cause that its residents are criminals. But if someone is closely associated with known criminals in the area, that fact can be used to help establish probable cause. The courts use the following criteria to decide whether probable cause exists to search and arrest specifically for drug-related crimes in certain locations:

1. The suspect is present in an area notorious for its drug trade.
2. The suspect is engaging in a sequence of events typical of drug transactions, for example, many brief hand-to-hand transactions conducted late at night.
3. The suspect attempts to escape after being confronted by police.
4. The suspect attempts to conceal the subject of his business.[53]

All the previously listed factors in conjunction with other information known to law enforcement and personal observations may be used to establish probable cause.[54]

Informants. Informants are people who give information to law enforcement about crime and criminals in exchange for a government benefit. A typical informant is a criminal who has been arrested and enters into a plea bargain with the government, either for reduced charges or for a lighter sentence that enables the person to stay on the streets and gather more information about criminal activity to help the police. Because of their willingness to trade information for their own freedom, informant information may be suspect because they have an incentive to accuse others in exchange for a get-out-of-jail-free card from the government. When information is used to establish probable cause for a warrant, the officer must show in the affidavit of probable cause supporting the warrant that the informant is reliable. Informant reliability is determined by a three-prong test:

1. The informant's basis of knowledge

   How did the informant learn the information about the target suspect?

2. The basis for believing that the informant is telling the truth

   i. If the informant is an ordinary citizen, he or she is considered inherently credible;
   ii. If the informant is a criminal, the government must show that the informant has given accurate information in the past that has led to the further investigation, arrests, or convictions of other suspects; and

3. Independent corroboration of the informant's information.

If the informant provided information that he witnessed the suspect manufacture and sell illegal drugs, for example, the officer must state that he corroborated the information by surveillance that established the fact that the suspect was engaged in making and selling drugs. In the chapter-opening case study, Beth would be deemed an inherently reliable informant because she is an ordinary citizen who has no reason to lie about her suspicions that Charlie is a spy. The agents also relied on their personal observations, collective knowledge, and reliable hearsay to determine that Charlie is spying for North Korea.

The Difference Between Informants and Anonymous Tips. Anonymous tips typically are insufficient to establish probable cause because the source refuses to be identified. Imagine if a vindictive roommate, Vinny, called the police department to report, anonymously, that his roommate Maki was an embezzler. If Maki was not an embezzler and Vinny simply wanted to use the police to harass Maki, police time would be wasted. Anonymous tips may be reliable if the tip is sufficiently detailed and if officers can independently corroborate the tip. An anonymous tip was found sufficient to establish probable cause in *Alabama v. White* (1990),[55] where an anonymous person called police and relayed the following information about Vanessa White: She would be leaving Lynwood Apartments driving a brown Plymouth station wagon with a broken taillight traveling to Dorsey's motel where she would be carrying a brown attaché case with an ounce of cocaine inside. Police followed White to the motel and she was arrested for the cocaine delivery. White challenged her conviction in appeal claiming the anonymous tip was insufficient probable cause, but the high Court found the officers had sufficiently verified the information provided and White's conviction was upheld.

On the other hand, in *Florida v. J. L.* (2000), police received an anonymous tip that a man would be standing at a bus station at a specific time and would be carrying a weapon.[56] Police went to the bus stop, saw a young man who fit the description, frisked him, and recovered the gun. The high Court overturned J. L.'s conviction on appeal, finding that the search for the gun was unreasonable because the anonymous tip was nothing more than "a man with a gun," no actual evidence of criminal activity, and, therefore, there was no legal justification for the stop. However, the high Court has held that if a 9-1-1 call to police reports a crime, the traceability of the caller makes the tip reliable to establish reasonable suspicion to make a traffic stop. In *Navarette v. California* (2014), a caller reported she had been run off the road by a truck driving erratically.[57] Police located the truck and, on making a *Terry* stop, smelled marijuana. A subsequent search discovered 30 pounds of marijuana. Justice Thomas wrote the majority opinion that under the totality of the circumstances under *Alabama v. White*, the officers had reasonable suspicion that the driver was drunk and the stop was legal. In dissent, Justice Scalia said the majority opinion was a "freedom-destroying cocktail consisting of 2 parts patent falsity," because people could call 9-1-1 with false information, which, pursuant to the majority decision, would grant police the authority to stop.

Springboard for Discussion

Given that many ordinary citizens fear retaliation from criminal suspects if they are known to report crime to the police, why does the law require more than an anonymous tip to establish probable cause?

Drug Courier Profile. The drug courier profile was developed by the federal Drug Enforcement Administration and is an abstract of characteristics found to be typical of persons transporting illegal drugs. The profile has been held a sufficient basis for a *Terry* stop but not probable cause. From a courtroom perspective, the government must be careful when law enforcement officers testify in drug cases. Officers testify as fact witnesses; that is, they tell the court about how they conducted their investigation. But officers also testify as quasi-experts about common characteristics about the drug trade based on their training and experience. In one case, *United States v. Espinoza-Valdez* (May 6, 2018),[58] a court overturned a defendant's conviction because the courier profile was the crux of the government's case. Rather than establish with proof that the defendant was part of a drug conspiracy, the government offered testimony about the structure of a typical drug organization and asked the jury to convict the defendant because he fit the courier profile. The court said, "A drug expert's testimony cannot substitute for witnesses who actually observed or participated in the illegal activity." In the courtroom, facts establishing a defendant's guilt are required to secure a conviction.

MAKING THE COURTROOM CONNECTION

The U.S. Supreme Court has said, "Responsible law enforcement officers will take care to learn what is required of them under Fourth Amendment precedent and will conform their conduct to these rules."[59] A review of state and federal case precedent reveals officers can often avoid mistakes in the field by simply slowing down and taking the time to ensure sources of probable cause are credible and there has been sufficient, corroborating investigation before relying on any confidential informant or anonymous tip. The majority of affidavits attached to arrest or search warrants are public records, and students should study them. Affidavits in federal cases are often road maps of how to develop probable cause through investigative techniques. Even

(Continued)

(Continued)

though many judges defer to officers and may simply sign the warrant because they trust the officer, ultimately, the officer is responsible for presenting the court with sufficient facts establishing probable cause and an error-free warrant to sign. To the extent practicable, prosecutors should work closely with officers during investigations and help write, if not actually write, the affidavit of probable cause based on the officers' collective knowledge to ensure completeness and sufficiency of a probable cause finding. The officer is the one swearing to the truth of the facts contained in the affidavit, but a prosecutor's help in drafting can help avoid legal error. For the defense, the burden is on counsel's investigative skills to challenge a probable cause determination, made more difficult in cases when informants are used to establish probable cause because their identity can remain confidential until called to testify at trial. Testing the sufficiency of probable cause is done at a pretrial hearing, called a *Franks* hearing.[60] To get a *Franks* hearing, defense counsel must make a showing with evidence, not merely make a claim, that law enforcement was intentionally deceptive in stating facts establishing probable cause, a high evidentiary burden to meet.

Supported by Oath or Affirmation

Typically, when a search warrant is prepared, a state or federal prosecutor works in conjunction with the investigating officer to produce an affidavit, a statement of facts legally sufficient to establish probable cause sworn under the pains and penalties of perjury in front of a magistrate or judge. As depicted in the example of a federal warrant on the student study site (edge.sagepub .com/jirard), the format of a federal search warrant does not allow much room to type in the pages of facts that might support a probable cause determination. Therefore, in the space on the face of the warrant typically is typed the words indicating that the affidavit is incorporated by reference, which means the facts establishing probable cause are "brought in" on the face of the warrant, making the warrant valid. Sometimes, too, the description of the things to be seized can be more than a page long. To satisfy the "particularity requirement" of the Fourth Amendment, this list of things to be seized must also be incorporated by reference into the information included on the actual face of the warrant.

Before the search or seizure, the officer takes the warrant and his affidavit in front of the magistrate, raises his right hand, and swears or affirms by oath or affirmation that the information contained in the warrant and affidavit is true to the best of his knowledge and belief. Requiring the officer to swear to the truth of the facts establishing probable cause not only impresses on the officer the solemnity of the court but may make the officer personally responsible if the facts supporting the issuance of the warrant turn out to be false.

The Neutral and Detached Magistrate

The Fourth Amendment requires the magistrate (judge) signing the warrant be neutral (i.e., not acting in favor of one party or not having a personal stake in the outcome of the case) and detached (having no prior knowledge of the facts of the case) as discussed in Chapter 1 to ensure that there is a sufficient legal basis to justify the search or arrest. Court decisions have held that if the magistrate has investigated the crime, serves as a part-time prosecutor, or actually participates in the search for which he signed the warrant, the magistrate's objectivity whether there is probable cause to search is compromised, and the warrant issued is defective. In *Coolidge v. New Hampshire* (1971),[61] a 14-year-old girl was found murdered and Coolidge was a suspect. While he was at the police station taking a lie detector test, police went to his home, where Coolidge's wife turned over guns and clothing he was wearing on the night of the murder. Two weeks later, the attorney general of New Hampshire, who had a dual role as a justice of the police, issued a search warrant for Coolidge's car, where officers found incriminating evidence in the trunk, linking Coolidge to the murder. Coolidge was convicted. Because the issuance of the warrant by a biased magistrate violated the warrant requirement and thus violated Coolidge's rights, his conviction was overturned.[62]

The Particularity Requirement

The Fourth Amendment commands that the warrant must "particularly describ[e] the place to be searched and the persons or things to be seized." As interpreted by the Supreme Court, the particularity requirement protects against general, exploratory searches and leaves "nothing . . . to the discretion of the officer executing the warrant."[63] Courts take an inflexible position on the particularity requirement and have invalidated warrants that insufficiently explained what officers were to seize. Likewise, the place to be searched must be described fully.

Rule of Law: Warrants must describe with specificity the place to be searched and the person or things to be seized to prevent officers from having to "guess" what to take.

Warrants have been found invalid when the place to be searched was described as a single-family residence and was, instead, an apartment building, for example. But if the warrant merely contains a typographical error (e.g., "231" instead of "321"), such errors do not compromise probable cause to search. "The test for determining the adequacy of the description of the location to be searched is whether the description is sufficient to enable the executing officer to locate and identify the premises with reasonable effort."[64] Below is an affidavit from a U.S. Treasury Department special agent establishing probable cause to search businesses, homes, mailboxes, computers, and financial records of BALCO Laboratories, a company linked to supplying steroids to enhance the performance of world-class and professional athletes. Note the specificity and detail the agent relates in his affidavit establishing probable cause to search the various locations and to seize specific evidence.[65]

In the chapter-opening case study, agents would have to obtain another warrant establishing probable cause to search Charlie's computer because of the vast quantity of information stored on a hard drive, as Agent Novitsky did in the BALCO affidavit. Searches conducted pursuant to warrants are limited to the items listed on the warrant.

What happens when officers are not specific about the information that they include both on the face of the warrant and in the supporting affidavit of probable cause? In *Groh v. Ramirez* (2004), the high Court found a federal agent was not entitled to qualified immunity and was personally liable (responsible) for damages (money) to the people whose house was the subject of the unlawful search.[66] The search warrant was defective in describing the things to be seized. Instead of listing the things to be seized on the face of the warrant, the agent listed the address of the property. The Court found that no reasonable officer would have executed such a facially deficient (obviously wrong by looking at it) warrant. The particularity requirement is what constrains law enforcement from deciding what to take while searching. How do courts determine if the particularity clause has been met or if the list of things to be seized is too broad? One

---

Affidavit Of Special Agent Jeff Novitzky In Support Of Request For Search Warrants

I, Jeff Novitzky, being duly sworn, hereby depose and state as follows:

Introduction

1. This affidavit is submitted in support of a request for the issuance of five search warrants for locations under the authority and control of Victor Conte, Jr. The five locations to be searched are . . . [Conte's business, residence, and private mailboxes].

2. This request for authorization to conduct searches at the above-referenced locations is based upon the development of facts which provide probable cause to believe that Victor Conte, Jr. and others are involved in a nationwide scheme to knowingly distribute athletic performance-enhancing drugs, including anabolic steroids, a federally controlled substance, to numerous elite professional athletes at a local, national and international level [in violation of federal law].

(Continued)

(Continued)

Affiant's Background

3. I am a Special Agent with the Internal Revenue Service, Criminal Investigation ("IRS-CI"), and have been so employed since 1993. During my 10 years with IRS-CI, I have conducted and/or participated in hundreds of criminal investigations involving income tax violations, money laundering violations, currency violations and other federal financial crimes.

Facts In Support Of Probable Cause

[Paragraphs 4–9 omitted]

Balco Laboratories, Inc. Background

10. On January 29, 2003, I spoke with Jaime Nazario, an employee of the Drug Enforcement Administration (DEA) in San Jose, California. Nazario ran the names of Victor Conte Jr. and Dr. Brian Halevie-Goldman [medical director of Balco Laboratories] through indices of authorized and registered controlled substance distributors that the DEA maintains. Nazario informed me that neither Conte nor Dr. Halevie-Goldman are currently authorized or registered through the DEA to distribute or prescribe controlled substances. Nazario further informed me that it is illegal for a doctor or anyone else to distribute or prescribe a controlled substance without authorization and registration with the DEA.

[Paragraphs 11–16 omitted]

Examination of Discarded Trash

17. Since September 3, 2002, I have performed, on approximately a weekly basis, an examination of the discarded garbage of Balco Laboratories Inc., located at 1520 Gilbreth Road in Burlingame, California. I have regularly retrieved the discarded garbage from a public-access parking lot where it is placed for pickup. . . . Following is a partial listing of items retrieved from the discarded trash of Balco Laboratories . . . along with the date the evidence was retrieved.

- A torn, empty box [that had contained] multiple vials of Serostin, a human growth hormone (9/3/02);

- A torn, empty box of 200 mg vial of testosterone (9/10/02); [Testosterone is an anabolic steroid and classified as a Schedule III controlled substance as listed in Title 21, U.S.C. §802] . . .

- At least eighty-four (84) empty, one-use syringe wrappers in various sizes (9/3/02 through 8/10/03); . . .

- A November/December 2002 issue of "Anabolic Insider," an underground steroid publication (12/16/02);

- Various small envelopes and letters from an elite track and field athlete, who is currently the United States champion in his event, including the following:

Vic, here is a check for the next cycl [sic]. I need it by the end of the week. [A cycle is a common phrase used for the administration of anabolic steroids because the users typically cycle their use on an on-and-off basis so that their bodies will not shut down the natural production of testosterone.]

Vic, here is $350, $300 for next + $50 for what I owed for last. Thanx.

[Paragraphs 18–39 omitted]

Emeric Delczeg

40. In the aforementioned interview of Conte in the November 13, 1998 article of "Testosterone" magazine, detailed earlier in this affidavit, Conte states: "A few of the older athletes feel that GH (growth hormone) supplementation has helped them extend their competitive career. I know a pro bodybuilder named Emeric Delczeg who's 47 years of age who supplements with GH . . . and he maintains a level of around 400 ng/ml. This is the level of a man twenty years younger."

41. On October 10, 2002, I received information from San Mateo County Narcotics Task Force (NTF) agent Ed Barberini that NTF had received information from a confidential informant that Emeric Delczeg was a steroid supplier to Balco Laboratories. Agent Barberini has informed me that the confidential informant who provided this information had pled guilty to felony steroid distribution charges a few years ago. Since the guilty plea, the informant has been providing information to the NTF on other individuals associated with steroids in an attempt to earn a reduced sentence in his criminal case. Agent Barberini has informed me that due to the cooperation provided by the informant, he has not done any jail time for his steroid conviction. The informant has never been paid by NTF. Agent Barberini has informed me that the informant has been deemed a reliable informant.

42. The informant told NTF that Delczeg, who is Bulgarian, obtains steroids and other performance-enhancing drugs from Europe and provides them to Balco in exchange for permission to sell a supplement on which Balco or its subsidiary, SNAC System Inc., owns licensing rights. In October 2002, the informant told NTF that Delczeg was in Europe to purchase steroids for Balco.

[Paragraphs 43–68 omitted]

Probable Cause to Search Computers

69. As detailed extensively in this affidavit, evidence has been collected showing that Conte and others use computers in furtherance of their criminal activities. In summary, Conte makes postings to an Internet message board regarding athletes and steroids, sends e-mails to athletes and coaches regarding performance-enhancing drugs and drug testing and has received e-mails from suspected athletic performance-enhancing drug suppliers of which a hard copy of such an e-mail was thrown out in Conte's discarded garbage. Because of these facts, I believe that probable cause exists to search any computers found on the physical locations of Conte's business and residence.

70. Based on my training and experience (which includes the execution of search warrants involving personal computers), as well as from consultation with Special Agent Michael Farley, Computer Investigative Specialist, I am aware that searching and seizing information from computers often requires agents to seize most or all electronic storage devices and the related peripherals to be searched later by a qualified computer expert in a laboratory or other controlled environment. This is true because of the following:

(A) Computer storage devices can store the equivalent of millions of pages of information. Additionally, a suspect may try to conceal criminal evidence by, for example, storing it in random order with deceptive file names. This may require searching authorities to examine all of the stored data to determine which particular files are evidence or instrumentalities of crime. This sorting process can take weeks or months, depending on the volume of the data stored, and it would be impractical to attempt this kind of data search on site.

[IV. omitted]

(Continued)

(Continued)

Conclusion

72. I believe that the foregoing facts presented in this affidavit present probable cause to believe that Victor Conte and others have committed violations of Title 21 U.S.C. §841, the possession with intent to distribute, and distribution, of anabolic steroids, and Title 18 U.S.C. §1956, the money laundering of profits earned from the drug distribution and mail fraud activities. Specifically this affidavit has presented evidence of: illegal anabolic steroid and other athletic performance-enhancing drug distribution to professional athletes, including the distribution of new, untested substances; the use of the mail to purchase epitestosterone, a substance used in the fraudulent defeat of athletic performance-enhancing drug tests; the withdrawal of over $480,000 over a period of less than two years from Conte's accounts while paying most business and personal expenses with bank checks from those accounts; and the depositing of large checks from numerous professional athletes into Conte's personal account instead of his business accounts, specifically at the request of Conte, constituting illegal money laundering transactions.

[Paragraph 73 omitted]

74. I declare under the penalty of perjury that the foregoing is true and correct and that this affidavit was executed at San Jose, California, on September _____, 2003.

_____

Jeff Novitzky

Special Agent

Internal Revenue Service

Criminal Investigation

Attachment A-1 Description of Location to Be Searched

Balco Laboratories/SNAC System Inc.

1520 Gilbreth Road

Burlingame, CA

Balco Laboratories and Snac System Inc. are businesses operated out of the same location in a commercial area in Eastern Burlingame. A blue sign reading Balco Laboratories is clearly posted above the entrance to the business. The numbers "1520" appear on a window just left of the main entryway into the facility facing Gilbreth Road.

Attachment B Items to Be Seized

1. All controlled substances and other athletic performance-enhancing drugs, substances and paraphernalia including: anabolic steroids, human growth hormone, erythropoietin (EPO), stimulants, other prescription drugs, drug, substance and syringe packaging and containers, mail packaging and receipts, syringes and syringe wrappers.

[Paragraphs 2–3 omitted]

4. All financial documents and business records referencing Victor Conte Jr., James Valente, Balco Laboratories Inc., SNAC System Inc., and other employees or agents of these businesses relating to the purchase and sale of anabolic steroids, syringes, epitestosterone, human growth hormone, erythropoietin, athletic performance-enhancing controlled substance and electronic mail, bank statements and records, wire transfer records, money order, official bank checks, ledgers, invoices, accounting and payroll documents, records detailing

the purchase of assets, documents detailing business expenses and documents relating to cash sources and cash expenditures from 1/1/94 through the present.

[Paragraph 5 omitted]

6. Address books, phone books, personal calendar, daily planners, journals, itineraries, rolodex indices and contact lists associated with Victor Conte, James Valente and any other employees or agents of Balco Laboratories and SNAC System, Inc.

[Paragraphs 7–8 omitted]

9. The terms "records," "documents," and "materials" include all of the items described in this Attachment in whatever form and by whatever means they have been created and/or stored. This includes any handmade, photographic, mechanical, electrical, electronic, and/or magnetic forms. It also includes items in the form of computer hardware, software, documentation, passwords, and/or data security devices.

a. Hardware—consisting of all equipment that can collect, analyze, create, display, convert, store, conceal, or transmit electronic, magnetic, optical, or similar computer impulses or data.

answer to the specificity question can be found in the U.S. Supreme Court case *Messerschmidt v. Millender* (2012).[67]

Augusta Millender lived in California and tried to help kids by being a foster mother, as she was to Jerry Ray Bowen. By the time he was an adult, Bowen had amassed a 17-page rap sheet (list of criminal charges and convictions) and was a known associate of a California street gang, the "Mona Park Crips." One day, Bowen tried to kill his ex-girlfriend, Shelly Kelly, by aiming and shooting at her car as she tried to escape Bowen's violence. Los Angeles police detective Curt Messerschmidt prepared both an arrest warrant for Bowen and a search warrant for Millender's house, an address that was associated with Bowen in computer files. The warrant was to search for guns, because Bowen had assaulted Kelly with a shotgun, but then Detective Messerschmidt listed in the warrant the following "gang-related" items to be seized:

Articles of evidence showing street gang membership or affiliation with any Street Gang to include but not limited to any reference to "Mona Park Crips," including writings or graffiti depicting gang membership, activity or identity. Articles of personal property tending to establish the identity of person [sic] in control of the premise or premises. Any photographs or photograph albums depicting persons, vehicles, weapons or locations, which may appear relevant to gang membership, or which may depict the item being sought and/or believed to be evidence in the case being investigated on this warrant, or which may depict evidence of criminal activity. Additionally to include any gang indicia that would establish the persons being sought in this warrant, affiliation or membership with the "Mona Park Crips" street gang.

The officers searched Millender's house and found and seized Millender's weapons. Three weeks later, Bowen was found hiding underneath a motel bed and arrested. Millender sued Detective Messerschmidt pursuant to 42 U.S.C. §1983 claiming, in part, the search conducted at her home was unreasonable. Millender's lawsuit stated any reasonable officer could see that the list of things to be seized (particularly for evidence of gang-related items) was too broad and, therefore, obviously illegal. Under the *Groh* precedent, Millender argued Detective Messerschmidt was not entitled to qualified immunity.

By an objective standard, probable cause to search Millender's house for guns existed because Bowen was a gang member who tried to kill someone. But did the probable cause extend to the generic evidence of gang membership, which, on its face, had nothing to do with Bowen's assault? Bowen's relationship with Kelly had been violent for a long time. What did his gang membership have to do with a domestic assault? The lower court agreed with Millender that the search was unreasonable, but on appeal, the U.S. Supreme Court found in the officer's favor.

In the chapter-opening case study, the warrant that listed Charlie's address in place of the things to be seized rendered the warrant inherently defective, and any agent serving the warrant may be personally responsible to Charlie in a civil lawsuit. Law enforcement officers are presumed to know the requirements of the Fourth Amendment.

The Service of the Warrant

Knock and Announce Requirement

To execute a warrant, officers must "knock and announce" their presence and use force to enter only if entry is refused. Federal law on the execution of warrants provides that:[68]

> The officer may break open any outer or inner door or window of a house, or any part of a house, or anything therein, to execute a search warrant, if, after notice of his authority and purpose, he is refused admittance or when necessary to liberate himself or a person aiding him in the execution of the warrant.

The average time to wait before forcing entry into a dwelling is affected by the circumstances known to the officers executing the search warrant. In *United States v. Banks* (2003), the Court determined it was reasonable to wait 15 to 20 seconds before kicking down a door to execute a warrant.[69] In *Banks*, Las Vegas officers working with federal agents executed a search warrant for evidence of drug dealing at the apartment of Mr. Banks. After the officers knocked and announced their presence, they broke down the front door with a battering ram just as Mr. Banks emerged from the shower, dripping wet. Banks was eventually convicted for possession of the weapons and cocaine found during the search, and on appeal, Banks argued that the 15 to 20 seconds the police waited before forced entry violated the Fourth Amendment's reasonableness clause. The Supreme Court disagreed. Holding that the totality of the circumstances determined the appropriate waiting period before using force is properly judged by officers on the scene who can properly assess the exigent or emergency circumstances, such as how quickly Banks could have flushed cocaine down the toilet or jumped out the back window, the 15- to 20-second wait was reasonable.

> Rule of Law: Police action during the execution of the warrant must be reasonable.

If the facts known to law enforcement prior to the execution of the warrant indicate that the officers' safety may be compromised by the knock and announce rule—for example, because of the nature of the suspected offense or known information about a suspect's prior convictions—then the officers can ask the issuing magistrate to issue a "no knock" on the warrant's face. This type of warrant allows officers to enter without announcement and may allow them to execute the search in the evening. Some state statutes provide for no-knock warrants in drug cases, but executing such warrants is dangerous because the occupants are often confused that it is law enforcement, and not armed criminals, who are breaking their door down in a forced entry. One U.S. Supreme Court pronouncement on the knock and announce rule is in the case *Hudson v. Michigan* (2006), in which the high Court found that even if the officers violated the knock and announce rule, which should lead to the operation of the exclusionary rule suppressing the evidence, the illegal drugs found in the case would be admissible because the knock and announce is a matter of courtesy, and the validity of the warrant and the authority to enter are not affected.[70]

Securing the Scene

> Rule of Law: For officer safety during the execution of a warrant, people found on the premises may be briefly detained.

Once officers are inside a person's home, what can officers do with the people who are found on the premises when they are executing the warrant? In *Michigan v. Summers* (1981), Summers was on the front steps of his house when police arrived to execute a search warrant for drugs.[71] While officers conducted the search, they detained Summers, who was eventually arrested, and drugs were found in his pocket when he was searched. The high Court held that the probable cause that sustains the warrant carries the authority to briefly detain people on the premises, reasoning that people on the premises may be involved in criminal activity justifying their detention. The length and condition of detention are situation specific.[72] The probable cause determination supporting the warrant will also forgive mistakes officers make in detaining people, such as a White couple detained when the arrest warrant was for African American suspects; even if the police know the people in the house are not the named suspects in the warrant, minimal detention of anyone on the premises for officer safety was warranted.[73]

APPLYING THE LAW TO THE FACTS

Is the Detention While Executing a Warrant Lawful?

The Facts: Police about to execute a search warrant witnessed two people leave the premises and drive away. Police followed and stopped the individuals one mile down the road. Officers ordered the men out of the car, handcuffed them, and told them they were not under arrest but were being detained pursuant to a search of the home. Officers brought the men back to the premises being searched. A cache of guns and drugs were found and used to convict Chunon Bailey. Was Bailey's initial detention one mile away from his home lawful?

The Law: No, the detention was not legal. The U.S. Supreme Court held in *Bailey v. United States* (2013) that under the *Michigan v. Summers* (1981) precedent, detention of others for officer safety is limited to the immediate area to be searched and does not apply to people who had left the premises at the time the police entered to search.[74]

The Return

Federal Rule of Criminal Procedure 41 requires the officer executing the warrant to "enter on its face the exact date and time it is executed." Next, the officer must "give a copy of the warrant and a receipt for the property taken to the person from whom, or from whose premises, the property was taken." If no one is home, the officer should leave a copy of the warrant and receipt for any property seized in a conspicuous location within the premises. The inventory of the property seized must be completed in the presence of another officer, who must verify its accuracy. Ideally, if the property owner is on the premises, he or she should sign the inventory acknowledging the removal of the property. The officer executing the warrant must return the warrant and swear that the inventory list is true in front of a magistrate, preferably the one who issued the warrant, indicated in the example of a federal warrant on the student study site (edge.sagepub.com/jirard). A return must occur even if no property is seized. The magistrate then files all papers associated with the warrant and the return with the court clerk in the jurisdiction where property was seized. The officers do not have to inform the property owner how to get his or her seized property back. The property owner may seek the return of the property by filing a motion in court in the district where the property was seized.

Scope of the Search

Generally, police can search pursuant to the warrant only those areas specified in the warrant. "If the place to be searched is identified by street number, the search is not limited to the dwelling house, but may also extend to the garage and other structures deemed to be within" the surrounding area of the house and yard.[75] If the warrant is specific about the place to be searched, the officers are limited to search in that area only. If the warrant is for contraband that can be easily hidden, such as drugs or illegal weapons, officers can search drawers, closets, and closed containers where the contraband may be found. A warrant to search a house does not extend to vehicles on the property, nor does a warrant to search a vehicle on the property extend to the buildings and homes on the property.

> **Rule of Law: The limits of the search are defined by the terms of the warrant itself.**

There is also no general "crime scene" exception to the warrant requirement, as held in *Mincey v. Arizona* (1978).[76] Once a crime scene has been secured, officers determine that no one needs medical aid, and no suspects are on the premises, a warrant is required for further search.

SUMMARY

1. You will be able to analyze Fourth Amendment problems. In early America, the king abused the colonists by seizing personal property by writs of assistance and general warrants allowed the king to confiscate press materials critical of his reign. The Fourth Amendment of the Bill of Rights prohibits unreasonable search, looking for evidence, and seizure, taking of evidence. In analyzing whether the government has complied with the law, the first step is to determine whether a government actor is involved. The second step is to determine whether an objective and subjective reasonable expectation of privacy exists, as held in *Katz v. United States* (1967). There is no privacy interest in abandoned property that a suspect throws away. The third step is to determine whether the government's search or seizure was "reasonable." The fourth step is to determine whether a warrant was required for the search and seizure or, if not, whether a well-recognized exception to the warrant requirement applies. The fifth step is to determine the remedy for the violation if the government has failed to comply with the Fourth Amendment, which is suppression of the evidence pursuant to the exclusionary rule and derivative evidence by operation of the fruit of the poisonous tree doctrine. The good faith exception may make admissible illegally-obtained evidence.

2. You will appreciate how Fourth Amendment analysis has changed with advancing technology. StingRays and dirtboxes, which simulate cell phone towers and intercept signals from private cell phones, do not require warrants when tracking movements in public, but if the tracking goes on for a long period of time, as in *United States v. Jones* (2012), or reveals intimate details and location inside the home, such as in *Kyllo v. United States* (2001) or *United States v. Karo* (1984), a warrant may be required, as to search electronic devices that contain your social DNA, as held in *Riley v. California* (2014). The third-party doctrine provides no privacy interest in information shared with third parties such as telephone companies that track phone numbers called in a pen register, but revealing a suspect's long-term location through monitoring cell tower signals requires a warrant per *Carpenter v. United States* (2018).

3. You will understand the role race may play in the intersection of the citizen–police encounter in assessing reasonable suspicion that criminal activity is afoot. Drug courier profiling has been allowed to provide reasonable suspicion but not probable cause. When the *Terry* case was decided in 1968, the high Court warned the practice of stopping and frisking might heighten tensions in minority communities, which happened when New York City adopted an aggressive stop and frisk policy, which may or may not justify a suspect running from the police, as the Massachusetts Supreme Court found in *Commonwealth v. Warren* (2016).

4. You will be able to distinguish the legal basis for a *Terry* stop, arrests, and claims of excessive force. A brief investigatory detention is also known as a *Terry* stop because of the case *Terry v. Ohio* (1968). The *Terry* stop allows officers to briefly detain people on the streets and ask questions based on reasonable suspicion that criminal activity is afoot—that a crime has been, is being, or will be committed. Reasonable suspicion is more than a hunch and is established by specific and articulable facts crime is happening. If, during a *Terry* stop, the officer has a reasonable belief that a person is armed, the officer can pat down the person's outer clothing for weapons only; the officer cannot conduct a full-blown search. A *Terry* stop can last only as long as the officer needs to confirm or dispel her reasonable suspicion that criminal activity is afoot. If the stop lasts longer, it is transformed into an arrest unsupported by probable cause, which is illegal. The same legal standard applies to *Terry* stops of automobiles. An arrest is a seizure of a person and requires an arrest warrant, unless it is conducted in a public place. To meet the constitutional requirements of the Fourth Amendment, the amount of force used to effectuate all arrests and seizures must be reasonable. Officers may not shoot to kill unarmed fleeing felons; that would be excessive force. In the context of high-speed chases, in which the police chase suspects in vehicles—chases that may end up harming or killing others or the suspects— courts use the same analysis of reasonable force under the Fourth Amendment.

5. You will be able to articulate the sources of probable cause and the procedure for obtaining and serving a warrant. A warrant is a legal document authorizing the government to search and seize based on probable cause that a suspect has or will commit a crime. Probable cause

means it is more likely than not that a specific offender committed a specific crime and may be established by officers' collective knowledge on the basis of reliable hearsay, informants, corroborated anonymous tips, witness statements, the officer's observations based on his or her training and experience, and presence in a high crime area that is not necessarily associated with race. In general, anonymous tips alone are not sufficient for probable cause and informants must be proven reliable. Searches conducted without a warrant are presumed to be unreasonable unless a well-recognized exception to the warrant requirement applies. The elements of the warrant requirement include probable cause connecting the person to be seized or the place to be searched to criminal activity and a description that explains with particularity the place to be searched and the things to be seized called the particularity requirement. In addition, the warrant must be issued under oath; that is, the officer must swear or affirm in front of the magistrate (judge) that the facts contained in the affidavit establishing the facts of probable cause are true to the best of the officer's knowledge and belief. The affidavit must be "incorporated by reference" on the front of the warrant's face. If by looking at the warrant the officer can tell it is facially deficient, civil liability may attach if the officer executes the bad warrant. Also, the warrant must be issued by a neutral and detached magistrate—a judge who has no prior extensive knowledge of the case and no personal stake in the outcome of the case. To execute a warrant, officers must knock and announce their presence and wait the amount of time the exigencies of the situation demand, in some cases as few as 15 to 20 seconds, before they conduct a forcible entry. On request, or by law in some states, officers can obtain a no-knock warrant in which officers do not have to announce who they are before they forcibly enter the premises on the basis that, if the officers do announce their presence before entry, the occupants may destroy evidence or compromise the safety of the officers.

Go back to the beginning of the chapter and reread the news excerpts associated with the learning objectives. Test yourself to determine if you can understand the material covered in the text in the context of the news.

KEY TERMS AND PHRASES

abandoned property 199
affidavit 206
anonymous tip 204
arrest warrant 201
collective knowledge 203
derivative evidence 188
dirtbox 193
excessive force 200
exclusionary rule 188
facially deficient 207
Fourth Amendment 186

fruit of the poisonous tree 188
general warrants 186
hunch 188
incorporated by reference 206
informant 204
knock and announce 212
no knock warrant 212
particularity requirement 207
pen register 191
probable cause 188
reasonable belief 195

reasonable expectation of privacy 188
reasonable force 200
reasonable suspicion 195
search 186
seizure 186
specific and articulable facts 195
StingRay 193
Terry stop 195
third-party doctrine 191
warrant 201
writs of assistance 186

PROBLEM-SOLVING EXERCISES

1. Police in Los Angeles, California, received information from the federal Drug Enforcement Administration (DEA) that a chemist was arriving from overseas with the express purpose of setting up a methamphetamine laboratory. With the help from an anonymous tip, officers identified Mr. Fletcher as he got off the plane and followed him to a hotel. Fletcher later met with Mr. Callahan and, under police surveillance, went to Callahan's house moving back and forth from the house to the backyard several times, behavior the officers believed to be suspicious. Officers got a search warrant and discovered 68 pounds of methamphetamine. Callahan complained officers lacked probable cause to search. The officers claim there was sufficient probable cause and, in the alternative, the good faith exception should apply and the drugs should be admissible. You are the judge. How will you decide the case? **(ROL: Probable cause, anonymous tips, "good faith" exception)**

2. In Indianapolis, police suspected that a man inside a motel room was mixing cocaine with additives in the bathroom. The suspect opened the motel door in response to the officers' knock. Six uniformed and armed officers were present. They asked if the suspect would

be willing to step outside the door and talk to them. When he refused and tried to close the door, one officer placed his foot inside the door preventing the suspect from closing it. Reluctantly, the man let the police in, whereupon, to sit on the bed, one officer moved a jacket, revealing a firearm on the bed. The man was arrested for illegally possessing a handgun. Was the entrance into the motel room and subsequent search legal? **(ROL: Reasonable expectation of privacy [objective, subjective];** *Katz, Olson, Carter, Byrd* **cases)**

3. Are the following descriptions of things to be seized listed in a hypothetical warrant sufficient to meet the particularity requirement of the Fourth Amendment?

a. An unknown make .38 caliber weapon, blue with a wood grip

b. Any and all videotapes made in violation of federal copyright laws

c. Any and all doctor's files concerning patients prescribed oxycodone

d. Items related to the smuggling, packaging, distribution, and use of controlled substances

e. All records or other information regarding the identification of the Gmail account holder, including name, address, telephone number, and any log-in IP address used

8

EXCEPTIONS TO THE WARRANT REQUIREMENT

G o to the end of the chapter. Skim the key terms and phrases and read the summary closely. Come back and look at the following news excerpts to focus your reading throughout the chapter to understand the law that establishes well-defined circumstances that excuse the government from first obtaining a warrant to search and seize. "Warrantless" searches and seizures are a number of judicially (judge-made) recognized exceptions to the legal requirement to obtain a warrant. In crafting the exceptions, the U.S. Supreme Court balanced the public's right to privacy against the state's legitimate goal to enforce the law and prevent crime. Although most warrant exceptions still require probable cause, there are other exceptions, such as a consensual search or sweeping for drugs on buses, trains, and airport luggage storage areas, or roadblocks for drunk drivers, that do not. The chapter begins with a hypothetical case study of Rick, Abigail, and Sabrina's exploits sitting in an apartment when the police come knocking. Follow the trio as they encounter the rules of law guiding warrantless searches and seizures presented throughout the chapter and connect their activities with the relevant section of text.

WHY THIS CHAPTER MATTERS TO YOU	THE LEARNING OBJECTIVES AS REFLECTED IN THE NEWS
After you have read this chapter: **Learning Objective 1:** You will be able to discuss the legal basis for all exceptions to the warrant requirement.	All across the country, Customs and Border Protection (CBP) agents are boarding buses—with Greyhound's consent—and subjecting riders to interrogation and detention . . . Greyhound has justified its cooperation with CBP with reference to a federal statute stating that, within a reasonable distance of the border, CBP agents may board vehicles without a warrant. But Greyhound has it wrong: This statute doesn't require Greyhound to grant CBP free rein over its property. As the Supreme Court has made clear with reference to this very law, "no Act of Congress can authorize a violation of the Constitution." . . . Statute or no statute, agents still need a warrant or Greyhound's consent to board its buses. (*Meadville Tribune* [PA], April 4, 2018)
Learning Objective 2: You will be able to recognize exigent circumstances justifying officer conduct in the field.	A federal appeals court says three officers who shot and killed a pair of dogs during a house search in Battle Creek acted "reasonably." . . . "There is no dispute that the shooting of Plaintiffs' dogs were severe intrusions given the emotional attachment between a dog and an owner," the court stated in the opinion. "On the other hand, insuring officer safety and preventing the destruction of evidence are particularly important governmental interests that the courts must strive to protect," the court added, saying the dogs "posed imminent threat to the officers." (WoodTV.com, February 20, 2016)

(Continued)

(Continued)

WHY THIS CHAPTER MATTERS TO YOU	THE LEARNING OBJECTIVES AS REFLECTED IN THE NEWS
Learning Objective 3: You will understand the limits of automobile searches and the protective sweep.	On January 2015, Anthony Ortiz was pulled over in Holyoke for his music being too loud. When an officer asked Ortiz if he had any drugs in the car, Ortiz allegedly said, "No, you can check." Police searched the cabin and then opened the car's hood. An officer removed the cap on the air filter and found two guns inside. The state supreme court ruled the search was illegal and the guns should be tossed out of evidence. Justices ruled that consenting to a search doesn't apply to under the hood of a vehicle. "The police come up to you and say, can I search your car, you are allowed to say no," [Lawyer] Newman said. (22News [MA], February 13, 2018)
Learning Objective 4: You will become knowledgeable about the law regulating warrantless drug, alcohol, and DNA seizures.	A Utah nurse who was unlawfully arrested for refusing to let police take a blood sample from an unconscious patient has received a $500,000 legal settlement from the city and her employer. A police body-camera video . . . showed a Salt Lake City police detective handcuffing the nurse at University of Utah Hospital and shoving her into an unmarked squad car, after she refused to let him draw blood from the patient without a warrant. (Reuters, November 1, 2017)
Learning Objective 5: You will be reintroduced to the exclusionary rule and understand good faith exceptions when mistakes are made in the field.	Notebooks seized from the apartment of former [University of Wisconsin-Madison] student Alec Cook, which prosecutors saw as evidence that he schemed to sexually assault women he met on campus, can't be used during any of Cook's trials, two judges wrote in a collaborative decision issued Friday. The first of the notebooks was discovered by police while they performed a limited search of Cook's apartment with his consent in October 2016, and the contents of that notebook led investigators to get a search warrant to more thoroughly search the apartment a few days later. The state has not established by clear and convincing evidence that the search of Mr. Cook's notebook fell within the scope of Mr. Cook's limited consent, nor has the state demonstrated that a different warrant exception applies. (*Daily Cardinal*, University of WI, January 2, 2018)

Chapter-Opening Case Study: Activity at the Apartment Complex

Police were investigating a report of a burglary at a multiunit apartment complex. As officers approached and knocked on the door of Apartment 2B, they heard suspicious activity behind the door, including the moving of heavy furniture, the increased volume of the television set, and frequent toilet flushing. Officer Lamont, suspecting illegal destruction of contraband, kicked open the door and saw Rick sitting on the couch and Abigail and Sabrina moving back and forth from one bedroom to the bathroom. **(Rule of Law [ROL]: Exigent circumstances means substantial risk of harm would arise if police delay obtaining a warrant.)** Rick, a juvenile, was allowed to leave. Officer Kennedy said, "I smell marijuana and where there are drugs, there are guns. I don't feel safe. I'm going to make a protective sweep." **(ROL: Protective sweep is done when there are specific and articulable facts indicating there are armed people on the premises justifying warrantless search for people.)** While making the sweep, Kennedy saw an 80-inch, wide-screen television and turned the television over to record the serial numbers to run through the stolen property database. **(ROL: Plain view: If officers on the scene legally and observe obvious contraband, the item may be seized; moving the item constitutes a search.)** While officers were not looking, Abigail snuck out of the apartment and was in her car attempting to start it and drive away. Officer Kennedy caught up with Abigail and ordered her to shut the engine off and exit the vehicle. Kennedy arrested Abigail on suspicion of drug activity and then searched her car for evidence of drugs. **(ROL: Search incident to an arrest (SITA) near a vehicle is justified when officers face a continuing threat to their safety or to preserve evidence related to arrest.)** As Kennedy finished searching the car, Sabrina approached. Officer Kennedy noticed a bulge in her jacket pocket and conducted a patdown (frisk) and manipulated the bulge before removing a wad of rolled bills wrapped in a rubber band. **(ROL: Plain feel: During a patdown, officers may remove obvious contraband.)** As Officer Kennedy was examining the bills, Sabrina pulled a weapon from her waistband and, laughing manically, ran into an apartment across the parking lot. Kennedy chased Sabrina into the apartment and arrested her. **(ROL: Hot pursuit allows for the warrantless entry into a home when fleeing a dangerous suspect.)** Rick returned to high school and, based on a rumor that he possessed illegal drugs based on his presence in Apartment 2B, school officials brought Rick into the bathroom and asked to shake out his undergarments in a search for drugs. A small bag of marijuana fell out of the waistband of Rick's pants. He was summarily suspended. **(ROL: School searches: There is a diminished expectation of privacy in a K–12 school setting, but all searches and seizures must be reasonable.)**

Did the officers and school officials act lawfully during the warrantless searches and seizures noted in chapter-opening case study?

WARRANTLESS SEARCHES AND SEIZURES

Consent

To meet the public safety and crime prevention goals, officers must approach people and ask questions, which is perfectly legal. Officers "do not violate the Fourth Amendment by merely approaching an individual on the street or other public place, by asking him if he is willing to answer some questions, by putting questions to him if the person is willing to listen, or by offering in evidence in a criminal prosecution his voluntary answers to such questions."[1] But if officers want to search something (e.g., a car, a purse, a house) and they do not have a warrant or probable cause, the law requires officers to obtain the owner's consent. **Consent** is asking someone to do something, and if the other party says yes, the yes can be legally binding. Giving officers consent to search means giving up an expectation of privacy; any evidence of illegal activity found during the search may be used against the person. To be legal, the consent must be voluntary and not the product of coercion, threat, or force.

> **Rule of Law: Legally valid consent to search must be voluntary and free from coercion.**

To determine whether the suspect has given officers voluntary consent to search, courts look at the totality of the circumstances, which are all facts surrounding the police–citizen encounter, and consider the following factors:

1. Knowledge of the right to refuse—officers need not tell citizen of this right[2]

2. Level of intelligence, age, and language skills[3]

3. Level of cooperation with authorities

4. Length of detention and nature of questioning by officers

5. Physical contact between the citizen and police

6. Any coercive tactics used by police

Once consent to search is given, police have the authority to search everything within a specific area, for example, the contents of a dresser if consent is given to search a bedroom. Even though a person may withdraw her consent and stop the police from searching further, it is logical that if police discover evidence of a crime or contraband during a consent search, then such discovery may give them probable cause to search further; rescinding consent to search at that point would be futile. When challenged in court, often through a motion to suppress evidence illegally seized, the government retains the burden by a preponderance of the evidence to prove that the suspect's consent was voluntary.

Submission to Authority Is Not Consent

Consent is not to be confused with **submission to authority**, which is when officers try to obtain a person's consent by saying resistance is futile because officers "have a warrant on the way." Obtaining consent by submission to authority is illegal. To distinguish between the two situations, let's examine two hypothetical situations. Officers receive information that Willy is suspected of selling drugs from his home. A lawful investigative technique is called a "**knock and talk**," where officers may be successful in obtaining the occupant's "apparent consent" by knocking on a suspect's door and asking to come inside. After gaining entry, the officers inform Willy that they're investigating information that drugs are in the house. The officers then ask for permission to search, and many people agree. Obtaining consent through the "knock and talk" is legal.[4]

If Willy gave consent to search during a "knock and talk," his consent would be legal. On the other hand, let's say police knock on Willy's door and ask for consent to search for drugs and Willy refuses. The police then say, "Do not bother saying no to us. We have a warrant on the way, so just let us inside." If Willy now allows the officers to search, he has not consented but has submitted to the officers' apparent legal authority (the warrant that is on its way) to enter.

> When a law enforcement officer claims authority to search a home under a warrant, he announces in effect that the occupant has no right to resist the search. The situation is indistinct with coercion [and where] there is coercion there cannot be consent.[5]

Deceiving citizens into granting consent because the police will search anyway preys on the public's ignorance that they have a right to refuse a search or that probable cause is required to search. If the court determines that the person merely submitted to police authority rather than willingly consented, then the evidence discovered as a result of the search may be inadmissible.

Lying to Obtain Consent. Lying to a suspect is a common investigative technique. As discussed in Chapter 9, during an interrogation it is lawful to lie to the suspect and tell him an eyewitness can place him at the scene of the crime, or his fingerprints or blood was discovered at the crime scene, or that a codefendant has confessed and blames the suspect. But lying to obtain consent to enter and search is not lawful, nor is it lawful to properly enter the home with consent and then lie about the object of the entry, for example, officers telling an occupant they are in the home to help someone with their taxes and yet surreptitiously searching for evidence of illegal tax filings.[6]

Informants often pose as someone else to induce suspects to commit crimes. Informants need not identify themselves as working with law enforcement. If a drug dealer willingly lets someone into her house to buy drugs, she cannot complain later that her consent to let the buyers in was "coerced" when she discovers one of her buyers is an informant.

Consent to Search Given by a Co-Occupant

The next question courts ask in deciding whether a person's consent was voluntary is the person's authority to give consent. If a person shares an apartment with two other people, called tenants in common, one person has the authority to give consent to search the common areas of the apartment that everyone shares, such as the living room, kitchen, and bathroom, but not the roommates' private bedrooms. Someone who shares an apartment has no authority to consent to search others' private areas, and a landlord does not have the authority to grant consent to search his tenants' rooms simply because he owns the property.[7] A lease or a hotel agreement grants the occupant exclusive "ownership" and privacy rights for the lease period. The officer's perspective guides the inquiry of whether any person lawfully inside the home has the apparent authority to give consent to search.[8]

Supreme Court case law allows joint tenants in common to refuse the authority to search where one tenant would grant such authority. In *Georgia v. Randolph* (2006), a married couple was going through a messy divorce, and the wife, Janet Randolph, gave police consent to search the house over her husband Scott's objection, which at the time was legally sufficient consent for police to search.[9] Officers discovered cocaine and used it to convict Scott of illegal possession. On appeal, Scott argued that his refusal of consent should have trumped his wife's consent. The U.S. Supreme Court agreed with Scott, stating "in the circumstances here at issue, a physically present co-occupant's stated refusal to permit entry prevails, rendering the warrantless search unreasonable and invalid as to him." The *Randolph* decision changed long-standing precedent allowing consent searches despite another tenant's objection.

What happens when the objecting co-tenant who refuses consent to search leaves the home and the consenting co-tenant remains? In 2012, police officers searching an apartment complex for a suspect in a gang-related incident heard a couple arguing behind a closed door. Police knocked, and a woman obviously in distress answered. The male occupant, later identified as Walter Fernandez, told the police to leave. When the officers realized that Fernandez was the suspect they were looking for, they arrested him. Police later returned to the apartment and received consent from Fernandez's girlfriend to search the apartment, seizing evidence used at trial to convict Fernandez on gang-related charges. Fernandez complained on appeal that, under the *Georgia v. Randolph* precedent, his refusal of consent to enter the apartment was superior to his girlfriend's permission for officers to enter and thus the ensuing search was unlawful. The U.S. Supreme Court disagreed with Fernandez, holding that when the objecting co-tenant leaves the premises for "an objectively reasonable reason," such as an arrest, the remaining co-tenant may give validly legal consent to search. Thus, if the objecting co-tenant leaves, his "no" travels with him, as the high Court decided in *Fernandez v. California* (2014).[10]

If officers believe the person granting consent to enter and search has the authority to grant consent, they may be granted immunity on their reasonable but mistaken belief.

No Consent Required to Search Those on Probation or Parole

Once convicted, the defendant is no longer "innocent" under the law and his rights and freedoms, while not abolished, may be severely curtailed. In *United States v. Knights* (2001), as a condition of probation, Knights had to submit to a search at any time.[11] Based on reasonable suspicion, Knights's probation officer searched his apartment and found evidence indicating intent to commit arson. The lower California state court found the search was conducted for investigative purposes rather than as a condition of probation and suppressed the evidence. On appeal, the U.S. Supreme Court reversed, holding that Knights's probation order stipulated as a condition of release that he could be searched at any time. The Court balanced the probationer's diminished right to privacy against the government's interest in crime prevention and held the search lawful. The Court noted that probation is still punishment and probationers "do not enjoy 'the absolute liberty'" of other citizens, and such searches serve the legitimate governmental interest of public safety. Similar justification also applies for searches of those on parole, which is early release from prison.[12]

Search Incident to an Arrest (SITA)

Once a suspect has been arrested based on probable cause, police do not need a warrant to conduct a search incident to an arrest (SITA), which is a full search of the suspect's person, clothing, and the area immediately within his control. Dispensing with the warrant requirement to search a recent arrestee guarantees officer safety and prevents the potential destruction of

Rule of Law: When two or more occupants have authority to search a common residence and one occupant refuses consent and says, "No," officers cannot search. But if the objecting occupant leaves, the "No" leaves with him, and police can return and search the residence.

Springboard for Discussion

Do you believe that people consent when police ask whether they can search their homes or cars because they are afraid their refusal might be interpreted as an admission of guilt? Why might people feel guilty for exercising the constitutional right to be free from unreasonable searches and seizures?

Rule of Law: Once a suspect is arrested, his person and the area within his immediate control are subject to lawful search.

evidence that the suspect could grab and dispose of quickly. The SITA presumes that the initial arrest was lawful. If there was no probable cause for the arrest, any contraband discovered in the subsequent search may be suppressed by operation of the exclusionary rule or the fruit of the poisonous tree doctrine. The case that set the legal standard for SITA is *Chimel v. California* (1969). Ted Chimel was a suspect in the burglary of a coin shop who was arrested inside of his house pursuant to an arrest warrant.[13] The police then searched Chimel's entire house for the next hour on the legal basis of the lawful arrest. In deciding that the search was unreasonable, the U.S. Supreme Court held that the police had gone too far. Law enforcement must consider two aspects in relation to SITA: (1) The search cannot reveal evidence to support the arrest. "Where the formal arrest followed quickly on the heels of the challenged search . . . we do not believe it particularly important that the search preceded the arrest rather than vice versa" so long as what the search disclosed was "not necessary to support probable cause to arrest."[14] (2) If the arrest occurs in a home, the SITA does not extend to the entire house. "If a search of a house is to be upheld as incident to an arrest, that arrest must take place inside the house . . . not somewhere outside—whether two blocks away, . . . twenty feet away, . . . or on the sidewalk near the front steps." Thus, even if the arrest does take place inside the house, the search incident to the arrest must be confined to the area within the arrestee's "immediate control," as held in *Vale v. Louisiana* (1970).[15] To get around the limitation of searching the immediate vicinity of the arrest in a home, officers may transport the handcuffed suspect from room to room, which allows a continuous "search [of] the area within the suspect's immediate control"—this is referred to as "portable *Chimel*." Although a handcuffed suspect cannot ostensibly reach a weapon to harm officers or destroy evidence, this has little significance to the portable *Chimel* analysis because suspects can, and do, escape from custody.

Automobile Searches

Probable Cause to Search Vehicle

On probable cause that the car contains evidence of a crime or contraband, the **automobile exception** allows a warrantless search justified by the car's mobility and by the myriad state regulations that control cars, such as licensing and inspection requirements that diminish an owner's expectation of privacy in the vehicle. The high Court has said,

> **Rule of Law:**
> The automobile exception allows warrantless searches of automobiles on probable cause because vehicles are mobile and obtaining a warrant would be impractical.

As an everyday occurrence, police stop and examine vehicles when license plates or inspection stickers have expired, or if other violations, such as exhaust fumes or excessive noise, are noted, or if headlights or other safety equipment are not in proper working order.[16]

In *Carroll v. United States* (1925), officers had probable cause that the suspect was delivering bootleg liquor and ripped the car's upholstery in the search.[17] The U.S. Supreme Court upheld the search because in the time it takes to secure a warrant, "the vehicle can be quickly moved out of the locality or jurisdiction in which the warrant must be sought"; the Court ruled the police can search the entire vehicle without a warrant.

Although vehicles are heavily regulated, drivers and passengers do not surrender their privacy rights simply by driving. The government's interest in conducting investigatory detentions or searches of vehicles must be balanced against the public's interest to be free from government intrusion. If police are surveilling a car parked in a driveway and officers have time to obtain a warrant to search, police do not have automatic authority to search simply because the car can be driven away.[18]

Officers believed a stolen motorcycle was parked in a driveway located next to a house. Officers believed Ryan Collins stole the motorcycle. The motorcycle was parked at the home of Collins's girlfriend and the mother of his child where he sometimes spent the night. Based on the automobile exception that a motorcycle can be driven away at any time, officers without a warrant walked up to the motorcycle, checked the identification number, confirmed the bike was stolen, and arrested Collins. Collins was convicted and on appeal argued that a warrant was required to search the area immediately surrounding the house—the curtilage—because a man's home is his castle, which enjoys the greatest Fourth Amendment protection. The U.S. Supreme Court agreed with him, holding that the automobile exception does not permit officers to encroach on curtilage without a warrant (*Collins v. Virginia*, 2018).[19]

Vehicle Search Incident to an Arrest

The Supreme Court has held that, when the driver or one of the passengers inside a car has been arrested based on probable cause, officers may search, without a warrant, the passenger compartment of the car (i.e., where people sit in the car). In *New York v. Belton* (1981), officers pulled over a car, ordered all the occupants out, and lawfully arrested them.[20] One officer searched the car and found a jacket on the floor with drugs inside one of the pockets. The jacket belonged to Roger Belton, who was convicted of drug possession charges. The Supreme Court found that, based on its decision in *Chimel v. California* (1969), a search of the area "within the immediate control of the arrestee" was lawful, and in a car this area encompassed the passenger compartment and any closed containers.

After the Court's decision in *Belton*, lower courts hearing appeals remained divided on the reach and scope of authority to search passenger compartments.[21] The question remained whether police could conduct a passenger compartment search pursuant to the *Belton* precedent if the driver had pulled over, parked, and moved out of his car before police initiated contact.[22] Marcus Thornton was driving when Officer Nichols ran a license plate check and discovered the plates did not match Thornton's car. Nichols pulled him over. Thornton parked his car, got out, and stood outside his car as Nichols approached. Thornton consented to a *Terry* frisk, and the officer found drugs. The ensuing search of his car revealed a weapon under the front seat. When Thornton challenged his conviction on drug and weapon charges, the Supreme Court found that Nichols had authority to conduct the search even though Thornton had left the vehicle before his arrest in *Thornton v. United States* (2004). The Court concluded that a SITA search of a car is lawful regardless of whether the police initiate contact with the suspect, as in *Belton*, or the suspect has left the car and initiated contact with the police, as did Marcus Thornton.[23]

Both the *Belton* and the *Thornton* cases were effectively curtailed when the U.S. Supreme Court decided *Arizona v. Gant* (2009), wherein the driver was arrested for driving with a suspended license and locked in a supervised police cruiser with no access to his vehicle.[24] In the warrantless search of Gant's car incident to his arrest, the police found guns and drugs, which were used to convict Gant. On appeal that the search of the car was illegal, the high Court held, in direct contradiction to *Belton* and a limitation of *Thornton*, that the police can only justifiably search an arrestee's car if

1. The suspect posed a continuing threat to officer safety, or

2. To preserve evidence of the crime of arrest.

In the field, the practical effect of the *Gant* ruling may be that officers, rather than placing a suspect in the back of a police cruiser, simply choose to handcuff the suspect and keep him next to the car, thereby creating a "continuing threat to officer safety," justifying the search. In the chapter-opening case study, Officer Kennedy's SITA search of Abigail's car was justified because of the arrest of drug activity and the belief drug evidence may be found in her vehicle.

Springboard for Discussion

The U.S. Supreme Court has often relied on the limited number of "well delineated" exceptions to the warrant requirement in allowing law enforcement to search and seize without appearing in front of a judge and raising their right hand and swearing or affirming that probable cause exists. Do you think the country's Founding Fathers had the listed warrant exceptions in mind when they drafted the Fourth Amendment?

Inventory Search

Probable cause is not necessary for police to conduct an inventory search of a suspect's property once it enters police custody. An **inventory search** is a warrantless official cataloguing of items seized, most often from automobiles impounded at police stations. Once a car has been

Rule of Law: For inventory searches to be valid, they should be conducted pursuant to department regulations.

impounded at the police station, the police must safeguard individual property from theft or destruction. The legal requirements for an inventory search are that police departments have established and followed rules and regulations for searching and cataloguing items. In *South Dakota v. Opperman* (1976), an illegally parked car was towed to a police lot and impounded. As officers conducted an inventory search of the vehicle's contents, they discovered marijuana in an unlocked glove compartment; the defendant was convicted of unlawful possession of drugs.[25] The defendant appealed on the basis that the officers needed a warrant to look in the glove compartment during the search, but the U.S. Supreme Court held that no warrant was required for inventory searches because such actions fell under the police "community caretaking" function to protect property and to protect the police from baseless allegations of theft. Inventory searches also protect the police by allowing them to discover potentially dangerous items that can harm them or others. The legal requirements for an inventory search of an automobile are as follows:

1. The search follows a lawful impoundment of the vehicle (or any other item in government custody),

2. The search is of a routine nature, and

3. The search may not be a pretext for evidence gathering.[26]

Police cannot and should not use inventory searches to conduct further investigation for which a warrant would be typically required. Nevertheless, if the inventory search is conducted pursuant to lawful regulations, the officers' subjective motives for conducting the search are irrelevant and any contraband found will be lawfully seized and admissible at trial. If contraband is discovered during an inventory search, then a more extensive search is permissible, but it still must be based on the impracticality of securing a warrant, as held in *Florida v. Meyers* (1984).[27]

APPLYING THE LAW TO THE FACTS

Is the Search Legal?

The Facts: An Arkansas state trooper responded to a 9-1-1 call regarding a road rage incident during which the driver of a sport utility vehicle (SUV) pulling a jet ski brandished a gun at the 9-1-1 caller. The officers found the SUV and arrested the driver, Justin Stegall, placing him in the back of a patrol vehicle. The officers began to inventory the contents of Stegall's vehicle before towing it. While searching the rear hatch of Stegall's SUV, the officers discovered weapons lodged between the back row of seats and the rear cargo floorboard. Stegall was convicted of unlawfully possessing an unregistered short-barreled rifle and argued the inventory search and SITA searches were illegal. Is Stegall correct?

The Law: No. First, officers may conduct an inventory search on the side of the road if such searches are a regular part of the way a particular department conducts business. Second, the two prongs of *Arizona v. Gant* (2009) allow a SITA search of a car for (1) officer safety and (2) to preserve evidence of arrest. Stegall was arrested for brandishing a weapon while driving; therefore, the inventory and SITA searches of the entire car were lawful (*United States v. Stegall*, 2017).[28]

Warrantless Search of Closed Containers

Probable Cause and Vehicles. Authority to search a car extends to search everything inside, including **closed containers** (e.g., purses, briefcases, consoles, glove boxes, and similar items designed to hold and conceal items). The limits of a warrantless search in a vehicle are not defined by the container, whether locked or unlocked, but by the object of the search and where the object might be found inside the car (*United States v. Ross*, 1982).[29] Handheld electronic devices are considered closed containers; however, based on the amount of data stored on cell phones, tablets, fitness trackers, and similar items that retrieve and collect personal information, the law requires a warrant to search unless exigent circumstances apply. The ability to remotely wipe the data from the device does not necessarily create an emergency justifying a warrantless search.

Consent and Vehicles. In *Florida v. Jimeno* (1991), Jimeno was stopped for a minor traffic violation and a police officer requested consent to search.[30] Jimeno said yes and that he "had nothing to hide." When the officer searched a brown paper bag on the floor and discovered a kilogram of cocaine, Jimeno was arrested and convicted on the drug charge. On appeal, Jimeno argued that the officer had no authority to open the paper bag. The high Court disagreed and said that the proper inquiry about the scope of Jimeno's consent was, first, what a typical person would have understood about why the officer was asking for consent and second, whether it was "reasonable for an officer to consider a suspect's general consent to a search of his car to include consent to examine a paper bag lying on the floor of the car," and the answer was yes. But the "objective reasonableness" standard that guides Fourth Amendment searches and seizures also applies to the scope of consent searches for such authority "is not limitless." As stated in *Jimeno*, "[i]t is very likely unreasonable to think that a suspect, by consenting to the search of his trunk, has agreed to the breaking open of a locked briefcase within the trunk."

Search Incident to Arrest. While *Chimel v. California* (1969) held that an arrestee and the area in his immediate control can be searched, lower courts have interpreted *Chimel* to allow the warrantless search of a locked container such as a purse or briefcase if found within his immediate control. A SITA associated with a car, as controlled by predicate circumstances articulated in *Arizona v. Gant* (2009), includes closed and locked containers "as well as luggage, boxes, bags, clothing, and the like," as stated in *New York v. Belton* (1981).[31]

Inventory Searches and Vehicles. During an inventory search, police officers may open a locked closed container to catalogue its contents, based on their assessment whether a specific container should be opened, as long as department policy allows officers to exercise discretion. (See *Florida v. Wells*, 1990, upholding suppression of marijuana found in a locked suitcase during an inventory search, because the police department had no policy regulating such searches, and leaving all discretion to line officers violated the Fourth Amendment).[32]

Dog Sniffs

Dog sniffs are nonintrusive and noninvasive on a citizen's privacy interests and therefore are not searches under the Fourth Amendment, but dog sniffs can provide the basis for probable cause to acquire the authority to search. If, during an investigative detention of a vehicle, a drug detection dog sniffs and alerts its handler to the presence of contraband, does the sniff constitute probable cause to search? In *Illinois v. Caballes* (2005), a canine unit officer overheard a call about a motorist speeding and responded to the scene.[33] The officer stopped the motorist, removed him from his car, and placed him in the officer's car. Later, a second canine unit officer arrived, and his dog went around Caballes's car and alerted to the presence of drugs in the trunk. The police searched the trunk and discovered drugs. Caballes was convicted and complained that there was no reasonable suspicion that a speeding motorist possessed drugs justifying the dog sniff. On appeal, the U.S. Supreme Court held that reasonable suspicion was not required to justify a dog sniff during a routine traffic stop and that the dog sniff established probable cause to search further, because a dog is only sniffing what is in public and his sniff is nonintrusive, a holding reaffirmed by *Florida v. Harris* (2013), where a dog who has been trained to detect narcotics can, under a totality of the circumstances approach, reliably alert to the presence of illegal drugs establishing probable cause to search.[34]

But let us remember Fourth Amendment case law (discussed in Chapter 7) that a man's home is his castle and is afforded under the law the highest level of protection from government intrusion. In *Florida v. Jardines* (2013), police received a tip that Jardines was conducting a marijuana grow operation at his home.[35] Officers brought a drug-detection dog to Jardines's house, where, walking up the driveway (the curtilage), the dog alerted to the presence of drugs. The officers secured a search warrant and seized marijuana plants from inside Jardines's home.

Jardines was convicted and argued on appeal that establishing probable cause through a dog sniff alone may be legal for a car but not at a home, and the high Court agreed. Even though there is no expectation of privacy in a smell, there is a heightened protection on one's property. Similarly, a federal appeals court held that dog sniffs outside apartment doors are insufficient to establish probable cause to search based on the privacy interests people have in their rented homes.[36] In sum, dog sniffs of a reliably trained dog can establish probable cause to search cars, but more than a dog sniff is required to establish probable cause to search a home or apartment.

Common Enterprise

A man having drinks in a bar, where the bartender was suspected of selling heroin and everyone at the bar was searched, successfully challenged the search, which revealed drugs in his pocket. The high Court held in *Ybarra v. Illinois* (1979), guilt by association is illegal. Simply because the man was in a bar where illegal activity was taking place did not give rise to the legal conclusion that he, too, was guilty.[37] But what about the small confines of a car that is stopped and searched and in which contraband is found? Can each passenger be held responsible for that contraband if no one speaks up and claims ownership when guilt by association is unlawful? The U.S. Supreme Court said yes, that officers had probable cause to arrest all occupants, even the occupants who claimed ignorance about the presence of contraband. Under the doctrine of **common enterprise** held in *Maryland v. Pringle* (2003), there is probable cause to make a warrantless arrest of everyone in a car where guns or drugs are found, unless one of the occupants claims responsibility.[38]

Driving Checkpoints

It is constitutional for law enforcement to establish roadblocks and **driving checkpoints** that are tactics to investigate crime, detect drunk drivers, and even check for people in the country without legal authority.[39] In *Illinois v. Lidster* (2004), officers conducted random vehicle stops to interview possible witnesses of a fatal hit-and-run of a 70-year-old man on a bicycle.[40] Robert Lidster was a drunk driver caught by the roadblock who challenged his conviction on the grounds that the investigatory checkpoint violated the Fourth Amendment's prohibition against unreasonable search and seizure. The high Court disagreed and said that such stops are "brief information-seeking" exchanges limited to crime detection. Because the intrusion on the drivers was minimal when weighed against the officers' community protection obligations, the stops were legal.

However, if the objective of the roadblock is to check for illegal drugs and not for drunk drivers or crime investigation, then such stops are illegal. Individualized suspicion that the driver or occupants are engaged in unlawful activity is generally required for a more invasive investigation. In *City of Indianapolis v. Edmond* (2000), the city set up vehicle checkpoints to intercept illegal drugs and conducted six checkpoints over a 4-month period, stopping 1,161 vehicles and arresting 104 motorists.[41] Fifty-five arrests were for drug-related crimes, and 49 were for offenses unrelated to drugs. The overall hit rate for drug arrests was approximately 9%. At each checkpoint approximately 30 officers stopped a predetermined number of vehicles. Motorists challenged the roadblocks on Fourth Amendment grounds. The U.S. Supreme Court agreed with the motorists that such drug checkpoints violated the Constitution.

> We have never approved a checkpoint program whose primary purpose was to detect evidence of ordinary criminal wrongdoing . . . There is no doubt that traffic in illegal narcotics creates social harms of the first magnitude . . . But the gravity of the threat alone cannot be dispositive of questions concerning what means law enforcement officers may employ to pursue a given purpose. . . . We are particularly reluctant to recognize exceptions to the general rule of individualized suspicion where governmental authorities primarily pursue their general crime control ends.

In your analysis of the legality of checkpoints and roadblocks, always balance the government's objective in conducting the stop with the level of government intrusion on the citizen's Fourth Amendment right to be free from unreasonable search and seizure.

Protective Sweep

To ensure officer safety, when police arrest someone in a home or approach a crime scene, can officers make a protective sweep by drawing their weapons and searching for other armed people who may pose a safety threat? The short answer is no. Only when officers have a reasonable belief based on specific and articulable facts that armed and dangerous people are present may the officers legally make a cursory sweep looking for them. In *Maryland v. Buie* (1990), police received a report of an armed robbery committed by two men. After finding one suspect and arresting him inside a house, they conducted a protective sweep for the other man, during which they discovered a red running suit reportedly worn by one of the robbers. The red running suit was introduced at trial and was part of the evidence used to convict Jerome Buie. In an unsuccessful motion to overturn his conviction, Buie claimed that the officers had no legal authority to roam around his home to conduct the protective sweep and, therefore, that the seizure of the running suit was unlawful, but the Supreme Court disagreed. Read the case excerpt below and determine if you agree with the high Court's reasoning.

> **Rule of Law: Officers must have specific and articulable facts that armed persons are on the premises to conduct a warrantless protective sweep to search where people can hide.**

MARYLAND V. BUIE, 494 U.S. 325 (1990)

Supreme Court of the United States

Justice White delivered the opinion of the Court. (7–2)

FACTS: On February 3, 1986, two men committed an armed robbery of a Godfather's Pizza restaurant in Prince George's County, Maryland. One of the robbers was wearing a red running suit. That same day, Prince George's County police obtained arrest warrants for respondent Jerome Edward Buie and his suspected accomplice in the robbery, Lloyd Allen. Buie's house was placed under police surveillance. On February 5, the police executed the arrest warrant for Buie. They first had a police department secretary telephone Buie's house to verify that he was home. The secretary spoke to a female first, then to Buie himself. Six or seven officers proceeded to Buie's house. Once inside, the officers fanned out through the first and second floors. Corporal James Rozar announced that he would "freeze" the basement so that no one could come up and surprise the officers. With his service revolver drawn, Rozar twice shouted into the basement, ordering anyone down there to come out. When a voice asked who was calling, Rozar announced three times: "This is the police, show me your hands."

Eventually, a pair of hands appeared around the bottom of the stairwell and Buie emerged from the basement. He was arrested, searched, and handcuffed by Rozar. Thereafter, Detective Joseph Frolich entered the basement "in case there was someone else" down there. He noticed a red running suit lying in plain view on a stack of clothing and seized it. The trial court denied Buie's motion to suppress

the running suit, stating in part: "The man comes out from a basement, the police don't know how many other people are down there. He is charged with a serious offense." The State introduced the running suit into evidence at Buie's trial. A jury convicted Buie.

ISSUE: [Was the protective sweep in Buie's home justified without a warrant?]

HOLDING: [Yes.] The Fourth Amendment permits a properly limited protective sweep in conjunction with an in-home arrest when the searching officer possesses a reasonable belief based on specific and articulable facts that the area to be swept harbors an individual posing a danger to those on the arrest scene.

REASONING: It goes without saying that the Fourth Amendment bars only unreasonable searches and seizures. Our cases show that in determining reasonableness, we have balanced the intrusion on the individual's Fourth Amendment interests against its promotion of legitimate governmental interests. Under this test, a search of the house or office is generally not reasonable without a warrant issued on probable cause. There are other contexts, however, where the public interest is such that neither a warrant nor probable cause is required.

That Buie had an expectation of privacy in those remaining areas of his house, however, does not mean such

(Continued)

(Continued)

rooms were immune from entry. In *Terry* [*v. Ohio* (1968)] and [*Michigan v. Long* (1983), vehicle search for weapons] we were concerned with the immediate interest of the police officers in taking steps to assure themselves that the persons with whom they were dealing were not armed with, or able to gain immediate control of, a weapon that could unexpectedly and fatally be used against them.

In the instant case, there is an analogous interest of the officers in taking steps to assure themselves that the house in which a suspect is being, or has just been, arrested is not harboring other persons who are dangerous and who could unexpectedly launch an attack. The risk of danger in the context of an arrest in the home is as great as, if not greater than, it is in an on-the-street or roadside investigatory encounter. Moreover, unlike an encounter on the street or along a highway, an in-home arrest puts the officer at the disadvantage of being on his adversary's "turf." An ambush in a confined setting of unknown configuration is more to be feared than it is in open, more familiar surroundings.

We agree with the State, as did the court below, that a warrant was not required [to search the house where Buie was found]. We also hold that as an incident to the arrest the officers could, as a precautionary matter and without probable cause or reasonable suspicion, look in closets and other spaces immediately adjoining the place of arrest from which an attack could be immediately launched. Beyond that, however, we hold that there must be articulable facts which, taken together with the rational inferences from those facts, would warrant a reasonably prudent officer in believing that the area to be swept harbors an individual posing a danger to those on the arrest scene.

CONCLUSION: The Fourth Amendment permits a properly limited protective sweep in conjunction with an in-home arrest when the searching officer possesses a reasonable belief based on specific and articulable facts that the area to be swept harbors an individual posing a danger to those on the arrest scene.

The holding in *Buie* identified two situations in which protective sweeps would be authorized. A protective sweep of spaces and closets "immediately adjoining the place of arrest from which an attack could be immediately launched" is justified without probable cause or reasonable suspicion. The second type of sweep requires reasonable suspicion that "the area to be swept harbors an individual posing a danger to those on the arrest scene" and is not a full search, but rather is limited to those "spaces where a person may be found." If police go to Johnny's house and arrest him in his bedroom, and the officers know that Johnny is part of an armed and dangerous drug-dealing ring, officers may conduct a protective sweep by looking under his bed or in his bedroom closets without probable cause or reasonable suspicion that armed people are hiding in ambush. But if, after arresting Johnny in the bedroom, police seek to conduct a protective sweep of the kitchen, bathroom, and garage, officers must point to specific and articulable facts that armed people are in the house. Their search would be limited to places where people could reasonably hide, such as in the hall closet, not inside the electric dishwasher. In the chapter-opening case study, when Officer Kennedy said she did not feel safe simply on the basis of smelling marijuana with no specific and articulable facts that armed and dangerous people were in the apartment, the legality of the protective sweep may turn on whether the reviewing court recognizes that drugs and guns go hand in hand. Although Officer Kennedy may have been justified in searching the rooms and closets for where armed people may hide, there was no authority to search for people in the refrigerator.

Plain View/Open Fields

If obvious contraband is in plain view (i.e., if anyone can see it without having to move or open anything) and if the officers are at the location legally with a warrant that does not list the contraband or under a legally recognized warrant exception, they may seize the item. There are two legal requirements to seize items in plain view:

1. The officer must have legal authority to be on the premises, and

2. The seized evidence must have a nexus/connection to a crime or be obvious contraband.

If the item is not obvious contraband, officers may not move or otherwise manipulate the item to discover its true identity. While investigating a shooting, police entered an apartment in a rundown area of town and discovered expensive stereo equipment. Officers turned the equipment over to record serial numbers; subsequent investigation revealed it was stolen property. The Court held that moving the equipment was a search unsupported by probable cause and it suppressed the evidence.[42] In the chapter-opening case study, Officer Kennedy's turning over the expensive television set to record serial numbers to run in the stolen property database constituted a search and the television could not be seized pursuant to the plain view exception because expensive electronics are not inherently criminal contraband, even if a person does not appear to be able to afford luxury goods.

Rule of Law: The language of the Fourth Amendment protects only "persons, houses, papers, and effects."

Open fields are typically patches of land over which one can fly in an airplane and see the contraband below, usually marijuana crops or methamphetamine laboratories often operated outside to reduce the potential of a fatal explosion from the combustible chemicals. Contraband discovered in an open field is subject to seizure without a warrant, because "open fields do not provide the setting for those intimate activities that the [Fourth] Amendment is intended to shelter from government interference or surveillance."[43] The Fourth Amendment is specifically limited to a person's "papers, effects, and houses," not things in the open for the public to see. Certain actions are not considered a search for plain-view purposes, such as using a flashlight to get a better view of an item.[44]

The area immediately surrounding a dwelling is called curtilage, and it retains Fourth Amendment privacy rights. People often wonder how far around the house curtilage extends. There is no set distance; it is simply a reasonable distance over which someone may expect to maintain privacy. Curtilage is also not defined by signs, fences, or "No Trespassing" warnings. The privacy interest in curtilage depends on the proximity to the structure. Four factors help define curtilage:[45]

1. The proximity of the home to the area claimed to be curtilage,

2. Whether the area claimed to be curtilage is within an enclosure surrounding the home,

3. The nature of the uses to which the curtilage is put, and

4. The steps taken to conceal the curtilage as a private area.

Property located outside of the curtilage may be treated as abandoned property. For example, if you place trash in a bin located next to your house, it is located within the curtilage and you retain a privacy interest in the trash. But once the garbage is placed out on the curb, it is outside the curtilage and considered abandoned. Law enforcement agents sometimes pose as garbage men, lawfully seize garbage, search it for incriminating evidence, as investigators did in the BALCO Laboratories investigation reported in the affidavit in Chapter 7.[46]

Plain Feel

Occasionally, while patting down suspects during a *Terry* stop, officers may feel what they believe to be contraband. Are they allowed to reach into the person's pocket and remove the item, under the logic that a person has no privacy right in things that are inherently illegal and a crime to possess? To permit officers to go into people's pockets unlawfully expands a *Terry* patdown into a full-blown search, but the plain feel exception to the warrant requirement is closely aligned with plain view and allows the officer to seize obvious contraband that he or she feels on a suspect. There are two conditions for the plain feel exception to the warrant requirement to apply:

1. The officer must lawfully be touching the person; and

2. Through the process of touching, the officer must have probable cause to believe that the object felt constitutes evidence of a crime or is obvious contraband.

Rule of Law: If, during a *Terry* patdown, an officer feels obvious contraband, the officer may seize it.

Other warrantless exceptions include plain smell and plain hearing, where smelling opium or marijuana or where statements overheard by officers without the benefit of enhanced listening devices may establish probable cause to search.[47] In *Minnesota v. Dickerson*, the Supreme Court found that manipulating a suspect's pocket for what the officer believed to be obvious crack cocaine was a search unsupported by probable cause, which is an illegal search. As you read the case below, ask yourself what the officers could have done to conduct a lawful search.

MINNESOTA V. DICKERSON, 508 U.S. 366 (1993)

Supreme Court of the United States

Justice White delivered the opinion of the Court. (6–3)

FACTS: On the evening of November 9, 1989, two Minneapolis police officers were patrolling an area on the city's north side in a marked squad car. At about 8:15 p.m., one of the officers observed respondent [Dickerson] leaving a 12-unit apartment building on Morgan Avenue North. The officer, having previously responded to complaints of drug sales in the building's hallways and having executed several search warrants on the premises, considered the building to be a notorious "crack house." According to testimony credited by the trial court, respondent began walking toward the police but, upon spotting the squad car and making eye contact with one of the officers, abruptly halted and began walking in the opposite direction.

His suspicion aroused, this officer watched as respondent turned and entered an alley on the other side of the apartment building. Based upon respondent's seemingly evasive actions and the fact that he had just left a building known for cocaine traffic, the officers decided to stop respondent and investigate further. The officers pulled their squad car into the alley and ordered respondent to stop and submit to a pat-down search. The search revealed no weapons, but the officer conducting the search did take an interest in a small lump in respondent's nylon jacket. The officer later testified: "As I pat-searched the front of his body, I felt a lump, a small lump, in the front pocket. I examined it with my fingers and it slid and it felt to be a lump of crack cocaine in cellophane."

ISSUE: Thus, the dispositive question before this Court is whether the officer who conducted the search was acting within the lawful bounds marked by *Terry* at the time he gained probable cause to believe that the lump in respondent's jacket was contraband?

HOLDING: [No. The search went beyond a *Terry* stop and was unlawful.]

REASONING: We have already held that police officers, at least under certain circumstances, may seize contraband detected during the lawful execution of a *Terry* search. In *Michigan v. Long* (1983), for example, police approached a man who had driven his car into a ditch and who appeared to be under the influence of some intoxicant. As the man moved to reenter the car from the roadside, police spotted a knife on the floorboard. The officers stopped the man, subjected him to a pat-down search, and then inspected the interior of the vehicle for other weapons. During the search of the passenger compartment, the police discovered an open pouch containing marijuana and seized it. This Court upheld the validity of the search and seizure under *Terry*. The Court held first that, in the context of a roadside encounter, where police have reasonable suspicion based on specific and articulable facts to believe that a driver may be armed and dangerous, they may conduct a protective search for weapons not only of the driver's person but also of the passenger compartment of the automobile. Of course, the protective search of the vehicle, being justified solely by the danger that weapons stored there could be used against the officers or bystanders, must be "limited to those areas in which a weapon may be placed or hidden." The Court then held: "If, while conducting a legitimate *Terry* search of the interior of the automobile, the officer should, as here, discover contraband other than weapons, he clearly cannot be required to ignore the contraband, and the Fourth Amendment does not require its suppression in such circumstances."

We also note that this Court's opinion in *Ybarra v. Illinois* (1979) appeared to contemplate the possibility that police officers could obtain probable cause justifying a seizure of contraband through the sense of touch.[48] In that case, police officers had entered a tavern and subjected its patrons to pat-down searches. While patting down the petitioner Ybarra, an "officer felt what he described as 'a cigarette pack with objects in it,'" seized it, and discovered heroin inside. The State argued that the seizure was constitutional because the officer obtained probable cause to believe that Ybarra was carrying contraband during a lawful *Terry* frisk. This Court rejected that argument on the grounds that "the initial frisk of

Ybarra was simply not supported by a reasonable belief that he was armed and presently dangerous," as required by *Terry*. The Court added: "since we conclude that the initial pat down of Ybarra was not justified under the Fourth and Fourteenth Amendments, we need not decide whether or not the presence on Ybarra's person of 'a cigarette pack with objects in it' yielded probable cause to believe that Ybarra was carrying any illegal substance." The Court's analysis does not suggest, and indeed seems inconsistent with, the existence of a categorical bar against seizures of contraband detected manually during a *Terry* pat-down search.

It remains to apply these principles to the facts of this case. [Dickerson] has not challenged the finding made by the trial court and affirmed by both the Court of Appeals and the State Supreme Court that the police were justified under *Terry* in stopping him and frisking him for weapons. . . . The State District Court did not make precise findings on this point, instead finding simply that the officer, after feeling "a small, hard object wrapped in plastic" in respondent's pocket, "formed the opinion that the object . . . was crack . . . cocaine." [The] District Court also noted that the officer made "no claim that he suspected this object to be a weapon," a finding affirmed on appeal (the officer "never thought the lump was a weapon"). The Minnesota Supreme Court, after "a close examination of the record," held that the officer's own testimony "belies any notion that he 'immediately'"

recognized the lump as crack cocaine. Rather, the court concluded, the officer determined that the lump was contraband only after "squeezing, sliding and otherwise manipulating the contents of the defendant's pocket"—a pocket which the officer already knew contained no weapon.

Under the State Supreme Court's interpretation of the record before it, it is clear that the court was correct in holding that the police officer in this case overstepped the bounds of the "strictly circumscribed" search for weapons allowed under *Terry*. Where, as here, "an officer who is executing a valid search for one item seizes a different item," this Court rightly "has been sensitive to the danger . . . that officers will enlarge a specific authorization, furnished by a warrant or an exigency, into the equivalent of a general warrant to rummage and seize at will." Here, the officer's continued exploration of respondent's pocket after having concluded that it contained no weapon was unrelated to "the sole justification of the search [under *Terry*] . . . the protection of the police officer and others nearby." It therefore amounted to the sort of evidentiary search that *Terry* expressly refused to authorize, and that we have condemned in subsequent cases.

CONCLUSION: Because this further search of [Dickerson's] pocket was constitutionally invalid, the seizure of the cocaine that followed is likewise unconstitutional.

If, during a *Terry* patdown, an officer must manipulate the item to identify it, then such manipulation is considered a search that can only be supported by probable cause. In the chapter-opening case study, Officer Kennedy's removal from Sabrina's pocket of a wad of rolled bills wrapped in a rubber band without knowing whether the money was contraband or otherwise connected to criminal activity was a search unsupported by probable cause, which is illegal.

Hot Pursuit

Hot pursuit allows officers to chase a suspect into a home without a warrant when the suspect may escape or pose a danger to the public if left on the street. A suspect cannot run from the police who have probable cause to arrest him and then thumb his nose at them from the doorway and shout, "You can't come in without a warrant!" before he dashes inside. The U.S. Supreme Court recognized police authority to arrest someone in hot pursuit without the need for a warrant in *Warden v. Hayden* (1967), where police had probable cause to believe that a robber was inside a house he had entered a few minutes before. They justified their warrantless entry of the home to arrest him on the basis of the exigent circumstances that he might flee or pose a danger to the public.[49] Even if a suspect was first seen in the doorway of his home and ran inside to escape arrest, officers could follow him inside in some jurisdictions under the basis of hot pursuit.

Springboard for Discussion

What would society look like if the high Court found in favor of the officers in *Minnesota v. Dickerson* (1993)? How intrusive would a *Terry* patdown become in an effort to "feel" whether or not a suspect possessed contraband, for example, at a fraternity party where officers were patting down partygoers hoping to find illegal drugs?

Rule of Law: The police need not stop a chase when they are in "hot pursuit" of a suspect who poses a danger to the community because the suspect enters a building, dwelling, or other structure.

Courts impose some limits on the hot pursuit exception to the warrant requirement:[50]

1. Officers must have probable cause to believe that the person they are chasing has committed a crime and is on the premises they are entering.

2. Officers must believe that the suspect will escape or harm others if he or she is not immediately arrested.

3. The initial power to arrest must be lawful, as in the plain view exception, and the officers must be on the premises legally for the ensuing search to be lawful.

4. Hot pursuit only applies to serious felonies and misdemeanors, not minor traffic offenses.

5. After the suspect has been arrested, the scope of the ensuing search may only be incident to that arrest and may not be expanded to areas where a warrant would be required.

In the chapter-opening case study, Officer Kennedy could chase Sabrina in hot pursuit into a different apartment without a warrant because she waved a weapon and posed an immediate danger to others.

Exigent Circumstances

Police must have probable cause that exigent or emergency circumstances exist that may justify a warrantless entry into a dwelling. **Exigent circumstances** occur when "a substantial risk of harm to the persons involved or to the law enforcement process would arise if the police delay a search or arrest until a warrant could be obtained."[51] If officers believe that someone inside a home is being injured, the exigency created by the need to protect others justifies warrantless entry into a home. In *Brigham City v. Stuart* (2006), officers approached a house and saw through a window what appeared to be people fighting, involving possible harm to a juvenile. Police rushed in to stop the violence based on the emergency that injured people may need help, and the Court held the warrantless entry lawful.[52] Similarly, in *Michigan v. Fisher* (2009), police responded to a report of a man "going crazy."[53] Officers approached a home and witnessed extensive property damage, fresh blood, and Jeremy Fisher inside screaming and throwing things. Fisher had barricaded the back door. When Officer Goolsby saw Fisher with a bandage on his hand, he pushed open the front door and entered the home. Goolsby left when Fisher pointed a gun at him. Fisher was charged with assault with a dangerous weapon and illegal possession of a firearm, but his motion to suppress the evidence was granted when the lower court held Officer Goolsby entered Fisher's home illegally. The U.S. Supreme Court, based on the *Brigham City* precedent, reversed the lower court and held Goolsby's entry was legal because he had "an objectively reasonable basis for believing" Fisher needed medical help or someone was in danger. The following factors are well recognized in evaluating the existence of exigent circumstances:

Rule of Law: Exigent circumstances are emergency circumstances that justify a warrantless search or seizure.

1. The time required to secure a warrant,

2. The reasonable belief that evidence will be destroyed if officers delay,

3. The safety of officers or the public if police delay acting, and

4. The suspect's awareness of police presence and likelihood of flight.[54]

What happens if the police, in the normal course in the performance of their duties, create exigent circumstances—would the officer's behavior then justify the warrantless entry into someone's apartment? In Lexington, Kentucky, police officers set up a controlled buy (use of an informant) of crack cocaine outside an apartment complex. After the purchase, officers followed the drug dealer inside the apartment building but lost him. As officers entered a breezeway, they heard a door shut and detected a very strong odor of burnt marijuana. The officers saw two apartments, one on the left and one on the right, and they did not know which apartment the suspect had entered. One of the uniformed officers approached the door and announced, "'This is the police' and as soon as [the officers] started banging on the door," they "could hear people inside moving," which led the officers to believe that drug-related evidence was about to be destroyed. Officers kicked in the door and saw marijuana and powder cocaine in plain view. In a subsequent search, they also discovered crack cocaine, cash, and drug paraphernalia. Was the warrantless entry into the apartment lawful pursuant to the exigent circumstances exception? Yes. In *Kentucky v. King* (2011), the Court held the conduct of the police prior to their entry into the apartment was entirely lawful because knocking on doors or asking questions does not constitute a search.[55] Officers did not violate the Fourth Amendment or threaten to do so when they knocked and then heard heavy shuffling noises; therefore, the exigent circumstances exception to the warrant requirement applies and the evidence can be used against the defendants.

In the chapter-opening case study, officers had a lawful right to knock on the door of Apartment 2B, and when they heard furniture moving and toilets flushing, the exigent circumstances exception justified their warrantless entry into the apartment.

MAKING THE COURTROOM CONNECTION

The burden remains with the government to prove police action was done lawfully. In the context of warrantless searches and seizures, the U.S. Supreme Court has a specific, limited list of exceptions the Court is not inclined to expand. The Court is deferential (submitting to another's authority) to the split-second decision making law enforcement officers must make in the field. If officer behavior in making warrantless searches is arguably reasonable under the totality of the circumstances, then courts will generally defer to the officers' discretion and not second-guess decisions made under the stress of interacting with suspects. A good rule of thumb for law enforcement to follow is if there is time to get a warrant, get one.

If defense counsel believe their client has a credible claim that the warrantless search and seizure was conducted without legal justification, they can consider filing a motion to suppress the evidence seized. Sometimes clients can testify at suppression hearings to the circumstances of the search. Even if the court denies the suppression motion and the case proceeds to trial, the government cannot use the client's testimony against him at trial. The logic of protecting a suspect from using his words against him at a later trial (assuming he does not testify at his later trial and change his story) is that the justice system can only discover officer misconduct (conducting an illegal search, e.g.) when the suspect is free to testify about the officer's conduct. If the prosecutor could use what the suspect said at a preliminary hearing against him at a later trial where he exercised his right to remain silent, official misconduct would go unreported and unpunished.

For correctional officers, a warrantless search within a jail or prison is standard practice. Prisoners' constitutional rights are subordinate to the ultimate goal of prison safety. Given the creativity of the inmates, family, and friends in sneaking contraband into prison, thorough and sometimes highly invasive searches are required. See Photo 8.1 of an x-ray of an inmate trying to smuggle a cell phone into prison through his digestive system.

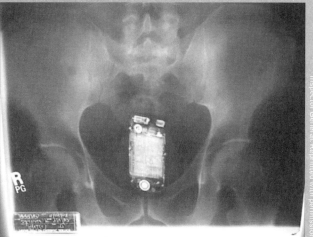

▶ Photo 8.1
Texas prisons in 2012 confiscated more than 900 cell phones, but not until 738 had been used inside the prison.

Texas Department of Criminal Justice, Office of the Inspector General. Reprinted with permission.

Breathalyzer and Blood Tests to Measure Blood Alcohol Content. A common example of exigent circumstances creating a need for a warrantless seizure is drunk-driving cases. The alcohol content in the bloodstream gradually dissipates after alcohol is consumed. If police suspect someone has been drinking and driving, especially late at night when the courts are closed and the burdens of securing a warrant are high, officers can take the suspect to a medical facility to draw blood to preserve the blood alcohol content (BAC) for possible later use at trial. In the case *Schmerber v. California*, 384 U.S. 757 (1966), Armando Schmerber was being treated at a hospital for injuries sustained in an accident when police directed the doctor to take a vial of Schmerber's blood as evidence. He was later convicted of driving under the influence and, on appeal, complained that the warrantless extraction of his blood violated the Fourth Amendment. The Supreme Court disagreed. The Court reasoned that the quick dissipation of alcohol from the suspect's bloodstream justified the exigency to act quickly because obtaining a warrant may take too much time.

The Court modified the *Schmerber* decision in *Missouri v. McNeely* (2013), where police officers took McNeely's blood without a warrant and used McNeely's BAC at trial to convict him of driving under the influence.[56] The high Court held that suspicion of drunk driving did not *per se* (on its face) create an emergency justifying the warrantless drawing of a suspect's blood. The determination whether an exigency existed required a totality of the circumstances analysis that must be resolved on a case-by-case basis. Drawing blood is greatly intrusive to a person's bodily integrity, but taking a breath sample is not, and a warrant is not required for a roadside breathalyzer test. In 2016, the Court held in *Birchfield v. North Dakota* that the Fourth Amendment permits warrantless breathalyzer tests incident to arrests for drunk driving because blowing into a tube is minimally invasive to the suspect's privacy interests.[57]

Body Cavity Searches. There are many situations in which courts must examine the circumstances surrounding **body cavity searches** (mouth, vagina, anus) and the seizure—or taking—of bodily fluids or stomach contents. The first prominent case in which the Supreme Court addressed the issue was *Rochin v. California* (1952). In this case, officers first tried to choke morphine tablets out of Richard Rochin's mouth. Then, when Rochin successfully swallowed the pills, officers took him to the hospital to pump his stomach for the evidence that would later be introduced at trial to convict him, a search the high Court said "shocks the conscience" and deemed unreasonable.

> **Rule of Law: Bodily intrusions by government officials are subject to the most protection under the Fourth Amendment, unless they occur at the country's borders or to inmates in prison.**

In *United States v. Montoya de Hernandez* (1985), Hernandez crossed the border and authorities believed she was a "drug mule," that is, hired to carry drugs across the border.[58] Before enhanced border security procedures after the September 11, 2001, terrorist attack, people (many young women) would swallow large quantities of drugs packed into the cut-off fingers of latex gloves tied and secured so the homemade "balloons" did not explode in the drug courier's belly. Hernandez told authorities that her stomach was swollen because she was pregnant, but officers did not believe her. Border patrol told Hernandez she could return to her home country, but she refused. Authorities detained her for over 12 hours until she passed 88 balloons of cocaine. Hernandez unsuccessfully sued, claiming her Fourth Amendment rights were violated, but the high Court rejected her claim stating, "Routine searches of the persons and effects of entrants [at the border] are not subject to any requirement of reasonable suspicion, probable cause, or a warrant . . . [O]ne's expectation of privacy [is] less at the border," which includes stomach contents.

In the jail setting, warrantless strip searches are also legal, even if the initial arrest was unlawful. In 2005, Albert Florence was a passenger in his BMW driven by his wife when she was pulled over for a traffic violation. A check for outstanding warrants revealed Albert was wanted for an outstanding traffic fine that he insisted was a mistake; he had paid the fine. Police arrested Florence and before placing him in a jail cell, conducted a strip search even though officials had no suspicion Florence was hiding weapons or contraband and the arresting offense was for a minor, nonviolent crime. Authorities moved Florence to another jail and before placing him in a cell, strip searched him again. After Florence was held for 7 days, he was released. Florence sued the officials at both jails under 42 U.S.C. §1983 (see Chapter 1 for the requirements of a civil claim), for a violation of his federal civil rights beginning with the mistaken information in the police database regarding the unpaid fine. The government responded that, for security purposes before they place a detainee in general population, a strip search is required. In *Florence v. Board of Chosen Freeholders of the County of Burlington* (2012), the U.S. Supreme Court found the strip searches legal, citing a common refrain in litigation over prison rules and regulations, that absent "substantial evidence showing their policies are an unnecessary or unjustified response to problems of jail security," the high Court would not interfere.[59]

DNA Collection. With advancing technology, a common area of litigation is the collection and storage of genetic information of convicted offenders for inclusion in computer databases. Is it a violation of the Fourth Amendment to collect blood for DNA typing where no exigency exists, and our genetic make-up determined at birth will remain relatively unchanged until death? The involuntary taking of a biological sample is a "search" under the Fourth Amendment, but if the **DNA collection** is done as part of the routine booking process when one has been charged with committing, or attempting to commit, a crime of violence, the collection of the sample without a warrant is legal. In 2009, Alonzo King was arrested for menacing a group of people with a shotgun. At his booking, Maryland law provided for the taking of a buccal (cheek) swab to obtain a tissue sample of DNA. King's DNA matched the biological evidence taken from a rape case, unsolved since 2003. King was convicted of the rape, sentenced to life without parole, and argued on appeal that the taking of his DNA was an unlawful search under the Fourth Amendment, but the U.S. Supreme Court disagreed in *Maryland v. King* (2013).[60] By a 5–4 vote, the Court weighed the relatively noninvasive procedure of obtaining a cheek swab with the legitimate law enforcement purpose of helping police solve crimes and said taking a swab was like "21st-century fingerprinting" and the taking of mug shots during the booking procedure. Moreover, the Maryland DNA Collection Act at issue in the case contains procedural safeguards to dispose of the DNA sample should the accused be found not guilty or is otherwise exonerated.[61]

APPLYING THE LAW TO THE FACTS

When Can the Government Collect DNA?

The Facts: Janice was being held in jail awaiting trial on robbery charges. She was called out of her cell ostensibly to meet with her attorney. Instead, deputies took Janice to a small room and asked for consent to take a buccal swab from her cheek to obtain a DNA sample. Janice refused, and officers restrained her and swabbed her cheek. When Janice complained, the government decided not to use the DNA results at trial. Janice then sued the jail for violating her Fourth Amendment rights and, in response, the government said the *Maryland v. King* (2013) precedent allows

for the collection of a suspect's biological evidence. Which side will win?

The Law: It's a toss-up. The Maryland case held collecting DNA as part of the routine booking process was much like taking fingerprints or mug shots. Here, Janice had been in jail for a period of time and awaiting trial. Where suspects have already been processed and are confined long enough to establish a prison routine, criminal justice professionals would likely need a warrant supported by probable cause that Janice committed a specific crime to obtain a DNA swab.[62]

Special Needs Searches

Special needs searches are those often justified by the unique nature of the regulatory activity justifying warrantless searches.

Drug Testing in Schools

Students have a lesser expectation of privacy in a school setting than in the general public, but they do not leave their constitutional rights at the steps of the schoolhouse door.[63] When school-teachers and administrators in Vernonia, Oregon, noticed increased drug use and disciplinary problems among students, the school board initiated a policy requiring student athletes, who were believed to be the leaders of the drug subculture, to undergo drug testing performed both at the beginning of their sport season and at least 10% of the time thereafter. The policy was implemented with the advice and consent of the parents. One student and his parents filed suit on Fourth Amendment grounds, and the U.S. Supreme Court decided in favor of the school district in *Vernonia School District 47J v. Acton* (1995).[64] The decision was made on the basis that the special needs for school discipline and the public safety needs in a school led to a decreased expectation of privacy for students; furthermore, the search was minimally invasive on the students' expectation of privacy. Associate Justice Sandra Day O'Connor dissented, finding that "suspicionless drug testing was not justified on the facts, since [drug testing situations are not] exceptions to the general view that mass suspicionless searches are *per se* unreasonable within the meaning of the Fourth Amendment."

Warrantless Searches for Drugs in Schools. The *Vernonia School District 47J* precedent balanced the government's interest in providing a drug-free school environment against the minimal intrusion of students giving urine samples as a requirement to play school sports; therefore, a search for drugs in school cannot be too invasive. In an Arizona middle school, school authorities received information that 13-year-old Savana Redding had shared with other students prescription-strength ibuprofen and over-the-counter naproxen (another type of pain reliever). School employees searched Savana's belongings and then took her into the bathroom. There Savana was ordered to strip down to her underwear and pull out the elastic band on her underpants and shake the straps of her bra, all in the hopes the hidden drugs would drop out of her undergarments: They found nothing. Savana sued the school district for conducting an unreasonable warrantless search in violation of the Fourth Amendment. School employees defended themselves based on qualified immunity. The high Court agreed with both parties. Justice Souter found the legal basis for Savana's search (rumors of prescription aspirin possession) could not justify the "quantum leap" from searching backpacks to "exposure of [a teenage girl's] intimate parts." On the other hand, as discussed in Chapter 1 on the liability of criminal justice actors when mistakes are made, the Court concluded in *Safford Unified School District #1 v. Redding* (2009) that the law governing the scope of searches on school property was "not clearly established" because lower courts had interpreted the school's authority to conduct such searches differently and, therefore, the Safford United School District employees were entitled to qualified immunity.[65]

Drug Testing of Government Employees

To work for or be promoted within some government agencies, employees must undergo drug testing based on the "special needs" of a safe workplace. When Customs Service employees challenged the Treasury Department's drug-testing program as a precondition to promotion eligibility, they lost their challenge. The Court held that the drug testing was legal because the drug results were not going to be used in criminal prosecutions; testing was necessary to promote drug-free people to positions of power; and the nature of the intrusion into personal privacy, providing a urine sample in a cup, was minimal.[66]

APPLYING THE LAW TO THE FACTS

Reasonable Search on School Grounds?

The Facts: A sheriff had a target list of 13 high school students suspected of drug possession. The sheriff and two deputies then went to the high school and spent hours as they searched 900 students by patting them down from head to toe as they faced their lockers. Many students complained the deputies had touched and groped their private areas. The search yielded nothing. Was the search reasonable?

The Law: No. The search was unreasonable and in November 2017, Worth County, Georgia, settled the resulting civil lawsuit with the affected students for $3 million. In the chapter-opening case study, the partial strip search of Rick in the school bathroom would likely be unreasonable, especially based on a "rumor" that Rick possessed drugs.

Searches of Government Property Used for Personal Business. In general, government employees have a lesser expectation of privacy in terms of the tools of their work (e.g., their desks, their offices, and computer files) than do employees who work for private corporations. Because government employees do not "own" the equipment they use, which was bought and paid for with tax dollars collected from the public, public employees cannot claim an absolute privacy right in work-related items as they would in their own personal computers and files. Jeff Quon was a police officer in the City of Ontario, California, who used his work-issued pager to send personal messages, some sexually explicit, to people not related to Quon's official duties. When an audit revealed that Quon had sent or received 456 messages during work hours in 1 month and no more than 57 were work related, Quon was disciplined. Quon sued, claiming a violation of his Fourth Amendment right to privacy. The U.S. Supreme Court found in favor of the police department in *City of Ontario v. Quon* (2010), holding that the "special needs" of the workplace justify warrantless searches that would otherwise be unreasonable when investigating "work-related misconduct."[67]

> **Rule of Law:** There is a diminished expectation of privacy for those who travel in public.

Airports/Subways/Buses

On July 22, 2005, in response to coordinated bombings on London's railway system, New York City implemented a random search procedure on its subways. Petitioners who rode the trains in New York challenged the mass suspicionless searches. The federal district court decided on December 5, 2005, that "the need to prevent a terrorist bombing of the New York City subway system is a governmental interest of the very highest order" that outweighed the minimal intrusion to passengers who used the 468 subway stations.[68] A similar rationale supports the heightened security in airports, and airport screening searches are legal administrative searches. The courts are clear that individuals who feel burdened by the brief intrusion on their liberty from using public trains and planes may travel by private means. But the changing nature of mass attacks using public conveyances justifies the suspicionless searches when weighed against the minimal government intrusion on a person's liberty interest to look into their personal bags.

In *United States v. Aukai* (2007), the federal court of appeals held that an airline passenger who successfully walks through the x-ray machine and is subjected to a "secondary screening" by a Transportation Security Administration officer cannot choose to forego the additional screening and abandon his flight.[69] Airport security was about to discover the contents of the pants pocket of defendant Aukai when he tried to leave the airport. When security found a methamphetamine pipe and Aukai was convicted of drug possession, he challenged the legality of the search. But the court found in favor of the government, stating "The constitutionality of an airport screening search, however, does not depend on consent . . . and requiring that a potential passenger be allowed to revoke consent to an ongoing airport security search makes little sense in a post–9/11 world." Courts today are more lenient in granting law enforcement the "special needs" authority to protect public transportation venues.

The high Court has found questioning passengers on buses and asking for consent to search does not trigger Fourth Amendment protections. Recall that if a reasonable person in the citizen's shoes would not feel free to leave or otherwise terminate the police encounter, then, under the Fourth Amendment, he has been "seized."[70] Two cases involving drug task force efforts to find drugs on buses illustrate the high Court's unwillingness to extend traditional privacy rights on public conveyances. In both cases, officers boarded busses in Florida, asked for tickets and identification, asked for and received consent to search, and found cocaine either in luggage or on the person.

In one case, *Florida v. Bostick* (1991), the high Court found the bus passengers were not seized and had free will to refuse the officer's request to search, and the drugs discovered were held admissible against the defendant. Similarly, in *United States v. Drayton* (2002), officers boarded a bus and stood in the aisle over two men, Christopher Drayton and Clifton Brown, Jr., asking to search their luggage, to which the men consented.[71] When the officer thought it strange that Drayton and Brown on a warm day were dressed in heavy, baggy clothing (although the bus trip started in Detroit, Michigan), the officer asked for permission to conduct a patdown and, again, Drayton and Brown said yes. The officer could not recall if he informed the men of their right to refuse his request.[72] When the men were found to have bundles of cocaine taped to their legs, they were arrested and claimed the search was illegal. The high Court found in favor of the officers, stating that Drayton and Brown could have terminated the encounter with the officer at any time, a finding some scholars disagree with considering a bus is a small confined space and an officer standing in the aisle blocking the exit would lead a reasonable person to feel "seized" and forced to comply.[73] But the "special needs" of safety on public conveyances often justifies the government's actions without first resorting to obtaining a warrant.

Border Searches

Even before the terrorist attacks on American soil on September 11, 2001 (9/11), America had a vested interest in protecting the integrity of its borders and there exists no probable cause requirement to search people entering the country. By willfully and lawfully entering the country, people consent to be searched. The waiving of these individual rights allows the government to maintain national security and combat international drug smuggling.

After 9/11, the Supreme Court was willing to allow greater latitude to officers at inspection stations at border crossings. In 2005, the Ninth Circuit held in *United States v. Cortez-Rocha* that removing and cutting open a truck's spare tire at the border was a reasonable search. Inspectors discovered over 42 kilograms of marijuana in a tire. The defendant argued that because the customs officials had no individualized suspicion that he was engaged in criminal activity, the evidence should be suppressed. The appeals court rejected the defendant's claims and focused on whether cutting the tire destroyed the vehicle. Finding that it did not, it deemed the search constitutional. Referring to earlier precedent in which the Court found the removal and dismantling of a vehicle's gas tank constitutional in *United States v. Flores-Montano* (2004), the justices analogized the spare tire to a closed container, which the agents, who the Court said were intelligent and respectful, should be free to inspect in furtherance of their duties.[74] Justice Thomas dissented and criticized the majority for giving "the government *carte blanche* to search and destroy all personal property at the border that does not affect vehicular operation." He concluded that, although safeguarding the border was of paramount concern, protection of Fourth Amendment rights remained a priority, especially in times "of great national distress."

The tension between a reduced expectation of privacy at the border, where warrantless searches are allowed, and the right to be free from unreasonably invasive searches is demonstrated below, a case excerpt of *United States v. Cotterman* (2013). Cotterman was a known sex offender who had his computer searched at the border. Agents discovered child pornography images, and Cotterman appealed on the basis that the search was unreasonable. The appellate court disagreed. The case was decided in 2013, before the *Riley v. California* (2014) case, holding that a warrant is required to search cell phones because a phone is a mini-computer stuffed with storage containing vast quantities of personal information (e.g., location history, contacts, e-mails).

UNITED STATES V. COTTERMAN, 709 F.3D 952 (9TH CIR. 2013)

FACTS: Howard Cotterman and his wife were driving home to the United States from a vacation in Mexico on Friday morning, April 6, 2007, when they reached the Lukeville, Arizona [border crossing]. During primary inspection by a border agent, the Treasury Enforcement Communication System (TECS) returned a hit for Cotterman as a sex offender—he had a 1992 conviction [sex crimes involving children]—and that he was potentially involved in child sex tourism. Because of the hit, Cotterman and his wife were referred to secondary inspection, where they were instructed to exit their vehicle and leave all their belongings in the car. The agents searched the vehicle and retrieved two laptop computers and three digital cameras. The agents allowed the Cottermans to leave the border crossing around 6 p.m., but retained the Cottermans' laptops and a digital camera [which the agents searched forensically] and found seventy-five images of child pornography within the unallocated space of Cotterman's laptop.

[The trial court suppressed the images of child pornography as seized as a result of an illegal border search, and the government appealed.]

ISSUE: [Was the warrantless forensic examination of the computer's hard drive unreasonable?]

HOLDING: [No.] Cotterman's TECS alert, prior child sex-related conviction, frequent travels, crossing from a country known for sex tourism, and collection of electronic equipment, plus the parameters of the Operation Angel Watch program, taken collectively, gave rise to reasonable suspicion of criminal activity.

REASONING: Every day more than a million people cross American borders, from the physical borders with Mexico and Canada to functional borders at airports such as Los Angeles (LAX), Honolulu (HNL), New York (JFK, LGA), and Chicago (ORD, MDW). As denizens of a digital world, they carry with them laptop computers, iPhones, iPads, iPods, Kindles, Nooks, Surfaces, tablets, Blackberries, cell phones, digital cameras, and more. These devices often contain private and sensitive information ranging from personal, financial, and medical data to corporate trade secrets. And, in the case of Howard Cotterman, child pornography.

Agents seized Cotterman's laptop at the U.S.-Mexico border in response to an alert based in part on a fifteen-year-old conviction for child molestation. The initial search at the border turned up no incriminating material. Only after Cotterman's laptop was shipped almost 170 miles away and subjected to a comprehensive forensic examination were images of child pornography discovered.

This watershed case implicates both the scope of the narrow border search exception to the Fourth Amendment's warrant requirement and privacy rights in commonly used electronic devices. The question we confront "is what limits there are upon this power of technology to shrink the realm of guaranteed privacy." *Kyllo v. United States* (2001). More specifically, we consider the reasonableness of a computer search that began as a cursory review at the border but transformed into a forensic examination of Cotterman's hard drive.

Computer forensic examination is a powerful tool capable of unlocking password-protected files, restoring deleted material, and retrieving images viewed on web sites. But while technology may have changed the expectation of privacy to some degree, it has not eviscerated it, and certainly not with respect to the gigabytes of data regularly maintained as private and confidential on digital devices. Our Founders were indeed prescient in specifically incorporating "papers" within the Fourth Amendment's guarantee of "[t]he right of the people to be secure in their persons, houses, papers, and effects." The papers we create and maintain not only in physical but also in digital form reflect our most private thoughts and activities.

Although courts have long recognized that border searches constitute a "historically recognized exception to the Fourth Amendment's general principle that a warrant be obtained," reasonableness remains the touchstone for a warrantless search. Even at the border, we have rejected an "anything goes" approach.

CONCLUSION: Because border agents had such a reasonable suspicion [that Cotterman was a sex tourist], we reverse the district court's order granting Cotterman's motion to suppress the evidence of child pornography obtained from his laptop.

A list summarizing the most notable exceptions to the warrant requirement and the probable cause requirement is found in Table 8.1.

Table 8.1 List of Warrant Exceptions		
Warrant Exceptions	Case Law	Probable Cause (P/C) Still Required?
Airports	*U.S. v. Davis* (1973)	Special needs, no P/C
Automobiles	*Carroll v. U.S.* (1925)	P/C the car contains contraband
Borders	*U.S. v. Flores-Montano* (2004)	Lower expectation of privacy entering the country, no P/C
Breathalyzer	*Birchfield v. North Dakota* (2016)	P/C needed for DUI arrest justifying breathalyzer

(Continued)

Table 8.1   (Continued)

Warrant Exceptions	Case Law	Probable Cause (P/C) Still Required?
Consent	*Schneckloth v. Bustamonte* (1973)	Must be voluntary, no P/C
Drug Testing in School	*Vernonia School District 47J v. Acton* (1995)	Special needs, no P/C
Exigent Circumstances	*Kentucky v. King* (2011)	Reasonable belief or P/C depending on circumstances
Hot Pursuit	*Warden v. Hayden* (1967)	P/C suspect committed dangerous felony
Inventory	*Colorado v. Bertine* (1987)	P/C needed for arrest justifying search
Open Fields	*Oliver v. U.S.* (1984)	Not covered by words of the Fourth Amendment
Plain View	*Texas v. Brown* (1983)	P/C needed to connect the evidence seized with a crime
Plain Feel	*Minnesota v. Dickerson* (1993)	Reasonable belief item to be seized is contraband
Protective Sweep	*Maryland v. Buie* (1990)	Specific and articulable facts indicating armed persons are on the premises
Search Incident to Arrest	*Chimel v. California* (1969)	P/C needed for arrest justifying search
Strip Search in Jail	*Florence v. Board of Chosen Freeholders* (2012)	P/C needed for arrest justifying search
Subways	*MacWade v. Kelly* (2006)	Special needs, no P/C

THE EXCLUSIONARY RULE AND THE GOOD FAITH EXCEPTION

The many steps in securing and executing a search or arrest warrant invite opportunities to make mistakes. In recognition of the government's investigative and judicial power to find and prosecute criminals, courts hold criminal justice officials to a higher ethical standard to know the law that guides their professional obligations. The exclusionary rule is a judge-made fix when officers obtain evidence in violation of the Fourth, Fifth, or Sixth Amendments. If criminal justice professionals do not follow the law, the court will not let the government profit by using illegally obtained evidence against the suspect. The analysis of the types of mistakes associated with search and seizure is guided by the Fourth Amendment's warrants and reasonableness clauses.

What if the police were merely doing their job and made a mistake? Should the innocent officer be punished by operation of the exclusionary rule and suppression of the evidence seized? In *United States v. Leon* (1984), police served a search warrant later found defective for lack of probable cause.[75] Though the exclusionary rule mandated the evidence retrieved unlawfully should be suppressed, the U.S. Supreme Court held the evidence admissible because the officers were acting in good faith. If the officers are acting in good faith, meaning that they had no unscrupulous motive or bad intent to gain an unfair advantage over the suspect or to advance the prosecution, there is no sense punishing the government by excluding the evidence seized.

The U.S. Supreme Court has devised a formula to determine if the exclusionary rule or its good faith exception applies, and it is a strict cost–benefit analysis. Excluding evidence against possibly guilty suspects extracts a high cost to society, and that cost must outweigh the benefit of suppressing the evidence to deter other professionals from violating the law. The Court has said,

> The basic insight of the *Leon* line of cases is that [the] deterrence benefits of exclusion "vary with the culpability of the law enforcement conduct" at issue. When the police exhibit "deliberate," "reckless," or "grossly negligent" disregard for Fourth Amendment rights, the *deterrent value of exclusion is strong* and tends to outweigh the resulting costs. But when the police act with an objectively "reasonable good-faith belief" that their conduct is lawful, or when their conduct involves only simple, "isolated" negligence, the "*deterrence rationale [of excluding evidence] loses much of its force,*" and exclusion [of evidence] cannot "pay its way"[76] [emphasis added].

Thus, the Court's formula is illustrated by the following chart describing the police conduct and the corresponding application of the exclusionary rule.

Table 8.2 The Exclusionary Rule as It Applies to Police Conduct	
Excluding the Evidence Is a Benefit That WILL Prevent Future Misconduct by the Police and They Will Be More Careful	**Excluding the Evidence Is a High Cost to Society In Letting the Guilty Go Free and Exclusion WILL NOT "Pay Its Way"**
Deliberate disregard for Fourth Amendment rights	Objectively reasonable, but mistaken, belief behavior was lawful
Reckless disregard for Fourth Amendment rights	Simple negligence
Grossly negligent disregard for Fourth Amendment rights	Isolated negligence

Moreover, based on the *Leon* precedent, officers can rely on the magistrate's signature on the face of the warrant indicating that the officer acted in good faith in securing the warrant and seizing the evidence. But there are four situations where courts will *rarely* find good faith in the Fourth Amendment context and may exclude the evidence preventing its use against the defendant at trial:

1. Magistrate relied on a deliberately false affidavit,

2. Magistrate was not neutral or detached,

3. No objective person could find probable cause exists from the facts presented, and

4. As in the *Groh v. Ramirez* (2004) case, where the warrant was invalid on its face.

The following material examines common mistakes with warrants and the attendant remedies.

Mistakes About the Law Supporting an Arrest

David Moore was in Virginia driving with a suspended license. Police mistakenly arrested Moore for the infraction, and the subsequent search revealed crack cocaine. In moving to suppress the drugs, Moore argued correctly that Virginia state law only allowed for the issuance of a summons for driving without a license, not an arrest. Are the drugs still admissible even though there was no legal justification for Moore's initial arrest? Yes, the high Court stated in *Virginia v. Moore* (2008), if the arrest was based on probable cause that a crime had been committed, the arrest is legal regardless of any state arrest statute.[77]

Similarly, officers in North Carolina believed a driver was suspicious because he "appeared stiff," and they pulled him over for driving with a broken brake light. The car's owner, Nicholas Heien, consented to the search of the car, which revealed cocaine. Driving with one operating tail light, however, was legal under state law and Heien won his motion to suppress the drugs. On appeal to the U.S. Supreme Court, the justices reversed the lower court's ruling in *Heien v. North Carolina* (2014), and found that reasonable suspicion to stop a motorist can rest on an officer's mistaken understanding of the law at the time of the stop, which, in this case, was an ambiguous state law defining "tail lights" or "rear lamps" and no court of law had interpreted the law giving police officers guidance.[78]

Mistakes in Whether Probable Cause Exists to Arrest

In Salt Lake City during an investigation into suspected methamphetamine production and distribution, officers were watching a suspected drug house when Edward Strieff came out and walked down the street. Officer Frackell approached and detained Strieff while running a check for any outstanding warrants. Strieff had a valid outstanding arrest warrant for a minor traffic violation that had occurred years earlier. Frackell arrested Strieff and, in conducting a search incident to arrest, discovered methamphetamine and drug paraphernalia later used to convict Strieff. The Utah Supreme Court overturned Strieff's conviction holding Frackell's initial stop of Strieff illegal, as there was no reasonable suspicion that criminal activity was afoot merely by Strieff coming out of a house under surveillance. On appeal, the U.S. Supreme Court reversed the state court decision in *Utah v. Strieff* (2016), and reinstated Strieff's conviction because the Court found a time and distance separation from the officer's initial illegal act (stopping Strieff in the street without reasonable suspicion) and the discovery of incriminating evidence (finding drugs and paraphernalia), rendering the evidence seized unlawfully admissible.[79] Justice Sotomayor's dissent in the *Strieff* case was discussed in Chapter 7.

Mistakes in Computer Databases Leading to an Arrest

In *Hudson v. Michigan* (2006), the Court stated that even if law enforcement has violated someone's Fourth Amendment's rights, there may not be a remedy. In *Herring v. United States* (2009), Bennie Herring came to the police department to retrieve something from his impounded truck. Herring was known to the police, and officers conducted a computer check for any outstanding warrants. Finding none, officers called a neighboring county to check if Herring had any outstanding warrants there. When the answer came back yes, Herring was arrested. In performing a search incident to arrest, police discovered drugs and a gun. Fifteen minutes after Herring's arrest, the neighboring county called to reveal there had been a mistake. The warrant the county believed was active had been recalled, and the information contained in the database was wrong. Herring argued that the contraband found as a result of his unlawful arrest should be suppressed.[80]

The high Court agreed with Herring that his arrest had been improper, but they did not find in his favor. The Court looked to its precedent, *Arizona v. Evans* (1995), where an arrest was made based on a county clerk's error in maintaining a warrant database.[81] In that case the Court said the evidence against Isaac Evans should be admissible because the deterrent effect of the exclusionary rule would not work to punish the police for a clerk's recordkeeping error. Herring argued that the *Evans* precedent should not apply to his case because the police, and not a clerk, made the mistake in arresting him, but the high Court disagreed. The Court said the exclusionary rule does not create a "personal constitutional right" for the citizen whose rights have been violated, and to exclude evidence "has always been our last resort, not our first impulse." The Court held the gun and drugs admissible and Herring's conviction was upheld.

In sum, if officers make mistakes that are merely negligent and not motivated by an impure motive, courts typically admit the evidence unlawfully seized. Conversely, the exclusionary rule is a high price to pay for officer misconduct, so courts are willing to exclude evidence at trial only if the officer's conduct was egregious, deserving of stiff punishment, and will likely deter other officers from committing the same misconduct.

SUMMARY

1. You will be able to discuss the legal basis for all exceptions to the warrant requirement. A search without a warrant is generally illegal, but there are many well-defined exceptions to the warrant requirement. Consent of the suspect to a search must be voluntary and must not be the product of a submission to authority. Deceit by undercover officers or informants is generally permissible to gain entry, but deceit by officers to gain consent or about the object of their search is not. A search incident to an arrest (SITA) may be conducted without a warrant and covers the person arrested and the area within his immediate control. For a SITA of a person arrested in or near his car, police must show the arrestee shows a continuing threat to officer safety or to preserve evidence of arrest. There are varying conditions to search closed containers depending on the nature of the initial citizen–police encounter.

2. You will be able to recognize exigent circumstances justifying officer conduct in the field. Generally, if the officers have time to secure a warrant, then they should do so unless exigent (emergency) circumstances are present—for instance, when there is a likelihood that evidence will be destroyed or evaporate or when the safety of the officers or the public is at issue. Additionally, officers who are in hot pursuit have a right to chase a fleeing suspect indoors without needing to obtain a warrant. If the place to be searched has a lower expectation of privacy than a home, for example, a car, or if the person's status allows the government to intrude on that person's privacy more freely, for example, if the person is a student, convict, or probationer, a warrant to search may not be required. Strip-searching students for drugs is generally too invasive, although certain body cavity searches for drugs may be reasonable, especially in confinement and at the border.

Because the language of the Fourth Amendment protects "persons, houses, papers, and effects," officers do not need a warrant to seize things in plain view, or based on plain feel, provided officers do not have to manipulate the object to discover its identity, as what happened in *Minnesota v. Dickerson* (1993), or items that are in open fields, provided that the officers are on the premises legally and the evidence to be seized is obvious contraband.

3. You will understand the limits of automobile searches and the protective sweep. Because automobiles are mobile and heavily regulated, officers need not secure a warrant to conduct searches if probable cause exists that the car contains contraband under the automobile exception. The auto exception does not justify a warrantless search of a home's curtilage for stolen vehicles (*Collins v. VA*, 2018). Due to the minimal intrusion on privacy interests and the government's need to stop drunk drivers or ask questions about recent crime, a warrant is not required at driving checkpoints, but random drug interdiction efforts require individualized suspicion and probable cause to search. Inventory searches must be conducted pursuant to a specific police protocol (although it need not be written) to be lawful. Dog sniffs are not a search but may supply probable cause to search a car, but not a home. Officers may conduct a protective sweep in a home based on specific and articulable facts that an armed and dangerous person is on the premises, as long as the area of the sweep is limited to the immediate area of the arrest and places within the premises where an armed person could be hiding, as happened in *Maryland v. Buie* (1990).

4. You will become knowledgeable about the law regulating warrantless drug, alcohol, and DNA seizures. Special needs searches involve the unique needs of law enforcement balanced against a lesser expectation of privacy based on someone's status as a student, a government employee, or a prisoner or probationer. Searches at airports, subways, buses and at the country's borders are examples of special needs searches to prevent random attacks on public conveyances, and at the border there is a lesser expectation of privacy in closed containers such as laptops, as illustrated by *United States v. Cotterman* (2013).

5. You will be reintroduced to the exclusionary rule and understand good faith exceptions when mistakes are made in the field. The exclusionary rule is a judge-made fix when officers obtain evidence in violation of the Fourth, Fifth, or Sixth Amendments to keep evidence out at a defendant's trial; the rule is designed to punish the police when they do not follow the law. Mistakes in the status of the law authorizing an arrest or computer databases about

the presence of active arrest warrants will be tolerated, as well as unlawful stops later justified by the discovery of an active warrant, as in *Utah v. Strieff* (2016). To justify the high societal cost of the exclusionary rule to suppress evidence against possibly guilty defendants, punishment of the police who engage in deliberate misconduct or who are grossly negligent must be applicable. Otherwise, for officers who commit simple acts of negligence or otherwise operate in good faith (no evil intent), courts are less likely to invoke the exclusionary rule and will not suppress the evidence illegally seized.

Go back to the beginning of the chapter and reread the news excerpts associated with the learning objectives. Test yourself to determine if you can understand the material covered in the text in the context of the news.

KEY TERMS AND PHRASES

automobile exception 222
body cavity search 234
border search 239
closed containers 224
common enterprise 226
consent 219
curtilage 229

DNA collection 235
dog sniff 225
driving checkpoint 226
exigent circumstances 232
hot pursuit 231
inventory search 224
knock and talk 220

open field 229
plain feel 229
plain view 228
protective sweep 227
search incident to an arrest 221
special needs searches 235
submission to authority 220

PROBLEM-SOLVING EXERCISES

1. Peter and Julie had a domestic incident on April 22, 2012. When police arrived at the residence, they observed Julie standing in front of the house on the sidewalk. She complained that she had gotten into a physical altercation with Peter. When Peter opened the door, the police officers pushed it open and chased Peter upstairs where he picked up one of his children and began to run into another room. The police deployed taser darts into Peter's back, causing him to drop his child, who sustained a head injury. Peter was then placed under arrest. Peter sued the officers for a violation of his Fourth Amendment rights. The officers responded that exigent circumstances justified their warrantless entry into Peter's home. Did the officers have legal authority to enter Peter's home under exigent circumstances? **(ROL: Exigent circmstances)**

2. The Bandidos and Cossacks were rival motorcycle gangs attending a local confederation of motorcycle clubs in Waco, Texas, in May 2015. The motorcycle club members met at a Twin Peaks Restaurant. There was a minor dispute about paying tribute (money) and paying proper respect among the gang members, and someone started shooting in the restaurant's parking lot. Nine people were killed, 18 seriously wounded, and 170 bikers were arrested with bond set at $1 million each. Police retrieved 100 guns and 100 other weapons. Many of the arrested bikers were law-abiding citizens who lost their jobs because of the arrests and complained they were arrested simply for wearing biker colors and not because the police had any probable cause that the bikers had committed a crime. In response, the prosecutor's office stated, "The act of engaging in organized crime was committed when these people showed up in our fair county with the intent to show themselves as a show of force."[82] You are a clerk to the judge deciding whether the warrantless arrests of all 170 men were legal. How would you advise the judge? **(ROL: Exigent circmstances, "no guilt by association," case *Ybarra v. Illinois*)**

3. Based on information received that a disgruntled high school student was "planning something big" at school in retaliation for being treated poorly by a fellow group of students, school administrators brought in bomb-sniffing dogs and had the dogs sniff all lockers. A dog alerted on the locker of student Patti Smith, and the principal opened her locker and found an ounce of marijuana. Smith has moved to suppress the marijuana on the basis that the school conducted an unlawful search. You are the judge. Should you grant or deny Smith's motion? **(ROL: Dog sniffs, special needs searches for drugs in schools)**

9

THE FIFTH AMENDMENT AND CONFESSIONS

G o to the end of the chapter. Come back and look at the following news excerpts to focus your reading throughout the chapter to understand *Miranda v. Arizona* (1966). Skim the key terms and phrases and read the summary closely. A brief history of the evolution of the *Miranda* rights is explored to give the student a perspective on the protections of the Fifth and Sixth Amendments. A courtroom perspective of how interrogations are conducted is provided. The chapter begins with a hypothetical case study of Al and Mike and Mike's travels through the interrogation process when he is suspected of killing Al. Follow Mike as he encounters the rules of law presented throughout the chapter and connect Mike's interrogation with the relevant section of text.

WHY THIS CHAPTER MATTERS TO YOU	THE LEARNING OBJECTIVES AS REFLECTED IN THE NEWS
After you have read this chapter: **Learning Objective 1:** You will understand when *Miranda* warnings must be given.	Does law enforcement have an obligation to reveal before reading *Miranda* rights to a suspect about to be questioned that he or she already has been charged? That is the issue before U.S. Middle District Judge Matthew W. Brann, who following a nearly two-hour hearing Thursday said he would decide in two weeks. His decision will determine the status of culpable statements that Leonard Maurice Lewis made to a postal inspector last Aug. 9 in his New York City residence after waiving his right to self-incrimination and having a lawyer present. Defense attorney E. J. Rymzsa contends those admissions should be suppressed because Lewis was unaware he had been indicted. If he had been, he likely would have requested an attorney before being questioned, he said. (PennLive, May 31, 2018)
Learning Objective 2: You will be familiar with the steps of interrogation to induce a confession.	As she voluntarily entered the police interrogation room in Moline, Illinois, four years ago, Dorothy Varallo-Speckeen thought she was there to help solve a child abuse case. She soon realized, however, that Detective Marcella O'Brien thought she, a then-22-year-old babysitter with no criminal record, had abused the child, a felony punishable by up to 30 years imprisonment. [O'Brien's] tactics . . . mirrored the Reid Technique of Interviewing and Interrogation. (*Globe Gazette* [IA], July 12, 2017)
Learning Objective 3: You will be able to identify the procedure for both invoking and waiving the rights protected by *Miranda*.	Malware reverse-engineer Marcus Hutchins—best known for his work in disabling the worldwide WannaCry ransomware infection—has tried to throw out phone transcripts and legal documents used against him by US prosecutors, who have accused him of computer crimes and fraud. Lawyers for

(Continued)

WHY THIS CHAPTER MATTERS TO YOU	THE LEARNING OBJECTIVES AS REFLECTED IN THE NEWS
	Hutchins, a British citizen, has asked a court to dismiss the Brits' Waiver of Miranda Rights form, and the transcript of a phone call made just after waiving his rights. [His lawyers argued,] "In conducting the custodial interrogation, the government coerced Mr. Hutchins, who was sleep-deprived and intoxicated, to talk. Moreover, because Mr. Hutchins is a citizen of the United Kingdom, where a defendant's post-arrest rights are very different than in the United States, he did not sufficiently understand any warnings he may have been given or rights being waived." (*The Register* [UK], May 16, 2018)
Learning Objective 4: You will be able to discuss the nature of the prohibited double interviewing process.	Judge John Agostini denied the motions to suppress information obtained from both defendants. Agostini found that Smith, in both of her interviews with police, understood her rights, verbalized she was willing to be interviewed and, in one case, signed her initials on a printed card next to each right. The defense asserted that the *Miranda* rights were described to Smith as a "little spiel" at one point, downplaying their seriousness, but Agostini said he accepts police testimony that the intention was for the interview to take a less formal tone. (*Daily Hampshire Gazette* [MA], March 9, 2018)
Learning Objective 5: You will be able to competently provide examples of *Miranda* exceptions and the use of statements taken in violation of *Miranda*.	Two Gloucester (MA) police detectives failed to read a child sexual abuse suspect his *Miranda* rights before asking him where his cell phone was during his arrest last year, prosecutors conceded during a hearing earlier this month. And as a result, they won't be allowed to use Richard Reardon's claims not to know where it had gone—and the fact that it was found under a cushion on the couch where police had asked Reardon to sit down while they looked for it—when his case goes to trial. They will still be allowed to use evidence found on Reardon's phone itself, however, Lawrence Superior Court Judge Jeffrey Karp ruled in a decision issued Tuesday. But that's only under a doctrine of "inevitable discovery"—the argument that police would have eventually found that phone as part of an arrest-related search for weapons or instruments of a crime. (*Salem News* [MA], April 25, 2018)

Chapter-Opening Case Study: The Story of Al and Mike

Al and Mike were friends who had worked in the accounting office of a big shipping company.[1] One day, Al disappeared, along with a large sum of cash from the accounting office safe. Officers focused their attention on Mike and invited him to the police station for an interview. Mike arrived and was escorted by two armed officers into a small, windowless room. **(Rule of Law [ROL]: Suspect is in custody when he feels he is not free to leave or otherwise terminate the police encounter.)** Officers locked the door and immediately confronted Mike with accusations that Mike killed Al and stole the money. **(ROL: Inbau and Reid, interrogation Step 1: Direct Confrontation)** The officers then constructed a "scenario" in which they advanced a "theme" that Mike killed Al spontaneously and stole the money as an afterthought. **(ROL: Step 2: Theme**

Development) Officers lied and told Mike his fingerprints were found at the crime scene and an eyewitness identified him leaving the crime scene. **(ROL: Trickery, deception, and lies are permissible interrogation techniques but not to secure a waiver of *Miranda* rights.)** Mike confessed to the theft from the safe and indicated that he was tired of talking, refused to talk any further, and said he wanted a lawyer. Police asked Mike whether he had any children. When Mike said he had a son who would turn 2 years old the following Saturday, the detective said, "Well, the time you're looking at means you're not going to see him until he's 17, and by then he'll have a new daddy. You have 1 minute to tell us the truth and this will be your last chance." **(ROL: Police must "scrupulously honor" a suspect's request for counsel or to have counsel present during questioning.)** Police arrested and charged Mike for the theft, and he was released on his own recognizance.

Two heavily armed officers visited Mike at home and asked if he would speak to them about Al. Mike invited the officers in and, eventually growing weary, confessed to killing Al. The investigators then gave Mike his rights pursuant to the Supreme Court's decision in *Miranda v. Arizona* (1966), and told Mike, "Okay, Mike, now I just want you to repeat what you just told us and I'm going to take notes this time." **(ROL: It is unlawful to first obtain an unwarned confession and then cleanse a subsequent confession by giving *Miranda* warnings.)** Mike then became hesitant to talk.

The investigator asked Mike, "Do you understand your rights, and are you willing to talk to me?" Mike stared back blankly. The investigator said, "Don't you feel guilty about killing your good friend Al?" Mike started to cry and said, "Yes, I did it." **(ROL: Silence is not a waiver of *Miranda* rights, but waiver can be implied by the suspect's conduct.)** At the suppression hearing, Mike claimed that his confession was inadmissible because Mike was in custody every time the officers interrogated him, officers did not honor Mike's request for counsel, and the double interviewing was unconstitutional. Will Mike win his arguments?

THE EVOLUTION OF *MIRANDA* WARNINGS

The Fifth and Sixth Amendments trace their origin to British common law. The Fifth Amendment was specifically enacted as a direct result of the colonists' experience under the British Crown when officials used torture to extract confessions. The amendment's mandate, "No person . . . shall be compelled in any criminal case to be a witness against himself," is commonly known as the privilege against self-incrimination. The Fifth Amendment forces the government to prove guilt with evidence other than what comes from the defendant's tongue.[2] At a criminal trial, the power of the defendant's own words introduced against him is unmistakable. Research on jury trials indicates that juries believe a defendant's confessions are tantamount to guilt for the crime and that "a confession is a conviction."[3] Popular myth assumes that innocent people do not confess to something they did not do. Furthermore, once a suspect has confessed, the weight of guilt is not easily overcome by new evidence of innocence, and some actors in the criminal justice system actively resist such evidence. The Fifth Amendment protects against compelled self-incrimination, but people are certainly free to confess to crimes that they commit. Many police training manuals and conferences discuss the science of inducing confessions through interrogation.

> Rule of Law:
> Interrogations of suspects are inherently coercive.

A confession alone is not enough evidence to support a conviction. At trial, the prosecution has the burden of proving the *corpus delicti*, which is the physical proof of a criminal offense, such as the body of a murder victim. The *corpus delicti* may not be established by a confession alone. The requirement of additional evidence other than a confession proving that the defendant committed a crime relies on our "long history of judicial experience with confessions and the realization that sound law enforcement requires police investigations which extend beyond the words of the accused."[4] A few prosecutions have been successful without a *corpus delicti*.

Interrogation Techniques

Captain Leaming, whose "Christian Burial Speech" induced a suspect to divulge the location of his victim's body in *Nix v. Williams* (1984), said,

> I didn't even know what those words [psychological coercion] meant, until I looked them up in the dictionary after I was accused of using it . . . Shucks, I was just being a good old-fashioned cop, the only kind I know how to be . . . I have never seen a prisoner physically abused, though I heard about those things in the early days . . . That type of questioning just doesn't work. They'll just resist harder. You have to butter 'em up, sweet talk 'em, use that—what's the word?—psychological coercion.[5]

Early court decisions often excluded confessions from trial because of their limited reliability and the known use of tricks, promises, threats, and physical violence to elicit the confession. When police forces became organized in the early 19th century, their interrogation techniques were crude and brutal. From the 1860s onward, documented interrogation techniques called the "third degree" included

> Rubbing lighted cigars against a suspect's arm or neck; lifting, kicking, squeezing a suspect's testicles; dragging, pulling, or lifting a woman by her hair; enlisting a dentist to grind down and drill into the nerves of a suspect's molars . . . giving someone the taps: at thirty-second intervals, the suspect was struck with a rubber hose on the side of the head [which caused] considerable pain; administering tear gas; and tightening a necktie to choking point.[6]

From the 1930s to the 1960s, the U.S. Supreme Court overturned convictions that resulted from confessions coerced from the defendants by police brutality, because such confessions violated the right to a fair trial. In *Brown v. Mississippi* (1936), the Supreme Court decided that confessions obtained after physical torture were inconsistent with the Fourteenth Amendment's Due Process Clause, not the Fifth Amendment's Self-Incrimination Clause. At the time of the *Brown* decision, the protections afforded citizens by the Bill of Rights applied only to actions taken by the federal government. Requiring the states to extend the same protections to the public took years and happened in a piecemeal manner. Because courts do not make law—only interpret it—the Court was left to continually use the Fourteenth Amendment's Due Process Clause to invalidate convictions based on confessions extracted by brutality. The Court overturned convictions based on confessions obtained after the defendants were kept naked for hours,[7] promised psychiatric care to gain their trust and extract incriminating statements,[8] told they would be lynched,[9] told that welfare agencies would take their children if they did not cooperate,[10] or moved to a secret location so family and friends could not intervene.[11]

It was not until the 1960s that the protection afforded suspects by the Fifth Amendment applied not just to the federal government's actions but also to actions taken by the states. The practice of incorporating the protections of the Bill of Rights to state defendants began with *Gideon v. Wainwright* (1963), in which the Court incorporated the Sixth Amendment right to counsel (access to a lawyer) at trial.[12] The Court decided in *Malloy v. Hogan* (1964) that the Fifth Amendment right against self-incrimination specifically prohibited the states from using compelled confessions against a defendant at trial.[13] *Malloy* inched the Court forward from *Gideon* and from *Mapp v. Ohio* (1961), which required the states to exclude illegally obtained evidence in criminal trials.[14]

The next step for due process protections via the Fourteenth Amendment came in the Court's decision in *Escobedo v. Illinois* (1964), which established for the first time the right to have counsel present during an interrogation if counsel had already been hired.[15] When Escobedo admitted some involvement in the murder, officers persisted in their questioning until Escobedo implicated himself further. By holding that Escobedo's confession was obtained illegally in violation of his Fifth and Sixth Amendment rights not to incriminate himself and to have an attorney present during questioning, the U.S. Supreme Court thus extended the *Mapp* exclusionary rule from the Fourth Amendment to evidence obtained as a result of improper police interrogations.

Voluntariness

A confession will be admissible against the defendant at trial only if, under the totality of the circumstances, the confession was given voluntarily. A confession is not considered legally voluntary if officers created pressure for the suspect to confess and if that pressure overbore the suspect's resistance to confessing. Some of the circumstances courts investigate in a totality analysis to determine voluntariness of the confession are[16]

> **Rule of Law: Confessions must be voluntary to be admissible as evidence against the defendant.**

1. Whether the suspect initiated contact with officers;

2. Suspect's age and history of drug and alcohol problems;

3. Suspect's physical problems, if any; and

4. Suspect's previous experience with the criminal justice system.

Mental illness alone is insufficient to render a confession involuntary. A floridly psychotic man confessed to murder even though his mental impairment prevented him from understanding the import of the *Miranda* warnings. The high Court held, in *Colorado v. Connelly* (1986), that absent police coercion, confessions are presumed voluntary.[17]

The Inbau and Reid Nine Steps of Interrogation

To resolve the question of when, exactly, a suspect had a right to a lawyer (either when charges are filed or during interrogation), the high Court consolidated four cases into one, *Miranda v. Arizona*, and held that the Fifth and Sixth Amendments apply to state criminal proceedings. The Court also stated that given the inherently coercive nature of the interrogation process, officers would have to inform suspects of their constitutional rights and the suspects would have to give up those rights before an interrogation could legally begin.

> **Rule of Law: An interrogation method designed to induce confessions may be used on suspects who officers believe are guilty.**

In the *Miranda* case, the Court criticized the interrogation technique developed by Inbau and Reid, who suggested using a nine-step approach to interrogate suspects believed to be guilty. The Court was adamant that an interrogation is accusatory in tone, is not a mere interview, and must not to be used on people believed to be innocent.[18] The nine steps are as follows.

Step 1: Direct Positive Confrontation

The first step to convince the suspect to confess is to confront the suspect with the interrogator's certainty that the suspect committed the crime. The interrogator must watch the suspect closely to see if the suspect looks away or avoids eye contact, actions that may indicate guilt. An innocent person may aggressively deny the false accusation, whereas the guilty party may react passively. The interrogator may focus on a suspect's good human nature, which may justify his commission of the crime or exaggerate his suspected involvement in the crime to obtain a reaction from the suspect minimizing his involvement.

Step 2: Theme Development

In Step 2, the interrogator attempts to gain the suspect's trust by creating a theme while also offering reasons for committing the crime that are morally reasonable or justifiable, allowing the suspect to place himself at the crime scene while minimizing his acts, culpability, and blame for the crime. In the chapter-opening case study, investigators used Steps 1 and 2 when they immediately called Mike a liar and then created a scenario with a theme that the crime happened with no forethought. The following is an excerpt from an officer's deposition (sworn testimony before trial to preserve testimony) showing how and why the officer created a certain theme during the interrogation of a murder suspect. The officer used the ploy of giving the suspect a reasonable scenario or theme that the victim died accidentally after rough sex, knowing that, legally, once the defendant confessed to murder, the "theme" he has bought into to minimize his blameworthiness is not enough to save him from conviction and possibly the death penalty. Here, the detective is being asked about his practice of reviewing crime scene photos and of coming up with a "scenario" with which to confront the suspect during the interrogation. The lawyer for Salazar is asking the detective questions and obtains an admission that creating "themes" could lead to false confessions, but the detective thinks Salazar admitted guilt because he was guilty. The prosecutor is present as well.

Florida v. Martin Salazar, 96-2169CF A02[19]

Deposition of Detective, June 3, 1996

Q. Now, you talk about a creative theme. What does that mean?

A. After looking at the crime scene photographs I decided that a possibility could be to speak to Mr. Salazar in relationship to a scenario that re-created the scene, which I thought after looking at the photographs might seem somewhat plausible to him, and this was created by me so I could use it as a tool to get him to tell the truth in relationship to what he did concerning the particular case.

Q. I'm not asking what always works, but is that the idea, you immediately hit them with the creative scenario?

A. No. With me looking at the photos it was obvious to me that those (police interviewers) that proceeded [sic] me were unsuccessful in getting Mr. Salazar to tell the truth. Looking at the crime scene photo book I created this scenario that looked plausible to me. And somebody that wasn't very skilled in knowing the ins and outs of the creative scenario, and these are words that I am using, what I did, I independently of anybody created this after looking at the crime scene photos.

I made up this scene of this bondage and autoerotic and all this other stuff and, if I presented that to Mr. Salazar, it may seem too plausible and only he could tell me if it was an accident or whether it was intentional. And Mr. Salazar, fortunately I think, bought into that scene, changed his negative way was and said, yes, he had tied an electrical cord around her neck, et cetera, et cetera.

Q. Where did you learn about this creative scenario, creative theme?

A. I just made it up one day.

Q. I don't mean the particular one, the theory of a creative theme or a—

A. I've been a policeman a long time, it's just something that you go to school and you just learn. I think the basic thing you do in an interview, you try to work whatever is plausible to get somebody to tell you the truth, just work within the confines of what the law allows you to do. I was just walking around after looking at the crime scene photo book and it just flashed in my mind that I would try that. . . .

I remember a case where I got a guy to confess to murder where he killed a Guatemalan guy. And I convinced him that he was an African-American guy, I convinced him that was okay because nobody cared about that Guatemalan guy and that makes people feel guilty, and you utilize that guilt and anxiety, and they'll feel better when they tell you they did. (I told him) nobody cares about that Guatemalan, people care about you, you're an American and he bought right into that, yeah, I really didn't mean to kill the guy in the robbery anyway. . . . Sure the consequences of them doing that is real significant if you know that they really want to tell you the truth and if you hit that right button.

Q. Detective, is there any danger when you use a creative theme or scenario that an individual who is innocent but recognizes the severity of the potential punishment they could be facing or its consequences of being charged with a crime and their family members, that they might buy into your scenario for reasons other than guilt?

A. Is it possible?

Q. Yeah.

A. It is possible, but not on this level case.

A. Why not on this level of a case?

> **A.** Because you can't buy into a scenario like that on a murder case. I mean you have to understand that the person that you're presenting the scenario to know that they committed the offense, that they're buying into the creative version of it and it's just not plausible to me. If you're talking about retail theft, petty theft, burglary, trespassers, something minor like that, most of those cases you wouldn't bother with a scenario. But it is possible somebody admitted to wrapping an electrical cord around somebody's neck in a voluntary sexual scenario, I don't think so.... It's just after you deal with murder and you raise the anxiety and you give them an out and most of the time they'll take it.
>
> The detective's deposition reveals that giving Salazar an escape hatch from the moral responsibility of murdering the woman intentionally was a powerful enough catalyst to produce a confession.

Step 3: Handling Denials

Inbau and Reid assert that criminals can commit crimes because they distort their motives for committing the crime. For example, in a child molestation case, the offender may describe his actions as showing love and affection for the child, or simply teaching the child about sex, a subject the offender asserts everyone needs to learn. The authors advocate suggesting "a less revolting and more morally acceptable motivation or reason for the offense than that which is known or presumed" so that interrogators can effectively handle the suspect's denials and invite him to keep talking.

Step 4: Overcoming Objections

A suspect's excuses are considered "objections" to the interrogator's unfailing belief in the suspect's guilt and to any proposed scenario into which the suspect may have not completely bought. To overcome these objections, officers should be aware that the suspect generates much less emotional anxiety for himself if he offers excuses as an alternative to outright denials. Suspects hope to deflect attention from their guilt by engaging in conversation designed to deflect suspicion, but when a suspect voices an objection he is clearly trying to conceal the truth. The investigator should let the suspect voice the objection and then turn the objection around to incorporate it back into the interrogation theme.

Let's take, for example, Step 2, theme development. Imagine during the Salazar case deposition excerpt that Salazar had objected to Detective Murphy's creative scenario of rough sex and said, "I wouldn't do a thing like that; I'm not a maniac." According to Inbau and Reid, Detective Murphy should first agree with Salazar and then turn his denial around, and say, for example, "Yes, I believe you are not a maniac, Salazar, and I know you are not the type of guy who would hurt women. That's why I know that you and the girl were having a consensual encounter when you both decided to try some rough stuff and it got out of hand" (return to theme that strangulation happened by accident).

Step 5: Procurement and Retention of a Suspect's Attention

After verbally engaging with officers, suspects may become emotionally withdrawn. At the signs of withdrawal, the investigator should move closer to the suspect as a sympathetic gesture, but the overall goal is to reestablish a psychological connection with the suspect to hold his attention.

Step 6: Handling the Suspect's Passive Mood

After realizing that his tactics and tricks of evasion and deflection are not working on the interrogator, the guilty suspect may grow passive and quiet. The officer should reestablish his theme and be alert for signs that the suspect is resigning himself to the fate that he has been caught and there is no use fighting the truth.

Step 7: Presenting an Alternative Question

"Which shall it be, the pie or the cake?" Inbau and Reid suggest that framing the dessert question as a choice to diners may produce more orders for sweets. The same technique applies to guilty suspects who, after becoming resigned to their fate that they cannot escape, can now buy into the alternative question, "Did you plan on pushing your husband off the ledge of the canyon since the day you got married, or did it pretty much happen on the spur of the moment because of the fight that you two had?" The alternative question is the result of developing the guilt-minimizing theme the suspect can buy into.

Step 8: Bringing the Suspect Into the Conversation

Once a suspect adopts an alternative explanation of the crime, it is imperative to immediately commit him to the details of and motive for the crime, which should then develop into a full confession. During this time, the interrogator should be alone with the suspect because the presence of others may stop the suspect from speaking freely.

Step 9: The Written Confession

Once an oral confession has been obtained, put it in writing and get it signed and witnessed as soon as possible. If the suspect can read and write, have the suspect write the confession in his own hand. To prove that the confession was voluntary, officers must show that the suspect voluntarily, intelligently, and knowingly waived his rights per *Miranda* and spoke freely; this is an easier argument to make when the confession is in the suspect's own handwriting. A summary of the nine steps of interrogation appears in Figure 9.1.

The *Miranda* Decision

> **Rule of Law:** *Miranda* warnings are judge-made interpretations of the Fifth and Sixth Amendments.

In March 1963, a young woman who worked at a refreshment stand in a movie theater in Phoenix, Arizona, was abducted by a man in a car and raped alongside the desert highway. Police arrested Ernesto Miranda, a 23-year-old laborer with a criminal past involving sex crimes, indecent exposure, attempted rape, and peeping into windows. The woman said that Miranda possibly looked like her attacker, but she wanted

Figure 9.1 Inbau and Reid's Nine Steps of Interrogation

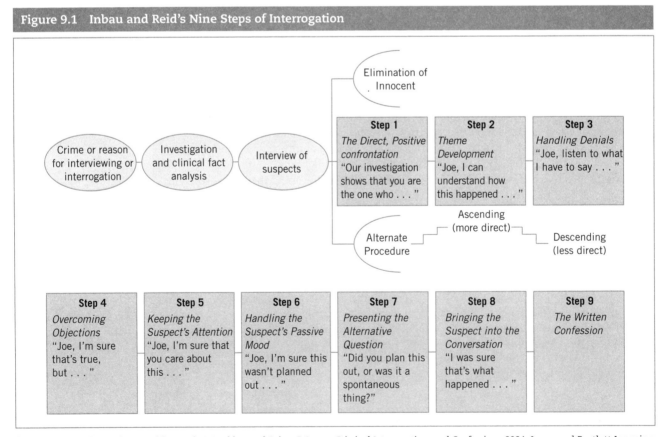

Source: Fred E. Inbau, John E. Reid, Joseph P. Buckley, and Brian C. Jayne. *Criminal Interrogations and Confessions*, 2004: Jones and Bartlett Learning, Burlington, MA. www.jblearning.com. Reprinted with permission.

to hear him speak before she made a positive identification. But Miranda had confessed before any further investigation. Miranda described the interrogation later as one in which he was kept awake for hours, threatened with a long prison term if he did not confess, and promised medical care to get him treatment for his problems. The police, on the other hand, testified at Miranda's trial that he confessed willingly and without any threats or promises. The Supreme Court decision was 5–4 in favor of Miranda and stood as a rejection of the practice of making suspects psychologically vulnerable to the point at which they confess simply to make the overbearing questioning stop. Read the case excerpt below and see if you agree with the Court's reasoning.

MIRANDA V. ARIZONA, 384 U.S. 436 (1966)

Supreme Court of the United States

Chief Justice Warren delivered the opinion of the Court. (5–4)

FACTS: In each [of the four cases consolidated to be heard on appeal], the defendant was questioned by police officers, detectives, or a prosecuting attorney in a room in which he was cut off from the outside world. In none of these cases was the defendant given a full and effective warning of his rights at the outset of the interrogation process. In all the cases, the questioning elicited oral admissions, and in three of them, signed statements as well which were admitted at their trials. They all thus share salient features—incommunicado interrogation of individuals in a police-dominated atmosphere, resulting in self-incriminating statements without full warnings of constitutional rights.

ISSUE: The constitutional issue we decide in each of these cases is the admissibility of statements obtained from a defendant questioned while in custody or otherwise deprived of his freedom of action in any significant way. We start here, as we did in [*Escobedo v. Illinois* (1964)], with the premise that our holding is not an innovation in our jurisprudence, but is an application of principles long recognized and applied in other settings.[20] We have undertaken a thorough re-examination of the *Escobedo* decision and the principles it announced, and we reaffirm it. That case was but an explication of basic rights that are enshrined in our Constitution—that "no person . . . shall be compelled in any criminal case to be a witness against himself," and that "the accused shall . . . have the Assistance of Counsel"—rights which were put in jeopardy in that case through official overbearing. These precious rights were fixed in our Constitution only after centuries of persecution and struggle. And in the words of Chief Justice Marshall, they were secured "for ages to come, and . . . designed to approach immortality as nearly as human institutions can approach it," *Cohens v. Virginia* (1821).[21]

HOLDING: Our holding briefly stated is this: the prosecution may not use statements, whether exculpatory or inculpatory, stemming from custodial interrogation of the defendant unless it demonstrates the use of procedural safeguards effective to secure the privilege against self-incrimination. By custodial interrogation, we mean questioning initiated by law enforcement officers after a person has been taken into custody or otherwise deprived of his freedom of action in any significant way. As for the procedural safeguards to be employed, unless other fully effective means are devised to inform accused persons of their right of silence and to assure a continuous opportunity to exercise it, the following measures are required.

Prior to any questioning, the person must be warned that he has a right to remain silent, that any statement he does make may be used as evidence against him, and that he has a right to the presence of an attorney, either retained or appointed. The defendant may waive effectuation of these rights, provided the waiver is made voluntarily, knowingly and intelligently. If, however, he indicates in any manner and at any stage of the process that he wishes to consult with an attorney before speaking there can be no questioning. Likewise, if the individual is alone and indicates in any manner that he does not wish to be interrogated, the police may not question him. The mere fact that he may have answered some questions or volunteered some statements on his own does not deprive him of the right to refrain from answering any further inquiries until he has consulted with an attorney and thereafter consents to be questioned.

REASONING: An understanding of the nature and setting of this in-custody interrogation is essential to our decisions today. The difficulty in depicting what transpires at such interrogations stems from the fact that in this country they have largely taken place incommunicado. From extensive factual studies undertaken in the early 1930's, including the famous Wickersham Report to Congress by a Presidential Commission, it is clear that police violence and the "third degree" flourished at that time.

(Continued)

(Continued)

In a series of cases decided by this Court long after these studies, the police resorted to physical brutality—beating, hanging, whipping—and to sustained and protracted questioning incommunicado in order to extort confessions. The Commission on Civil Rights in 1961 found much evidence to indicate that "some policemen still resort to physical force to obtain confessions." The use of physical brutality and violence is not, unfortunately, relegated to the past or to any part of the country. Only recently in Kings County, New York, the police brutally beat, kicked and placed lighted cigarette butts on the back of a potential witness under interrogation for the purpose of securing a statement incriminating a third party.

Again we stress that the modern practice of in-custody interrogation is psychologically rather than physically oriented . . . [T]his Court has recognized that coercion can be mental as well as physical, and that the blood of the accused is not the only hallmark of an unconstitutional inquisition. [The Court recites a number of police interrogation tactics deemed inherently coercive, including the Inbau and Reid manual.] The potentiality for compulsion is forcefully apparent, for example, in [a lower court decision] *Miranda*, where the indigent Mexican defendant was a seriously disturbed individual with pronounced sexual fantasies, and in *Stewart*, in which the defendant was an indigent Los Angeles Negro who had dropped out of school in the sixth grade. To be sure, the records do not evince overt physical coercion or

patent psychological ploys. The fact remains that in none of these cases did the officers undertake to afford appropriate safeguards at the outset of the interrogation to insure that the statements were truly the product of free choice. It is obvious that such an interrogation environment is created for no purpose other than to subjugate the individual to the will of his examiner. This atmosphere carries its own badge of intimidation. To be sure, this is not physical intimidation, but it is equally destructive of human dignity.

The current practice of incommunicado interrogation is at odds with one of our Nation's most cherished principles—that the individual may not be compelled to incriminate himself. Unless adequate protective devices are employed to dispel the compulsion inherent in custodial surroundings, no statement obtained from the defendant can truly be the product of his free choice.

CONCLUSION: We have concluded that without proper safeguards the process of in-custody interrogation of persons suspected or accused of crime contains inherently compelling pressures which work to undermine the individual's will to resist and to compel him to speak where he would not otherwise do so freely. In order to combat these pressures and to permit a full opportunity to exercise the privilege against self-incrimination, the accused must be adequately and effectively apprised of his rights and the exercise of those rights must be fully honored.

Notice that the Court's reasoning in *Miranda* is deductive (based on logical inference):

1. The Constitution's no compelled self-incrimination clause protects citizens from convicting themselves through forced confessions,

2. Common police interrogation techniques are inherently coercive and designed to compel self-incrimination, and

3. Procedural safeguards in the form of warnings about the right to remain silent and to have the assistance of counsel during questioning are necessary to ameliorate (ease) the compulsory aspects of police interrogation.

Even though the *Miranda* decision is a judge-made rule to protect the people from the overbearing nature of government power, the high Court has recognized that the warnings have become part of our national dialogue and are not to be overturned (*Dickerson v. United States*, 2000).[22]

Rule of Law: *Miranda* warnings are required during custodial interrogations.

The *Miranda* Warnings and When to Advise

There are no magic words that are required when advising a suspect of his rights pursuant to the *Miranda* case. The warnings need not be read from a card, and a suspect does not have to sign a piece of paper indicating that he received and understood the warnings. If the warnings have "touched all of the bases required by *Miranda*," the warnings will be adequate.[23] The so-called warnings are the following:

1. You have the right to remain silent.

2. Anything you say can and will be used against you in a court of law.

3. You have a right to have an attorney present during questioning.

4. If you cannot afford an attorney, one will be appointed to represent you.

The warnings need not be given in the same exact language time after time. In *Florida v. Powell* (2010), officers gave the defendant a semblance of the rights but specifically said Powell could have an attorney "if and when you go to court." Powell was convicted and complained that the rights conveyed did not indicate he could have an attorney present during questioning, which is what *Miranda* provides. The high Court disagreed with Powell's interpretation of the right. Read the case excerpt below and see if you agree.

FLORIDA V. POWELL, 599 U.S. 50 (2010)

United States Supreme Court

Justice Ginsburg delivered the opinion of the Court. (7–2)

FACTS: After arresting respondent Powell, but before questioning him, Tampa Police read him their standard *Miranda* form, stating, *inter alia*: "You have the right to talk to a lawyer before answering any of our questions" and "you have the right to use any of these rights at any time you want during this interview." Powell then admitted he owned a handgun found in a police search. He was charged with possession of a weapon by a convicted felon in violation of Florida law. The trial court denied Powell's motion to suppress his inculpatory [proving guilt] statements, which was based on the contention that the *Miranda* warnings he received did not adequately convey his right to the presence of an attorney during questioning.

HOLDING: Advice that a suspect has "the right to talk to a lawyer before answering any of [the law enforcement officers'] questions," and that he can invoke this right "at any time . . . during the interview" satisfies *Miranda*.

REASONING: *Miranda* requires that a suspect "be warned prior to any questioning . . . that he has the right to the presence of an attorney." While the warnings prescribed by *Miranda* are invariable, this Court has not dictated the words in which the essential information must be conveyed. *See, e.g., California v. Prysock* (1981). In determining whether police warnings were satisfactory . . . The inquiry is simply whether the warnings reasonably "convey to [a suspect] his rights as required by Miranda." *Duckworth v. Eagan* (1989).

CONCLUSION: The warnings Powell received satisfy this standard. By informing Powell that he had "the right to talk to a lawyer before answering any of [their] questions," the Tampa officers communicated that he could consult with a lawyer before answering any particular question. And the statement that Powell had "the right to use any of [his] rights at any time [he] wanted during the interview" confirmed that he could exercise his right to an attorney while the interrogation was underway. In combination, the two warnings reasonably conveyed the right to have an attorney present, not only at the outset of interrogation, but at all times.

Custody

The *Miranda* warnings need only be given to a suspect before a custodial interrogation. Under the totality of the circumstances, courts will ask, "First, what were the circumstances surrounding the interrogation; and, second, given those circumstances, would a reasonable person have felt that he or she was not at liberty to terminate the interrogation and leave?" as stated in *Thompson v. Keohane* (1995).[24] In the chapter-opening case study, Mike may be in **custody** if the officers in a small windowless room behind a locked door make clear that Mike is not free to leave.

A different analysis applies when the two officers visit Mike at home—presumably Mike would feel in control to consent or withdraw from the interview. To make the custody determination, courts will examine the following nonexhaustive list of factors:

> **Rule of Law:** If a suspect feels trapped by police presence and that belief is objectively reasonable (i.e., other people would believe the same thing), he or she is in custody.

1. The duration of the detention,
2. The nature and degree of the pressure applied to detain the suspect,
3. The suspect's age and previous experience with law enforcement,
4. The physical surroundings and location of the questioning, and
5. The language and posture of the officer(s) doing the questioning.[25]

What the public may perceive as being in custody (e.g., being incarcerated in prison) is not necessarily true under the law. Remember that courts, in deciding criminal law and procedure issues, are always balancing the government's interest in protecting public safety against a suspect's constitutional due process rights to liberty and freedom. In *Maryland v. Shatzer* (2010), Shatzer was in prison and interrogated about sexually molesting his son. When read his *Miranda* warnings, Shatzer invoked his right to counsel.[26] Three years later, officers returned to prison and again asked Shatzer about child abuse allegations; this time he admitted the abuse and then asked for an attorney. Shatzer was convicted; he complained on appeal that he had never left the prison and was still in "custody"; therefore, officers could not come back and question him without an attorney present. The U.S. Supreme Court disagreed with Shatzer's custody analysis, finding that after an inmate acclimates to an institutional routine, a prison can be considered a "home." The Court carved out a new timetable and held the police could come back and reinitiate questioning after a suspect has asked for a lawyer as long as there has been a 14-day break in custody between the first and second attempt. Although Shatzer had been in prison for years between the first and second interrogations, there had been a sufficient break in "custody" to make his confession admissible.

Similarly, in *Howes v. Fields* (2012), the Court held a prisoner who was escorted from his cell to a small room surrounded by guards could have asked to return to his cell at any time and was, therefore, not in custody requiring *Miranda* warnings before he was interrogated.

HOWES V. FIELDS, 565 U.S. 499 (2012)

Supreme Court of the United States

Justice Alito Delivered the Opinion of the Court. (6–3)

FACTS: While serving a sentence in a Michigan jail, Randall Fields was escorted by a corrections officer to a conference room where two sheriff's deputies questioned him about allegations that, before he came to prison, he had engaged in sexual conduct with a 12-year-old boy. In order to get to the conference room, Fields had to go down one floor and pass through a locked door that separated two sections of the facility. Fields arrived at the conference room between 7 p.m. and 9 p.m. and was questioned for between five and seven hours. At the beginning of the interview, Fields was told that he was free to leave and return to his cell. Later, he was again told that he could leave whenever he wanted. The two interviewing deputies were armed during the

interview, but Fields remained free of handcuffs and other restraints. The door to the conference room was sometimes open and sometimes shut. About halfway through the interview, after Fields had been confronted with the allegations of abuse, he became agitated and began to yell.

Fields testified that one of the deputies, using an expletive, told him to sit down and said that "if [he] didn't want to cooperate, [he] could leave." Fields eventually confessed to engaging in sex acts with the boy. According to Fields' testimony at a suppression hearing, he said several times during the interview that he no longer wanted to talk to the deputies, but he did not ask to go back to his cell prior to the end of the interview.

When he was eventually ready to leave, he had to wait an additional 20 minutes or so because a corrections officer had to be summoned to escort him back to his cell, and he did not return to his cell until well after the hour when he generally retired. At no time was Fields given *Miranda* warnings or advised that he did not have to speak with the deputies.

The State of Michigan charged Fields with criminal sexual conduct. Relying on *Miranda*, Fields moved to suppress his confession, but the trial court denied his motion. Over the renewed objection of defense counsel, one of the interviewing deputies testified at trial about Fields' admissions. The jury convicted Fields of two counts of third-degree criminal sexual conduct, and the judge sentenced him to a term of 10 to 15 years of imprisonment.

ISSUE: [Was the interview in the conference room a "custodial interrogation" within the meaning of *Miranda*?]

HOLDING: [No.]

REASONING: In *Illinois v. Perkins* (1990),[27] where we upheld the admission of un-Mirandized statements elicited from an inmate by an undercover officer masquerading as another inmate, we noted that "[t]he bare fact of custody may not in every instance require a warning *even when the suspect is aware that he is speaking to an official, but we do not have occasion to explore that issue here*" [emphasis in original]. Instead, we simply "rejected the argument that *Miranda* warnings are required whenever a suspect is in custody in a technical sense and converses with someone who happens to be a government agent."

Most recently, in *Maryland v. Shatzer* (2010), we expressly declined to adopt a bright-line rule for determining the applicability of *Miranda* in prisons. *Shatzer* considered whether a break in custody ends the presumption of involuntariness and, if so, whether a prisoner's return to the general prison population after a custodial interrogation constitutes a break in *Miranda* custody. In considering the latter question, we noted first that "we have *never* decided whether incarceration constitutes custody for *Miranda* purposes, and have indeed explicitly declined to address the issue." The answer to this question, we noted, would "depend upon whether [incarceration] exerts the coercive pressure that *Miranda* was designed to guard against—the 'danger of coercion [that] results from the *interaction* of custody and official interrogation.'"

Miranda adopted a "set of prophylactic measures" designed to ward off the "inherently compelling pressures of custodial interrogation," but *Miranda* did not hold that such pressures are always present when a prisoner is taken aside and questioned about events outside the prison walls. Indeed, *Miranda* did not even establish that police questioning of a suspect at the station house is always custodial (*Oregon v. Mathiason*, 1977).[28]

In sum, our decisions do not clearly establish that a prisoner is always in custody for purposes of *Miranda* whenever a prisoner is isolated from the general prison population and questioned about conduct outside the prison.

In determining whether a person is in custody in this sense, the initial step is to ascertain whether, in light of "the objective circumstances of the interrogation . . . a reasonable person (would) have felt he or she was not at liberty to terminate the interrogation and leave."[29] And in order to determine how a suspect would have "gauge[d]" his "freedom of movement," courts must examine "all of the circumstances surrounding the interrogation." Relevant factors include the location of the questioning, its duration, statements made during the interview, the presence or absence of physical restraints during the questioning, and the release of the interviewee at the end of the questioning.

Determining whether an individual's freedom of movement was curtailed, however, is simply the first step in the analysis, not the last. Not all restraints on freedom of movement amount to custody for purposes of *Miranda*. We have "decline[d] to accord talismanic power" to the freedom-of-movement inquiry, and have instead asked the additional question whether the relevant environment presents the same inherently coercive pressures as the type of station house questioning at issue in *Miranda*. "Our cases make clear . . . that the freedom-of-movement test identifies only a necessary and not a sufficient condition for *Miranda* custody."

There are at least three strong grounds for this conclusion. First, questioning a person who is already serving a prison term does not generally involve the shock that very often accompanies arrest. In the paradigmatic *Miranda* situation—a person is arrested in his home or on the street and whisked to a police station for questioning—detention represents a sharp and ominous change, and the shock may give rise to coercive pressures. A person who is "cut off from his normal life and companions," and abruptly transported from the street into a "police-dominated atmosphere," may feel coerced into answering questions.

By contrast, when a person who is already serving a term of imprisonment is questioned, there is usually no such change. "Interrogated suspects who have previously been convicted of crime live in prison." *Maryland v. Shatzer* (2010). For a person serving a term of incarceration, we reasoned in *Shatzer*, the ordinary restrictions of prison life, while no doubt unpleasant, are expected and familiar and thus do not involve the same "inherently compelling pressures" that are often present when a suspect is yanked from familiar surroundings in the outside world and subjected to interrogation in a police station.

Second, a prisoner, unlike a person who has not been sentenced to a term of incarceration, is unlikely to be lured into speaking by a longing for prompt release. When a

(Continued)

person is arrested and taken to a station house for interrogation, the person who is questioned may be pressured to speak by the hope that, after doing so, he will be allowed to leave and go home. On the other hand, when a prisoner is questioned, he knows that when the questioning ceases, he will remain under confinement.

Third, a prisoner, unlike a person who has not been convicted and sentenced, knows that the law enforcement officers who question him probably lack the authority to affect the duration of his sentence. And "where the possibility of parole exists," the interrogating officers probably also lack the power to bring about an early release. "When the suspect has no reason to think that the listeners have official power over him, it should not be assumed that his words are motivated by the reaction he expects from his listeners." Under such circumstances, there is little "basis for the assumption that a suspect . . . will feel compelled to speak by the fear of reprisal for remaining silent or in the hope of [a] more lenient treatment should he confess."

In short, standard conditions of confinement and associated restrictions on freedom will not necessarily implicate the same interests that the Court sought to protect when it afforded special safeguards to persons subjected to custodial interrogation. Thus, service of a term of imprisonment, without more, is not enough to constitute *Miranda* custody.

It is true that taking a prisoner aside for questioning may necessitate some additional limitations on his freedom of movement. A prisoner may, for example, be removed from an exercise yard and taken, under close guard, to the room where the interview is to be held. But such procedures are an ordinary and familiar attribute of life behind bars. Escorts and special security precautions may be standard procedures regardless of the purpose for which an inmate is removed from his regular routine and taken to a special location. For example, ordinary prison procedure may require such measures when a prisoner is led to a meeting with an attorney.

Finally, we fail to see why questioning about criminal activity outside the prison should be regarded as having a significantly greater potential for coercion than questioning under otherwise identical circumstances about criminal activity within the prison walls. In both instances, there is the potential for additional criminal liability and punishment. If anything, the distinction would seem to cut the other way, as an inmate who confesses to misconduct that occurred within the prison may also incur administrative penalties, but even this is not enough to tip the scale in the direction of custody. "The threat to a citizen's Fifth Amendment rights that *Miranda* was designed to neutralize" is neither mitigated nor magnified by the location of the conduct about which questions are asked.

"Fidelity to the doctrine announced in *Miranda* requires that it be enforced strictly, but only in those types of situations in which the concerns that powered the decision are implicated." Confessions voluntarily made by prisoners in other situations should not be suppressed. "Voluntary confessions are not merely a proper element in law enforcement, they are an unmitigated good, essential to society's compelling interest in finding, convicting, and punishing those who violate the law."

The record in this case reveals that respondent was not taken into custody for purposes of *Miranda*. To be sure, respondent did not invite the interview or consent to it in advance, and he was not advised that he was free to decline to speak with the deputies. The following facts also lend some support to respondent's argument that *Miranda*'s custody requirement was met: The interview lasted for between five and seven hours in the evening and continued well past the hour when respondent generally went to bed; the deputies who questioned respondent were armed; and one of the deputies, according to respondent, "used a very sharp tone."

Because he was in prison, respondent was not free to leave the conference room by himself and to make his own way through the facility to his cell. Instead, he was escorted to the conference room and, when he ultimately decided to end the interview, he had to wait about 20 minutes for a corrections officer to arrive and escort him to his cell. But he would have been subject to this same restraint even if he had been taken to the conference room for some reason other than police questioning; under no circumstances could he have reasonably expected to be able to roam free. And while respondent testified that he "was told . . . if I did not want to cooperate, I needed to go back to my cell," these words did not coerce cooperation by threatening harsher conditions. Returning to his cell would merely have returned him to his usual environment. See *Shatzer* ("Interrogated suspects who have previously been convicted of crime live in prison. When they are released back into the general prison population, they return to their accustomed surroundings and daily routine—they regain the degree of control they had over their lives prior to the interrogation").

Taking into account all of the circumstances of the questioning—including especially the undisputed fact that respondent was told that he was free to end the questioning and to return to his cell—we hold that respondent was not in custody within the meaning of *Miranda*.

The judgment of the Court of Appeals is reversed.

Interrogation

Interrogation is express questioning or its functional equivalent by the police or other government agents that is designed to elicit incriminating information. Express questioning is easy to define as interrogation, for example, "When did you buy the gun to kill your neighbor?" The functional equivalent of interrogation is defined as "any words or actions . . . that the police should know are reasonably likely to elicit an incriminating response from the suspect." Distinguishing between police banter and psychological ploys designed to get the suspect to talk may be difficult. Let's take, for example, two suspects who are arrested for intravenous drug use, and the police want to find evidence of their crimes (i.e., drugs and syringes) that the suspects buried in undisclosed locations. The police also know the suspects have the protection of counsel, preventing the police from interrogating them. In both cases, two officers take the suspect for a ride in a police car and engage in a discussion among themselves designed to be overheard by the suspect.

The officers talk with each other and talk about the vulnerability of children and how, if police fail to find the drugs and syringes, children may be hurt. It works! The suspects both talk and lead the police to the evidence that incriminates them at trial. Did the police interrogate the suspects? The U.S. Supreme Court has said only if the police *knew* a suspect was specifically susceptible to covert emotional appeals to protect children would the Court classify the police conversation as interrogation. If the officers had their discussion and did *not* know a suspect had specific feelings about the vulnerability of children, then the conversation would not be considered an interrogation and any evidence retrieved will be admissible at trial. The two divergent holdings are represented by *Brewer v. Williams* (1977), where Detective Leaming told the suspect not to talk but then gave the "Christian Burial speech."[30] When the suspect talked, it was deemed an interrogation because the police knew the suspect was deeply religious and exploited his beliefs to get the suspect to talk. In contrast, in *Rhode Island v. Innis* (1980), a suspect in the armed robbery of a cab driver was in the back of a police car as detectives had a conversation about what a shame it would be if handicapped children in the area came upon the hidden shotgun and hurt themselves.[31] One of the detectives said, "God forbid one of them might find a weapon with shells and they might hurt themselves," whereupon the suspect led officers to the location of the weapon. Finding the conversation *not* an interrogation, the Court said the police had no knowledge that Innis had a particular sensitivity to children with disabilities, so Innis's confession was voluntary.

Springboard for Discussion

The Court makes a distinction in the *Howes* case between those who are in prison for a long time, feeling like home, and those in jail briefly. Does the length of time matter to the person detained? If a person is incarcerated, does he ever "feel" as if he is not in "custody" for the purposes of *Miranda*?

> **Rule of Law:**
> Interrogation is express questioning, or its functional equivalent, by law enforcement agents designed to elicit incriminating responses from a suspect.

MAKING THE COURTROOM CONNECTION

The developing law on custodial interrogations has steadily remained on the side of the government. Civil libertarians bemoan the seeming eradication of the layers of protection for suspects. (Why would someone have to speak to exercise their right to remain silent?) But the constant drum of news stories about false identifications and false confessions increases the level of responsibility on the government to adhere to the constitutional bedrock principles of due process and fairness and equity. "To whom much is given, much is required," and the arsenal available at the prosecutor's disposal requires sobriety and restraint, especially with vulnerable citizens who remain at risk, particularly in the pretrial stage of the criminal trial process. For defense counsel, there is clear and concise advice to give clients and

(Continued)

(Continued)

to inform the public when giving legal education talks about rights when police want to question citizens.

> If you want to remain silent, speak up and say, "I don't wish to speak!"

> If you want a lawyer, even if the court appoints one, ask for one and say, "I want a lawyer!"

> If you want to waive your rights and talk, say so and say, "Yes, I understand my rights and give them up willingly!"

The right to counsel is a personal right and the suspect must assert the right, not the lawyer on behalf of the client.

In a correctional setting, one of the interesting aspects of the *Maryland v. Shatzer* (2010) and *Howes v. Fields* (2012) decisions is the U.S. Supreme Court finding a prisoner who is obviously in custody (incarcerated) may be deemed not in custody because of the routine nature of prison life. While incarcerated, prisoners follow a set schedule of meals, recreation, in-prison employment, visits, and routine medical care. When interrogating inmates, courts will examine whether the one interrogated was taken from what could be considered part of his normal routine, or whether the inmate just arrived to the prison setting and has yet to adjust. The more recent and the less time in prison, the more a court will find the *Miranda* warnings required before taking an inmate's statement.

Juveniles and *Miranda*

The U.S. Supreme Court has held that the test of whether someone feels she is in custody is an objective one; that is, a court will look at the circumstances surrounding the police–citizen encounter and determine whether it is objectively (according to everyone else) reasonable that a person would not feel free to leave or otherwise terminate the encounter with officers. The high Court's decisions have evolved whether officers should consider a suspect's age in deciding whether the suspect feels she is in custody.

In one case, 17-year-old Michael Alvarado was invited to the police station to talk with officers about what Alvarado knew about a recent robbery and murder. Police did not give the teenager *Miranda* warnings before talking to him. On appeal, Alvarado stated that he was in custody and warnings should have been given. The high Court disagreed, because Alvarado came to the station on his own volition, he was not told he was under arrest, and he could have left (*Yarborough v. Alvarado*, 2004).[32] The Court revisited the age issue when a 13-year-old seventh grader was taken from his social studies classroom by a uniformed officer and questioned in a school administrator's office for 30 to 45 minutes about a spate of recent neighborhood robberies. After he confessed, the officer informed the juvenile that he was free to leave and could refuse to answer questions. Adjudicated delinquent, his appeal made it to the high Court where the justices held, in *J.D.B. v. North Carolina* (2011), that a suspect's age is a relevant factor in making a determination whether someone is in custody.[33]

Rule of Law: "*Miranda* forbids coercion, not mere strategic deception . . . Ploys to mislead a suspect or lull him into a false sense of security that do not rise to the level of compulsion or coercion to speak are not within *Miranda's* concerns."[34]

Trickery and Deceit in Interrogations

The U.S. Supreme Court required officers to inform a suspect of his rights prior to a custodial interrogation because of the coercion inherent during the police questioning process. The giving of the *Miranda* warnings and the suspect's waiving of his rights must be free from coercion or **trickery and deceit**, but once a suspect agrees to speak, the high Court has refused to condemn a number of tactics developed to invite the suspect to confess, such as lying to a suspect that, among other things, his fingerprints or DNA has been found at the crime scene; that results of a polygraph indicate deception when the suspect maintained his innocence; that an accomplice has confessed and put the blame on the suspect; or faking sympathy with the suspect and agreeing that the suspect's motives for the crime were necessary because, somehow, the victim "deserved" the outcome.

Springboard for Discussion

Why do people confess to crimes they have never committed? What remedy would you propose to eliminate the possibility of false confessions?

Whereas scholars have decried trickery in interrogations because it leads vulnerable suspects to falsely confess, particularly the mentally infirm or juveniles, the high Court has consistently reaffirmed the value of getting guilty suspects to confess their crimes and, absent egregious misconduct,[35] lying to a suspect who has already waived his rights remains legal. In the chapter-opening case study, the officers lying to Mike in telling him his fingerprints and an eyewitness connecting Mike to the crime scene is a permissible technique to invite the guilty to confess.

INVOKING THE RIGHTS PURSUANT TO *MIRANDA*

The Court created the *Miranda* warnings to prevent police misconduct in pressuring suspects to confess. Typically, a suspect receives warnings per *Miranda* when he is under suspicion of committing a crime and before any charges have been brought or court proceedings begun.

Invoking the Right to Remain Silent

If, after hearing the *Miranda* warnings, a suspect indicates he wants to stop talking or wants a lawyer, officers must "**scrupulously honor**" the suspect's right and stop the interrogation immediately. The officers cannot continue questioning the suspect, attempt to change his mind, convince him to continue talking, or frighten him by saying this is his last chance to help himself and cut a deal. In the chapter-opening case study, officers did not, as the law requires, immediately stop interrogating Mike once he stated he wanted a lawyer. Officers cannot try to cajole a suspect into talking by saying that he would talk if he had nothing to hide or this is the suspect's last chance to tell his side of the story.[36] If, after invoking *Miranda* rights, the suspect wishes to talk, he can initiate further communication, exchanges, or conversations with the police, but *Miranda* warnings should be renewed and a new waiver of rights obtained.

> **Rule of Law:** *Miranda* case law, as developed since 2009, places an affirmative duty on a suspect to exercise both his right to remain silent and his right to counsel.

Reinterrogation After Invoking the Right to Remain Silent

If the officers honor the suspect's right to remain silent and wait for a period of time (some courts say at least 2 hours), they may come back and try to speak to the suspect again.[37] If, after invoking his right to remain silent, the suspect indicates he wishes to speak, officers must renew the *Miranda* warnings and obtain a legally valid waiver of rights.

Reinterrogation After Invoking the Right to a Lawyer

If the suspect, instead, invokes his right to counsel, another attempt at interrogation or law enforcement contact may occur only when counsel is present, whether or not the accused has consulted counsel, as the high Court found in *Minnick v. Mississippi* (1990), where the defendant's capital murder conviction was reversed after defendant requested a lawyer, met with a lawyer, and then law enforcement reinitiated interrogation and defendant confessed.[38] Once a suspect has requested a lawyer and is in custody, law enforcement cannot come back and try to speak to the suspect because the Court does not want the government to "badger" a defendant into waiving his previously asserted *Miranda* rights and start talking; this is known as the *Edwards* rule.[39] The *Edwards* rule protects a suspect "by presuming his *post-assertion* [after invoking *Miranda*] statements to be involuntary, even where the suspect executes a waiver and his statements would be considered voluntary under traditional standards" [emphasis added]. This rule "protects a suspect's voluntary choice *not* to speak outside his lawyer's presence."[40]

The *Edwards* rule applies only while the suspect is in custody, because "when a defendant is not in custody, he is in control, and need only . . . walk away to avoid police badgering." If there is at least a 14-day break in custody from the first interrogation to the second one, officers may return and try to interrogate again after renewing *Miranda* warnings and waiver.[41]

Invoking the Right to Have Counsel Present During Questioning

The *Miranda* rights to remain silent and to have a lawyer present during questioning stem from the Fifth Amendment telling the government that no citizen shall be "compelled to be a witness against himself," meaning the government cannot force a suspect to tell on himself, to give from his mouth the government the evidence it needs to convict. Although the Fifth Amendment says nothing about a lawyer, the Court has held to protect the "no forced self-incrimination" right that citizens may need counsel present during questioning as a buffer against police coercion during interrogation. On the other hand, the right to a lawyer protected by the Sixth Amendment is to ensure fairness in the adversarial criminal trial process, a recognition that the suspect is outnumbered at trial, facing the overwhelming power of the government trained to convict, sentence, and possibly execute.

The Difference Between Miranda *Right to Counsel and the Sixth Amendment Right to Counsel.* The Sixth Amendment states that "in all criminal prosecutions, the accused shall enjoy the right . . . to have the Assistance of Counsel for his defense." The high Court has interpreted the Sixth Amendment "to assure that in any criminal prosecution, the accused shall not be left to his own devices in facing the prosecutorial forces or organized society."[42] The Sixth Amendment right to counsel attaches by way of the initiation of adversary proceedings, such as

1. Arraignment,

2. The initiation of formal charges by way of information or indictment, or

3. A preliminary hearing.[43] Unlike the *Miranda* right to counsel, the Sixth Amendment right to counsel is "offense specific" which means the right only attaches to the crime charged, discussed more fully in Chapter 10.

Once a person has been charged with a crime, different constitutional protections apply, as represented in Figure 9.2, where the *Miranda* train veers off on another track once a person has been charged.

> **Rule of Law: *Miranda* is a two-step process: the giving of the rights and a waiver of those rights.**

Waiving the Rights Pursuant to *Miranda*

Before the prosecutor can introduce a statement made by the defendant incriminating him, the government must prove that

1. Officers gave the suspect *Miranda* warnings, and

2. The suspect waived (gave up) those rights voluntarily, intelligently, and knowingly.

The test for a legal waiver of *Miranda* rights is also two-pronged. The government must prove that the suspect

a. Understood the rights given up by the waiver, and

b. Voluntarily waived those rights.[44]

The waiver of *Miranda* rights must be voluntary, intelligent, and knowing, which means the following:

1. Voluntary: Police use no physical violence, coercion, threats, or promises.

2. Intelligent: Suspect understands the function of the rights, which are to remain silent and to have counsel present during questioning

3. Knowing: Suspect appreciates the consequences of giving up *Miranda* protections; for example, he understands that if he speaks to officers, anything he says can be used against him in court at his trial.[45]

Figure 9.2 The *Miranda* Train

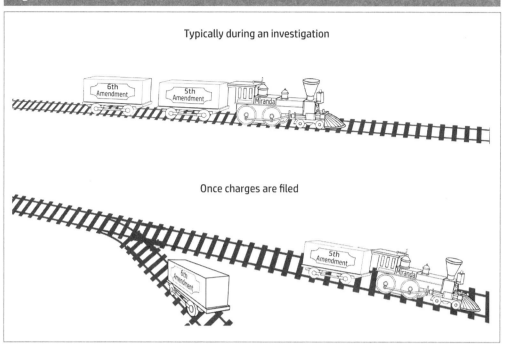

To determine the validity of the waiver of the rights pursuant to *Miranda*, courts look at the totality of the circumstances of the interrogation. As the high Court said of waiving *Miranda* protections in *Moran v. Burbine* (1986),[46]

> First the relinquishment of the right must have been voluntary . . . the product of free and deliberate choice rather than intimidation, coercion or deception. Second, the waiver must have been made with a full awareness both of the nature of the right being abandoned and the consequences of the decision to abandon it.

Common sense dictates that factors unique to the suspect affect her understanding of the waiver, such as her mental state, level of intelligence or presence of a learning disability, intellectual disability (formerly referred to as mental retardation), age, former involvement with the criminal justice system, use of illegal narcotics or other intoxicants, knowledge of English as a native or foreign tongue, and amount of time that elapsed between the giving of *Miranda* and the actual questioning. But in the field these factors make little or no difference in evaluating whether or not the suspect knew and understood both the rights and the consequences of giving them up.

Waiver can be implied by the suspect's conduct. In *North Carolina v. Butler* (1979), the suspect Butler had robbed gas stations and was brought into the police station for questioning.[47] Butler was given *Miranda* warnings and made incriminating statements. He was convicted. On appeal, Butler said he had not directly given an oral waiver of his rights. The *Miranda* case explicitly stated a suspect's silence is not a waiver. But the high Court found the police could rely on Butler's actions of talking and answering questions as an "implied waiver" of his rights. The Court said,

> An explicit statement of waiver is not invariably necessary to support a finding that the defendant waived the right to remain silent or the right to counsel guaranteed by the *Miranda* case. In at least some cases, waiver can be clearly inferred from the actions and words of the person interrogated.

The reasoning in the *Butler* case about implied waivers of *Miranda* rights was further expanded in *Berghuis v. Thompkins* (2010).[48] Thompkins was given *Miranda* warnings and interrogated about a fatal shooting. He was largely silent during the 3-hour interrogation but never indicated he wished to remain silent or wished to cease the interrogation. Toward the end of questioning, the following exchange took place: Detective Helgert asked Thompkins, "Do you believe in God?" and Thompkins said, "Yes," as his eyes "welled up with tears." The detective then asked, "Do you pray to God?" and "Do you pray to God to forgive you for shooting that boy down?" Thompkins answered "Yes" to both questions. The high Court determined that this limited exchange indicated Thompkins had waived his right to remain silent based on certain findings.

> Thompkins understood his *Miranda* rights . . . Thompkins' answer to Detective Helgert's question about whether Thompkins prayed to God for forgiveness for shooting the victim is a "course of conduct indicating waiver" of the right to remain silent. *North Carolina v. Butler* (1979). If Thompkins wanted to remain silent, he could have said nothing in response to Helgert's questions, or he could have unambiguously invoked his *Miranda* rights and ended the interrogation . . . The fact that Thompkins made a statement about three hours after receiving a *Miranda* warning does not overcome the fact that he engaged in a course of conduct indicating waiver. This is confirmed by the fact that before then Thompkins had given sporadic answers to questions throughout the interrogation. [Moreover], there is no evidence that Thompkins' statement was coerced.

In the chapter-opening case study, Mike's actions and words, on being asked if he felt guilty for killing Al, could be construed as an "implied waiver" of his rights per *Miranda*. Officers should always strive to get a suspect to execute a written waiver, as illustrated in Figure 9.3, although getting the suspect to sign any form in the *Miranda* context is not legally required.

The defendant does not have to sign a waiver for it to be effective. If the defendant thinks that he has not confessed unless he has signed something, his confession is still valid. In *Connecticut v. Barrett*, 479 U.S. 523 (1987), the Supreme Court held that an oral confession need not be suppressed when, after *Miranda* warnings, the suspect agreed to speak to the police but indicated that he would not make a written statement without his lawyer present. The Court reasoned that the police do not have to ignore a suspect's willingness to speak. "The fact that officials took the opportunity provided by Barrett to obtain an oral confession is quite consistent with the Fifth Amendment. *Miranda* gives the defendant a right to choose between speech and silence, and Barrett chose to speak."

Figure 9.3 *Miranda* Waiver Form

Notification and Waiver of Rights

Before we ask you questions, you must **understand your rights**.

They are:

You have the right to remain silent.

Anything you say can and will be used against you in a court of law.

You have the right to talk to an attorney for advice before we ask you any questions and to have an attorney present during questioning.

If you cannot afford an attorney, one will be provided for you before any questioning.

If you decide to answer questions now without an attorney present, you have the right to stop talking at any time.

You also have the right to stop talking at any time until you confer with counsel.

Waiver of Rights

I have read this statement of my rights and understand my rights. I am willing to make a statement and answer questions. I do not want an attorney at this time. No promises or threats have been made to me to cooperate and no pressure or coercion of any kind has been used against me. I am _____ years of age and have completed the _____ grade. _____ is my first language.

_____

Signature

_____

Witness

Place:

Date:

Time:

APPLYING THE LAW TO THE FACTS

Can Police Conduct Negate a *Miranda* Waiver?

The Facts: After signing a *Miranda* rights waiver form, Dante was being interrogated by Detective Schuster. Dante asked Schuster if she thought he should get a lawyer, and Schuster said, "I can't answer that." Dante then asked Schuster what she thought were the pros and cons of hiring a lawyer. For pros, Shuster said a lawyer would "protect your rights." For cons, Shuster said, "I'm going to want to ask you questions and he's going to tell you [that] you can't answer me." Shuster also told Dante that "honesty is not going to hurt you." Dante then confessed and was convicted based in part on his confession. On appeal, Dante claimed his confession was not voluntary because of the conversation he had with Detective Shuster. Will Dante win his argument?

The Law: Yes, Dante will win. Telling Dante that having a lawyer present would mean he could not answer incriminating questions goes against the purpose of *Miranda*, which is to protect a suspect's right against self-incrimination, and the phrase "honesty won't hurt you" goes against the *Miranda* warning that anything you say can be used against you in court. See *Hart v. Attorney General of the State of Florida* (2003).[49]

Silence is not a waiver of *Miranda* rights, but silence after a suspect receives *Miranda* warnings may be used against a suspect. For instance, police brought suspect Genovevo Salinas to the police station, but he was not in custody and was free to leave at any time; officers asked questions about Salinas's involvement in the killing of two brothers. When Salinas was asked whether shotgun shells found at the crime scene would match his shotgun, he shrugged and said nothing. At his murder trial, the prosecutor introduced his silence as evidence of his guilt, and Salinas was convicted. On appeal Salinas complained that introducing his silence violated his right against self-incrimination, but the U.S. Supreme Court disagreed and said, "Before [Salinas] could rely on the privilege against self-incrimination, he was required to invoke it" (*Salinas v. Texas*, 2013).[50]

Students should be careful to distinguish the legal use of a suspect's pretrial silence as an admission of guilt from the illegal use of a defendant's silence at trial as an admission of guilt. A defendant has a Fifth Amendment right not to speak at trial, and the judge will instruct the jury that no negative inference may be drawn from his exercise of his constitutional right. The high Court said the Fifth Amendment "forbids either comment by the prosecution on the accused's silence or instructions by the court that such silence is evidence of guilt" (*Griffin v. California*, 1965).[51] A summary chart of when the *Miranda* warnings must be given and how the waiver works is illustrated in Figure 9.4. For a confession to be admissible against a defendant at trial, it must be voluntary. The government

▶ **Photo 9.1**

Mug shot of Ernesto Miranda

Figure 9.4 Summary of *Miranda* Protections and Waiver

Miranda v. Arizona (1966)

I. APPLIES ONLY TO CUSTODIAL INTERROGATION

1. Custody = Person does not feel free to leave

   a. Imprisonment alone does not necessarily constitute *Miranda* custody:

   > *Maryland v. Shatzer* (2010);

   > *Howes v. Fields* (2012)

2. Interrogation = Questioning designed to eliminate incriminating information, or its functional equivalent
   Rhode Island v. Innis (1980)

II. GIVING THE WARNINGS

The gist is ok, no need to read from a card: *Duckworth v. Eagan* (1989)

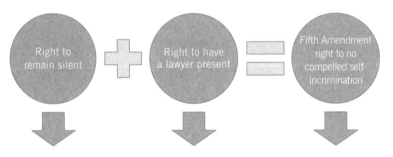

3. Invoke = **Must Be Clear** and Must "Scrupulously Honor"

Berghuis v. Thompkins (2010) *Miranda v. Arizona* (1966) *Michigan v. Mosely* (1975)

III. WAIVING THE RIGHTS

4. Waiver Must be **VIK Voluntary** – free from physical violence, threats, promises

   > **Intelligent** – understand what the rights mean

   > **Knowing** – aware of the consequences of giving up your rights

   a. Waiver cannot be based on silence alone: *Miranda v. Arizona*, (1966)

   b. Waiver can be implied from actions and circumstances: *North Carolina v. Butler* (1979)

   c. After Waiver, request for counsel **Must Be Clear**: *Davis v. United States* (1994) (many courts also apply *Davis* to pre-waiver cases)

---

has awesome power during an interrogation (small windowless room, social isolation, psychological pressure). The giving and waiving of *Miranda* rights is equivalent to voluntariness of the confession.

The Prohibition Against Double Interviewing. An additional *Miranda* rights issue is the "double interviewing" of suspects, a technique common in many jurisdictions prior to 2004. Double interviewing is to get friendly with the suspect before giving *Miranda* warnings in the hope that the suspect confesses. After the suspect confesses, *Miranda* warnings are given to "cleanse" or "sanitize" the subsequent confession for use at trial.

In the suspect's mind, there may be no difference between the "friendly" conversation and subsequent confession, and the "sanitized" confession that can be introduced as evidence. In 2004, the high Court declared in *Missouri v. Seibert*, reprinted in part on the following page, that the double interviewing technique was unconstitutional. The law now requires investigators to give *Miranda* warnings immediately to all those in custodial interrogation settings.

MISSOURI V. SEIBERT, 542 U.S. 600 (2004)

Supreme Court of the United States

Justice Souter delivered the opinion of the Court. (5–4)

FACTS: Patrice Seibert's 12-year-old son Jonathan had cerebral palsy, and when he died in his sleep she feared charges of neglect because of bedsores on his body. In her presence, two of her teenage sons and two of their friends devised a plan to conceal the facts surrounding Jonathan's death by incinerating his body in the course of burning the family's mobile home, in which they planned to leave Donald Rector, a mentally ill teenager living with the family, to avoid any appearance that Jonathan had been unattended. Seibert's son Darian and a friend set the fire, and Donald died. Five days later, the police awakened Seibert at 3 a.m. at a hospital where Darian was being treated for burns.

In arresting [Seibert], Officer Kevin Clinton followed instructions . . . that he refrain from giving *Miranda* warnings. After Seibert had been taken to the police station and left alone in an interview room for 15 to 20 minutes, [Rolla, Missouri, officer Richard Hanrahan] questioned her without *Miranda* warnings for 30 to 40 minutes, squeezing her arm and repeating "Donald was also to die in his sleep." After Seibert finally admitted she knew Donald was meant to die in the fire, she was given a 20-minute coffee and cigarette break. Officer Hanrahan then turned on a tape recorder, gave Seibert the *Miranda* warnings, and obtained a signed waiver of rights from her. He resumed the questioning with "Ok, 'trice [Patrice], we've been talking for a little while about what happened on Wednesday the twelfth, haven't we?" and confronted her with her prewarning statements.

After being charged with first-degree murder for her role in Donald's death, Seibert sought to exclude both her prewarning and postwarning statements. At the suppression hearing, Officer Hanrahan testified that he made a "conscious decision" to withhold *Miranda* warnings, thus resorting to an interrogation technique he had been taught: question first, then give the warnings, and then repeat the question "until I get the answer that she's already provided once." He acknowledged that Seibert's ultimate statement was "largely a repeat of information . . . obtained" prior to the warning.

ISSUE: [Was Seibert's confession improperly admitted as evidence at her trial when her rights per *Miranda* were violated by the double interviewing technique?]

HOLDING: [Yes. Seibert's conviction was overturned.]

REASONING: Seibert argues that her second confession should be excluded from evidence under the doctrine known by the metaphor of the "fruit of the poisonous tree," developed in the Fourth Amendment context in *Wong Sun*

v. United States (1963): evidence otherwise admissible but discovered as a result of an earlier violation is excluded as tainted, lest the law encourage future violations. But the Court in [*Oregon v. Elstad* (1985)] rejected the *Wong Sun* fruits doctrine for analyzing the admissibility of a subsequent warned confession following "an initial failure . . . to administer the warnings required by *Miranda*." In *Elstad*, "a simple failure to administer the warnings, unaccompanied by any actual coercion or other circumstances calculated to undermine the suspect's ability to exercise his free will" did not "so taint the investigatory process that a subsequent voluntary and informed waiver is ineffective for some indeterminate period. Though *Miranda* requires that the unwarned admission must be suppressed, the admissibility of any subsequent statement should turn in these circumstances solely on whether it is knowingly and voluntarily made." . . .

After all, the reason that question-first [without reading the suspect *Miranda* warnings] is catching on is as obvious as its manifest purpose, which is to get a confession the suspect would not make if he understood his rights at the outset; the sensible underlying assumption is that with one confession in hand before the warnings, the interrogator can count on getting its duplicate, with trifling additional trouble. Upon hearing warnings only in the aftermath of interrogation and just after making a confession, a suspect would hardly think he had a genuine right to remain silent, let alone persist in so believing once the police began to lead him over the same ground again.

A more likely reaction on a suspect's part would be perplexity about the reason for discussing rights at that point, bewilderment being an unpromising frame of mind for knowledgeable decision. What is worse, telling a suspect that "anything you say can and will be used against you," without expressly excepting the statement just given, could lead to an entirely reasonable inference that what he has just said will be used, with subsequent silence being of no avail. Thus, when *Miranda* warnings are inserted in the midst of coordinated and continuing interrogation, they are likely to mislead and "depriv[e] a defendant of knowledge essential to his ability to understand the nature of his rights and the consequences of abandoning them." *Moran v. Burbine* (1986). By the same token, it would ordinarily be unrealistic to treat two spates of integrated and proximately conducted questioning as independent interrogations subject to independent evaluation simply because *Miranda* warnings formally punctuate them in the middle. . . .

CONCLUSION: The judgment of the Supreme Court of Missouri [suppressing the confession] is affirmed.

In the chapter-opening case study, after officers get Mike to confess before "cleansing" the confession by giving *Miranda* warnings is unlawful.

Exceptions to the Giving of *Miranda* Warnings

Miranda warnings are required only in custodial interrogations, so if the suspect is either not in custody or not being asked questions designed to elicit incriminating information, *Miranda* does not apply. The goal of *Miranda* is prophylactic (preventive) in nature to prevent police coercion in overbearing a suspect's will to confess. There is no Fifth Amendment protection against giving blood samples, fingerprints, and photographs for identification purposes; giving handwriting samples; being forced to read a statement so a witness may hear a suspect's voice; or the filming of a videotape showing the defendant's drunken and slurred speech and stumbling steps at time of arrest. In certain situations, such protection from coercion to self-incriminate oneself is not required, such as:

- **Volunteered statements**. These are statements given spontaneously and not as a result of any police questioning, for example, admitting the location of contraband even though no one asked.

- **Public safety questions**. As an example, consider "Where's the gun?" The answer may be incriminating, but the officer's goal to protect the public safety outweighs the individual's privilege not to self-incriminate.[52]

- **Questioning by ordinary citizens**. Questions by ordinary people do not require *Miranda* warnings because the protections of the Bill of Rights apply only against government actors.

- **Routine booking questions**. Questions that ask name, age, date of birth, height, and weight do not constitute custodial interrogation, even if the answers to the booking questions are incriminating (e.g., "Identify your tattoos"), *Pennsylvania v. Muniz* (1990).[53]

- **Crime scene investigation questions**. Questions designed to learn facts to aid in the investigation do not need to be preceded by *Miranda* warnings.

- ***Terry* stops and routine traffic stops**. Brief investigatory detentions do not implicate the coercive concerns of a custodial interrogation.

- **Undercover officers and informants**. An undercover agent or civilian working on behalf of the government in an undercover situation need not disclose his identity and need not warn suspects of *Miranda* warnings because police coercion is not present. Be careful to distinguish if a suspect has been formally charged and requested counsel; those working undercover may then only passively listen and not actively elicit incriminating information.

- **Individuals on probation or parole.** Offenders on probation or parole may be ordered to give information as a condition of their release status.

WHEN *MIRANDA* IS VIOLATED

Physical Evidence Remains Admissible

Miranda warnings are given to protect a suspect's right against coercive government action to obtain spoken confessions. If, as a result of a *Miranda* violation, officers discover physical evidence, such as contraband or evidence of a crime, the evidence is not poisoned fruit and is admissible. The case *United States v. Patane* (2004) illustrates these distinctions between the constitutional protections and the protections of the judge-made remedies of the exclusionary rule and *Miranda* warnings. When police gave Patane his *Miranda* warnings before questioning about gun possession as a felon, Patane stopped officers and said, "I know my rights." Patane was eventually convicted and argued on appeal that the gun should have been suppressed as fruit of the poisonous tree from the officers' faulty giving of *Miranda* warnings. The high Court agreed that the *Miranda* warnings were flawed because a citizen cannot abrogate (take away) an officer's legal duty to do her job, and officers should have continued giving Patane *Miranda* warnings despite Patane's insistence he already knew his rights. But the Court held the gun admissible because *Miranda* warnings are to protect against forcing a person to say something incriminating, not to suppress physical evidence that may be derived from a *Miranda* violation.

Springboard for Discussion

There are many exceptions to giving *Miranda* warnings. Do you agree with the list of exceptions, or do you think citizens should be given *Miranda* warnings whenever police ask them questions?

UNITED STATES V. PATANE, 542 U.S. 630 (2004)

Supreme Court of the United States

Justice Thomas delivered the opinion of the Court. (5–4)

FACTS: In June 2001, Samuel Francis Patane was arrested for harassing his ex-girlfriend, Linda O'Donnell. He was released on bond, subject to a temporary restraining order that prohibited him from contacting O'Donnell. Patane apparently violated the restraining order by attempting to telephone O'Donnell. On June 6, 2001, Officer Tracy Fox of the Colorado Springs Police Department began to investigate the matter. On the same day, a county probation officer informed an agent of the Bureau of Alcohol, Tobacco, and Firearms (ATF), that Patane, a convicted felon, illegally possessed a .40 Glock pistol. The ATF relayed this information to Detective Josh Benner, who worked closely with the ATF. Together, Detective Benner and Officer Fox proceeded to Patane's residence. After reaching the residence and inquiring into Patane's attempts to contact O'Donnell, Officer Fox arrested Patane for violating the restraining order. Detective Benner attempted to advise Patane of his *Miranda* rights but got no further than the right to remain silent. At that point, Patane interrupted, asserting that he knew his rights, and neither officer attempted to complete the warning. Detective Benner then asked Patane about the Glock. Patane was initially reluctant to discuss the matter, stating: "I am not sure I should tell you anything about the Glock because I don't want you to take it away from me." Detective Benner persisted, and Patane told him that the pistol was in his bedroom. Patane then gave Detective Benner permission to retrieve the pistol. Detective Benner found the pistol and seized it.

ISSUE: [W]hether a failure to give a suspect the warnings prescribed by *Miranda v. Arizona*, 384 U.S. 436 (1966),

requires suppression of the physical fruits of the suspect's unwarned but voluntary statements.

HOLDING: [No. Physical evidence derived from unwarned statements is admissible.]

REASONING: Our cases also make clear the related point that a mere failure to give *Miranda* warnings does not, by itself, violate a suspect's constitutional rights or even the *Miranda* rule ("failure to give a *Miranda* warning does not, without more, establish a completed violation when the unwarned interrogation ensues"). This, of course, follows from the nature of the right protected by the Self-Incrimination Clause, which the *Miranda* rule, in turn, protects. It is "a fundamental trial right." It follows that police do not violate a suspect's constitutional rights (or the *Miranda* rule) by negligent or even deliberate failures to provide the suspect with the full panoply of warnings prescribed by *Miranda*. Potential violations occur, if at all, only upon the admission of unwarned statements into evidence at trial. And, at that point, "[t]he exclusion of unwarned statements . . . is a complete and sufficient remedy" for any perceived *Miranda* violation.

Similarly, because police cannot violate the Self-Incrimination Clause by taking unwarned though voluntary statements, an exclusionary rule cannot be justified by reference to a deterrence effect on law enforcement. . . . Our decision not to apply *Wong Sun* to mere failures to give *Miranda* warnings was sound at the time *Tucker* and *Elstad* were decided, and we decline to apply *Wong Sun* to such failures now.

The Court of Appeals ascribed significance to the fact that, in this case, there might be "little [practical] difference between Patane's confessional statement" and the

(Continued)

actual physical evidence. The distinction, the court said, "appears to make little sense as a matter of policy." But, putting policy aside, we have held that "the word 'witness' in the constitutional text limits the" scope of the Self-Incrimination Clause to testimonial evidence. The Constitution itself makes the distinction. And although it is true that the Court requires the exclusion of the physical fruit of actually coerced statements, it must be remembered that statements taken without sufficient *Miranda*

warnings are presumed to have been coerced only for certain purposes and then only when necessary to protect the privilege against self-incrimination. For the reasons discussed above, we decline to extend that presumption further.

CONCLUSION: We reverse the judgment of the Court of Appeals [suppressing the gun] and remand the case for further proceedings consistent with this opinion.

Inevitable Discovery

The exclusionary rule has two primary exceptions: the inevitable discovery and independent source doctrines. Under the inevitable discovery rule, a court may admit illegally obtained evidence if investigators would have eventually discovered the evidence close in time to the initial illegal retrieval. The rule had a tortured history in the case *Nix v. Williams* (1984).[54] In that case, mentally ill offender Williams had kidnapped and killed a 10-year-old girl. Police were informed by Williams's lawyer not to talk to him without the lawyer's presence. As officers transported Williams from a county jail, the officer gave Williams what is known as the "Christian Burial Speech" with Williams sitting in the back of the cruiser. Officers knew Williams to be a religious man. Detective Leaming said to Williams,

> **Rule of Law:** If the tainted evidence would have been found inevitably despite the initial illegality that poisoned the tree, it is admissible.

I want to give you something to think about while we're traveling down the road . . . They are predicting several inches of snow for tonight, and I feel that you yourself are the only person that knows where this little girl's body is . . . and if you get a snow on top of it you yourself may be unable to find it. And since we will be going right past the area [where the body is] on the way to Des Moines, I feel that we could stop and locate the body, that the parents of this little girl should be entitled to a Christian burial for the little girl who was snatched away from them on Christmas [E]ve and murdered. . . . [A]fter a snow storm [we may not be] able to find it at all.

Leaming told Williams he knew that the girl's body was in the area of Mitchellville—a town they would be passing on the way to Des Moines. Leaming concluded his speech by saying, "I do not want you to answer me. Just think about it." Williams then directed the officers to the location of the victim's body, which was in the general vicinity where a search party had been looking.

On appeal from his death sentence, the court found Leaming's burial speech to be a Sixth Amendment violation of Williams's right to counsel. Because Leaming committed a constitutional violation under the Sixth Amendment right to counsel rather than a failure to give *Miranda* warnings, the girl's body was excluded as evidence by operation of the fruit of the poisonous tree doctrine. That is, the tainted "confession" contaminated the base of the tree, which then poisoned the tree's fruit, which was Williams's disclosure of the victim's location; the little girl's body was excluded from trial. After a retrial and more appeals, the U.S. Supreme Court heard the case and held that because the search party already in progress would have "inevitably discovered" the girl's body, the body should be admitted into evidence as an exception to the exclusionary rule.

Independent Source

Another exclusionary rule exception, independent source, permits illegally obtained evidence to be introduced at trial if it was discovered through a source not connected with the initial illegality.[55] For example, during an investigation into drug dealing, police entered a warehouse unlawfully without a warrant and discovered bales of marijuana. Some officers kept the warehouse under surveillance while others went to secure the warrant to search the warehouse. In the officer's affidavit establishing probable cause to search the warehouse, he did not mention that the police had already entered the warehouse illegally. The warrant was issued, and the drug dealers were caught. At trial, the defendants challenged the initial illegality at the warehouse that formed the basis of probable cause. The U.S. Supreme Court found that the officer's knowledge came from an "independent source" regardless of the unlawful search because the illegal search was not used as the basis for the warrant.[56] In another case in which stolen goods were illegally seized and suppressed by operation of the exclusionary rule, testimony about the goods was admissible because the witnesses' knowledge about the crime was an "independent source" and therefore fit the exception to the exclusionary rule.[57] The rationale of the independent source exception was explained by the high Court this way:

> [T]he interest of society in deterring unlawful police conduct and the public interest in having juries receive all probative evidence of a crime are properly balanced by putting the police in the same, not a worse, position that they would have been in if no police error or misconduct had occurred. . . . When the challenged evidence has an independent source, exclusion of such evidence would put the police in a worse position than they would have been in absent any error or violation (*Nix v. Williams*, 1984).[58]

Collateral Uses of Excluded Evidence

Use of evidence that was obtained in violation of a suspect's *Miranda* rights might still be used in certain circumstances because *Miranda* is a judge-made prophylactic rule. Such tainted evidence may still be introduced against a defendant in federal civil tax proceedings, *habeas corpus* proceedings, grand jury proceedings, deportation proceedings, parole revocation, and sentencing hearings. If a confession is excluded from trial because of a failure to read *Miranda* warnings to the suspect, the confession may still be used against the defendant if he or she takes the stand and specifically contradicts his or her previous confession. To allow a defendant to benefit at the expense of the state's mistake by changing her story and committing perjury is untenable.[59]

On the other hand, if police coerced the suspect to confess or obtained the confession in violation of the Sixth Amendment right to counsel, the confession must be suppressed for all purposes. The high Court held, in *Mincey v. Arizona* (1978), that it is a violation of due process to use a coerced confession not only to prove guilt, but for any purpose at trial, including impeaching the defendant with his own perjury on the witness stand, because the defendant's due process rights to a fair trial will have been fatally compromised.[60]

> **Rule of Law: Evidence is admissible if discovered through an independent source unrelated to the initial illegality.**

SUMMARY

1. You will understand when *Miranda* warnings must be given. *Miranda v. Arizona* (1966) held that for a suspect to properly exercise his constitutional right not to incriminate himself and to have counsel present during questioning, he had to be apprised of his rights before any custodial interrogation. Custody means the suspect believes he is not free to leave, and interrogation is when law enforcement agents ask questions, or their functional equivalent, intended to elicit incriminating information. Being incarcerated in a prison does not necessarily mean the suspect is in custody because long-term imprisonment may make a person as comfortable as in his own home, even

though he has no freedom of movement within the prison environment, as established by *Howes v. Fields* (2012).

2. You will be familiar with the steps of interrogation to induce a confession. There are many interrogation techniques, but Inbau and Reid's manual recommends nine steps of interrogation to induce guilty suspects to confess. Trickery in interrogations is proper, but deceit in obtaining a *Miranda* waiver is not. To be admissible in court, a confession must be voluntary.

3. You will be able to identify the procedure for both invoking and waiving the rights protected by *Miranda*.

The giving of *Miranda* warnings does not have to be exact. As long as officers deliver the "gist" of what the warnings mean in terms of the right to remain silent and to have an attorney, courts are satisfied, as in *Florida v. Powell* (2010). If a suspect invokes the right to remain silent, all questioning must cease, but police may reinitiate interrogation after rewarning the suspect with *Miranda*. If a suspect who is in custody invokes the right to have an attorney present, all questioning must stop until the suspect has had an opportunity to consult with counsel. To be valid, the state must prove a *Miranda* waiver was voluntary, intelligent, and knowing. Silence will not suffice as a waiver, but a waiver can be implied from a suspect's actions and words. To be admitted, a confession must have been given voluntarily; if it was produced through police coercion, it will be suppressed and cannot be used for any purpose.

4. You will be able to discuss the nature of the prohibited double interviewing process. The law, as recognized by *Missouri v. Seibert* (2004), prohibits double interviewing, which is the practice of extracting a confession, then providing *Miranda* warnings, and then asking the suspect to repeat the confession. Statements taken in violation of *Miranda* must be suppressed by operation of the exclusionary rule, but exclusion does not apply to physical evidence because the Fifth Amendment protects only against self-incriminating statements, and such statements can be used to impeach (challenge) a defendant when the defendant testifies and changes her story at trial.

5. You will be able to competently provide examples of *Miranda* exceptions and the use of statements taken in violation of *Miranda*. Exceptions in which *Miranda* does not apply include questions involving public safety, routine booking, crime scene investigation, ordinary citizens, lawful traffic stops, and investigatory detentions. Volunteered and spontaneous confessions are always admissible because there is no government compulsion to speak. Physical evidence taken in violation of *Miranda* warnings remains admissible because such evidence does not implicate the Fifth Amendment's right to be free from compelled self-incrimination, as in *United States v. Patane* (2004).

Go back to the beginning of the chapter and reread the news excerpts associated with the learning objectives. Test yourself to determine if you can understand the material covered in the text in the context of the news.

KEY TERMS AND PHRASES

confession 247
corpus delicti 247
custody 255
Fifth Amendment 247
functional equivalent 259

Inbau and Reid nine steps 249
independent source 270
inevitable discovery 270
interrogation 259
invoking *Miranda* 261

scrupulously honor 261
trickery and deceit 260
voluntary, intelligent,
 and knowing waiver 262

PROBLEM-SOLVING EXERCISES

1. On October 28, 2016, a complaint was filed alleging that Hazel burglarized a Walgreens Store in Lincoln, Nebraska (the "state case"). Hazel got an attorney. On January 19, 2017, Hazel was indicted in federal court for stealing from ATM machines (the "federal case"). On the morning of February 1, 2017, Hazel was processed out of the county jail and transported to the federal building for her arraignment in the federal case. At the federal building, Hazel was greeted by FBI Special Agent Saad for an interview. Saad gave Hazel *Miranda* warnings; she signed a waiver form and made incriminating statements. Hazel tried to suppress her statements, claiming that Agent Saad could not question her without an attorney on the federal case because she had an attorney for the state case. You are the judge. Will you suppress Hazel's statements? **(ROL: *Miranda* right to counsel)**

2. During a custodial interrogation about a shooting, the officers read the suspect *Miranda* warnings and he competently waived his rights. Officer Smith then said to the suspect that this was his "last chance" to "distance himself" from the crime by admitting that he was present during the shooting. The officers said it was clear the suspect was simply in "the wrong place at the wrong time." One officer said, "The district attorney is going to see this. The judge is going to see this, and ultimately the jury is going to see this, and when they hear you spinning this tale, you're not helping yourself. So, tell the story of what happened out there. If you didn't pull the trigger, now's the chance for you to tell your story." The suspect confessed, and later moved to suppress his confession, claiming coercion. The government said the confession was voluntary. Which side will win? **(ROL: Voluntariness, trickery)**

10

THE SIXTH AMENDMENT
Counsel and Trial Rights

G o to the end of the chapter. Skim the key terms and phrases and read the summary closely. Come back and look at the following news excerpts to focus your reading throughout the chapter to understand the Sixth Amendment as it relates to the right to counsel at critical stages of the adversary process, the right to represent oneself at trial, and the right to challenge government witnesses through the Confrontation Clause. Also discussed is venue selection for the location of trial. Discussed elsewhere in the text are the other Sixth Amendment provisions (counsel in the pretrial identification process, speedy trial, and jury selection in Chapter 2; the right to counsel during interrogations conducted pursuant to *Miranda v. Arizona* [1966] in Chapter 9). The chapter begins with a hypothetical case study of Gary, who is in prison and needs a lawyer before trial. Follow Gary as he encounters the Sixth Amendment protections presented throughout the chapter and connect the situations Gary encounters with the relevant section of text.

WHY THIS CHAPTER MATTERS TO YOU	THE LEARNING OBJECTIVES AS REFLECTED IN THE NEWS
After you have read this chapter: **Learning Objective 1:** Discuss the constitutional foundation of the right to counsel.	More than 50 years ago, *Gideon v. Wainwright* was argued before the U.S. Supreme Court. The high Court unanimously ruled that state courts are required to provide legal counsel for those defendants accused of a crime who cannot afford a lawyer. The right to effective counsel for indigent defense may be in peril. When it comes to legal services, you get what you pay for, and Pennsylvania, for instance, pays nothing. Pennsylvania stands alone among the 50 states in its steadfast refusal to allocate any money in the state budget for indigent criminal defense. Instead, it is up to each Pennsylvania county to design, and pay for, a system to provide legal representation to the poor. (*The Times* [PA], May 16, 2018)
Learning Objective 2: You will understand how indigent defendants obtain counsel.	A court has allowed George Zimmerman to use a public defender in his alleged stalking case after he filed documents saying he's $2.5 million in debt and has zero income. Zimmerman is facing stalking accusations in his latest legal woes since his 2013 acquittal in the shooting death of Trayvon Martin. Details of his finances were filed in a Seminole County court to support his request for a public defender. In the documents, he lists that he's unemployed and has $0 in assets including cash, bank accounts and equity on property. Zimmerman is accused of repeatedly threatening and harassing Dennis Warren. Warren is a private investigator who was hired by a production company that was working on a documentary about Martin's life. Deputies said Zimmerman called Warren 55 times, left 36 voicemails, texted him 67 times and sent 27 emails over a nine-day span. (www.wqad.com [FL], May 24, 2018)

(Continued)

(Continued)

WHY THIS CHAPTER MATTERS TO YOU	THE LEARNING OBJECTIVES AS REFLECTED IN THE NEWS
Learning Objective 3: Identify when the right to counsel attaches and the significance of its relationship to *Miranda v. Arizona*.	[Massachusetts'] highest court says drivers suspected of operating under the influence are not entitled to consult an attorney before deciding whether to take a breath test. The justices ruled that the point at which a suspect decides whether or not to take a breath test "occurs at the evidence gathering stage," which is not a "critical point" in the criminal process—and therefore the suspect does not need to be advised of their right to an attorney prior to making that decision. "It is well settled that the right to counsel under the Sixth Amendment does not attach until the occurrence of critical stages at or after the initiation of adversary judicial proceedings, whether that be by formal charge, preliminary hearing, indictment, information, or arraignment," the ruling reads. (wbur.news [MA], August 15, 2016)
Learning Objective 4: You will appreciate how the Sixth Amendment guarantees autonomy to defendants during the criminal trial process.	The Indiana Court of Appeals has rebuked a Lake Superior Court judge for seemingly not knowing that a criminal defendant always has the right to proceed to trial without the assistance of an attorney. According to court records, Judge Diane Boswell repeatedly told a defendant who announced his intent to fire his public defender that he did not have a right to represent himself, that she decided he could not represent himself, and even asked where the defendant had heard or read about the right to represent himself. Records also show that during a discussion at the bench, Boswell required prosecutors provide a citation and legal explanation about a defendant's right to self-representation, and how a defendant's request to waive his right to counsel must be made. (nwi.com [IN], February 8, 2018)
Learning Objective 5: Understand how the Sixth Amendment works at trial through the Confrontation Clause.	In an Akron, Ohio, courtroom this week, a Charlotte man charged with recruiting for ISIS retains the constitutional right to confront his accusers. But one of the witnesses testifying against Erick Hendricks will be wearing a disguise. In an unusual ruling last month, U.S. District Judge John Adams has cleared the way for an undercover FBI agent to hide his identity by using a pseudonym and altering his appearance when he's in the courtroom. Under normal circumstances, the Sixth Amendment would guarantee Hendricks a public trial. Instead, only the judge, jury, Hendricks and his attorneys, government prosecutors and essential clerical staff will be allowed to hear the agent's testimony in person. (*Charlotte* [NC] *Observer*, March 8, 2018)

Chapter-Opening Case Study: Gary Needs a Lawyer

While Gary was on probation for illegal gambling, he produced a "dirty urine," a positive drug test result for marijuana. Officers arrested Gary and charged him with illegal drug use. Gary met with his lawyer, but the government revoked his probation and placed him in prison to serve the remaining 2 years of his sentence. After 6 months, officers came to the prison to speak to Gary. He was escorted from his cell into a small room. Officers closed the door and started to ask Gary questions about a murder the officers were investigating. Gary told them he had a lawyer, and officers left. Three weeks later, police came back and tried to talk to Gary again. **(Rule of Law [ROL]: Police may reinitiate interrogation after a 14-day break in custody.)** Gary then confessed to the murder. **(ROL: Sixth Amendment right to counsel is offense specific; police can ask questions about other crimes.)**

The murder charge was sensational and negative press coverage about Gary's presumed guilt was relentless. Before trial, Gary brought a motion to suppress his confession to murder because he was represented by counsel and argued, therefore, the police should not have been able to interrogate him without his lawyer being present. Gary also filed a motion for a change of venue based on the press creating a negative bias in the potential jury pool before Gary's trial. **(ROL: Venue—trial should be held in the district where the crime occurred.)** The court denied Gary's motions. At trial, Gary's lawyer was obviously high on drugs and refused to ask questions or cross-examine any of the state's witnesses against Gary. **(ROL: Ineffective assistance of counsel means the attorney's performance fell below that of a reasonable attorney; ROL: Confrontation Clause means the defendant can challenge the witnesses against him.)** Midway through the trial, Gary asked the judge if he could represent himself. After a colloquy during which the court established Gary understood the risks of self-representation, the judge allowed Gary to be his own counsel. **(ROL: Defendants can represent themselves at trial.)** Paying homage to the adage, "a man who represents himself has a fool for a client," Gary was convicted and argued his confession was obtained unlawfully, his change of venue motion should have been granted, and his lawyer was ineffective. Will Gary win his appeal?

THE SIXTH AMENDMENT
AS DUE PROCESS PROTECTION

The Sixth Amendment Protects All Other
Rights Associated With Fair and Equitable Justice

The Sixth Amendment provides:

> In all criminal prosecutions, the accused shall enjoy the right to a speedy and public trial, by an impartial jury of the state and district wherein the crime shall have been committed, which district shall have been previously ascertained by law, and to be informed of the nature and cause of the accusation; to be confronted with the witnesses against him; to have compulsory process for obtaining witnesses in his favor, and to have the assistance of counsel for his defense.

Law Professors Erwin Chemerinsky and Laurie Levenson have broken down the Sixth Amendment to its basic parts:

> In all criminal prosecutions—criminal cases, not in *habeas corpus* proceedings

> The accused—means formal charges have been filed, not pretrial (generally)

> Enjoy the right to—at common law, there was no right to counsel in certain cases

> Assistance of counsel—what is the minimal standard of competent counsel?[1]

As discussed in Chapter 1, due process as conceived in the Constitution was designed to protect the public from the government's awesome power. When the legislative or executive branch seeks to deprive a person of life, liberty, or property, a lawyer's help is required to assist the regular person in battle against the government, which has many prosecutorial weapons at its disposal: law enforcement who can obtain warrants to search and seize, crime labs to test evidence, and the power to generate testimony by granting plea bargains to codefendants. The Sixth Amendment's right to counsel protects all due process rights and more. Because the Bill of Rights, when enacted, did not apply to the states, the U.S. Supreme Court was left to use the concept of due process to fix miscarriages of justice. Due process is the portal through which all other rights to ensure a fair trial—from the time the defendant is first charged with the crime through sentencing and appeal—are protected. The high Court invalidated a number of state criminal cases for violating the due process trial rights of the defendants through a series of death-penalty cases featuring African American defendants. Author Michael Klarman writes about these cases:

> In *Moore v. Dempsey*, the Supreme Court interpreted the Due Process Clause of the Fourteenth Amendment to forbid criminal convictions obtained through mob-dominated trials. In *Powell v. Alabama*, the Court ruled that the Due Process Clause requires state appointment of counsel in capital cases and overturned convictions where defense counsel had been appointed the morning of trial. In *Norris v. Alabama*, the Court reversed a conviction under the Equal Protection Clause where blacks had been intentionally excluded from juries. . . . In *Brown v. Mississippi*, the Court construed the Due Process Clause to forbid criminal convictions extracted through torture."[2]

Slowly, through the doctrine of incorporation, the U.S. Supreme Court through the Fourteenth Amendment's Due Process Clause made most of the Bill of Rights applicable to the states.[3] But before the Sixth Amendment was incorporated, the high Court analyzed the common law development of the right to counsel.

The Constitutional Requirements to the Assistance of Counsel at Trial

As discussed in Chapter 1, cases provide a snapshot in time of why the rules of criminal law and procedure are so important to the public's perception of fairness in the government's administration of justice. As Klarman says, some cases are celebrated for fidelity to equal protection and the rule of law: The state case on appeal to the U.S. Supreme Court that was the basis of the *Powell v. Alabama* (1932) is a travesty of justice. Nine Black youths were accused of raping two White women while they were riding a train through the South. The defendants were arrested in Alabama, and became known as the "Scottsboro boys," which was a loose basis for the classic book by Harper Lee, *To Kill a Mockingbird*. The defendants ranged in age from 13 to 19 years old. The press coverage preyed on racist stereotypes, as one headline read, "All Negroes positively identified by girls and one White boy who was held prisoner with pistol and knives while nine Black fiends committed revolting crime."[4] The "Black on White" rape trope has been used to justify violence against African Americans since 1892 when anti-lynching activist Ida B. Wells wrote in *Southern Horrors*, "The South is shielding itself behind the plausible screen of defending the honor of its women."[5] The myth is so strong that it motivated Dylann Roof, featured in this chapter on the right to represent oneself at trial, to shoot and kill six women and three men at Bible study on June 17, 2015, at the historically Black Emanuel A.M.E. Church in Charleston, South Carolina. In his confession explaining his motivation for the mass shooting, Roof said,

> Well I had to do it because . . . somebody had to do something. Because you know Black people are killing White people every day on the streets. And they rape, they rape White women, a hundred White women a day. That's [a] FBI statistic from 2005. You know, that's ten years ago. It might even be more now. Who knows?[6]

The "Scottsboro Boys" were indicted for rape, a capital offense, and 6 days later went to trial that lasted 1 day. From all accounts, the trial was a sham. Finding it difficult to find lawyers willing to represent the defendants, a lawyer who had been contacted about the boys' plight came from Chattanooga, Tennessee, and met his clients on the day of trial. One local attorney assisted. At trial the victims, Victoria Price and Ruby Bates, lied about what happened on the train. Their lies were revealed after trial when Bates admitted she had committed perjury. According to UMKC.com, defense counsel called only one witness, a court employee, to testify that public celebration outside the courthouse when each guilty verdict was read could be heard inside the courthouse as the jury decided the fate of the remaining defendants.

The defendants were convicted and sentenced to death. The Alabama Supreme Court upheld all the sentences except for Eugene Williams, who at age 13 was a juvenile and should not have been tried as an adult under Alabama law. The Alabama court reasoned as long as the defendants had not been lynched, justice under fluid and ever-changing criminal procedure rules was served. The U.S. Supreme Court overturned the defendants' convictions holding that if a fair trial means anything, having the assistance of counsel is a requirement. As you read the case excerpt below, pay close attention to the Court's historical narrative of counsel's role in guaranteeing a defendant's due process rights.

POWELL V. ALABAMA, 287 U.S. 45 (1932)

U.S. Supreme Court

Justice Sutherland delivered the opinion of the Court. (7–2)

FACTS: The record shows that on the day when the offense is said to have been committed, these defendants, together with a number of other negroes, were upon a freight train on its way through Alabama. On the same train were seven white boys and the two white girls. A fight took place between the negroes and the white boys, in the course of which the white boys, with the exception of one named Gilley, were thrown off the train. A message was sent ahead, reporting the fight and asking that every negro be gotten off the train. The participants in the fight, and the two girls, were in an open gondola car. The two girls testified that each of them was assaulted by six different negroes in turn, and they identified the seven defendants as having been among the number. None of the white boys was called to testify, with the exception of Gilley, who was called in rebuttal.

Before the train reached Scottsboro, Alabama, a sheriff's posse seized the defendants and two other negroes. Both girls and the negroes then were taken to Scottsboro, the county seat. Word of their coming and of the alleged assault had preceded them, and they were met at Scottsboro by a large crowd. The sheriff thought it necessary to call for the militia to assist in safeguarding the prisoners. It is perfectly apparent that the proceedings, from beginning to end, took place in an atmosphere of tense, hostile and excited public sentiment. During the entire time, the defendants were closely confined or were under military guard. The record does not disclose their ages, except that one of them was nineteen; but the record clearly indicates that most, if not all, of them were youthful, and they are constantly referred to as "the boys." They were ignorant and illiterate. All of them were residents of other states, where alone members of their families or friends resided.

HOLDING: Under the circumstances disclosed, we hold that defendants were not accorded the right of counsel in

any substantial sense. To decide otherwise, would simply be to ignore actualities.

REASONING: The Constitution of Alabama provides that in all criminal prosecutions the accused shall enjoy the right to have the assistance of counsel; and a state statute requires the court in a capital case, where the defendant is unable to employ counsel, to appoint counsel for him. The state supreme court held that these provisions had not been infringed, and with that holding we are powerless to interfere. The question, however, which it is our duty, and within our power, to decide, is whether the denial of the assistance of counsel contravenes the due process clause of the Fourteenth Amendment to the federal Constitution.

If recognition of the right of a defendant charged with a felony to have the aid of counsel depended upon the existence of a similar right at common law as it existed in England when our Constitution was adopted, there would be great difficulty in maintaining it as necessary to due process. Originally, in England, a person charged with treason or felony was denied the aid of counsel, except in respect of legal questions which the accused himself might suggest. At the same time parties in civil cases and persons accused of misdemeanors were entitled to the full assistance of counsel. After the revolution of 1688, the rule was abolished as to treason, but was otherwise steadily adhered to until 1836, when by act of Parliament the full right was granted in respect of felonies generally.

An affirmation of the right to the aid of counsel in petty offenses, and its denial in the case of crimes of the gravest character, where such aid is most needed, is so outrageous and so obviously a perversion of all sense of proportion that the rule was constantly, vigorously and sometimes passionately assailed by English statesmen and lawyers. As early as 1758, Blackstone, although recognizing that the rule was settled at common law, denounced it as not in keeping with the rest of the humane treatment of prisoners by the English law. "For

(Continued)

(Continued)

upon what face of reason," he says, "can that assistance be denied to save the life of a man, which yet is allowed him in prosecutions for every petty trespass?" One of the grounds upon which Lord Coke defended the rule was that in felonies the court [the Judge] itself was counsel for the prisoner . . . [but this] rule was rejected by the colonies [so, too, the English common law that denied accused felons the right to counsel]. It thus appears that in at least twelve of the thirteen colonies . . . the right to counsel [was] fully recognized in all criminal prosecutions, save that in one or two instances the right was limited to capital offenses or to the more serious crimes; and this court seems to have been of the opinion that this was true in all the colonies.

The Sixth Amendment, in terms, provides that in all criminal prosecutions the accused shall enjoy the right "to have the assistance of counsel for his defense." The fact that the right involved is of such a character that it cannot be denied without violating those "fundamental principles of liberty and justice which lie at the base of all our civil and political institutions," is obviously one of those compelling considerations which must prevail in determining whether it is embraced within the due process clause of the Fourteenth Amendment, although it be specifically dealt with in another part of the federal Constitution. Evidently this court, in the later cases enumerated, regarded the rights there under consideration as of this fundamental character. . . . it is possible that some of the personal rights safeguarded by the first eight Amendments against National action may also be safeguarded against state action, because a denial of them would be a denial of due process of law. If this is so, it is not because those rights are enumerated in the first eight Amendments, but because they are of such a nature that they are included in the conception of due process of law.

While the question has never been categorically determined by this court, a consideration of the nature of the right and a review of the expressions of this and other courts, makes it clear that the right to the aid of counsel is of this fundamental character. It never has been doubted by this court, or any other so far as we know, that notice and hearing are preliminary steps essential to the passing of an enforceable judgment, and that they, together with a legally competent tribunal having jurisdiction of the case, constitute basic elements of the constitutional requirement of due process of law. The words of Webster, so often quoted, that by "the law of the land" is intended "a law which hears before it condemns," have been repeated in varying forms of expression in a multitude of decisions. What, then, does a hearing include? Historically and in

practice, in our own country at least, it has always included the right to the aid of counsel when desired and provided by the party asserting the right. The right to be heard would be, in many cases, of little avail if it did not comprehend the right to be heard by counsel.

Even the intelligent and educated layman has small and sometimes no skill in the science of law. If charged with crime, he is incapable, generally, of determining for himself whether the indictment is good or bad. He is unfamiliar with the rules of evidence. Left without the aid of counsel he may be put on trial without a proper charge, and convicted upon incompetent evidence, or evidence irrelevant to the issue or otherwise inadmissible. He lacks both the skill and knowledge adequately to prepare his defense, even though he had a perfect one. He requires the guiding hand of counsel at every step in the proceedings against him. Without it, though he be not guilty, he faces the danger of conviction because he does not know how to establish his innocence. If that be true of men of intelligence, how much more true is it of the ignorant and illiterate, or those of feeble intellect. If in any case, civil or criminal, a state or federal court were arbitrarily to refuse to hear a party by counsel, employed by and appearing for him, it reasonably may not be doubted that such a refusal would be a denial of a hearing, and, therefore, of due process in the constitutional sense. The state decisions which refer to the matter, invariably recognize the right to the aid of counsel as fundamental in character. In the light of the facts outlined in the forepart of this opinion . . . we think the failure of the trial court to give them reasonable time and opportunity to secure counsel was a clear denial of due process.

All that it is necessary now to decide, as we do decide, is that in a capital case, where the defendant is unable to employ counsel, and is incapable adequately of making his own defense because of ignorance, feeble mindedness, illiteracy, or the like, it is the duty of the court, whether requested or not, to assign counsel for him as a necessary requisite of due process of law; and that duty is not discharged by an assignment at such a time or under such circumstances as to preclude the giving of effective aid in the preparation and trial of the case. The duty of the trial court to appoint counsel under such circumstances is clear, as it is clear under circumstances such as are disclosed by the record here; and its power to do so, even in the absence of a statute, can not be questioned. Attorneys are officers of the court, and are bound to render service when required by such an appointment.

CONCLUSION: The judgments must be reversed and the causes remanded for further proceedings not inconsistent with this opinion.

Government Appointment of Counsel

As illuminated by the *Powell* decision, America has always taken the right to counsel seriously and particularly for those charged with serious crimes. The colonies rejected English common law that provided the judge, and not retained counsel, represented those accused of felonies. But the question remained after the *Powell* case of who, exactly, did have the right to appointed counsel? Federal courts provided counsel in capital cases and so, too, did many states. In state courts, judges appointed counsel in noncapital cases only if the resulting trial would be so "offensive to the common and fundamental ideas of fairness and right," as held in *Betts v. Brady* (1942).[7] In the *Betts* case, the Court held that due process did not demand the appointment of counsel for defendants who could not afford to hire a lawyer. Then came Clarence Gideon.

Clarence Gideon was charged with breaking and entering at a Florida pool hall in June 1961. An eyewitness identified Gideon as the culprit. At trial facing felony charges, Gideon requested a lawyer and the judge said he could not appoint an attorney to represent Gideon.

> **The court**: Mr. Gideon, I am sorry, but I cannot appoint Counsel to represent you in this case. Under the laws of the State of Florida, the only time the Court can appoint Counsel to represent a Defendant is when that person is charged with a capital offense. I am sorry, but I will have to deny your request to appoint Counsel to defend you in this case.

> **Gideon**: The United States Supreme Court says I am entitled to be represented by Counsel.

Gideon did the best he could representing himself by making arguments, examining witnesses, and professing his innocence. Convicted and sentenced to 5 years in the state penitentiary, Gideon handwrote his own appeal to the U.S. Supreme Court, reprinted in Figure 10.1, stating that, as he understood the Sixth Amendment, he had a right to a lawyer's help at trial.

The U.S. Supreme Court found in Gideon's favor establishing for the first time the right to counsel for anyone facing jail time in *Gideon v. Wainwright* (1963), and if the defendant was indigent and could not afford counsel, the state would have to provide one as a measure of due process.[8] The Court said, "The right of one charged with crime to counsel may not be deemed fundamental and essential to fair trials in some countries, but it is in ours." The *Gideon* holding changed the landscape of criminal defense. Once states had to provide lawyers for all defendants facing jail time, lawmakers had to decide how counsel would be appointed. Studies indicate about three quarters of defendants are represented by court-appointed counsel that comprise

1. Lawyers employed by public defender offices, state or federal;

2. Lawyers in private practice appointed by the court on a case-by-case basis; and

3. Lawyers who contract with the court to represent clients, often for a flat rate fee.

Public defenders share with prosecutors the desire to protect the public—the prosecutor by convicting guilty defendants and the defense counsel by ensuring the government meets its burden fairly and does not convict the innocent or award an excessive punishment to the guilty. Public defenders must take any and all clients who qualify for appointment of counsel based on their financial status. There are obviously more defendants who need representation than there are public defenders to represent them. High-profile litigation and media coverage over

Springboard for Discussion

Recall from our discussion in Chapter 1 about procedural due process where people can accept the outcome of their case more readily if they have been treated with kindness and respect throughout the judicial process. What role does having competent counsel play in procedural justice?

> **Rule of Law: The right to counsel extends to all, rich or poor, citizen or alien, alike.**

Figure 10.1 *Gideon v. Wainwright* SCOTUS Petition

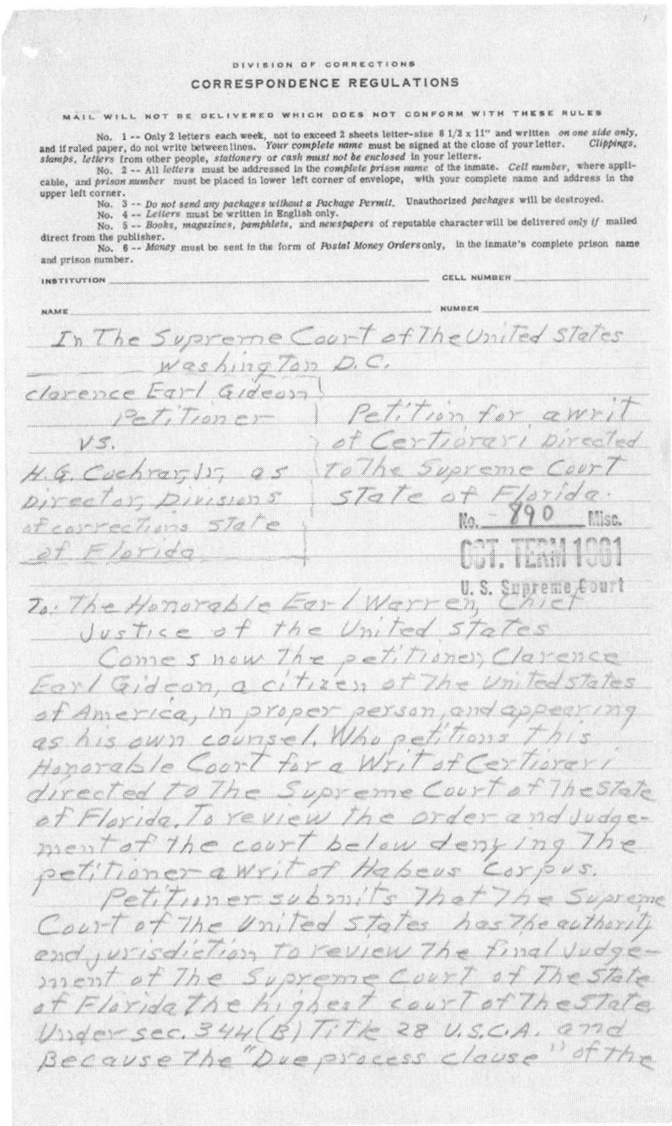
DIVISION OF CORRECTIONS

CORRESPONDENCE REGULATIONS

MAIL WILL NOT BE DELIVERED WHICH DOES NOT CONFORM WITH THESE RULES

No. 1 -- Only 2 letters each week, not to exceed 2 sheets letter-size 8 1/2 x 11" and written *on one side only*, and if ruled paper, do not write between lines. *Your complete name* must be signed at the close of your letter. *Clippings, stamps, letters* from other people, *stationery* or *cash must not be enclosed* in your letters.

No. 2 -- All *letters* must be addressed in the *complete prison name* of the inmate. *Cell number*, where applicable, and *prison number* must be placed in lower left corner of envelope, with your complete name and address in the upper left corner.

No. 3 -- *Do not send any packages without a Package Permit.* Unauthorized *packages* will be destroyed.

No. 4 -- *Letters* must be written in English only.

No. 5 -- *Books, magazines, pamphlets,* and *newspapers* of reputable character will be delivered *only if* mailed direct from the publisher.

No. 6 -- *Money* must be sent in the form of *Postal Money Orders* only, in the inmate's complete prison name and prison number.

INSTITUTION ______ CELL NUMBER ______

NAME ______ NUMBER ______

In The Supreme Court of The United States
Washington D.C.
clarence Earl Gideon
Petitioner | Petition for a writ
vs. | of Certiorari Directed
H.G. Cochran, Jr, as | to The Supreme Court
Director, Divisions | State of Florida.
of corrections State | No. 890 Misc.
of Florida | OCT. TERM 1961
U.S. Supreme Court

To: The Honorable Earl Warren, Chief
Justice of the United States
Comes now the petitioner, Clarence
Earl Gideon, a citizen of The United States
of America, in proper person, and appearing
as his own counsel. Who petitions this
Honorable Court for a Writ of Certiorari
directed to The Supreme Court of The State
of Florida, To review the order and Judge-
ment of the court below denying The
petitioner a writ of Habeus Corpus.
Petitioner submits That The Supreme
Court of The United States has The authority
and jurisdiction to review The final Judge-
ment of The Supreme Court of The State
of Florida the highest court of The State
Under sec. 344(B) Title 28 U.S.C.A. and
Because the "Due process clause" of the

Source: National Archives Catalog. Records of the Supreme Court of the United States, 1772–2007. Appellate Jurisdiction Case Files, 1792–2015. Appellate Jurisdiction Case File *Gideon v. Wainright*.

the number of clients and caseload demands paint a grim picture of the public defender's ability to provide a vigorous defense.[9] Although state funding for prosecutors' offices remains a priority, the right to a speedy trial is often compromised by a lack of funding for state defense counsel. All lawyers have an ethical obligation not to take on too many cases, because a heavy caseload can compromise representation of each client. When public defender offices are at their maximum capacity or there is a conflict of interest in representing codefendants charged with the same crime, the court usually appoints lawyers in private practice to represent the accused. Often, private lawyers make money representing businesses in corporate transactions and may have little to no criminal trial experience. Yet, all lawyers are duty bound to accept the court appointment to represent an indigent client, which, for private counsel, is often at a much lower hourly rate than they can charge their clients in private practice. Many big law firms located in major cities will often dedicate a young associate's time to *pro bono* (for free] representation in indigent defense.

The state of Louisiana has been particularly willful in not providing sufficient funds for indigent defense. In *State v. Peart* (1993), a defendant with multiple charges involving robbery, rape, and murder was appointed counsel for all charges except the murder.[10] The lawyer petitioned the court for funds for investigation and expert witnesses but was denied. In its decision, the Louisiana Supreme Court found that the state had a "general pattern" of "chronic underfunding of indigent defense programs in most areas of the state," and said that relying for a source of money fees collected from criminal and traffic tickets was insufficient. The Court concluded,

> If legislative action is not forthcoming and indigent defense reform does not take place, this Court, in the exercise of its constitutional and inherent power and supervisory jurisdiction, may find it necessary to employ the more intrusive and specific measures it has thus far avoided to ensure that indigent defendants receive reasonably effective assistance of counsel.

The problem has persisted for years unabated. In *Louisiana v. Boyer* (2011) the state court of appeals found that Jonathan Boyer awaiting trial for 7 years from his time of arrest unreasonable, even if part of the delay was due to Boyer asking for continuances.[11] The court said,

> The length of the delay in the instant case was presumptively prejudicial. Defendant was arrested on March 8, 2002, and indicted on June 6, 2002, for first degree murder. The charge was reduced in May 2007 to second degree murder. He was convicted of second degree murder and armed robbery with a firearm on September 29, 2009, more than seven years after his arrest. Defendant was incarcerated the entire time. The largest part of the delay involved the "funding crisis" experienced by the State

of Louisiana. It is the court's duty to identify funds and the state's duty to fund the defense, which may involve large amounts of money in first degree murder cases, particularly where the death penalty is sought, as was in the current case.

The issue with underfunded defense systems is that the quality of representation for the defendants who need it most is often severely compromised. Payment is not only for a lawyer's time preparing and trying the case but also for ancillary costs, such as investigators, postage, gas to interview witnesses, photocopying, and any medical examination required of the defendant, particularly of his mental state to judge competency and other *mens rea* defenses, illustrated by Vermont law reprinted here, in part.

Vermont Statutes Annotated Title 13, §5231 Right to representation, services and facilities

(a) A needy person who is being detained by a law enforcement officer without charge or judicial process, or who is charged with having committed or is being detained under a conviction of a serious crime, is entitled:

    (1) To be represented by an attorney to the same extent as a person having his or her own counsel; and

    (2) To be provided with the necessary services and facilities of representation . . .

(b) The attorney, services and facilities, and court costs shall be provided at public expense to the extent that the person, at the time the court determines need, is unable to provide for the person's payment without undue hardship.

The requirement that the state have to pay for services related to an indigent defendant's preparation for trial was established in the case *Ake v. Oklahoma* (1985). Ake had murdered two people while he was obviously mentally ill.[12] Facing capital murder charges, Ake's lawyer requested a state-funded psychiatric examination, and the court denied the motion. Ake was convicted and sentenced to death, but on appeal the U.S. Supreme Court held the Fourteenth Amendment's Due Process Clause required the state to pay. The Court reasoned that an indigent defendant cannot get a fair trial if the state limits his ability to present a complete defense.

Springboard for Discussion

What are some of the consequences of an underfunded and under-staffed public defender office? Do you think indigent defendants may feel pressured to plead guilty if they fear the state will not fully fund a vigorous defense?

INVOKING THE RIGHT TO COUNSEL

The Sixth Amendment Prevents "Deliberate Elicitation" of Incriminating Statements

As discussed in Chapter 9 on the warnings of the right to remain silent and the right to have counsel present during a custodial interrogation pursuant to the requirements of *Miranda v. Arizona* (1966), the Sixth Amendment right to a lawyer attaches at the beginning of adversarial proceedings between the government and suspect, "whether by way of formal charge, preliminary hearing, indictment, information, or arraignment."[13] Many of the legal rules discussed with respect to *Miranda* (e.g., the request for, or waiver of, counsel) apply equally to the Sixth Amendment. There is a distinction between the Fifth and Sixth Amendment rights to counsel during an investigation before charges are brought against a suspect, but in the field, defendants who have been charged and have a lawyer rarely agree to be interrogated. Typically, once represented by counsel, the burden has been on law enforcement to communicate only through counsel, and not with the defendant directly, or at least notify counsel when police wish to have contact with the client. The Sixth Amendment recognizes the lawyer's role as the intermediary, the "medium" between the government and the public.

Rule of Law: The Sixth
Amendment right to
counsel attaches at the
beginning of adversary
proceedings.

Moreover, relatively recent U.S. Supreme Court decisions have blurred the distinction between when counsel is required under the Fifth or the Sixth Amendments, and even experienced attorneys have a hard time explaining the difference. There is much overlap in the cases discussed here and in Chapter 9. For example, in analyzing the "psychological coercion" of Detective Leaming's "Christian Burial Speech" in getting the defendant Robert Williams to disclose the location of his 10-year-old murder victim, Pamela Powers, the case involved not only what constituted an "interrogation" but also the defendant's Sixth Amendment's right to counsel. Williams, who had escaped from a mental institution, abducted Pamela in Des Moines, Iowa, but he was found 160 miles away in Davenport. Before the detectives retrieved Williams for the ride back to Des Moines, a warrant had been issued and he had been arraigned and spoke to counsel: The adversary process had begun. If police violate a suspect's right to counsel because adversary proceedings have begun, the prosecution cannot use the defendant's incriminating statements to prove his guilt.

In *Massiah v. United States* (1964), the defendant Winston Massiah conspired with others to smuggle drugs into the country.[14] Massiah and others were caught; he was indicted and retained counsel. Without Massiah's knowledge, one of his codefendants began cooperating with the authorities. On behalf of the government pursuant to a plea deal for leniency in sentencing, this codefendant began surreptitiously tape-recording Massiah's incriminating statements. At trial, the tape-recorded statements were introduced over Massiah's objection. The question before the U.S. Supreme Court was whether the government had violated Massiah's right to counsel because he already had an attorney when the informant's tape recording of Massiah occurred. The high Court overturned Massiah's conviction and held that if a suspect has already been indicted for a crime, the government cannot "deliberately elicit" incriminating information from the defendant. In contrast, if police merely place an informant in the defendant's cell who passively listens while the accused makes incriminating statements, there is no Sixth Amendment violation when the informant discloses what he has heard to the police. It is important to remember that the constitutional restrictions concerning search, seizure, and confessions apply only to the government and its agents, including informants and others working on the government's behalf; the restrictions do not apply to private citizens.[15] Because Detective Leaming's burial speech "deliberately elicited" from Williams incriminating information, his Sixth Amendment right to counsel was violated and his conviction overturned.[16]

If the right to counsel attaches only by reading the *Miranda* warnings, a different analysis applies. The Court created the *Miranda* warnings to prevent police officer misconduct in pressuring suspects to confess. Typically, a suspect receives warnings per *Miranda* when he is under suspicion of committing a crime and before any charges have been brought or court proceedings begun. Legal scholar James Tomkovicz explains the difference between the Sixth Amendment's constitutional basis for the exclusionary rule under *Massiah* versus the prophylactic measures of the exclusionary rule under *Miranda*:

> *Massiah* exclusion is akin to the suppression of statements under the Due Process and Self-Incrimination Clauses. Like those two guarantees, the Sixth Amendment safeguards an interest in not being convicted as a result of government methods deemed unfair by our Constitution. All three provisions [Fourth, Fifth and Sixth Amendments] are violated—and trials are unfair—when the evidentiary products of those methods are used to convict. When the state's pretrial conduct is of a sort that would be forbidden at trial, all three guarantees are enforced by constitutional rights to exclusion, not judicially developed exclusionary rules or remedies designed to prevent future wrongs or to guard against risks of present wrongs.[17]

In sum, Tomkovicz is saying that the exclusion of evidence obtained in violation of a Sixth Amendment right to counsel is based on the constitutional guarantees of due process and a right to a fair trial, while excluding evidence obtained in violation of the judge-made *Miranda* rule to give warnings is done so judges can punish and deter police misconduct.

There is one more significant difference to note here. Unlike the right to counsel under the *Miranda* decision, the Sixth Amendment right to counsel is "offense specific," which means that if the suspect is arraigned or indicted for drugs, officers cannot ask questions about drugs but can ask questions about other crimes, such as murder, that they believe the suspect has committed, as held in *Texas v. Cobb* (2001).[18] Cobb had confessed to committing a burglary but denied any involvement in the disappearance from the home of a woman and child. Cobb retained counsel for the burglary, and when his father notified police that Cobb had confessed to killing the victims, officers came to interrogate Cobb. Cobb waived his rights, confessed, was convicted, and was sentenced to death. On appeal, he argued that because he had counsel for the burglary and the murders were part of the same course of criminal conduct, his right to an attorney had been violated. The high Court disagreed and found the Sixth Amendment right to counsel "offense specific." The test to determine whether a continuing course of conduct will result in one or many different offenses, courts look to the elements of each offense and the statutes to prosecute each. If the conduct fits different statutory definitions of crime, they are not the same offense.[19] In the chapter-opening case study, it was permissible for officers to ask Gary questions about the murder, because he had an attorney for the drug-based probation violation only; these were two, distinct and separate crimes.

What follows here informs the student of the law separating the amendments with respect to the right to counsel but focuses on what the criminal justice professional must know to do his or her job properly, from a courtroom perspective. Typically, the difference focuses on

1. Whether the suspect's status has changed by being charged with a crime;

2. Whether law enforcement can use an informant to elicit incriminating information from the suspect, once charged; and

3. Whether the suspect is in custody.

Analyzing the right to counsel is often intertwined with the right to be free from compelled self-incrimination. If the suspect is not subject to custodial interrogation and, instead, is walking about freely on the streets, courts will presume the suspect could always walk away from police-initiated contact when approached for an interview.

Figure 10.2 illustrates the differences between the Fifth and Sixth Amendment rights to counsel.

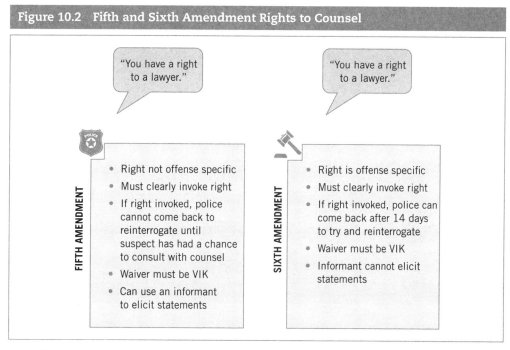

Figure 10.2   Fifth and Sixth Amendment Rights to Counsel

"You have a right to a lawyer."

"You have a right to a lawyer."

FIFTH AMENDMENT

- Right not offense specific
- Must clearly invoke right
- If right invoked, police cannot come back to reinterrogate until suspect has had a chance to consult with counsel
- Waiver must be VIK
- Can use an informant to elicit statements

SIXTH AMENDMENT

- Right is offense specific
- Must clearly invoke right
- If right invoked, police can come back after 14 days to try and reinterrogate
- Waiver must be VIK
- Informant cannot elicit statements

Icon credits: © iStock.com/Olga Kashurina, © iStock.com/SergeiKorolko.

Note: VIK = voluntary, intelligent, and knowing.

Invoking and Waiving the Right to Counsel

Counsel is appointed usually at the defendant's first appearance to hear the charges he's facing. On the filing of a financial disclosure form, the judge determines that the defendant is indigent and, therefore, eligible for state-funded counsel. Once the adversarial process has begun and a defendant has the right to have counsel at all critical stages of the criminal trial process, the government is then limited in trying to talk or otherwise elicit information from the defendant.

> **Rule of Law: To invoke the right to counsel, the defendant must affirmatively speak.**

Prior to 2009, once a defendant was represented by counsel, police could not attempt to get that defendant to waive his rights and submit to an interview, but the rule changed with the Court's decision in *Montejo v. Louisiana* (2009) below. Jesse Montejo was charged with capital murder in Louisiana, and the court appointed counsel. Officers then took Montejo from jail to look for the murder weapon, after which he wrote a letter of apology to the victim's wife. The letter was introduced against Montejo at trial, and he was convicted and sentenced to death. On appeal, Montejo said because counsel had been appointed, under the law, officers should *not* have approached him to talk. Montejo was correct under the high Court's prior rulings, but in his case before the Court, the Court removed one layer of protection for criminal defendants by overruling *Michigan v. Jackson* (1986), which presumed any statements taken from a defendant represented by counsel who was not present during the interview were involuntary.[20] Today after the *Montejo* decision, until a defendant invokes his right to counsel, the police may initiate contact, give *Miranda* warnings, and see if the defendant will waive his right to counsel and speak to law enforcement.

MONTEJO V. LOUISIANA, 556 U.S. 778 (2009)

Supreme Court of the United States

Justice Scalia delivered the opinion of the Court. (5–4)

FACTS: Petitioner Jesse Montejo was arrested on September 6, 2002, in connection with the robbery and murder of Lewis Ferrari, who had been found dead in his own home one day earlier. Suspicion quickly focused on Jerry Moore, a disgruntled former employee of Ferrari's dry cleaning business. Police sought to question Montejo, who was a known associate of Moore.

Montejo waived his rights under *Miranda v. Arizona* (1966),[21] and was interrogated at the sheriff's office by police detectives through the late afternoon and evening of September 6 and the early morning of September 7. During the interrogation, Montejo repeatedly changed his account of the crime, at first claiming that he had only driven Moore to the victim's home, and ultimately admitting that he had shot and killed Ferrari in the course of a botched burglary. These police interrogations were videotaped.

On September 10, Montejo was brought before a judge for what is known in Louisiana as a "72-hour hearing"—a preliminary hearing required under state law. Although the proceedings were not transcribed, the minute record indicates what transpired: "The defendant being charged

with First Degree Murder, Court ordered No Bond set in this matter. Further, the Court ordered the Office of Indigent Defender be appointed to represent the defendant."

Later that same day, two police detectives visited Montejo back at the prison and requested that he accompany them on an excursion to locate the murder weapon (which Montejo had earlier indicated he had thrown into a lake). After some back-and-forth, the substance of which remains in dispute, Montejo was again read his *Miranda* rights and agreed to go along; during the excursion, he wrote an inculpatory letter of apology to the victim's widow. Only upon their return did Montejo finally meet his court-appointed attorney, who was quite upset that the detectives had interrogated his client in his absence. At trial, the letter of apology was admitted over defense objection. The jury convicted Montejo of first-degree murder, and he was sentenced to death.

ISSUE: ["Whether after the right to counsel has attached and counsel has been appointed, the defendant must take affirmative steps to "accept" the appointment in order to secure the protection of the Sixth Amendment and preclude a police-initiated interrogation."[22]]

HOLDING: [Yes. The defendant must take affirmative steps to invoke the right to counsel.] *Michigan v. Jackson* should be and now is overruled.

REASONING: *Michigan v. Jackson* (1986) held that "if police initiate interrogation after a defendant's assertion, at an arraignment or similar proceeding, of his right to counsel, any waiver of the defendant's right to counsel for that police-initiated interrogation is invalid." Under the rule adopted by the Louisiana Supreme Court, a criminal defendant must request counsel, or otherwise "assert" his Sixth Amendment right at the preliminary hearing, before the *Jackson* protections are triggered. If he does so, the police may not initiate further interrogation in the absence of counsel. But if the court on its own appoints counsel, with the defendant taking no affirmative action to invoke his right to counsel, then police are free to initiate further interrogations provided that they first obtain an otherwise valid waiver by the defendant of his right to have counsel present.

This rule would apply well enough in States that require the indigent defendant formally to request counsel before any appointment is made, which usually occurs after the court has informed him that he will receive counsel if he asks for it. That is how the system works in Michigan, for example, whose scheme produced the factual background for this Court's decision in *Michigan v. Jackson*. Jackson, like all other represented indigent defendants in the State, had requested counsel in accordance with the applicable state law.

But many States follow other practices. In some two dozen, the appointment of counsel is automatic upon a finding of indigency and in a number of others, appointment can be made either upon the defendant's request or *sua sponte* [on its own] by the court. Nothing in our *Jackson* opinion indicates whether we were then aware that not all States require that a defendant affirmatively request counsel before one is appointed; and of course we had no occasion there to decide how the rule we announced would apply to these other States.

The Louisiana Supreme Court's answer to that unresolved question is troublesome. The central distinction it draws—between defendants who "assert" their right to counsel and those who do not—is exceedingly hazy when applied to States that appoint counsel absent request from the defendant. How to categorize a defendant who merely asks, prior to appointment, whether he will be appointed counsel? Or who inquires, after the fact, whether he has been? What treatment for one who thanks the court after the appointment is made? And if the court asks a defendant whether he would object to appointment, will a quick shake of his head count as an assertion of his right?

To the extent that the Louisiana Supreme Court's rule also permits a defendant to trigger *Jackson* through the "acceptance" of counsel, that notion is even more mysterious: How does one affirmatively accept counsel appointed by court order? An indigent defendant has no right to choose his counsel, *United States v. Gonzalez-Lopez* (2006),[23] so it is hard to imagine what his "acceptance" would look like, beyond the passive silence that Montejo exhibited.

It is worth emphasizing first what is *not* in dispute or at stake here. Under our precedents, once the adversary judicial process has been initiated, the Sixth Amendment guarantees a defendant the right to have counsel present at all "critical" stages of the criminal proceedings. Interrogation by the State is such a stage.[24] Our precedents also place beyond doubt that the Sixth Amendment right to counsel may be waived by a defendant, so long as relinquishment of the right is voluntary, knowing, and intelligent.[25]

[A] defendant who does not want to speak to the police without counsel present need only say as much when he is first approached and given the *Miranda* warnings. At that point, not only must the immediate contact end, but "badgering" by later requests is prohibited. If that regime suffices to protect the integrity of "a suspect's voluntary choice not to speak outside his lawyer's presence" before his arraignment, it is hard to see why it would not also suffice to protect that same choice after arraignment, when Sixth Amendment rights have attached. And if so, then *Jackson* is simply superfluous.

CONCLUSION: In sum, when the marginal benefits of the *Jackson* rule are weighed against its substantial costs to the truth-seeking process and the criminal justice system, we readily conclude that the rule does not "pay its way" *United States v. Leon* (1984)[26] [and the *Jackson* precedent is overturned].

The significance of the *Montejo* decision is to conflate the Fifth and Sixth Amendment rights to counsel. Prior to *Montejo*, if the suspect had counsel, whether by hiring a lawyer or the court appointing counsel, officers could not approach the suspect in an effort to have the suspect waive his right to counsel and talk to police. After *Montejo*, even if a suspect has counsel, officers can approach the suspect and attempt to get him to waive his right to counsel and speak. Presumably, the opportunity to approach the suspect lasts up until the time of trial. For a defendant in custody for whom the Sixth Amendment right to counsel has attached and been asserted, if the police try and interview him and he refuses, police must wait 14 days before they can come back and ask the defendant to waive his rights and speak (*Maryland v. Shatzer*, 2010).[27] Similar to the reasoning in the *Montejo* case, the high Court has said if people do not wish to speak to the police, they need only say so and decline the invitation. In the chapter-opening case study, Gary was in prison and represented by counsel when he initially refused to speak with police. When the officers returned 3 weeks later and Gary confessed, he was left without a viable claim that the officers violated his right to counsel.

In most cases, officers are giving *Miranda* warnings when they approach defendants as the mechanism for defendants to waive their rights and talk. The high Court said in *Patterson v. Illinois* (1997), a waiver of the right to counsel under *Miranda* was equally sufficient for waiver of the Sixth Amendment right to counsel.[28] Waiver must be VIK (voluntary, intelligent, and knowing); that is, the person must be aware of the purpose of the rights' protections and understand the consequences of giving up those protections, such as anything they say can be used against them in a court of law. But *Miranda* is a prophylactic right, protecting people from the overbearing method of an interrogation so they do not feel compelled to confess. Waiving counsel under the Sixth Amendment has implications beyond interrogation, as it protects rights before, during, and after trial.

THE CRIMINAL CASE

Venue

The U.S. Constitution and many state constitutions provide that a criminal trial shall be held in the state, district, or county where the crime occurred. The rationale for trying the case in the place where the crime was committed ensures that the people most affected in the community have a chance to see justice served and the defendant can have access to witnesses and evidence that are geographically close by. In the founding days of the Republic, when the colonies were still under British rule, Parliament revived a law that allowed a colonist accused of treason to be brought back to England for trial. Faced with the prospect of defending themselves away from the emotional and financial support of their families, the colonists protested. As one legal scholar noted, "For any accused, trial at a distant location would be inconvenient and expensive. For an accused of limited means, trial at a distant location could, in effect, mean a complete inability to present a defense to a charge."[29] Author Andrew Leipold has stated that this turmoil "led to the vicinage [neighborhood, near dwelling] provision in the Sixth Amendment, mandating that the jury be drawn from the 'State and district' where the crime occurred."[30]

Often judges hold evidentiary hearings before a jury is selected to allow both sides to introduce evidence in the form of opinion polls or newspaper stories that indicate media saturation about the case has tainted the local jury pool. In this situation, potential jurors may already believe the defendant is guilty and ignore the presumption of innocence because of the "facts" of the case they have learned through the newspapers and television coverage. This happened in the Missouri case of Kenneth Baumruk, who shot and killed his wife in a St. Louis County courthouse. Baumruk filed a motion to change venue away from St. Louis, but the trial judge said no. Baumruk was later tried on capital murder charges for that killing in the very same courthouse where the shooting occurred. Finding that trying the defendant at the crime scene was unconscionable, the court awarded Baumruk a new trial, where he was found guilty of first-degree murder and, again, sentenced to death. In November 2014, Baumruk died in prison, awaiting execution.

> **Rule of Law:** The rule of venue mandates that the trial take place in the district where the crime occurred.

In the chapter-opening case study, Gary's motion for a change of venue was likely properly denied, because negative press does not necessarily rise to the level of anti-defendant saturation to completely bias the entire jury pool (see discussion in Chapter 2 about Boston Marathon bomber Dzhokhar Tsarnaev's unsuccessful change of venue motion).

MISSOURI V. BAUMRUK, 85 S.W.3D 644 (2002)

Supreme Court of Missouri

Justice Wolff delivered the opinion of the court.

FACTS: On May 5, 1992, Kenneth Baumruk and his wife, Mary, were scheduled for a hearing in the St. Louis County circuit court for [marriage] dissolution of marriage. Baumruk carried two .38 caliber handguns in his brief case to court that day. Before the scheduled hearing, the attorney for Baumruk's wife, Scott Pollard, discovered that he had a conflict of interest because he had represented [Kenneth] Baumruk in a previous dissolution. Judge Hais decided to make a record in open court and determined that the case would proceed only if both Mary and Kenneth Baumruk waived the conflict.

After Judge Hais administered the oath to Mary and Kenneth Baumruk, Pollard examined Mary regarding the conflict, and she stated that she wanted Pollard to remain as her attorney. Baumruk then reached into his brief case and retrieved the two handguns, stood and shot Mary in the neck. Baumruk turned toward Pollard, shooting him in the chest. He then shot [his own] attorney [Garry] Seltzer in the chest and, when Seltzer turned to run, Baumruk shot him in the back. Next, Baumruk walked around the counsel table, put the gun near his wife's head and shot her again, killing her. Judge Hais escaped through the door behind his bench as Baumruk shot at him and pursued him.

As Baumruk proceeded down the hall outside of the courtroom, bailiff Fred Nicolay pushed a clerk and two attorneys into another judge's chambers and closed and locked the door. Baumruk then shot Nicolay in the shoulder and ran out into the hall. Baumruk then shot at a police officer and then shot and wounded a security officer. Police officers in the courthouse fired weapons at Baumruk, hitting him nine times. Two of the wounds were to his head. St. Louis media provided extensive coverage of the incident, describing it as a "rampage," "shooting spree" and "mayhem" that "terrorized hundreds of people." In the media reports, several hundred citizens filled the streets around the courthouse, and more gazed down on the scene from their office windows. Quotes in the media compared the scene to a fire fight in Vietnam. Hundreds were reported to have watched paramedics wheel Baumruk and the victims from the courthouse to ambulances.

After the shooting, the St. Louis County courthouse, which previously had not had metal detectors and other extensive security, received immediate attention. The number of security guards was doubled and metal detectors were installed. Media coverage, which was massive, centered not only on the shootings, but also on domestic violence, concealed weapons, and the fears of domestic relations lawyers and clients. Several years after the incident, a poll indicated that approximately 70% of the county residents still remembered Baumruk's shootings at the courthouse. [In 1998, after much legal wrangling over Baumruk's competency to stand trial due to his brain injury,] the St. Louis County prosecutor obtained an 18-count indictment that included murder in the first degree in the death of Mary Baumruk. [Baumruk filed a motion for a change of venue].

ISSUE: [Was it an abuse of discretion by the judge in St. Louis County not to grant Baumruk's change of venue motion?]

HOLDING: [Yes. Baumruk's motion to change venue should have been granted.]

REASONING: Whether to grant or deny a change of venue is within the discretion of the trial court. That ruling will not be disturbed unless it was a clear abuse of discretion. This discretion is abused when the record shows that the inhabitants of the county are so prejudiced against the defendant that a fair trial cannot occur in that county. However, the question is not whether the community remembers the case but whether the actual jurors of the case have fixed opinions such that they could not judge impartially whether the defendant was guilty. There must be a "pattern of deep and bitter prejudice" or a "wave of public passion" such that the seating of an impartial jury is impossible. A change of venue is required when it is necessary to assure the defendant a fair and impartial trial.

Six years after the shootings, in 1998, and three years before Baumruk's trial, a poll conducted by political scientist Dr. Kenneth Warren found that about 70% of St. Louis County residents remembered the shooting incident that occurred at the courthouse. Dr. Warren's 1998 poll found that, of those who had heard about the shootings, over 80% said that Baumruk was definitely guilty and about 18% indicated that he was "probably guilty." Although the poll was conducted three years before the 2001 trial, most of its findings are consistent with the examination of prospective jurors when the case was brought for trial. Sixty-three of the 99 people who appeared for jury service said they had heard about the case in the

(Continued)

(Continued)

media. Eight of the 12 jurors who ultimately sat on Baumruk's jury remembered the incident. One of the jurors acknowledged that, as a result of the media reports, he believed Baumruk was guilty.[31]

This required sense or appearance of neutrality is illustrated by *Turner v. Louisiana* (1965), where two key witnesses for the state also served as the bailiffs attending the jury during the three-day trial. Even though the bailiffs assured the judge that they had not communicated with the jurors about the case, the Court found such an association between the jurors and two key prosecution witnesses, especially when those witnesses were deputy sheriffs, was wrong and undermined the basic guarantees of trial by jury. This is not just a pretrial publicity, improper venue case. At its core, this case raises a serious question as to the "impartiality of the adjudicator" because of the environment in which the trial was held. The jurors were aware that the courtroom in which they sat was the same as the crime scene and that the building in which they entered every day of trial was the scene of the terrifying events. The prosecutor emphasized the point, appealing to "the citizens of this county" to punish Baumruk "for what he did in this courthouse."

Jurors cannot be asked to place themselves in the shoes of the victims. Here, the jurors arrived at the courthouse and entered through metal detectors that had been installed as a direct result of Baumruk's shooting spree. Jurors walked the same halls and used the same elevators, stairwells, and escalators that were used by escaping victims. The trial was held in a courtroom nearly identical to the courtroom that was the scene of the crime. The jurors, in effect, sat at the murder scene while determining guilt or innocence and the penalty to be imposed. The right to jury trial guarantees a fair trial by a panel of impartial, "indifferent" jurors. *Irvin v. Dowd* (1961).[32] Failure to give the accused a fair hearing violates the minimal standards of due process. The verdict must be based on the evidence that is developed at trial regardless of the heinousness of the crime or the apparent guilt of the offender. This Court's constitutional duty, as set forth in decisions of the United States Supreme Court and this Court, is to assure that a defendant receives a fair and impartial trial. No such assurance is possible where the jurors were influenced by pretrial publicity and by the atmosphere of the trial setting. The jurors, for the entire duration of their service, were invited to relive Baumruk's reign of terror and to identify with his victims at the very place where the events took place.

CONCLUSION: The judgment is reversed, and the case is remanded with instruction to the trial court to grant the change of venue.

APPLYING THE LAW TO THE FACTS

Should the Venue Be Changed?

The Facts: Sam Sheppard was a physician charged in 1954 with murdering his wife, Marilyn. Before trial, many damaging news stories were published confirming community suspicions that the doctor was guilty. Newspapers also printed the names of prospective jurors, who began to receive mail about the case. Three months before trial, a televised inquest into the cause of Marilyn Sheppard's death was held in a school gymnasium in front of hundreds of people. Sheppard was convicted. Should the court have granted Sheppard's change of venue motion?

The Law: Yes. The appeals court granted Sheppard's *habeas corpus* petition granting him a new trial because his due process rights were violated by the extensive local negative pretrial publicity.[33]

The Right to Control the Criminal Case

The Right to Self-Represent at Trial

The Sixth Amendment gives the right to counsel, but what if a defendant wants to represent herself—is that right guaranteed by the Constitution? The Supreme Court held in *Faretta v. California* (1975), that although not explicitly stated, the Sixth Amendment does confer such a right on the defendant.[34] The law favors granting of the right, but the court must establish that the defendant is aware of what she is doing and aware of what she is giving up by representing herself. Like a guilty plea colloquy where the judge and defendant engage in a conversation to ensure the defendant is making certain choices affecting his constitutional rights voluntarily, intelligently, and knowingly (VIK), there is a colloquy before granting a defendant's right to represent herself. The factors that the court examines before granting the defendant the **right to self-representation** are

> **Rule of Law:** The defendant, and not the lawyer, has the ultimate control over important decisions in her case.

1. The timing of the request,

2. Whether the request was made to delay the case,

3. Whether the case is so complicated that assistance of a trained lawyer is required, and

4. Whether the defendant is mentally incompetent and incapable of legally waiving the right to counsel.

In a 2015 hate-crime case that gripped the nation, Dylann Roof, who participated in Bible study at a historically Black church, shot and killed nine parishioners and wounded two others. You will recall from Chapter 2, a death-penalty trial is bifurcated and conducted in two stages: the first to determine guilt and the second to determine the sentence limited to death or life without parole. Roof was found guilty of 33 charges related to the shooting. Prior to the beginning of the sentencing phase, Roof insisted on representing himself. Roof had well-documented conflict with his attorneys and complained in writing to the federal prosecutors that his counsel were the "sneakiest people I ever met" for wanting to introduce mental health evidence in mitigation at his trial. Figure 10.3 shows the first page of his letter.

Figure 10.3   Dylann Roof's Handwritten Letter to the Prosecutors

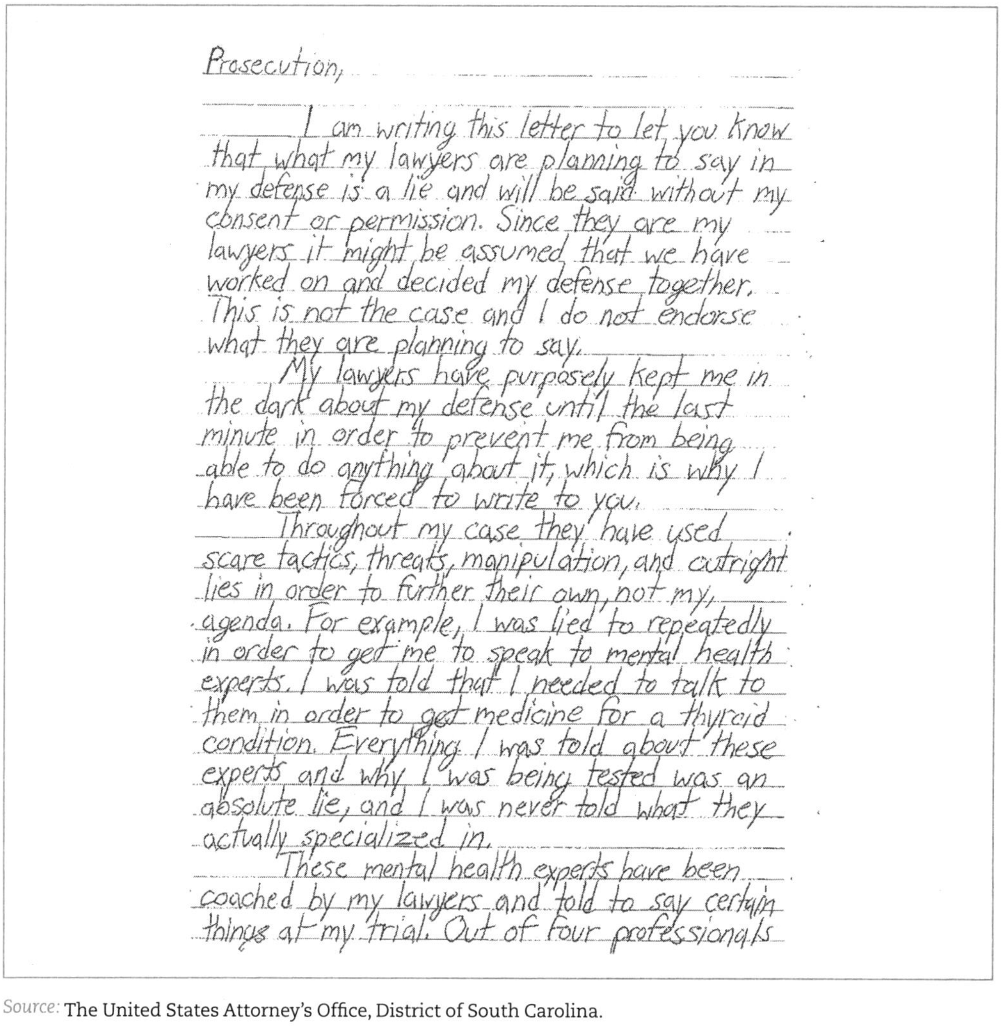

Source: The United States Attorney's Office, District of South Carolina.

CHAPTER 10 • THE SIXTH AMENDMENT   289

To determine whether Roof understood the risk of representing himself, the colloquy illustrates the four factors the judge examined before granting Roof's wish to forego counsel. The judge ultimately granted Roof's request and allowed Roof's attorneys to act as standby counsel for Roof to consult during the courtroom proceedings.

Colloquy Between Judge Richard Gergel and Dylann Roof

January 2, 2017 Charleston, South Carolina

JUDGE: Mr. Roof, you and I — I end up asking you a lot of questions. Some of these you may have heard before. But I think it's important to establish your understanding of things. Let's — one of the issues here is, are you competent to stand trial, and there is another issue of whether you are competent to self-represent. Even though you are, you understand you have a choice. Even if you are competent to self-represent, you recognize you have the right to have counsel. You understand that, don't you?[35]

ROOF: Yes.

JUDGE: And I know from listening to those videotapes that your grandfather and your parents, both of them have urged you to allow Mr. Bruck to continue to represent you, correct?

ROOF: Yes.

JUDGE: And how many times have I told you that? Too many to count, huh?

ROOF: Yes.

JUDGE: But I've also told you that I respect your constitutional right to self-represent if that is what you want to do, and I view it, as I've said many times, as a bad decision, but a bad decision you have a right to make. You do understand you have a right to counsel, do you not, sir?

ROOF: Yes, I understand.

JUDGE: And you understand that if you changed your mind, Mr. Bruck is in a position to immediately resume representing you. You understand that, don't you?

ROOF: Yes.

JUDGE: And I've told you many times that though I know you have differences with Mr. Bruck because you have goals different than him in some ways — Dr. Ballenger described those, I think, very ably. There is no doubt — I just want to share my view — there is no doubt that he wants to help you. It is very clear to me he wants to help you. And it is also clear to me that you are better served with the jury hearing all the evidence. And that evidence is not just the mental health evidence, but the — for instance, the evidence of Father John, who has met with you 100 hours, who says why you have hope. That is one of the mitigating factors that has been asserted that you may change your views. That's your decision. I just was very moved by Father John and his devotion to come see you for all those hours; and, you know, I can't make you call him as a witness, but perhaps you could work out something where he could testify in areas even if you self-represent that might allow the jury to hear from him. Do you continue to have your view that you wish to waive your right to counsel and to self-represent? Does that continue to be your view?

ROOF:	Yes.
JUDGE:	And today is the 2nd, so we are running out of time here. You are confident that is your view that you wish to self-represent? [**Factor 1: the timing of the request; Factor 2: whether the request was made to delay the case**]
ROOF:	Yes.
JUDGE:	And you clearly are asking me to allow you to continue your self-representation; is that right?
ROOF:	Yes.
JUDGE:	You understand, of course, as we have talked about before, that Mr. Bruck has a great deal more experience than you do in handling capital cases. You understand that?
ROOF:	Yes.
JUDGE:	And he has been highly successful in saving defendants from the death penalty. You understand that? [**Factor 3: Whether a case is so complicated that assistance of a trained lawyer is required**]
ROOF:	Yes.
JUDGE:	Now, I know you have talked to your family. You talked to Mr. Bruck and others. You've gotten the — the advice from me. Have you weighed all that advice very carefully?
ROOF:	Yes.
JUDGE:	You have thought about it hard?
ROOF:	Yes.
JUDGE:	This is not a rash decision on your part, is it?
ROOF:	No.
JUDGE:	But you wish to waive your right to counsel and to self-represent, no ifs, ands, or buts; is that right?
ROOF:	That's right . . . .
JUDGE:	Dr. Ballenger described that your primary goal was not surviving the death penalty itself, but to preserve your own view regarding why you committed these crimes. Did he get that right?
ROOF:	Yes, he got that part right. And he also talked about preserving a reputation.
JUDGE:	Yes.
ROOF:	And I would like to comment on that if I could.
JUDGE:	Please do.
ROOF:	I told you I think at the last competency hearing that I don't actually have a reputation to preserve because nobody likes me, including other white nationalists, but in my view, what my lawyers wanted to do is — I have like a corpse of a reputation, and they want to burn it. You see, they just want to — I already don't have a reputation, and then they just want to make it worse. So it's not really about preserving a reputation.

(Continued)

(Continued)

JUDGE:	But you understand — and I know because I recognize — I did this intentionally this morning. I want to make it clear to you the content of this hearing is going to be made public. I mean, I don't want you to think, "Oh, if I just don't have a lawyer, it will all be kept a secret." . . . I wanted you to have a chance to tell the jury what you wish and not to hear it secondhand. You understand that?
ROOF:	Yes . . .
JUDGE:	. . . Did Dr. Ballenger [mental health professional who evaluated Roof to determine if Roof were competent to stand trial] get it right that you were trying to commit the most outrageous crime you could?
ROOF:	Yes, that's right.
JUDGE:	And you could see how a jury might react to that?
ROOF:	Yes, I can see it.
JUDGE:	Now, you made a decision not to offer witnesses in the sentencing phase. Would you do this for me: Would you meet with Father John one more time and see if you can't at least talk to him about — y'all might get somewhere where you might consider offering his testimony? . . .
JUDGE:	Okay. I just think it should not — withstanding your differences on other issues — that is not a mental health issue, you know. It's a different issue. You — and the issue of whether you are going to examine or cross-examine witnesses, you know you have the right to do that, correct?
ROOF:	Right. And I — I intend to cross-examine the witnesses from the jail, but not the victim impact witnesses. That's my —
JUDGE:	Because you think that would be counterproductive?
ROOF:	Yes, and I just couldn't do it.
JUDGE:	But in terms of — for instance, Agent Hamski might testify. Is it possible you would cross-examine him?
ROOF:	It would depend on what he said.
JUDGE:	You are not eliminating other witnesses who may testify other than the victim witnesses?
ROOF:	No.
JUDGE:	And your present plan, though you can change, is to make an opening and closing statement?
ROOF:	(Nodding.)
JUDGE:	Is that correct?
ROOF:	That's right.
JUDGE:	Standby counsel had also thought about having family members testify. You don't wish to have any family members testify?
ROOF:	Absolutely not.

JUDGE:	How about prison officials to talk about good behavior in the jail?
ROOF:	No.
JUDGE:	You don't want them?
ROOF:	No.
JUDGE:	You recognize that in a death penalty case one advantage the defendant has is he only needs one juror not to vote for death. Do you understand that?
ROOF:	Yes, I understand.
JUDGE:	And that is why usually defendants defer to their lawyers who look for opportunities to persuade one or more jurors, and you recognize, Mr. Roof, I take it, that by eliminating certain witnesses, you may be reducing the risk you could get that one vote. Do you understand that? **[Factor 3: Case complexity explained]**
ROOF:	Yes, I understand.
JUDGE:	And though you understand that, why do you insist on not offering that mental health evidence? **[Factor 4: Whether the defendant is incompetent and therefore cannot VIK waive the right to counsel]**
ROOF:	Because it's all a bunch of lies, and just like I refuted everything to Dr. Ballenger, I could pick those reports apart all day long. It's just the basic issues that it's not true other than the ones that I agreed to, social anxiety, and like I said, I think — I read the DSM avoidant personality disorder. I think I absolutely have that. My point is I am not opposed to a diagnosis if it's true. I'm opposed to an untrue diagnosis.
JUDGE:	Dr. Ballenger describes you as — a predominant explanation for your difficulties with your lawyers and your view about not offering mental health evidence is that you really are not ashamed of what you did. You are proud of what you did.
ROOF:	Right. And that was putting words in my mouth. I think that is a little bit —
JUDGE:	You tell me the proper words.
ROOF:	Well, I mean I'm not going to say that is necessarily wrong. I just think it's a little bit strong. To say "proud" is a little bit —
JUDGE:	You don't deny it?
ROOF:	Right.
JUDGE:	You are not ashamed of it?
ROOF:	Right.
JUDGE:	You are not remorseful about it?
ROOF:	Right.
JUDGE:	You avow yourself to a political prisoner like a Muslim Jihadist in Israel. Is that a fair analogy?

(Continued)

(Continued)	
ROOF:	Or anywhere.
JUDGE:	Or anywhere. Is that a fair analogy?
ROOF:	Yes, that is fair.
JUDGE:	And because your lawyers don't wish to offer that view, and you do, is that a major point of your differences with your counsel?
ROOF:	Well, see, that is the thing. It's not — I'm not necessarily intending to offer that view. It's just — I'm not sure. It's just — I'm not planning on saying that. That's what I'm saying.
JUDGE:	Okay. But in terms of the differences with your lawyers, you don't want the explanation of why you went into the Emanuel Church to be that you were mentally ill?
ROOF:	That's right.
MR. BRUCK [Court-appointed defense counsel]:	If Your Honor please, I would ask the defendant's answers to the questions, the affirmative answers about being proud or not having remorse, those be stricken on the grounds of they are beyond the scope of the competency evaluation. I understand why the Court asked them.
JUDGE:	I'm asking because they could go to competency issues, because what you have attributed, Mr. Bruck, to be signs of mental illness, Dr. Ballenger, the Court's examiner, has expressed they are based upon Mr. Roof's political views, and I sought to confirm those. Because they are not what I would normally encounter or you, I needed to confirm that. I respectfully deny your request to strike those. I think they are appropriate to ask.
MR. BRUCK:	If I may place on the record part of the basis of my objection is that there is no Fifth Amendment protection at a competency hearing; and therefore, the protection is limited.
JUDGE:	You see, you make it difficult. You bring a competency challenge, and I have to address it. And I can't take this with one arm tied behind my back. I've got to hear — I have appointed a court examiner who says, "No, it's not mental illness. It is a deep, almost pathological feelings about a certain race of people." And I need to confirm that. And that is what I have just done.
MR. BRUCK:	I wish to note the objection.
JUDGE:	Your objection is noted. I do it with no pleasure.
. . . JUDGE:	Are you confident in your ability to self-represent?
ROOF:	Yes.
JUDGE:	After the closing argument, there will be a closing charge by the Court, and I will submit before the end of the case a proposed closing charge, and I will again mention as I did at the opening charge that you can meet with standby counsel, that they will have a right to prepare documents in response as long as you sign it just like you did before.

	After the closing charge, the jury will deliberate and reach a verdict on the death penalty issue. And as we discussed, one of the potential verdicts you understand is death?
ROOF:	Yes, I understand.
JUDGE:	And you understand the dangers and consequences of self-representation?
ROOF:	Yes, I understand.
JUDGE:	And not withstanding that, you continue to express to this Court your desire to waive counsel and to represent yourself through the balance of this case; is that correct?
ROOF:	That's correct.

At the sentencing phase of his trial, Roof vacillated between representing himself and having his court-appointed counsel represent him. On January 11, 2017, the jury returned a death verdict.

The Right to Assert Innocence at Trial

The status of the law prior to 2018 in terms of a lawyer making decisions and the client agreeing to the lawyer's strategy, particularly in admissions of guilt was stated in the case *Florida v. Nixon* (2004), where Joe Nixon tied his victim to a tree and burned her alive. Nixon confessed and faced the death penalty at trial.[36] Nixon's appointed counsel, given the overwhelming evidence, decided to admit guilt at trial, introduce evidence that Nixon was mentally deranged and plead for mercy to spare his life. When presented with the lawyer's strategy, Nixon neither agreed nor disagreed. After Nixon was convicted and sentenced to death, he claimed ineffective assistance of counsel. The high Court found in the state's favor and defined four important decisions a client gets to make in his case, "whether to plead guilty, waive a jury, testify in his or her own behalf, or take an appeal," and noting that clients and ethical rules typically defer litigation strategy decisions to the lawyer, found Nixon's counsel was not ineffective.

In contrast to the *Nixon* case, in *McCoy v. Louisiana* (2018), defendant Robert McCoy explicitly objected to his lawyer's choice to admit McCoy's guilt in a triple homicide and, like Nixon's attorney, introduced evidence of mental instability and pleaded for mercy to spare his life. When his lawyer admitted McCoy's guilt at trial, McCoy spoke out and complained. He then took the stand and said he was innocent. When McCoy was sentenced to death, he appealed on the grounds that his attorney conceded guilt without McCoy's consent. The U.S. Supreme Court found in his favor, holding that, unlike Nixon who never said yay or nay to his lawyer's strategy of admitting his guilt, McCoy maintained his innocence from the first day to the last, and the lawyer's strategic choices could not override his client's wishes. Read the case excerpt below and see if you agree with the Court's reasoning.

MCCOY V. LOUISIANA, 584 U.S. ___ (2018)

Supreme Court of the United States

Justice Ginsburg delivered the opinion of the Court. (6–3)

FACTS: Petitioner Robert McCoy was charged with murdering his estranged wife's mother, stepfather, and son.

McCoy pleaded not guilty to first-degree murder, insisting that he was out of State at the time of the killings and that corrupt police killed the victims when a drug deal went wrong. Although he vociferously insisted on his

(Continued)

innocence and adamantly objected to any admission of guilt, the trial court permitted his counsel, Larry English, to tell the jury, during the trial's guilt phase, McCoy "committed [the] three murders." English's strategy was to concede that McCoy committed the murders, but argue that McCoy's mental state prevented him from forming the specific intent necessary for a first-degree murder conviction. Over McCoy's repeated objection, English told the jury McCoy was the killer and that English "took [the] burden off of [the prosecutor]" on that issue. McCoy testified in his own defense, maintaining his innocence and pressing an alibi difficult to fathom. The jury found him guilty of all three first-degree murder counts. At the penalty phase, English again conceded McCoy's guilt, but urged mercy in view of McCoy's mental and emotional issues. The jury returned three death verdicts. Represented by new counsel, McCoy unsuccessfully sought a new trial. The Louisiana Supreme Court affirmed the trial court's ruling that English had authority to concede guilt, despite McCoy's opposition.

HOLDING: The Sixth Amendment guarantees a defendant the right to choose the objective of his defense and to insist that his counsel refrain from admitting guilt, even when counsel's experienced-based view is that confessing guilt offers the defendant the best chance to avoid the death penalty.

REASONING: The Sixth Amendment guarantees to each criminal defendant "the Assistance of Counsel for his defence." The defendant does not surrender control entirely to counsel, for the Sixth Amendment, in "grant[ing] to the accused personally the right to make his defense," "speaks of the 'assistance' of counsel, and an assistant, however expert, is still an assistant." *Faretta v. California* (1975). The lawyer's province is trial management, but some decisions are reserved for the client—including whether to plead guilty, waive the right to a jury trial, testify in one's own behalf, and forgo an appeal. Autonomy to decide that the objective of the defense is to assert innocence belongs in this reserved-for-the-client category. Refusing to plead guilty in the face of overwhelming evidence against her, rejecting the assistance of counsel, and insisting on maintaining her innocence at the guilt phase of a capital trial are not strategic choices; they are decisions about what the defendant's objectives in fact are.

Counsel may reasonably assess a concession of guilt as best suited to avoiding the death penalty, as English did here. But the client may not share that objective. He may wish to avoid, above all else, the opprobrium attending admission that he killed family members, or he may hold life in prison not worth living and prefer to risk death for any hope, however small, of exoneration. Thus, when a client makes it plain that the objective of "his defence" is to maintain innocence of the charged criminal acts and pursue an acquittal, his lawyer must abide by that objective and may not override it by conceding guilt.

CONCLUSION: The Court's ineffective-assistance-of-counsel jurisprudence, see *Strickland v. Washington*, 466 U.S. 668, does not apply here, where the client's autonomy, not counsel's competence, is in issue. To gain redress for attorney error, a defendant ordinarily must show prejudice. But here, the violation of McCoy's protected autonomy right was complete when the court allowed counsel to usurp control of an issue within McCoy's sole prerogative. Violation of a defendant's Sixth Amendment-secured autonomy has been ranked "structural" error; when present, such an error is not subject to harmless-error review. McCoy must therefore be accorded a new trial without any need first to show prejudice.

MAKING THE COURTROOM CONNECTION

One of the difficulties in criminal defense is representing a client who may have delusions (false fixed beliefs) about how the crime was committed or how law enforcement has used the client as a scapegoat for other crimes. For instance, Aileen Wournos, who was put to death by the state of Florida in 2001 for killing seven men, believed that law enforcement knew Aileen was committing murder because, in her words, she was a "hitchhiking hooker," and the state allowed her to keep killing to "clean the streets." Law enforcement did, however, justify some of Aileen's paranoia that she was being used by others when some officers sold their rights to the story of their investigation while the investigation was ongoing potentially compromising the investigation to fit their business contracts for a sensational story about Aileen. The problem in representing a delusional client is the client may want the lawyer to advance certain theories at trial that have no basis in reality or prevent the lawyer from introducing evidence of the client's mental infirmity. Ted Kaczynski was on trial in federal court for mailing bombs that killed three and wounded others. Known as the "Unabomber," Kaczynski had lived in a remote cabin in Montana and blamed technology for society's ills. His lawyers wanted to introduce mental illness as a defense, but Ted refused and pleaded guilty to prevent his lawyers from implying he was "crazy." Kaczynski then appealed on the grounds he was "forced" to plead guilty because of the fight with his lawyers. With the *McCoy v. LA* (2018) ruling, the defense counsel must cede to the client's wishes to maintain his innocence.

Ultimately, the defendant must live the consequences of his choices in a criminal case, whether to plead guilty, take a plea bargain, or go to trial. It is his decision to make. In the chapter-opening case study, Gary was found competent to represent himself midtrial, but it is always a risk to act as one's own counsel.

Ineffective Assistance of Counsel

The introduction of requiring a lawyer for all defendants naturally increased the complexity of the litigation. Equality means providing competent counsel. If the attorney's performance before and during trial falls below the standard of a minimally competent attorney, the defendant may have grounds for a successful appeal of his conviction based on a claim of ineffective assistance of counsel. The legal standard that a defendant must meet to prove that his counsel fell below the standard of a reasonable attorney was expressed by the U.S. Supreme Court in *Strickland v. Washington* (1984), where the defendant must show that

1. Counsel's performance was deficient. This requires showing that counsel made errors so serious that counsel was not functioning as the "counsel" guaranteed the defendant by the Sixth Amendment.

2. The deficient performance prejudiced the defense. This requires showing that counsel's errors were so serious as to deprive the defendant of a fair trial, a trial whose result is reliable.

Unless a defendant can meet the dual prongs of *Strickland*, it cannot be said that the conviction resulted from a breakdown in the adversary process that renders the result unreliable.[37]

The law presumes every attorney who passes the bar examination and is admitted to practice in state or federal jurisdiction is qualified to represent clients. However, over the years, the number of death-row inmates found to have exceptionally poor counsel has led many states and the American Bar Association to require a certain level of proficiency and expertise to represent men and women facing the death penalty at trial or on appeal. But defendants typically have a high bar to hurdle in proving their lawyer rendered ineffective assistance of counsel. In one well-known case, a Texas appellate court and the federal Court of Appeals for the Fifth Circuit upheld the death sentence of Calvin Burdine, even though his lawyer slept through substantial portions of the trial.[38] Burdine was on trial for the 1983 killing and robbery of his former roommate W. T. "Dub" Wise. Responding to the public outrage over the appellate courts' ruling that a lawyer who sleeps through a capital murder case is competent counsel, the federal appeals court reheard Burdine's appeal and reversed itself, saying an "unconscious counsel equates to no counsel at all" and holding "a trial is unfair if the accused is denied counsel at a critical stage of his trial," citing *United States v. Cronic* (1984).[39] Burdine eventually pleaded guilty and received three life sentences.

Notably in Burdine's case, his trial lawyer Mr. Cannon had testified at a hearing that he was not sleeping but merely concentrating with his eyes closed. Students should be aware, when a defendant raises a claim counsel was ineffective, the defendant waives the attorney client privilege and the court holds an evidentiary hearing where the attorney gets a chance to respond to the defendant's claim. If the attorney claims that decisions made at trial were part of a

Springboard for Discussion

Imagine you are a defense counsel with a challenging client. You know the law and think you know what is in the best interest of the client, especially in a capital murder case. How would you handle your emotions if your client made certain choices and the case had a negative outcome? Is it enough to realize that the Constitution guarantees the "assistance" of counsel and not the "control" by counsel?

Rule of Law: The defense counsel's performance must be that of a reasonable attorney.

bigger litigation strategy, then courts are reluctant to find he was ineffective. Lawyers are legally ineffective when no reasonable attorney would have made the same or similar choices. For instance, in *Padilla v. Kentucky* (2010), the U.S. Supreme Court held it was ineffective counsel to not warn noncitizen clients of the possible deportation consequences in pleading guilty. That is, in advising a client to accept a plea bargain to plead guilty in exchange for reduced charges or sentence, reasonable attorneys would warn clients who are not U.S. citizens that a guilty plea is a conviction under the law, and convictions typically trigger deportation proceedings.[40] In the chapter-opening case study, Gary's lawyer was ineffective because his performance was deficient because he was high on drugs, and his unwillingness to question any of the state's witnesses likely prejudiced the outcome of Gary's trial, because Gary felt compelled to ultimately represent himself.

The Sixth Amendment's Confrontation Clause

The Sixth Amendment guarantees that "in all criminal prosecutions, the accused shall enjoy the right . . . to be confronted with the witnesses against him." The Confrontation Clause requires the witness to come forward and face the defendant, and the defendant has a right to confront the witness through the mechanism of cross-examination. If the defendant does not have a chance to cross-examine the witness, the witness's statements cannot be used against him. For example, in 2004 Michael Crawford attacked a man who had allegedly tried to rape Crawford's wife. Crawford claimed self-defense, and police took a tape recording of Crawford's wife making a statement that threw into question Crawford's version of events. At trial, the wife refused to testify based on marital privilege, and the prosecutor introduced her tape-recorded statement against her husband. Crawford was convicted, but he won on appeal in *Crawford v. Washington* (2004) where the U.S. Supreme Court said if a witness makes a statement before trial and disappears or is unavailable to testify (Mrs. Crawford had a right to refuse to testify against her husband based on marital privilege), then only if the defendant had actually confronted the witness pretrial will the statement be admissible against him at trial.[41] So, only if Michael Crawford's attorney had cross-examined his wife while making the tape-recorded statement right after the attack would the taped statement been admissible against him at trial. Because Crawford did not have an opportunity to cross-examine his wife at the time she made the tape-recorded statement at the police station, and because she was unavailable at defendant Crawford's trial because she refused to testify, his conviction was overturned for a Confrontation Clause violation.[42] In the chapter-opening case study, Gary's lawyer did not exercise Gary's right to confront witnesses when he refused to question any of the state's witnesses who were testifying against Gary.

> **Rule of Law:**
> **Defendants exercise their Sixth Amendment Confrontation Clause rights by cross-examining witnesses.**

The *Crawford* case changed the legal landscape of Confrontation Clause issues. If a statement or document sought to be introduced against a defendant at trial is "testimony," then such evidence will *not* be admitted unless the defendant had an opportunity to cross-examine the person making the statement or creating the document. If the evidence is "nontestimonial," it is admissible at trial without the defendant having the opportunity to "confront" the witnesses before trial. Table 10.1 gives a summary of *Crawford v. Washington* (2004) and its progeny (cases derived from the original precedent) regarding when, and when not, the Sixth Amendment's Confrontation Clause is violated by the admission of evidence at trial.

Child Witnesses in Sex Abuse Cases. What happens when the witness is too traumatized to come into court and confront the defendant? Does the defendant's Sixth Amendment right to confront witnesses against him outweigh the witness's discomfort in coming into court? The question most often arises in child sexual molestation cases in which the entire dynamic of the abuse is the ultimate control of the child, either by threatening the child if the child discloses the abuse or, in a strange twist, in making the child believe that whatever affection is supplied by the offender will stop, and that the family will dissolve, if the child discloses. To ask the child to come and testify as the defendant "stares down" the child may create problems for the child. In 1988, the United States Supreme Court held that a screen separating the defendant from the

Table 10.1 Summary of *Crawford v. Washington* (2004)

People's Statements

Crawford v. Washington, 541 U.S. 36 (2004) Testimonial evidence requires cross-examination to be admissible at trial	**Confrontation Clause violation** to admit tape recording of wife's inculpatory statement against husband with no opportunity for cross-examination
Davis v. Washington, 547 U.S. 813 (2006) Emergency conversations such as 9-1-1 calls are nontestimonial evidence, which is admissible without cross-examination	**No Confrontation Clause violation** to admit 9-1-1 call at intimate partner violence trial against man charged with assaulting woman where woman failed to testify despite no opportunity to cross-examine her
Giles v. California, 554 U.S. 353 (2008) Prosecution sought to admit 9-1-1 call detailing abuse at murder trial of abuse victim's ex-boyfriend	**No Confrontation Clause violation** if one of the defendant's intents in killing victim was to make her unavailable to testify against him; statement is admissible under the doctrine of forfeiture by wrongdoing
Michigan v. Bryant, 562 U.S. 344 (2011) Police find man who has been shot and who identifies his assailant held statements nontestimonial because of ongoing emergency	**No Confrontation Clause violation** to admit statements of a murder victim identifying his assailant as statements were nontestimonial given the ongoing emergency
Ohio v. Clark, 135 S.Ct. 2173 (2015) Three-year-old boy who identified mother's boyfriend as the source of his injuries admissible	**No Confrontation Clause violation** where boy did not testify at trial but his statements about who abused him admitted at trial because such identification to teachers are nontestimonial because they are not made for the purposes of trial

Laboratory Reports

Melendez-Diaz v. Massachusetts, 557 U.S. 305 (2009)	**Confrontation Clause violation** to admit a lab report documenting a test of submitted drugs without the testimony of the technician who performed that lab analysis
Bullcoming v. New Mexico, 131 S.Ct. 2705 (2011)	**Confrontation Clause violation** to admit surrogate testimony by lab supervisor who did not conduct the lab test for submitted drugs and did not interpret lab results

witness violated the defendant's right to confront the witness face-to-face in *Coy v. Iowa* (1988).[43] But 2 years later in 1990, the Court allowed the use of closed-circuit television to deliver the testimony of a child because the protection of a vulnerable witness was an important government interest. The defendant's rights were protected because he could communicate with his attorney who cross-examined the witness (*Maryland v. Craig*, 1990).[44]

The rationale of the Confrontation Clause is to allow the jury to judge the credibility of the witness. The jury may conclude that a chronic drug addict who has a hard time remembering details is less reliable than a witness who has never used drugs. The ability to conduct cross-examination is critical to expose a witness's weaknesses. But the state does not get to use alternative means of testimony in every child sex abuse case by saying the child would have a hard time testifying in court. The state has to make a showing to the judge, usually before the child testifies and out of the presence of the jury, that the child will suffer severe emotional harm by having to confront the defendant in court. Such evidence can be developed from personal and professional testimony of those who have had contact with the victim and presumably have helped the victim overcome some of the effects of the abuse. Federal law has codified when the court can order the closed-circuit testimony if the child is unable to testify in open court. This can be done when one of the following circumstances is found:

1. The child is afraid of the defendant, specifically because of the threats used to keep sexual abuse secret.

2. The expert testimony establishes that the child would suffer emotional harm from testifying in the presence of the defendant.

3. The child suffers from a possible mental infirmity.

4. The behavior of the defendant or defense counsel makes the child unable to continue testifying in open court.

The defendant's constitutional Confrontation Clause rights are typically superior to any statute designed to protect witnesses. For example, under rape shield statutes enacted to protect sexual assault victims from unnecessary humiliation during cross-examination, one exception to the law is if the defendant's Confrontation Clause rights demand a particular line of questioning (see the discussion about rape shield in Chapter 4).

The Right to Appointed Counsel on Appeal

Recall in the seminal case *Gideon v. Wainwright* (1963), the U.S. Supreme Court held constitutional due process required the state appoint counsel for those who cannot afford an attorney. All other rights a defendant has is largely dependent on a lawyer's advice and counsel. What about after conviction, when the defendant no longer enjoys the presumption of innocence? Does the right of counsel still apply on appeal? The answer is it depends on which appeal we are talking about. In the typical appellate process, once a defendant is convicted, she has one appeal as a matter of right. That is, if convicted of murder in state court, she has a right to appeal to the state's highest court. Beyond that first right to appeal, any other appeal becomes discretionary; that is, the defendant may choose to pursue further appeals or not. The right to counsel attaches only for the first appeal of right.

The U.S. Supreme Court decided that a state must appoint counsel for the first appeal as required under the Fourteenth Amendment, as decided in *Douglas v. California* (1963), because the state has created appellate courts as "an integral part of the . . . system for finally adjudicating the guilt or innocence of a defendant" (*Griffin v. Illinois*, 1956). Therefore, the court system deciding appeals must comply with the Fourteenth Amendment's demands of due process and equal protection. Beyond the first appeal as of right are discretionary appeals and writs of *habeas corpus* where the now-convicted defendant is asking higher courts to review both the trial and first appellate court decisions. Court-appointed counsel is not required beyond the first appeal of right, as held in *Ross v. Moffitt* (1974), because the first appeal is looking at the sufficiency of evidence and possible errors that led to conviction, whereas discretionary appeals and *habeas corpus* petitions are generally examining the legality of the prisoner's incarceration.

SUMMARY

1. Discuss the constitutional foundation of the right to counsel. Historically, America broke from the English common law rule that only judges, and not lawyers, represented those accused of felonies. In *Powell v. Alabama* (1932), decided before the Sixth Amendment had been incorporated to apply to the states, the high Court recognized the appointment of counsel was crucial to meet the Fourteenth Amendment's due process requirement

of a fair trial. In *Gideon v. Wainwright* (1963), the Court extended the right to counsel to those who could not afford to hire a lawyer and required the states fund indigent defense to meet the due process requirement of a fair trial.

2. You will understand how indigent defendants obtain counsel. Defendants who need counsel fill out a financial form establishing their eligibility for appointed counsel. Many states have funded public defender offices dedicated to indigent defense. Private counsel can be appointed by the court to represent indigent clients, and some lawyers contract with the court to provide a set of indigent defense services for a flat fee. Defendants who cannot afford counsel are eligible for a state-funded attorney on their first appeal of right but not further discretionary appeals or *habeas corpus* petitions. Chronic underfunding for indigent defense threatens the quality of representation of the poor.

3. Identify when the right to counsel attaches and the significance of its relationship to *Miranda v. Arizona*. The right to counsel is different under the Fifth Amendment pursuant to *Miranda v. Arizona* (1966), and the Sixth Amendment, with technical legal distinctions that remain confusing for the lay person. *Miranda* is a prophylactic designed to protect suspects from overbearing interrogations. The Sixth Amendment is to protect defendants, once they have been charged, from the government's overbearing prosecutorial tools throughout trial to appeals. One protection is venue selection as in the case of *Missouri v. Baumruk* (2002) where the appeals court held refusing to change the trial venue from the courthouse where the defendant killed his wife and wounded others was an abuse of discretion. Recent changes in the law, specifically in *Montejo v. Louisiana* (2009), now requires a defendant represented by counsel to affirmatively invoke his right to counsel during an attempted custodial interrogation. Should the defendant request counsel, officers may come back and try to reinterrogate after a 14-day break pursuant to the holding in *Maryland v. Shatzer* (2010). If a defendant represented by counsel is not in custody, he is not being "interrogated" and can choose whether or not to speak to officers without the benefit of counsel. Waiver of counsel remains the same under both *Miranda* and the Sixth Amendment, it must be VIK—voluntary (without coercion), intelligent (aware of the consequences of giving up the right), and knowing (knowing what the right protects).

4. You will appreciate how the Sixth Amendment guarantees autonomy to defendants during the criminal trial process. A defendant has a right to self-representation after the court determines through a colloquy that he knows the risks and, if he so chooses, to be represented by competent counsel. To prove ineffective assistance of counsel, the defendant must show his attorney's performance falls below that of a reasonable attorney and such deficient performance altered the outcome of the case against the defendant. Typically, the law defers to the lawyer to make strategic decisions about the conduct of the defense at a criminal trial, but under *McCoy v. Louisiana* (2018), no lawyer may admit guilt over the client's express intent to assert his innocence.

5. Understand how the Sixth Amendment's Confrontation Clause works. The Sixth Amendment's Confrontation Clause, which guarantees the defendant's right to confront witnesses against him through the process of cross-examination, has been expanded by recent U.S. Supreme Court case law. Prior to the high Court's decision in *Crawford v. Washington* (2004), if hearsay statements had some indicia of reliability and the witness was unavailable, the statement could be used against the defendant at trial. Since the *Crawford* decision, hearsay of unavailable witnesses is admissible only if the defendant had an opportunity to cross-examine that witness before he or she became unavailable. The Confrontation Clause does not apply to nontestimonial evidence, such as 9-1-1 calls or a child's report to his teacher that he is being abused. At trial in child abuse cases, certain concessions may be made to accommodate the children who may fear the defendant abuser if the state has shown through expert testimony that the child will suffer mental harm if the child faces the defendant and defense counsel has the opportunity to cross-examine the child.

Go back to the beginning of the chapter and reread the news excerpts associated with the learning objectives. Test yourself to determine if you can understand the material covered in the text in the context of the news.

KEY TERMS AND PHRASES

Confrontation Clause 298
deliberate elicitation 282

first appeal of right 300
ineffective assistance of counsel 297

right to self-representation 289
Sixth Amendment 275

1. Randy and Vonny were co-conspirators involved in a drug distribution conspiracy. Randy was caught by police officers and made a deal that allowed him to remain on the street and act as an informant. Right before the investigation was about to end and Randy's role as an informant was about to be exposed, Randy gave a statement to police detailing his role in the conspiracy, and then he died. At Vonny's trial, the state sought to introduce Randy's statement made to police before he died. On the basis of his Sixth Amendment Confrontation Clause right, what objections, if any, can Vonny make to the admission of Randy's statement? **(ROL: Confrontation Clause)**

2. Nicole and Shania were contemplating robbing the local bank. They purchased handguns and tools to break into the bank's vault. As they approached the bank's entrance, they became afraid and started to run away, but astute police officers noticed their suspicious behavior, chased after the women, and arrested them. The officers notified the prosecutor, who wrote an information charging both women with attempted robbery. The women filled out forms that indicated they were indigent and in need of appointed counsel. They appeared before the judge, who read the charges aloud in court and appointed counsel for each woman. The women were returned to jail and placed in separate cells. Police came to see Shania and asked if she would like to speak to them. They read Shania her *Miranda* rights, but she said nothing, and the officers left. In Nicole's cell, police placed an informant, Ellie. Ellie struck up a conversation with Nicole and asked, "What did you do to get yourself in this mess?" Nicole told Ellie about the plot to rob the bank. Before trial, both women raised claims that their Sixth Amendment right to counsel had been violated. Are they correct? **(ROL: *Montejo* and *Massiah* precedents)**

3. Jackson was private counsel appointed to represent Joey on kidnapping charges. When Joey spoke about the case, he insisted that the victim, Betsy, was secretly in love with him and went with Joey willingly across state lines. Joey had a mental health history for stalking. Betsy told police that Joey had abducted her from a crowded parking lot. Many eyewitnesses had seen Betsy screaming and struggling before Joey forced her into the car and sped away. Jackson thought Joey's best move at trial would be to admit the facts of the case and to hire an expert to inform the jury of Joey's delusions. Joey insisted he was innocent but did not object to Jackson's trial strategy. Jackson asked the court for funds to have Joey psychologically evaluated before trial, but the judge said Jackson had already spent his allotted indigency defense funds, and there was no more state money. At trial, Jackson admitted to the jury that Joey was guilty but asked for mercy based on Joey's medical condition. Joey was convicted and appealed on the basis of ineffective assistance of counsel because Jackson admitted his guilt and because the court refused to pay for medical services. Will Joey win his appeal? **(ROL: *Nixon*, *McCoy*, and *Ake* precedents; ineffective assistance of counsel claims)**

PART IV

THE PERSONAL

Offender-Specific Punishment

11

THE FIRST AMENDMENT AND CRIMINAL LAW

G o to the end of the chapter. Skim the key terms and phrases and read the summary closely. Come back and look at the following news excerpts to focus your reading throughout the chapter to understand First Amendment freedoms and expression protected from criminal punishment. Some speech is not protected by the First Amendment and can be suppressed (censored and kept from the public); this speech includes words that incite violence, pose a clear and present danger, or are obscene. The chapter begins with a hypothetical case study of James, who is at a rally protesting the removal of a statue of Confederate General Robert E. Lee in a Virginia park. Follow James as he encounters the First Amendment principles presented throughout the chapter and connect his activities with the relevant section of text.

WHY THIS CHAPTER MATTERS TO YOU	THE LEARNING OBJECTIVES AS REFLECTED IN THE NEWS
After you have read this chapter: **Learning Objective 1:** You will be able to competently discuss the difference between protected and unprotected speech.	The FBI had received tips from concerned citizens over the content of Louie's shooter Alex Tilghman's YouTube posts, but considered it a matter of free speech. "The caller reported concerns about a YouTube channel associated with the subject, but did not report any potential threat of violence and did not have any knowledge of the subject possessing any weapons. Based on this information, and following our standard protocol, no further investigation was warranted," according to a statement released by the FBI. Tilghman was shot to death by citizens after he opened fire on customers outside Louie's on Lake Hefner [Oklahoma]. (newsok.com, May 29, 2018)
Learning Objective 2: You will understand the significance of symbolic speech and how to achieve public order without suppressing speech and expression.	The NFL and the owners of its 32 teams enacted a new policy that no longer requires players to be on the sideline for the playing of the national anthem before games, but does empower teams to discipline players who protest publicly during that time. The league's new position, the latest development in a controversy that began with Colin Kaepernick kneeling during the anthem in 2016 and became more heated last fall . . . leaves wide discretion to discipline players for acts deemed disrespectful during the anthem. (*Washington Post*, May 24, 2018)
Learning Objective 3: You will be able to properly identify obscenity.	Richard Alan Wellbeloved-Stone pleaded guilty to one count of production of child pornography. Wellbeloved-Stone, a former high school teacher in Charlottesville, was discovered by law enforcement after chatting online with an undercover agent from the United Kingdom about sexually abusing a young child. A search warrant executed at Wellbeloved-Stone's home recovered several images of child pornography produced by Wellbeloved-Stone of at least two young minor victims. (Thai News Service, April 30, 2018)

WHY THIS CHAPTER MATTERS TO YOU	THE LEARNING OBJECTIVES AS REFLECTED IN THE NEWS
Learning Objective 4: You will be able to articulate the legal restrictions on free speech rights in public schools, employment, and prisons.	The lawsuit . . . claims that the boy was disciplined for engaging "in a respectful, silent, and peaceful expression of his political views" by wearing a Firearms Policy Coalition t-shirt to school. The shirt invokes the constitution and themes dating back to the American Revolution, with the words "Don't Tread On Me" and a coiled rattlesnake (familiar elements of the Gadsden flag) flanked by references to the United States of America ("USA") and the Second Amendment ("2A"). According to the plaintiffs, the student's teacher . . . directed him to remove the FPC shirt, claiming that it violated the school's dress code. (ForTraders.com, April 24, 2018)
Learning Objective 5: You will be able to make sense of the limits of a secular government's relationship with religion with respect to criminal law and procedure.	Since 2012, Morris County [NJ] has provided more than $4.6 million to 12 churches in the form of historic preservation grants, a readily available source of money to fix facades, stained glass windows and aging roofs. But a unanimous decision by the New Jersey Supreme Court found that public money could no longer be used by churches, citing a clause in the State Constitution expressly forbidding it, a decision that could reverberate beyond New Jersey and reignite a national debate over the separation of church and state. (*New York Times*, April 24, 2018)

Chapter-Opening Case Study: "Unite the Right" Rally, Charlottesville, Virginia, August 11–12, 2017

James is a White supremacist who has advocated the overthrow of the government. On Friday night, August 11, 2017, James joined a group of friends in Charlottesville, Virginia, to protest the city's planned removal of the statue of Confederate General Robert E. Lee. **(Rule of Law [ROL]: The First Amendment guarantees the right to peaceably assemble.)** Carrying lighted tiki torches replicating the Nazi nighttime rallies during World War II, the crowd burned a cross and chanted "Jews will not replace us," offending many spectators. **(ROL: The First Amendment prohibits the government from engaging in viewpoint discrimination.)** The next day, James and others rallied around General Lee's statue while counterprotesters, including members of Black Lives Matter and Antifa (anti-fascists), screamed and yelled insults and racial epithets at each other. **(ROL: Fighting words are those that inflict injury by their very utterance; unprotected speech.)** Police watched as the groups clashed. From his side of the street, James yelled, "You call it terrorism. I call it patriotism. You hear me? Die! Free speech or die America, you got no safe place." **(ROL: Clear and present danger must incite imminent lawlessness; unprotected speech.)** Heather Heyer was killed when a man drove his car into the crowd. **(ROL: The First Amendment protects hate speech; hate crimes that hurt people are illegal.)** Commenting on the weekend's events, a probation officer in a neighboring state posted to her personal Facebook page a comment about African Americans saying, "I'm almost to the point of wanting them all segregated on one side of town . . . Maybe the 50s and 60s were really onto something."[1] The probation officer was fired and claimed her free speech rights were violated **(ROL: Public employees' free speech rights are limited to work-related issues.)**

James returned home. To ensure everyone in the community knew James's views, he bought his sixth-grade daughter, Amy, a Confederate flag T-shirt, which she wore to school. The principal found the T-shirt offensive and told Amy to turn the shirt inside out; she refused and was expelled. **(ROL: "It can hardly be argued that either students or teachers shed their constitutional rights to freedom of speech or expression at the schoolhouse gate."[2])** Back at his house, James's 21-month-old baby Max was burning with fever. James relied on his religious beliefs that prayer and peyote heal all sickness. **(ROL: The First Amendment protects the free exercise of religion.)** Because he was stressed, James began to collect pornography. James was arrested for his activities described here. In his defense to the charges, he has claimed the protections of the First Amendment. How will James's case be resolved?

PROTECTED SPEECH

In the early colonies, the king licensed all printers, and those who complained of his governance in the press were prosecuted for seditious libel, which is advocating "the overthrow of the government by force or violence." The First Amendment was drafted and enacted as a direct result of abuses by the Crown. The First Amendment lists five rights and provides

> Congress shall make no law respecting an establishment of religion, or prohibiting the free exercise thereof; or abridging [taking away] the freedom of speech, or of the press; or the right of the people peaceably to assemble, and to petition the Government for a redress [fix] of grievances.

As Supreme Court Justice Louis Brandeis said, in 1927 about the First Amendment, in a case upholding the conviction of Charlotte Whitney for founding the Communist Labor Party of America and advocating the violent overthrow of the government:

> Those who won our liberty . . . believed liberty to be the secret of happiness and courage to be the secret of liberty. They believed that freedom to think as you will and to speak as you think are means indispensable to the discovery and spread of political truth; that without free speech and assembly, discussion would be futile; that with them, discussion affords ordinary adequate protection against the dissemination of noxious doctrine; that *the greatest menace to freedom is an inert people; that public discussion is a political duty*; and that this should be a fundamental principle of the American government[3] (emphasis added).

Rule of Law: The First Amendment protects speech, even speech that is unpopular and offensive (such as in political protest or pornography), as well as expressive conduct such as burning a cross or the flag.

The First Amendment is the basis for democracy's strength in that it promotes the voice of a free America. If people are legally protected when they express unpopular or even offensive ideas, democracy flourishes. The Constitution allows people to be as hateful as they want and protects those who express views others may find racist, derogatory toward religion, or debasing to those of a certain gender or sexual identity. Be mindful, though, that physical acts of violence directed toward others as hate crimes are illegal.

How to Analyze the First Amendment

The first step in analyzing First Amendment problems is to determine if the government is trying to regulate speech. The First Amendment regulates government conduct, not private conduct. If a sports broadcaster makes an incendiary comment and is fired by the private company that owns the media outlet, her First Amendment rights were not violated because she signed a contract that allows the employer to control the employment relationship. Different analysis is required if a public school expels a student because of something she said in the student newspaper because a public school is a government agency.

Rule of Law: The government cannot suppress speech based on its content or the viewpoint the speech represents.

Content-Based Regulation of Speech

Speech is broadly defined as a message communicated by words or associated expressive conduct, such as giving a speech at a political rally or flashing high beams to warn oncoming drivers there is a speed trap located ahead.[4] The government, as a representative of all people, cannot suppress speech because it disagrees with the message conveyed, called content-based regulation or viewpoint discrimination. If the government passed a law that stated everyone must stand during the playing of the National Anthem or go to jail, the law would be punishing the "viewpoint," of those who refused to stand the sitting as an act of protest. When a person challenges a law based on the argument that it infringes on fundamental rights and freedoms, courts employ a strict scrutiny, an analysis in which a court examines under the most powerful of microscopes the government's motive for enacting restrictive laws. To survive strict scrutiny, the government must have enacted the law to achieve a compelling state interest (CSI), which is for the benefit of public health, safety, and welfare. Laws enacted to carry out government objectives must also be narrowly tailored, enacted to address a discrete problem and employ the least restrictive means, which means written to place the minimal burden on personal freedoms. The court analyzes laws that infringe on constitutional rights, particularly those regulations infringing on the First Amendment, to determine if the law

1. Is necessary to achieve a CSI,

2. Is narrowly tailored to achieve the CSI, and

3. Is the least restrictive means to achieving the CSI.

For instance, Massachusetts has a CSI to protect people going in and out of clinics that provide a number of reproductive services to women, including abortion services. To implement the CSI of clinic access, the state government enacted a law creating a 35-feet "buffer zone" around the clinic entrance where members of the public could not legally cross. Those who tried to dissuade women from entering the clinics with "pro-life counseling" sued the state, arguing that the buffer zone infringed on their First Amendment freedom of speech. The U.S. Supreme Court found in favor of the protesters in *McCullen v. Coakley* (2014), holding the law enacting the buffer zone was not "narrowly tailored" and was not the "least restrictive means" to achieve the state's CSI protecting those going in and out of the clinics.[5] Massachusetts's CSI placed too heavy a burden on people's free speech rights to dissuade women from going inside the clinic, and, therefore, the law was illegal, the high Court said. Then again, there are times where a CSI does outweigh individual rights, such as in the chapter-opening case study. James has a First Amendment right to pray over a sick child, but the government's CSI in protecting the health and welfare of children outweighs religious freedom, and James could not use religion as a defense for neglecting Max's medical needs.

An example of impermissible content-based regulation of speech is the case *Alvarez v. United States*, reprinted in part on the following page, where Congress passed a law making lying about one's military service a crime. Wearing or appropriating medals or other military accolades one has not rightfully earned is a serious breach of military protocol that many service members consider dishonorable conduct. When Mr. Alvarez lied and claimed he was a Medal of Honor winner, he was prosecuted under the federal law making such speech a crime, but the U.S. Supreme Court held that the federal law was an illegal content-based suppression of speech. The government cannot prosecute you because they do not like what you are saying, even if what you are saying is untrue.

The *Alvarez* case cites as precedent the *Snyder v. Phelps* (2011) case, which relates to funeral protests. The Westboro Baptist Church of Kansas, which largely comprises the members of Fred Phelps's family, began protesting outside of military funerals celebrating the service member's death as just deserts for the military's protection of a morally corrupt United States. The church particularly took issue with American society's acceptance of homosexuality. If a service member died in the name of protecting America, church members held signs outside the funeral that said, "Thank God for Dead Soldiers," "You're Going to Hell," and "God Hates You," suggesting divine retribution and causing emotional distress for mourners. The father of a fallen Marine Corps corporal successfully sued the church for emotional distress when they protested at his son's

UNITED STATES V. ALVAREZ, 132 S.CT. 2537 (2012)

Supreme Court of the United States

Justice Kennedy delivered the opinion of the Court. (6–3)

FACTS: Lying was his habit. Xavier Alvarez, the respondent here, lied when he said that he played hockey for the Detroit Red Wings and that he once married a starlet from Mexico. But when he lied in announcing he held the Congressional Medal of Honor, respondent ventured onto new ground; for that lie violates a federal criminal statute, the Stolen Valor Act of 2005. 18 U.S.C. §704.

In 2007, [Alvarez] attended his first public meeting as a board member of the Three Valley Water District Board. The board is a governmental entity with headquarters in Claremont, California. He introduced himself as follows: "I'm a retired marine of 25 years. I retired in the year 2001. Back in 1987, I was awarded the Congressional Medal of Honor. I got wounded many times by the same guy." None of this was true. For all the record shows, respondent's statements were but a pathetic attempt to gain respect that eluded him. The statements do not seem to have been made to secure employment or financial benefits or admission to privileges reserved for those who had earned the Medal. [Alvarez] was indicted under the Stolen Valor Act for lying about the Congressional Medal of Honor at the meeting.

ISSUE: [Will Alvarez's conviction be overturned because his lying about winning the Medal of Honor was made a crime by federal law, the Stolen Valor Act?]

HOLDING: [Yes. The Stolen Valor Act is invalid under the First Amendment.]

RATIONALE: This is the second case in two Terms requiring the Court to consider speech that can disparage, or attempt to steal, honor that belongs to those who fought for this Nation in battle. *See Snyder v. Phelps* (2011) (hateful protests by the Westboro Baptist Church directed at the funeral of a serviceman who died in Iraq legal under the First Amendment). Here the statement that the speaker held the Medal was an intended, undoubted lie.

[Alvarez] challenges the [Stolen Valor Act] as a content-based suppression of pure speech, speech not falling within any of the few categories of expression where content-based regulation is permissible. The Government defends the statute as necessary to preserve the integrity and purpose of the Medal, an integrity and purpose it contends are compromised and frustrated by the false statements the statute prohibits. It argues that false statements "have no First Amendment value in themselves," and thus "are protected only to the extent needed to avoid chilling fully protected speech." Although the statute covers [Alvarez's] speech, the Government argues that it leaves breathing room for protected speech, for example speech which might criticize the idea of the Medal or the importance of the military. The Government's arguments cannot suffice to save the statute.

Permitting the government to decree this speech [Alvarez's lie about being a Medal of Honor winner] to be a criminal offense, whether shouted from the rooftops or made in a barely audible whisper, would endorse government authority to compile a list of subjects about which false statements are punishable. Our constitutional tradition stands against the idea that we need Oceania's Ministry of Truth. *See G. Orwell, Nineteen Eighty-Four* (1949). Were this law to be sustained, there could be an endless list of subjects the National Government or the States could single out [to suppress]. Where false claims are made to effect a fraud or secure moneys or other valuable considerations, say offers of employment, it is well established that the Government may restrict speech without affronting the First Amendment.

But the Stolen Valor Act is not so limited in its reach. Were the Court to hold that the interest in truthful discourse alone is sufficient to sustain a ban on speech, absent any evidence that the speech was used to gain a material advantage, it would give government a broad censorial power unprecedented in this Court's cases or in our constitutional tradition.

The mere potential for the exercise of that [abuse of] power casts a chill, a chill the First Amendment cannot permit if free speech, thought, and discourse are to remain a foundation of our freedom.

CONCLUSION: The Nation well knows that one of the costs of the First Amendment is that it protects the speech we detest as well as the speech we embrace. Though few might find [Alvarez's] statements anything but contemptible, his right to make those statements is protected by the Constitution's guarantee of freedom of speech and expression. The Stolen Valor Act infringes upon speech protected by the First Amendment [and the statute is, therefore, unlawful].

funeral. On appeal, the U.S. Supreme Court reversed the father's monetary award and found in favor of the church, stating,

> Speech is powerful. It can stir people to action, move them to tears of both joy and sorrow, and—as it did here—inflict great pain. On the facts before us, we cannot react to that pain by punishing the speaker. As a Nation we have chosen a different course—to protect even hurtful speech on public issues to ensure that we do not stifle public debate. That choice requires that we shield Westboro from tort liability [responsibility for personal injury] for its picketing in this case.[6]

In response to the perceived injury to those attending the funeral of a friend or loved one who would have to gaze on a nearby protest, the federal government and many states enacted laws restricting protests to hours before and after the funeral and at 300 feet away from the funeral, called time, manner, place restrictions.

When the country's Founding Fathers wrote the First Amendment they protected the public square as the embodiment of where true democracy thrived. Today's public forum is anyplace people can engage in the "marketplace of ideas," including parks, streets, and the Internet. Speech in a public forum is one of the hallmarks of our democracy. "The privilege [of access to] the streets and parks for communication of views on national questions may be regulated in the interest of all; [but] it must not, in the guise of regulation, be abridged or denied."[7] As the high Court has said,

> A function of free speech under our system of government is to invite dispute. It may indeed best serve its high purpose when it induces a condition of unrest, creates dissatisfaction with conditions as they are, or even stirs people to anger. Speech is often provocative and challenging. It may strike at prejudices and preconceptions and have profound unsettling effects as it presses for acceptance of an idea.[8]

When the government tries to restrict public speech, courts will examine if the regulation is aimed at the speech's content or merely imposing time, manner, and place restrictions on the speech.

Time, Manner, and Place Restrictions

The government often defers to its right to control the time (at 10 a.m., not 2 a.m.), manner (a bullhorn, not concert speakers), and place (a public park, not a private driveway) speech takes place.[9] A time, manner, and place (TMP) restriction is when the government can legally regulate delivery of the speech to eliminate a public nuisance without reference to the speech's content or message. To be legal, a regulation must meet a three-part test:[10]

1. It must be "justified without reference to the content of the regulated speech."

2. It must be narrowly tailored.

3. It must leave open alternative channels for communication of the information.

To reduce citizen complaints that rock concerts in the city were too loud, the New York City government made musicians use city-provided

Springboard for Discussion

The U.S. Supreme Court found in favor of the Westboro Baptist Church's signs that many find offensive for display at a military funeral. What would society look like if the high Court found in favor of the military family? How would courts determine the legality of speech based on the listener's sensitivity to the message?

> **Rule of Law: The government cannot suppress protected speech because of its content, but it may enact time, manner, and place restrictions.**

Springboard for Discussion

Imagine that it is the year 2028. Congress has passed a law that would abolish the First Amendment, and the Supreme Court has interpreted the law as legal. What would society look like, especially American newspapers, television shows, documentaries, and political discourse? Give specific examples of the types of speech and expression you think the government might want to suppress.

equipment and speakers. Rock artists challenged the city's regulation, arguing that restriction of their volume infringed on the groups' rights to freedom of expression, but they lost. The court decided the city's CSI in protecting the public from a loud nuisance was a valid TMP restriction because the regulation was the least restrictive means to meet the government's CSI.

The Internet as a Public Forum. The Founding Fathers could not have foreseen the Internet and the global possibilities of communication and cross-fertilization of ideas, protest, and speech, which are the hallmarks of democracy. North Carolina law makes it a felony for a registered sex offender "to access a commercial social networking Web site where the sex offender knows that the site permits minor children to become members or to create or maintain personal Web pages."[11] Lester Packingham, who was a 21-year-old college student when he engaged in sexual relations with a 13-year-old, was required to register as a sex offender for 30 years. Packingham, a North Carolina resident, celebrated a parking ticket dismissal on Facebook and was charged with violating the law banning social media access for sex offenders. Packingham then sued the state claiming the Internet is today's public forum that he had a First Amendment right to access. The state replied that banning sex offenders from social media protected vulnerable children from online exploitation. The U.S. Supreme Court found in the defendant's favor in *Packingham v. North Carolina* (2017). The Court said about Twitter, LinkedIn, and Facebook, which have 1.79 billion users:

> These websites can provide perhaps the most powerful mechanisms available to a private citizen to make his or her voice heard. They allow a person with an Internet connection to become a town crier with a voice that resonates farther than it could from any soapbox.[12]

Given the amount of activity that occurs on social media (e.g., job searches, family updates, updates on current events), prohibiting some from using the Internet would foreclose their participation in the "vast democratic forums of the Internet" that defines American liberty.[13]

Vagueness

A law is unconstitutionally **vague** if people fear going to jail because the law is so unclear that people have to guess what conduct or speech is illegal. Vague laws have a "**chilling effect**"—like a bucket of cold water—on free speech because of the uncertainty of what speech is punishable. Vagueness may invalidate a criminal law for either of two independent reasons. First, it may fail to provide the kind of notice that will enable ordinary people to understand what conduct it prohibits; second, it may authorize and even encourage arbitrary and discriminatory enforcement. For example, there was a California law "that requires persons who loiter or wander on the streets to provide a 'credible and reliable' identification and to account for their presence when requested by a police officer." The high Court invalidated the loitering law because the law gave too much power to police officers to stop individuals for vaguely defined reasons, and could unconstitutionally infringe on the public's rights to freedom of movement.[15] The doctrine of invalidating laws under the doctrine of vagueness stems from the procedural due process requirement of fair notice to the public of what conduct is prohibited and will be punished (see "Principle of Legality" discussion in Chapter 3).

Rule of Law: A vague law "is so unclearly defined that persons of common intelligence must necessarily guess at its meaning and differ as to its application."[14]

Expressive Conduct

In the 1960s, many young men were drafted to war in Southeast Asia. To protest, many burned their draft cards despite a federal law that made criminal the willful and knowing mutilation or destruction of a draft card. David O'Brien burned his card, was arrested and convicted, and appealed to the U.S. Supreme Court that he had a First Amendment right to symbolic expression (i.e., burning the card expressed his protest). The high Court rejected O'Brien's argument by weighing the government's CSI in maintaining a wartime draft against the minimal suppression of O'Brien's particular act of protest. The government was not silencing O'Brien; he could express himself in many, alternative ways (*United States v. O'Brien*, 1968).[16]

Flag Desecration

A powerful form of symbolic speech is burning the American flag in protest. In *Texas v. Johnson* (1989), the U.S. Supreme Court struck down a Texas statute that outlawed flag burning.[17] Justice Kennedy, in a concurring opinion, said people would be unhappy with the Court's opinion that it is perfectly lawful to burn the flag, especially those "who have had the singular honor of carrying the flag into battle." But Kennedy continued that "it is poignant but fundamental that the flag protects those who hold it in contempt," which means it is the freedom that the flag represents that gives people the right to desecrate (treat disrespectfully) it; the flag is where we get the power to burn it. In response to the *Johnson* decision, the federal government enacted the Flag Protection Act of 1989 that punished anyone who "knowingly mutilates, defaces, physically defiles, burns, maintains on the floor or ground, or tramples upon any flag of the United States," but the act was declared illegal because it suppressed speech and expression based on the content of the speech.[18] Many states still have laws in force that make it a crime to desecrate a flag, but considering U.S. Supreme Court precedent, such laws appear constitutionally infirm. Delaware's desecration law with respect to defacing a national flag is one example.

> Delaware Code Annotated, Title 11, Chapter 5, §1331
>
> Desecration; class A misdemeanor.
>
> > A person is guilty of desecration if the person intentionally defaces, damages, pollutes or otherwise physically mistreats any public monument or structure, any place of worship, the national flag or any other object of veneration by the public or a substantial segment thereof, in a public place and in a way in which the actor knows will outrage the sensibilities of persons likely to observe or discover the actions.

Cross Burning

Burning a cross is expressive speech protected by the First Amendment. Statutes that try to punish cross burning as symbolic hate speech typically fail on either vagueness or overbreadth grounds because such a law would punish speech based on its content. In *Virginia v. Black* (2003), a state law that outlawed cross burning was upheld as constitutional because the statute specifically made cross burning "fighting words," which are "words by their very utterance inflict injury or incite an immediate breach of the peace," and enjoy no protection under the First Amendment. The Virginia statute recites,

> It shall be unlawful for any person or persons, with the intent of intimidating any person or group of persons, to burn, or cause to be burned, a cross on the property of another, a highway or other public place. Any person who shall violate any provision of this section shall be guilty of a Class 6 felony. Any such burning of a cross shall be *prima facie* [on its face] evidence of an intent to intimidate a person or group of persons.

In the *Virginia v. Black* case, White men drove a truck onto the property of the African American Jubilee family in the middle of the night and burned a cross in the yard. Read the history of cross burning in America provided in the excerpt of *Virginia v. Black*, reprinted in part on the following pages. Cross burning is a protected form of expression, but once it crossed the line and was done to intimidate or harass others, cross burning became fighting words that the government could legally suppress.

Rule of Law: Freedom of speech includes freedom of expression, such as cross and flag burning.

Rule of Law: It is legal to burn a cross as expressive speech. It is not legal to burn a cross with the intent to intimidate others.

VIRGINIA V. BLACK, 538 U.S. 343 (2003)

Supreme Court of the United States

Justice O'Connor delivered the opinion of the Court. (5–4)

REASONING: Cross burning originated in the 14th century as a means for Scottish tribes to signal each other.[19] Sir Walter Scott used cross burnings for dramatic effect in "The Lady of the Lake," where the burning cross signified both a summons and a call to arms.[20] Cross burning in this country, however, long ago became unmoored from its Scottish ancestry. Burning a cross in the United States is inextricably intertwined with the history of the Ku Klux Klan. The first Ku Klux Klan began in Pulaski, Tennessee, in the spring of 1866. Although the Ku Klux Klan started as a social club, it soon changed into something far different. The Klan fought Reconstruction and the corresponding drive to allow freed blacks to participate in the political process. Soon the Klan imposed "a veritable reign of terror" throughout the South.[21] The Klan employed tactics such as whipping, threatening to burn people at the stake, and murder.[22] The Klan's victims included blacks, southern whites who disagreed with the Klan, and "carpetbagger" northern whites.

The activities of the Ku Klux Klan prompted legislative action at the national level. In 1871, "President Grant sent a message to Congress indicating that the Klan's reign of terror in the Southern States had rendered life and property insecure." In response, Congress passed what is now known as the Ku Klux Klan Act. *See* "An Act to enforce the Provisions of the Fourteenth Amendment to the Constitution of the United States, and for other Purposes," 17 Stat. 13 (now codified at 42 U.S.C. §§1983, 1985, and 1986). President Grant used these new powers to suppress the Klan in South Carolina, the effect of which severely curtailed the Klan in other States as well. By the end of Reconstruction in 1877, the first Klan no longer existed.

The genesis of the second Klan began in 1905, with the publication of Thomas Dixon's *The Clansmen: An Historical Romance of the Ku Klux Klan.* Dixon's book was a sympathetic portrait of the first Klan, depicting the Klan as a group of heroes "saving" the South from blacks and the "horrors" of Reconstruction. Although the first Klan never actually practiced cross burning, Dixon's book depicted the Klan burning crosses to celebrate the execution of former slaves. Cross burning thereby became associated with the first Ku Klux Klan. When D.W. Griffith turned Dixon's book into the movie *The Birth of a Nation* in 1915, the association between cross burning and the Klan became indelible. Soon thereafter, in November 1915, the second Klan began.

From the inception of the second Klan, cross burnings have been used to communicate both threats of violence and messages of shared ideology. The first initiation ceremony occurred on Stone Mountain near Atlanta, Georgia. While a 40-foot cross burned on the mountain, the Klan members took their oaths of loyalty. This cross burning was the second recorded instance in the United States. The first known cross burning in the country had occurred a little over one month before the Klan initiation, when a Georgia mob celebrated the lynching of Leo Frank by burning a "gigantic cross" on Stone Mountain that was "visible throughout."

The new Klan's ideology did not differ much from that of the first Klan. As one Klan publication emphasized, "We avow the distinction between [the] races . . . and we shall ever be true to the faithful maintenance of White Supremacy and will strenuously oppose any compromise thereof in any and all things." Violence was also an elemental part of this new Klan. By September 1921, the *New York World* newspaper documented 152 acts of Klan violence, including 4 murders, 41 floggings, and 27 tar-and-featherings.

Often, the Klan used cross burnings as a tool of intimidation and a threat of impending violence. For example, in 1939 and 1940, the Klan burned crosses in front of synagogues and churches. After one cross burning at a synagogue, a Klan member noted that if the cross burning did not "shut the Jews up, we'll cut a few throats and see what happens." In Miami in 1941, the Klan burned four crosses in front of a proposed housing project, declaring, "We are here to keep n****rs out of your town . . . When the law fails you, call on us." And in Alabama in 1942, in "a whirlwind climax to weeks of flogging and terror," the Klan burned crosses in front of a union hall and in front of a union leader's home on the eve of a labor election. These cross burnings embodied threats to people whom the Klan deemed antithetical to its goals. And these threats had special force given the long history of Klan violence.

The Klan continued to use cross burnings to intimidate after World War II. In one incident, an African-American "school teacher who recently moved his family into a block formerly occupied only by whites asked the protection of city police . . . after the burning of a cross in his front yard." And after a cross burning in Suffolk, Virginia during the late 1940's, the Virginia Governor stated that he would "not allow any of our people of any race to be subjected to terrorism or intimidation in any form by the Klan or any other organization."[23] These incidents of cross burning, among others, helped prompt Virginia to enact its first version of the cross-burning statute in 1950.

The decision of this Court in *Brown v. Board of Education* (1954), along with the civil rights movement of the 1950's and 1960's, sparked another outbreak of Klan violence. These acts of violence included bombings, beatings, shootings, stabbings, and mutilations. Members of the

Klan burned crosses on the lawns of those associated with the civil rights movement, assaulted the Freedom Riders, bombed churches, and murdered blacks as well as whites whom the Klan viewed as sympathetic toward the civil rights movement.

For its own members, the cross was a sign of celebration and ceremony. During a joint Nazi-Klan rally in 1940, the proceeding concluded with the wedding of two Klan members who "were married in full Klan regalia beneath a blazing cross." On March 26, 1960, the Klan engaged in rallies and cross burnings throughout the South in an attempt to recruit 10 million members. Later in 1960, the Klan became an issue in the third debate between Richard Nixon and John Kennedy, with both candidates renouncing the Klan. After this debate, the Klan reiterated its support for Nixon by burning crosses. And cross burnings featured prominently in Klan rallies when the Klan attempted to move toward more nonviolent tactics to stop integration. In short, a burning cross has remained a symbol of Klan ideology and of Klan unity.

To this day, regardless of whether the message is a political one or whether the message is also meant to intimidate, the burning of a cross is a "symbol of hate." And while cross burning sometimes carries no intimidating message, at other times the intimidating message is the *only* message conveyed. For example, when a cross burning is directed at a particular person not affiliated with the Klan, the burning cross often serves as a message of intimidation, designed to inspire in the victim a fear of bodily harm. Moreover, the history of violence associated with the Klan shows that the possibility of injury or death is not just hypothetical. The person who burns a cross directed at a particular person often is making a serious threat, meant to coerce the victim to comply with the Klan's wishes unless the victim is willing to risk the wrath of the Klan.

In sum, while a burning cross does not inevitably convey a message of intimidation, often the cross burner intends that the recipients of the message fear for their lives. And when a cross burning is used to intimidate, few if any messages are more powerful.

In the chapter-opening case study, James could legally participate in symbolic tiki torch burning as a message of social identity.

UNPROTECTED SPEECH

Certain types of speech enjoy no protection under the First Amendment. Although our democracy cherishes and values the marketplace of ideas to advocate change through public discourse and discussion, there are some types of speech that cross the line and can be criminalized. Not covered in this chapter is commercial speech, discussed in the *Alvarez* case, such as false advertising for financial gain, which the government may regulate to protect the public.

Rule of Law: The government may suppress unprotected speech and expression because it enjoys no protection under the First Amendment; such unprotected speech and expression include fighting words, true threats, and obscenity.

Fighting Words

Walter Chaplinsky was a Jehovah's Witness who was handing out pamphlets and, according to the case, attracted a "restless" crowd as he denounced all religion as a "racket." When he was arrested, he called the city marshal a "G** damned racketeer" and "a damned Fascist" and included the whole government of Rochester, New Hampshire. He was convicted under a statute that said no person "shall address any offensive, derisive or annoying word to any person who is lawfully in any street or other public place, nor call him by any offensive or derisive name."

Chaplinsky's conviction was upheld by a unanimous U.S. Supreme Court, who found the fascist epithets "likely to provoke the average person to retaliation, and thereby cause a breach of the peace."[24] Thirty years later, in *Cohen v. California* (1971), Cohen wore a jacket with the slogan "F*** the draft" in a Los Angeles courthouse where women and children were present. He was charged under the statute that made criminal the intentional "disturbing the peace or quiet of any . . . person [by] offensive conduct," and convicted. In overturning his conviction, the U.S. Supreme Court explained that Cohen's message was not obscene, that the people in the courthouse were not a "captive audience" because they could walk out if they wanted to.[25] The Court said that the function of the First Amendment

Rule of Law: Fighting words are those words, which "by their very utterance inflict injury or tend to incite an immediate breach of the peace."

was to "remove governmental restraints for the arena of public discussion." It is difficult to draw the line between protected free speech and unprotected "fighting words."

A juvenile, John M., was adjudicated delinquent for calling two African American women a derogatory racial epithet meant to slur Black people and, on appeal, he claimed the First Amendment protected his speech. The Arizona Court of Appeals disagreed and in citing *Cohen v. California* (1971), defined John M.'s use of the "N word" as "likely to provoke violent reaction when addressed to the ordinary citizen."[26] Similarly, a man engaged in sidewalk evangelizing called a woman a "whore," "harlot" and "jezebel" over 30 times in six minutes. In upholding his conviction for disorderly conduct, the court found his speech "easily characterized as resort to epithets and personal abuse which inflict injury by their very utterance."[27]

Conversely, screaming at police officers or otherwise interrupting officers in the performance of their duties is not always criminal. One man was arrested for yelling at a police officer, "Why don't you pick on somebody your own size?" and prosecuted under a statute that made it a crime "for any person wantonly to curse or revile or to use obscene or opprobrious language toward or with reference to any member of the city police while in the actual performance of his duty."[28]

The U.S. Supreme Court held the statute overbroad and stated law enforcement officers should be immune to provocation when the public curses and condemns them because "a properly trained officer may reasonably be expected to 'exercise a higher degree of restraint' than the average citizen, and thus be less likely to respond belligerently to 'fighting words.'"[29]

Clear and Present Danger

From the draft for World War I, well-known socialist Charles Schenck was convicted under the Espionage Act of 1917 for handing out flyers to draftees urging them to resist the "involuntary servitude" of the draft. The high Court upheld Schenck's conviction saying "the character of every act depends upon the circumstances in which it is done." Although Schenck's act of distributing flyers calling for insubordination to the government would pose no harm in peacetime, during war, the same speech posed a "clear and present danger" to the safety and security of the United States and could be suppressed. The high Court said whereas a man might yell "Fire!" in the privacy of his home and no one would get hurt, the First Amendment would never "protect a man in falsely shouting fire in a theatre and causing a panic."[30]

> **Rule of Law:** A "clear and present" danger incites the public to imminent, lawless action.

In *Brandenburg v. Ohio* (1969), the "clear and present danger" test evolved to whether the speech invited others to "imminent lawless action."[31] Brandenburg was a Ku Klux Klan leader who advocated violence as a way to motivate political change. He was convicted under a Ohio statute for advocating "the duty, necessity, or propriety of crime, sabotage, violence, or unlawful methods of terrorism as a means of accomplishing industrial or political reform."[32] The U.S. Supreme Court overturned Brandenburg's conviction and held Ohio's law invalid because Brandenburg's speech calling for political reform, even if by violence, was protected. On the other hand, if Brandenburg were calling on the public to immediately commit lawless acts, then his speech would be unprotected.

That same year, Vernon Watts, an 18-year-old African American, protesting the Vietnam conflict near the Washington Monument said to a crowd, "If they ever make me carry a rifle, the first man I want to get in my sights is L.B.J. [President Lyndon Baines Johnson]. They are not going to make me kill my black brothers," and the crowd laughed in response. Watts was convicted under a 1917 statute making it a crime to threaten the life of the president. Like Brandenburg, the high Court overturned Watts's conviction because there was no "incitement to imminent lawless action" and no basis to sustain the conviction (*Watts v. United States*, 1969).[33] Watts's threat was conditional—only if sent to Vietnam (the condition) would Watts endanger Johnson's life (the threat), and his speech was hyperbole (exaggeration no one would believe). Indeed, everyone in the crowd laughed, indicating no one took Watts's threat seriously.

> **Rule of Law:** A "true threat" communicates a threat to commit violence to identifiable people.

A similar type of unprotected speech is the true threat. In the *Virginia v. Black* case in this chapter, U.S. Supreme Court Justice Sandra Day O'Connor defined "true threats" as

those statements where the speaker means to communicate a serious expression of an intent to commit an act of unlawful violence to a particular individual or group of individuals. The speaker need not actually intend to carry out the threat. Rather, a prohibition on true threats protect[s] individuals from the fear of violence and from the disruption that fear engenders, in addition to protecting people from the possibility that the threatened violence will occur.

If someone directs a threat to a person or group with the intent of putting them in fear of bodily harm or death, it is a true threat, similar to a terroristic threat, and not free speech. As one commentator states, "Courts often have trouble determining whether violent expression should be evaluated under the 'incitement to imminent lawless action' standard or under a true-threats line of analysis."[34] In the chapter-opening case study, James calling out "free speech or die America" would likely qualify as hyperbole and not a criminal true threat or call to imminent lawless action from the crowd.

Obscenity

Since the advent of photography there has been a market for sexually stimulating photographs of naked men and women. There has been much litigation over the definition of obscene written material or photographic work designed to arouse or excite the viewer sexually. The difficulty in agreeing on one solid definition is best exemplified by U.S. Supreme Court Justice Potter Stewart, who said about obscenity, "I know it when I see it."[36] The legal test courts use today to establish whether a book, movie, piece of art, or other expressive conduct is obscene was enunciated by the Supreme Court in *Miller v. California* (1973).[37] If the work is judged obscene, it is not protected by the Constitution and the government has the right to suppress it and keep it from the public. In this case, Marvin Miller mailed sexually explicit brochures from Los Angeles, California, and was arrested and convicted under California state obscenity law when an elderly woman received one of Miller's mailings, complete with graphic depictions of sexual content on the cover. The high Court overturned Miller's conviction and enunciated a three-part test used to define obscenity. Pursuant to the *Miller* test, the judge or jury at trial must determine whether

> Rule of Law: Obscene material portrays sex in a manner appealing to a "prurient interest," which is a shameful and morbid interest in nudity, sex, or excretion.[35]

1. "The average person applying contemporary community standards" would find the work, taken as a whole, appeals to the prurient interest [defined as "a shameful or morbid interest in nudity, sex, or excretion]";[38]

2. The work depicts or describes, in a patently offensive way, sexual conduct specifically defined by the applicable state law; and

3. The work, taken as a whole, lacks serious literary, artistic, political, or scientific value.

Georgia's obscenity law defines patently sexually offensive material to include perverted intercourse, masturbation, bestiality, sexual acts of torture, and the lewd exhibition of the genitals.[39]

The distinction between obscene material that is illegal and material that an individual may legally possess in his or her home went one step further in *New York v. Ferber* (1982).[40] In *Ferber*, the high Court allowed the state of New York to outlaw child pornography even if such pornography was not defined as obscene under the *Miller* test. As the high Court said in *Ferber*, "The prevention of sexual exploitation and abuse of children constitutes a government objective of surpassing importance." Protecting children from sexual exploitation was a major piece of the Court's decision in *Osborne v. Ohio* (1990), in which the Court made even mere possession of child pornography illegal.[41] One child pornography victim described the lasting damage knowing the photographs can forever circulate in public, never to be retracted or removed:

> The pictures that were taken when I was so young are still out there. Who knows where they are and how many people have seen them. I wonder if they will show up when I least expect it. I am away from the abuse now, but know that someone could be pleasuring himself while looking at my pictures or showing them to kids.[42]

With the advances in technology from motion pictures, to home video cameras, the World Wide Web, webcams, digital processors, scanners, and home photoshop software, it has been difficult to stop the proliferation of child pornography.[43] In the chapter-opening case study, James could legally collect pornography depicting adults, but pornography that meets the three prongs of the *Miller* test would be deemed obscene and illegal to purchase or possess.

Overbroad Doctrine

Invoking the overbreadth doctrine is one of the most effective ways the U.S. Supreme Court can protect freedom of speech. A law is overbroad in First Amendment analysis if it criminalizes both protected and unprotected speech. An example of a hate speech law that failed on overbreadth grounds is in the case *R.A.V. v. City of St. Paul* (1992), where the hate crime ordinance provided,

> Whoever placed on public property or private property a symbol, object, appellation, characterization or graffiti, including, but not limited to, a burning cross or Nazi swastika, *which one knows or has reasonable grounds to know arouse anger, alarm or resentment in others* [fighting words] on the basis of race, color, creed, religion or gender commits disorderly conduct and shall be guilty of a misdemeanor.[44] (emphasis added)

Teenage defendants taped broken chair legs together into a cross and burned it inside the fenced yard of an African American family, acts that are criminal as trespass or arson. But the teenagers were prosecuted under the hate crimes ordinance instead. Teenager R.A.V. (initials were used to protect his juvenile identity) was convicted under the ordinance, and the U.S. Supreme Court overturned his conviction because the ordinance discriminated on the basis of a person's viewpoint. The law was overbroad because it lawfully prohibited fighting words as those which arouse "anger, alarm or resentment in others," but the statute unlawfully criminalized speech made "on the basis of race, color, creed, religion or gender," which is protected.

Another example of an overbroad law is when Congress enacted the Child Pornography Prevention Act (CPPA) in 1996,[45] which sought to add to the definition of child pornography "any visual depiction, including any photograph, film, video, picture, or computer or computer-generated image or picture" that "is or appears to be of a minor engaging in sexually explicit conduct." The law was challenged because it criminalized access to computer-generated pornography that involved no real children. The U.S. Supreme Court struck down that provision of the CPPA as overbroad. Figure 11.1 illustrates the overbroad statute struck down in the *Ashcroft* case. Read the case excerpt on the following pages and see if you agree with the Court's reasoning.

Rule of Law: An overbroad law punishes both legal and illegal speech and is, therefore, an illegal law.

Figure 11.1 Venn Diagram of Overbroad Law

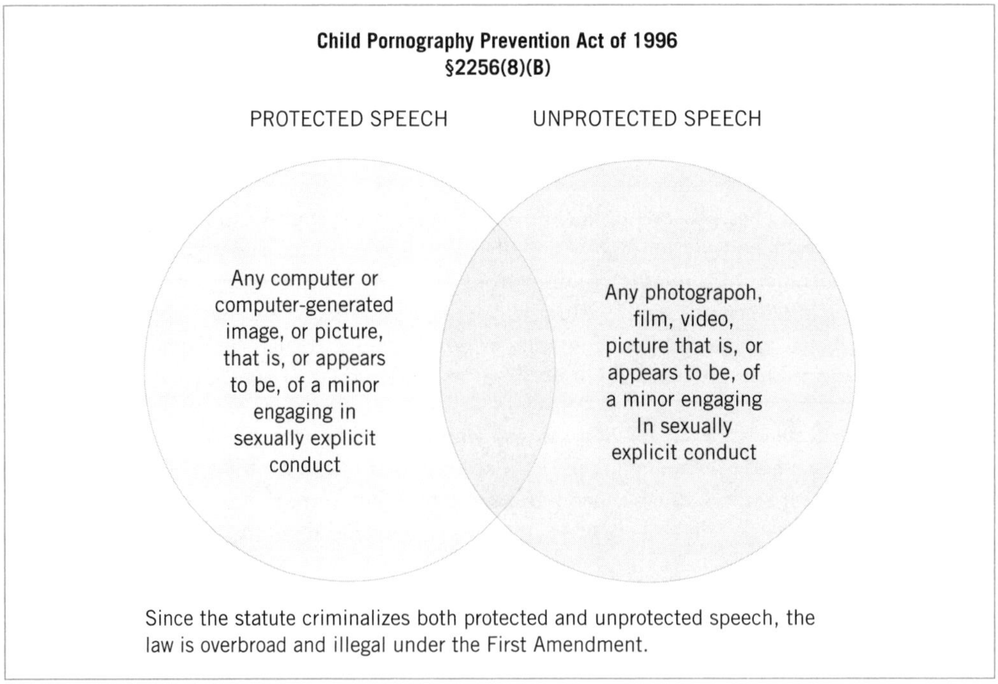

Child Pornography Prevention Act of 1996
§2256(8)(B)

PROTECTED SPEECH   UNPROTECTED SPEECH

Any computer or computer-generated image, or picture, that is, or appears to be, of a minor engaging in sexually explicit conduct

Any photograpoh, film, video, picture that is, or appears to be, of a minor engaging In sexually explicit conduct

Since the statute criminalizes both protected and unprotected speech, the law is overbroad and illegal under the First Amendment.

ASHCROFT V. FREE SPEECH COALITION, 535 U.S. 234 (2002)

Supreme Court of the United States

Justice Kennedy delivered the opinion of the Court. (6–3)

ISSUE: We consider in this case whether the Child Pornography Prevention Act of 1996 (CPPA), 18 U.S.C. §2251 et seq. [et seq. = and more], abridges the freedom of speech. The CPPA extends the federal prohibition against child pornography to sexually explicit images that appear to depict minors but were produced without using any real children. The statute prohibits, in specific circumstances, possessing or distributing these images, which may be created by using adults who look like minors or by using computer imaging. The new technology, according to Congress, makes it possible to create realistic images of children who do not exist. . . .

HOLDING: The prohibitions of [the CPPA] are overbroad and unconstitutional.

REASONING: By prohibiting child pornography that does not depict an actual child, the statute goes beyond *New York v. Ferber* (1982), which distinguished child pornography from other sexually explicit speech because of the State's interest in protecting the children exploited by the production process. As a general rule, pornography can be banned only if obscene, but under *Ferber*, pornography showing minors can be proscribed whether or not the images are obscene under the definition set forth in *Miller v. California* (1973).[46] *Ferber* recognized that "the *Miller* standard, like all general definitions of what may be banned as obscene, does not reflect the State's particular and more compelling interest in prosecuting those who promote the sexual exploitation of children."

Before 1996, Congress defined child pornography as the type of depictions at issue in *Ferber*, images made using actual minors. 18 U.S.C. §2252 (1994 ed.). The CPPA retains that prohibition at 18 U.S.C. §2256(8)(A) and adds three other prohibited categories of speech, of which the first, §2256(8)(B), and the third, §2256(8)(D), are at issue in this case. Section 2256(8)(B) prohibits "any visual depiction, including any photograph, film, video, picture, or computer or computer-generated image or picture" that "is, or appears to be, of a minor engaging in sexually explicit conduct." The prohibition on "any visual depiction" does not depend at all on how the image is produced. The section captures a range of depictions, sometimes called "virtual child pornography," which include computer-generated images, as well as images produced by more traditional means. For instance, the literal terms of the statute embrace a Renaissance painting depicting a scene from

classical mythology, a "picture" that "appears to be, of a minor engaging in sexually explicit conduct." The statute also prohibits Hollywood movies, filmed without any child actors, if a jury believes an actor "appears to be" a minor engaging in "actual or simulated . . . sexual intercourse." §2256(2).

These images do not involve, let alone harm, any children in the production process; but Congress decided the materials threaten children in other, less direct, ways. Pedophiles might use the materials to encourage children to participate in sexual activity. "[A] child who is reluctant to engage in sexual activity with an adult, or to pose for sexually explicit photographs, can sometimes be convinced by viewing depictions of other children 'having fun' participating in such activity." Furthermore, pedophiles might "whet their own sexual appetites" with the pornographic images, "thereby increasing the creation and distribution of child pornography and the sexual abuse and exploitation of actual children." Under these rationales, harm flows from the content of the images, not from the means of their production.

The First Amendment commands, "Congress shall make no law . . . abridging the freedom of speech." The government may violate this mandate in many ways, but a law imposing criminal penalties on protected speech is a stark example of speech suppression. The CPPA's penalties are indeed severe. A first offender may be imprisoned for 15 years. §2252A(b)(1). A repeat offender faces a prison sentence of not less than 5 years and not more than 30 years in prison. While even minor punishments can chill protected speech, this case provides a textbook example of why we permit facial challenges to statutes that burden expression. With these severe penalties in force, few legitimate movie producers or book publishers, or few other speakers in any capacity, would risk distributing images in or near the uncertain reach of this law. The Constitution gives significant protection from overbroad laws that chill speech within the First Amendment's vast and privileged sphere.

Under this principle, the CPPA is unconstitutional on its face if it prohibits a substantial amount of protected expression. The sexual abuse of a child is a most serious crime and an act repugnant to the moral instincts of a decent people. In its legislative findings [justifying the enacting of the CCPA], Congress recognized that there are subcultures of persons who harbor illicit desires for children and commit criminal acts to gratify the impulses. Congress also found that surrounding the serious offenders are those who flirt with these impulses and trade pictures and written accounts of sexual activity with young

(Continued)

(Continued)

children. Congress may pass valid laws to protect children from abuse, and it has, e.g., 18 U.S.C. §§2241, 2251.

The prospect of crime, however, by itself does not justify laws suppressing protected speech—"Among free men, the deterrents ordinarily to be applied to prevent crime are education and punishment for violations of the law, not abridgment of the rights of free speech." It is also well established that speech may not be prohibited because it concerns subjects offending our sensibilities."—"The fact that society may find speech offensive is not a sufficient reason for suppressing it" [and] "In evaluating the free speech rights of adults, we have made it perfectly clear that 'sexual expression which is indecent but not obscene is protected by the First Amendment'" [because] "The fact that protected speech may be offensive to some does not justify its suppression."

As a general principle, the First Amendment bars the government from dictating what we see or read or speak or hear. The freedom of speech has its limits; it does not embrace certain categories of speech, including defamation, incitement, obscenity, and pornography produced with real children. While these categories may be prohibited without violating the First Amendment, none of them includes the speech prohibited by the CPPA.

The CPPA prohibits speech despite its serious literary, artistic, political, or scientific value. The statute proscribes the visual depiction of an idea—that of teenagers engaging in sexual activity—that is a fact of modern society and has been a theme in art and literature throughout the ages. Both themes—teenage sexual activity and the sexual abuse of children—have inspired countless literary works. William Shakespeare created the most famous pair of teenage lovers, one of whom is just 13 years of age. See Romeo and Juliet, act I, sc. 2, l. 9 ("She hath not seen the change of fourteen years"). In the drama, Shakespeare portrays the relationship as something splendid and innocent, but not juvenile. The work has inspired no less than 40 motion pictures, some of which suggest that the teenagers consummated their relationship [e.g., the movie Romeo and Juliet (B. Luhrmann director, 1996)].

Shakespeare may not have written sexually explicit scenes for the Elizabethan audience, but were modern directors to adopt a less conventional approach, that fact alone would not compel the conclusion that the work was obscene.

Contemporary movies pursue similar themes. Last year's Academy Awards featured the movie, Traffic, which was nominated for Best Picture.[47] The film portrays a teenager, identified as a 16-year-old, who becomes addicted to drugs. The viewer sees the degradation of her addiction, which in the end leads her to a filthy room to trade sex for drugs. The year before, American Beauty won the Academy Award for Best Picture.[48] In the course of the movie, a teenage girl engages in sexual relations with her teenage boyfriend, and another yields herself to the gratification of a middle-aged man. The film also contains a scene where, although the movie audience understands the act is not taking place, one character believes he is watching a teenage boy performing a sexual act on an older man.

Whether or not the films we mention violate the CPPA, they explore themes within the wide sweep of the statute's prohibitions. If these films, or hundreds of others of lesser note that explore those subjects, contain a single graphic depiction of sexual activity within the statutory definition, the possessor of the film would be subject to severe punishment without inquiry into the work's redeeming value.

CONCLUSION: The Government may not suppress lawful speech as the means to suppress unlawful speech. Protected speech does not become unprotected merely because it resembles the latter. The Constitution requires the reverse. "The possible harm to society in permitting some unprotected speech to go unpunished is outweighed by the possibility that protected speech of others may be muted...." The overbreadth doctrine prohibits the Government from banning unprotected speech if a substantial amount of protected speech is prohibited or chilled in the process.

The Court in *Ashcroft* recognized the competing interests in preventing the sexual exploitation of children with the First Amendment rights that allow adults to consume pornographic materials. The Court rejected Congress's argument that computer-generated child pornography could be used by adults to lure children into committing sex acts; the same could be said for gifts or candy. But the harm in censoring materials on the basis that children and sex were present in the same work could lead to the slippery slope of the government outlawing Shakespeare or the movie *American Beauty*, because those works allude to sexual conduct with minors, a result the Court found untenable.

APPLYING THE LAW TO THE FACTS

Is the Law Overbroad?

The Facts: Congress passed a law making it a crime to buy or sell recordings of "conduct in which a living animal is intentionally maimed, mutilated, tortured, wounded or killed." Robert Stephens was convicted under the Animal Crush Video Prohibition Act of 2010, 18 U.S.C. §48, enacted to punish those who made or sold videos where women wearing stiletto heels, for the sexual pleasure of those watching, crush under their feet small animals to death. Stephens sold videos of pit bull dogs fighting and was convicted under the law. On appeal, he challenged the animal crush law as overbroad because the law criminalized the protected speech of people who kill animals in making lawful hunting and fishing videos as well as the unprotected speech of torturing animals on film. Is the anti-crush law illegal because it violates the First Amendment?

The Law: Yes, the law is overbroad. The U.S. Supreme Court found in favor of Stephens (8–1) noting that all 50 states had animal cruelty laws on the books to prosecute those who made or sold "crush" videos, and as written, the anti-crush law could unlawfully punish hunters and fishermen who videotaped their exploits.[49]

Post-*Ashcroft* Developments to Regulate Child Pornography

In response to the *Ashcroft* decision, Congress enacted the Prosecutorial Remedies and Other Tools to end the Exploitation of Children Today Act of 2003 (PROTECT Act), a collection of statutes enacted to prevent child abuse.[50] Remember from the discussion in Chapter 1, the hook for federal jurisdiction over crimes not uniquely federal, such as counterfeiting, is the Constitution's Commerce Clause. The new statutes did not criminalize the possession of child pornography but the child pornography that had been disseminated across state lines, most often through computer transmission. Dwight Whorley, a man already on probation for child pornography charges, was at work at a Virginia state agency when he downloaded Japanese anime child pornography. He was convicted under one portion of the PROTECT Act, 18 U.S.C. §1466A.

---

18 U.S.C. §1466A. Obscene visual representations of the sexual abuse of children

(a) In general. Any person who, in a circumstance described in subsection (d), knowingly produces, distributes, receives, or possesses with intent to distribute, a visual depiction of any kind, including a drawing, cartoon, sculpture, or painting, that—

(1) (A) depicts a minor engaging in sexually explicit conduct; and

(B) is obscene; or

(2) (A) depicts an image that is, or appears to be, of a minor engaging in graphic bestiality, sadistic or masochistic abuse, or sexual intercourse, including genital-genital, oral-genital, anal-genital, or oral-anal, whether between persons
of the same or opposite sex; and

(B) lacks serious literary, artistic, political, or scientific value; or attempts or conspires to do so, shall be subject to [criminal] penalties . . .

Whorley unsuccessfully claimed that cartoon children involved in depictions of sexual activity with cartoon adults did not harm any real children and, under the *Ashcroft* precedent, the statute was illegal. The appeals court disagreed, holding Whorley's conviction valid because under the three-prong *Miller* test, the anime was obscene. One defendant who successfully challenged the

PROTECT Act's ban on child-porn anime was Christopher Handley. Handley received in the mail at his home in Iowa drawings of cartoon children engaged in sexual acts. He successfully challenged portions of the PROTECT Act as overbroad because the statute did not fully incorporate the *Miller* test's requirement to examine the challenged work "taken as a whole" before making an obscenity determination.[51] Despite invalidating those provisions of the PROTECT Act, there was sufficient evidence to convict Handley and he was sentenced to 6 months in jail.

SPECIAL FIRST AMENDMENT ISSUES

Juveniles, Schools, and Free Speech

Students' free speech rights were first recognized in the 1940s when Jehovah Witnesses sued the school for forcing their children to participate in the morning ritual of reciting the Pledge of Allegiance; pledging to a symbol ran afoul of their religious beliefs.[52] Finding in favor of the students, the Court said that the government could not "compel" speech from the public. The contours of student rights were further defined in *Tinker v. Des Moines Independent Community School District* (1969), where students who wore black armbands to protest the Vietnam conflict were suspended.[53] The U.S. Supreme Court held in favor of the students' free speech rights and said in a memorable quote, "It can hardly be argued that either students or teachers shed their constitutional rights to freedom of speech or expression at the schoolhouse gate." The Court said student speech and expression should be allowed unless it materially and "substantially disrupted" the school's educational mission. In the chapter-opening case study, James's daughter, Amy, is expelled when she refuses to turn her Confederate flag T-shirt inside out because the principal believes the shirt is offensive. Unless the principal can show Amy's speech (i.e., the message on the shirt) substantially disrupted the school's educational mission by, for example, distracting all classrooms, Amy's expulsion is unlawful.

> **Rule of Law: Schools may limit the free speech rights of its juvenile students.**

In later cases, however, the Court limited the protections of *Tinker*, for example, in *Bethel School District No. 403 v. Fraser*, where the Court upheld the disciplining of a student who gave a speech at a school assembly peppered with sexual innuendo.[54] The Court ruled that the school had the power to regulate student speech or conduct that is "vulgar" or "offensively lewd" because such speech would seriously interfere with the ability of the school to meet its educational mission.

In *Morse v. Frederick* (2007), as the 2002 Olympic Torch passed the high school as students were assembled outside, student Joseph Frederick unfurled a banner, "BONG HiTS 4 JESUS," meant as a joke. Principal Morse confiscated the banner, destroyed it, and suspended Frederick. The case made its way to the high Court because of the tension between a student's free speech rights and the school's ability to educate students without undue interference.[55] The U.S. Supreme Court found in favor of the school.

The Court viewed the banner as advocating the use of illegal drugs and held, "Because schools may take steps to safeguard those entrusted to their care from speech that can reasonably be regarded as encouraging illegal drug use, the school officials in this case did not violate the First Amendment by confiscating the pro-drug banner and suspending Frederick." The dissent saw the case as being not about drugs, but about free speech, and questioned whether a banner that said "Wine sips 4 Jesus" could be constitutionally banned because it promoted alcohol use, which poses similar, if not greater, danger to students.

Recent federal court rulings on regulating student speech has particular importance for free speech rights with the marriage of widespread student social media access and the number of threats of violence directed at schools, teachers, and administrators. The constitutional test articulated in *Tinker* that student speech is allowed in school if not a "substantial disruption" to the educational mission has been extended to a student's off-campus speech if a student's message transmits threats of violence that cause concern, alarm, and fear at the school campus for which the school is directly responsible to prevent.

A high school sophomore kept a diary describing a wish list describing specific acts of violence against the school community. In upholding the student's suspension, the federal court of appeals stated, "School administrators must be permitted to react quickly and decisively to address a threat of physical violence . . . without worrying that they will have to face years of litigation second-guessing their judgment as to whether the threat posed a real risk of substantial disturbance."[56] The challenge for school administrators seeking to punish students for their speech by suspension or expulsion is to determine, often on short notice, the threat level created by the speech.[57]

APPLYING THE LAW TO THE FACTS

Can a Student Who Is Not on School Grounds Be Suspended for Posting on Social Media a Rap Song Deemed Offensive?

The Facts: A high school student at home posted to a social media site a rap song he wrote, threatening two school coaches because the student heard a report the coaches had molested female students. The relevant four lyrics were

1. "betta watch your back / I'm a serve this n****, like I serve the junkies with some crack";

2. "Run up on T-Bizzle / I'm going to hit you with my rueger";

3. "you f***** with the wrong one / going to get a pistol down your mouth / Boww"; and

4. "middle fingers up if you want to cap that n**** / middle fingers up / he get no mercy n****."

The student's use of "rueger" [sic] references a firearm manufactured by Sturm, Ruger & Co.; to "cap" someone is slang for "shoot." And the "n word" reference was written with an "a" ending. The student was suspended and challenged the school's action, claiming his free speech rights as protected by *Tinker* were violated. Who will win, the student or the school?

The Law: The school wins. The student named the coaches, described the violence, and admitted that the specific intent in making the song was to reach the school community. The school board was within its rights to predict the song's "substantial disruption" at school because of the song's threatening, intimidating, and harassing language.[58]

Student Codes of Conduct and Free Speech

Many schools and universities have codes of conduct that seek to guide student behavior to act appropriately within the school environment. Students who attend a private school or university consent to the school's rules and regulations. For example, Bob Jones University in South Carolina banned its students from interracial dating because God created people differently;[59] students who attended the university agreed to constrict their freedom to associate. At public institutions, the analysis of the government trying to censor speech receives greater scrutiny. To cultivate a welcoming environment, conduct codes often try and limit hateful or racist speech. Students will suffer disciplinary action if they display "unauthorized or obscene, offensive, or obstructive signs at school-sponsored concerts, sporting games, and social-cultural events,"[60] or commit "acts of intolerance" that demonstrate a "malicious intention" toward others.[61] The terms *offensive* and *intolerance* have been found vague and overbroad, and in violation of the First Amendment.

On the other hand, codes that have "prohibited individuals from engaging in conduct that would intimidate, harass, threaten, or assault any person engaged in lawful activities on campus" have been held to be valid when punishing a student who wrote in a journal kept for class about his sexual fantasies involving his female professor.[62] From a courtroom perspective, if schools try to restrict student speech in a public forum in an effort to make everyone "play nice," the code of conduct may be illegal, but for those students who harass others in the campus community directly, the code's prohibition of such speech and acts will likely be upheld as valid.

Rule of Law: On conviction and remand to the government's custody, a prisoner's First Amendment rights are limited.

Prisoners

In Pennsylvania, one prison disallowed certain reading materials—nonreligious newspapers and magazines—for inmates who were classified as especially disruptive and resistant to other disciplinary measures. The prison deemed these materials to be rewards as an incentive for these particularly "bad" prisoners to show better behavior. The prisoners challenged the prison censorship of reading materials. The U.S. Supreme Court decided against the prisoners in *Beard v. Banks* (2006) and held that courts should defer to the legitimate prison objectives of maintaining internal security, including using access to reading materials as an incentive for compliant behavior.[63]

With respect to the freedom of religion in prison, Gregory Holt's beard reflected the depth of his devotion to faith. The Religious Land Use and Institutionalized Persons Act of 2000 (RLUIPA), 42 U.S.C.S. §2000 et seq. prohibits government from imposing a burden on the religious practices of those incarcerated in jails and prisons unless the government's action is the least restrictive means of achieving a CSI. Gregory Holt sued the Arkansas prison as violating his rights under the RLUIPA for not allowing him to grow a beard. The prison justified its policy that no inmate shall have facial hair on the safety need to quickly identify prisoners. The U.S. Supreme Court rejected the state's argument finding that the prison could take photos of the inmate with and without facial hair and the mandated half-inch length precluded the likelihood that the prisoner would hide contraband in his short beard (*Holt v. Hobbs*, 2015).[64]

MAKING THE COURTROOM CONNECTION

With the special populations of juveniles in schools or those incarcerated in prisons, prosecutors must assess the institutional goals and needs and whether or not the school or prison can articulate a CSI to limit First Amendment rights. Typically, courts will defer to an institution. But be wary of blanket prohibitions on constitutionally protected behaviour, as courts may deem the regulation overbroad in punishing otherwise non-disruptive behavior. Counsel defending juveniles in free speech cases will want to challenge the legality of school-issued discipline of the student drawing the distinction between actionable speech (lewd, vulgar, harassing, intimidating, menacing) and acceptable speech (political viewpoints, wearing shirts emblazoned with political messages). In representing prisoners, counsel must fight the institution's right to suppress a wide range of speech and conduct under the umbrella of "the safety and security of staff and inmates," when the prison may accommodate prisoner's rights with more staff oversight and management.

For those working in prisons and jails, one of the most significant areas of government regulation is of a prisoner's freedom of association. In California prisons with large gang populations, the Department of Corrections justified segregating prisoners based on race as an officer and inmate safety issue. The high Court struck down the policy because the prison violated the Constitution by not treating everyone equally under law (*Johnson v. California*, 2005).[65] The other common claim involves the visitation rights of a prisoner's children. A blanket policy keeping children from parents is unconstitutional, but the needs of institutional security outweigh a prisoner's First Amendment right to associate with his or her kids.[66] In determining the whether the prison policy meets constitutional mandates, correctional administrators should ensure policies are narrowly tailored to meet the legitimate prison interest and determine whether any alternative methods exist for the prisoner's exercise of the rights allegedly infringed.

Public Employees

Public employees, such as those who work in law enforcement, courts, and corrections, have free speech rights, but they are limited. As the famous judge Oliver Wendell Holmes said in 1892 upholding restrictions on a policeman's ability to participate in politics, "The petitioner may have a constitutional right to talk politics, but he has no constitutional right to be a policeman."[67] Criminal justice professionals represent "the people," and an employee's personal views may reflect negatively on the agency mission and lead to discipline or termination. The U.S. Supreme Court said in a case holding no First Amendment violation where a deputy district attorney claimed he was not promoted for criticizing the legitimacy of a warrant,

Rule of Law: Public employees have a free speech right to criticize the workplace as long as the speech is a "matter of public concern."

> When a citizen enters government service, the citizen by necessity must accept certain limitations on his or her freedom. . . . Public employees, moreover, often occupy trusted positions in society. When they speak out, they can express views that contravene governmental policies or impair the proper performance of governmental functions. (*Garcetti v. Ceballos*, 2006)[68]

Under the *Garcetti* **test**, the public employee's speech will be protected if

1. The speech is made pursuant to the employee's official job duties,

2. The speech "relates to a matter of public concern" (school teacher wrongfully fired for writing a letter to the editor criticizing the school board's spending decisions),[69] and

3. In the balance between the employee's free speech rights and the boss's ability to run an efficient agency, the agency continues to operate smoothly.

Today's free speech at work cases often involve social media postings and the burden such posts, if inflammatory, place on the agency's trust within the community. In the chapter-opening case study, the probation officer could be legally fired for her racially derogatory Facebook post because her comments were not related to improving the work environment and the public she serves could legitimately question whether she would treat everyone equally under the law.[70]

FREEDOM OF ASSOCIATION

The First Amendment does not explicitly mention freedom of association, but the U.S. Supreme Court has interpreted such a right. If the individual can do it legally by himself, so, too, can he do it with others. For the government to restrict a group's right to associate, it must be shown that

1. The government interest is compelling, and

2. The government's objective cannot be achieved by less restrictive means.

Lawmakers have been aggressive in trying to stop gang members from associating with one another. Robust illegal drug trade and deadly gang violence are closely related. States passed laws that prohibited gang members from gathering and punished those gangs that did. In *City of Chicago v. Morales* (1999), the high Court examined the ordinance that "prohibits 'criminal street gang members' from loitering in public places.[71] Under the ordinance, if a police officer observes a person whom he reasonably believes to be a gang member loitering in a public place with one or more persons, he shall order them to disperse. Anyone who does not promptly obey such an order has violated the ordinance." The Court concluded that the ordinance unlawfully included a great deal of harmless behavior: In any public place in Chicago, persons in the company of a gang member may be ordered to disperse if their purpose is not apparent to an officer. Moreover, the ordinance's loitering definition—"to remain in any one place with no apparent purpose"—gave officers absolute discretion to determine what activities constitute loitering, which violates the principle of legality, discussed in Chapter 3.

Rule of Law: Everyone has a First Amendment right to associate with others.

FREEDOM OF RELIGION

Rule of Law: The Establishment Clause means anyone can "establish" a house of worship and the government cannot deny a religion's legitimacy without investigation.

Establishment Clause

The freedom of religion expressed in the First Amendment is two pronged: It protects both the establishment of religion and the exercise (practice) of religion. The so-called Establishment Clause has been interpreted to separate church and state so that neither entity is involved in the other's affairs. The test for whether a law has an impermissible religious objective is called the *Lemon* test, enunciated in *Lemon v. Kurtzman* (1971):

1. The challenged statute must have a secular (nonreligious) legislative purpose,

2. The statute's principal or primary effect must be one that neither advances nor inhibits religion, and

3. The statute must not foster an excessive government entanglement with religion.[72]

In 2005, the U.S. Supreme Court noted that the *Lemon* test was applied in a piecemeal fashion and was not helpful in deciding the case before it, *Van Orden v. Perry* (2005). In the *Van Orden* case, the Court was asked to decide whether a display of the religious tenets of the Ten Commandments at the Texas state capitol violated the separation of church and state. The Court found that the display was one of several monuments and historical markers representing a part of state history, so the monument survived the Establishment Clause challenge. On the same day the *Van Order* decision was announced, the Court reached an opposite result in *McCreary County v. ACLU of Kentucky* (2005), where the high Court was asked to rule on the legality of the placement of gold-framed copies of the Ten Commandments in the hallways of Kentucky courthouses.[73] The Court upheld the removal of the displays because county governments cannot promote certain religious displays over others. But not all cases where there appears an excessive entanglement of government and religion are decided on the side of a strict separation of church and state. Many state-sponsored functions, such as school sporting and graduation events, begin or end with a moment of reflection and prayer.

The town of Greece, New York, opened every session of their board meeting, where they discussed and passed ordinances that affected the community, with a prayer. Two town members complained that the prayers violated the Establishment Clause, but the high Court disagreed in *Greece v. Galloway* (2014), stating that the federal Congress and many state legislatures have been praying before meetings since the country's inception.[74] In finding in favor of the town of Greece, the Court noted a variety of faiths represented at the meetings and no government official coerced people to participate.

Exercise Clause

Rule of Law: The Exercise Clause means anyone can worship (exercise) however they please, subject to criminal laws penalizing hurting people physically or sexually.

Whereas religious beliefs enjoy absolute protection under the First Amendment, religious practices that offend societal norms or subvert the social order can be regulated.[75] The government may regulate certain religious practices, for example, by outlawing polygamy, incest, drug use, or murder in religious ceremonies. But the government may not infringe on religious practices simply because only a minority of people practice a particular faith.[76] In the *Church of the Lukumi Babalu Aye* case, reprinted in part on the following pages, the city government passed ordinances that appeared facially valid (documents that appear legal "on their face") but, on strict scrutiny review, were enacted to only apply to the Santerian religion, which sacrificed chickens as a valid exercise of their worship practices. Read the case excerpt carefully and take note of the lawmakers' comments to gain public support for the ordinances.

CHURCH OF THE LUKUMI BABALU AYE, INC. V. CITY OF HIALEAH, 508 U.S. 520 (1993)

Supreme Court of the United States

Justice Kennedy delivered the opinion of the Court. (9–0)

FACTS: This case involves practices of the Santeria religion, which originated in the 19th century. When hundreds of thousands of members of the Yoruba people were brought as slaves from western Africa to Cuba, their traditional African religion absorbed significant elements of Roman Catholicism. The resulting syncretion, or fusion, is Santeria, "the way of the saints." The Santeria faith teaches that every individual has a destiny from God, a destiny fulfilled with the aid and energy of the orishas. The basis of the Santeria religion is the nurture of a personal relation with the orishas, and one of the principal forms of devotion is an animal sacrifice. The sacrifice of animals as part of religious rituals has ancient roots. Animal sacrifice is mentioned throughout the Old Testament, and it played an important role in the practice of Judaism before destruction of the second Temple in Jerusalem. In modern Islam, there is an annual sacrifice commemorating Abraham's sacrifice of a ram in the stead of his son.

According to Santeria teaching, the orishas are powerful but not immortal. They depend for survival on the sacrifice. Sacrifices are performed at birth, marriage, and death rites, for the cure of the sick, for the initiation of new members and priests, and during an annual celebration. Animals sacrificed in Santeria rituals include chickens, pigeons, doves, ducks, guinea pigs, goats, sheep, and turtles. The animals are killed by the cutting of the carotid arteries in the neck. The sacrificed animal is cooked and eaten, except after healing and death rituals.

Petitioner Church of the Lukumi Babalu Aye, Inc. (Church), is a not-for-profit corporation organized under Florida law in 1973. The Church and its congregants practice the Santeria religion. In April 1987, the Church leased land in the city of Hialeah, Florida, and announced plans to establish a house of worship as well as a school, cultural center, and museum [with the goal] to bring the practice of the Santeria faith, including its ritual of animal sacrifice, into the open. The prospect of a Santeria church in their midst was distressing to many members of the Hialeah community, and the announcement of the plans to open a Santeria church in Hialeah prompted the city council to hold an emergency public session on June 9, 1987.

First, the city council adopted Resolution 87-66, which noted the "concern" expressed by residents of the city "that certain religions may propose to engage in practices which are inconsistent with public morals, peace or safety," and declared that "the City reiterates its commitment to a prohibition against any and all acts of any and all religious groups which are inconsistent with public morals, peace or safety."

Next, the council approved an emergency ordinance, Ordinance 87-40, which incorporated in full, except as to penalty, Florida's animal cruelty laws. Among other things, the incorporated state law subjected to criminal punishment "whoever . . . unnecessarily or cruelly . . . kills any animal." The city council responded at first with a hortatory [strong urging] enactment, Resolution 87-90, that noted its residents' "great concern regarding the possibility of public ritualistic animal sacrifices" and the state law prohibition. The resolution declared the city policy "to oppose the ritual sacrifices of animals" within Hialeah and announced that any person or organization practicing animal sacrifice "will be prosecuted."

In September 1987, the city council adopted three substantive ordinances addressing the issue of religious animal sacrifice. Ordinance 87-52 defined "sacrifice" as "to unnecessarily kill, torment, torture, or mutilate an animal in a public or private ritual or ceremony not for the primary purpose of food consumption," and prohibited owning or possessing an animal "intending to use such animal for food purposes." It restricted application of this prohibition, however, to any individual or group that "kills, slaughters or sacrifices animals for any type of ritual, regardless of whether or not the flesh or blood of the animal is to be consumed."

Declaring, moreover, that the city council "has determined that the sacrificing of animals within the city limits is contrary to the public health, safety, welfare and morals of the community," the city council adopted Ordinance 87-71 [which] provided that "it shall be unlawful for any person, persons, corporations or associations to sacrifice any animal within the corporate limits of the City of Hialeah, Florida."

The final Ordinance, 87-72, defined "slaughter" as "the killing of animals for food" and prohibited slaughter outside of areas zoned for slaughterhouse use. All ordinances and resolutions passed the city council by unanimous vote. Violations of each of the four ordinances were punishable by fines not exceeding $500 or imprisonment not exceeding 60 days, or both.

(Continued)

(Continued)

ISSUE: [Do city ordinances regulating animal sacrifice, but effectively prohibiting only sacrifice as practiced by a particular religion, violate the First Amendment's free exercise of religion clause?]

HOLDING: [Yes.]

REASONING: The Free Exercise Clause of the First Amendment, which has been applied to the States through the Fourteenth Amendment, provides that "Congress shall make no law respecting an establishment of religion, or prohibiting the free exercise thereof . . . ." In addressing the constitutional protection for free exercise of religion, our cases establish the general proposition that a law that is neutral and of general applicability need not be justified by a compelling [state] interest [CSI] even if the law has the incidental effect of burdening a particular religious practice.[77] A law failing to satisfy these requirements must be justified by a [CSI] and must be narrowly tailored to advance that interest. These ordinances fail. . . .

In our Establishment Clause cases, we have often stated the principle that the First Amendment forbids an official purpose to disapprove of a particular religion or of religion in general. Indeed, it was "historical instances of religious persecution and intolerance that gave concern to those who drafted the Free Exercise Clause."[78] To determine the object of a law, we must begin with its text, for the minimum requirement of neutrality is that a law **not** discriminate on its face. . . . The record in this case compels the conclusion that suppression of the central element of the Santeria worship service was the object of the ordinances. That the ordinances were enacted "'because of,' not merely 'in spite of'" their suppression of Santeria religious practice, is revealed by the events preceding their enactment.

The minutes and taped excerpts of the June 9 session, both of which are in the record, evidence significant hostility exhibited by residents, members of the city council, and other city officials toward the Santeria religion and its practice of animal sacrifice. When Councilman Martinez, a supporter of the ordinances [suppressing Santeria], stated that in prerevolution Cuba "people were put in jail for practicing this religion," the audience applauded. Other statements by members of the city council were in a similar vein . . . [when Martinez] . . . questioned: "If we could not practice this [religion] in our home-land [Cuba], why bring it to this country?"

Councilman Cardoso said that Santeria devotees at the Church "are in violation of everything this country stands for." Councilman Mejides indicated that he was "totally against the sacrificing of animals" and distinguished kosher slaughter because it had a "real purpose." The "Bible says we are allowed to sacrifice an animal for consumption," he continued, "but for any other purposes, I don't believe that the Bible allows that." The president of the city council, Councilman Echevarria, asked: "What can we do to prevent the Church from opening?"

Various Hialeah city officials made comparable comments. The chaplain of the Hialeah Police Department told the city council that Santeria was a sin, "foolishness," "an abomination to the Lord," and the worship of "demons." He advised the city council: "We need to be helping people and sharing with them the truth that is found in Jesus Christ." He concluded: "I would exhort you . . . not to permit this Church to exist." The city attorney commented that Resolution 87-66 indicated: "This community will not tolerate religious practices which are abhorrent to its citizens. . . ." Similar comments were made by the deputy city attorney. This history discloses the object of the ordinances [was religiously motivated to suppress the Santeria worshippers].

CONCLUSION: The ordinances had as their object the suppression of religion. These ordinances are not neutral, and the court below committed clear error in failing to reach this conclusion. Reversed.

The *Hialeah* case is important because it illustrates the high Court's strict scrutiny approach when governments seek to suppress First Amendment freedoms claiming a superior CSI. We know through the city ordinances' exemption of hunters, kosher slaughterhouses, and exterminators, Hialeah's purported CSI in forbidding "animal cruelty" was not, as the representatives said, public safety. When Councilman Cardoso said the Santerians "are in violation of everything this country stands for," he exposed the pretext that the public safety ordinances were enacted not to protect the community but for religious suppression of a faith with whom the larger community did not agree. From a courtroom perspective represented in Figure 11.2, the case was resolved with the Santerians' free exercise rights outweighing Hialeah's purported CSI, because the lawmakers exposed their discriminatory intent before enacting the laws.

Figure 11.2 Santerians' Scales of Justice

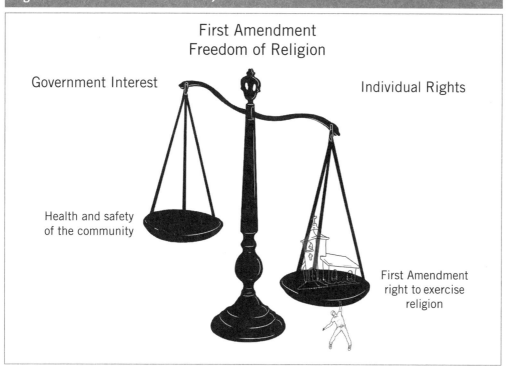

First Amendment
Freedom of Religion

Government Interest

Individual Rights

Health and safety
of the community

First Amendment
right to exercise
religion

SUMMARY

1. You will be able to competently discuss the difference between protected and unprotected speech. The First Amendment provides that "Congress shall make no law . . . abridging freedom of speech," which includes expressive conduct. If the government regulates speech on the basis of its content—where "content" means "what you are saying" (criticizing the government, e.g.)—then citizens may feel that their free speech rights have been "chilled." Vague laws have a chilling effect on free speech rights. The law prevents content-based restrictions and viewpoint discrimination, unless there is a compelling state interest (CSI) in regulating the speech. The government regulation must be the least restrictive means and narrowly tailored to not burden speech, but the government can place time, manner, and place restrictions on speech. People have a right to be free from annoyances in the middle of the night, for example, but speech cannot be censored merely because the speech is offensive to some people. Two doctrines that protect speech are the overbroad doctrine, which invalidates laws that proscribe

protected and unprotected speech, and the vagueness doctrine, which says that if people of reasonable intelligence have to guess at the meaning of the law's words, it is void.

2. You will understand the significance of symbolic speech and how to achieve public order without suppressing speech and expression. Fighting words are words that, by their very utterance, inflict injury or incite immediate violence; as such, they are not protected by the First Amendment. Other speech that is unprotected is speech that poses a clear and present danger, which is a call to incite immediate lawless activity or a true threat, which does not have to be carried out to be illegal. Expressive conduct conveys an idea that is protected as legal. Activities such as nude dancing, wearing a jacket that swears at the military draft, burning the flag, or being a Nazi and holding a public march through a town heavily populated by Holocaust survivors—although all may be considered offensive— are legal. Cross burning is legal if it is not meant to intimidate, and the *Virginia v. Black* (2003) case gives a

good history of why cross burning is specifically meant to intimidate minorities. Speech in a public forum is given special protections because the First Amendment encourages discourse in the "marketplace of ideas."

3. You will be able to properly identify obscenity. Pornography, which includes photographs or movies that depict adults engaged in sexual activity or sexually provocative poses, is protected speech and is legal under the First Amendment. Child pornography, which depicts minors engaged in sexual activity with each other or with adults, is unprotected speech by the First Amendment, except if computer generated such as in the *Ashcroft v. Free Speech* (2002) case, a holding that has been since modified by federal law criminalizing all obscene depictions of sex with minors. The test for obscenity, known as the *Miller* test, defines a work as obscene if, by contemporary community standards, it depicts work that appeals to a prurient interest, is patently offensive sexually, and taken as a whole lacks serious literary, artistic, political, or scientific value. If the photograph, book, movie, or other work meets all three prongs of the *Miller* test, it is obscene and the government may suppress it and censor it from the public.

4. You will be able to articulate the legal restrictions on free speech rights in public schools, employment, and prisons. Students do not give up their free speech rights at the schoolhouse gate, but the government has an interest in regulating behavior that undermines the educational mission. University speech codes on college campuses must be narrowly tailored when colleges seek to promote diversity without suppressing the free speech rights of students to express hatred for people based on their race, gender, or sexual orientation. Prisoners have limited First Amendment rights, but the prison must have a legitimate CSI to infringe on the freedom of prisoners to read certain material or to grow a short beard in religious observance. Public employees under the *Garcetti* test have free speech rights if their speech is made in their official capacity, is related to a public concern, and does not interfere with the smooth running of the agency.

5. You will be able to make sense of the limits of a secular government's relationship with religion with respect to criminal law and procedure. The Establishment Clause and the Exercise Clause of the First Amendment give protection to religious beliefs, but the government can restrict certain religious practices that contravene societal duties and are subversive to good order. The *Lemon* test is used to test Establishment Clause violations, and laws will be held invalid if they are not secular, advance or inhibit religion, or foster an excessive entanglement with religion. Strict scrutiny is used to analyze laws that burden religion as discovered in the *Church of the Lukumi Babalu Aye* (1993) case that showed the city council was impermissibly suppressing an unfavored religious practice.

Go back to the beginning of the chapter and reread the news excerpts associated with the learning objectives. Test yourself to determine if you can understand the material covered in the text in the context of the news.

KEY TERMS AND PHRASES

chilling effect 310
clear and present danger 314
compelling state interest 307
content-based regulations 307
Establishment Clause 324
Exercise Clause 324
expressive conduct 306
facially valid 324
fighting words 311

First Amendment 306
Garcetti test 323
least restrictive means 307
Lemon test 324
Miller test 315
narrowly tailored 307
obscenity 315
overbroad 316
protected speech 306

prurient interest 315
public forum 309
speech 306
strict scrutiny 307
time, manner, and place restriction 309
true threats 314
unprotected speech 314
vague 310
viewpoint discrimination 307

PROBLEM-SOLVING EXERCISES

1. The Delaware Breach of the Peace statute provides the following:

Whoever placed on public or private property a symbol, object, appellation, including but not limited to, a burning cross, Nazi swastika, a stuffed doll in likeness of any elected official, which one knows or has reasonable grounds to know arouses anger, alarm or resentment in others, shall be guilty of a felony.

John Smith, a devout member of the Santeria church, made a stuffed doll in the likeness of the local mayor and in one of the local university's free speech zones, hung the doll in a tree and lit it on fire. At Smith's trial, he appeared in court wearing chicken feathers and the judge told him to take them off.[79] Smith refused and said he was wearing the feathers to honor his god, Icarus. The judge held Smith in contempt. Discuss any defenses to the felony and contempt charges Smith may have. **(ROL: Compelling state interest [CSI], overbroad, First Amendment Exercise Clause)**

2. Mary opposed the United States' military operations overseas. She went to a public park and stood on a grassy knoll and began addressing a group of 12 to 15 people. Mary said, "Let's demand accountability from the government. If members of the administration won't pull our troops out of the Middle East, let's assemble and detonate bombs and plant them outside of all the military bases until the government has to withdraw from Iraq." No one listening responded to Mary's speech, but one listener waved in approval. Mary was arrested under a state statute that prohibited "advocating insurrection against the federal government." Mary claims she has a complete defense in the First Amendment. Is Mary correct? **(ROL: True threat, clear and present danger)**

3. After a well-publicized hate killing on public transit in a major northwest city, protest organizations that identify as "alt-right" (alternative right-wing political perspective) planned a freedom of speech rally and a rally "against Sharia law and for human rights" planned by the group "ACT for America" that called itself "the NRA [National Rifle Association] of national security." In light of the city's mourning for the victims, the mayor called for the revocation of permits for the rallies to take place in the city's public parks claiming that, if held according to plan, many people would be injured and incited to riot. The group claimed their First Amendment rights to peaceably assemble outweighed the mayor's fear. Which side will win and why? **(ROL: First Amendment right to peaceably assemble, protected speech)**

4. The chair of the county government board of supervisors launched a Facebook page where county business was publicized and discussed. The chair actively solicited comments asking the community to "please let me know what you're thinking about what's going on" in the county. One community member, Brian, posted on the county's page criticizing the board and alleging corruption. In response, the chair blocked Brian so he could no longer post on the county's page claiming that Brian's posts were derogatory and, therefore, inappropriate. Did the chair violate Brian's First Amendment rights? **(ROL: Content-based regulation of speech)**

12

DEFENSES

Go to the end of the chapter. Skim the key terms and phrases and read the summary closely. Come back and look at the following news excerpts to focus your reading throughout the chapter to understand the law ensuring punishments are fair, accepted by society, and tailored to the individual offender, which is what recognizing defenses guarantees. In this chapter you will learn about defenses based on excuse, which concedes the crime was wrong but tells you why the offender did it (e.g., the offender was too drunk to know what was going on). You will also learn about defenses based on justification that the crime was committed but it was right to commit, such as killing in self-defense. The chapter begins with a case excerpt from a death-penalty client, Freddie Hall, which recounts the heinous way some intellectually disabled children are treated counterbalanced with the heinous crimes they commit as adults, reflecting society's struggles with recognizing defenses and fashioning an appropriate punishment for the offender.

WHY THIS CHAPTER MATTERS TO YOU	THE LEARNING OBJECTIVES AS REFLECTED IN THE NEWS
After you have read this chapter: **Learning Objective 1:** You will be able to articulate the public policy reasons for recognizing defenses.	The legal term is *entrapment*. 20 men were arrested on sex charges after they thought they were talking to an underage girl. This type of undercover operation is just one of hundreds law enforcement officers are using to catch would-be sexual offenders online. But how the officers reel in the suspects could be illegal, in some cases. The line between entrapment and really good investigation is whether the idea to commit the crime began in the mind of the accused, or in the mind of law enforcement. (WTVM.com [TX], May 7, 2018)
Learning Objective 2: You will understand how defenses are raised before and at trial.	Facing a mountain of circumstantial evidence in the first-degree murder trial of former New England Patriots star Aaron Hernandez, the defense team took a gamble during its closing argument. They claimed Hernandez witnessed his PCP-addled associates Ernest Wallace and Carlos Ortiz fatally shoot 27-year-old Odin Lloyd at a North Attleborough, Massachusetts, industrial park on June 17, 2013. The move backfired and stunned members of the jury that ultimately convicted Hernandez on Wednesday on first-degree murder and gun charges. Worse, the admission strengthened the prosecution's circumstantial case that otherwise lacked a murder weapon, a cooperative eyewitness or a solid motive. The gamble, along with the defense's last-minute presentation of an alternative narrative for Lloyd's murder, undid weeks of effective tactics from Hernandez' all-star defense team, legal experts said. "They put an end to any question about it, any doubt the jury could have raised in the deliberation room, by just coming straight out in the closing arguments and saying he was there." "Biggest blunder. Never should have been said." (*International Business Times*, April 16, 2015)

WHY THIS CHAPTER MATTERS TO YOU	THE LEARNING OBJECTIVES AS REFLECTED IN THE NEWS
Learning Objective 3: You will appreciate the defenses based on excuse and variations of the *mens rea*–based defenses, such as infancy and insanity.	The Portland man arrested in Woodburn after allegedly attacking several people with a machete in January 2017 will rely on a guilty except for insanity defense (GEI) according to court documents. Alan Brock, then 29, was arrested by Woodburn police and charged with multiple counts of attempted murder, robbery and assault. He was ruled unfit to proceed to a trial in July 2017 and was admitted to Oregon State Hospital for treatment of his mental illness. Brock's attorney Steven Walls gave notice of his defendant's intent to rely upon GEI defense in a court hearing April 10, 2018. A GEI defense attempts to prove that a defendant did not know what he or she was doing was wrong when crimes were committed. (*Woodburn Independent* [OR], April 25, 2018)
Learning Objective 4: You will successfully distinguish defenses based on justification.	The Minnesota Court of Appeals dismissed the state of Minnesota's appeal to allow climate activists charged for shutting down a petroleum pipeline the chance to present evidence to explain their actions. In 2016, defendants Annette Klapstein and Emily Johnston drove to the remote town of Leonard, Minnesota, and used bolt cutters to break the lock on a gate and shut down a pipeline valve to stop the flow of tar. The activists were charged with several felonies or misdemeanors [and] sent notice that they would be using the "necessity defense," to express "their individual perceptions of the necessity of their actions in preventing environmental harm." (LegalNewsLine, May 7, 2018)
Learning Objective 5: You will be able to identify the differences between self-defense, battered woman syndrome, and defense of others and property.	Thirteen years in prison haven't dimmed Nancy Seaman's memory of the morning she killed her husband. At trial, Seaman's co-workers testified they had seen her with a black eye and other physical injuries. One of her sons testified he witnessed her being abused by his father. Seaman, a stay-at-home mom for most of her marriage, told jurors she was emotionally and physically abused throughout the decades they spent together. She went to the police twice, but never filed a report. The abuse worsened as she earned her teaching degree and her husband lost his job, and escalated when he discovered she planned to leave him, she said. It never took much to trigger the abuse, Seaman said. "It could be the tone of my voice, the look on my face, some thought he imagined I was having. It became my routine to repair kicked-in doors, damaged drywall, broken furniture, smashed glassware. It was a way of denying the violence, covering up the evidence of it, and going about life as if nothing had ever happened." (NBC News [MI], April 26, 2018)

Chapter-Opening Case Study:
The Public Policy Reasons to Recognize Defenses

Freddie Lee Hall's siblings testified that there was something "very wrong" with him as a child. Hall was "slow with speech and . . . slow to learn." He "walked and talked long after his other brothers and sisters" and had "great difficulty forming his words." Hall's upbringing appeared to make his deficits in adaptive functioning all the more severe. Hall was raised, in the words of the sentencing judge, "under the most horrible family circumstances imaginable."

Although "teachers and siblings alike immediately recognized [Hall] to be significantly mentally retarded . . . this retardation did not garner any sympathy from his mother, but rather caused much scorn to befall him." Hall was "constantly beaten because he was 'slow' or because he made simple mistakes." His mother "would strap [Hall] to his bed at night, with a rope thrown over a rafter. In the morning, she would awaken Hall by hoisting him up and whipping him with a belt, rope, or cord." Hall was beaten "ten or fifteen times a week sometimes." His mother tied him "in a 'croaker' sack, swung it over a fire, and beat him," "buried him in the sand up to his neck to 'strengthen his legs,'" and "held a gun on Hall . . . while she poked [him] with sticks."

The jury, notwithstanding this testimony, voted to sentence Hall to death, and the sentencing court adopted the jury's recommendation. [Hall had been convicted along with Mack Ruffin when in 1978 they both kidnapped, raped, and killed Karol Hurst who was 21 and pregnant and killed Sheriff's Deputy Lonnie Coburn who was trying to arrest the pair at a convenience store robbery]. The court found that there was "substantial evidence in the record" to support the finding that "Freddie Lee Hall has been mentally retarded his entire life." Yet the court also "suspected that the defense experts [were] guilty of some professional overkill," because "nothing of which the experts testified could explain how a psychotic, mentally-retarded, brain damaged, learning-disabled, speech-impaired person could formulate a plan whereby a car was stolen and a convenience store was robbed." The sentencing court went on to state that, even assuming the expert testimony to be accurate, "the learning disabilities, mental retardation, and other mental difficulties . . . cannot be used to justify, excuse or extenuate the moral culpability of the defendant in this cause" (*Hall v. Florida,* 2014).[1]

HOW DEFENSES ARE RAISED

The Public Policy Reasons to Recognize Defenses

Human nature favors the value of the victim's life when weighed against the defendant's life. Public opinion often rejects criminal defenses because such defenses seemingly place the victim and defendant on equal footing. Who among us can advocate a defense by which someone may "get away" with murder? Yet a defendant's actions are sometimes excused. Suffering from a mental illness can interfere with daily functioning and may lead one to victimize others. Or a defendant's actions are sometimes justified, for example, killing an aggressor in self-defense. One legal scholar has described the difference between the two types of defenses this way: "A justification speaks to the rightness of the act; an excuse, to whether the actor is accountable for a concededly wrongful act."[2]

This chapter examines the basic defenses in criminal law and how they operate to relieve a criminal actor from a certain or specific punishment under the law.

Table 12.1 Defenses Based on Excuse and Justification	
Excuse "What I did is wrong, but I should not be in trouble because I have an excuse."	**Justification** "What I did is wrong, but I should not be in trouble because what I did is justified."
Consent	Necessity
Mistake	Self-defense
Infancy	Defense of others
Intoxication	Imperfect self-defense
Duress	Battered woman syndrome
Mens rea–based defenses	Entrapment

In a criminal trial, the government, represented by the prosecution, carries the burden of proof to prove every element of an offense beyond a reasonable doubt. The burden of proof remains with the prosecution always. Under common law, the burden of proving "affirmative defenses—indeed, 'all circumstances . . . of justification, excuse or alleviation'—rested on the defendant."[3] The term *burden of proof* encompasses two intertwined and similar concepts: the burden of production and the burden of persuasion.

Burden of Production and Persuasion

If the defense chooses to raise a defense during trial, she has what is called the burden of production, which is the minimum amount of evidence the judge will consider sufficient to warrant a jury instruction (discussed in Chapter 2). For instance, if Akeno wanted to assert the defense that she was too intoxicated to form the specific intent for first-degree murder (willful, premeditated, and deliberate), she would have to introduce sufficient evidence that she was drunk. Evidence might be testimony by the bartender and friends; observations by the police officers who witnessed her slurred speech, stumbling gait, and the alcohol smell on her breath; or testimony by the physician who noted her blood alcohol level when he drew a sample. Introducing alcohol-related evidence would allow the judge to give the jury an intoxication instruction that would read "if you find the defendant was intoxicated to negate specific intent *mens rea* for the crime of murder. . . ." If Akeno, instead, just sat quietly at trial, confident that everyone knew she was drunk when she committed the crime, but introduced no evidence, the judge could not instruct the jury on the intoxication defense because making a bold statement at trial unsupported by evidence is legally insufficient. Akeno would not have met her burden of production.

For some defenses, the defendant must notify the prosecution that he intends to raise those defenses at trial, for example, an alibi or mental health defense, to give the prosecution an opportunity to rebut the defense. In many jurisdictions, if a defendant raises a mental health defense, he must be examined by a state doctor or forfeit his right to assert the defense. The U.S. Supreme Court held that no Fifth Amendment prohibition against "compelled self-incrimination" applies in state-ordered mental status evaluations and the results can be used against the defendant to rebut a diminished capacity defense, as in *Kansas v. Cheever* (2013), where the state was allowed to use a court-ordered evaluation to rebut defendant's methamphetamine intoxication defense.[4] State laws differ over the amount of evidence required to sustain the burden of production for affirmative defenses. Some states require a preponderance of evidence standard, which typically means 51% on a scale from 1 to 100; others demand a clear and convincing standard, which is more than a preponderance but less than beyond a reasonable doubt; and others require a beyond reasonable doubt standard. State law also varies on how the burden of production might shift between defense and prosecution, most notably with the law of self-defense.[5] The practice in most states is once a defendant raises self-defense, the burden shifts to the state to prove that the defendant did *not* act in self-defense. At all times, however, the burden of proving each and every element of the crime, regardless of the defense raised, remains with the government.[6]

The burden of persuasion means the responsibility at trial to convince the jury to find in your favor. As with any evidence at trial, the jury is free to disregard the defense raised or to give the defense great weight. Recognizing a defense typically results in an acquittal for the defendant, or at least a reduced sentence.

Alibi

Having an alibi is a complete defense; if the judge or jury accepts the defense as true, the defendant will be acquitted and go home. An alibi defense means that, at the time the crime occurred, the defendant was somewhere else and can prove it. If the crime happened in Phoenix, Arizona, while the defendant was on the Great Wall of China, and the defendant can prove his whereabouts with plane tickets, photographs, and eyewitnesses, then the defendant will be acquitted. If successfully raised, an alibi defense disproves the government's contention that the defendant is the perpetrator of the crime. Prior to trial, as in the case of insanity, the defendant has an affirmative obligation to notify the government that she intends to raise such a defense at trial to give the government an opportunity to disprove it. If the state confirms the defendant's alibi, there may be no need for a trial.

Statute of Limitations

A statute of limitations places limits, defined by legislators, on the time during which an action can be brought in both civil and criminal cases. A statute of limitations can be a defense to certain crimes because the prosecutor failed to file charges within the time frame defined by law. Many states have different statutes of limitations for various crimes, but there is no limitation for the crime of murder. Statutes of limitations can be tolled (stopped) by certain events, such as the suspect's leaving the jurisdiction and running away from the administration of justice.

> **Rule of Law: A statute of limitations is a specific time in which to bring charges for a crime; there is no statute of limitations for the crime of murder.**

Statutes of limitation cannot be retroactively applied in a manner that violates the Constitution's *ex post facto* clause, which prohibits criminalizing conduct that was not a crime when it was committed. Stogner was indicted in California for sex-related child abuse that occurred for close to twenty years, from 1955 to 1973. When the alleged abuse took place, the statute of limitations for prosecuting such crimes was 3 years from the date the crime took place. California later amended its sex abuse statute of limitations laws because of the typically long delay between the acts of molestation and eventual victim disclosure. Stogner complained that enlarging the statute of limitations after he had allegedly committed the crimes was unfair, and the high Court agreed, holding California's amended law violated the Constitution and Sogner's due process rights (*Stogner v. California*, 2003).[7]

COMPETENCY

Competency means that the defendant possesses the mental faculties required to be a meaningful participant in all stages of the criminal trial process, from initial arrest, through sentencing, to execution via the death penalty if applicable. To be competent under the law and thereby ensuring public confidence in the criminal trial process, a defendant must meet two prongs:

1. Understand the nature of the court proceedings against him, and

2. Be able to assist his counsel in his defense.[8]

> **Rule of Law: Due process requires that a defendant understand the complex dynamics of a trial and be able to assist in his defense throughout the entire criminal trial process.**

Understanding the complexity of the court proceedings includes knowing the roles of the prosecutor, judge, and defense counsel; the consequences of exercising the right to remain silent or to testify at trial; and the consequences of a conviction. The defendant must also be able to help his lawyer defend him by identifying defense witnesses or talking about trial strategy. If one prong is missing, the defendant is not competent.[9]

Forcible Medication to Restore Competency

Often, jails and prisons substitute for mental health facilities, and mind-altering medication is dispensed to control a mentally ill inmate's behavior. Having a mental illness is not a crime. But what happens when an inmate refuses to take medication and be placed into what some observers call a "chemical straitjacket"? Does an inmate have a constitutional right to be free from being forcibly medicated, ingesting drugs against his will? If we imagine the scales of justice, on one side is the government's interest in bringing an offender to trial or, if in prison, to protect himself and fellow inmates; on the other side is the offender's constitutional liberty not to be forcibly medicated. The legal analysis differs whether an offender is awaiting trial or has already been convicted.

In *Washington v. Harper* (1990), a prisoner was suffering from psychosis (break from reality) and was entitled to a hearing before being forcibly medicated,[10] if an independent body determined that the prisoner was

1. A danger to himself and others, and

2. Such medication was in the inmate's best interest.

The U.S. Supreme Court said in *Harper*, "The forcible injection of medication into a nonconsenting person's body represents a substantial interference with that person's liberty." Whereas the *Harper* decision focused on a convicted defendant remanded to custody in a prison, the analysis is different when medication might interfere with a defendant's presentation at trial. In 1987, David Riggins was charged with robbery and murder and had experienced psychotic episodes. He was treated with thioridazine (Mellaril), a strong antipsychotic drug that can produce noticeable zombie-like side effects. Riggins wanted to discontinue the medication prior to trial to let the jury see his true mental condition, but the trial judge refused. The jury rejected Riggins's insanity defense, convicted him of murder and sentenced him to death. The U.S. Supreme Court overturned his conviction in *Riggins v. Nevada* (1992), and vacated his death sentence on the basis that once Riggins asked to be taken off the medication, the state had to establish the medical necessity for forcing him to continue.[11]

The high Court further refined the legal standard for forcible medication in 2003 with the appeal of a St. Louis dentist, Charles Sell, who was charged with insurance fraud and was deemed incompetent to stand trial. Through a long series of legal proceedings, the government sought to forcibly medicate Sell to restore him to competency to stand trial. The U.S. Supreme Court heard Sell's motion to resist "artificial competence" and determined the state must meet the following criteria to forcibly medicate a defendant:

1. Defendant must be charged with a serious crime.

2. Proposed treatment will get defendant to meet the two-prong test for competency.

3. The drug's side effects will not impair the defendant's due process right to a fair trial.

4. The drugs are "medically appropriate" for the defendant's illness.

Based on his incompetency to stand trial, Sell was eventually incarcerated longer than if he had been tried and convicted of the charged offenses.

Springboard for Discussion

According to a 2014 Treatment Advocacy Center report:

> American prisons and jails housed an estimated 356,268 inmates with severe mental illness in 2012—on par with the population of Anchorage, Alaska, or Trenton, New Jersey. That figure is more than 10 times the number of mentally ill patients in state psychiatric hospitals in the same year— about 35,000 people.[12]

Many mentally ill inmates are consigned to solitary confinement for their safety. Is this fair?

DEFENSES BASED ON EXCUSE

Consent

Consent is the willing participation of the actor. For some crimes, the consent of the alleged victim may influence the *mens rea* of the defendant. There are crimes in which consent is a defense to the offender's liability, most notably for the crime of rape, in which the victim's nonconsent is an essential element of the crime. Typically, whether the victim consented to the act giving rise to criminal liability is no defense; for example, it is not a valid defense in a murder case that the victim begged to be killed. Likewise, agreeing to become a fraternity or sorority pledge does not mean that one consents to alcohol poisoning or other initiation rites that may lead to serious bodily injury or death.

Rule of Law: Consent is a complete defense.

Rule of Law: Mistakes
of fact or law can be
defenses in limited-fact
situations.

Mistake

Everybody makes mistakes. In criminal law, mistakes that negate *mens rea* excuse criminal liability. The Model Penal Code provides the general outline of the defense:

Model Penal Code §2.04

Ignorance or mistake as to a matter of fact or law is a defense if:

a. The ignorance or mistakes negatives [negates, eliminates] the purpose, knowledge, belief, recklessness or negligence required to establish a material element of the offense.

There are two types of mistakes: mistakes in fact and mistakes in law, similar to the discussion of impossibility defenses (factual and legal) in Chapter 4's discussion of attempt crimes.[13] A mistake of fact is when the offender takes certain action, believing certain facts to be true that, on later discovery, are found not to be true, thus saving the offender from liability. Consider the case of a man who shoots another man in the head to kill him, not recognizing that his victim is already dead from a heart attack. Factually, it is a defense that you cannot kill the dead, but that fact may not relieve the attacker of an attempted murder charge.

Mistakes of law arise from a misperception whether a "legal norm" has been enacted or abolished.[14] An example of the two mistakes is illustrated by a felon-in-possession case. Neva Snyder was convicted in California of possessing a concealed firearm, a crime for a convicted felon. Snyder claimed she believed her initial conviction for selling marijuana was only a misdemeanor, because after her conviction she had registered to vote and voted, a right forbidden to felons. California law provides that if a suspect has acted under a "mistake of fact," she cannot be guilty of a crime because she had no criminal intent. "Mistakes of law," on the other hand, are rarely a defense because public welfare and safety require people have some knowledge of right and wrong, even if people are unfamiliar with legal details. Regardless of what Snyder believed about whether she was a felon forbidden to have a gun, it was a mistake of law, not fact, and her conviction was upheld.[15]

Infancy

Each state has different laws addressing the proper treatment of children in the legal system. Infancy as a defense means that, due to his or her young age, the defendant could not have possessed the requisite state of *mens rea* to commit certain crimes. Despite the differences among the jurisdictions, there are general rules of applicability to keep in mind when examining an infancy defense. One general rule is the rule of presumptions. A presumption is a device in the law that suggests conclusions about certain facts. Under common law, there was a legal presumption that children under the age of 7 had no capacity to form *mens rea*, a guilty mind.[16] The presumption that children age 7 and younger cannot form *mens rea* is irrebuttable. An irrebuttable presumption is irrefutable and cannot be overcome by additional evidence. For example, in 2001 first-grader Kayla Rollins was shot and killed by a 6-year-old classmate. Under the law, the child who shot her could not be prosecuted, because under the law a young child is incapable of forming the requisite *mens rea* (purposeful, knowing, reckless, or negligent) to be held responsible, despite the community's outrage over the killing and desire to bring a criminal prosecution.

A rebuttable presumption means that other facts can overcome the presumption. Children between the ages of 8 and 14 do not have the capacity to form *mens rea* is a rebuttable presumption that can be overcome by evidence that the child had the capacity to appreciate the criminality of his conduct, which means the offender knew what he was doing was wrong.[17] On March 24, 1998, two boys—Andrew Golden, 11, and Mitchell Johnson, 13—broke a window to reach in and release two locks at Golden's grandparents' house, where they stole four pistols, three rifles, and one Remington .30-06 deer hunting rifle with a high-powered telescope on top. The boys went to Westside Middle School in Jonesboro, Arkansas, and perched behind a grassy knoll outside the school. Golden crept down to the school and pulled a fire alarm, then ran back to the knoll and where Johnson was waiting for him. When the schoolyard filled with children, Golden and Mitchell fired into the crowd. They killed four female children and a teacher, shooting the teacher, Shannon Wright, twice. Nine other children and another teacher were wounded.

Under the common law, there is a rebuttable presumption that the boys could *not* form *mens rea* to kill, but the prosecution could overcome that presumption by showing that the boys were aware of the criminality of their conduct by planning the killings, taking steps to achieve their criminal aims, and running away from the crime scene after the shootings. The boys were found "delinquent," the Arkansas equivalent to guilty after the judge rejected the boys' insanity and incompetency pleas. State law only provided for the boys to be held until they reached the age of 18 years,[18] but additional federal gun charges allowed the boys to be kept confined until they reached 21 years of age. Mitchell Johnson was released from a federal detention facility in August 2005 but was indicted on gun and theft charges for separate criminal acts and sentenced to a term of imprisonment. Golden was released from custody in 2007.[19]

The defense of infancy should not be confused with juvenile delinquency and juvenile court matters. Children older than age 14 can form *mens rea* and are typically brought before juvenile courts. However, according to some state jurisdictions, juveniles charged with serious crimes such as murder or rape may be transferred to adult court. Even if juveniles commit murder before the age of 18 and are transferred to adult court, they are not eligible for the death penalty, even if they would be adults at the time of the execution, as decided by *Roper v. Simmons* (2005).[20]

Intoxication

Dependent on the jurisdiction, a state may or may not recognize intoxication as a defense to committing a crime. Intoxication means that one's central nervous system is affected by the ingestion of toxic substances, most commonly alcohol or drugs, both illegal and prescription. The state must recognize the defense for it to be valid. For example, Missouri does not recognize voluntary intoxication due to drugs or alcohol as a defense.

> **Rule of Law:** Intoxication can result from the use of alcohol or drugs and may be voluntary or involuntary (e.g., a person could be unaware that someone put an intoxicating agent in a drink or food).

Missouri Revised Statutes §562.076

> A person who is in an intoxicated or drugged condition, whether from alcohol, drugs or other substance, is criminally responsible for conduct, unless such condition is involuntarily produced and deprived him or her of the capacity to know or appreciate the nature, quality or wrongfulness of his or her conduct.

In contrast, Pennsylvania does allow the intoxication defense to reduce the specific intent of first-degree murder to the general intent of third-degree murder.

Title 18 Pennsylvania Consolidated Statutes §308

> [N]either voluntary intoxication nor voluntary drugged condition is a defense to a criminal charge, nor may evidence of such conditions be introduced to negative the element of intent of the offense, *except* that evidence of such intoxication or drugged condition of the defendant may be offered by the defendant whenever it is relevant to reduce murder from a higher degree to a lower degree of murder.

Federal law also allows the defendant to introduce evidence that he was impaired by intoxicants if it creates reasonable doubt that the defendant had the specific intent to commit the crime. Virtually all jurisdictions recognize the defense of involuntary intoxication, in which the defendant was unknowingly drugged and committed a crime.

Duress

Duress in common law excused the actions of a criminal when those actions were compelled by threats from another human being because the defendant is acting without free will. The elements of the duress defense are

1. Imminent threat of serious bodily injury or death,

2. The apparent ability to carry out the threat, and

3. No reasonable opportunity to escape the harm other than to commit the crime.

Rule of Law: Duress is being forced to commit a crime by threat of bodily harm or death.

Courts hold that the threat must be immediate, not in the distant or even near future. The avenue of escape must be foreclosed to the defendant for the defense to be valid. Often an opportunity not taken to get help and escape the threat of harm will negate the defense. In *United States v. Solano* (1993), the defendant was charged with methamphetamine production.[21] Solano claimed he committed the crime because of threats to his life and the lives of his family, but his defense failed when it was shown that he possessed the precursors to make the drug even after the individual threatening him had died.

Keisha Dixon lied when she filled out paperwork to purchase more than one handgun at different gun shows; lying to purchase firearms is a federal crime. The purchase of guns at gun shows is typically less regulated by federal law than the purchase of firearms from a licensed dealer. At trial, Dixon said she committed the crime only because her boyfriend had threatened that if she did not, he would bring violence on her and her children. The jury did not believe her. On appeal, the high Court said,

> Like the defense of necessity, the defense of duress does not negate a defendant's criminal state of mind when the applicable offense requires a defendant to have acted knowingly or willfully; instead, it allows the defendant to "avoid liability. . . because coercive conditions or necessity negates a conclusion of guilt even though the necessary *mens rea* was present." Since [the defendant did not prove her duress defense by a preponderance of the evidence standard], her conviction is affirmed.[22]

Duress is never a defense to murder of an innocent person. If the defendant was approached by a man who said, "Go kill a high-ranking executive at the bank or I'll kidnap and torture your children," the defense of duress would be unavailable to her at her murder trial.

APPLYING THE LAW TO THE FACTS

When May a Defendant Make a Successful Duress Defense?

The Facts: On August 28, 2003, a man entered a bank with a bomb collar around his neck. When police stopped him, he claimed that an unknown assailant had placed the bomb around his neck and was waiting nearby to detonate the bomb if he did not rob the bank. Is duress a reasonable defense?

The Law: Yes, the elements for a successful duress defense have been met. The offender was forced to commit a crime under the threat of physical harm or death. This example is drawn from the true story of Brian Wells and an attempted robbery in Erie, Pennsylvania. Police apprehended Wells and while waiting for the bomb squad to diffuse the collar bomb, it exploded and killed Wells.[23]

Diminished Capacity

Writer Nina Bernstein has written about unclaimed bodies buried on New York City's Hart Island, but she could just as easily be commenting about the multitude of defendants in the criminal justice system when she observes, "Bad childhoods, bad choices or just bad luck—the chronic calamities of the human condition figure in many of these narratives. Here are the harshest consequences of mental illness, addiction or families scattered or distracted by their own misfortunes."[24] Suffering a bad childhood is not a precursor to a life of crime, early trauma is a risk factor for future mental impairment. The defense of diminished capacity means the defendant was suffering from impaired mental functioning or a mental defect that interfered with his ability to form *mens rea* to commit the crime. Mental disease or defect can be "any mental abnormality regardless of its medical label, origin, or source" and includes "congenital and traumatic mental conditions as well as disease" but excludes certain conditions, such as abnormal sexual conduct manifested by repeated criminal or otherwise antisocial conduct, and drug and alcohol abuse unaccompanied by psychosis.[25] A common manifestation of mental illness is the suffering from delusions, which are false fixed beliefs that are unrelentingly persistent. Diminished capacity can be nonorganic, such as intoxication, or organic, such as a malfunction in brain chemistry. There are three distinct categories of organic diminished capacity: mental illness, insanity, and intellectual disability.

There is no insanity without mental illness, but many who are mentally ill are not insane. Intellectual disability (formerly referred to as mental retardation) is not mental illness or insanity. The distinction between the three categories of *mens rea* defenses is important because those who are insane or intellectually disabled are exempt from the death penalty as punishment, whereas the mentally ill remain eligible for execution.

M'Naghten Test for Insanity

The issue of whether a defendant was "insane" at the time of the commission of his crime has been hotly debated in criminal law for decades. The defense of insanity is a legal question, not a medical or psychological one. That is, lawmakers decide on the definition of insanity. Some states, such as Kansas, Montana, Idaho, and Utah, have abolished the defense altogether but still allow evidence of a defendant's defective *mens rea* at the time of the commission of the crime. Meanwhile, the federal government has amended its definition and the burden of proof for such a claim on at least three occasions since the 1950s.[26] There are many permutations of the insanity defense and other defenses that are based on diminished or impaired *mens rea*. This section examines the most widely recognized of those defenses.

> Rule of Law: Insanity means that the defendant could not appreciate the nature of his conduct or did not think what he was doing was wrong.

The standard legal test for insanity was named after Daniel M'Naghten (alternative spellings include McNaughton), who came to believe that the British prime minister, later known as the "Father of Modern Policing," Robert Peel, was part of a conspiracy to kill him. In 1843, M'Naghten waited outside No. 10 Downing Street, intending to kill Peel, but he mistakenly killed Peel's secretary, Edward Drummond. M'Naghten was held not responsible for Drummond's murder "by reason of insanity." British lords enunciated what is now known as the M'Naghten test, which states the defendant is legally insane, if

1. At the time the accused committed the crime,

2. He was suffering under such a defect of reason caused by a mental illness that he

   a. Could not tell the difference between right and wrong, or

   b. Could not appreciate the criminality of his conduct.

It is important to note that a person could be suffering from an extreme mental illness and yet still know the difference between right or wrong, which would make the person legally sane. In June 2001, in Houston, Texas, housewife Andrea Yates said goodbye to her husband Rusty as he left for work at the nearby National Aeronautics and Space Administration (NASA) facility. Then she proceeded to systematically drown her four sons and one daughter. She described chasing down her oldest son, Noah, as he ran for his life after seeing his four siblings laid out on the bed. As Noah lay lifeless in the tub, Andrea called the police and her husband to report something had happened to the children. At her first trial, her counsel entered a plea of not guilty by reason of insanity, as Andrea's motive for the drownings was to save the children's souls because "they would burn in hell if she did not kill them while they were still innocents."

Despite Andrea's extensive psychiatric history that included in-patient hospitalizations and treatment with powerful antipsychotic medication, the jury found her legally sane because her decision to wait for Rusty to leave for work before killing the children and her immediate call to authorities after the drownings indicated that she clearly knew right from wrong. Yate's conviction was overturned and at her second trial in the summer of 2006, the jury found her not guilty by reason of insanity and she was sentenced to life in prison. A representative insanity law is illustrated by Illinois law:

---

720 Illinois Consolidated Statutes 5/6-2 Insanity

(a) A person is not criminally responsible for conduct if at the time of such conduct, as a result of mental disease or mental defect, he lacks substantial capacity to appreciate the criminality of his conduct.

(b) The terms "mental disease" or "mental defect" do not include an abnormality manifested only by repeated criminal or otherwise antisocial conduct.

(c) A person who, at the time of the commission of a criminal offense, was not insane but was suffering from a mental illness, is not relieved of criminal responsibility for his conduct and may be found guilty but mentally ill.

(d) For purposes of this Section, "mental illness" or "mentally ill" means a substantial disorder of thought, mood, or behavior which afflicted a person at the time of the commission of the offense and which impaired that person's judgment, but not to the extent that he is unable to appreciate the wrongfulness of his behavior.

(e) When the defense of insanity has been presented during the trial, the burden of proof is on the defendant to prove by clear and convincing evidence that the defendant is not guilty by reason of insanity. However, the burden of proof remains on the State to prove beyond a reasonable doubt each of the elements of each of the offenses charged, and, in a jury trial where the insanity defense has been presented, the jury must be instructed that it may not consider whether the defendant has met his burden of proving that he is not guilty by reason of insanity until and unless it has first determined that the State has proven the defendant guilty beyond a reasonable doubt of the offense with which he is charged.

Durham Rule

In 1954 Chief Judge David Bazelon of the D.C. Court of Appeals wrote his famous decision in *Durham v. United States* (1954), which temporarily replaced the M'Naghten test for insanity.[27] The *Durham* rule says the defendant was not criminally responsible for his behavior because it was produced by a "mental disease or defect," which is a profound mental illness. The *Durham* rule did not work in court largely because it elevated psychiatric testimony over the jury's role to determine whether the defendant had the requisite *mens rea* for the crime. In addition, alcoholics, compulsive gamblers, and other addicts used the rule with great success to escape criminal responsibility. The *Durham* rule was overturned in *United States v. Brawner* (1972) which proposed an insanity rule recognized as the ALI Substantial Capacity Test.[28]

ALI Substantial Capacity Test

The American Legal Institute (ALI), authors of the Model Penal Code, introduced as part of the Code the **ALI Substantial Capacity Test,** which held a defendant was not responsible for his act if, at the time of the offense, as the result of mental disease or defect, he lacked "substantial capacity either to appreciate the criminality of his conduct or to conform his conduct to the requirements of the law." In these cases, defendants could be found not guilty by reason of insanity. Approximately half the state jurisdictions that allow a defendant to raise an insanity defense use the M'Naghten definition of insanity, while the other half employ the ALI definition. The typical evidentiary burden of production for insanity in most jurisdictions is by clear and convincing evidence.

The federal government amended the law allowing the use of an insanity plea in federal courts after the trial of John W. Hinckley, Jr. Hinckley claimed he was insane during his attempt to assassinate President Ronald Reagan in Washington, D.C., on March 31, 1981, when he shot not only the president but three others as well. One victim, Press Secretary James Brady, was the inspiration for the gun control law, the "Brady Bill." The evidence presented at trial revealed that Hinckley, a failed college student from an upper-class family, had a history of mental disturbance. He had become fixated on the actress Jodie Foster, who, at age 13, had starred as a teenage prostitute in the movie *Taxi Driver* (1976). In this movie, actor Robert De Niro plays taxi cab driver Travis Bickle, who attempts to assassinate a political figure as a claim to fame. Hinckley stalked Foster while she was an undergraduate at Yale University and tried to assassinate Reagan to impress Foster and win her affection.

The federal law, at the time Hinckley went to trial, used the ALI definition of insanity and placed the burden of proof on the prosecution. That is, once the defendant claimed he was not guilty by reason of insanity, the prosecution had to disprove his claim. After Hinckley's acquittal, the government changed the law and passed the Insanity Defense Reform Act of 1984, 18 U.S.C. §4241 et seq., which, like most jurisdictions that retain the insanity defense, place the affirmative burden on the defendant to prove his claim.

Guilty but Mentally Ill

By finding the defendant guilty but mentally ill (GBMI), 13 states allow a jury to conclude that a defendant remains criminally responsible, while acknowledging his criminal behavior was most likely caused by mental illness. The GBMI verdict does not necessarily replace the verdict of guilty by reason of insanity but supplements it in the states that use it. The GBMI statute in Pennsylvania follows.

Title 18 Pennsylvania Consolidated Statutes §314 Guilty but Mentally Ill

(a) <u>General Rule</u> A person who timely offers a defense of insanity in accordance with the Rules of Criminal Procedure may be found "guilty but mentally ill" at trial if the trier of fact [jury or judge in a nonjury trial] finds, beyond a reasonable doubt, that the person is guilty of an offense, was mentally ill at the time of the commission of the offense and was *not* legally insane at the time of the commission of the offense . . . (emphasis added)

(b) <u>(omitted)</u>

(c) Definitions

(1) "Mentally ill." One who as a result of mental disease or defect, lacks substantial capacity either to appreciate the wrongfulness of his conduct or to conform his conduct to the requirements of the law. . . .

(d) Common law M'Naghten's Rule preserved—Nothing in this section shall be deemed to repeal or otherwise abrogate the common law defense of insanity (M'Naghten's Rule) in effect in this Commonwealth on the effective date of this section.

If the defendant receives a GBMI verdict, it is hoped that the defendant will be placed in a correctional facility that treats mentally ill convicts. John E. DuPont of the family that owns the DuPont chemical company was suffering from paranoid schizophrenia for years before he killed Olympic wrestler David Schultz while Schultz was coaching wrestlers at DuPont's state-of-the-art wrestling center. DuPont's jury returned a GBMI verdict, and he was transferred to the correctional facility in Camp Hill, Pennsylvania, specifically for the mental treatment he would receive. In 2010, DuPont died in custody.

Irresistible Impulse

Sometimes the defendant is cognizant of the wrongfulness of his conduct but, because of a defect or mental illness, he cannot control his actions. Such behavior allows for an irresistible impulse defense that the offender could not control his impulses to cause harm—that he had no emotional brakes between his irrational thoughts and resulting criminal conduct. In an 1834 case, the judge instructed the jury that if they found that the defendant's "mind was such that he retained the power of discriminating, or to leave him conscious [that] he was doing wrong, a state of mind in which at the time of the deed he was free to forbear, or to do the act, he is responsible as a sane man."[29] Another popular definition of irresistible impulse states that an offender would commit the crime even if he had a "policeman at his elbow."[30]

Intellectual Disability

Those defendants who are intellectually disabled (formerly called mentally retarded) pose a unique problem for assessing criminal responsibility. The diagnosis of intellectual disability involves

1. Typically an IQ (intelligence quotient) of 70 or below;

2. Significant limitations in two or more areas of adaptive functioning, measured by "conceptual, social, and practical skills," such as using money, telling time, navigating public transportation, following the rules, protecting oneself from exploitation or victimization; and

3. Symptoms must manifest themselves before the age of 18.

The high Court has held that a straight IQ cutoff of 70 or below to determine intellectual disability is unconstitutional, because the tests have a 5-point (plus or minus) variance range and medical professionals use a holistic, whole-person approach to diagnosis disability.[31] One cannot tell who is intellectually disabled simply by looking at them. They have no unique facial features, and they can navigate some aspects of life; for example, they can marry, have children, have jobs where they perform rote activities, learn to drive (although not necessarily obtain a driver's license), and have friendships. On closer inspection, though, the intellectually disabled can be gullible, naïve, and follow without question those in leadership positions. Appropriate punishment for the intellectually disabled who commit serious crimes is an issue. As the trial court said in *Hall v. Florida* (2014) featured in the chapter-opening case study "the learning disabilities, mental retardation, and other mental difficulties . . . cannot be used to justify, excuse or extenuate the moral culpability of the defendant in this cause," while the U.S. Supreme Court said in reviewing the case on appeal, the three primary goals of punishment – deterrence, rehabilitation and retribution – are never met by "executing a person with intellectual disability."

States differ over the definition of *intellectual disability*. The high Court decided the intellectually disabled are exempt from the death penalty but left to the states the discretion to make the rules to define and determine if a defendant is, actually, disabled. A summary of behaviors professionals examine to measure intellectual functioning and adaptive behavior is shown in Figure 12.1.

Giving discretion to the states to define intellectual disability may subject the disabled to an unacceptable risk of execution. In 2004, after the U.S. Supreme Court decision in *Atkins v. Virginia* (2002) declaring the execution of the "mentally retarded" to be cruel and unusual punishment in violation of the Eighth Amendment, the Texas Court of Criminal Appeals said in *Ex parte Briseno* (2004):

> Most Texas citizens might agree that Steinbeck's Lennie should, by virtue of his lack of reasoning ability and adaptive skills, be exempt. But, does a consensus of Texas citizens agree that all persons who might legitimately qualify for assistance under the social services definition of mental retardation be exempt from an otherwise constitutional penalty?

Figure 12.1 Intellectual Functioning Skills

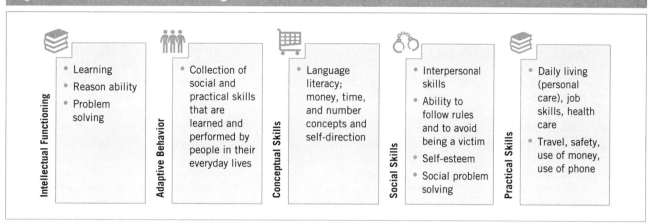

The fictional character Lennie in John Steinbeck's novel *Of Mice and Men* has a mild mental disability and he likes to pet soft things but ends up killing them, including a woman who let Lennie pet her hair. What the Texas court is asking is if someone has been receiving social security disability for a diagnosis of mental retardation, do a majority of Texans agree that the "Lennies" of the world should be "exempt from an otherwise constitutional [death] penalty?"[32] Since the *Briseno* court did not find receiving social services for intellectual disability was enough to define one as disabled enough to be spared from capital punishment, the court came up with seven questions, known as the *Briseno* factors, which sought to distinguish the image in popular culture of the disabled as children in need of constant supervision from those who could willingly plan and execute brutal killings. The factors are the following:

1. Did those who knew the person best during the developmental stage—his family, friends, teachers, employers, authorities— think he was mentally retarded at that time, and, if so, act in accordance with that determination?

2. Has the person formulated plans and carried them through, or is his conduct impulsive?

3. Does his conduct show leadership, or does it show that he is led around by others?

4. Is his conduct in response to external stimuli rational and appropriate, regardless of whether it is socially acceptable?

5. Does he respond coherently, rationally, and on point to oral or written questions, or do his responses wander from subject to subject?

6. Can the person hide facts or lie effectively in his own or others' interests?

7. Putting aside any heinousness or gruesomeness surrounding the capital offense, did the commission of that offense require forethought, planning, and complex execution of purpose?

In 1980 Texas, 20-year-old Bobby Moore robbed a grocery store and shot a store clerk to death. He was convicted and sentenced to death. In 2014, the postconviction court held an evidentiary hearing and determined Moore was intellectually disabled and recommended resentencing to life without parole. A higher reviewing court disagreed because the postconviction court did not properly consider the seven *Briseno* factors. Moore appealed, and the U.S. Supreme Court overturned the *Briseno* factors in *Moore v. Texas* (2017), excerpted on the following page, because the factors were not based on current medical standards to determine intellectual disability.

MOORE V. TEXAS, 137 S.CT. 1039 (2017)

Supreme Court of the United States

Justice Ginsburg delivered the opinion of the Court. (5–3 [only 8 justices ruled])

REASONING: In concluding that Moore did not suffer significant adaptive deficits, the [state appellate court] overemphasized Moore's perceived adaptive strengths [such as Moore] lived on the streets, mowed lawns, and played pool for money. Moore's adaptive strengths, in the [state appellate court]'s view, constituted evidence adequate to overcome the considerable objective evidence of Moore's adaptive deficits.

But the medical community focuses the adaptive-functioning inquiry on adaptive *deficits* [not strengths] ("significant limitations in conceptual, social, or practical adaptive skills [are] not outweighed by the potential strengths in some adaptive skills");[33] (inquiry should focus on "[d]eficits in adaptive functioning"; deficits in only one of the three adaptive-skills domains suffice to show adaptive deficits)[34]; ("Intellectually disabled persons may have 'strengths in social or physical capabilities, strengths in some adaptive skill areas, or strengths in one aspect of an adaptive skill in which they otherwise show an overall limitation.'")

The [state appellate court]'s attachment to the seven *Briseno* evidentiary factors . . . impeded its assessment of Moore's adaptive functioning. By design and in operation, the *Briseno* factors "create an unacceptable risk that persons with intellectual disability will be executed." After observing that persons with "mild" intellectual disability might be treated differently under clinical standards than under Texas' capital system, the [state appellate court] defined its objective as identifying the "consensus of *Texas citizens*" on who "should be exempted from the death penalty." Mild levels of intellectual disability, although they may fall outside Texas citizens' consensus, nevertheless remain intellectual disabilities, and States may not execute anyone in "the *entire category* of [intellectually disabled] offenders."

Skeptical of what it viewed as "exceedingly subjective" medical and clinical standards, the [state appellate court] in *Briseno* advanced lay perceptions of intellectual disability.

Briseno asks, for example, "Did those who knew the person best during the developmental stage—his family, friends, teachers, employers, authorities—think he was mentally retarded at that time, and, if so, act in accordance with that determination?" Addressing that question here, the [state appellate court] referred to Moore's education in "normal classrooms during his school career," his father's reactions to his academic challenges, and his sister's perceptions of Moore's intellectual abilities. But the medical profession has endeavored to counter lay stereotypes of the intellectually disabled. Those stereotypes, much more than medical and clinical appraisals, should spark skepticism.

The *Briseno* factors are an outlier, in comparison both to other States' handling of intellectual-disability pleas and to Texas' own practices in other contexts. (consensus in the States provides "objective indicia of society's standards in the context of the Eighth Amendment").

No state legislature has approved the use of the *Briseno* factors or anything similar. In the 12 years since Texas adopted the factors, only one other state high court and one state intermediate appellate court have authorized their use. Indeed, Texas itself does not follow *Briseno* in contexts other than the death penalty. For example, the [requirement Texas defends here that Moore show his intellectual and adaptive deficits were related] is conspicuously absent from the standards the State uses to assess students for intellectual disabilities.[35] And even within Texas' criminal-justice system, the State requires the intellectual-disability diagnoses of juveniles to be based on "the latest edition of the DSM."[36] Texas cannot satisfactorily explain why it applies current medical standards for diagnosing intellectual disability in other contexts, yet clings to superseded [obsolete] standards when an individual's life is at stake.

CONCLUSION: The [state appellate court] failed adequately to inform itself of the "medical community's diagnostic framework," [to properly assess Moore's intellectual disability]. Because [the *Briseno* precedent] pervasively infected the [Texas court's] analysis, the decision of that court cannot stand.

MAKING THE COURTROOM CONNECTION

Police officers face enormous pressures on the job and difficult choices how to handle mentally ill offenders or those incapacitated by drugs and alcohol, who may pose a risk of danger to themselves or others. Officers need training on how to recognize certain disorders as well as involvement in community crisis intervention teams that are specifically trained in specialized mental health issues to respond appropriately to persons in need. A prosecutor's job as a representative of the people is to seek justice, not convictions, and care is required to properly assess how to adjudicate defendants with mental illness or intellectual disabilities.

Defense counsel should always consider psychological assessment in preparing a defense regardless of how a client presents himself. Some clients may, at all cost, resist being labeled mentally ill. Some defendants go to great lengths to prevent their defense counsel from raising a defense of insanity or some other mental defect that would save the defendant from a harsher charge based on

the ability to form *mens rea*. Counsel may face certain challenges in exploring mental health issues without the client's cooperation, but the courts require making the effort.

Correctional officers should be aware that suicide is the number one cause of death among inmates in local jails and one of the top five causes of death in state prisons.[37] Given a persistent lack of funding for adequate medical care in both public and private prisons, a common solution is to place the mentally ill in solitary confinement, which may actually worsen their mental health. Research indicates those suffering from mental illness without also suffering from drug dependence are no more violent than the general population. [38]

On remand with the Texas Court of Criminal Appeals held on June 6, 2018, that Bobby Moore failed to prove intellectual disability and remained eligible for execution.

Not Guilty by Reason of Mental Defect

Many defendants who successfully claim some type of mental defect defense are sent to a mental hospital for treatment. Some are later transferred to prison or serve their sentences in the psychiatric ward of a prison until their conditions improve, at which time they may be transferred to general population. The U.S. Supreme Court held that a defendant who was acquitted of a criminal offense by reason of insanity could be confined to a mental institution until he has regained his sanity or is no longer a danger to himself or others, even if that commitment time turns out to be longer than any sentence he might have received had he been sentenced to the original crime.[39] To determine whether the defendant is competent to be released, the mental institution holds a review hearing on the status of the offender, who may be conditionally released back into society. John Hinckley, discussed earlier in this chapter as the would-be assassin of President Reagan, was released from custody in 2016 and now lives with his mother in Williamsburg, Virginia. Hinckley has been medically cleared as no longer suffering from dangerous mental illness, but he still must comply with court-ordered supervision.[40]

DEFENSES BASED ON JUSTIFICATION

Necessity

Necessity as a defense means that the offender had to choose between committing the crime or suffering harm to himself, choosing the lesser of two evils. The development of the defense was first raised in the seminal case *Regina v. Dudley and Stephens* (1884), concerning three sailors and a cabin boy who were on a lifeboat after their ship sank.[41] After 12 days adrift with no food or water, two of the older men, Thomas Dudley and Edward Stephens, killed 17-year-old cabin boy Richard Parker, ate his flesh and drank his blood. After Dudley and Stephens were rescued, the Crown charged them with murder. They offered the defense of necessity, explaining that they had chosen the lesser of two evils—eating the boy or dying themselves. The court recognized the dire circumstances of the men at sea but found them guilty of murder. After the sailors were convicted, Queen Victoria later reduced their death sentences to 6 months' imprisonment.

> **Rule of Law: Necessity is the defense of choosing the lesser of two evils.**

The elements of the necessity defense are as follows:

1. The offender was faced with two evils and chose the lesser of them.
2. The offender acted to prevent imminent harm.

3. There was a relationship between his conduct and the harm to be avoided.

4. There were no legal alternatives.

The crux of the necessity defense is that the threat of harm to the victim must be immediate. A review of federal cases finds the necessity defense has been rejected in cases in which (a) a felon charged with possession of a firearm claimed necessity because he had to take the gun away from his girlfriend's son, who was threatening suicide; (b) marijuana smokers were treating their glaucoma with the drug; (c) Central American illegal aliens were traveling through the country by underground railroad because the Immigration and Naturalization Service and courts would not judiciously hear their cases; (d) antinuclear protesters destroyed infrastructure associated with nuclear energy; and (e) individuals brought the illegal drug laetrile into the United States to treat cancer patients.[42] The defense must introduce sufficient evidence that there were no safer alternatives to choosing the lesser evil.

Self-Defense

> **Rule of Law: One has a right to use reasonable force to repel an attack on oneself or others.**

Self-defense is the right to defend oneself against force, injury, or death by meeting it with equal force. The law does not require an individual being attacked to accept the attack out of fear of being criminally responsible for harming his or her attacker. Self-defense is a complete defense. That is, if a victim of a deadly attack kills the attacker, the victim will spend no time in jail, because the killing will be justifiable homicide. But there are certain requirements that must be met to assert a valid self-defense claim. The successful self-defense claim has the following elements:

1. The victim was confronted

2. With an immediate physical threat

3. And had to use a reasonable amount of force

4. To repel the attack.

The prevailing view under the common law and in modern statutes is that, under an objective analysis which asks what others would think, not only the person being attacked, was the force used by the victim must have been reasonable to repel the attack. The other qualifying factor for the victim to use force is that the threat of physical harm must be imminent. If a professional basketball player who stands over 7 feet tall and weighs approximately 300 pounds approaches to slap a man who is a little over 5 feet tall and weighs 115 pounds, can the smaller man stab the larger man to death as a defensive measure and claim that he believed that one slap from the larger man would send him through the door? No; using deadly force would be justified only if the smaller man reasonably believed that such force was necessary to prevent great bodily harm or death.

Deadly Force. When a person is confronted with a show of force sufficient to put his life in danger, it is justified to use deadly force to repel such an attack. The legal analysis of a self-defense claim involving deadly force often focuses on the person's "reasonable belief" that killing the attacker was the only way to prevent dying at the hands of the aggressor.

Duty to Retreat and Defense of Property. The castle doctrine says, "A man's house is his castle—for where shall a man be safe if it be not in his house?" The doctrine is legal recognition that a person's home is where he should feel the safest and have legal license to defend himself vigorously[43] and declares there is no duty to retreat and run away when confronted in one's home. As Justice Benjamin Cardozo wrote in 1914, no man is bound to retreat if attacked inside his home for he "may stand his ground and resist the attack."[44] When people are confronted within their own homes, the legal rules about the amount of force they may use to protect themselves and their property become different. In this scenario, the use of deadly force is defensible if it is reasonable to use force to repel the attack, if a reasonable amount of force is used, and if, in most, but not all, jurisdictions, the victim tries to resolve the situation by using a nondeadly alternative prior to using deadly force.

Under the **defense of property** doctrine, an individual may use force to protect his or her home but not deadly force to defend solely property. The law frowns on taking an irreplaceable life in defense of property, which can always be replaced. Also, rigging booby traps to protect property is unlawful because "to employ mechanical devices imperils the life of children, firemen, and policemen acting within the scope of their employment, and others" and poses an unacceptable risk of harm to innocents rather than the unwanted intruder.[45]

Duty to Retreat and "Stand Your Ground" Laws. One cannot rightly claim that an act of violence was necessary in self-defense if one had the option to retreat or run away from the threat. The issue of retreat usually arises only when deadly force is used, and to make a claim of justifiable self-defense, typically, there was no retreat possible. But what happens when the person being attacked could run away, but chooses to stand their ground and kill the attacker instead? The **"no retreat" doctrine** has been viable in English common law since the 17th century, justifying the killing of an aggressor as a necessity in defense of self. The legal justification to kill someone rather than running away received national media attention with the killing of teenager Trayvon Martin in Sanford, Florida, in February 2012. Although the defendant was acquitted on a traditional self-defense claim, he was not arrested until 2 months after killing the teenager because under Florida's "**stand your ground**" law, once a self-defense claim is raised, the government must introduce enough evidence to disprove the victim's belief deadly force was justified, which is the similar burden at trial.[46] If the government cannot prove the defendant did *not* act in self-defense, the defendant most likely will be acquitted. The Florida law provides the following:

Florida Statute §776.012. Use or threatened use of force in defense of person

(1) A person is justified in using or threatening to use force, except deadly force, against another when and to the extent that the person reasonably believes that such conduct is necessary to defend himself or herself or another against the other's imminent use of unlawful force. A person who uses or threatens to use force in accordance with this subsection does *not* have a duty to retreat before using or threatening to use such force.

(2) A person is justified in using or threatening to use deadly force if

    i. He or she reasonably believes that using or threatening to use such force is necessary to prevent imminent death or great bodily harm to himself or herself or another or to prevent the imminent commission of a forcible felony.

    ii. A person who uses or threatens to use deadly force in accordance with this subsection does not have a duty to retreat and has the right to stand his or her ground if the person using or threatening to use the deadly force is not engaged in a criminal activity and is in a place where *he or she has a right to be* (emphasis added).

In "stand your ground" jurisdictions, according to research examining homicide rates before and after the law's enactment, the language that a person can use deadly force in any place where "he or she has a right to be," has led to an increase in homicide rates.[47]

Defense of Others

In certain situations, a person may raise the **defense of others**, which is a self-defense claim on behalf of another who is being attacked. The amount of force one can used is the same as if standing in the victim's shoes, but it must be reasonable. If someone comes upon an old woman being attacked, the person could repel the attacker as if he were standing in the old woman's shoes. A messenger came upon two men beating a younger man. The messenger thought that the younger man needed assistance, so he entered the fray and broke one of the attackers' legs. The older men were plainclothes detectives making a lawful arrest, and the messenger was convicted of assault. In reversing his conviction, the appellate court said, "Had the facts been as he thought them, he would have been a hero and not condemned as a criminal actor." The higher court then reversed the appeals court [reinstating the conviction], and said,

> [O]ne who goes to the aid of a third person does so at his own peril. While the doctrine [of defense of others by standing in their shoes adopted by] the court below may have support in some states, we feel that such a policy would *not* be conducive to an orderly society . . . [T]he right of a person to defend another ordinarily should *not be greater than* such person's right to defend himself[48] (emphasis added).

Thus, since the man being arrested could not have broken the plainclothes police officer's leg, neither could his would-be rescuer.

Imperfect Self-Defense

In the law the term *imperfect* means incomplete or defective. In the context of self-defense, if the force used was disproportionate, the self-defense claim may fail. Imperfect self-defense is raised when the force used to repel an attack was unreasonable under the circumstances. Peterson was inside his house when Keitt came to steal windshield wipers from an abandoned car on Peterson's property. Peterson approached Keitt with a gun, and Keitt approached Peterson with a raised wrench. Peterson warned Keitt not to take another step, then shot Keitt to death. On appeal for a conviction of manslaughter, Peterson claimed that the trial court was in error in *not* giving a jury instruction that he had a right to use deadly force to save himself from serious bodily harm or death, the threat posed by Keitt. The court upheld Peterson's conviction and said that, even though Keitt may have been the aggressor in coming to the property to steal, Peterson was not entitled to use more force than was necessary to repel the attack.

> One cannot support a claim of self-defense by a self-generated necessity to kill. The right of homicidal self-defense is granted only to those free from fault in the difficulty; it is denied slayers who incite the fatal attack, encourage the fatal quarrel or otherwise promote the necessitous occasion for taking life.[49]

As for Peterson, a claim of self-defense that is imperfect will reduce what would normally be a murder charge to manslaughter because the perpetrator does not possess the requisite *mens rea* for an intentionally premeditated and deliberate murder.

Battered Woman Syndrome

Battered woman syndrome was a term created by psychologist Lenore Walker to describe a type of self-defense whose focus is on the victim's inability to perceive threats of violence in the same reasonable frame of mind as someone who is not in a battering relationship. Anyone can be a battered person, and battering can take place in all types of relationships: parent–child, grandparent–grandchild, and same-sex partners, for example. The syndrome is often used in court to explain why a victim has killed his or her abuser when the abuser was not posing an immediate threat of harm. In 1984, Walker introduced the cycle of violence to explain to lay people how post-traumatic stress disorder may result from relentless intimate partner violence. The cycle of violence has three phases that repeat in an abusive relationship. The multifaceted nature of intimate partner violence is represented by the power and control wheel in Figure 12.2. The professionals who created the wheel said this:

> Over several months in 1984, staff at the [Duluth, Minnesota] Domestic Abuse Intervention Program (DAIP) convened focus groups of women who had been

battered. We listened to heart-wrenching stories of violence, terror and survival. After listening to these stories and asking questions, we documented the most common abusive behaviors or tactics that were used against these women. These tactics chosen for the wheel are those that were most universally experienced by battered women.

Battering is one form of domestic or intimate partner violence. It is characterized by the pattern of actions that an individual uses to intentionally control or dominate his intimate partner. That is why the words "power and control" are in the center of the wheel. A batterer systematically uses threats, intimidation, and coercion to instill fear in his partner. These behaviors are the spokes of the wheel. Physical and sexual violence holds it all together - this violence is the rim of the wheel.

Figure 12.2   The Power and Control Wheel

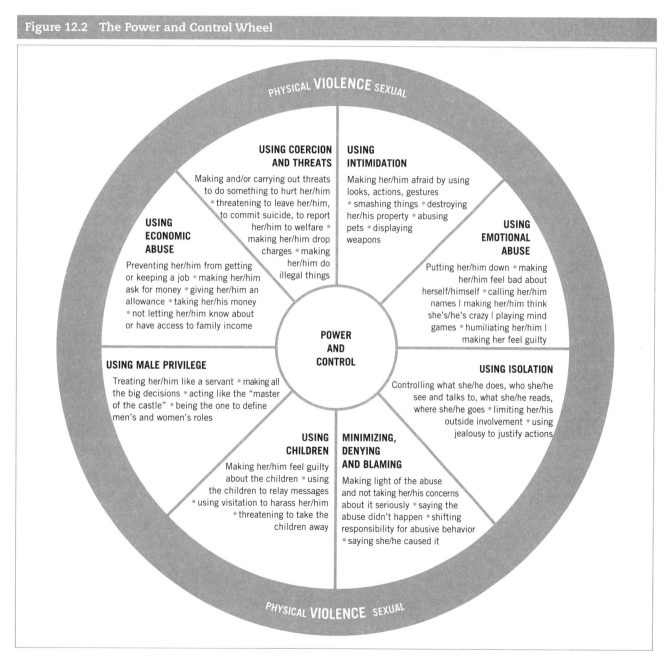

Source: Domestic Abuse Intervention Programs, 202 East Superior Street, Duluth, MN 55802. www.theduluthmodel.org

Phase 1: Tension-building phase: When two people fall in love, they see each other through rose-colored glasses; everything about the other person seems wonderful. In a relationship in which violence is used as a means of control, the couple will eventually enter the first phase in a cycle of violence, the tension-building phase, during which one partner begins to belittle and criticize the other about appearance, housekeeping or lovemaking skills, or ability to be a good parent. This phase is usually characterized by minor acts of violence, such as pinches, slaps, or pulling of the hair. **Phase 2: Acute battering incident**: The second phase is an acute battering incident in which the victim is severely beaten and may need medical care. **Phase 3: Honeymoon phase**: The third phase is the most peaceful phase during which the batterer may apologize, bring gifts home as a token of contrition, blame the beating on an intoxicated or drugged state, and make promises never to do it again. In time, the cycle of violence repeats. Note that those who work in domestic violence say many survivors "have never and will never" experience the "honeymoon phase." The psychology of a battering relationship is unique, and popular culture holds many myths about battering victims that contribute to the victims' sense of isolation. The biggest myth is that a domestic violence victim can leave a relationship at any time. Many victims have been threatened with death to themselves, children, and pets if they leave, and they are fully aware that if they stay in the abusive relationship, it is only a matter of time before an acute battering incident occurs again.

In the case reprinted in part below, Carol Stonehouse was a Pennsylvania police officer who suffered abuse at the hands of her one-time boyfriend, William Welsh. Despite having a good claim to self-defense, Stonehouse was convicted and the issue on appeal was whether her lawyer was negligent in not finding an expert witness to testify about the dynamics unique to a battering relationship; the court said yes. Jurors tend to cling to myths about domestic violence. In particular, male jurors have difficulty believing the level of threat a battered woman feels and why, if afraid, she would remain in an abusive partnership.[50]

PENNSYLVANIA V. STONEHOUSE,
555 A.2D 772 (1989)

Supreme Court of Pennsylvania

Justice Larsen delivered the opinion of the court.

FACTS: On the morning of March 17, 1983, Appellant[51] [Carol Stonehouse] shot and killed William Welsh. The events culminating in Welsh's death are so bizarre that one would be tempted to dismiss them as the stuff of pulp fiction were it not for the corroboration of disinterested witnesses and for the fact that the literature on the "battered woman syndrome" is replete with similar cases. The chronology of events leading to Welsh's death are as follows. In March of 1980, less than a month after Stonehouse completed her training as a police cadet and assumed her duties as a police officer in the City of Pittsburgh, Stonehouse met Welsh. Welsh was married at that time and had served as a Pittsburgh police officer for approximately twenty years. Stonehouse had been twice divorced. The two began dating shortly after they met. Within the first three months of their relationship, Welsh broke into Stonehouse's apartment once and, shortly thereafter, made such a nuisance of himself by banging on her door late at night, that she called the police. That incident was treated as a "domestic" by the officers, who knew Welsh, and no police report was filed. Stonehouse attributed Welsh's behavior to a drinking problem and continued dating him. Welsh was possessive and demanding with respect to his relationship with Stonehouse. By the fall of 1980, whenever Stonehouse did not do what he told her to do, Welsh would let the air out of the tires of her car. This occurred as often as two or three times a week. Welsh admitted doing this, but insisted that Stonehouse would never be able to prove he was doing it.

Arguments began to occur with some frequency, and, after one such argument, Welsh was able to enter Stonehouse's secured apartment building and place flowers outside her door. Welsh told Stonehouse the flowers were for her funeral. Welsh also put sugar in the gas tank of Stonehouse's car, and on many occasions he would take Stonehouse's car and move it, or he would pull the ignition wires. It was also in the fall of 1980, that Welsh began to harass

Stonehouse by telephoning her late at night. Welsh justified his acts of vandalism and harassment by stating to Stonehouse that she "deserved it." In the summer of 1981, Stonehouse's landlord did not renew Stonehouse's lease because of Welsh and the arguments that were disturbing the other tenants. When Stonehouse prepared to move from her apartment, Welsh came in, broke a box of dishes, and left without saying a word. Welsh left [harassing] notes everywhere for Stonehouse—on her car, at work, at the spa, and he started to follow her everywhere she went. Welsh continued to harass Stonehouse by filling her dresser drawers with water, soaking the clothes in her closet, and leaving beer bottles all over her apartment. One night, after Stonehouse's daughter and grandchild moved out at the end of 1981, Welsh turned on the gas in Stonehouse's apartment. Stonehouse became quite ill, but Welsh woke her in the morning with all the windows open, saying "I couldn't do it to you this time, you bitch. I'll do it the next time." Welsh continued to follow Stonehouse everywhere, and he continued to enter her apartment at night.

In September of 1982, Stonehouse filed harassment charges against Welsh with a magistrate. At the hearing, witnesses testified about Welsh breaking Stonehouse's doors and following her, and appearing uninvited at social events to which Stonehouse had been invited. Welsh admitted harassing Stonehouse and admitted breaking her nose. Welsh was ordered to stay away from Stonehouse for sixty days. At that time, Stonehouse dated another man briefly. Welsh gave the man's estranged wife Stonehouse's name, address and phone number and warned the man not to see Stonehouse, saying "Remember, you got kids." Welsh also followed Stonehouse and that man on a date and threatened Stonehouse's companion with a gun. At the next hearing before the magistrate in November, 1982, the charges were dismissed because Welsh had not been harassing Stonehouse.

When Stonehouse returned to her residence she found that Welsh had again wrecked and defiled her apartment. There were seventeen knife slashes in Stonehouse's waterbed. The water damaged the apartment on the first floor occupied by another tenant, and . . . flowed into the basement of the building. Drapes had been slashed or torn off the windows and stuffed into the toilet. Stonehouse's clothes were soaking in the bathtub with beet juice and hot water. Cleaning supplies, cold cream, lotion, food and potting soil were smeared all over the walls, windows, floors, mirrors and rugs. Curtain rods and racks were torn off the walls. The back door was off its hinges, and every closet was emptied, every piece of furniture upset. Stonehouse filed a police report, but did not pursue charges against Welsh with the magistrate because Welsh convinced her that his friends would say he had been elsewhere that night.

On March 16, 1983, the night before the shooting, Stonehouse drove to a friend's house. Welsh followed in his vehicle, tailgating Stonehouse and bumping into the rear of her car at traffic lights. Stonehouse and her woman friend went to a lounge and had a few drinks. Welsh appeared there, so Stonehouse and her friend left and went to an after hours club. Stonehouse spoke briefly with an old friend and neighbor, Steve Owens. Welsh, who had followed Stonehouse to the club and who also knew Owens, asked Stonehouse: "Are you going to take him home tonight, slut?" Stonehouse took her woman friend home shortly thereafter at about 4 or 5 in the morning, and returned to her apartment to prepare for bed.

Steve Owens went, uninvited, to Stonehouse's apartment and, shortly thereafter, Welsh began kicking the front door. Stonehouse did not go to the door, but she became quite upset, realizing that Welsh was "going to do something." Welsh then went to the back door and started kicking and banging on it. Knowing that Welsh would be able to break in the back door, Stonehouse went to the door holding a gun at her side and let Welsh in. There was a struggle for the gun. Welsh took the gun from Stonehouse, but Stonehouse and Owens were able to retrieve the gun from Welsh. Owens testified that Welsh appeared to be "wild-eyed" and was not "the person that I had known." Welsh immediately left, and within seconds, Welsh threw a brick through the window of Stonehouse's car, prompting a neighbor to remark to her son: "He really looks like he's mad today." Stonehouse called the police, and Owens left to get cigarettes as they waited for the police to arrive.

Stonehouse knew Welsh would return because he always returned, so she stepped out onto the back porch to look for him, not wanting to be caught with her guard down. As she leaned over the railing, Stonehouse saw Welsh on the ground below aiming his gun at her. Believing that she heard a shot, Stonehouse fired her gun twice. One of the bullets entered Welsh at the top of his right shoulder and exited near his clavicle, severing a major artery. At the time of his death, Welsh's blood alcohol level was .14. Welsh was found dead beside his van with the fingers of his left hand wrapped around the grip and trigger of a .357 Magnum revolver that had not been fired.

On September 14, 1983, a jury convicted Stonehouse of murder of the third degree . . . and Stonehouse was sentenced to seven to fourteen years imprisonment on July 25, 1984.

ISSUE: [Was Stonehouse's] trial counsel . . . ineffective in failing to request a jury instruction that would require the jury to consider the cumulative effects of psychological and physical abuse when assessing the reasonableness of a battered person's fear of imminent danger of death or serious bodily harm with respect to a claim of self-defense?

(Continued)

HOLDING: [Yes.] The trial court did not instruct the jury as to the legal relevance of the history of abuse presented at trial on behalf of Stonehouse. The failure of counsel to request this instruction was clearly erroneous under the law of this Commonwealth.

REASONING: When evidence of self-defense arises from any source, the Commonwealth must *disprove self-defense beyond a reasonable doubt* (emphasis added). To sustain that burden, the Commonwealth must prove that (1) the defendant did not reasonably believe that he or she was in danger of death or serious bodily injury; (2) the defendant provoked the use of force; or (3) the defendant had a duty to retreat and retreat was possible with complete safety. The trial court herein properly determined that Stonehouse had no duty to retreat. Nor was there any serious contention that Stonehouse provoked the attack on her by Welsh on the morning of March 17. [note 5- The prosecutor attempted to show that Stonehouse deliberately provoked Welsh's attacks by talking with and dating other men.] The only issue remaining, therefore, was whether Stonehouse had a reasonable belief that she was in imminent danger.

In *Commonwealth v. Watson* (1981),[52] this Court stated that "[where] there has been physical abuse over a long period of time, the circumstances which assist the court in determining the reasonableness of a defendant's fear of death or serious injury at the time of a killing include the defendant's familiarity with the victim's behavior in the past." Thus, the jury should have been apprised of the fact that the abuse Stonehouse suffered for three years was to be considered by the jury with respect to the reasonableness of Stonehouse's fear of imminent danger of death or serious bodily injury. Stonehouse's trial counsel had no reasonable basis for failing to request such a charge to the jury, and the absence of the charge was prejudicial to Stonehouse in that the jury likely would have found Stonehouse not guilty of murder of the third degree if such an instruction had been given.

In addition, Stonehouse asserts that her trial counsel was ineffective in failing to present expert testimony regarding the characteristics of the victims of psychological and physical abuse, where uncontradicted testimony revealed that Stonehouse was the victim of such abuse, and the jury, without the aid of expert testimony, rendered a verdict based upon erroneous myths concerning the victims of such abuse. This is the issue that *amici* [plural of *amicus*, meaning friend (of the court)] framed in terms of the "battered woman syndrome."

It has long been the law of this Commonwealth that "expert testimony is admissible in all cases, civil and criminal alike, when it involves explanations and inferences not within the range of ordinary training,

knowledge, intelligence and experience." Because the battered woman syndrome is not within the ordinary training, knowledge, intelligence, and experience of jurors, we believe that expert testimony regarding battered women is admissible as the basis for proving justification in the use of deadly force where the defendant has been shown to be a victim of psychological and physical abuse. "A battered woman is a woman who is repeatedly subjected to any forceful physical or psychological behavior by a man in order to coerce her to do something he wants her to do without any concern for her rights." Walker, *The Battered Woman* at xv (1979). Battered women have been compared to hostages, prisoners of war, and concentration camp victims,[53] and the battered woman syndrome is recognized as a post-traumatic stress disorder.

It is widely acknowledged that commonly held beliefs about battered women are subject to myths that ultimately place the blame for battering on the battered victim. For example, battered women are generally considered to be masochists who derive pleasure from being abused. This myth was exploited by the prosecutor in the instant case when he asked Stonehouse if she was "a willing participant in the activities that went on between [her] and William Welsh," and when he stressed to the jury in his closing argument that if Stonehouse had truly been an innocent victim she could have put an end to the relationship. Similarly, this myth was given credence by the Superior Court which determined that Stonehouse's assertion of self-defense was unreasonable because of "[t]he continued relationship between Stonehouse and the victim." These "blame the victim" myths enable juries to remain oblivious to the fact that battering is not acceptable behavior, and such myths do not begin to address why battered women remain in battering relationships.

Other myths commonly believed about battered women are that battered women are uneducated and have few job skills and that the police can protect the battered woman. These myths were also exploited by the prosecutor, who introduced testimony that detailed the police training Stonehouse had received, implying that her training made her incapable of being victimized by a batterer, and who argued to the jury that Stonehouse could have been rescued, if she had wanted to be rescued, by a law enforcement system ready, willing and able to protect women who are victims of domestic violence. [note 10- An additional myth advanced by the prosecutor was that Stonehouse used weapons to defend herself and having used weapons did not conform to the stereotype of battered women who suffer their beatings passively. Although there are battered women who do not defend themselves and die as a result of their injuries, the fact that a woman attempts to defend herself from a beating does not make her any less a battered woman when her attempts do not stop the repeated episodes of physical and emotional abuse.]

To the contrary, researchers have shown that many battered women are highly competent workers and successful career women, who include among their ranks doctors, lawyers, nurses, homemakers, politicians and psychologists. Moreover, statistics have shown that police departments do not make arrests as often in domestic assault cases as they do in nondomestic assault cases. *See also* testimony of Pittsburgh Police Lieutenant Michael Conroy, who was one of the first officers to arrive at Stonehouse's apartment on the morning of the shooting: "Any type of a domestic disturbance—very, very seldom is ever a police report made." A properly qualified expert would have been able to assail these myths and to inform the jury that battered women are nearly always subject to intense sexual jealousy which leads them to isolate themselves socially. Expert testimony would reveal that battered women view batterers "as omnipotent in terms of their ability to survey their women's activities," and that there are reasons for battered women's reluctance to seek help from others, such as fear, embarrassment, and the inability of police to respond in ways that are helpful to the battered women. Expert testimony would also have shown that among battered women who kill, the final incident that precipitates the killing is viewed by the battered woman as "more severe and more life-threatening than prior incidents."

On the basis of such expert testimony, the jury could have found that Stonehouse herein was a battered woman and that, like most battered women, Stonehouse was isolated and justifiably believed that no one could help her solve her predicament except herself. It was clear from the evidence presented at trial that Welsh's colleagues in the police department did little to protect Stonehouse from Welsh's surveillance, harassment, acts of vandalism, and assaults. Yet, the prosecutor argued to the jury that the lack of adequate police protection in this instance had less of a bearing on Stonehouse's sense of isolation than it did on the Commonwealth's theory that Stonehouse must not have really been a helpless victim of battering.

There was no reasonable basis for trial counsel not to call an expert witness to counter the erroneous battered woman myths upon which the Commonwealth built its case. Thus, trial counsel was ineffective, and the absence of such expert testimony was prejudicial to Stonehouse in that the jury was permitted, on the basis of unfounded myths, to assess Stonehouse's claim that she had a reasonable belief that she faced a life-threatening situation when she fired her gun at Welsh.

CONCLUSION: [We] reverse the order of Superior Court which affirmed the judgment of sentence, and we remand for a new trial consistent with this opinion.

At retrial in March 1990, before a judge alone, Stonehouse was acquitted. She was then reinstated to the Pittsburgh police force and awarded $129,000 in back pay.[54] In 1996, the Department of Justice released a report on introducing domestic violence evidence at criminal trials and concluded "the term 'battered woman syndrome' is no longer useful or appropriate" and expert testimony now refers to "battering and its effects." A representative example of the updated terminology is found in California's evidence law:

California Evidence Code §1107. Admissibility of expert evidence regarding intimate partner battering

(a) In a criminal action, expert testimony is admissible by either the prosecution or the defense regarding intimate partner battering and its effects, including the nature and effect of physical, emotional, or mental abuse on the beliefs, perceptions, or behavior of victims of domestic violence, except when offered against a criminal defendant to prove the occurrence of the act or acts of abuse which form the basis of the criminal charge. Given the continuing nature of the threat of violence, the proper criminal justice response for those found guilty of committing intimate partner violence is often incarceration. Treatment for those who batter focuses on elevating the self-esteem of the abuser to eliminate their use of violence as a means of keeping people close to them. Violence is a learned response to internal conflict and can be unlearned. Therapy for the abuser should extend beyond "anger management" classes to involve workshops designed to elevate feelings of self-worth so if a relationship does end, the abuser may realize he or she can survive rejection.[55]

> **Rule of Law:**
> Entrapment is when outrageous government conduct induces a person, who was not otherwise predisposed, to commit a crime.

Entrapment

If the government uses outrageous conduct to get otherwise innocent people to commit crimes, the defense of entrapment may prevail. The entrapment defense most often arises in criminal cases in which undercover officers pose as criminals and offer opportunities or otherwise induce defendants to commit crimes. Two tests are used to determine whether a defendant has been entrapped by the government: the objective and the subjective test. The U.S. Supreme Court discussed the subjective test in *Sorrells v. United States* (1932), in which a government agent asked Sorrells to procure liquor during the Prohibition Era when it was illegal to do so.[56] On the agent's third request, Sorrells did procure liquor and was convicted for the offense. On appeal, Sorrells argued that the judge should have given a jury instruction on the entrapment defense. The Supreme Court agreed with Sorrells and held the entrapment defense can be raised if, under the defendant's personal subjective perception, "the criminal design *originates* with the officials of the government, and they *implant* in the mind of an innocent person the disposition to commit the alleged offense and induce its commission in order that they might prosecute" (emphasis added).

Most jurisdictions follow the *Sorrells* approach, which focuses on the defendant's state of mind and whether the government overcame his will in convincing the defendant to commit the crime. The objective test for entrapment does not focus on the defendant's mind, but asks whether the government's outrageous conduct induced a reasonable law-abiding person to commit a crime; did the government make the defendant an "offer he couldn't refuse"?

For a look at both objective and subjective tests at work, examine the reasoning used by the Florida Court in *State v. Laing* (2016), where a 15-year-old girl was caught by school resource officers making out with Laing, her 19-year-old boyfriend. A detective took the girl's phone and, posing as her, made arrangements to meet Laing for sexual relations, a crime defined as statutory rape. When Laing showed up expecting to have sexual relations, he was arrested and charged with traveling to meet a minor for unlawful sexual activity and lewd computer solicitation of a child. The trial court dismissed the charges, finding that Laing was entrapped by the government. In the opinion reprinted in part below, the Florida court reinstated the charges, finding that under either the subjective or objective test for entrapment under Florida law, Laing acted willingly.

In popular culture on shows such as *To Catch a Predator*, suspects who seek to engage children for sexual activity who discover the "child" is an undercover police officer often raise the defense of entrapment. Depending on state jurisdiction, a subjective test focuses on whether the suspect would have engaged in the criminal activity regardless of the sting operation, or the objective test focuses on whether the government's outrageous conduct invited an otherwise law-abiding citizen to commit a crime he would not otherwise commit.

STATE V. LAING, 182 SO.3D 812 (2016)

District Court of Appeal of Florida, Fourth District

The State of Florida (the "State") appeals an order granting Jamal Rashad Laing's ("[Laing]") motion to dismiss the charges of traveling to meet a minor for unlawful sexual activity ("count I") and lewd computer solicitation of a child ("count II"). We find that the trial court erred in granting [Laing]'s motion to dismiss the charges under both the subjective and objective standards of entrapment, and reverse.

FACTS: On October 9, 2013, a school resource officer observed Laing inside a parked car in a local park with a minor female ("S.G."). According to the resource officer, Laing was on top of S.G., kissing her. At the time, Laing was nineteen years old and S.G. was fifteen. After the officer intervened and spoke with S.G., she told him that during the consensual encounter Laing attempted to touch her hip, breast, and groin areas. The officer released Laing without arresting him after a warrant check came back clean.

The resource officer then transported S.G. back to school to interview her. During the interview, she told him that she and Laing had multiple conversations after meeting on Facebook, and that Laing had picked her up that day after school. It was also revealed that Laing and S.G. had exchanged nude pictures of themselves in those Facebook conversations. S.G. showed the resource officer her phone containing numerous text messages between herself and Laing, and in one message Laing specifically stated that he wanted S.G. to perform oral sex on him.

The case then was turned over to a detective with the Indian River County Sheriff's Office for further investigation, who discovered that Laing had no criminal history. Laing did not call, text, or otherwise try to contact S.G. during the week following their encounter.

Using S.G.'s phone, the detective initiated contact with Laing on October 16 by texting him the word "hey." Laing responded by asking if S.G. had gotten in trouble for the incident. After some innocent conversation between Laing and the detective posing as S.G., Laing asked S.G. if she thought they would have had sex if they had not been interrupted. The detective responded "maybe," and inquired whether or not the fact that she was only fifteen would have been a problem for Laing. When questioned as to why she was asking him that question, the detective responded (as S.G.) that it was to make sure Laing was comfortable with her age, and that it was not a problem with her if it was not a problem with him. Laing stated that he did not care about her age.

Laing then texted that he had been ready to have sex with S.G. during the first encounter, to which the detective responded, "too bad that cop showed up." Laing replied that he knew they should not have gone to the park, and that they should have gone to a different location. In response, the detective told Laing, "I no [sic] a place where nobody would see us." Arrangements then were made to have Laing meet S.G. at a restaurant the following day. Laing confirmed he would meet S.G., and stated that he wanted her to perform oral sex on him. He also stated that he would show up only if she would give him some gas money. Laing was arrested upon his arrival at the restaurant.

ISSUE: [Was Laing entrapped by the government?]

HOLDING: [No.]

REASONING: The Entrapment Defense

In Florida, the defense of entrapment is bifurcated into *objective and subjective* variants (emphasis added): There are two different theories of entrapment. "*Objective* entrapment analysis focuses on the conduct of law enforcement" and "operates as a bar to prosecution in those instances where the government's conduct 'so offends decency or a sense of justice' that it amounts to a denial of due process." *Subjective* entrapment, on the other hand, "is applied in the absence of egregious law enforcement conduct and focuses on inducement of the accused based on an apparent lack of predisposition to commit the offense." . . .

(2) A person prosecuted for a crime shall be acquitted if the person proves by a preponderance of the evidence that his or her criminal conduct occurred as a result of an entrapment. The issue of entrapment shall be tried by the trier of fact [the jury].

Objective Due Process Standard

In considering objective entrapment, courts must look to the totality of the circumstances, focusing on "whether the government conduct 'so offends decency or a sense of justice that judicial power may not be exercised to obtain a conviction. . . . It is a balancing test; the court must weigh the rights of the defendant against the government's need to combat crime." The justification lies in stunting prosecutions premised upon "methods offending one's sense of justice." Objective entrapment also exists where law enforcement otherwise employs impermissible tactics to create the offense.

[Laing] argues that the detective's conduct in this case was egregious because the agent initiated contact with him via text message. However, creating nothing more than an opportunity to commit a crime is not prohibited (no due process violation where law enforcement set up a sting operation in which a decoy entered an online chat room purporting to be a minor, waited for someone to solicit sexual activity, and allowed the defendant to set up a meeting intending to engage in sexual activity with a 13-year-old); (undercover officer's conduct in approaching the defendant at a gay bar and telling the defendant that he liked to "party," which he explained as meaning the use of cocaine, was not so outrageous as to warrant dismissal of charges against the defendant for providing crystal meth to the officer).

We have held in previous cases that repeated calls alone, absent any showing of threats or promises, is insufficient to constitute entrapment. Here, there is no evidence that the detective prodded or coerced Laing into submitting to pressure to have sex with an underage female. Nor was there any type of law enforcement misconduct that we previously have stated violates a defendant's due process rights by ensnaring the defendant to commit a crime, regardless of his predisposition.

Subjective Standard

Application of the subjective standard codified in section 777.201 requires a three-part test:

(Continued)

(1) "whether an agent of the government induced the accused to commit the offense charged"

(2) if so, "whether the accused was predisposed to commit the offense charged, and

(3) "whether the entrapment evaluation should be submitted to a jury."

The first two [parts] involve questions of fact and differing burdens of proof, and the third [part] addresses whether the issue of entrapment must be submitted to the jury or whether the issue can be decided by the judge as a matter of law.

Texting the word "hey" to Laing after a week of no contact with the victim is wholly insufficient to constitute inducement. There was no evidence in this case that the detective induced Laing to agree to a sexual encounter. Rather, it was Laing who proposed meeting the minor

once again to engage in the unlawful acts that previously had been interrupted, after the detective mentioned that he knew of a more private area. Laing guided the conversation to sex on his own volition; the detective's innocuous text message to start the conversation with Laing did not amount to a concerted effort to lure him into committing a crime, and neither did his statement regarding knowledge of a more secluded location. Therefore, Laing was not induced [to commit the crime].

CONCLUSION: Because the evidence shows that law enforcement did not induce Laing to commit the crimes charged, we need not address the other prongs of the subjective entrapment test. We reverse the trial court's dismissal of counts I and II on the grounds that neither objective nor subjective entrapment existed as a matter of law, and remand for proceedings consistent with this opinion.

Reversed and Remanded.

SUMMARY

1. You will be able to articulate the public policy reasons for recognizing defenses. The reasons society recognizes defenses is to ensure that all sentences meet the minimal threshold of not running afoul of the Eighth Amendment's ban on cruel and unusual punishment. Fairness in criminal justice requires recognizing that some people are not completely responsible for their actions or the crimes that they commit.

2. You will understand how defenses are raised before and at trial. Alibi means the offender can prove they were far away when the crime was committed, and consent means the victim agreed to the alleged crime; both are complete defenses based on excuse. The statute of limitations prevents the state from prosecuting some crimes because too much time has passed since the time the act occurred. There is no statute of limitations for the crime of murder. Defenses are generally affirmative defenses and must be raised by the defendant, who has the burden of production (producing enough evidence to allow the issue to go to the jury) and the burden of persuasion (convincing the jury that it is more likely than not that the defense is valid). At every stage in the criminal trial process, a defendant must be competent, which means he understands the legal proceedings and is able to assist his counsel in his defense. Some defendants may be forcibly medicated to restore

them to competency if medically necessary and in their best interest.

3. You will appreciate the defenses based on excuse and variations of the *mens rea*–based defenses, such as infancy and insanity. The mistake of law and mistake of fact are generally unavailable to defendants. When they are available for certain crimes, it is the jury's responsibility to resolve the issue whether such mistakes negate the *mens rea* required to find the defendant guilty of the crime charged. Duress is when a person is compelled to commit a crime by another person who poses a serious immediate threat to the victim's own life. There are different *mens rea* defenses that recognize a defendant's diminished capacity, such as intoxication where drugs and alcohol impair mental functioning. The M'Naghten test for insanity provides that if at the time the defendant committed the crime he was suffering under such defect of reason that he could not tell the difference between right and wrong, or he could not appreciate the criminality of his conduct, then he is legally insane and not responsible for his criminal acts. Variations of diminished capacity defenses include the irresistible impulse defense, which recognizes that the defendant may have no emotional brakes to resist the impulse to commit a crime; the ALI substantial capacity test, which is a defense if the defendant was unable to conform his

conduct to the requirements of the law; and the guilty but mentally ill (GBMI) defense, which gives juries an alternative to finding the defendant insane while still recognizing that the defendant's mental defect may have been the genesis of his criminal conduct. Infancy means there is an irrebuttable presumption that children up to age 7 have no *mens rea*, but a rebuttable presumption for children ages 8 through 14 by showing the child could appreciate the criminality of her conduct. Determining intellectual disability requires a flexible approach based on intelligence tests and adaptive functioning skills but should not rely on stereotypes common in popular culture, as reflected in the *Moore v. Texas* (2017) case that rejected the seven *Briseno* factors as not properly rooted in science.

4. You will successfully distinguish defenses based on justification. Sometimes people act out of necessity and choose the lesser of two evils. When one is facing an attack, one can respond in self-defense or in the defense of others or property depending upon the circumstances. Generally, one cannot use deadly force to protect solely property because human life is worth more than items one can purchase. Entrapment alleges that outrageous government conduct induced someone who is not otherwise predisposed to commit a criminal act, as rejected in *State v. Laing* (2016).

5. You will be able to identify the differences between self-defense, battered woman syndrome, and defense of others and property. A third justification for criminal acts is self-defense, when someone is threatening bodily harm or death and the victim has the legal right to use the same amount of force to repel the attack. A victim may act in the defense of others as well, or defend property with less than deadly force, provided that the victim complies with the retreat laws applicable in his state jurisdiction. In "stand your ground" jurisdictions, a person is allowed to use deadly force without retreat if there is a reasonable belief of a deadly threat. Battered woman syndrome is not necessarily a defense but rather a compilation of psychological reactions formed as a result of suffering repeated cycles of emotional and physical abuse that make the victim believe they must kill even if no immediate threat to life exists, as in *Pennsylvania v. Stonehouse* (1989). Evidence of battered woman syndrome is usually introduced through expert testimony at trial; the phrase used more often now is "battering and its effects" to eliminate the connotation that a "syndrome" is a pathology.

Go back to the beginning of the chapter and reread the news excerpts associated with the learning objectives. Test yourself to determine if you can understand the material covered in the text in the context of the news.

KEY TERMS AND PHRASES

ALI substantial capacity test 340
alibi 333
appreciate the criminality
  of his conduct 336
battered woman syndrome 348
burden of persuasion 333
burden of production 333
competency 334
cycle of violence 348
defense of others 347
defense of property 347

delusion 339
diminished capacity 339
duress 338
entrapment 354
guilty but mentally ill 341
imperfect self-defense 348
infancy 336
intellectual disability 342
intoxication 337
irrebuttable presumption 336
irresistible impulse 342

mental disease or defect 339
mistake of fact 336
mistake of law 336
M'Naghten test 339
necessity 345
"no retreat" doctrine 347
psychosis 335
rebuttable presumption 336
self-defense 346
stand your ground 347
statute of limitations 334

PROBLEM-SOLVING EXERCISES

1. John was a small-time cocaine dealer. One of his customers, Owen, was caught by federal drug agents. To negotiate for a less severe sentence, Owen cooperated with the government and continued buying drugs from John. The agents set up audio and video surveillance of John, and Owen continued to purchase small quantities of cocaine but began to insist that John procure at least one kilogram of cocaine for Owen to buy. It took repeated requests and many months, but John finally secured the kilogram for Owen. On delivery day, agents discovered John in the car with the kilogram on his lap. At John's trial for cocaine distribution, he raised the defense of entrapment. Will he be successful? **(ROL: Entrapment)**

2. Juliet was driving Romeo home when she swerved in front of a car driven by Paris. Paris swerved to avoid a crash with

Juliet but was very angry and started to follow Juliet on the roadway, yelling profanities out of his window. At an intersection with a stop sign, Paris, who was 6 feet, 3 inches and 260 pounds, jumped out of his car, approached Juliet's car, and dragged her from behind the steering wheel. Paris starting kicking Juliet, who was an average-size woman. Romeo, who was 5 feet, 2 inches and 130 pounds, jumped out of Juliet's car to help her and yelled at Paris to stop. When Paris would not stop, Romeo pulled a pistol out of his coat pocket and fired a warning shot in the air, telling Paris he would shoot him if Paris did not stop. Paris stopped kicking Juliet and started coming toward Romeo and Romeo shot him in the arm. Romeo has been charged with aggravated battery. Does Romeo have a defense? (ROL: Self-defense and defense of others)

3. Defendant was 13 years old when he sexually assaulted his neighbor by breaking into her home, threatening her with a mop handle, and fondling her breasts. The defendant was evaluated before trial and found to have an IQ of 72 and an inability to count money, read, or navigate a schedule for public transportation. A psychologist found that defendant suffered from impaired brain functioning that made him "more impulsive" than other juveniles his age and noted the defendant came from an impoverished background. The defendant told the psychologist he thought the victim was his "girlfriend," who was just playing hard to get when she would not open the door when he knocked. The victim had never met the defendant. What defenses can the defendant raise? (ROL: Infancy, intellectual disability, insanity)

13

SENTENCING AND APPEALS

Go to the end of the chapter. Skim the key terms and phrases and read the summary closely. Come back and look at the following news excerpts to focus your reading throughout the chapter to understand the law to ensure punishments are fair and accepted by society. The guilty judgment allows the government to restrict the person's liberty by putting her in prison or placing her on probation and parole where the court retains jurisdiction over the offender until the sentence has been completed. The chapter also examines "actual innocence" claims and the *writ of habeas corpus* to bring postconviction issues to the court's attention. The chapter begins with a case excerpt highlighting the intersection of technology and the government's sentencing decisions. Many terms in this chapter have been used and defined in previous chapters.

WHY THIS CHAPTER MATTERS TO YOU	THE LEARNING OBJECTIVES AS REFLECTED IN THE NEWS
After you have read this chapter: **Learning Objective 1:** You will be able to understand how society determines cruel and unusual punishment.	A federal jury awarded $1 million to two former Florida inmates who were repeatedly sexually assaulted by a correctional officer while in custody at Bay County Jail in Panama City in 2013. On Monday evening, the jury found that the inmates' treatment while under the protection of the Bay County Sheriff's Office (BCSO) constituted cruel and unusual punishment and required the sheriff's office to pay the large damages. The jury found that other jail staff, including the warden [Anglin], had known for months that one of their officers posed a threat to female inmates. Anglin's failure to act on the threat caused the rape of the two women. (*Miami Herald*, March 2, 2018)
Learning Objective 2: You will be able to distinguish between the types of sentences, such as mandatory minimum sentences and sex offender registries.	New Jersey's highest court has ruled a portion of Megan's Law unconstitutional because it requires juveniles to remain listed on the state's sex offender registry for life. The unanimous Supreme Court decision found placing such a lifetime requirement on child offenders violated their due process rights under the state constitution [because] registration requirements may impede a juvenile's rehabilitative efforts. The ruling concerned a defendant identified only as C.K., who was convicted of sexually assaulting his adopted brother. The court reverted to an older requirement that allows juvenile sex offenders to apply to be removed from the registry after 15 years. (NJ.com, April 25, 2018)

(Continued)

WHY THIS CHAPTER MATTERS TO YOU	THE LEARNING OBJECTIVES AS REFLECTED IN THE NEWS
Learning Objective 3: You will be able to understand suspended sentences, such as probation and parole.	Meek Mill has been released from prison following an order from the Philadelphia Supreme Court. The rapper, whose legal name is Robert Rihmeek Williams, served an up-to-four-year sentence for violating probation stemming from a 2008 conviction on drug and gun counts. He has been in jail since last November. The Philadelphia District Attorney's (D.A.) office acknowledged that circumstances surrounding the original conviction might lead to it being reversed [because Meek's] arresting officer Reginald V. Graham gave false testimony. Graham was the only government witness during [Meek's] trial and was part of the search warrant that produced the alleged evidence against the rapper. (*Rolling Stone*, April 24, 2018)
Learning Objective 4: Identify the bifurcated death-penalty trial and sentencing process.	Hamstrung by troubles with lethal injection—gruesomely botched attempts, legal battles and growing difficulty obtaining the drugs—states are looking for alternative ways to carry out the death penalty. High on the list for some is a method that has never been used before: inhaling nitrogen gas. Oklahoma, Alabama and Mississippi have authorized nitrogen for executions and are developing protocols to use it, which represents a leap into the unknown. There is no scientific data on executing people with nitrogen, leading some experts to question whether states, in trying to solve old problems, may create new ones. (*New York Times*, May 7, 2018)
Learning Objective 5: You will be able to summarize the legal requirements for *habeas corpus* review and claims of "actual innocence."	Judge Missey proposed that, if the Missouri Supreme Court disagreed with his analysis regarding Robinson's "free standing" claim of innocence, the Court should consider his "gateway" claim of actual innocence. The "gateway" threshold has a lesser burden of proof than "free standing" actual innocence and allows courts to examine previously unraised claims of constitutional errors at trial [such as] the State's presentation of the perjured testimony of Jason Richison . . . and the prosecutor should have corrected the presentation of the evidence at trial. (*Southeast Missourian*, May 4, 2018)

Chapter-Opening Case Study: Risk Assessment and Sentencing

Wisconsin v. Loomis, Case No. 2015AP157-CR (July 2016)

The facts of this case are not in dispute. The State contends that Loomis was the driver in a drive-by shooting. It charged him with five counts, all as a repeater: (1) First degree recklessly endangering safety; (2) Attempting to flee or elude a traffic officer; (3) Operating a motor vehicle without the owner's consent; (4) Possession of a firearm by a felon of a short-barreled shotgun or rifle. He waived his right to trial and entered a guilty plea to only two of the less severe charges, attempting to flee a traffic officer and operating a motor vehicle without the owner's consent (the other charges will be dismissed, but read into the record at sentencing) ...

Although [Loomis] denies he had any role in the shooting, and only drove the car after the shooting occurred, the State believes he was the driver of the car when the shooting happened. The State will leave any appropriate sentence to the Court's discretion, but will argue aggravating [make worse] and mitigating [make less severe] factors. After accepting Loomis's plea, the circuit court ordered a presentence investigation. The Presentence Investigation Report (PSI) included an attached COMPAS **risk assessment** [risk=chances/assessment=evaluation]. COMPAS is a risk-need assessment tool designed by Northpointe, Inc. to provide decisional support for the Department of Corrections when making placement decisions, managing offenders, and planning treatment. The COMPAS risk assessment is based on information gathered from the defendant's criminal file and an interview with the defendant.

A COMPAS [Correctional Offender Management Profiling for Alternative Sanctions] report consists of a risk assessment designed to predict recidivism (released from criminal sanctions and committing another crime) and a separate needs assessment for identifying program needs in areas such as employment, housing and substance abuse. The risk assessment portion of COMPAS generates risk scores displayed in the form of a bar chart, with three bars that represent pretrial recidivism risk, general recidivism risk, and violent recidivism risk. Each bar indicates a defendant's level of risk on a scale of one to ten.

As the PSI explains, risk scores are intended to predict the general likelihood that those with a similar history of offending are either less likely or more likely to commit another crime following release from custody. However, the COMPAS risk assessment does not predict the specific likelihood that an individual offender will reoffend. Instead, it provides a prediction based on a comparison of information about the individual to a similar data group.

Loomis's COMPAS risk scores indicated that he presented a high risk of recidivism on all three bar charts. His PSI included a description of how the COMPAS risk assessment should be used and cautioned against its misuse, instructing that it is to be used to identify offenders who could benefit from interventions and to target risk factors that should be addressed during supervision.

Ultimately, the [trial judge] referenced the COMPAS risk score along with other sentencing factors in ruling out [making unavailable] probation:

> You're identified, through the COMPAS assessment, as an individual who is at high risk to the community. In terms of weighing the various factors, I'm ruling out probation because of the seriousness of the crime and because your history, your history on supervision, and the risk assessment tools that have been utilized, suggest that you're extremely high risk to re-offend [recidivate].

Loomis filed a motion for postconviction relief requesting a new sentencing hearing. He argued that the circuit court's consideration of the COMPAS risk assessment at sentencing violated his due process rights. How should the court rule on Loomis's motion?

SENTENCING PROCESS

Cruel and Unusual Punishment

The purpose of punishment is to protect society and punish offenders, as explored in Chapter 1 and highlighted by legal scholar Kent Greenawalt:

> Why should wrongdoers be punished? Most people might respond simply that they deserve it or that they should suffer in return for the harm they have done. A simple retributivist justification provides a philosophical account corresponding to these feelings; someone who has violated the rights of others should be penalized, and punishment restores the moral order that has been breached by the original wrongful act.[1]

Within the realm of sanctions imposed by the state are a wide range of punishments, but all sentencing decisions must be particular and individualized for each convict. There are especially harsh punishments, such as mandatory minimum sentences that require the convict to serve no less than a specified number of years in prison, "three-strikes" laws that impose a life sentence on conviction of a third felony, life imprisonment without parole (LWOP), and execution. As the chapter-opening case study indicates, courts

Rule of Law: The Eighth Amendment's ban against cruel and unusual punishment requires society punish the offender, not the crime.

are now turning to artificial intelligence algorithms (computer calculations), such as COMPAS, to help judges make sentencing decisions.

What constitutes cruel and unusual punishment must be measured by a proportionality review to ensure people who commit similar crimes receive similar sentences. The Constitution's Eighth Amendment provides "Excessive bail shall not be required, nor excessive fines imposed, nor cruel and unusual punishments inflicted."

Sometimes, proportionality is based on the severity of the crime charged. For example, in the case *Harmelin v. Michigan* (1991), reprinted in part below, a young student with no criminal history was sentenced to life imprisonment for possessing more than 650 grams of cocaine. The primary issue for the U.S. Supreme Court on appeal was whether a life sentence for a first-time drug offense constituted cruel and unusual punishment? The high Court said Harmelin's sentence was legal because state lawmakers who represent the will of the voters have adjudged drug crimes as appropriately severe to carry a life sentence.

HARMELIN V. MICHIGAN, 501 U.S. 957 (1991)

United States Supreme Court

Justice Scalia announced the decision of the Court. (5–4)

FACTS: [Harmelin] was convicted of possessing 672 grams of cocaine and sentenced to a mandatory term of life in prison without possibility of parole.

ISSUE: [Harmelin] claims that his sentence is unconstitutionally "cruel and unusual" for two reasons: first, because it is "significantly disproportionate" to the crime he committed; second, because the sentencing judge was statutorily required to impose it, without taking into account the particularized circumstances of the crime and of the criminal.

HOLDING: The sentence is affirmed.

REASONING: Most historians agree that the "cruell and unusuall Punishments" provision of the English Declaration of Rights was prompted by the abuses attributed to the infamous Lord Chief Justice Jeffreys of the King's Bench during the Stuart reign of James II. They do not agree, however, on which abuses. Jeffreys is best known for presiding over the "Bloody Assizes" following the Duke of Monmouth's abortive rebellion in 1685; a special commission led by Jeffreys tried, convicted, and executed hundreds of suspected insurgents. Some have attributed the Declaration of Rights provision to popular outrage against those proceedings. But the vicious punishments for treason decreed in the Bloody Assizes (drawing and quartering, burning of women felons, beheading, disemboweling, etc.) were common in that period—indeed, they were specifically authorized by law and remained so for many years afterwards.

[Harmelin] claims that his sentence violates the Eighth Amendment for a reason in addition to its alleged disproportionality. He argues that it is "cruel and unusual" to impose a mandatory sentence of such severity, without any consideration of so-called mitigating factors such as, in his case, the fact that he had no prior felony convictions. He apparently contends that the Eighth Amendment requires Michigan to create a sentencing scheme whereby life in prison without possibility of parole is simply the most severe of a range of available penalties that the sentencer may impose after hearing evidence in mitigation and aggravation . . . this claim has no support in the text and history of the Eighth Amendment.

CONCLUSION: We have drawn the line of required individualized sentencing at capital cases, and see no basis for extending it further. The judgment of the Michigan Court of Appeals is affirmed.

Justice Stevens, with whom Justice Blackmun joins, dissenting:

[A] mandatory sentence of life imprisonment without the possibility of parole does share one important characteristic of a death sentence: The offender will never regain his freedom. Because such a sentence does not even purport to serve a rehabilitative function, the sentence must rest on a rational determination that the punished "criminal conduct is so atrocious that society's interest in deterrence and retribution wholly outweighs any considerations of reform or rehabilitation of the perpetrator." Serious as this defendant's crime was, I believe it is irrational to conclude that every similar offender is wholly incorrigible.

The following are typical steps in the sentencing process, but students should research the procedures followed in their respective state jurisdictions.

Presentence Investigation

To determine the appropriate sentence, the pretrial services or probation officer conducts a presentence investigation to collect all important information concerning the background, character, and conduct of a person convicted of an offense which a court "may receive and consider for the purpose of imposing an appropriate sentence,"[2] such as defendant's family history, educational background and achievements, economic status, employment history, medical history, and history of drug use. The probation officer verifies the convict's background information by calling relevant references such as employers and family members, reviews the nature of the charges and the circumstances surrounding the crime, and makes a recommendation about the appropriate sentence in the case. The information is collected in a presentence report, which is generally not available to the public.

Usually a probation officer interviews the convict. Defense counsel should attend this interview and counsel her client because some of the statements made by the defendant may be used against her at sentencing. Under the Federal Sentencing Guidelines, relevant conduct, which is criminal conduct associated with the offense but not charged as a crime, may be used to enhance a sentence.[3] For example, members of a drug conspiracy sold methamphetamine on eight, different transactions. Mr. Figueroa was involved only in three of the sales. In the presentence investigation, the probation officer attributed all eight sales to Figueroa as relevant conduct related to his sentencing. Because drug sentences are often determined on the overall weight of drugs sold, Figueroa's guideline sentence doubled. On appeal, the court overturned Figueroa's sentence because the trial judge failed to make factual findings about how much weight for which Figueroa was ultimately responsible. Figueroa was lucky because, generally, relevant conduct defines the "scope of behavior" attributable to the defendant and can be used against him in determining a criminal sentence, which is usually longer than he would have originally received.[4]

The presentence investigation incorporates all the information gathered by the probation officer and is presented to the prosecutor, defense counsel, and judge. In determining an appropriate sentence, a judge is not necessarily limited to the information contained in the presentence investigation; "a judge may appropriately conduct an inquiry broad in scope, largely unlimited either as to the kind of information he may consider, or the source from which it may come."[5] A judge may legally consider any and all testimony adduced at trial or by the guilty plea, including any of the defendant's statements or testimony. In the chapter-opening case study, the appellate court found using the COMPAS risk assessment tool permissible in fashioning Loomis's sentence but found relying on COMPAS exclusively (rather than merely considering the score) to impose the sentence is improper.

Springboard for Discussion

If you were a state legislator charged with managing your state's entire budget, would you adopt a punitive or rehabilitative philosophy of punishment? Can you think of programs within your state that reflect each sentencing purpose?

The Sentencing Hearing

Prior to the actual imposition of a sentence, the court holds a sentencing hearing during which the judge hears arguments from both the prosecution and the defense and may accept additional evidence in aggravation or in mitigation. As discussed in Chapter 1, courts allow victims to make an impact statement to the court reflecting the pain and suffering caused by the offender. In *Payne v. Tennessee* (1991), Chief Justice Rehnquist stated that if courts refused victims an opportunity to speak prior to a defendant's sentencing, it "deprives the State of the full moral force of its evidence and may prevent the jury from having before it all the information necessary to determine the proper punishment."[6]

The judge also hears the allocution, the defendant's statement to the court before sentence is imposed. In the Boston Marathon bomber's case featured in Chapter 2 as an illustration of the criminal trial process, the defendant, Dzhokhar Tsarnaev, addressed the court before formal imposition of a death sentence on June 24, 2015:

> The Prophet Muhammad, peace and blessings be upon him, said that if you do not—if you are not merciful to Allah's creation, Allah will not be merciful to you, so I'd like to now apologize to the victims, to the survivors. Immediately after the bombing, which

I am guilty of—if there's any lingering doubt about that, let there be no more. I did do it along with my brother.

I learned of some of the victims. I learned their names, their faces, their age. And throughout this trial more of those victims were given names, more of those victims had faces, and they had burdened souls. Now, all those who got up on that witness stand and that podium related to us—to me—I was listening—the suffering that was and the hardship that still is, with strength and with patience and with dignity. Now, Allah says in the Qur'an that no soul is burdened with more than it can bear, and you told us just how unbearable it was, how horrendous it was, this thing I put you through.

After allocution, the judge pronounces a sentence and imposes a penalty for the offense. If the defendant has been convicted of multiple charges such as robbery and kidnapping, a judge may impose concurrent sentences, all sentences running together, or consecutive sentences, allowing the sentence for robbery to run and, when time served, implementing the sentence for the kidnapping. Federal judges need not wait for a consecutive sentence to run and may impose successive sentences based on the anticipation of when state sentences, not yet imposed, may conclude.[7] Concurrent jurisdiction is simultaneous federal and state power to hear a case, even though only one sovereign (government) typically prosecutes the case.

TYPES OF SENTENCES

Sentence Should Reflect Offender's Culpability

The American public is diverse, and the jail and prison population reflect the culture's differences. No two offenders commit a crime for the same reason. The Eighth Amendment requires criminal sentences reflect the offender's culpability.

Determinate and Indeterminate Sentences

Determinate sentencing involves the imposition of fixed or flat prison time. Determinate sentences, much like the three-strikes laws described in this chapter, increase the prison population and the attendant strain on resources within the prison, including security, medical care, and rehabilitation. Such sentences reflect the public's wariness of the presumed revolving door at the prison gate. In contrast, in indeterminate sentencing, the judge imposes a sentencing range, for example, 2 to 20 years, and if the prisoner exhibits good behavior in prison, he may be released early by a parole board. Indeterminate sentencing was largely responsible for the enactment of tough sentencing reforms in the 1980s. In *Mistretta v. United States* (1989), the U.S. Supreme Court said that in enacting the Federal Sentencing Guidelines, Congress concluded that rehabilitation was a failed corrections philosophy and that indeterminate sentencing "was a serious impediment to an evenhanded and effective operation of the criminal justice system."[8] The result of the uncertainty produced by indeterminate sentences was the enactment of guideline sentencing schemes enacted in all jurisdictions to achieve uniformity in sentencing.

Federal Sentencing Guidelines

In 1984, Congress enacted the Comprehensive Crime Control Act and the Sentencing Reform Act.[9] This legislation set mandatory minimum sentences for drug crimes and also authorized the creation of the U.S. Sentencing Commission, which promulgated the first set of codified sentencing guidelines for federal trial courts. The commission's mandate was stated in pertinent part,

> The Comprehensive Crime Control Act of 1984 foresees guidelines that will further the basic purpose of criminal punishment by deterring crime, incapacitating the offender, providing just punishment, and rehabilitating the offender. It delegates to the Commission broad authority to review and rationalize the federal sentencing process.

The commission drafted the Federal Sentencing Guidelines, which were then passed into law by Congress in 1987 to minimize sentencing disparities based on jurisdiction or offender characteristics. The guidelines assigned numbers for each crime and each type of criminal history and, as critics contended, reduced federal sentencing to a mathematical calculation rather than an individual sentence. The guidelines made all sentences determinate and eliminated the system of parole whereby prisoners, in exchange for good behavior, had their sentences reduced by 15% for any sentence over a year. A convict subject to sentencing under the Federal Sentencing Guidelines may also be subject to "mandatory minimum" sentences. If an offender would otherwise be eligible for a 21-month sentence under the guidelines for selling 100 grams of heroin, she will nonetheless serve a 5-year mandatory minimum based on federal drug laws. An example of how to determine a sentence under the guidelines is illustrated by Figure 13.1 and by the following narrative.

Let's imagine famous Chicago gangster Al "Scarface" Capone and his cohorts are convicted under a series of offenses related to racketeering, such as drug dealing, sex trafficking, larceny, and murder. Every federal crime for which someone can be sentenced is listed in Chapter 2 of the Federal Sentencing Guidelines and is assigned a corresponding base offense level (BOL), from 1 to 43. If the crime has certain aggravating circumstances making the crime worse, we add levels, and if there are mitigating circumstances diminishing the offender's culpability, we subtract offense levels. We then must determine a person's criminal history points, also in Chapter 4 of the guidelines. Referring to the sentencing table in Figure 13.1, we add offense levels to get the appropriate number down the left column and the number of criminal history points 1 to 13 or more to fit into the appropriate criminal history category, I through VI. For criminal history, the numbers under each category represents the number of points; for example, criminal history category IV means an offender has 7, 8, or 9 criminal history points. To determine the appropriate sentence, we follow where the base offense levels intersect with the criminal history category to calculate the sentencing range of months in prison.

Starting at the bottom of Figure 13.1 (#1), Al Capone could be found guilty of conspiracy to commit murder because the head of criminal gangs often kills rivals (think Chicago's 1929 St. Valentine's Day massacre in which seven men were massacred, presumably on order by Capone). The guidelines at §2A1.5 provide that if, as a result of the conspiracy to commit murder, a death results, the BOL is 43; because the sentence BOL is life in prison, Capone's criminal history category does not matter. Capone's lieutenant in the gang is running a prostitution ring that involves minors (#2), guidelines at §2G1.3. The lieutenant starts at BOL 24 and for being a ring leader of five or more people §3B1.1, we add another 4 levels (totalling BOL 28). The lieutenant also has a criminal history; he had previously received two sentences, one for at least 6 months imprisonment and one for 13 months in prison for a total of 5 criminal history points. Go across the top of the sentencing table and find that 5 criminal history points places him in category III. BOL 28 intersects with criminal history level III at 97 to 121 months imprisonment.

The gang's secretary (#3) was stealing money, guidelines at §2B1.1. An offense level for larceny starts at BOL 6, but because the gang was so profitable and earned more than $9.5 million, we add 20 levels (to BOL 26). And because the secretary's crime resulted in substantial hardship to one or more victims, as most gangs cause great public harm, we add another 2 levels (to BOL 28). But because the secretary felt bad and decided to accept responsibility and plead guilty, we reduce her BOL by 3 for a final offense level of 25. Because she has no criminal history points, she is in category I, which intersects with BOL 25 at 57 to 71 months imprisonment.

The worker bees at the bottom of the gang pyramid (#4) sold marijuana, which, according to the drug table, guidelines at §2D1.1, for an amount of at least 20 kilograms but not more than 40 kilograms, starts at BOL 16. If in committing their drug crimes they bribed police, which is common for gang members, add 2 levels, or used a firearm, add 2 levels. If some soldiers were only minor participants in the gang's overall operation, the court could pursuant to §3B1.2 reduce their offense levels by 4. Their ultimate sentence would depend on the number of criminal history points each accrued by committing prior bad acts. The federal guidelines are used for illustrative purposes here. Most state jurisdictions have patterned their sentencing schemes on a guideline-based template.

Enhancing a Sentence

From the time of their enactment in 1987 until 2005, the Federal Sentencing Guidelines were mandatory and bound all defendants tried and convicted in federal court. On appeal, courts examined whether trial judges had sentenced within the guideline range for a particular crime. Essentially, the guidelines made judges into no more than accountants who counted points on a mathematical grid to determine an appropriate sentence, but U.S. Supreme Court decisions have made significant changes in guidelines law starting with the *Apprendi* decision.

In 1994, George and Martha Washington, an African American couple, moved into Derry township in New Jersey. One neighbor, Charles Apprendi, Jr., decided to welcome the Washingtons by shooting .38 caliber bullets through their living room window. In *Apprendi v. New Jersey* (2000), the sentencing judge found that Apprendi's crime was triggered by his racial bias against the Washingtons, and under the "hate crime enhancement," 2 years were added to Apprendi's sentence, which was already the maximum for his offense.[10] On appeal, the U.S. Supreme Court decided that the judge's action in increasing the sentence violated Apprendi's Sixth Amendment right to a jury trial. The Court held, "Other than the fact of prior conviction, any fact that increases the penalty for a crime beyond the prescribed statutory maximum must be submitted to a jury, and proved beyond a reasonable doubt."

The Court reasoned that when the judge, as in Apprendi's case, makes findings of fact (such as Apprendi was motivated by racial hatred) that lead to increased prison time, this action deprives the defendant of his right to a jury trial as guaranteed by the Sixth Amendment. Because of the *Apprendi* ruling, many sentences across the country that had been enhanced solely by a judge

Figure 13.1 How to Calculate a Federal Guideline Sentence

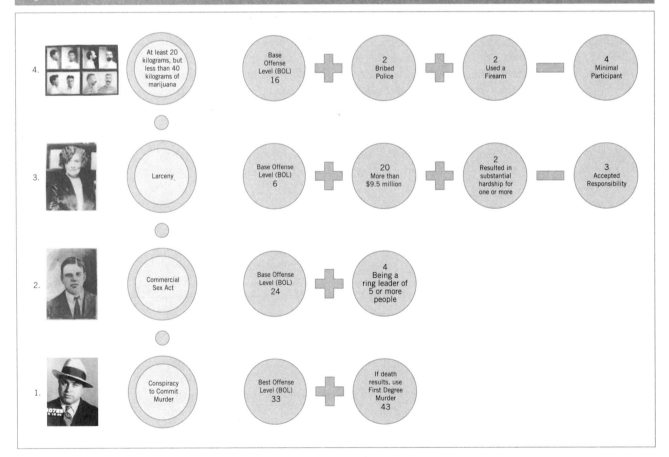

SENTENCING TABLE
(in months of imprisonment)

	Offense Level	Criminal History Category (Criminal History Points)					
		I (0 or 1)	II (2 or 3)	III (4,5,6)	IV (7,8,9)	V (10,11,12)	VI (13 or more)
	1	0-6	0-6	0-6	0-6	0-6	0-6
	2	0-6	0-6	0-6	0-6	0-6	1-7
	3	0-6	0-6	0-6	0-6	2-8	3-9
	4	0-6	0-6	0-6	2-8	4-10	6-12
Zone A	5	0-6	0-6	1-7	4-10	6-12	9-15
	6	0-6	1-7	2-8	6-12	9-15	12-18
	7	0-6	2-8	4-10	8-14	12-18	15-21
	8	0-6	4-10	6-12	10-16	15-21	18-24
	9	4-10	6-12	8-14	12-18	18-24	21-27
Zone B	10	6-12	8-14	10-16	15-21	21-27	24-30
	11	8-14	10-16	12-18	18-24	24-30	27-33
	12	10-16	12-18	15-21	21-27	27-33	30-37
Zone C	13	12-18	15-21	18-24	24-30	30-37	33-41
	14	15-21	18-24	21-27	27-33	33-41	37-46
	15	18-24	21-27	24-30	30-37	37-46	41-51
#4 Soldiers	16	21-27	24-30	27-33	33-41	41-51	46-57
	17	24-30	27-33	30-37	37-46	46-57	51-63
	18	27-33	30-37	33-41	41-51	51-63	57-71
	19	30-37	33-41	37-46	46-57	57-71	63-78
	20	33-41	37-46	41-51	51-63	63-78	70-87
	21	37-46	41-51	46-57	57-71	70-87	77-96
	22	41-51	46-57	51-63	63-78	77-96	84-105
	23	46-57	51-63	57-71	70-87	84-105	92-115
	24	51-63	57-71	63-78	77-96	92-115	100-125
#3 Secretary	25	57-71	63-78	70-87	84-105	100-125	110-137
	26	63-78	70-87	78-97	92-115	110-137	120-150
	27	70-87	78-97	87-108	100-125	120-150	130-162
#2 Lieutenant	28	78-97	87-108	97-121	110-137	130-162	140-175
	29	87-108	97-121	108-135	121-151	140-175	151-188
	30	97-121	108-135	121-151	135-168	151-188	168-210
	31	108-135	121-151	135-168	151-188	168-210	188-235
	32	121-151	135-168	151-188	168-210	188-235	210-262
	33	135-168	151-188	168-210	188-235	210-262	235-293
	34	151-188	168-210	188-235	210-262	235-293	262-327
	35	168-210	188-235	210-262	235-293	262-327	292-365
	36	188-235	210-262	235-293	262-327	292-365	324-405
	37	210-262	235-293	262-327	292-365	324-405	360-life
	38	235-293	262-327	292-365	324-405	360-life	360-life
	39	262-327	292-365	324-405	360-life	360-life	360-life
	40	292-365	324-405	360-life	360-life	360-life	360-life
	41	324-405	360-life	360-life	360-life	360-life	360-life
	42	360-life	360-life	360-life	360-life	360-life	360-life
#1 Al Capone	43	life	life	life	life	life	life

making determinations as to the aggravating circumstances, were reduced. Today under *Apprendi*, either a jury has to find facts that would enhance a sentence or the defendant would have to agree to the facts when he pleaded guilty.

The high Court then decided *Blakely v. Washington* (2004).[11] Ralph Blakely, Jr., kidnapped his wife and terrorized his teenage son in the state of Washington. He entered into a plea agreement in federal court, and the judge decided to lengthen Blakely's sentence based on certain aggravating factors during Blakely's commission of the crime. Blakely appealed the actions of the judge that made his sentence longer. His case made it to the Supreme Court, which decided in Blakely's favor. The Court held that the *Apprendi* precedent required any factor that enhanced a defendant's sentence must be found by a jury or admitted during a guilty plea, conditions not present in Blakely's case. The ultimate outcome of Blakely's case was that judges could not enhance a defendant's sentence at their own discretion, for such action violated the defendant's Sixth Amendment rights to a fair trial. The significance of this ruling is that most determinate sentencing schemes were now in peril of being held unconstitutional if they allowed the judge alone to increase the sentence after a defendant had been found guilty by a jury or pleaded guilty to sufficient facts.

Next, the Court decided *United States v. Booker* (2005).[12] Because of a jury conviction on drug charges, Freddie Booker was facing 210 to 262 months (17½–22 years) in prison, but the judge found additional relevant facts at sentencing and increased Booker's sentence to 30 years imprisonment. The federal court of appeals held that such a sentence enhancement was directly in violation of the *Apprendi* precedent. The high Court found that the judge's actions increasing Booker's sentence violated his Sixth Amendment right to have a jury find sentencing enhancements beyond a reasonable doubt. The Court also made the Federal Sentencing Guidelines advisory rather than mandatory, returning some discretion to the federal judges to impose appropriate sentences. Federal judges are still required to base their sentences on guideline calculations, but the sentence may now fall within a minimum and maximum range of punishment defined by applicable law.

Judges, Juries, and the Death-Penalty Sentence. When a state court judge determined that Timothy Ring should receive the death penalty for murder, armed robbery, and related charges, the U.S. Supreme Court said that due to *Apprendi*'s implication for a defendant's Sixth Amendment right to a fair trial, the aggravating factors that made Ring eligible for the death penalty could be legally determined only by a jury, not a judge. Because of the Supreme Court's decision in *Ring v. Arizona* (2002), applying the *Apprendi* ruling to cases where a judge, and not a jury, found the aggravating factors supporting a death sentence, 150 death-row inmates across the country whose cases were in the first stages of their appeals had their death sentences commuted to life without the possibility of parole.[13] For the death-row inmates who had their aggravating circumstances found by a judge and not a jury,[14] but whose appeals were final, the high Court held in *Schriro v. Summerlin* (2004), that the *Ring* decision was not retroactive, and they remained condemned to death.[15] Justice Breyer, dissenting from the decision *not* to retroactively apply the *Ring* holding, said,

> Certainly the ordinary citizen will not understand the difference. That citizen will simply witness two individuals, both sentenced through the use of unconstitutional procedures, one individual going to his death, the other saved, all through an accident of timing. How can the Court square this spectacle with what it has called the "vital importance to the defendant and to the community that any decision to impose the death sentence be, and appear to be, based on reason"?

The high Court's precedent on whether their decisions apply retroactively to cases already decided depends on whether the holding announces a "watershed procedural rule."[16]

The Fair Sentencing Act of 2010. One of the unforeseen consequences of the Federal Sentencing Guidelines was that, with respect to sentencing for possession of powder cocaine versus crack cocaine, 1 gram of crack was treated as the equivalent of 100 grams of powder cocaine. Crack is a diluted form of cocaine in which additives are mixed with the powder cocaine, boiled, and dried to create a powerful stimulant. The Fair Sentencing Act of 2010, (FSA), 124 Stat. 2372, was enacted to reduce the disparity by increasing the penalties for powder cocaine. Crack was mainly used by inner-city dwellers, and 85% of the crack defendants were African American.[17] As in many sentencing issues and whether or not new changes in the law are retroactive, the FSA applies to defendants who committed a crack cocaine crime before the FSA went into effect but were sentenced after its effective date in 2010. The FSA applies to everyone sentenced after it was enacted no matter when they committed the crime (*Dorsey v. United States*, 2012).[18]

Mandatory Minimum Sentences

In response to society's growing dissatisfaction with the perception that the criminal justice system was ineffective in dealing appropriately with offenders, many laws were enacted that were designed to impose stringent punishment for offenders who were traditionally treated less harshly, such as first-time drug offenders. Particularly in response to the so-called War on Drugs, states began to enact mandatory minimum sentences for which the offender must serve a minimum term of incarceration before any consideration of release. Given that most of the offenders were low-level members of drug conspiracies who carried all the risk of transporting the drugs, and minimum sentences of 5 and 10 years were now determined on the weight of the drugs that the conspiracy sold, the prison population swelled. One New York state judge observed that

> faced with what it found to be a high recidivism rate in drug-related crimes, an inadequate response to less severe punishment, and an insidiously growing drug abuse problem, the Legislature could reasonably shift the emphasis to other penological purposes, namely, isolation and deterrence.[19]

In a survey of Commonwealth of Pennsylvania Common Plea Judges on mandatory Minimum Sentencing Statutes released on October 4, 2006, one state court judge reiterated what U.S. Supreme Court Associate Justice Kennedy had to say about mandatory minimum schemes. The Justice criticized the transfer of sentencing decisions from an independent judiciary to a prosecutor who could simply notify the defendant, or put him on "notice" of his intent to seek a mandatory minimum, which might induce the defendant to plead guilty to a lesser charge. The state judge wrote that such a transfer of power upset the balance of justice, and added in an anonymous statement,

> The most pungent issue, however, involves the odor that arises from the prosecutors' use of their legislatively created and judicially sanctioned thumb screw. If mandatory minimum sentencing statutes are dependent for their imposition upon "notice" by the Commonwealth, the government is free to use the notice as the sword of Damocles,[20] forcing the accused to relinquish the most sacred rights guaranteed by our Constitutions. Under the guise of "evidentiary considerations," district attorneys are free to use the threat of mandatory imprisonment to coerce defendants out of exercising rights to suppress evidence (bad searches) and even to extract a guilty plea from an otherwise innocent accused to avoid certain incarceration.

The primary complaint among the Pennsylvania judges surveyed was that mandatory minimum sentences did not allow them to fashion appropriate sentences for the specific and unique facts of each case presented before them, which resulted in real miscarriages of justice. They noted that whereas the will of the people through the legislature has the authority to define crimes, grade them as felonies, and define the degrees of felonies and misdemeanors, the one-size-fits-all approach of mandatory minimums robs the spirit of justice from her course. The majority of survey respondents believed that mandatory minimum sentences did not help the administration of justice, but a few judges did praise the seeming uniformity of the sentences.

On the federal level, Congress directed the U.S. Sentencing Commission to conduct a study of mandatory minimum sentencing in the federal criminal justice system. The commission found in its 2011 report that mandatory minimum sentences protect the public and achieve uniformity, noting that for offenses where a mandatory minimum sentence was not the law, there was wide disparity in sentences imposed.[21] The current political focus has been on systemic criminal justice reform to reduce prison populations to save state and federal budgets, and rethinking the efficacy of mandatory minimum sentencing is one piece of that calculus.[22]

Rule of Law: A suspended sentence can be reinstated if the defendant fails to live up to the conditions for release set by the court.

Suspended Sentences

In certain cases, judges have discretion to suspend or delay the imposition of a sentence of confinement to a penal institution. A **suspended sentence** imposes a term of incarceration that is not executed unless and until the convict violates certain restrictions and conditions set by the court—for example, avoiding known felons in the community. If the convict fails to meet the conditions, the judge can order the offender return to prison and serve the remainder of the original sentence. Two types of suspended sentences are probation and parole, commonly known as community supervision. According to the Bureau of Justice Statistics, by the end of 2015, there were approximately 4.65 million people, or 1 in 53 adults, in the country on some form of probation, parole, or other type of post-prison supervision.[23]

Probation. **Probation** is a suspended sentence whereby a convicted offender is released into the community subject to control and supervision by a probation agency. Probation is often granted without a convict serving any term of imprisonment. Research indicates that men are more likely to be on probation for crimes against the public, such as weapons offenses, drunk driving, and traffic offenses, whereas women are sentenced to probation most often for offenses relating to property, such as stealing. For certain serious crimes in many jurisdictions, such as murder or kidnapping, the granting of probation as a sentence without jail time is prohibited. Misdemeanor crimes, on the other hand, usually receive a sentence of straight probation. Once on a probationary status, an offender will go to prison only if he or she violates the terms of probation, such as using illegal drugs when a condition of remaining in the community is no drug use. Probationers are also subject to unannounced home visits and warrantless searches and seizures of their persons and homes. If the probationer violates the terms of probation, her probation officer usually presents to a judge a warrant detailing the violations and asking for a probation-revocation hearing. The probationer has a right to counsel at the hearing, and the result may be a warning, the imposition of more stringent conditions, or revocation of probation.

Parole. **Parole** is an early release from prison with certain conditions the offender must meet to stay out of jail, such as seeking employment and submitting to testing for illegal drug use. Recommendations for release on parole are usually made by a parole board, typically composed of political appointees of the state governor or other elected official. The primary criticism of parole boards is that there are no formal requirements for the members who sit in judgment of prisoners and the board may be unduly influenced by public opinion about a specific convict. The goal of parole is for the government to keep a close and watchful eye on the convict as she makes her way back into society while retaining the ability to return her to prison if she fails to meet the parole conditions, which mirror many of the conditions for those on probation (e.g., drug testing, curfews, looking for and keeping a job). As the punishment trend moved toward "get tough on crime" incarceration models and moved away from rehabilitation, some states abolished parole altogether, whereas others, including the federal government, renamed parole "supervised release."[24]

APPLYING THE LAW TO THE FACTS

Can an Offender Make Mistakes While on Probation?

The Facts: A woman had originally been sentenced to a term of probation on misdemeanor assault charges stemming from an altercation at a manicurist shop over a dispute about how much money she owed. There were additional battery charges when she resisted arrest. The defendant had moved residences without securing permission, had briefly left the state without notifying her parole officer, had been rearrested for an altercation over a cell phone, and had withdrawn from court-ordered anger management. Should the judge put the defendant in jail?

The Law: Yes. Based on the defendant's numerous instances of noncompliance with the court-ordered conditions of probation, the judge revoked probation and imposed the original 12-month sentence of imprisonment on the original assault charge.[25]

Three-Strikes Laws

In the 1990s, society became fatigued with the revolving door of prison for repeat offenders. As a play on the baseball expression "three strikes, you're out," **"three-strikes" laws** were enacted to sentence a defendant more severely—for terms up to life in prison—on conviction for a third serious crime. In the case *Lockyer v. Andrade* (2003), the defendant stole $150 worth of videotapes, which, under California law, was his "third strike"—meaning that the theft was his third conviction—calling for a mandatory sentence of two consecutive terms of 25 years to life in prison.[26] On appeal, the U.S. Supreme Court rejected Andrade's argument that his sentence was excessive. Relying on its precedent in *Harmelin v. Michigan*, reprinted on page 373, the high Court held that states were allowed the freedom to administer their police function by enacting tough sentences on conviction for certain crimes. According to author and sentencing expert Michael Tonry, mandatory life sentences for people who have not killed anyone "often keep offenders in prison long after it makes incapacitative sense—because crime, especially violent crime is a young man's game and older prisoners age out of their violent proclivities."[27] Many states, particularly California, have started to reevaluate three-strikes laws. California is the only state that allows a nonviolent crime to constitute a third strike. Offenders with nonviolent third strikes, such as Andrade the video thief, make up close to 60% of third-strike offenders in California. The result for California is a prison system bloated with aged and infirm prisoners who will spend the rest of their natural lives decaying at public expense.

Megan's Laws

Megan's Law is a federal law aimed at controlling "sexually violent predators" through a system of community registration and notification. All states now have some form of Megan's Law. The legal implications of Megan's Laws are twofold: the designation of an offender as a sexual predator and the procedures to notify the community of the offender's presence. A review of New Jersey's Megan's Law indicates how it works. First, sex offenders are notified by the court or by mail of their duty to register with local law enforcement.[28] Offenders fill out a sexual offender registration form listing their name, address, make of car, license plate number, and physical description, as well as the specifics of the sex offense, and include a photograph. They are then separated into three tiers based on their perceived risk of reoffending. Tier ranking dictates who in the community must be notified that the offender lives in the neighborhood. The classifications and notification scheme are as follows:

1. Tier 1: low risk to reoffend: notify law enforcement only.

2. Tier 2: moderate risk to reoffend: notify law enforcement, schools, and community organizations likely to encounter the offender.

3. Tier 3: high risk to reoffend: notify law enforcement, schools, organizations, and members of the public.

Judges can alter an offender's tier classification number, and some offenders introduce expert testimony to have their tier number (and hence, the level of community notification) lowered. Anyone convicted of a sex offense by trial or guilty verdict in New Jersey is subject to the process previously described. The law excludes community notification for some sex offenders, most notably incest offenders. The exemption follows from the erroneous argument that those who prey on children in their own homes are not "predatory" and are unlikely to molest outside of the home. The court refused to notify schools that an incest offender lived close by on the justification that

> [the offender's] acts arose from a trusting relationship between him and his victims. They were not predatory in the sense of the Guidelines that he placed himself in a household which included these children in order to offend against them. Nothing in the evidence suggest[s] that he is given to prowling schoolyards or other areas serving children.[29]

The U.S. Supreme Court has upheld the constitutionality of registration, notification of community,[30] and the civil commitments of sexual offenders after they have served their prison punishment for their crimes. In *Kansas v. Hendricks* (1997), the Court held that laws allowing for the civil commitment of sex offenders were "non-punitive, remedial legislation," not punishment.[31] If a dangerous sex offender is about to be released from prison, many laws allow for the involuntary civil commitment of the offender in a mental hospital. Because the high Court has held such commitment as treatment, not punishment, the offender may be held indefinitely pursuant to regular reassessment of the offender by physicians.

Sex Offender Registration and Notification Act (SORNA). One problem with enforcement of laws to regulate sex offenders is the inability to track offenders once released in our highly mobile society. Congress tried to fix the problem of sex offender tracking by amending the Adam Walsh Child Protection and Safety Act of 2006[32] to create a national database of offenders so that, presumably, anyone could find a registered sex offender regardless of state of residence. The mandates of SORNA require sex offenders who must register notify local law enforcement who then enter the offender's information into the national database. But most national efforts that require labor from state employees often have little or no funding attached to pay people to get the job done, as discussed in Chapter 1 on the federal government requiring states run background checks for firearm purchases. SORNA is an unfunded federal mandate, so national compliance has been slow.

Juveniles and Sentencing

One of the criticisms of SORNA is that the law includes sex offender registration for juvenile offenders when the juvenile justice model is based on restorative justice.[33] Juvenile justice initially developed because, historically, if a child, 6 years or older, committed a crime, "it was natural for authorities to apply traditional adult criminal law remedies to a variety of juvenile misbehavior."[34] The birth of reformist thought that children deserved special treatment within the justice system is traced to Chicago courts in 1899. The early movement in juvenile justice was to remove from the jails and penitentiaries children who had committed criminal acts. Based on the concept that children were, indeed, people not yet fully formed mentally and socially, the early juvenile justice movement sought to establish an alternative track of justice for children who could be rehabilitated and returned to society. The juvenile system entrusted great discretion to judges who could decide whether to commit juveniles to reformatories or continue incarcerating them.[35] The historian David Tanenhaus traces the struggle between the judicial branch's extension of its law enforcement role and the development of juvenile justice by reformers who wanted the courts to have a positive impact on the lives of disadvantaged children. But the lumbering progress of training competent probation officers, the lack of standards and procedures classifying juveniles not only based on age but also on type and severity of crime committed, and the inherent corruption of patronage appointments to sensitive positions within the developing juvenile court system created community backlash against a system desperate for public support.[36]

America's fear of the juvenile delinquent, as constructed by popular culture in the 1950s, has been traced to many different variables in American life, such as the rise of the independent woman outside the home, fear of the atomic age, anxiety of family disruption by the rebellious teen, and racial integration.[37] The societal structure was changing, and adults grew uncomfortable over the dress and social habits of their teenagers. The panic of youthful delinquency in the 1950s, at least one researcher has noted on the federal level, allowed lawmakers to entertain ideas of rehabilitation and crime prevention rather than an excessive punitive response.[38] In 1953, the congressional inquiry into the causes of delinquency was led by Senator Estes Kefauver's Chairmanship of the Subcommittee on Delinquency. The subcommittee received letters from constituents that believed the rise of uncontrollable adolescents to "progressive education, to fluoridated water, to communism, labor unions, working mothers, and racial integration."[39] The trend of the era was to punish juveniles for status crimes—those acts that would only be prosecuted because of the juvenile's status as a minor (e.g., curfew crimes).

Studies indicate that media portrayal of specific crime problems are often reliable bellwethers for ultimate change in the penal codes. For instance, media saturation in the 1980s of stories about babies born addicted to crack had a direct correlation to the enactment of mandatory sentencing laws for drug crimes. According to media scholars, coverage of crime and justice issues tend to "rearrange political priorities [that move] the gamut of criminal justice issues higher up the list of legislative business."[40] The 1980s gave us the term *superpredator,* referring to juvenile criminals that led to many states lowering the age at which juveniles could be tried as adults and increasing tenfold the number of juveniles who could be sentenced to life without parole.

Life Without Parole for Juveniles. Responses to crime often revolve around spectacular events that grab national media attention, and the rising clamor in the late 1980s about superpredators resulted in an increase in the award of LWOP sentences and the rare death sentence for those 16-year-olds tried as an adult. In 2003, the U.S. Supreme Court outlawed the death penalty for juveniles who commit murder, even if tried as an adult, reasoning in *Roper v. Simmons* (2003), that the entire concept of juvenile justice is based on the immaturity and impulsivity of the child's mind; thus, death for juveniles violated the Eighth Amendment's prohibition on cruel and unusual punishment. By 2010, Terrance Graham, who at age 16 had been sentenced to LWOP for robbery (while already on probation for robbery), was one of the 123 juveniles who had been sentenced to LWOP for a nonhomicide offense and one of the 77 juvenile lifers in Florida.

When Graham's case made it to the high Court in 2010, the Court held in *Graham v. Florida* (2010), that having outlawed the death penalty for juveniles, the most severe punishment was now LWOP and under a proportionality review, LWOP for those who did not kill could not withstand scrutiny under the Eighth Amendment.[41] The Court said, "A 16-year-old and a 75-year-old each sentenced to life without parole receive the same punishment in name only," and decided juveniles sentenced to LWOP should be given a "meaningful opportunity" for release by having a parole hearing. The juvenile sentenced to LWOP having killed no one might not be released for crimes they had committed, 10, 20, 30, or 40 years ago, but the Court said they should at least have a chance. In 2012, the U.S. Supreme Court revisited the LWOP decision for juveniles, but this time in *Miller v. Alabama* (2012), reprinted in part on the following pages, for those LWOP juveniles who had committed murder, ultimately deciding that they, too, deserved a parole hearing at least once in their lives. Read the case excerpt and see if you agree with the Court's reasoning.

MILLER V. ALABAMA, 567 U.S. 460 (2012)

Supreme Court of the United States

Justice Kagan delivered the opinion of the Court. (5–4)

FACTS: In November 1999, petitioner Kuntrell Jackson, then 14 years old, and two other boys decided to rob a video store. En route to the store, Jackson learned that one of the boys, Derrick Shields, was carrying a sawed-off shotgun in his coat sleeve. Jackson decided to stay outside when the two other boys entered the store. Inside, Shields pointed the gun at the store clerk, Laurie Troup, and demanded that she "give up the money." Troup refused. A few moments later, Jackson went into the store to find Shields continuing to demand money. At trial, the parties disputed whether Jackson warned Troup that "[w]e ain't playin'," or instead told his friends, "I thought you all was playin.'" When Troup threatened to call the police, Shields shot and killed her. The three boys fled empty-handed.

Arkansas law gives prosecutors discretion to charge 14-year-olds as adults when they are alleged to have committed certain serious offenses. *See* Arkansas Code Annotated 9-27-318(c) (1988). The prosecutor here exercised that authority by charging Jackson with capital felony murder and aggravated robbery. Jackson moved to transfer the case to juvenile court, but after considering the alleged facts of the crime, a psychiatrist's examination, and Jackson's juvenile arrest history (shoplifting and several incidents of car theft), the trial court denied the motion, and an appellate court affirmed. A jury later convicted Jackson of both crimes. Noting that "in view of [the] verdict, there's only one possible punishment," the judge sentenced Jackson to life without parole.

Like Jackson, petitioner Evan Miller was 14 years old at the time of his crime. Miller had by then been in and out of foster care because his mother suffered from alcoholism

(Continued)

(Continued)

and drug addiction and his stepfather abused him. Miller, too, regularly used drugs and alcohol; and he had attempted suicide four times, the first when he was 6 years old.

One night in 2003, Miller was at home with a friend, Colby Smith, when a neighbor, Cole Cannon, came to make a drug deal with Miller's mother. The two boys followed Cannon back to his trailer, where all three smoked marijuana and played drinking games. When Cannon passed out, Miller stole his wallet, splitting about $300 with Smith. Miller then tried to put the wallet back in Cannon's pocket, but Cannon awoke and grabbed Miller by the throat. Smith hit Cannon with a nearby baseball bat, and once released, Miller grabbed the bat and repeatedly struck Cannon with it. Miller placed a sheet over Cannon's head, told him "I am God, I've come to take your life," and delivered one more blow. The boys then retreated to Miller's trailer, but soon decided to return to Cannon's to cover up evidence of their crime. Once there, they lit two fires. Cannon eventually died from his injuries and smoke inhalation.

Alabama law required that Miller initially be charged as a juvenile, but allowed the District Attorney (D. A.) to seek removal of the case to adult court. The D. A. did so, and the juvenile court agreed to the transfer after a hearing. Citing the nature of the crime, Miller's "mental maturity," and his prior juvenile offenses (truancy and "criminal mischief"), the Alabama Court of Criminal Appeals affirmed. The State accordingly charged Miller as an adult with murder in the course of arson. That crime (like capital murder in Arkansas) carries a mandatory minimum punishment of life without parole. See Alabama Code 13A-5-40(a)(9), 13 A-6-2(c) (1982).

ISSUE: [Does sentencing juveniles who kill to life without parole violate the Eighth Amendment's prohibition against cruel and unusual punishment?]

HOLDING: [Yes. Juveniles should have a chance at a hearing to determine if the possibility of parole is possible.]

REASONING: The Eighth Amendment prohibition of cruel and unusual punishment "guarantees individuals the right not to be subjected to excessive sanctions." That right, we have explained, "flows from the basic precept of justice that punishment for crime should be graduated and proportioned" to both the offender and the offense. As we noted the last time we considered life-without-parole sentences imposed on juveniles, "[t]he concept of proportionality is central to the Eighth Amendment." And we view that concept less through a historical prism than according to "the evolving standards of decency that mark the progress of a maturing society."

The cases before us implicate two strands of precedent reflecting our concern with proportionate punishment. The first has adopted categorical bans on sentencing practices based on mismatches between the culpability of a class of offenders and the severity of a penalty. So, for example, we have held that imposing the death penalty for nonhomicide crimes against individuals, or imposing it on mentally retarded defendants, violates the Eighth Amendment. See *Kennedy v. Louisiana* (2008) [no death penalty for rape of a child who lives]; *Atkins v. Virginia* (2002) [mentally retarded exempt from the capital punishment].[42] Several of the cases in this group have specially focused on juvenile offenders, because of their lesser culpability. Thus, *Roper* held that the Eighth Amendment bars capital punishment for children, and *Graham* concluded that the Amendment also prohibits a sentence of life without the possibility of parole for a child who committed a nonhomicide offense. *Graham* further likened life without parole for juveniles to the death penalty itself, thereby evoking a second line of our precedents. In those cases, we have prohibited mandatory imposition of capital punishment, requiring that sentencing authorities consider the characteristics of a defendant and the details of his offense before sentencing him to death.

Roper and *Graham* emphasized that the distinctive attributes of youth diminish the penological justifications for imposing the harshest sentences on juvenile offenders, even when they commit terrible crimes. Because "[t]he heart of the retribution rationale" relates to an offender's blameworthiness, "the case for retribution is not as strong with a minor as with an adult." Nor can deterrence do the work in this context, because "the same characteristics that render juveniles less culpable than adults"—their immaturity, recklessness, and impetuosity—make them less likely to consider potential punishment. Similarly, incapacitation could not support the life-without-parole sentence in *Graham*: Deciding that a "juvenile offender forever will be a danger to society" would require "mak[ing] a judgment that [he] is incorrigible"—but "incorrigibility is inconsistent with youth." And for the same reason, rehabilitation could not justify that sentence. Life without parole "forswears altogether the rehabilitative ideal." It reflects "an irrevocable judgment about [an offender's] value and place in society," at odds with a child's capacity for change.

Graham concluded from this analysis that life-without-parole sentences, like capital punishment, may violate the Eighth Amendment when imposed on children. To be sure, *Graham*'s flat ban on life without parole applied only to nonhomicide crimes, and the Court took care to distinguish those offenses from murder, based on both moral culpability and consequential harm. But none of what it said about children—about their distinctive (and transitory) mental traits and environmental vulnerabilities—is crime-specific. Those features are evident in the same way, and to the same degree, when (as in both cases here) a botched robbery turns into a killing. So *Graham*'s reasoning implicates any life-without-parole sentence imposed on a juvenile, even as its categorical bar relates only to nonhomicide offenses.

Most fundamentally, *Graham* insists that youth matters in determining the appropriateness of a lifetime of incarceration without the possibility of parole. And in other contexts as well, the characteristics of youth, and the way they weaken rationales for punishment, can render a life-without-parole sentence disproportionate. "An offender's age," we made clear in *Graham*, "is relevant to the Eighth Amendment," and so "criminal procedure laws that fail to take defendants' youthfulness into account at all would be flawed. The Chief Justice, concurring in the judgment, made a similar point. Although rejecting a categorical bar on life-without-parole sentences for juveniles, he acknowledged "*Roper's* conclusion that juveniles are typically less culpable than adults," and accordingly wrote that "an offender's juvenile status can play a central role" in considering a sentence's proportionality. (*Graham's* "youth is one factor, among others, that should be considered in deciding whether his punishment was unconstitutionally excessive").

CONCLUSION: Here, the confluence of these two lines of precedent leads to the conclusion that mandatory life-without-parole sentences for juveniles violate the Eighth Amendment.

The *Miller* case holding juveniles get a hearing to determine suitability for release was held to retroactively apply to all juvenile offenders sentenced under mandatory life without parole sentences in the *Montgomery v. Louisiana* (2016) case, where Henry Montgomery had been sentenced to life at age 17 for the shooting death of a sheriff's deputy and had been incarcerated in Louisiana since 1963.[43] In February 2018, the parole board denied the 71-year-old Montogomery's bid for early release.

MAKING THE COURTROOM CONNECTION

Corrections officials are responsible for implementing the sentence imposed. All prisoners entering prison are assessed for risk of violence, mental health needs, and physical disorders. Officers must also tend to administrative tasks, such as helping the prisoner set up a commissary account to buy toiletries or snacks and documenting an approved list of visitors. Most of the important information about a prisoner comes from the sentencing process.

A courtroom perspective of litigation surrounding the behavior of correctional officers often underscores the level of stress officers face every day. There are affirmative legal duties placed on officers pursuant to the federal Prison Rape Elimination Act of 2003, to prevent and accurately report on incidents of sexual assault behind the prison walls.[44] Then, there's the stress of prison work itself. A 2013 Portland State University study on the health of Oregon prison guards found that officers as a group "are overworked, sleep-deprived, continually exhausted, fearful on the job, and speak ill of their work once they get outside the walls." The level of stress suffered by officers can lead to poor decision making and prisoner maltreatment. Oregon responded by initiating a mindfulness meditation and group discussion series in an effort to reduce the prevalence of post-traumatic stress disorder (PTSD), which the officers suffer at a rate three times greater than the general population. Those going into the corrections field must make taking care of one's physical and mental health a top priority and key to career longevity.[45]

Law enforcement officers can have a great impact on the sentencing recommendation for a convict made by prosecutors and accepted by the judge. During an investigation, officers learn the level of culpability of specific defendants and have first-hand knowledge of the evidence that will or will not support charges brought by the prosecutor and any plea bargain eventually accepted by the judge. Officers often stay with a case through the initial investigation through the final appeal and are often available to "fill in the gaps" of any information missing from the written records. For prosecutors, a common practice in determining an appropriate sentence for an offender involves "charge bargaining." That is, because 90% of all criminal cases are resolved by guilty plea, the prosecutor retains great discretion to affect the ultimate sentence imposed by the judge in choosing what charges to bring. Defense counsel must take care during the presentence process, during which probation and parole officers conduct interviews for reports submitted to the judge, to help the bench determine an appropriate sentence. Defendants are to be truthful during court-initiated interviews but may unwittingly admit to facts that increase their exposure to harsher sentences. Counsel should prepare for the presentence investigation diligently to argue to the judge how much weight to give certain information in the presentence investigation in determining an appropriate sentence for the client.

Expungement of Sentences, Pardons, and Executive Clemency

Several states allow for the expungement of certain offenses to be sealed from the defendant's record, which means sealed from public view or destroyed. Usually first-time offenders who successfully complete a rehabilitative effort are eligible for record expungement, as are people who were arrested but never convicted or those who successfully completed alternative diversion programs. In the U.S. Supreme Court decision *Dickerson v. New Banner Institute, Inc.* (1983), the Court reviewed the wide variety of expungement statutes in the states by observing that

> some are applicable only to young offenders [Michigan] . . . some [are] available only to persons convicted of certain offenses [New Jersey], others, however, permit expunction of a conviction for any crime including murder [Massachusetts]. Some are confined to first offenders [Oklahoma]; [s]ome are discretionary [Minnesota] while others provide for automatic expunction under certain circumstances [Arizona]. The statutes vary in the language to describe what they do. Some speak of expunging the conviction, others of "sealing" the file or of causing the dismissal of the charge. The statutes also differ in their actual effect. Some are absolute; others are limited. Only a minority address questions such as whether the expunged conviction may be considered in sentencing for a subsequent offense or in setting bail on a later charge, or whether the expunged conviction may be used for impeachment purposes, or whether the convict may deny the fact of his conviction.[46]

Students should research the law in their respective jurisdictions to determine what type of statute applies to offenders in their home states.

A pardon is an action by the chief executive (for the federal government it is the president, whereas for the states, it is the governor) that wipes the slate clean for someone charged or convicted of a crime. Article II of the U.S. Constitution gives the president the authority "to grant Reprieves and Pardons for Offenses against the United States, except in Cases of Impeachment," commonly called the Pardons Clause. Writer Samuel Morison noted, "The president may, and occasionally does, pardon individuals after the commission of an offense, but prior to their being convicted of any specific crime, in which event a pardon would not only preclude the imposition of punishment for the pardoned offense, but would obviously forestall the creation of any record of a conviction."[47]

THE DEATH PENALTY

This text has discussed the death penalty throughout the chapters for its effects on the criminal trial process. Discussed here are the mechanics of the death-penalty process. Since biblical times death as punishment has been deemed legally appropriate for certain crimes. The death penalty is capital punishment. Examples of capital punishment abound in the Bible. In Genesis, God annihilated all life except for those creatures on Noah's ark and destroyed Sodom and Gomorrah because of rampant sin. During the time of Moses, God carried out the plague of death for all first-born sons of Egypt. The death penalty was given for crimes regarded as trivial today, such as disrespecting one's parents or taking the animals out of the barn too soon. From religion we get the concept of *lex talionis* ("a life for a life").

Modern death-penalty jurisprudence began with the case *Furman v. Georgia* (1972), in which the U.S. Supreme Court declared the death penalty illegal and invalidated all death statutes nationwide.[48] Finding that the lack of statutes guiding jury decision making resulted in death sentences that were "wanton and freakishly imposed," the Court concluded that the death penalty violated the Eighth Amendment. In response to the *Furman* decision, state legislatures went to work giving more structure to death-penalty laws. When these newly constituted death laws came before the Supreme Court for review in *Gregg v. Georgia* (1976), the high Court reinstated death as legal punishment.[49] The major difference in the new laws was the bifurcated (two-stage) trial process with one innocence phase and then a sentencing phase.

Contrary to public belief, most money associated with the death penalty is not through the years of appeals. Rather, the meter starts running once the prosecutor decides to seek the death penalty as more resources for investigation, lawyers, experts, jury selection, and jury sequestration are required to ensure the due process guarantees of a fair trial. In many cases, such costs can be avoided because many defendants agree to plead guilty to a life without parole sentence, a relatively inexpensive procedure that involves bringing the defendant to the courthouse to plead guilty in front of a judge. James Holmes who in 2012 killed 12 and wounded 70 in a theater shooting in Aurora, Colorado, agreed to plead guilty to all charges in exchange for life without parole sentence, but the prosecutor refused and insisted on seeking the death penalty. The cost associated with Holmes's case was over $2 million even before the trial began.[50] Ultimately, the jury could not unanimously agree on whether to impose the death penalty, and the law required Holmes receive a life without parole sentence.

> **Rule of Law: Potential jurors who are unwilling to impose a death sentence are legally ineligible to hear and decide death-penalty cases.**

Death Qualification of the Jury

The process of picking a jury in a death-penalty case is called death qualification, first discussed in Chapter 2. For potential jurors to be picked to hear a death-penalty case, they must express willingness during *voir dire* to impose a death sentence on the defendant. If moral or religious reasons prevent a venireperson from seriously considering imposing a death sentence, the person is legally unqualified to hear the case. The first U.S. Supreme Court cases that challenged the exclusion of jurors who were opposed to the death penalty from sitting on death-penalty cases were *Witherspoon v. Illinois* (1968) and *Wainwright v. Witt* (1985).[51] If a juror's views on the imposition of the death penalty "prevent or substantially impair the performance of his duties as a juror in accordance with his instructions and his oath," then he cannot sit in such a case. If a potential juror were asked during *voir dire* whether he could impose a death sentence, and he answered "no, not under any circumstances," then he would be excused from jury duty; such potential jurors are called "'*Witherspoon*' or '*Witt*' Excludables."

U.S. Supreme Court Associate Justices Brennan and Marshall disagreed that people morally opposed to the death penalty should be excluded from jury service on death cases. In their statement of dissention from the majority holdings, they said,

> Like the death-qualified juries that the prosecution can now mold to its will to enhance the chances of victory, this Court increasingly acts as the adjunct of the State and its prosecutors in facilitating efficient and expedient conviction and execution irrespective of the Constitution's fundamental guarantees. One can only hope that this day too will soon pass.

Studies show that death-qualified juries are more likely to convict defendants and more likely to believe the state's witnesses over the defendant's witnesses.[52] These findings make sense: If only jurors who are willing to sentence the defendant to death get on the jury, then evidence of guilt may be a foregone conclusion in their minds. Jurors may already be thinking of an appropriate sentence before they hear a single witness testify or see one piece of tangible evidence introduced. In 2007, the U.S. Supreme Court reaffirmed the *Witherspoon/Witt* excludable analysis in *Uttecht v. Brown* (2007).[53] Defendant Uttecht was sentenced to death in Washington State and appealed on the grounds that one potential juror was removed from the panel because he stated that he could not impose a death sentence. In a 5–4 decision, the high Court held that the trial judge had the authority to determine the qualifications of potential death jurors and that appellate courts should defer to those judges.

Bifurcated Sentencing Procedure

The high Court stated in *Furman v. Georgia* (1972) that the death penalty may be fairly imposed on criminal defendants in which the sentencing authority receives information relevant to

The American death penalty has become a punishment restricted by geography. Five states are responsible for the most executions since the death penalty was reinstated in 1976: Texas, Virginia, Oklahoma, Florida, and Missouri. Do you think the chances of receiving capital punishment on a conviction of first-degree murder should be dependent on jurisdiction?

deciding the proper sentence and receives guidelines on how to use that information. The bifurcated, two-phase death-penalty trial upheld as constitutional in *Gregg v. Georgia* (1976) is used in every death-penalty jurisdiction today and both "minitrials" are heard by the same jury. The first stage of a death trial is the innocence phase, in which the prosecution has the burden of proving beyond a reasonable doubt the defendant guilty of first-degree murder. If the jury returns a guilty verdict on the murder charge, the trial proceeds to the second sentencing phase in which the jury determines whether life in prison without parole (LWOP) or death is the appropriate sentence. By a guilty finding in the first phase of a death-penalty trial, the defendant will likely die in jail—the only question is when. In most death jurisdictions, a life sentence leaves no possibility of parole or early release. In deciding between awarding a death or LWOP sentence, some states ask jurors to conduct their own risk assessment and consider the "future dangerousness" of the defendant. In those states, the U.S. Supreme Court has held that jurors must be informed that LWOP means the defendant will not leave prison until he dies of old age or other causes, as held in *Shafer v. South Carolina* (2001). Studies show, however, when LWOP is an alternative to the death penalty and properly explained that LWOP means the defendant will not leave prison, support for the death penalty drops.[54]

The sentencing phase is a minitrial in which the prosecutor must prove beyond a reasonable doubt that there was at least one aggravating circumstance making the defendant eligible for the death penalty. The defendant often offers mitigating circumstances, such as his age or that the murder was committed under extreme emotional duress. These circumstances do not excuse the crime but do explain the characteristics of the defendant when he committed the crime and may sway the jury to award a sentence of LWOP. The jury weighs aggravators against mitigators to arrive at a sentence. In *Kansas v. Marsh* (2006), the U.S. Supreme Court held that where the aggravating and mitigating circumstances were of equal weight, a state could still make it mandatory for the jury to impose a death sentence.[55] Michael Marsh killed a woman and her baby and was sentenced to death. In Kansas, if the aggravators are of equal weight to the mitigators, the jury has no discretion and is required under the law to award a death sentence. On appeal, Marsh's complaint was that the statutory scheme created an "unconstitutional presumption in favor of death." The U.S. Supreme Court said that even if Marsh's argument was true, it was within the police power of state legislatures to determine that state's sentencing procedures, the same rationale that upheld Harmelin's life sentence for a first-time drug offense in the case presented on page 373.

New Evidence of Innocence and Exonerations

The U.S. Supreme Court has recognized the right of inmates on death row to challenge their convictions based on new evidence, and recent decisions have exonerated previously convicted defendants. In its 5–3 decision, the Court held that new evidence, including DNA test results, raised sufficient doubt to merit a new hearing for Tennessee death-row inmate Paul House, sentenced to death for the rape and murder of his neighbor. Writing for the majority in his case, *House v. Bell* (2006), Justice Kennedy declared, "Although the issue is close, we conclude that this is the rare case where—had the jury heard all the conflicting testimony—it is more likely than not that no reasonable juror viewing the record as a whole would lack reasonable doubt."[56] The Court identified three aspects of House's case that, when considered as a whole, qualified him to gain access to a *habeas corpus* hearing in federal court. The first piece of new evidence was recent DNA test results indicating that House was not the source of semen found in the murder victim; the source was instead the victim's husband. Second, new statements from three witnesses linked the victim's husband to the crime. Lastly, the reliability of blood evidence presented at House's trial was called into question.[57]

A similar case where the issue was how to treat new evidence in death cases was that of Randy Lee Guzek, who was found guilty in Oregon of capital murder and sentenced to death. On appeal, the Oregon Supreme Court affirmed Guzek's conviction but vacated his sentence and ordered a new sentencing hearing.[58] When the case came before the U.S. Supreme Court, the issue was whether Oregon could limit the admission of evidence exonerating Guzek if Guzek failed to introduce such evidence at his original trial. The Court held in the state's favor and held that such limitation of introducing new evidence did not violate a capital defendant's constitutional rights.

Competency to Be Executed

Societal standards on death as a just punishment for certain crimes has informed the U.S. Supreme Court's evolving standards of decency standard. If society viewed death as too harsh a sentence for the crime of rape, as shown by the fact that many death-penalty states were not executing rapists, then the high Court would remove rape from the list of crimes that could make an offender death-eligible. In the case *Coker v. Georgia* (1977), the Supreme Court held "the death penalty, which is unique in its severity and irrevocability, is an excessive penalty for the rapist who, as such, does not take human life."[59] Since *Coker*, the death penalty has been reserved for murder convictions, and attempts by states to impose the death penalty for child rapists who did not kill have been held unconstitutional (*Kennedy v. Louisiana*, 2008).

Based on the evolving decency standard, the high Court exempted mentally retarded offenders from the death penalty. In *Atkins v. Virginia* (2002), Daryl Atkins had been convicted of abduction, armed robbery, and capital murder in the state of Virginia, but he appealed his sentence on the grounds that he was mentally retarded (his IQ [intelligence quotient] was 59 when the average IQ is 100).[60] In 1989, the Supreme Court had rejected challenges from retarded offenders that they should be exempt from the death penalty because of their disability.[61] But by the time Atkins's case came before the Court, the Court cited that many of the death-penalty states had, over the years, exempted the retarded from state death statutes. Given the evolving standard of decency across the country with respect to death-penalty jurisprudence, the U.S. Supreme Court, too, held that executing the retarded violated the Eighth Amendment's prohibition on cruel and unusual punishment.

Based on the *Atkins* decision, Christopher Simmons, who had been sentenced to death for the rape and murder of Shirley Crook, appealed to the U.S. Supreme Court on the grounds that the evolving standards of decency, based on a "national consensus against the execution of juvenile offenders," required that the Court exempt from eligibility for the death sentence those who committed murder before they reached their 18th birthday. The Court agreed and reasoned that adulthood began at age 18, when people become eligible to vote, join the armed forces, serve on juries, enter into legally binding contracts, and marry without parental consent. So, the age of 18 should also be the demarcation age to receive a death sentence, and any juveniles who commit first-degree murder are ineligible to receive the death penalty.[62]

> Rule of Law: The Eighth Amendment protects society's weak and young from the death penalty.

In 1986, the U.S. Supreme Court ruled in *Ford v. Wainwright* (1986) that it was cruel and unusual punishment to execute the insane.[63] The Court did not spell out a specific standard to determine insanity, but Justice Powell's concurring opinion stated that the Constitution required that a condemned man about to be executed must be able to recognize what exactly he is being punished for. As reporter Emily Bazelon has said, "A defendant can be executed as long as he shows some rational understanding that he is about to die, and why."[64] The Court revisited this standard in its 2007 decision in the case of *Panetti v. Quarterman* (2007).[65] Scott Panetti murdered his in-laws in 1992 in front of his wife and 3-year-old child. He was sentenced to death after he represented himself. He was schizophrenic and claimed "that his body had been taken over by an alter ego he called Sarge Ironhorse and that demons were bent on killing him for his Christian beliefs."[66] He showed up to court wearing western shirts and cowboy boots, alleged that President Kennedy had healed his wounds with coconut milk during World War II, tried to subpoena Jesus, refused to take the medication that kept his psychosis at bay, and insisted that he was being executed in retaliation for preaching the gospel. The high Court remanded the case, holding that the lower court had used too narrow a standard to determine Panetti's insanity and eligibility for execution. On remand, the state court refused to give Panetti's lawyer money or time to have Panetti properly evaluated. The federal appellate court ordered the lower to court to give Panetti's lawyers the resources he needed.[67]

APPLYING THE LAW TO THE FACTS

Can the State Force a Defendant to Become Competent to Be Executed?

The Facts: A young man convicted and sentenced to death began to exhibit signs of schizophrenia during his appeals process, which lasted 24 years. At one point, he decided to stop taking his medication and was rendered incompetent. The state applied for a court order to forcibly medicate the prisoner. His lawyers argued that it was not in the prisoner's best interest to be forcibly medicated to restore him to competency so that the state could then execute him. Which side will win?

The Law: The state. If the medication of a prisoner is necessary, even if it is to restore competency so that the prisoner may be executed, the state has a right to forcibly medicate that prisoner.[68]

The Execution Process

Even after they have exhausted their regular appeals, death-row inmates can pursue their legal challenges to lethal injection as a civil rights action. Thirty-five out of the 36 death-penalty states have typically used a lethal injection combination of drugs of, first, sodium thiopental, which acts as anesthesia, then, pancuronium bromide, which causes suffocation by paralyzing the muscles, and, finally, potassium chloride, which stops the heart. On April 16, 2008, the U.S. Supreme Court decided *Baze v. Rees*, in which two Kentucky death-row inmates challenged the lethal injection process as a violation of the Eighth Amendment's ban on cruel and unusual punishment because the condemned prisoner could suffer acute pain through the process if the first sedative drug is administered improperly.[69] The Court upheld the chemical cocktail execution method even if it resulted in pain because it "does not establish the sort of 'objectively intolerable risk of harm' that qualifies as cruel and unusual" under the Eighth Amendment; the Constitution does not demand the elimination of all risk of pain "either by accident or as an inescapable consequence of death."

After *Baze* was decided, international pharmaceutical companies refused to sell their drugs to American prisons because of "misusing" the drugs to kill. States devised alternative drug cocktails. Oklahoma tried to execute two prisoners on April 29, 2014. Executing Clayton Lockett for the murder of Stephanie Neiman took 40 minutes; news reports called Oklahoma's attempt a "botched execution." State officials called off Charles Warner's execution that day, and Oklahoma death-row inmates challenged the new drug protocol as violating the Eighth Amendment, specifically substituting midazolam for sodium thiopental. The high Court found in the government's favor.

> First, the prisoners failed to identify a known and available alternative method of execution that entails a lesser risk of pain, a requirement of all Eighth Amendment method-of-execution claims. Second, the District Court did not commit clear error when it found that the prisoners failed to establish that Oklahoma's use of a massive dose of midazolam in its execution protocol entails a substantial risk of severe pain.

The Court went on to note no one is guaranteed a pain-free death and to find in the death-row inmates' favor would be to declare the death penalty unconstitutional, which the Court was unwilling to do (*Glossip v. Gross*, 2015).[70] Recent movements in death-penalty states are to return to the gas chamber, electric chair, and firing squad as preferred methods of execution. On August 14, 2018, in a first for the country, Nebraska executed Carey Moore who had been on death row for 39 years for murdering two cab drivers in 1979 with an injection of drugs that included the deadly opioid fentanyl.[71] Most attempts to discover what the states are doing with their lethal drug supply are hidden by state law requiring such information remain secret.[72]

THE APPELLATE PROCESS

Motion for a New Trial and First Appeal

Appellate court rules for each state and the federal government dictate the appeals process for each sovereign. Typically, the first step a defendant takes after conviction is to file with the trial judge a motion for a new trial alleging mistakes the prosecutor and judge made at trial. Most motions for a new trial are denied as a matter of routine unless "the interests of justice so require."[73] A defendant has a period of time defined by statute in which to file a motion for a new trial based on newly discovered evidence—that is, evidence that the defendant could not, with due diligence and his utmost effort, have discovered before or during his trial. Otherwise, the time limitation on the filing of a motion for a new trial on grounds other than new evidence is approximately one week.

Typically, defense counsel must preserve an issue for an appeal by raising and making the appropriate objections at trial. For example, after a motion to suppress the defendant's confession is denied, once the prosecution seeks to introduce the defendant's confession, the defense counsel must object to preserve the issue of the confession's admissibility for appeal. If the defense counsel does not object to evidence at trial and other trial issues that operate to the detriment of the defendant's due process rights to a fair trial, then the issue has been lost for appeal purposes. There are some situations in which the defense lawyer's failure to object is such a gross deviation from the reasonable standard of care for defense counsel that an appellate court might find such deviance a "plain error" and grant the defendant appellate relief on that basis, as discussed later.

By law, a court must hear a first appeal of right. The highest court in Maryland is mandated by law to hear appeals in death-penalty cases, appeals in legislative redistricting cases, cases concerning removal of certain public officers, and certifying certain questions of law. For all other types of appeals, the court has discretion whether to issue a *writ of certiorari* to entertain the appeal, called a discretionary appeal. If a court declines to hear a discretionary appeal, it need not give any reason for its refusal. The appointment of counsel for indigent convicts pursuing their appeals has been litigated frequently. If the appeal is a right established by law and the client is indigent, the state must appoint counsel.[74] If the appeal is discretionary on the part of the defendant, the state need not provide counsel.

If the defendant is claiming that his federal constitutional rights have been violated, he must be heard by all applicable state courts and exhaust his remedies before becoming eligible for an audience in federal court. Even at the state level, courts do not want to be in the position of making a decision that may conflict with another court. The exhaustion of remedies requirement is formalized and highly structured for a reason. Defendants must squeeze all available review out of one court before being allowed access to a higher court. Such formal processing makes sense: The system wants cases resolved at the lowest level and with the least use of judicial resources. The same reasoning applies to appeals: If a lower court can answer the question and address the issue, there is no reason to go forward. This is one reason death-penalty appeals may take a long time to process through no fault of the defendant. If a lower appellate court decides to return the case back to the trial court again, the procedure starts anew. All death cases are eligible for federal appellate review because of the constitutional issues involved, specifically the Eighth Amendment's ban on cruel and unusual punishment.

Before or during trial, very few issues can be appealed to a higher court. To prevent the delay that an appeal could cause during a trial in federal court and in most state jurisdictions, the trial must be completed and the decision final before an appellate court will review a conviction. The final judgment rule requires that appeals be heard only on issues that had been completely decided, but there are exceptions. The U.S. Supreme Court declared that an exception to the final judgment rule could be made for decisions that "finally determine claims of right separable from and collateral to, rights asserted in the action [that are] too important to be denied review and too independent of the cause itself to require that appellate consideration be deferred until the whole case is adjudicated."[75] An exception to the final judgment rule is called the collateral order doctrine and allows appeal from a judgment that

1. Leaves no doubt on an issue in the case,

2. Is not related to whether or not the defendant is innocent or guilty, and

3. Cannot be appealed once a final judgment has entered in the case.

An order committing a defendant to a federal medical facility for an examination or requiring a defendant to be forcibly medicated, for instance, is immediately appealable under the collateral order doctrine. In each of these cases, the decision is unrelated to the defendant's guilt, the defendant cannot appeal the order once the trial is over, and the order leaves no doubt about an issue in the case (here, the mental status of the defendant).[76] Under the collateral order doctrine, motions relying on the double jeopardy protection of the Fifth Amendment and motions to reduce excessive bail are immediately appealable, but not motions to dismiss on the basis of speedy trial violations or motions to suppress evidence.[77]

An interlocutory appeal is made before the case has been finally decided. Courts are reluctant to entertain appeals in the middle of a trial because of the delay in the process. A common issue that defendants wish to appeal before the trial is over is the suppression of evidence. Such interlocutory appeals are not allowed until after trial. "Promptness in the dispatch of the criminal business of the courts is by all recognized as in the highest degree desirable. Greater expedition is demanded by a wholesome public opinion. Delays in the prosecution of criminal cases are numerous and lengthy enough without sanctioning appeals that are not plainly authorized by statute."[78]

The rationale for the final judgment rule is that many evidence suppression issues cannot be properly decided without developing all the evidence through a full trial, although federal law allows the prosecution to file an interlocutory appeal of a trial judge's denial of exclusion of evidence.

Writ of *Habeas Corpus*

Another avenue for a court to review the legality of a defendant's sentence is by filing a *habeas corpus* petition, which literally means "you have the body." A *habeas corpus* petition asks either a state or federal court to review the legality of the defendant's detention and imprisonment. The *writ of habeas corpus* is provided for in the Constitution, Art. I, Sec. 9, which provides in part,

> The Privilege of the Writ of Habeas Corpus shall not be suspended, unless when in Cases of Rebellion or Invasion the public Safety may require it.

Famously, President Abraham Lincoln in 1861 suspended *habeas corpus* during the Civil War for prisoners from Maryland based on the fear they would successfully challenge their detention and rejoin Confederate forces.

In the federal system, 28 U.S.C. §2254 allows a state prisoner to file a *writ of habeas corpus* in federal court "only on grounds that the prisoner's confinement violates the Constitution, laws or treaties of the United States." Because the writ is limited to constitutional claims, courts are careful not to usurp the balance of power between federal and state adjudication of claims and disposition of criminal cases, which is the province of the state police power.

State prisoners must exhaust all state appellate remedies before filing a *habeas* petition to federal courts. In *Anderson v. Harless* (1982), the defendant was convicted at a trial court in Michigan and filed a direct appeal to the intermediate Michigan Court of Appeals on the basis that the judge erred in giving jury instructions.[79] The appellate court confirmed Harless's conviction. Then he appealed to the highest appellate court in the state, the Michigan Supreme Court, which also affirmed his conviction. Harless filed a *habeas* petition with the federal district court, the trial court, which issued a writ finding in his favor, but the U.S. Supreme Court reversed the trial court's decision.

The high Court held that Harless had not exhausted his state appellate remedies because he changed the basis of his appeal. The Supreme Court stated that the new claim had not been properly addressed by the state court below, and that failure rendered his *habeas* claim defective. The reasoning behind the Court's decision is that *habeas* is an extraordinary writ and federal courts want to give state courts a fair "opportunity to apply controlling legal principles to the facts bearing on [her] constitutional claim."[80]

Standard for Granting *Habeas* Review

As stated, federal *habeas* law requires the defendant to first exhaust his state court appeals by presenting his claims to the state courts. "Common *habeas corpus* claims include Sixth Amendment claims of ineffective assistance of counsel, Fifth Amendment claims concerning statements obtained in violation of *Miranda v. Arizona* (1966), prosecutorial misconduct, significant judicial error, and claims of insufficient evidence."[81] Under a *habeas* **standard of review**, a court examines the legality of the defendant's confinement. The court does not review the defendant's conviction but the lawfulness of his custody. Justice Frankfurter, in his separate opinion in *Brown v. Allen* (1953),[82] stated,

> Insofar as [federal *habeas*] jurisdiction enables federal district courts to entertain claims that State Supreme Courts have denied rights guaranteed by the United States Constitution, it is not a case of a lower court sitting in judgment on a higher court. It is merely one aspect of respecting the Supremacy Clause of the Constitution whereby federal law is higher than State law.

Habeas law was changed dramatically by the enactment, under President Clinton, of the **Antiterrorism and Effective Death Penalty Act of 1996 (AEDPA)**,[83] which limits the number of federal *habeas* petitions filed by convicts, limits the filing and granting of more than one successive *habeas* petition based on the same set of facts or circumstances, and severely circumscribes access to federal *habeas* review from death-row inmates. The U.S. Supreme Court has upheld the limits on second successive *habeas* writs on the basis that the convict has access to appellate relief but not limitless access to the judicial system. Moreover, when reviewing *habeas corpus* claims, the high Court has limited the federal court reviewing the prisoner's claim to the record that was before the state court at the time the lower court made its decision, as held in *Cullen v. Pinholster* (2011).[84] Unfortunately for many prisoners, limitations on the evidence a higher appellate court can review benefits the government and not those confined.

Habeas Corpus and Actual Innocence

Does the fact, as the defendant claims, that he is actually innocent raise a constitutional claim sufficient to grant *habeas corpus* review? According to the case *Herrera v. Collins* (1993), the answer is no.[85] Herrera was sentenced to death for killing two Texas police officers. After numerous appeals, he raised in a *habeas corpus* petition the fact that affidavits (sworn statements) tended to prove that he was actually innocent of the crime. The U.S. Supreme Court declined to grant his *habeas* petition, reasoning that the petition could not be heard because no constitutional issue was raised.

In Herrera's *habeas* petition, he attached affidavits that claimed the actual murderer was his deceased brother. In rejecting his claim, the U.S. Supreme Court held that **actual innocence** claims never form the basis for federal relief "absent an independent constitutional violation occurring in the underlying state criminal proceeding." In other words, if the defendant had a constitutionally error-free trial, the fact that he may actually be innocent would *not* meet the threshold requirement for obtaining federal *habeas* review. Even if Herrera were factually innocent, he had no independent constitutional claim to satisfy the *habeas* standard of review. In 1992, Herrera was executed, still protesting his innocence. There is an exception to the *Herrera* ruling, however. In recognizing the possible **manifest injustice**, such as the execution of an innocent person that may accrue in death-penalty cases where the defendant discovers exculpatory evidence well after the statute of limitations expires to bring such claims, the U.S. Supreme Court has held that an actual innocence claim may circumvent AEDPA's 1-year statute of limitations. In *McQuiggen v. Perkins* (2013), the Court said that "actual innocence, if proved, serves as a gateway through which a petitioner may pass."[86]

Springboard for Discussion

Should sentencing decisions take the defendant's entire life into account, or focus more on the crime charged and the harm caused? Which aspect of the defendant's life is more predictive of a defendant's risk of committing future harm, the defendant's background or the crime committed?

APPLYING THE LAW TO THE FACTS

Should *Habeas Corpus* Review Be Granted?

The Facts: A defendant allegedly stabbed a fellow prison inmate to death. Three eyewitnesses testified at his death-penalty trial claiming to have seen the defendant stab the other inmate in the back. Over a 15-year period, all three witnesses recanted their testimony, claiming that they were forced or tricked into testifying. There was no other physical evidence connecting the defendant to the crime. Can the defendant get *habeas* review on his claim of "actual innocence?"

The Law: No. Under the *Herrera* standard, the defendant cannot secure *habeas corpus* review on a "free standing" claim (unrelated to any constitutional violation at trial) of

innocence. In the case of Joseph Amrine, his conviction had been upheld in both state and federal appeals. According to the Eighth Circuit Court of Appeals, Amrine had "not shown actual innocence entitling him to review of his procedurally barred claims [because of elapsed time] or that his constitutional rights were violated" despite recantations from the three eyewitnesses to the murder and the lack of physical evidence linking Amrine to the crime.

Claiming it would be a "manifest injustice" to execute an innocent man, the Missouri Supreme Court ordered Amrine released, and he walked out after 18 years on death row for a murder he did not commit.

SUMMARY

1. You will be able to understand how society determines cruel and unusual punishment. The Eighth Amendment requires society to punish the offender and not the crime. The high Court held in *Harmelin v. Michigan* (1991) that a state has police power to determine sentences, so long as the sentences are not cruel and unusual, which is often determined by a proportionality review comparing a defendant's sentence with others similarly sentenced. Before sentencing, the court orders a presentence investigation in which all relevant information about the offender is compiled in a presentence report for the judge to impose an appropriate sentence. Later, at a sentencing hearing, the judge will hear sentencing recommendations from the prosecutor and the defense counsel, any victim-impact testimony, and the defendant's allocution before imposing sentence. Relevant conduct related to the crime charged may be a factor in the ultimate sentence imposed and courts are turning to technology, such as the COMPAS algorithm program to conduct risk assessment for offenders for help in fashioning an appropriate sentence, as in *Wisconsin v. Loomis* (2016).

2. You will be able to distinguish between the different types of sentences, such as mandatory minimum sentences and sex offender registries. The main types of sentences are indeterminate, which is a range of years, and determinate, which is a fixed number of years. As the War on Drugs became a popular focus of law enforcement and crime control efforts in the late 1970s and early 1980s, so, too, did the legislative response to enact mandatory minimum sentences, the minimum (least) amount of time an offender

will serve for committing certain crimes, mainly moving a certain weight of drugs. Also, part of the justice reform movement was the transfer of sentencing discretion away from judges by the enactment of sentencing guidelines, such as the Federal Sentencing Guidelines, a grid that formulates sentences in terms of months of incarceration based on the severity of the crime and the offender's criminal history. U.S. Supreme Court decisions have made the federal guidelines advisory and not mandatory as they once were. Sentences for different crimes may be consecutive, which means the sentences run one after the other, or concurrent, which means the sentences run all at the same time. The Fair Sentencing Act of 2010 reduced the 100:1 powder cocaine/crack disparity in sentencing. At one point, judges could enhance a criminal sentence if the crime had certain aggravating circumstances. The high Court held in *Apprendi v. New Jersey* (2000) that any fact that is used to increase (enhance) a defendant's must be found by a jury beyond a reasonable doubt, a finding that also applies to death-penalty cases in *Ring v. Arizona* (2002) and *Hurst v. Florida* (2016). Punitive reforms such as "three-strikes" legislation allows for offenders who commit three serious or violent felonies to be sentenced to life without parole, which the U.S. Supreme Court has said does not violate the Eighth Amendment's prohibition against cruel and unusual punishment. Megan's Laws, which require community notification and registration of sex offenders, are also constitutional, as is the civil commitment of holding sex offenders in mental hospitals after the termination of their sentence because, as the Supreme Court has said, such incarceration at a hospital is treatment and not "punishment." New registration requirements are in effect because of the SORNA legislation. Juveniles traditionally are exempt from adult-like sentencing because young people should be given a chance to rehabilitate. Mandatory life without parole sentences for juveniles are unconstitutional for nonhomicide cases (*Graham v. Florida*, 2010) and for homicide cases per *Miller v. Alabama* (2012), which is retroactive for all juveniles sentenced to LWOP per *Montgomery v. Louisiana* (2016).

3. You will be able to understand suspended sentences. One type of suspended sentence is probation, the release of the offender into the community under specific restrictions, often given to offenders for committing misdemeanors. Another type of suspended sentence is parole, in which an offender serving an indeterminate sentence can reduce the time he spends in prison through good behavior.

4. You will be able to identify the bifurcated death-penalty trial and sentencing process. Capital punishment has been recognized as a legal punishment since the founding of the country. The expenses in a death-penalty trial are incurred before and during trial, not necessarily on appeal. The process whereby a jury is selected for a death-penalty case is called death qualification and examines whether each potential juror is willing to impose the death penalty. Death-penalty cases are bifurcated into two minitrials with one jury. The first part of the trial is to determine whether the defendant is guilty; if the jury finds the defendant guilty, the second minitrial is a sentencing hearing during which the same jury will determine whether the defendant lives or dies. At the sentencing phase of a capital trial, the state must introduce aggravating circumstances that make the defendant eligible for the death penalty—that is, death is appropriate punishment only for murder, but some murders are aggravated (the murder of a child or a police officer, e.g.), and these make death an available punishment for the defendant. In contrast, the defendant offers mitigating circumstances, which is anything that would tend to explain, not excuse, the defendant's conduct surrounding the murder. Case law allows states to force juries to return a death sentence if mitigating and aggravating circumstances are equally weighted. The lethal injection process has been challenged in court, unsuccessfully, as states have to find alternatives because of a lack of drugs used in the process. Moreover, states are seeking to keep information related to the execution process a state secret unavailable to public scrutiny. One must be competent to be executed; juveniles, the intellectually disabled, and the insane are exempt from execution.

5. You will be able to summarize the legal requirements for *habeas corpus* review and claims of "actual innocence." The first step for a defendant on being found guilty is to file a motion for a new trial. Appeal rules are set by state and federal appellate rules, and most allow appeals only when cases are finished, called the final judgment rule. The final judgment rule prevents the system from being bogged down. An exception to the final judgment rule is

the collateral order doctrine, which gives a defendant the chance to appeal certain issues that will be moot when the trial is over. An appeal is generally a motion to a court higher than the trial court asking for review of the legality of the conviction based on the sufficiency of the evidence or the incorrect application of law. There are two types of appeals. An interlocutory appeal is filed before or during trial and is granted under very limited circumstances because to delay the judicial process while appeals of minor issues take place would grind the system to a halt. A final appeal is taken after the trial is over and can only be taken pursuant to the final judgment rule that the case is finally over. Every defendant convicted at trial gets one appeal of right as a matter of law, whereby the appellate court must hear the first appeal filed by the defendant; it is usually a direct appeal to the next highest court in the appellate structure. The next type of appeal is a discretionary appeal, discretionary not because the convict may or may not file the second appeal, but because the appellate court can choose—has discretion—to hear the appeal. The U.S. Supreme Court only hears discretionary appeals, those cases it chooses. Some cases, especially death sentences, have mandatory appeal provisions where the highest appellate court in the state must review the defendant's conviction, even if the defendant never files an appeal.

The first standard of review an appellate court will use in deciding whether to affirm (uphold) or reverse (undo) the defendant's conviction is whether the error at trial was substantial and significant enough to violate the defendant's right to a fair trial—whether, had the error not occurred, the outcome of the trial would have been different. Also, before a higher court of appeal will take a case from a lower court of appeals, the defendant must have exhausted all remedies at the lower court. The Antiterrorism and Effective Death Penalty Act of 1996 (AEDPA) limits the number of appeals that can be filed by individuals convicted of capital murder and limits successive *habeas* petitions based on the same set of facts or circumstances. A free-standing claim of actual innocence—that a defendant has been wrongfully convicted and is "actually innocent" of the crime—will not be heard by an appeals court; the claim must accompany a constitutional violation at court, but if a "manifest injustice" will result in the conviction and execution of an innocent man, the prisoner may circumvent AEDPA's 1-year statute of limitations for filing *habeas corpus* writs. Executive clemency or pardons are always available to those convicted of a crime by the chief executive of the federal or respective state government, and expungement of a criminal record is often available, particularly for misdemeanor crimes.

Go back to the beginning of the chapter and reread the news excerpts associated with the learning objectives. Test yourself to determine if you can understand the material covered in the text in the context of the news.

actual innocence 383
allocution 363
Antiterrorism and Effective Death
    Penalty Act of 1996 (AEDPA) 383
bifurcated trial 378
capital punishment 376
collateral order doctrine 381
concurrent sentences 364
consecutive sentences 364
cruel and unusual 362
determinate sentencing 364

evolving standards of decency 379
exhaustion of remedies 381
expungement 376
Fair Sentencing Act 368
Federal Sentencing Guidelines 365
final judgment rule 381
indeterminate sentencing 364
interlocutory appeal 382
mandatory minimum sentence 369
manifest injustice 383
Megan's Laws 371

pardon 376
parole 370
presentence investigation 363
presentence report 363
probation 370
proportionality review 362
relevant conduct 363
risk assessment 361
sentencing hearing 363
suspended sentence 370
"three-strikes" laws 371

PROBLEM-SOLVING EXERCISES

1. William Page was convicted by a federal jury of possessing 16 kilograms of cocaine and faced a prison term under the Federal Sentencing Guidelines of 121 to 151 months incarceration. At the sentencing hearing, the judge determined that Page was responsible for the distribution of an additional 150 kilograms of cocaine, which would increase his sentence to 188 to 235 months. After the hearing, the judge on his own accord decided to increase Page's sentence. Page appealed based on the U.S. Supreme Court rulings on judge-issued sentencing enhancements. If you were the appellate judge, how would you rule? **(ROL: *Apprendi v. New Jersey* precedent)**

2. Florida's three-strikes law allows anyone convicted three times for certain felonies, including aggravated stalking, child abuse, and murder, to be sentenced to life without parole. Billy, who has two prior convictions, one for aggravated stalking and one for child abuse, now faces a driving under the influence accident in which a victim was killed. The prosecutor could charge Billy with murder, making him eligible for three-strikes sentencing, but the prosecutor likes Billy and agrees to a plea bargain whereby Billy will plead guilty to reckless driving and serve a sentence of 2 years. When the victim's family members learn of the plea deal, they are furious and appeal to a judge for help invalidating the prosecutor's decision. Can the prosecutor willingly and knowingly lower charges to avoid three-strikes sentencing? Does your answer change if the offender is subject to mandatory minimum sentencing depending on the offense charged? **(ROL: "Three-strikes," mandatory minimum sentences)**

3. Tammy was on probation for robbery. One of her probation conditions was that she stay away from known felons. At Thanksgiving dinner, both Tammy and her cousin Terrell, who had just been released from prison on a gun charge, showed up to dinner at her mother's house. Tammy and Terrell smoked some marijuana together in her car. Tammy's parole officer, who happened to be in the neighborhood for her own turkey celebration, saw Tammy behind the wheel. The probation officer ordered Tammy out of the car, conducted a search, and learned that Terrell was a felon. The next business day, the probation officer filed a petition asking the court to find Tammy in violation of her probation conditions, revoke her suspended sentence, and send her to jail for 2 years. Does Tammy have any defenses? **(ROL: Probation, suspended sentences)**

4. You Be the Judge

   1. Precedent: *Apprendi v. New Jersey* (2000): The Sixth Amendment requires that any fact that is going to increase a defendant's sentence must be admitted by him in a guilty plea or determined by a jury.

   2. Precedent: *Ring v. Arizona* (2002): Based on the *Apprendi* holding, state laws in death-penalty jurisdictions that allow the judge, alone, to impose the death penalty after a jury trial are invalid.

   3. You Decide: Timothy Hurst killed Cynthia Harrison, his coworker, in a robbery attempt at the fast food restaurant where the two worked. Under Florida law, death can be imposed if "findings by the court that such person shall be punished by death." Hurst was sentenced to death because the jury could recommend a sentence, but the judge, alone, ultimately imposed the death penalty. Hurst appealed.

   Which side will win? You decide. Answer at endnote.[87]

The Constitution of the United States of America

We the People of the United States, in Order to form a more perfect Union, establish Justice, insure domestic Tranquility, provide for the common defence, promote the general Welfare, and secure the Blessings of Liberty to ourselves and our Posterity, do ordain and establish this Constitution for the United States of America.

ARTICLE I

Section 1. All legislative Powers herein granted shall be vested in a Congress of the United States, which shall consist of a Senate and House of Representatives.

Section 2. (1) The House of Representatives shall be composed of Members chosen every second Year by the People of the several States, and the Electors in each State shall have the Qualifications requisite for Electors of the most numerous Branch of the State Legislature.

(2) No Person shall be a Representative who shall not have attained to the age of twenty-five Years, and been seven Years a Citizen of the United States, and who shall not, when elected, be an Inhabitant of that State in which he shall be chosen.

(3) Representatives and direct Taxes shall be apportioned among the several States which may be included within this Union, according to their respective Numbers, which shall be determined by adding to the whole Number of free Persons, including those bound to Service for a Term of Years, and excluding Indians not taxed, three fifths of all other Persons. The actual Enumeration shall be made within three Years after the first Meeting of the Congress of the United States, and within every subsequent Term of ten Years, in such Manner as they shall by Law direct. The Number of Representatives shall not exceed one for every thirty Thousand, but each State shall have at Least on Representative; and until such enumeration shall be made, the State of New Hampshire shall be entitled to chuse three, Massachusetts eight, Rhode Island and Providence Plantations one, Connecticut five, New York six, New Jersey four, Pennsylvania eight, Delaware one, Maryland six, Virginia ten, North Carolina five, South Carolina five, and Georgia three.

(4) When vacancies happen in the Representation from any State, the Executive Authority thereof shall issue Writs of Election to fill such Vacancies.

(5) The House of Representatives shall chuse their Speaker and other Officers; and shall have the sole Power of Impeachment.

Section 3. (1) The Senate of the United States shall be composed of two Senators from each State, chosen by the Legislature thereof, for six Years; and each Senator shall have one Vote.

(2) Immediately after they shall be assembled in Consequence of the first Election, they shall be divided as equally as may be into three Classes. The Seats of the Senators of the first Class shall be vacated at the Expiration of the Second Year, of the second

Class at the Expiration of the fourth Year, and of the third class at the Expiration of the sixth Year, so that one third may be chosen every second Year; and if Vacancies happen by Resignation, or otherwise, during the Recess of the Legislature of any State, the Executive thereof may make temporary Appointments until the next Meeting of the Legislature, which shall then fill such Vacancies.

(3) No Person shall be a Senator who shall not have attained to the Age of thirty Years, and been nine Years a Citizen of the United States, and who shall not, when elected, be an Inhabitant of that State for which he shall be chosen.

(4) The Vice President of the United States shall be President of the Senate, but shall have no Vote, unless they be equally divided.

(5) The Senate shall chuse their other Officers, and also a President pro tempore, in the Absence of the Vice President, or when he shall exercise the Office of the President of the United States.

(6) The Senate shall have the sole Power to try all Impeachments. When sitting for that Purpose, they shall be on Oath or Affirmation. When the President of the United States is tried, the Chief Justice shall preside: And no Person shall be convicted without the Concurrence of two thirds of the Members present.

(7) Judgment in Cases of Impeachment shall not extend further than to removal from Office, and disqualification to hold and enjoy any Office of honor, Trust or Profit under the United States: but the Party convicted shall nevertheless be liable and subject to Indictment, Trial, Judgment and Punishment, according to Law.

Section 4. (1) The Times, Places and Manner of holding Elections for Senators and Representatives, shall be prescribed in each State by the Legislature thereof; but the Congress may at any time by Law make or alter such Regulations, except as to the Places of chusing Senators.

(2) The Congress shall assemble at least once in every Year, and such Meeting shall be on the first Monday in December, unless they shall by Law appoint a different Day.

Section 5. (1) Each House shall be the Judge of the Elections, Returns and Qualifications of its own Members, and a Majority of each shall constitute a Quorum to do Business; but a smaller Number may adjourn from day to day, and may be authorized to compel the Attendance of absent Members, in such Manner, and under such Penalties as each House may provide.

(2) Each House may determine the Rules of its Proceedings, punish its members for disorderly Behaviour, and, with the Concurrence of two thirds, expel a Member.

(3) Each House shall keep a Journal of its Proceedings, and from time to time publish the same, excepting such Parts as may in their Judgment require Secrecy; and the Yeas and Nays of the Members of either House on any question shall, at the Desire of one fifth of those Present, be entered on the Journal.

(4) Neither House, during the Session of Congress, shall, without the Consent of the other, adjourn for more than three days, nor to any other Place than that in which the two Houses shall be sitting.

Section 6. (1) The Senators and Representatives shall receive a Compensation for their Services, to be ascertained by Law, and paid out of the Treasury of the United States. They shall in all cases, except Treason, Felony and Breach of the Peace, be privileged from Arrest during their Attendance at the Session of their respective Houses, and in going to and returning from the same; and for any Speech or Debate in either House, they shall not be questioned in any other Place.

(2) No Senator or Representative shall, during the Time for which he was elected, be appointed to any civil Office under the Authority of the United States, which shall have

been created, or the Emoluments whereof shall have been encreased during such time; and no Person holding any Office under the United States, shall be a Member of either House during his Continuance in Office.

Section 7. (1) All Bills for raising Revenue shall originate in the House of Representatives; but the Senate may propose or concur with Amendments as on other Bills.

(2) Every Bill which shall have passed the House of Representatives and the Senate, shall, before it become a Law, be presented to the President of the United States; If he approve he shall sign it, but if not he shall return it, with his Objections to that House in which it shall have originated, who shall enter the Objections at large on their Journal, and proceed to reconsider it. If after such Reconsideration two thirds of that House shall agree to pass the Bill, it shall be sent, together with the Objections, to the other House, by which it shall likewise be reconsidered, and if approved by two thirds of that House, it shall become a law. But in all such Cases the Votes of both Houses shall be determined by Yeas and Nays, and the Names of the Persons voting for and against the Bill shall be entered on the Journal of each House respectively. If any Bill shall not be returned by the President within ten Days (Sunday excepted) after it shall have been presented to him, the Same shall be a Law, in like Manner as if he had signed it, unless the Congress by their Adjournment prevent its Return, in which Case it shall not be a Law.

(3) Every Order, Resolution, or Vote to which the Concurrence of the Senate and House of Representatives may be necessary (except on a question of Adjournment) shall be presented to the President of the United States; and before the Same shall take Effect, shall be approved by him, or being disapproved by him, shall be repassed by two thirds of the Senate and House of Representatives, according to the Rules and Limitations prescribed in the Case of a Bill.

Section 8. (1) The Congress shall have Power to lay and Collect Taxes, Duties, Imposts and Excises, to pay the Debts and provide for the common Defence and general Welfare of the United States; but all Duties, Imposts and Excises shall be uniform throughout the United States;

(2) To borrow Money on the credit of the United States;

(3) To regulate Commerce with foreign Nations, and among the several States, and with the Indian Tribes;

(4) To establish a uniform rule of Naturalization, and uniform Laws on the subject of Bankruptcies throughout the United States;

(5) To coin Money, regulate the Value thereof, and of foreign Coin, and to fix the Standard of Weights and Measures;

(6) To provide for the Punishment of counterfeiting the Securities and current Coin of the United States;

(7) To establish Post Offices and post Roads;

(8) To promote the Progress of Science and useful Arts, by securing for limited Times to Authors and Inventors the exclusive Right to their respective Writings and Discoveries;

(9) To constitute Tribunals inferior to the supreme Court;

(10) To define and punish Piracies and Felonies committed on the high Seas, and Offenses against the Law of Nations;

(11) To declare War, grant Letters of Marque and Reprisal, and make Rules concerning Captures on Land and Water;

(12) To raise and support Armies, but no Appropriation of Money to that Use shall be for a longer Term than two Years;

(13) To provide and maintain a Navy;

(14) To make Rules for the Government and Regulation of the land and naval Forces;

(15) To provide for calling forth the Militia to execute the Laws of the Union, suppress Insurrections and repel Invasions;

(16) To provide for organizing, arming, and disciplining, the Militia, and for governing such Part of them as may be employed in the Service of the United States, reserving to the States respectively, the Appointment of the Officers, and the Authority of training the Militia according to the discipline prescribed by Congress;

(17) To exercise exclusive Legislation in all Cases whatsoever, over such District (not exceeding ten Miles square) as may, by Cession of particular States, and the Acceptance of Congress, become the Seat of the Government of the United States, and to exercise like Authority over all Places purchased by the Consent of the Legislature of the State in which the Same shall be, for the Erection of Forts, Magazines, Arsenals, dock-Yards, and other needful Buildings;-- And

(18) To make all Laws which shall be necessary and proper for carrying into Execution the foregoing Powers, and all other Powers vested by this Constitution in the Government of the United States, or in any Department or Officer thereof.

Section 9. (1) The Migration or Importation of such Persons as any of the States now existing shall think proper to admit, shall not be prohibited by the Congress prior to the Year one thousand eight hundred and eight, but a Tax or Duty may be imposed on such Importation, not exceeding ten dollars for each Person.

(2) The Privilege of the Writ of Habeas Corpus shall not be suspended unless when in Cases of Rebellion or Invasion the public Safety may require it.

(3) No Bill of Attainder or ex post facto Law shall be passed.

(4) No Capitation, or other direct, Tax shall be laid, unless in Proportion to the Census or Enumeration herein before directed to be taken.

(5) No Tax or Duty shall be laid on Articles exported from any State.

(6) No Preference shall be given by any Regulation of Commerce or Revenue to the Ports of one State over those of another; nor shall Vessels bound to, or from, one State, be obliged to enter, clear or pay Duties in another.

(7) No Money shall be drawn from the Treasury, but in Consequence of Appropriations made by Law; and a regular Statement and Account of the Receipts and Expenditures of all public Money shall be published from time to time.

(8) No Title of Nobility shall be granted by the United States: And no Person holding any Office of Profit or Trust under them, shall, without the Consent of the Congress, accept of any present, Emolument, Office, or Title, of any kind whatever, from any King, Prince or foreign State.

Section 10. (1) No State shall enter into any Treaty, Alliance, or Confederation; grant Letters of Marque and Reprisal; coin Money; emit Bills of Credit; make any Thing but gold and silver Coin a Tender in Payment of Debts; pass any Bill of Attainder, ex post facto Law, or Law impairing the Obligation of Contracts, or grant any Title of Nobility.

(2) No State shall, without the Consent of Congress, lay any Imposts or Duties on Imports or Exports, except what may be absolutely necessary for executing its inspection Laws: and the net Produce of all Duties and Imposts, laid by any State on Imports or Exports, shall be for the Use of the Treasury of the United States; and all such Laws shall be subject to the Revision and Controul of the Congress.

(3)   No state shall, without the Consent of Congress, lay any Duty of Tonnage, keep Troops, or Ships of War in time of Peace, enter into any Agreement or Compact with another State, or with a foreign Power, or engage in War, unless actually invaded, or in such imminent Danger as will not admit of Delay.

ARTICLE II

Section 1. (1) The Executive Power shall be vested in a President of the United States of America. He shall hold his Office during the Term of four Years, and, together with the Vice President, chosen for the same Term, be elected, as follows:

(2)   Each state shall appoint, in such Manner as the Legislature thereof may direct, a Number of Electors, equal to the whole Number of Senators and Representatives to which the State may be entitled in the Congress: but no Senator or Representative, or Person holding an Office of Trust or Profit under the United States, shall be appointed an Elector.

The Electors shall meet in their respective States, and vote by Ballot for two Persons, of whom one at least shall not be an Inhabitant of the same State with themselves. And they shall make a List of all the Persons voted for, and of the Number of Votes for each; which List they shall sign and certify, and transmit sealed to the Set of the Government of the United States, directed to the President of the Senate. The President of the Senate shall, in the presence of the Senate and House of Representatives, open all the Certificates, and the Votes shall then be counted. The Person having the greatest Number of Votes shall be the President, if such Number be a Majority of the whole Number of Electors appointed; and if there be more than one who have such Majority, and have an equal Number of Votes, then the House of Representatives shall immediately chuse by Ballot one of them for President; and if no Person have a Majority, then from the five highest on the List the said House shall in like Manner chuse the President. But in chusing the President, the Votes shall be taken by States, the Representation from each State having one Vote; a quorum for this Purpose shall consist of a Member or Members from two thirds of the States, and a Majority of all the States shall be necessary to a Choice. In every Case, after the Choice of the President, the Person having the greatest Number of Votes of the Electors shall be the Vice President. But if there should remain two or more who have equal Votes, the Senate shall chuse from them by Ballot the Vice President.

(3)   The Congress may determine the Time of chusing the Electors, and the Day on which they shall give their Votes; which Day shall be the same throughout the United States.

(4)   No Person except a natural born Citizen, or a Citizen of the United States, at the time of the Adoption of this Constitution, shall be eligible to the Office of President; neither shall any Person be eligible to that Office who shall not have attained to the Age of thirty-five years, and been fourteen Years a Resident within the United States.

(5)   In Case of the Removal of the President from Office, or of his Death, Resignation, or Inability to discharge the Powers and Duties of the said Office, the Same shall devolve on the Vice President, and the Congress may by Law provide for the Case of Removal, Death, Resignation or Inability, both of the President and Vice President, declaring what Officer shall then act as President, and such Officer shall act accordingly, until the Disability be removed, or a President shall be elected.

(6)   The President shall, at stated Times, receive for his Services, a Compensation, which shall neither be increased nor diminished during the Period for which he shall have been elected, and he shall not receive within that Period any other Emolument from the United States, or any of them.

(7)   Before he enter on the Execution of his Office, he shall take the following Oath or Affirmation:"I do solemnly swear (or affirm) that I will faithfully execute the Office of President of the United States, and will to the best of my Ability, preserve, protect and defend the Constitution of the United States."

Section 2. (1) The President shall be Commander in Chief of the Army and Navy of the United States, and of the Militia of the several States, when called into the actual Service of the United States; he may require the Opinion, in writing, of the principal Officer in each of the executive Departments, upon any Subject relating to the Duties of their respective Offices, and he shall have Power to grant Reprieves and Pardons for Offenses against the United States, except in Cases of Impeachment.

(2) He shall have Power, by and with the Advice and Consent of the Senate, to make Treaties, provided two thirds of the Senators present concur; and he shall nominate, and by and with the Advice and Consent of the Senate, shall appoint Ambassadors, other public Ministers and Consuls, Judges of the supreme Court, and all other Officers of the United States, whose Appointments are not herein otherwise provided for, and which shall be established by Law: but the Congress may by Law vest the Appointment of such inferior Officers, as they think proper, in the President alone, in the Courts of Law, or in the Heads of Departments.

(3) The President shall have Power to fill up all Vacancies that may happen during the Recess of the Senate, by granting Commissions which shall expire at the End of their next Session.

Section 3. He shall from time to time give to the Congress Information of the State of the Union, and recommend to their Consideration such Measures as he shall judge necessary and expedient; he may, on extraordinary Occasions, convene both Houses, or either of them, and in Case of Disagreement between them, with Respect to the Time of Adjournment, he may adjourn them to such Time as he shall think proper; he shall receive Ambassadors and other public Ministers; he shall take Care that the Laws be faithfully executed, and shall Commission all the Officers of the United States.

Section 4. The President, Vice President and all Civil Officers of the United States, shall be removed from Office on Impeachment for, and Conviction of, Treason, Bribery, or other high Crimes and Misdemeanors.

ARTICLE III

Section 1. The judicial Power of the United States, shall be vested in one supreme Court, and in such inferior Courts as the Congress may from time to time ordain and establish. The Judges, both of the supreme and inferior Courts, shall hold their Offices during good Behaviour, and shall, at stated Times, receive for their Services, a Compensation, which shall not be diminished during their Continuance in Office.

Section 2. (1) The judicial Power shall extend to all Cases, in Law and Equity, arising under this Constitution, the Laws of the United States, and Treaties made, or which shall be made, under their Authority;—to all Cases affecting Ambassadors, other public Ministers and Consuls;—to all Cases of admiralty and maritime Jurisdiction;—to Controversies to which the United States shall be a party;—to Controversies between two or more States;—between a State and Citizens of another States;—between Citizens of different States;—between Citizens of the same State claiming Lands under Grants of different States, and between a State, or the Citizens thereof, and foreign States, Citizens or Subjects.

(2) In all cases affecting Ambassadors, other public Ministers and Consuls, and those in which a State shall be Party, the supreme Court shall have original Jurisdiction. In all the other Cases before mentioned, the supreme Court shall have appellate Jurisdiction, both as to Law and Fact, with such Exceptions, and under such Regulations as the Congress shall make.

(3) The Trial of all Crimes, except in Cases of Impeachment, shall be by Jury; and such Trial shall be held in the State where the said Crimes shall have been committed; but when not committed within any State, the Trial shall be at such Place or Places as the Congress may by Law have directed.

Section 3. (1) Treason against the United States, shall consist only in levying War against them, or in adhering to their Enemies, giving them Aid and Comfort. No Person shall be convicted of Treason unless on the Testimony of two Witnesses to the same overt Act, or on Confession in open Court.

(2) The Congress shall have Power to declare the Punishment of Treason, but no Attainder of Treason shall work Corruption of Blood, or Forfeiture except during the Life of the Person attained.

ARTICLE IV

Section 1. Full Faith and Credit shall be given in each State to the public Acts, Records, and judicial Proceedings of every other State. And the Congress may by general Laws prescribe the Manner in which such Acts, Records and Proceedings shall be proved, and the Effect thereof.

Section 2. (1) The Citizens of each State shall be entitled to all privileges and Immunities of Citizens in the several States.

(2) A Person charged in any State with Treason, Felony, or other Crime, who shall flee from Justice, and be found in another State, shall on Demand of the executive Authority of the State from which he fled, be delivered up, to be removed to the state having Jurisdiction of the Crime.

(3) No Person held to Service of Labour in one State, under the Laws thereof, escaping into another, shall, in Consequence of any Law or Regulation therein, be discharged from such Service or Labour, but shall be delivered up on Claim of the Party to whom such Service or Labour may be due.

Section 3. (1) New States may be admitted by the Congress into this Union; but no new State shall be formed or erected within the Jurisdiction of any other State; nor any State be formed by the Junction of two or more States, or Parts of States, without the Consent of the Legislatures of the States concerned as well as of the Congress.

(2) The Congress shall have power to dispose of and make all needful Rules and Regulations respecting the Territory or other Property belonging to the United States; and nothing in this Constitution shall be so construed as to Prejudice any Claims of the United States, or of any particular State.

Section 4. The United States shall guarantee to every State in this Union a Republican Form of Government, and shall protect each of them against Invasion; and on Application of the Legislature, or of the Executive (when the Legislature cannot be convened) against domestic Violence.

ARTICLE V

The Congress, whenever two thirds of both Houses shall deem it necessary, shall propose Amendments to this Constitution, or, on the Application of the Legislatures of two thirds of the several States, shall call a Convention for proposing Amendments, which, in either Case, shall be valid to all Intents and Purposes, as Part of this Constitution, when ratified by the Legislatures of three fourths of the several States, or by Conventions in three fourths thereof, as the one or the other Mode of Ratification may be proposed by the Congress; Provided that no Amendment which may be made prior to the Year One thousand eight hundred and eight shall in any Manner affect the first and fourth Clauses in the Ninth Section of the first Article; and that no State, without its Consent, shall be deprived of its equal Suffrage in the Senate.

ARTICLE VI

(1) All Debts contracted and Engagements entered into, before the Adoption of this Constitution, shall be as valid against the United States under this Constitution, as under the Confederation.

(2) This Constitution, and the Laws of the United States which shall be made in Pursuance thereof; and all Treaties made, or which shall be made, under the Authority of the United States, shall be the supreme Law of the Land; and the Judges in every State shall be bound thereby, any Thing in the Constitution or Laws of any State to the Contrary notwithstanding.

(3) The Senators and Representatives before mentioned, and the Members of the several State Legislatures, and all executive and judicial Officers, both of the United States and of the several States, shall be bound by Oath or Affirmation, to support this Constitution; but no religious Test shall ever be required as a Qualification to any Office or public Trust under the United States.

ARTICLE VII

The Ratification of the Conventions of nine States, shall be sufficient for the Establishment of this Constitution between the States so ratifying the Same.

ARTICLES IN ADDITION TO, AND AMENDMENT OF, THE CONSTITUTION OF THE UNITED STATES OF AMERICA, PROPOSED BY CONGRESS, AND RATIFIED BY THE SEVERAL STATES, PURSUANT TO THE FIFTH ARTICLE OF THE ORIGINAL CONSTITUTION.

Amendment I (1791)

Congress shall make no law respecting an establishment of religion, or prohibiting the free exercise thereof; or abridging the freedom of speech, or of the press; or the right of the people peaceably to assemble, and to petition the Government for a redress of grievances.

Amendment II (1791)

A well regulated Militia, being necessary to the security of a free state, the right of the people to keep and bear Arms, shall not be infringed.

Amendment III (1791)

No Soldier shall, in time of peace be quartered in any house, without the consent of the Owner, nor in time of war, but in a manner to be prescribed by law.

Amendment IV (1791)

The right of the people to be secure in their persons, houses, papers, and effects, against unreasonable searches and seizures, shall not be violated, and no Warrants shall issue, but upon probable cause, supported by Oath or affirmation, and particularly describing the place to be searched, and the persons or things to be seized.

Amendment V (1791)

No person shall be held to answer for a capital, or otherwise infamous crime, unless on a presentment or indictment of a Grand Jury, except in cases arising in the land or naval forces, or in the Militia, when in actual service in time of War or public danger; nor shall any person be subject for the same offence to be twice put in jeopardy of life or limb; nor shall be compelled in any criminal case to be a witness against himself, nor be deprived of life, liberty, or property, without due process of law; nor shall private property be taken for public use, without just compensation.

Amendment VI (1791)

In all criminal prosecutions, the accused shall enjoy the right to a speedy and public trial, by an impartial jury of the State and district wherein the crime shall have been committed, which district shall have been previously ascertained by law, and to be informed of the nature and cause of the accusation; to be confronted with the witnesses against him; to have compulsory process for obtaining witnesses in his favor, and to have the Assistance of Counsel for his defence.

Amendment VII (1791)

In Suits at common law, where the value in controversy shall exceed twenty dollars, the right of trial by jury shall be preserved, and no fact tried by a jury, shall be otherwise re-examined in any Court of the United States, than according to the rules of the common law.

Amendment VIII (1791)

Excessive bail shall not be required, nor excessive fines imposed, nor cruel and unusual punishments inflicted.

Amendment IX (1791)

The enumeration in the Constitution, of certain rights, shall not be construed to deny or disparage others retained by the people.

Amendment X (1791)

The powers not delegated to the United States by the Constitution, nor prohibited by it to the States, are reserved to the States respectively, or to the people.

Amendment XI (1798)

The Judicial power of the United States shall not be construed to extend to any suit in law or equity, commenced or prosecuted against one of the United States by Citizens of another State, or by Citizens or Subjects of any Foreign State.

Amendment XII (1804)

The Electors shall meet in their respective states and vote by ballot for President and Vice-President, one of whom, at least, shall not be an inhabitant of the same state with themselves; they shall name in their ballots the person voted for as President, and in distinct ballots the person voted for as Vice-President, and they shall make distinct lists of all persons voted for as President, and of all persons voted for as Vice-President, and of the number of votes for each, which lists they shall sign and certify, and transmit sealed to the seat of the government of the United States, directed to the President of the Senate;--The President of the Senate shall, in the presence of the Senate and House of Representatives, open all the certificates and the votes shall then be counted;--The person having the greatest number of votes for President, shall be the President, if such number be a majority of the whole number of Electors appointed; and if no person have such majority, then from the persons having the highest numbers not exceeding three on the list of those voted for as President, the House of Representatives shall choose immediately, by ballot, the President. But in choosing the President, the votes shall be taken by states, the representation from each state having one vote; a quorum for this purpose shall consist of a member or members from two-thirds of the states, and a majority of all the states shall be necessary to a choice. And if the House of Representatives shall not choose a President whenever the right of choice shall devolve upon them, before the fourth day of March next following, then the Vice-President shall act as President, as in the case of the death or other constitutional disability of the President— The person having the greatest number of votes as Vice-President, shall be the Vice-President, if such number be a majority of the whole number of Electors appointed, and if no person have a majority, then from the two highest numbers on the list, the Senate shall choose the Vice-President; A quorum for the purpose shall consist of two-thirds of the whole number of Senators, and a majority of the whole number shall be necessary to a choice. But no person constitutionally ineligible to the office of President shall be eligible to that of Vice-President of the United States.

Amendment XIII (1865)

Section 1. Neither slavery nor involuntary servitude, except as a punishment for crime whereof the party shall have been duly convicted, shall exist within the United States, or any place subject to their jurisdiction.

Section 2. Congress shall have power to enforce this article by appropriate legislation.

Amendment XIV (1868)

Section 1. All persons born or naturalized in the United States and subject to the jurisdiction thereof, are citizens of the United States and of the State wherein they reside. No State shall make or enforce any law which shall abridge the privileges or immunities of citizens of the United States; nor shall any State deprive any person of life, liberty, or property, without due process of law; nor deny to any person within its jurisdiction the equal protection of the laws.

Section 2. Representatives shall be apportioned among the several States according to their respective numbers, counting the whole number of persons in each State, excluding Indians not taxed. But when the right to vote at any election for the choice of electors for President and Vice-President of the United States, Representatives in Congress, the Executive and Judicial officers of a State, or the members of the Legislature thereof, is denied to any of the male inhabitants of such State, being twenty-one years of age, and citizens of the United States, or in any way abridged, except for participation in rebellion, or other crime, the basis of representation therein shall be reduced in the proportion which the number of such male citizens shall bear to the whole number of male citizens twenty-one years of age in such State.

Section 3. No person shall be a Senator or Representative in Congress, or elector of President and Vice-President, or hold any office, civil or military, under the United States, or under any State, who, having previously taken an oath, as a member of Congress, or as an officer of the United States, or as a member of any State legislature, or as an executive or judicial officer of any State, to support the Constitution of the United States, shall have engaged in insurrection or rebellion against the same, or given aid or comfort to the enemies thereof. But Congress may by a vote of two-thirds of each House, remove such disability.

Section 4. The validity of the public debt of the United States, authorized by law, including debts incurred for payment of pensions and bounties for services in suppressing insurrection or rebellion, shall not be questioned. But neither the United States nor any State shall assume or pay any debt or obligation incurred in aid of insurrection or rebellion against the United States, or any claim for the loss or emancipation of any slave; but all such debts, obligations and claims shall be held illegal and void.

Section 5. The Congress shall have power to enforce, by appropriate legislation, the provisions of this article.

Amendment XV (1870)

Section 1. The right of citizens of the United States to vote shall not be denied or abridged by the United States or by any State on account of race, color, or previous condition of servitude.

Section 2. The Congress shall have power to enforce this article by appropriate legislation.

Amendment XVI (1913)

The Congress shall have power to lay and collect taxes on incomes, from whatever source derived, without apportionment among the several States, and without regard to any census or enumeration.

Amendment XVII (1913)

The Senate of the United States shall be composed of two Senators from each State, elected by the people thereof, for six years; and each Senator shall have one vote. The electors in each State shall have the qualifications requisite for electors of the most numerous branch of the State legislatures.

When vacancies happen in the representation of any State in the Senate, the executive authority of such State shall issue writs of election to fill such vacancies: *Provided*, That the legislature of any State may empower the executive thereof to make temporary appointments until the people fill the vacancies by election as the legislature may direct.

This amendment shall not so be construed as to affect the election or term of any Senator chosen before it becomes valid as part of the Constitution.

Amendment XVIII (1919)

Section 1. After one year from the ratification of this article the manufacture, sale, or transportation of intoxicating liquors within, the importation thereof into, or the exportation thereof from the United States and all territory subject to the jurisdiction thereof for beverage purposes is hereby prohibited.

Section 2. The Congress and the several States shall have concurrent power to enforce this article by appropriate legislation.

Section 3. This article shall be inoperative unless it shall have been ratified as an amendment to the Constitution by the legislatures of the several States, as provided in the Constitution, within seven years from the date of the submission hereof to the States by the Congress.

Amendment XIX (1920)

The right of citizens of the United States to vote shall not be denied or abridged by the United States or by any State on account of sex.

Congress shall have power to enforce this article by appropriate legislation.

Amendment XX (1933)

Section 1. The terms of the President and Vice President shall end at noon on the 20th day of January, and the terms of Senators and Representatives at noon on the 3d day of January, of the years in which such terms would have ended if this article had not been ratified; and the terms of their successors shall then begin.

Section 2. The Congress shall assemble at least once in every year, and such meeting shall begin at noon on the 3d day of January, unless they shall by law appoint a different day.

Section 3. If, at any time fixed for the beginning of the term of the President, the President elect shall have died, the Vice President elect shall become President. If a President shall not have been chosen before the time fixed for the beginning of his term, or if the President elect shall have failed to qualify, then the Vice President elect shall act as President until a President shall have qualified; and the Congress may by law provide for the case wherein neither a President elect nor a Vice President elect shall have qualified, declaring who shall then act as President, or the manner in which one who is to act shall be selected; and such person shall act accordingly until a President or Vice President shall have qualified.

Section 4. The Congress may by law provide for the case of the death of any of the persons from whom the House of Representatives may choose a President whenever the right of choice shall have devolved upon them, and for the case of the death of any of the persons from whom the Senate may choose a Vice President whenever the right of choice shall have devolved upon them.

Section 5. Sections 1 and 2 shall take effect on the 15th day of October following the ratification of this article.

Section 6. This article shall be inoperative unless it shall have been ratified as an amendment to the Constitution by the legislatures of three-fourths of the several States within seven years from the date of its submission.

Amendment XXI (1933)

Section 1. The eighteenth article of amendment to the Constitution of the United States is hereby repealed.

Section 2. The transportation or importation into any State, Territory or possession of the United States for delivery or use therein of intoxicating liquors, in violation of the laws thereof, is hereby prohibited.

Section 3. This article shall be inoperative unless it shall have been ratified as an amendment to the Constitution by conventions in the several States, as provided in the Constitution, within seven years from the date of the submission hereof to the States by the Congress.

Amendment XXII (1951)

Section 1. No person shall be elected to the office of the President more than twice, and no person who has held the office of President, or acted as President, for more than two years of a term to which some other person was elected President shall be elected to the office of President more than once. But this Article shall not apply to any person holding the office of President when this Article was proposed by Congress, and shall not prevent any person who may be holding the office of President, or acting as President, during the term within which this Article becomes operative from holding the office of President or acting as President during the remainder of such term.

Section 2. This article shall be inoperative unless it shall have been ratified as an amendment to the Constitution by the legislatures of three-fourths of the several States within seven years from the date of its submission to the States by the Congress.

Amendment XXIII (1961)

Section 1. The District constituting the seat of Government of the United States shall appoint in such manner as Congress may direct:

A number of electors of President and Vice President equal to the whole number of Senators and Representatives in Congress to which the District would be entitled if it were a State, but in no event more than the least populous State; they shall be in addition to those appointed by the States, but they shall be considered, for the purposes of the election of President and Vice President, to be electors appointed by a State; and they shall meet in the District and perform such duties as provided by the twelfth article of amendment.

Section 2. The Congress shall have power to enforce this article by appropriate legislation.

Amendment XXIV (1964)

Section 1. The right of citizens of the United States to vote in any primary or other election for President or Vice President, for electors for President or Vice President, or for Senator or Representative in Congress, shall not be denied or abridged by the United States or any State by reason of failure to pay poll tax or other tax.

Section 2. The Congress shall have power to enforce this article by appropriate legislation.

Amendment XXV (1967)

Section 1. In case of the removal of the President from office or of his death or resignation, the Vice President shall become President.

Section 2. Whenever there is a vacancy in the office of the Vice President, the President shall nominate a Vice President who shall take office upon confirmation by a majority vote of both Houses of Congress.

Section 3. Whenever the President transmits to the President pro tempore of the Senate and the Speaker of the House of Representatives his written declaration that he is unable to discharge the powers and duties of his office, and until he transmits to them a written declaration to the contrary, such powers and duties shall be discharged by the Vice President as Acting President.

Section 4. Whenever the Vice President and a majority of either the principal officers of the executive departments or of such other body as Congress may by law provide, transmit to the President pro tempore of the Senate and the Speaker of the House of Representatives their written declaration that the President is unable to discharge the powers and duties of his office, the Vice President shall immediately assume the powers and duties of the office as Acting President.

Thereafter, when the President transmits to the President pro tempore of the Senate and the Speaker of the House of Representatives his written declaration that no inability exists, he shall resume the powers and duties of his office unless the Vice President and a majority of either the principal officers of the executive department or of such other body as Congress may by law provide, transmit within four days to the President pro tempore of the Senate and the Speaker of the House of Representatives their written declaration that the President is unable to discharge the powers and duties of his office. Thereupon Congress shall decide the issue, assembling within forty-eight hours for that purpose if not in session. If the Congress, within twenty-one days after receipt of the latter written declaration, or, if Congress is not in session, within twenty-one days after Congress is required to assemble, determines by two-thirds vote of both Houses that the President is unable to discharge the powers and duties of his office, the Vice President shall continue to discharge the same as Acting President; otherwise, the President shall resume the powers and duties of his office.

AMENDMENT XXVI (1971)

Section 1. The right of citizens of the United States, who are eighteen years of age or older, to vote shall not be denied or abridged by the United States or by any State on account of age.

Section 2. The Congress shall have power to enforce this article by appropriate legislation.

AMENDMENT XXVII (1992)

No law, varying the compensation for the services of the Senators and Representatives, shall take effect, until an election of representatives shall have intervened.

APPENDIX B

Selected Excerpts From the Model Penal Code

American Legal Institute, 1962

PART I

GENERAL PROVISIONS

ARTICLE 1. PRELIMINARY

§ 1.04. Classes of Crimes; Violations.

(1) An offense defined by this Code or by any other statute of this State, for which a sentence of [death or of] imprisonment is authorized, constitutes a crime. Crimes are classified as felonies, misdemeanors or petty misdemeanors.

(2) A crime is a felony if it is so designated in this Code or if persons convicted thereof may be sentenced [to death or] to imprisonment for a term which, apart from an extended term, is in excess of one year.

(3) A crime is a misdemeanor if it is so designated in this Code or in a statute other than this Code enacted subsequent thereto.

(4) A crime is a petty misdemeanor if it is so designated in this Code or in a statute other than this Code enacted subsequent thereto or if it is defined by a statute other than this Code which now provides that persons convicted thereof may be sentenced to imprisonment for a term of which the maximum is less than one year.

(5) An offense defined by this Code or by any other statute of this State constitutes a violation if it is so designated in this Code or in the law defining the offense or if no other sentence than a fine, or fine and forfeiture or other civil penalty is authorized upon conviction or if it is defined by a statute other than this Code which now provides that the offense shall not constitute a crime. A violation does not constitute a crime and conviction of a violation shall not give rise to any disability or legal disadvantage based on conviction of a criminal offense.

(6) Any offense declared by law to constitute a crime, without specification of the grade thereof or of the sentence authorized upon conviction, is a misdemeanor.

(7) An offense defined by any statute of this State other than this Code shall be classified as provided in this Section and the sentence that may be imposed upon conviction thereof shall hereafter be governed by this Code.

Model Penal Code, Copyright @ 1985 by the American Law Institute. Reproduced with permission. All rights reserved.

§ 1.05. All Offenses Defined by Statute; Application of General Provisions of the Code.

(1) No conduct constitutes an offense unless it is a crime or violation under this Code or another statute of this State.

(2) The provisions of Part I of the Code are applicable to offenses defined by other statutes, unless the Code otherwise provides.

(3) This Section does not affect the power of a court to punish for contempt or to employ any sanction authorized by law for the enforcement of an order or a civil judgment or decree.

***

§ 1.12. Proof Beyond a Reasonable Doubt; Affirmative Defenses; Burden of Proving Fact When Not an Element of an Offense; Presumptions.

(1) No person may be convicted of an offense unless each element of such offense is proved beyond a reasonable doubt. In the absence of such proof, the innocence of the defendant is assumed.

(2) Subsection (1) of this Section does not:

(a) require the disproof of an affirmative defense unless and until there is evidence supporting such defense; or

(b) apply to any defense which the Code or another statute plainly requires the defendant to prove by a preponderance of evidence.

(3) A ground of defense is affirmative, within the meaning of Subsection (2) (a) of this Section, when:

(a) it arises under a section of the Code which so provides; or

(b) it relates to an offense defined by a statute other than the Code and such statute so provides; or

(c) it involves a matter of excuse or justification peculiarly within the knowledge of the defendant on which he can fairly be required to adduce supporting evidence.

(4) When the application of the Code depends upon the finding of a fact which is not an element of an offense, unless the Code otherwise provides:

(a) the burden of proving the fact is on the prosecution or defendant, depending on whose interest or contention will be furthered if the finding should be made; and

(b) the fact must be proved to the satisfaction of the Court or jury, as the case may be.

(5) When the Code establishes a presumption with respect to any fact which is an element of an offense, it has the following consequences:

(a) when there is evidence of the facts which give rise to the presumption, the issue of the existence of the presumed fact must be submitted to the jury, unless the Court is satisfied that the evidence as a whole clearly negatives the presumed fact; and

(b) when the issue of the existence of the presumed fact is submitted to the jury, the Court shall charge that while the presumed fact must, on all the evidence, be proved beyond a reasonable doubt, the law declares that the jury may regard the facts giving rise to the presumption as sufficient evidence of the presumed fact.

(6) A presumption not established by the Code or inconsistent with it has the consequences otherwise accorded it by law.

§ 1.13. General Definitions.

In this Code, unless a different meaning plainly is required:

(1) "statute" includes the Constitutional and a local law or ordinance of a political subdivision of the State;

(2) "act" or "action" means a bodily movement whether voluntary or involuntary;

(3) "voluntary" has the meaning specified in Section 2.01;

(4) "omission" means a failure to act;

(5) "conduct" means an action or omission and its accompanying state of mind, or, where relevant, a series of acts and omissions.

(6) "actor" includes, where relevant, a person guilty of an omission;

(7) "acted" includes, where relevant, "omitted to act";

(8) "person," "he" and "actor" include any natural person and, where relevant, a corporation or an unincorporated association;

(9) "element of an offense" means (i) such conduct or (ii) such attendant circumstances or (iii) such a result of conduct as

    (a) is included in the description of the forbidden conduct in the definition of the offense; or

    (b) establishes the required kind of culpability; or

    (c) negatives an excuse or justification for such conduct; or

    (d) negatives a defense under the statute of limitations; or

    (e) establishes jurisdiction or venue;

(10) "material element of an offense" means an element that does not relate exclusively to the statute of limitations, jurisdiction, venue or to any other matter similarly unconnected with (i) the harm or evil, incident to conduct, sought to be prevented by the law defining the offense, or (ii) the existence of a justification or excuse for such conduct;

(11) "purposely" has the meaning specified in Section 2.02 and equivalent terms such as "with purpose," "designed" or "with design" have the same meaning;

(12) "intentionally" or "with intent" means purposely;

(13) "knowingly" has the meaning specified in Section 2.02 and equivalent terms such as "knowing" or "with knowledge" have the same meaning;

(14) "recklessly" has the meaning specified in Section 2.02 and equivalent terms such as "recklessness" or "with recklessness" have the same meaning;

(15) "negligently" has the same meaning specified in Section 2.02 and equivalent terms such as "negligence" or "with negligence" have the same meaning;

(16) "reasonably believes" or "reasonable belief" designates a belief which the actor is not reckless or negligent in holding.

ARTICLE 2. GENERAL PRINCIPLES OF LIABILITY

§ 2.01. Requirement of Voluntary Act;
Omission as Basis of Liability; Possession as an Act.

(1) A person is not guilty of an offense unless his liability is based on conduct which includes a voluntary act or the omission to perform an act of which he is physically capable.

(2) The following are not voluntary acts within the meaning of this Section:

    (a) a reflex or convulsion;

    (b) a bodily movement during unconsciousness or sleep;

    (c) conduct during hypnosis or resulting from hypnotic suggestion;

    (d) a bodily movement that otherwise is not a product of the effort or determination of the actor, either conscious or habitual.

(3) Liability for the commission of an offense may not be based on an omission unaccompanied by action unless:

    (a) the omission is expressly made sufficient by the law defining the offense; or

    (b) a duty to perform the omitted act is otherwise imposed by law.

(4) Possession is an act, within the meaning of this Section, if the possessor knowingly procured or received the thing possessed or was aware of his control thereof for a sufficient period to have been able to terminate his possession.

§ 2.02. General Requirements of Culpability.

(1) *Minimum Requirements of Culpability.* Except as provided in Section 2.05, a person is not guilty of an offense unless he acted purposely, knowingly, recklessly or negligently, as the law may require, with respect to each material element of the offense.

(2) *Kinds of Culpability Defined.*

    (a) *Purposely.*

A person acts purposely with respect to a material element of an offense when:

    (i) if the element involves the nature of his conduct or a result thereof, it is his conscious object to engage in conduct of that nature or to cause such a result; and

    (ii) if the element involves the attendant circumstances, he is aware of the existence of such circumstances or he believes or hopes that they exist.

    (b) *Knowingly.*

A person acts knowingly with respect to a material element of an offense when:

    (i) if the element involves the nature of his conduct or the attendant circumstances, he is aware that his conduct is of that nature or that such circumstances exist; and

    (ii) if the element involves a result of his conduct, he is aware that it is practically certain that his conduct will cause such a result.

    (c) *Recklessly.*

A person acts recklessly with respect to a material element of an offense when he consciously disregards a substantial and unjustifiable risk that the material element exists or will result from his conduct. The risk must be of such a nature and degree that, considering the nature and purpose of the actor's conduct and the circumstances known to him, its disregard involves a gross deviation from the standard of conduct that a law-abiding person would observe in the actor's situation.

    (d) *Negligently.*

A person acts negligently with respect to a material element of an offense when he should be aware of a substantial and unjustifiable risk that the material element exists or will result from his conduct. The risk must be of such a nature and degree that the actor's failure to perceive it, considering the nature and purpose of his conduct and the circumstances known to him, involves a gross deviation from the standard of care that a reasonable person would observe in the actor's situation.

(3) *Culpability Required Unless Otherwise Provided.*

When the culpability sufficient to establish a material element of an offense is not prescribed by law, such element is established if a person acts purposely, knowingly or recklessly with respect thereto.

(4) *Prescribed Culpability Requirement Applies to All Material Elements.*

When the law defining an offense prescribes the kind of culpability that is sufficient for the commission of an offense, without distinguishing among the material elements thereof, such provision shall apply to all the material elements of the offense, unless a contrary purpose plainly appears.

(5) *Substitutes for Negligence, Recklessness and Knowledge.*

When the law provides that negligence suffices to establish an element of an offense, such element also is established if a person acts purposely, knowingly or recklessly. When recklessness suffices to establish an element, such element also is established if a person acts purposely or knowingly. When acting knowingly suffices to establish an element, such element also is established if a person acts purposely.

(6) *Requirement of Purpose Satisfied if Purpose Is Conditional.*

When a particular purpose is an element of an offense, the element is established although such purpose is conditional, unless the condition negatives the harm or evil sought to be prevented by the law defining the offense.

(7) *Requirement of Knowledge Satisfied by Knowledge of High Probability.*

When knowledge of the existence of a particular fact is an element of an offense, such knowledge is established if a person is aware of a high probability of its existence, unless he actually believes that it does not exist.

(8) *Requirement of Willfulness Satisfied by Acting Knowingly.*

A requirement that an offense be committed willfully is satisfied if a person acts knowingly with respect to the material elements of the offense, unless a purpose to impose further requirements appears.

(9) *Culpability as to Illegality of Conduct.*

Neither knowledge nor recklessness or negligence as to whether conduct constitutes an offense or as to the existence, meaning or application of the law determining the elements of an offense is an element of such offense, unless the definition of the offense or the Code so provides.

(10) *Culpability as Determinant of Grade of Offense.*

When the grade or degree of an offense depends on whether the offense is committed purposely, knowingly, recklessly or negligently, its grade or degree shall be the lowest for which the determinative kind of culpability is established with respect to any material element of the offense.

§ 2.03. Causal Relationship Between Conduct and Result; Divergence Between Result Designed or Contemplated and Actual Result or Between Probable and Actual Result.

(1) Conduct is the cause of a result when:

  (a) it is an antecedent but for which the result in question would not have occurred; and

  (b) the relationship between the conduct and result satisfies any additional causal requirements imposed by the Code or by the law defining the offense.

(2) When purposely or knowingly causing a particular result is an element of an offense, the element is not established if the actual result is not within the purpose or the contemplation of the actor unless:

  (a) the actual result differs from that designed or contemplated, as the case may be, only in the respect that a different person or different property is injured or affected or that the injury or harm designed or contemplated would have been more serious or more extensive than that caused; or

  (b) the actual result involves the same kind of injury or harm as that designed or contemplated and is not too remote or accidental in its occurrence to have a [just] bearing on the actor's liability or on the gravity of his offense.

(3) When recklessly or negligently causing a particular result is an element of an offense, the element is not established if the actual result is not within the risk of which the actor is aware or, in the case of negligence, of which he should be aware unless:

  (a) the actual result differs from the probable result only in respect that a different person or different property is injured or affected or that the probable injury or harm would have been more serious or more extensive than that caused; or

  (b) the actual result involves the same kind of injury or harm as the probable result and is not too remote or accidental in its occurrence to have a [just] bearing on the actor's liability or on the gravity of his offense.

(4) When causing a particular result is a material element of an offense for which absolute liability is imposed by law, the element is not established unless the actual result is a probable consequence of the actor's conduct.

§ 2.04. Ignorance or Mistake.

(1) Ignorance or mistake as to a matter of fact or law is a defense if:

  (a) the ignorance or mistake negatives the purpose, knowledge, belief, recklessness or negligence required to establish a material element of the offense; or

  (b) the law provides that the state of mind established by such ignorance or mistake constitutes a defense.

(2) Although ignorance or mistake would otherwise afford a defense to the offense charged, the defense is not available if the defendant would be guilty of another offense had the situation been as he supposed. In such case, however, the ignorance or mistake of the defendant shall reduce the grade and degree of the offense of which he may be convicted to those of the offense of which he would be guilty had the situation been as he supposed.

(3) A belief that conduct does not legally constitute an offense is a defense to a prosecution for that offense based upon such conduct when:

  (a) the statute or other enactment defining the offense is not known to the actor and has not been published or otherwise reasonably made available prior to the conduct alleged; or

(b) he acts in reasonable reliance upon an official statement of the law, afterward determined to be invalid or erroneous, contained in (i) a statute or other enactment; (ii) a judicial decision, opinion or judgment; (iii) an administrative order or grant of permission; or (iv) an official interpretation of the public officer or body charged by law with responsibility for the interpretation, administration or enforcement of the law defining the offense.

(4) The defendant must prove a defense arising under Subsection (3) of this Section by a preponderance of evidence.

§ 2.05. When Culpability Requirements Are Inapplicable to Violations and to Offenses Defined by Other Statutes; Effect of Absolute Liability in Reducing Grade of Offense to Violation.

(1) The requirements of culpability prescribed by Sections 2.01 and 2.02 do not apply to:

(a) offenses which constitute violations, unless the requirement involved is included in the definition of the offense or the Court determines that its application is consistent with effective enforcement of the law defining the offense; or

(b) offenses defined by statutes other than the Code, insofar as a legislative purpose to impose absolute liability for such offenses or with respect to any material element thereof plainly appears.

(2) Notwithstanding any other provision of existing law and unless a subsequent statute otherwise provides:

(a) when absolute liability is imposed with respect to any material element of an offense defined by a statute other than the Code and a conviction is based upon such liability, the offense constitutes a violation; and

(b) although absolute liability is imposed by law with respect to one or more of the material elements of an offense defined by a statute other than the Code, the culpable commission of the offense may be charged and proved, in which event negligence with respect to such elements constitutes sufficient culpability and the classification of the offense and the sentence that may be imposed therefor upon conviction are determined by Section 1.04 and Article 6 of the Code.

§ 2.06. Liability for Conduct of Another; Complicity.

(1) A person is guilty of an offense if it is committed by his own conduct or by the conduct of another person for which he is legally accountable, or both.

(2) A person is legally accountable for the conduct of another person when:

(a) acting with the kind of culpability that is sufficient for the commission of the offense, he causes an innocent or irresponsible person to engage in such conduct; or

(b) he is made accountable for the conduct of such other person by the Code or by the law defining the offense; or

(c) he is an accomplice of such other person in the commission of the offense.

(3) A person is an accomplice of another person in the commission of an offense if:

(a) with the purpose of promoting or facilitating the commission of the offense, he

(i) solicits such other person to commit it; or

(ii) aids or agrees or attempts to aid such other person in planning or committing it; or

(iii) having a legal duty to prevent the commission of the offense, fails to make proper effect so to do; or

(b) his conduct is expressly declared by law to establish his complicity.

(4) When causing a particular result is an element of an offense, an accomplice in the conduct causing such result is an accomplice in the commission of that offense, if he acts with the kind of culpability, if any, with respect to that result that is sufficient for the commission of the offense.

(5) A person who is legally incapable of committing a particular offense himself may be guilty thereof, if it is committed by the conduct of another person for which he is legally accountable, unless such liability is inconsistent with the purpose of the provision establishing his incapacity.

(6) Unless otherwise provided by the Code or by the law defining the offense, a person is not an accomplice in an offense committed by another person if:

(a) he is a victim of that offense; or

(b) the offense is so defined that his conduct is inevitably incident to its commission; or

(c) he terminates his complicity prior to the commission of the offense and

(i) wholly deprives it of effectiveness in the commission of the offense; or

(ii) gives timely warning to the law enforcement authorities or otherwise makes proper effort to prevent the commission of the offense.

(7) An accomplice may be convicted on proof of the commission of the offense and of his complicity therein, though the person claimed to have committed the offense has not been prosecuted or convicted or has been convicted of a different offense or degree of offense or has an immunity to prosecution or conviction or has been acquitted.

***

§ 2.08. Intoxication.

(1) Except as provided in Subsection (4) of this Section, intoxication of the actor is not a defense unless it negatives an element of the offense.

(2) When recklessness establishes an element of the offense, if the actor, due to self-induced intoxication, is unaware of a risk of which he would have been aware had he been sober, such unawareness is immaterial.

(3) Intoxication does not, in itself, constitute mental disease within the meaning of Section 4.01.

(4) Intoxication which (a) is not self-induced or (b) is pathological is an affirmative defense if by reason of such intoxication the actor at the time of his conduct lacks substantial capacity either to appreciate its criminality [wrongfulness] or to conform his conduct to the requirements of law.

(5) *Definitions.* In this Section unless a different meaning plainly is required:

(a) "intoxication" means a disturbance of mental or physical capacities resulting from the introduction of substances into the body;

(b) "self-induced intoxication" means intoxication caused by substances which the actor knowingly introduces into his body, the tendency of which to cause intoxication he know or ought to know, unless he introduces them pursuant to medical advice or under such circumstances as would afford a defense to a charge of crime;

(c) "pathological intoxication" means intoxication grossly excessive in degree, given the amount of the intoxicant, to which the actor does not know he is susceptible.

§ 2.09. Duress.

(1) It is an affirmative defense that the actor engaged in the conduct charged to constitute an offense because he was coerced to do so by the use of, or a threat to use, unlawful force against his person or the person of another, which a person of reasonable firmness in his situation would have been unable to resist.

(2) The defense provided by this Section is unavailable if the actor recklessly placed himself in a situation in which it was probable that he would be subjected to duress. The defense is also unavailable if he was negligent in placing himself in such a situation, whenever negligence suffices to establish culpability for the offense charged.

(3) It is not a defense that a woman acted on the command of her husband, unless she acted under such coercion as would establish a defense under this Section. [The presumption that a woman, acting in the presence of her husband, is coerced is abolished.]

(4) When the conduct of the actor would otherwise be justifiable under Section 3.02, this Section does not preclude such defense.

***

§ 2.11. Consent.

(1) *In General.*

The consent of the victim to conduct charged to constitute an offense or to the result thereof is a defense if such consent negatives an element of the offense or precludes the infliction of the harm or evil sought to be prevented by the law defining the offense.

(2) *Consent to Bodily Harm.*

When conduct is charged to constitute an offense because it causes or threatens bodily harm, consent to such conduct or to the infliction of such harm is a defense if:

(a) the bodily harm consented to or threatened by the conduct consented to is not serious; or

(b) the conduct and the harm are reasonably foreseeable hazards of joint participation in a lawful athletic contest or competitive sport; or

(c) the consent establishes a justification for the conduct under Article 3 of the Code.

(3) *Ineffective Consent.*

Unless otherwise provided by the Code or by the law defining the offense, assent does not constitute consent if:

(a) it is given by a person who is legally incompetent to authorize the conduct charged to constitute the offense; or

(b) it is given by a person who by reason of youth, mental disease or defect or intoxication is manifestly unable or known by the actor to be unable to make a reasonable judgment as to the nature or harmfulness of the conduct charged to constitute the offense; or

(c) it is given by a person whose improvident consent is sought to be prevented by the law defining the offense; or

(d) it is induced by force, duress or deception of a kind sought to be prevented by the law defining the offense.

***

§ 2.13. Entrapment.

(1) A public law enforcement official or a person acting in cooperation with such an official perpetrates an entrapment if for the purpose of obtaining evidence of the commission of an offense, he induces or encourages another person to engage in conduct constituting such offense by either:

    (a) making knowingly false representations designed to induce the belief that such conduct is not prohibited; or

    (b) employing methods of persuasion or inducement which create a substantial risk that such an offense will be committed by persons other than those who are ready to commit it.

(2) Except as provided in Subsection (3) of this Section, a person prosecuted for an offense shall be acquitted if he proves by a preponderance of evidence that his conduct occurred in response to an entrapment. The issue of entrapment shall be tried by the Court in the absence of the jury.

(3) The defense afforded by this Section is unavailable when causing or threatening bodily injury is an element of the offense charged and the prosecution is based on conduct causing or threatening such injury to a person other than the person perpetrating the entrapment.

ARTICLE 3. GENERAL PRINCIPLES OF JUSTIFICATION

§ 3.01. Justification an Affirmative Defense; Civil Remedies Unaffected.

(1) In any prosecution based on conduct which is justifiable under this Article, justification is an affirmative defense.

(2) The fact that conduct is justifiable under this Article does not abolish or impair any remedy for such conduct which is available in any civil action.

§ 3.02. Justification Generally: Choice of Evils.

(1) Conduct which the actor believes to be necessary to avoid harm or evil to himself or to another is justifiable, provided that:

    (a) the harm or evil sought to be avoided by such conduct is greater than that sought to be prevented by the law defining the offense charged; and

    (b) neither the Code nor other law defining the offense provides exceptions or defenses dealing with the specific situation involved; and

    (c) a legislative purpose to exclude the justification claimed does not otherwise plainly appear.

(2) When the actor was reckless or negligent in bringing about the situation requiring a choice of harms or evils or in appraising the necessity for his conduct, the justification afforded by this Section is unavailable in a prosecution for any offense for which recklessness or negligence, as the case may be, suffices to establish culpability.

§ 3.03. Execution of Public Duty.

(1) Except as provided in Subsection (2) of this Section, conduct is justifiable when it is required or authorized by:

    (a) the law defining the duties or functions of a public officer or the assistance to be rendered to such officer in the performance of his duties; or

    (b) the law governing the execution of legal process; or

    (c) the judgment or order of a competent court or tribunal; or

    (d) the law governing the armed services or the lawful conduct of war; or

    (e) any other provision of law imposing a public duty.

(2) The other sections of this Article apply to:

    (a) the use of force upon or toward the person of another for any of the purposes dealt with in such sections; and

    (b) the use of deadly force for any purpose, unless the use of such force is otherwise expressly authorized by law or occurs in the lawful conduct of war.

(3) The justification afforded by Subsection (1) of this Section applies:

    (a) when the actor believes his conduct to be required or authorized by the judgment or direction of a competent court or tribunal or in the lawful execution of legal process, notwithstanding lack of jurisdiction of the court or defect in the legal process; and

    (b) when the actor believes his conduct to be required or authorized to assist a public officer in the performance of his duties, notwithstanding that the officer exceeded his legal authority.

§ 3.04. Use of Force in Self-Protection.

(1) *Use of Force Justifiable for Protection of the Person.*
Subject to the provisions of this Section and of Section 3.09, the use of force upon or toward another person is justifiable when the actor believes that such force is immediately necessary for the purpose of protecting himself against the use of unlawful force by such other person on the present occasion.

(2) *Limitations on Justifying Necessity for Use of Force.*

    (a) The use of force is not justifiable under this Section:

        (i) to resist arrest which the actor knows is being made by a peace officer, although the arrest is unlawful; or

        (ii) to resist force used by the occupier or possessor of property or by another person on his behalf, where the actor knows that the person using the force is doing so under a claim of right to protect the property, except that this limitation shall not apply if:

            (1) the actor is a public officer acting in the performance of his duties or a person lawfully assisting him therein or a person making or assisting him therein or a person making or assisting in a lawful arrest; or

            (2) the actor has been unlawfully dispossessed of the property and is making a re-entry or recaption justified by Section 3.06; or

            (3) the actor believes that such force is necessary to protect himself against death or serious bodily harm.

(b) The use of deadly force is not justifiable under this Section unless the actor believes that such force is necessary to protect himself against death, serious bodily harm, kidnapping or sexual intercourse compelled by force or threat; nor is it justifiable if:

    (i) the actor, with the purpose of causing death or serious bodily harm, provoked the use of force against himself in the same encounter; or

    (ii) the actor knows that he can avoid the necessity of using such force with complete safety by retreating or by surrendering possession of a thing to a person asserting a claim of right thereto or by complying with a demand that he abstain from any action which he has no duty to take, except that:

        (1) the actor is not obliged to retreat from his dwelling or place of work, unless he was the initial aggressor or is assailed in his place of work by another person whose place of work the actor knows it to be; and

        (2) a public officer justified in using force in the performance of his duties or a person justified in using force in his assistance or a person justified in using force in making an arrest or preventing an escape is not obliged to desist from efforts to perform such duty, effect such arrest or prevent such escape because of resistance or threatened resistance by or on behalf of the person against whom such action is directed.

(c) Except as required by paragraphs (a) and (b) of this Subsection, a person employing protective force may estimate the necessity thereof under the circumstances as he believes them to be when the force is used, without retreating, surrendering possession, doing any other act which he has no legal duty to do or abstaining from any lawful action.

(3) *Use of Confinement as Protective Force.* The justification afforded by this Section extends to the use of confinement as protective force only if the actor takes all reasonable measures to terminate the confinement as soon as he knows that he safely can, unless the person confined has been arrested on a charge of crime.

§ 3.05. Use of Force for the Protection of Other Persons.

(1) Subject to the provisions of this Section and of Section 3.09, the use of force upon or toward the person of another is justifiable to protect a third person when:

    (a) the actor would be justified under Section 3.04 in using such force to protect himself against the injury he believes to be threatened to the person whom he seeks to protect; and

    (b) under the circumstances as the actor believes them to be, the person whom he seeks to protect would be justified in using such protective force; and

    (c) the actor believes that his intervention is necessary for the protection of such other person.

(2) Notwithstanding Subsection (1) of this Section:

    (a) when the actor would be obliged under Section 3.04 to retreat, to surrender the possession of a thing or to comply with a demand before using force in self-protection, he is not obliged to do so before using force for the protection of another person, unless he knows that he can thereby secure the complete safety of such other person; and

    (b) when the person whom the actor seeks to protect would be obliged under Section 3.04 to retreat, to surrender the possession of a thing or to comply with a demand if he knew that he could obtain complete safety by so doing, the actor is obliged to try to cause him to do so before using force in his protection if the actor knows that he can obtain complete safety in that way; and

(c) neither the actor nor the person whom he seeks to protect is obliged to retreat when in the other's dwelling or place of work to any greater extent than in his own.

§ 3.06. Use of Force for the Protection of Property.

(1) *Use of Force Justifiable for the Protection of Property.*

Subject to the provisions of this Section and of Section 3.09, the use of force upon or toward the person of another is justifiable when the actor believes that such force is immediately necessary:

(a) to prevent or terminate an unlawful entry or other trespass upon land or a trespass against or the unlawful carrying away of tangible, movable property, provided that such land or movable property is, or is believed by the actor to be, in his possession or in the possession of another person for whose protection he acts; or

(b) to effect an entry or re-entry upon land or to retake tangible movable property, provided that the actor believes that he or the person by whose authority he acts or a person from whom he or such other person derives title was unlawfully dispossessed of such land or movable property and is entitled to possession, and provided, further, that:

(i) the force is used immediately or on fresh pursuit after such dispossession; or

(ii) the actor believes that the person against whom he uses force has no claim of right to the possession of the property and, in the case of land, the circumstances, as the actor believes them to be, are of such urgency that it would be an exceptional hardship to postpone the entry or re-entry until a court order is obtained.

(2) *Meaning of Possession.*

For the purposes of Subsection (1) of this Section:

(a) a person who has parted with the custody of property to another who refuses to restore it to him is no longer in possession, unless the property is movable and was and still is located on land in his possession;

(b) a person who has been dispossessed of land does not regain possession thereof merely by setting foot thereon;

(c) a person who has a license to use or occupy real property is deemed to be in possession thereof except against the licensor acting under claim of right.

(3) *Limitations on Justifiable Use of Force.*

(a) *Request to Desist.*

The use of force is justifiable under this Section only if the actor first requests the person against whom such force is used to desist from his interference with the property, unless the actor believes that:

(i) such request would be useless; or

(ii) it would be dangerous to himself or another person to make the request; or

(iii) substantial harm will be done to the physical condition of the property which is sought to be protected before the request can effectively be made.

(b) *Exclusion of Trespasser.*

The use of force to prevent or terminate a trespass is not justifiable under this Section if the actor knows that the exclusion of the trespasser will expose him to substantial danger of serious bodily harm.

(c) *Resistance of Lawful Re-entry or Recaption.*
  The use of force to prevent an entry or re-entry upon land or the recaption of moveable property is not justifiable under this Section, although the actor believes that such re-entry or recaption is unlawful, if:

  (i) the re-entry or recaption is made by or on behalf of a person who was actually dispossessed of the property; and

  (ii) it is otherwise justifiable under paragraph (1) (b) of this Section.

(d) *Use of Deadly Force.*
  The use of deadly force is not justifiable under this Section unless the actor believes that:

  (i) the person against whom the force is used is attempting to dispossess him of his dwelling otherwise than under a claim of right to its possession; or

  (ii) the person against whom the force is used is attempting to commit or consummate arson, burglary, robbery or other felonious theft or property destruction and either:

    (1) has employed or threatened deadly force against or in the presence of the actor; or

    (2) the use of force other than deadly force to prevent the commission or the consummation of the crime would expose the actor or another in his presence to substantial danger of serious bodily harm.

(4) *Use of Confinement as Protective Force.*
  The justification afforded by this Section extends to the use of confinement as protective force only if the actor takes all reasonable measures to terminate the confinement as soon as he knows that he can do so with safety to the property, unless the person confined has been arrested on a charge of crime.

(5) *Use of Device to Protect Property.*
  The justification afforded by this Section extends to the use of a device for the purpose of protecting property only if:

  (a) the device is not designed to cause or known to create a substantial risk of causing death or serious bodily harm; and

  (b) the use of the particular device to protect the property from entry or trespass is reasonable under the circumstances, as the actor believes them to be; and

  (c) the device is one customarily used for such a purpose or reasonable care is taken to make known to probable intruders the fact that it is used.

(6) *Use of Force to Pass Wrongful Obstructor.*
  The use of force to pass a person whom the actor believes to be purposely or knowingly and unjustifiably obstructing the actor from going to a place to which he may lawfully go is justifiable, provided that:

  (a) the actor believes that the person against whom he uses force has no claim or right to obstruct the actor; and

  (b) the actor is not being obstructed from entry or movement on land which he knows to be in the possession or custody of the person obstructing him, or in the possession or custody of another person by whose authority the obstructor acts, unless the circumstances, as the actor believes them to be, are of such urgency that it would not be reasonable to postpone the entry or movement on such land until a court order is obtained; and

(c) the force used is not greater than would be justifiable if the person obstructing the actor were using force against him to prevent his passage.

§ 3.07. Use of Force in Law Enforcement.

(1) *Use of Force Justifiable to Effect an Arrest.*
   Subject to the provisions of this Section and of Section 3.09, the use of force upon or toward the person of another is justifiable when the actor is making or assisting in making an arrest and the actor believes that such force is immediately necessary to effect a lawful arrest.

(2) *Limitations on the Use of Force.*

   (a) The use of force is not justifiable under this Section unless:
      (i) the actor makes known the purpose of the arrest or believes that it is otherwise known by or cannot reasonably be made known to the person to be arrested; and
      (ii) when the arrest is made under a warrant, the warrant is valid or believed by the actor to be valid.

   (b) The use of deadly force is not justifiable under this Section unless:

      (i) the arrest is for a felony; and
      (ii) the person effecting the arrest is authorized to act as a peace officer or is assisting a person whom he believes to be authorized to act as a peace officer; and
      (iii) the actor believes that the force employed creates no substantial risk of injury to innocent persons; and
      (iv) the actor believes that:
         (1) the crime for which the arrest is made involved conduct including the use or threatened use of deadly force; or
         (2) there is a substantial risk that the person to be arrested will cause death or serious bodily harm if his apprehension is delayed.

(3) *Use of Force to Prevent Escape from Custody.*
   The use of force to prevent the escape of an arrested person from custody is justifiable when the force could justifiably have been employed to effect the arrest under which the person is in custody, except that a guard or other person authorized to act as a peace officer is justified in using any force, including deadly force, which he believes to be immediately necessary to prevent the escape of a person from a jail, prison, or other institution for the detention of persons charged with or convicted of a crime.

(4) *Use of Force by Private Person Assisting an Unlawful Arrest.*

   (a) A private person who is summoned by a peace officer to assist in effecting an unlawful arrest, is justified in using any force which he would be justified in using if the arrest were lawful, provided that he does not believe the arrest is unlawful.

   (b) A private person who assists another private person in effecting an unlawful arrest, or who, not being summoned, assists a peace officer in effecting an unlawful arrest, is justified in using any force which he would be justified in using if the arrest were lawful, provided that
      (i) he believes the arrest is lawful, and
      (ii) the arrest would be lawful if the facts were as he believes them to be.

(5) *Use of Force to Prevent Suicide or the Commission of a Crime.*

(a) The use of force upon or toward the person of another is justifiable when the actor believes

that such force is immediately necessary to prevent such other person from committing suicide, inflicting serious bodily harm upon himself, committing or consummating the commission of a crime involving or threatening bodily harm, damage to or loss of property or a breach of the peace, except that:

(i) any limitations imposed by the other provisions of this Article on the justifiable use of force in self-protection, for the protection of others, the protection of property, the effectuation of an arrest or the prevention of an escape from custody shall apply notwithstanding the criminality of the conduct against which such force is used; and

(ii) the use of deadly force is not in any event justifiable under this Subsection unless:

(1) the actor believes that there is a substantial risk that the person whom he seeks to prevent from committing a crime will cause death or serious bodily harm to another unless the commission or the consummation of the crime is prevented and that the use of such force presents no substantial risk of injury to innocent persons; or

(2) the actor believes that the use of such force is necessary to suppress a riot or mutiny after the rioters or mutineers have been ordered to disperse and warned, in any particular manner that the law may require, that such force will be used if they do not obey.

(b) The justification afforded by this Subsection extends to the use of confinement as

preventive force only if the actor takes all reasonable measure to terminate the confinement as soon as he knows that he safely can, unless the person confined has been arrested on a charge of crime.

ARTICLE 4. RESPONSIBILITY

§ 4.01. Mental Disease or Defect Excluding Responsibility.

(1) A person is not responsible for criminal conduct if at the time of such conduct as a result of mental disease or defect he lacks substantial capacity either to appreciate the criminality [wrongfulness] of his conduct or to conform his conduct to the requirements of law.

(2) As used in this Article, the terms "mental disease or defect" do not include an abnormality manifested only by repeated criminal or otherwise anti-social conduct.

§ 4.02. Evidence of Mental Disease or Defect Admissible When Relevant to Element of the Offense; [Mental Disease or Defect Impairing Capacity as Ground for Mitigation of Punishment in Capital Cases].

(1) Evidence that the defendant suffered from a mental disease or defect is admissible whenever it is relevant to prove that the defendant did or did not have a state of mind which is an element of the offense.

[(2) Whenever the jury or the Court is authorized to determine or to recommend whether or not the defendant shall be sentenced to death or imprisonment upon conviction, evidence that the capacity of the defendant to appreciate the criminality [wrongfulness] of his conduct or to conform his conduct to the requirements of law was impaired as a result of mental disease or defect is admissible in favor of sentence of imprisonment.]

§ 4.03. Mental Disease or Defect Excluding Responsibility Is Affirmative Defense; Requirement of Notice; Form of Verdict and Judgment When Finding of Irresponsibility Is Made.

(1) Mental disease or defect excluding responsibility is an affirmative defense.

(2) Evidence of mental disease or defect excluding responsibility is not admissible unless the defendant, at the time of entering his plea of not guilty or within ten days thereafter or at such later time as the Court may for good cause permit, files a written notice of his purpose to rely on such defense.

(3) When the defendant is acquitted on the ground of mental disease or defect excluding responsibility, the verdict and the judgment shall so state.

§ 4.04. Mental Disease or Defect Excluding Fitness to Proceed.

No person who as a result of mental disease or defect lacks capacity to understand the proceedings against him or to assist in his own defense shall be tried, convicted or sentenced for the commission of an offense so long as such incapacity endures.

§ 4.05. Psychiatric Examination of Defendant with Respect to Mental Disease or Defect.

(1) Whenever the defendant has filed a notice of intention to rely on the defense of mental disease or defect excluding responsibility, or there is reason to doubt his fitness to proceed, or reason to believe that mental disease or defect of the defendant will otherwise become an issue in the cause, the Court shall appoint at lease one qualified psychiatrist or shall request the Superintendent of the _____ Hospital to designate at least one qualified psychiatrist, which designation may be or include himself, to examine and report upon the mental condition of the defendant. The Court may order the defendant to be committed to a hospital or other suitable facility for the purpose of the examination for a period of not exceeding sixty days or such longer period as the Court determines to be necessary for the purpose and may direct that a qualified psychiatrist retained by the defendant be permitted to witness and participate in the examination.

(2) In such examination any method may be employed which is accepted by the medical profession for the examination of those alleged to be suffering from mental disease or defect.

(3) The report of the examination shall include the following:

(a) a description of the nature of the examination;

(b) a diagnosis of the mental condition of the defendant;

(c) if the defendant suffers from a mental disease or defect, an opinion as to his capacity to understand the proceedings against him and to assist in his own defense;

(d) when a notice of intention to rely on the defense of irresponsibility has been filed, an opinion as to the extent, if any, to which the capacity of the defendant to appreciate the [wrongfulness] of his conduct or to conform his conduct to the requirements of law was impaired at the time of the criminal conduct charged; and

(e)   when directed by the Court, an opinion as to the capacity of the defendant to have a particular state of mind which is an element of the offense charged.

If the examination cannot be conducted by reason of the unwillingness of the defendant to participate therein, the report shall so state and shall include, if possible, an opinion as to whether such unwillingness of the defendant was the result of mental disease or defect.

The report of the examination shall be filed [in triplicate] with the clerk of the Court, who shall cause copies to be delivered to the district attorney and to counsel for the defendant.

§ 4.08. Legal Effect of Acquittal on the Ground of Mental Disease or Defect Excluding Responsibility; Commitment; Release or Discharge.

(1) When a defendant is acquitted on the ground of mental disease or defect excluding responsibility, the Court shall order him to be committed to the custody of the Commissioner of Mental Hygiene [Public Health] to be placed in an appropriate institution for custody, care and treatment.

(2) If the Commissioner of Mental Hygiene [Public Health] is of the view that a person committed to his custody, pursuant to paragraph (1) of this Section, may be discharged or released on condition without danger to himself or to others, he shall make application for the discharge or release of such person in a report to the Court by which such person was committed and shall transmit a copy of such application and report to the prosecuting attorney of the county [parish] from which the defendant was committed. The Court shall thereupon appoint at least two qualified psychiatrists to examine such person and to report within sixty days, or such longer period as the Court determines to be necessary for the purpose, their opinion as to his mental condition. To facilitate such examination and the proceedings thereon, the Court may cause such person to be confined in any institution located near the place where the Court sits, which may hereafter be designated by the Commissioner of Mental Hygiene [Public Health] as suitable for the temporary detention of irresponsible persons.

(3) If the Court is satisfied by the report filed pursuant to paragraph (2) of this Section and such testimony of the reporting psychiatrists as the Court deems necessary that the committed person may be discharged or released on condition without danger to himself or others, the Court shall order his discharge or his release on such conditions as the Court determines to be necessary. If the Court is not so satisfied, it shall promptly order a hearing to determine whether such person may safely be discharged or released. Any such hearing shall be deemed a civil proceeding and the burden shall be upon the committed person to prove that he may safely be discharged or released. According to the determination of the Court upon the hearing, the committed person shall thereupon be discharged or released on such conditions as the Court determines to be necessary, or shall be recommitted to the custody of the Commissioner of Mental Hygiene [Public Health], subject to discharge or release only in accordance with the procedure prescribed above for a first hearing.

(4) If, within [five] years after the conditional release of a committed person, the Court shall determine, after hearing evidence, that the conditions of release have not been fulfilled and that for the safety of such person or for the safety of others his conditional release should be revoked, the Court shall forthwith order him to be recommitted to the Commissioner of Mental Hygiene [Public Health], subject to discharge or release only in accordance with the procedure prescribed above for a first hearing.

(5) A committed person may make application for his discharge or release to the Court by which he was committed, and the procedure to be followed upon such application shall be the same as that prescribed above in the case of an application by the Commissioner of Mental Hygiene [Public Health]. However, no such application by a committed person need be considered until he has been

confined for a period of not less than [six months] from the date of the order of commitment, and if the determination of the Court be adverse to the application, such person shall not be permitted to file a further application until [one year] has elapsed from the date of any preceding hearing on an application for his release or discharge.

§ 4.09. Statements for Purposes of Examination or Treatment Inadmissible Except on Issue of Mental Condition.

A statement made by a person subjected to psychiatric examination or treatment pursuant to Sections 4.05, 4.06 or 4.08 for purposes of such examination or treatment shall not be admissible in evidence against him in any criminal proceeding on any issue other than that of his mental condition but it shall be admissible upon that issue, whether or not it would otherwise be deemed a privileged communication [unless such statement constitutes an admission of guilt of the crime charged].

§ 4.10. Immaturity Excluding Criminal Conviction; Transfer of Proceedings to Juvenile Court.

(1) A person shall not be tried for or convicted of an offense if:

    (a) at the time of the conduct charged to constitute the offense he was less than sixteen years of age [in which case the Juvenile Court shall have exclusive jurisdiction]; or

    (b) at the time of the conduct charged to constitute the offense he was sixteen or seventeen years of age, unless:

        (i) the Juvenile Court has no jurisdiction over him, or,

        (ii) the Juvenile Court has entered an order waiving jurisdiction and consenting to the institution of criminal proceedings against him.

(2) No court shall have jurisdiction to try or convict a person of an offense if criminal proceedings against him are barred by Subsection (1) of this Section. When it appears that a person charged with the commission of an offense may be of such an age that criminal proceedings may be barred under Subsection (1) of this Section, the Court shall hold a hearing thereon, and the burden shall be on the prosecution to establish to the satisfaction of the Court that the criminal proceeding is not barred upon such grounds. If the Court determines that the proceeding is barred, custody of the person charged shall be surrendered to the Juvenile Court, and the case, including all papers and processes relating thereto, shall be transferred.

ARTICLE 5. INCHOATE CRIMES

§ 5.01. Criminal Attempt.

(1) *Definition of Attempt.* A person is guilty of an attempt to commit a crime if, acting with the kind of culpability otherwise required for commission of the crime, he:

    (a) purposely engages in conduct which would constitute the crime if the attendant circumstances were as he believes them to be; or

    (b) when causing a particular result is an element of the crime, does or omits to do anything with the purpose of causing or with the belief that it will cause such result without further conduct on his part; or

    (c) purposely does or omits to do anything which, under the circumstances as he believes them to be, is an act or omission constituting a substantial step in a course of conduct planned to culminate in his commission of the crime.

(2) *Conduct Which May Be Held Substantial Step Under Subsection (1)(c).*
Conduct shall not be held to constitute a substantial step under Subsection (1)(c) of this Section unless it is strongly corroborative of the actor's criminal purpose. Without negativing the sufficiency of other conduct, the following, if strongly corroborative of the actor's criminal purpose, shall not be held insufficient as a matter of law:

(a) lying in wait, searching for or following the contemplated victim of the crime;

(b) enticing or seeking to entice the contemplated victim of the crime to go to the place contemplated for its commission;

(c) reconnoitering the place contemplated for the commission of the crime;

(d) unlawful entry of a structure, vehicle or enclosure in which it is contemplated that the crime will be committed;

(e) possession of materials to be employed in the commission of the crime, which are specially designed for such unlawful use or which can serve no lawful purpose of the actor under the circumstances;

(f) possession, collection or fabrication of materials to be employed in the commission of the crime, at or near the place contemplated for its commission, where such possession, collection or fabrication serves no lawful purpose of the actor under the circumstances;

(g) soliciting an innocent agent to engage in conduct constituting an element of the crime.

(3) *Conduct Designed to Aid Another in Commission of a Crime.* A person who engages in conduct designed to aid another to commit a crime which would establish his complicity under Section 2.06 if the crime were committed by such other person, is guilty of an attempt to commit the crime, although the crime is not committed or attempted by such other person.

(4) *Renunciation of Criminal Purpose.* When the actor's conduct would otherwise constitute an attempt under Subsection (1)(b) or (1)(c) of this Section, it is an affirmative defense that he abandoned his effort to commit the crime or otherwise prevented its commission, under circumstances manifesting a complete and voluntary renunciation of his criminal purpose. The establishment of such defense does not, however, affect the liability of an accomplice who did not join in such abandonment or prevention.

Within the meaning of this Article, renunciation of criminal purpose is not voluntary if it is motivated, in whole or in part, by circumstances, not present or apparent at the inception of the actor's course of conduct, which increase the probability of detection or apprehension or which make more difficult the accomplishment of the criminal purpose. Renunciation is not complete if it is motivated by a decision to postpone the criminal conduct until a more advantageous time or to transfer the criminal effort to another but similar objective or victim.

§ 5.02. Criminal Solicitation.

(1) *Definition of Solicitation.* A person is guilty of solicitation to commit a crime if with the purpose of promoting or facilitating its commission he commands, encourages or requests another person to engage in specific conduct which would constitute such crime or an attempt to commit such crime or which would establish him complicity in its commission or attempted commission.

(2) *Uncommunicated Solicitation.* It is immaterial under Subsection (1) of this Section that the actor fails to communicate with the person he solicits to commit a crime if his conduct was designed to effect such communication.

(3) *Renunciation of Criminal Purpose.* It is an affirmative defense that the actor, after soliciting another person to commit a crime, persuaded him not to do so or otherwise prevented the commission of the crime, under circumstances manifesting a complete and voluntary renunciation of his criminal purpose.

§ 5.03. Criminal Conspiracy.

(1) *Definition of Conspiracy.* A person is guilty of conspiracy with another person or persons to commit a crime if with the purpose of promoting or facilitating its commission he:

    (a) agrees with such other person or persons that they or one of more of them will engage in conduct which constitutes such crime or an attempt or solicitation to commit such crime; or

    (b) agrees to aid such other person or persons in the planning or commission of such crime or of an attempt or solicitation to commit such crime.

(2) *Scope of Conspiratorial Relationship.* If a person guilty of conspiracy, as defined by Subsection (1) of this Section, knows that a person with whom he conspires to commit a crime has conspired with another person or persons to commit the same crime, he is guilty of conspiring with such other person or persons, whether or not he knows their identity, to commit such crime.

(3) *Conspiracy With Multiple Criminal Objectives.* If a person conspires to commit a number of crimes, he is guilty of only one conspiracy so long as such multiple crimes are the object of the same agreement or continuous conspiratorial relationship.

(4) *Joinder and Venue in Conspiracy Prosecutions.*

    (a) Subject to the provisions of paragraph (b) of this Subsection, two or more persons charged with criminal conspiracy may be prosecuted jointly if:

        (i) they are charged with conspiring with one another; or

        (ii) the conspiracies alleged, whether they have the same or different parties, are so related that they constitute different aspects of a scheme or organized criminal conduct.

    (b) In any joint prosecution under paragraph (a) of this Subsection:

        (i) no defendant shall be charged with a conspiracy in any county [parish or district] other than one in which he entered into such conspiracy or in which an overt act pursuant to such conspiracy was done by him or by a person with whom he conspired; and

        (ii) neither the liability of any defendant nor the admissibility against him of evidence of acts or declarations of another shall be enlarged by such joinder; and

        (iii) the Court shall order a severance or take a special verdict as to any defendant who so requests, if it deems it necessary or appropriate to promote the fair determination of his guilt or innocence, and shall take any other proper measures to protect the fairness of the trial.

(5) *Overt Act.* No person may be convicted of conspiracy to commit a crime, other than a felony of the first or second degree, unless an overt act in pursuance of such conspiracy is alleged and proved to have been done by him or by a person with whom he conspired.

(6) *Renunciation of Criminal Purpose.* It is an affirmative defense that the actor, after conspiring to commit a crime, thwarted the success of the conspiracy, under circumstances manifesting a complete and voluntary renunciation of his criminal purpose.

(7) *Duration of Conspiracy.* For purposes of Section 1.06 (4):

    (a) conspiracy is a continuing course of conduct which terminates when the crime or crimes which are its object are committed or the agreement that they be committed is abandoned by the defendant and by those with whom he conspired; and

    (b) such abandonment is presumed if neither the defendant nor anyone with whom he conspired does any overt act in pursuance of the conspiracy during the applicable period of limitation; and

(c) if an individual abandons the agreement, the conspiracy is terminated as to him only if and when he advises those with whom he conspired of his abandonment or he informs the law enforcement authorities of the existence of the conspiracy and of his participation therein.

§ 5.04. Incapacity, Irresponsibility or Immunity of Party to Solicitation or Conspiracy.

(1) Except as provided in Subsection (2) of this Section, it is immaterial to the liability of a person who solicits or conspires with another to commit a crime that:

(a) he or the person whom he solicits or with whom he conspires does not occupy a particular position or have a particular characteristic which is an element of such crime, if he believes that one of them does; or

(b) the person whom he solicits or with whom he conspires is irresponsible or has an immunity to prosecution or conviction for the commission of the crime.

(2) It is a defense to a charge of solicitation or conspiracy to commit a crime that if the criminal object were achieved, the actor would not be guilty of a crime under the law defining the offense or as an accomplice under Section 2.06 (5) or 2.06 (6)(a) or (b).

§ 5.05. Grading of Criminal Attempt, Solicitation and Conspiracy; Mitigation in Cases of Lesser Danger; Multiple Convictions Barred.

(1) *Grading.* Except as otherwise provided in this Section, attempt, solicitation and conspiracy are crimes of the same grade and degree as the most serious offense which is attempted or solicited or is an object of the conspiracy. An attempt, solicitation or conspiracy to commit a [capital crime or a] felony of the first degree is a felony of the second degree.

(2) *Mitigation.* If the particular conduct charged to constitute a criminal attempt, solicitation or conspiracy is so inherently unlikely to result or culminate in the commission of a crime that neither such conduct nor the actor presents a public danger warranting the grading of such offense under this Section, the Court shall exercise its power under Section 6.12 to enter judgment and impose sentence for a crime of lower grade or degree or, in extreme cases, may dismiss the prosecution.

(3) *Multiple Convictions.* A person may not be convicted of more than one offense defined by this Article for conduct designed to commit or to culminate in the commission of the same crime.

§ 5.06. Possessing Instruments of Crime; Weapons.

(1) *Criminal Instruments Generally.* A person commits a misdemeanor if he possesses any instrument of crime with purpose to employ it criminally. "Instrument of crime" means:

(a) anything specially made or specially adapted [sic] for criminal use; or

(b) anything commonly used for criminal purposes and possessed by the actor under circumstances which do not negative unlawful purpose.

(2) *Presumption of Criminal Purpose from Possession of Weapon.* If a person possesses a firearm or other weapon on or about his person, in a vehicle occupied by him, or otherwise readily available for use, it shall be presumed that he had the purpose to employ it criminally, unless:

(a) the weapon is possessed in the actor's home or place of business;

(b) the actor is licensed or otherwise authorized by law to possess such weapon; or

(c) the weapon is of type commonly used in lawful sport.

"Weapon" means anything readily capable of lethal use and possessed under circumstances not manifestly appropriate for lawful uses which it may have; the term includes a firearm which is not loaded or lacks a clip or other component to render it immediately operable, and components which can readily be assembled into a weapon.

(3) *Presumptions as to Possession of Criminal Instruments in Automobiles.* Where a weapon or other instrument of crime is found in an automobile, it is presumed to be in the possession of the occupant if there is but one. If there is more than one occupant, it shall be presumed to be in the possession of all, except under the following circumstances:

(a) where it is found upon the person of one of the occupants;

(b) where the automobile is not a stolen one and the weapon or instrument is found out of view in a glove compartment, car trunk, or other enclosed customary depository, in which case it shall be presumed to be in the possession of the occupant or occupants who own or have authority to operate the automobile;

(c) in the case of a taxicab, a weapon or instrument found in the passenger's portion of the vehicle shall be presumed to be in the possession of all the passengers, if there are any, and, if not, in the possession of the driver.

§ 5.07. Prohibited Offensive Weapons.

A person commits a misdemeanor if, except as authorized by law, he makes, repairs, sells, or otherwise deals in, uses or possesses any offensive weapon. "Offensive weapon" means any bomb, machine gun, sawed-off shotgun, firearm specially made or specially adapted for concealment or silent discharge, any blackjack, sandbag, metal knuckles, dagger, or other implement for the infliction of serious bodily injury which serves no common lawful purpose. It is a defense under this Section for the defendant to prove by a preponderance of evidence that he possessed or dealt with the weapon solely as a curio or in a dramatic performance, or that he possessed it briefly in consequence of having found it or taken it from an aggressor, or under circumstances similarly negativing any purpose or likelihood that the weapon would be used unlawfully. The presumptions provided in Section 5.06(3) are applicable to prosecutions under this Section.

PART II

DEFINITION OF SPECIFIC CRIMES

Offenses Involving Danger to the Person

ARTICLE 210. CRIMINAL HOMICIDE

§ 210.0. Definitions.

In Articles 210-213, unless a different meaning plainly is required:

(1) "human being" means a person who has been born and is alive;

(2) "bodily injury" means physical pain, illness or any impairment of physical condition;

(3) "serious bodily injury" means bodily injury which creates a substantial risk of death or which causes serious, permanent disfigurement, or protracted loss or impairment of the function of any bodily member or organ;

(4) "deadly weapon" means any firearm, or other weapon, device, instrument, material or substance, whether animate or inanimate, which in the manner it is used or is intended to be used is known to be capable of producing death or serious bodily injury.

§ 210.1. Criminal Homicide.

(1) A person is guilty of criminal homicide if he purposely, knowingly, recklessly or negligently causes the death of another human being.

(2) Criminal homicide is murder, manslaughter, or negligent homicide.

§ 210.2. Murder.

(1) Except as provided in Section 210.3(1)(b), criminal homicide constitutes murder when:

(a) it is committed purposely or knowingly; or

(b) it is committed recklessly under circumstances manifesting extreme indifference to the value of human life. Such recklessness and indifference are presumed if the actor is engaged or is an accomplice in the commission of, or an attempt to commit, or flight after committing, or attempting to commit robbery, rape or deviate sexual intercourse by force or threat of force, arson, burglary, kidnapping or felonious escape.

(2) Murder is a felony of the first degree [but a person convicted of murder may be sentenced to death, as provided in Section 210.6]. (The brackets are meant to reflect the fact that the Institute took no position on the desirability of the death penalty. . .)

§ 210.3. Manslaughter.

(1) Criminal homicide constitutes manslaughter when:

(a) it is committed recklessly; or

(b) a homicide which would otherwise be murder is committed under the influence of extreme mental or emotional disturbance for which there is a reasonable explanation or excuse. The reasonableness of such explanation or excuse shall be determined from the viewpoint of a person in the actor's situation under the circumstances as he believes them to be.

(2) Manslaughter is a felony of the second degree.

§ 210.4. Negligent Homicide.

(1) Criminal homicide constitutes negligent homicide when it is committed negligently.

(2) Negligent homicide is a felony of the third degree.

§ 210.5. Causing or Aiding Suicide.

(1) *Causing Suicide as a Criminal Homicide.* A person may be convicted of criminal homicide for causing another to commit suicide only if he purposely causes such suicide by force, duress or deception.

(2) *Aiding or Soliciting Suicide as an Independent Offense.* A person who purposely aids or solicits another to commit suicides is guilty of a felony of the second degree if his conduct causes such suicide or an attempted suicide, and otherwise of a misdemeanor.

(1) *Death Sentence Excluded.* When a defendant is found guilty of murder, the Court shall impose sentence for a felony of the first degree if it is satisfied that:

(a) none of the aggravation circumstances enumerated in Subsection (3) of this Section was established by the evidence at the trial or will be established if further proceedings are initiated under Subsection (2) of this Section; or

(b) substantial mitigating circumstances, established by the evidence at the trial, call for leniency; or

(c) the defendant, with the consent of the prosecuting attorney and the approval of the Court, pleaded guilty to murder as a felony of the first degree; or

(d) the defendant was under 18 years of age at the time of the commission of the crime; or

(e) the defendant's physical or mental condition calls for leniency; or

(f) although the evidence suffices to sustain the verdict, it does not foreclose all doubt respecting the defendant's guilt.

(2) *Determination by Court or by Court and Jury.* Unless the Court imposes sentence under Subsection (1) of this Section, it shall conduct a separate proceeding to determine whether the defendant should be sentenced for a felony of the first degree or sentenced to death. The proceeding shall be conducted before the Court alone if the defendant was convicted by a Court sitting without a jury or upon his plea of guilty or if the prosecuting attorney and the defendant waive a jury with respect to sentence. In other cases it shall be conducted before the Court sitting with the jury which determined the defendant's guilt or, if the Court for good cause shown discharges that jury, with a new jury empaneled for the purpose.

In the proceeding, evidence may be presented as to any matter that the Court deems relevant to sentence, including but not limited to the nature and circumstances of the crime, the defendant's character, background, history, mental and physical condition and any of the aggravating or mitigating circumstances enumerated in Subsections (3) and (4) of this Section. Any such evidence not legally privileged, which the Court deems to have probative force, may be received, regardless of its admissibility under the exclusionary rules of evidence, provided that the defendant's counsel is accorded a fair opportunity to rebut any hearsay statements. The prosecuting attorney and the defendant or his counsel shall be permitted to present argument for or against sentence of death.

The determination whether sentence of death shall be imposed shall be in the discretion of the Court, except that when the proceeding is conducted before the Court sitting with a jury, the Court shall not impose sentence of death unless it submits to the jury the issue whether the defendant should be sentenced to death or to imprisonment and the jury returns a verdict that the sentence should be death. If the jury is unable to reach a unanimous verdict, the Court shall dismiss the jury and impose sentence for a felony of the first degree.

The Court, in exercising its discretion as to sentence, and the jury, in determining upon its verdict, shall take into account the aggravating and mitigating circumstances enumerated in Subsections (3) and (4) and any other facts that it deems relevant, but it shall not impose or recommend sentence of death unless it finds one of the aggravating circumstances enumerated in Subsection (3) and further finds that there are no mitigating circumstances sufficiently substantial to call for leniency. When the issue is submitted to the jury, the Court shall so instruct and also shall inform the jury of the nature of the sentence of imprisonment that may be imposed, including its implication with respect to possible release upon parole, if the jury verdict is against sentence of death.

Alternative formulation of Subsection (2):

(2) *Determination by Court.* Unless the Court imposes sentence under Subsection (1) of this Section, it shall conduct a separate proceeding to determine whether the defendant should be sentenced for a felony of the first degree or sentenced to death. In the proceeding, the Court, in

accordance with Section 7.07, shall consider the report of the presentence investigation and, if a psychiatric examination has been ordered, the report of such examination. In addition, evidence may be presented as to any matter that the Court deems relevant to sentence, including but not limited to the nature and circumstances of the crime, the defendant's character, background, history, mental and physical condition and any of the aggravating or mitigating circumstances enumerated in Subsections (3) and (4) of this Section. Any such evidence not legally privileged, which the Court deems to have probative force, may be received, regardless of its admissibility under the exclusionary rules of evidence, provided that the defendant's counsel is accorded a fair opportunity to rebut any hearsay statements. The prosecuting attorney and the defendant or his counsel shall be permitted to present argument for or against sentence of death.

The determination whether sentence of death shall be imposed shall be in the discretion of the Court. In exercising such discretion, the Court shall take into account the aggravating and mitigating circumstances enumerated in Subsections (3) and (4) and any other facts that it deems relevant but shall not impose sentence of death unless it finds one of the aggravating circumstances enumerated in Subsection (3) and further finds that there are no mitigating circumstances sufficiently substantial to call for leniency.

(3) *Aggravating Circumstances.*

(a) The murder was committed by a convict under sentence of imprisonment.

(b) The defendant was previously convicted of another murder or of a felony involving the use or threat of violence to the person.

(c) At the time the murder was committed the defendant also committed another murder.

(d) The defendant knowingly created a great risk of death to many persons.

(e) The murder was committed while the defendant was engaged or was an accomplice in the commission of, or an attempt to commit, or flight after committing or attempting to commit robbery, rape or deviate sexual intercourse by force or threat of force, arson, burglary or kidnapping.

(f) The murder was committed for the purpose of avoiding or preventing a lawful arrest or effecting an escape from lawful custody.

(g) The murder was committed for pecuniary gain.

(h) The murder was especially heinous, atrocious or cruel, manifesting exceptional depravity.

(4) *Mitigating Circumstances.*

(a) The defendant has no significant history of prior criminal activity.

(b) The murder was committed while the defendant was under the influence of extreme mental or emotional disturbance.

(c) The victim was a participant in the defendant's homicidal conduct or consented to the homicidal act.

(d) The murder was committed under circumstances which the defendant believed to provide a moral justification or extenuation for his conduct.

(e) The defendant was an accomplice in a murder committed by another person and his participation in the homicidal act was relatively minor.

(f) The defendant acted under duress or under the domination of another person.

(g) At the time of the murder, the capacity of the defendant to appreciate the criminality [wrongfulness] of his conduct or to conform his conduct to the requirements of law was impaired as a result of mental disease or defect or intoxication.

(h) The youth of the defendant at the time of the crime.

ARTICLE 211. ASSAULT; RECKLESS ENDANGERING; THREATS

§ 211.0. Definitions.

In this Article, the definitions given in Section 210.0 apply unless a different meaning plainly is required.

§ 211.1. Assault.

(1) *Simple Assault.* A person is guilty of assault if he:

    (a) attempts to cause or purposely, knowingly or recklessly causes bodily injury to another; or

    (b) negligently causes bodily injury to another with a deadly weapon; or

    (c) attempts by physical menace to put another in fear of imminent serious bodily injury.

Simple assault is a misdemeanor unless committed in a fight or scuffle entered into by mutual consent, in which case it is a petty misdemeanor.

(2) *Aggravated Assault.* A person is guilty of aggravated assault if he:

    (a) attempts to cause serious bodily injury to another, or causes such injury purposely, knowingly or recklessly under circumstances manifesting extreme indifference to the value of human life; or

    (b) attempts to cause or purposely or knowingly causes bodily injury to another with a deadly weapon.

Aggravated assault under paragraph (a) is a felony of the second degree; aggravated assault under paragraph (b) is a felony of the third degree.

§ 211.2. Recklessly Endangering Another Person.

A person commits a misdemeanor if he recklessly engages in conduct which places or may place another person in danger of death or serious bodily injury. Recklessness and danger shall be presumed where a person knowingly points a firearm at or in the direction of another, whether or not the actor believed the firearm to be loaded.

§ 211.3. Terroristic Threats.

A person is guilty of a felony of the third degree if he threatens to commit any crime of violence with purpose to terrorize another or to cause evacuation of a building, place of assembly, or facility of public transportation, or otherwise to cause serious public inconvenience, or in reckless disregard of the risk of causing such terror or inconvenience.

ARTICLE 212. KIDNAPPING AND RELATED OFFENSES; COERCION

§ 212.0. Definitions.

In this Article, the definitions given in section 210.0 apply unless a different meaning plainly is required.

§ 212.1. Kidnapping.

A person is guilty of kidnapping if he unlawfully removes another from his place of residence or business, or a substantial distance from the vicinity where he is found, or if he unlawfully confines another for a substantial period in a place of isolation, with any of the following purposes:

    (a) to hold for ransom or reward, or as a shield or hostage; or

    (b) to facilitate commission of any felony or flight thereafter; or

    (c) to inflict bodily injury on or to terrorize the victim or another; or

    (d) to interfere with the performance of any governmental or political function.

Kidnapping is a felony of the first degree unless the actor voluntarily releases the victim alive and in a safe place prior to trial, in which case it is a felony of the second degree. A removal or confinement is unlawful within the meaning of this Section if it is accomplished by force, threat or deception, or, in the case of a person who is under the age of 14 or incompetent, if it is accomplished without the consent of a parent, guardian or other person responsible for general supervision of his welfare.

§ 212.2 Felonious Restraint.

A person commits a felony of the third degree if he knowingly:

    (a) restrains another unlawfully in circumstances exposing him to risk of serious bodily injury; or

    (b) holds another in a condition of involuntary servitude.

§ 212.3. False Imprisonment.

A person commits a misdemeanor if he knowingly restrains another unlawfully so as to interfere substantially with his liberty.

§ 212.4. Interference with Custody.

    (1) *Custody of Children.* A person commits an offense if he knowingly or recklessly takes or entices any child under the age of 18 from the custody of its parent, guardian or other lawful custodian, when he has no privilege to do so. It is an affirmative defense that:

        (a) the actor believed that his action was necessary to preserve the child from danger to its welfare; or

        (b) the child, being at the time not less than 14 years old, was taken away at its own instigation without enticement and without purpose to commit a criminal offense with or against the child.

Proof that the child was below the critical age gives rise to a presumption that the actor knew the child's age or acted in reckless disregard thereof. The offense is a misdemeanor unless the actor, not being a parent or person in equivalent relation to the child, acted with knowledge that his conduct would cause serious alarm for the child's safety, or in reckless disregard of a likelihood of causing such alarm, in which case the offense is a felony of the third degree.

    (2) *Custody of Committed Persons.* A person is guilty of a misdemeanor if he knowingly or recklessly takes or entices any committed person away from lawful custody when he is not privileged to do so. "Committed person" means, in addition to anyone committed under juvenile warrant, any orphan, neglected or delinquent child, mentally defective or insane person, or other dependent or incompetent person entrusted to another's custody by or through a recognized social agency or otherwise by authority of law.

§ 212.5. Criminal Coercion.

(1) *Offense Defined.* A person is guilty of criminal coercion if, with purpose unlawfully to restrict another's freedom of action to his detriment, he threatens to:

    (a) commit any criminal offense; or

    (b) accuse anyone of a criminal offense; or

    (c) expose any secret tending to subject any person to hatred, contempt or ridicule, or to impair his credit or business repute; or

    (d) take or withhold action as an official, or cause an official to take or withhold action.

It is an affirmative defense to prosecution based on paragraphs (b), (c) or (d) that the actor believed the accusation or secret to be true or the proposed official action justified and that his purpose was limited to compelling the other to behave in a way reasonably related to the circumstances which were the subject of the accusation, exposure or proposed official action, as by desisting from further misbehavior, making good a wrong done, refraining from taking any action or responsibility for which the actor believes the other disqualified.

(2) *Grading.* Criminal coercion is a misdemeanor unless the threat is to commit a felony or the actor's purpose is felonious, in which cases the offense is a felony of the third degree.

ARTICLE 213. SEXUAL OFFENSES.

§ 213.0. Definitions.

In this Article, unless a different meaning plainly is required:

(1) the definitions given in Section 210.0 apply;

(2) "sexual intercourse" includes intercourse per os or per anum, with some penetration however slight; emission is not required;

(3) "deviate sexual intercourse" means sexual intercourse per os or per anum between human beings who are not husband and wife, and any form of sexual intercourse with an animal.

§ 213.1. Rape and Related Offenses.

(1) *Rape.* A male who has sexual intercourse with a female not his wife is guilty of rape if:

    (a) he compels her to submit by force or by threat of imminent death, serious bodily injury, extreme pain or kidnapping, to be inflicted on anyone; or

    (b) he has substantially impaired her power to appraise or control her conduct by administering or employing without her knowledge drugs, intoxicants or other means for the purpose of preventing resistance; or

    (c) the female is unconscious; or

    (d) the female is less than 10 years old.

Rape is a felony of the second degree unless

    (i) in the course thereof the actor inflicts serious bodily injury upon anyone, or

    (ii) the victim was not a voluntary social companion of the actor upon the occasion of the crime and had not previously permitted him sexual liberties, in which cases the offenses is a felony of the first degree.

(2) *Gross Sexual Imposition.* A male who has intercourse with a female not his wife commits a felony of the third degree if:

(a) he compels her to submit by any threat that would prevent resistance by a woman of ordinary resolution; or

(b) he knows that she suffers from a mental disease or defect which renders her incapable of appraising the nature of her conduct; or

(c) he knows that she is unaware that a sexual act is being committed upon her or that she submits because she mistakenly supposes that he is her husband.

§ 213.2. Deviate Sexual Intercourse by Force or Imposition.

(1) *By Force or Its Equivalent.*

A person who engages in deviate sexual intercourse with another person, or who causes another to engage in deviate sexual intercourse, commits a felony of the second degree if:

(a) he compels the other person to participate by force or by threat of imminent death, serious bodily injury, extreme pain or kidnapping, to be inflicted on anyone; or

(b) he has substantially impaired the other person's power to appraise or control his conduct, by administering or employing without the knowledge of the other person drugs, intoxicants or other means for the purpose of preventing resistance; or

(c) the other person is unconscious; or

(d) the other person is less than 10 years old.

(2) *By Other Imposition.*

A person who engages in deviate sexual intercourse with another person, or who causes another to engage in deviate sexual intercourse, commits a felony of the third degree if:

(a) he compels the other person to participate by any threat that would prevent resistance by a person of ordinary resolution; or

(b) he knows that the other person suffers from a mental disease or defect which renders him incapable of appraising the nature of his conduct; or

(c) he knows that the other person submits because he is unaware that a sexual act is being committed upon him.

§ 213.3. Corruption of Minors and Seduction.

(1) *Offense Defined.* A male who has sexual intercourse with a female not his wife, or any person who engages in deviate sexual intercourse or causes another to engage in deviate sexual intercourse, is guilty of an offense if:

(a) the other person is less than [16] years old and the actor is at least [4] years older than the other person; or

(b) the other person is less than 21 years old and the actor is his guardian or otherwise responsible for general supervision of his welfare; or

(c) the other person is in custody of law or detained in a hospital or other institution and the actor has supervisory or disciplinary authority over him; or

(d) the other person is a female who is induced to participate by a promise of marriage which the actor does not mean to perform.

(2) *Grading.* An offense under paragraph (a) of Subsection (1) is a felony of the third degree. Otherwise an offense under this section is a misdemeanor.

§ 213.4. Sexual Assault.

A person who has sexual contact with another not his spouse, or causes such other to have sexual contact with him, is guilty of sexual assault, a misdemeanor, if:

(1) he knows that the conduct is offensive to the other person; or

(2) he knows that the other person suffers from a mental disease or defect which renders him or her incapable of appraising the nature of his or her conduct; or

(3) he knows that the other person is unaware that a sexual act is being committed; or

(4) the other person is less than 10 years old; or

(5) he has substantially impaired the other person's power to appraise or control his or her conduct, by administering or employing without the other's knowledge drugs, intoxicants or other means for the purpose of preventing resistance; or

(6) the other person is less than [16] years old and the actor is at least [four] years older than the other person; or

(7) the other person is less than 21 years old and the actor is his guardian or otherwise responsible for general supervision of his welfare; or

(8) the other person is in custody of law or detained in a hospital or other institution and the actor has supervisory or disciplinary authority over him.

Sexual contact is any touching of the sexual or other intimate parts of the person for the purpose of arousal or gratifying sexual desire.

§ 213.5. Indecent Exposure.

A person commits a misdemeanor if, for the purpose of arousing or gratifying sexual desire of himself or of any person other than his spouse, he exposes his genitals under circumstances in which he knows his conduct is likely to cause affront or alarm.

§ 213.6. Provisions Generally Applicable to Article 213.

(1) *Mistake as to Age.* Whenever in this Article the criminality of conduct depends on a child's being below the age of 10, it is no defense that the actor did not know the child's age, or reasonably believed the child to be older than 10. When criminality depends on the child's being below a critical age other than 10, it is a defense for the actor to prove by a preponderance of the evidence that he reasonably believed the child to be above the critical age.

(2) *Spouse Relationships.* Whenever in this Article the definition of an offense excludes conduct with a spouse, the exclusion shall be deemed to extend to persons living as man and wife, regardless of the legal status of their relationship. The exclusion shall be inoperative as respects spouses living apart under a decree of judicial separation. Where the definition of an offense excludes conduct with a spouse or conduct by a woman, this shall not preclude conviction of a spouse or woman as accomplice in a sexual act which he or she causes another person, not within the exclusion, to perform.

(3) *Sexually Promiscuous Complainants.* It is a defense to prosecution under Section 213.3, and paragraphs (6), (7) and (8) of Section 213.4 for the actor to prove by a preponderance of the evidence that the alleged victim had, prior to the time of the offense charged, engaged promiscuously in sexual relations with others.

(4) *Prompt Complaint.* No prosecution may be instituted or maintained under this Article unless the alleged offense was brought to the notice of public authority within [3] months of its occurrence or, where the alleged victim was less than [16] years old or otherwise incompetent to make complaint, within [3] months after a parent, guardian or other competent person specially interested in the victim learns of the offense.

(5) *Testimony of Complainants.* No person shall be convicted of any felony under this Article upon the uncorroborated testimony of the alleged victim. Corroboration may be circumstantial. In any prosecution before a jury for an offense under this Article, the jury shall be instructed to evaluate the testimony of a victim or complaining witness with special care in view of the emotional involvement of the witness and the difficulty of determining the truth with respect to alleged sexual activities carried out in private.

OFFENSES AGAINST PROPERTY

ARTICLE 220. ARSON, CRIMINAL MISCHIEF, AND OTHER PROPERTY DESTRUCTION

§ 220.1. Arson and Related Offenses.

(1) *Arson.* A person is guilty of arson, a felony of the second degree, if he starts a fire or causes an explosion with the purpose of:

(a) destroying a building or occupied structure of another; or

(b) destroying or damaging any property, whether his own or another's to collect insurance for such loss. It shall be an affirmative defense to prosecution under this paragraph that the actor's conduct did not recklessly endanger any building or occupied structure of another or place any other person in danger of death or bodily injury.

(2) *Reckless Burning or Exploding.* A person commits a felony of the third degree if he purposely starts a fire or causes an explosion, whether on his own property or another's, and thereby recklessly:

(a) places another person in danger of death or bodily injury; or

(b) places a building or occupied structure of another in danger of damage or destruction.

(3) *Failure to Control or Report Dangerous Fire.* A person who knows that a fire is endangering life or a substantial amount of property of another and fails to take reasonable measures to put out or control the fire, when he can do so without substantial risk to himself, or to give a prompt fire alarm, commits a misdemeanor if:

(a) he knows that he is under an official, contractual, or other legal duty to prevent or combat the fire; or

(b) the fire was started, albeit lawfully, by him or with his assent, or on property in his custody or control.

(4) *Definitions.* "Occupied structure" means any structure, vehicle or place adapted for overnight accommodation or persons, or for carrying on business therein, whether or not a person is actually present. Property is that of another, for the purposes of this section, if anyone other than the actor has a possessory or proprietary interest therein. If a building or structure is divided into separately occupied units, any unit not occupied by the actor is an occupied structure of another.

§ 220.2. Causing or Risking Catastrophe.

(1) *Causing Catastrophe.* A person who causes a catastrophe by explosion, fire, flood, avalanche, collapse of building, release of poison gas, radioactive material or other harmful or destructive force or substance, or by any other means of causing potentially widespread injury or damage, commits a felony of the second degree if he does so purposely or knowingly, or a felony of the third degree if he does so recklessly.

(2) *Risking Catastrophe.* A person is guilty of a misdemeanor if he recklessly creates a risk of catastrophe in the employment of fire, explosives or other dangerous means listed in Subsection (1).

(3) *Failure to Prevent Catastrophe.* A person who knowingly or recklessly fails to take reasonable measures to prevent or mitigate a catastrophe commits a misdemeanor if:

    (a) he knows that he is under an official, contractual or other legal duty to take such measures; or

    (b) he did or assented to the act causing or threatening the catastrophe.

§ 220.3. Criminal Mischief.

(1) *Offense Defined.* A person is guilty of criminal mischief if he:

    (a) damages tangible property of another purposely, recklessly, or by negligence in the employment of fire, explosives, or other dangerous means listed in Section 220.2 (1); or

    (b) purposely or recklessly tampers with tangible property of another so as to endanger person or property; or

    (c) purposely or recklessly causes another to suffer pecuniary loss by deception or threat.

(2) *Grading.* Criminal mischief is a felony of the third degree if the actor purposely causes pecuniary loss in excess of $5,000 or a substantial interruption or impairment of public communication, transportation, supply of water, gas or power, or other public service. It is a misdemeanor if the actor purposely causes pecuniary loss in excess of $100, or a petty misdemeanor if he purposely or recklessly causes pecuniary loss in excess of $25. Otherwise criminal mischief is a violation.

ARTICLE 221. BURGLARY AND OTHER CRIMINAL INTRUSION.

§ 221.0. Definitions.

In this Article, unless a different meaning plainly is required:

(1) "occupied structure" means any structure, vehicle or place adapted for overnight accommodation of persons, or for carrying on business therein, whether or not a person is actually present.

(2) "night" means the period between thirty minutes past sunset and thirty minutes before sunrise.

§ 221.1. Burglary.

(1) *Burglary Defined.* A person is guilty of burglary if he enters a building or occupied structure, or separately secured or occupied portion thereof, with purpose to commit a crime therein, unless the premises are at the time open to the public or the actor is

licensed or privileged to enter. It is an affirmative defense to prosecution for burglary that the building or structure was abandoned.

(2) *Grading.* Burglary is a felony of the second degree if it is perpetrated in the dwelling of another at night, or if, in the course of committing the offense, the actor:

   (a) purposely, knowingly or recklessly inflicts or attempts to inflict bodily injury on anyone; or

   (b) is armed with explosives or a deadly weapon.
   An act shall be deemed "in the course of committing" an offense if it occurs in an attempt to commit the offense or in flight after the attempt or commission.

(3) *Multiple Convictions.* A person may not be convicted both for burglary and for the offense which it was his purpose to commit after the burglarious entry or for an attempt to commit that offense, unless the additional offense constitutes a felony of the first or second degree.

§ 221.2. Criminal Trespass.

(1) *Buildings and Occupied Structures.* A person commits an offense if, knowing that he is not licensed or privileged to do so, he enters or surreptitiously remains in any building or occupied structure, or separately secured or occupied portion thereof. An offense under this Subsection is a misdemeanor if it is committed in a dwelling at night. Otherwise it is a petty misdemeanor.

(2) *Defiant Trespasser.* A person commits an offense if, knowing that he is not licensed or privileged to do so, he enters or remains in any place as to which notice against trespass is given by:

   (a) actual communication to the actor; or

   (b) posting in a manner prescribed by law or reasonably likely to come to the attention of intruders; or

   (c) fencing or other enclosure manifestly designed to exclude intruders.

An offense under this Subsection constitutes a petty misdemeanor if the offender defies an order to leave personally communicated to him by the owner of the premises or other authorized person. Otherwise it is a violation.

(3) *Defenses.* It is an affirmative defense to prosecution under this Section that:

   (a) a building or occupied structure involved in an offense under Subsection (1) was abandoned; or

   (b) the premises were at the time open to members of the public and the actor complied with all lawful conditions imposed on access to or remaining in the premises; or

   (c) the actor reasonably believed that the owner of the premises, or other person empowered to license access thereto, would have licensed him to enter or remain.

ARTICLE 222. ROBBERY

§ 222.1. Robbery

(1) *Robbery Defined.* A person is guilty of robbery if, in the course of committing a theft, he:

   (a) inflicts serious bodily injury upon another; or

(b) threatens another with or purposely puts him in fear of immediate serious bodily injury; or

(c) commits or threatens immediately to commit any felony of the first or second degree.

An act shall be deemed "in the course of committing a theft" if it occurs in an attempt to commit theft or in flight after the attempt or commission.

(2) *Grading.* Robbery is a felony of the second degree, except that it is a felony of the first degree if in the course of committing the theft the actor attempts to kill anyone, or purposely inflicts or attempts to inflict serious bodily injury.

ARTICLE 223. THEFT AND RELATED OFFENSES

§ 223.0. Definitions.

In this Article, unless a different meaning plainly is required:

(1) "deprive" means:

(a) to withhold property of another permanently or for so extended a period as to appropriate a major portion of its economic value, or with intent to restore only upon payment of reward or other compensation; or

(b) to dispose of the property so as to make it unlikely that the owner will recover it.

(2) "financial institution" means a bank, insurance company, credit union, building and loan association, investment trust or other organization held out to the public as a place of deposit of funds or medium savings or collective investment.

(3) "government" means the United States, any State, county, municipality, or other political unit, or any department, agency or subdivision of any of the foregoing, or any corporation or other association carrying out the functions of government.

(4) "movable property" means property the location of which can be changed, including things growing on, affixed to, or found in land, and documents although the rights represented thereby have no physical location. "Immovable property" is all other property.

(5) "obtain" means:

(a) in relation to property, to bring about a transfer or purported transfer of a legal interest in the property, whether to the obtainer or another; or

(b) in relation to labor or service, to secure performance thereof.

(6) "property" means anything of value, including real estate, tangible and intangible personal property, contract rights, choses-in-action and other interests in or claims to wealth, admission or transportation tickets, captured or domestic animals, food and drink, electric or other power.

(7) "property of another" includes property in which any person other than the actor has an interest which the actor is not privileged to infringe, regardless of the fact that the actor also has an interest in the property and regardless of the fact that the other person might be precluded from civil recovery because the property was used in an unlawful transactions or was subject to forfeiture as contraband. Property in possession of the actor shall not be deemed property of another who has only a security interest therein, even if legal title is in the creditor pursuant to a conditional sales contract or other security agreement.

§ 223.1. Consolidation of Theft Offenses; Grading; Provisions Applicable to Theft Generally.

(1) *Consolidation of Theft Offenses.* Conduct denominated theft in this Article constitutes a single offense. An accusation of theft may be supported by evidence that it was committed in any manner that would be theft under this Article, notwithstanding the specification of a different manner in the indictment or information, subject only to the power of the Court to ensure fair trial by granting a continuance or other appropriate relief where the conduct of the defense would be prejudiced by lack of fair notice or by surprise.

(2) *Grading of Theft Offenses.*

(a) Theft constitutes a felony of the third degree if the amount involved exceeds $500, or if the property stolen is a firearm, automobile, airplane, motorcycle, motorboat or other motor-propelled vehicle, or in the case of theft by receiving stolen property, if the receiver is in the business of buying or selling stolen property.

(b) Theft not within the preceding paragraph constitutes a misdemeanor, except that if the property was not taken from the person or by threat, or in breach of a fiduciary obligation, and the actor proves by a preponderance of the evidence that the amount involved was less than $50, the offense constitutes a petty misdemeanor.

(c) The amount involved in a theft shall be deemed to be the highest value, by any reasonable standard, of the property or services which the actor stole or attempted to steal. Amounts involved in thefts committed pursuant to one scheme or course of conduct, whether from the same person or several persons, may be aggregated in determining the grade or the offense.

(3) *Claim of Right.* It is an affirmative defense to prosecution for theft that the actor:

(a) was unaware that the property or service was that of another; or

(b) acted under an honest claim of right to the property or service involved or that he had a right to acquire or dispose of it as he did; or

(c) took property exposed for sale, intending to purchase and pay for it promptly, or reasonably believing that the owner, if present, would have consented.

(4) *Theft from Spouse.* It is no defense that theft was from the actor's spouse, except that misappropriation of household and personal effects, or other property normally accessible to both spouses, is theft only if it occurs after the parties have ceased living together.

§ 223.3. Theft by Unlawful Taking or Disposition.

(1) *Movable Property.* A person is guilty of theft if he unlawfully takes, or exercises unlawful control over, movable property of another with purpose to deprive him thereof.

(2) *Immovable Property.* A person is guilty of theft if he unlawfully transfers immovable property of another or any interest therein with purpose to benefit himself or another not entitled thereto.

§ 223.3. Theft by Deception.

A person is guilty of theft if he purposely obtains property of another by deception. A person deceives if he purposely:

(1) creates or reinforces a false impression, including false impression as to law, value, intention or other state of mind; but deception as to a person's intentions to perform a promise shall not be inferred from the fact alone that he did not subsequently perform the promise; or

(2)   prevents another from acquiring information which would affect his judgment of a transaction; or

(3)   fails to correct a false impression which the deceiver previously created or reinforced, or which the deceiver knows to be influencing another to whom he stands in a fiduciary or confidential relationship; or

(4)   fails to disclose a known lien, adverse claim or other legal impediment to the enjoyment of property which he transfers or encumbers in consideration for the property obtained, whether such impediment is or is not valid, or is or is not a matter of official record.

The term "deceive" does not, however, include falsity as to matters having no pecuniary significance, or puffing by statements unlikely to deceive ordinary persons in the group addressed.

§ 223.4. Theft by Extortion.

A person is guilty of theft if he obtains property of another by threatening to:

(1)   inflict bodily injury on anyone or commit any other criminal offense; or

(2)   accuse anyone of a criminal offense; or

(3)   expose any secret tending to subject any person to hatred, contempt or ridicule, or to impair his credit or business repute; or

(4)   take or withhold action as an official, or cause an official to take or withhold action; or

(5)   bring about or continue a strike, boycott or other collective unofficial action, if the property is not demanded or received for the benefits of the group in whose interest the actor purports to act; or

(6)   testify or provide information or withhold testimony or information with respect to another's legal claim or defense; or

(7)   inflict any other harm which would not benefit the actor.

It is an affirmative defense to prosecution based on paragraphs (2), (3) or (4) that the property obtained by threat of accusation, exposure, lawsuit or other invocation of official action was honestly claimed as restitution or indemnification for harm down in the circumstances to which such accusation, exposure, lawsuit or other official action relates, or as compensation for property or lawful services.

§ 223.5. Theft of Property Lost, Mislaid, or Delivered by Mistake.

A person who comes into control of property of another that he knows to have been lost, mislaid, or delivered under a mistake as to the nature or amount of the property or the identity of the recipient is guilty of theft if, with purpose to deprive the owner thereof, he fails to take reasonable measures to restore the property to a person entitled to have it.

§ 223.6. Receiving Stolen Property.

(1)   *Receiving.* A person is guilty of theft if he purposely receives, retains, or disposes of moveable property of another knowing that it has been stolen, or believing that it has probably been stolen, unless the property is received, retained, or disposed with purpose to restore it to the owner. "Receiving" means acquiring possession, control or title, or lending on the security of the property.

(2) *Presumption of Knowledge.* The requisite knowledge or belief is presumed in the case of a dealer who:

    (a) is found in possession or control of property stolen from two or more persons on separate occasions; or

    (b) has received stolen property in another transaction within the year preceding the transaction charged; or

    (c) being a dealer in property of the sort received, acquires it for a consideration which he knows is far below its reasonable value.

"Dealer" means a person in the business of buying or selling goods including a pawnbroker.

§ 223.7. Theft of Services.

(1) A person is guilty of theft if he purposely obtains services which he knows are available only for compensation, by deception or threat, or by false token or other means to avoid payment for the service. "Services" include labor, professional service, transportation, telephone or other public service, accommodation in hotels, restaurants or elsewhere, admission to exhibitions, use of vehicles or other movable property. Where compensation for service is ordinarily paid immediately upon the rendering for such service, as is the case of hotels and restaurants, refusal to pay or absconding without payment or offer to pay gives rise to a presumption that the service was obtained by deception as to intention to pay.

(2) A person commits theft if, having control over the disposition of service, of others, to which he is not entitled, he knowingly diverts such services to his own benefit or to the benefit of another not entitled thereto.

§ 223.8. Theft by Failure to Make Required Disposition of Funds Received.

A person who purposely obtains property upon agreement, or subject to a known legal obligation, to make specified payment or other disposition, whether from such property or its proceeds or from his own property to be reserved in equivalent amount, is guilty of theft if he deals with the property obtained as his own and fails to make the required payment or disposition. The foregoing applies notwithstanding that it may be impossible to identify particular property as belonging to the victim at the time of the actor's failure to make the required payment or disposition. An officer or employee of the government or of a financial institution is presumed:

    (i) to know any legal obligation relevant to his criminal liability under this Section, and

    (ii) to have dealt with the property as his own if he fails to pay or account upon lawful demand, or if an audit reveals a shortage or falsification of accounts.

ARTICLE 224. FORGERY AND FRAUDULENT PRACTICES

§ 224.0. Definitions.

In this Article, the definitions given in Section 223.0 apply unless a different meaning plainly is required.

§ 224.1. Forgery.

    (1) *Definition.* A person is guilty of forgery if, with purpose to defraud or injure anyone, or with knowledge that he is facilitating a fraud or injury to be perpetrated by anyone, the actor:

(a) alters any writing of another without his authority; or

(b) makes, completes, executes, authenticates, issues or transfers any writing so that it purports to be the act of another who did not authorize that act, or to have been executed at a time or place or in a numbered sequence other than was in fact the case, or to be a copy of an original when no such original existed; or

(c) utters any writing which he knows to be forged in a manner specified in paragraphs (a) or (b). "Writing" includes printing or any other method of recording information, money, coins, tokens, stamps, seals, credit cards, badges, trademarks, and other symbols of value, right, privilege, or identification.

(2) *Grading.* Forgery is a felony of the second degree if the writing is or purports to be part of an issue of money, securities, postage or revenue stamps, or other instruments issued by the government, or part of an issue of stock, bonds or other instruments representing interest in or claims against any property or enterprise. Forgery is a felony of the third degree if the writing is or purports to be a will, deed, contract, release, commercial instrument, or other document evidencing, creating, transferring, altering, terminating, or otherwise affecting legal relations. Otherwise forgery is a misdemeanor.

§ 224.5. Bad Checks.

A person who issues or passes a check or similar sight order for the payment of money, knowing that it will not be honored by the drawee, commits a misdemeanor. For the purposes of this Section as well as in any prosecution for theft committed by means of a bad check, an issuer is presumed to know that the check or order (other than a postdated check or order) would not be paid, if:

(1) the issuer had no account with the drawee at the time the check or order was issued; or

(2) payment was refused by the drawee for lack of funds, upon presentation within 30 days after issue, and the issuer failed to make good within 10 days after receiving notice of that refusal.

§ 224.8. Commercial Bribery and Breach of Duty to Act Disinterestedly.

(1) A person commits a misdemeanor if he solicits, accepts or agrees to accept any benefit as consideration for knowingly violating or agreeing to violate a duty of fidelity to which he is subject as:

(a) partner, agent or employee of another;

(b) trustee, guardian, or other fiduciary;

(c) lawyer, physician, accountant, appraiser, or other professional adviser or informant;

(d) officer, director, manager or other participant in the direction of the affairs of an incorporated or unincorporated association; or

(e) arbitrator or other purportedly disinterested adjudicator or referee.

(2) A person who holds himself out to the public as being engaged in the business of making disinterested selection, appraisal, or criticism of commodities or services commits a misdemeanor if he solicits, accepts or agrees to accept any benefit to influence his selection, appraisal or criticism.

(3) A person commits a misdemeanor if he confers, or offers or agrees to confer, any benefit the acceptance of which would be criminal under this Section.

OFFENSES AGAINST THE FAMILY

ARTICLE 230. OFFENSES AGAINST THE FAMILY

§ 230.1. Bigamy and Polygamy.

(1) *Bigamy.* A married person is guilty of bigamy, a misdemeanor, if he contracts or purports to contract another marriage, unless at the time of the subsequent marriage:

    (a) the actor believes that the prior spouse is dead; or

    (b) the actor and the prior spouse have been living apart for five consecutive years throughout which the prior spouse was not known by the actor to be alive; or

    (c) a Court has entered a judgment purporting to terminate or annul any prior disqualifying marriage, and the actor does not know that judgment to be invalid; or

    (d) the actor reasonably believes that he is legally eligible to remarry.

(2) *Polygamy.* A person is guilty of polygamy, a felony of the third degree, if he marries or cohabits with more than one spouse at a time in purported exercise of the right of plural marriage. The offense is a continuing one until all cohabitation and claim of marriage with more than one spouse terminates. This Sections does not apply to parties to a polygamous marriage, lawful in the country of which they are residents or nationals, while they are in transit through or temporarily visiting this State.

(3) *Other Party to Bigamous or Polygamous Marriage.* A person is guilty of bigamy or polygamy, as the case may be, if he contracts or purports to contract marriage with another knowing that the other is thereby committing bigamy or polygamy.

§ 230.2. Incest.

A person is guilty of incest, a felony of the third degree, if he knowingly marries or cohabits or has sexual intercourse with an ancestor or descendant, a brother or sister of whole or half blood [or an uncle, aunt, nephew or niece of whole blood]. "Cohabit" means to live together under the representation or appearance of being married. The relationships referred to herein include blood relationships without regard to legitimacy, and relationship of parent and child by adoption.

§ 230.4. Endangering Welfare of Children.

A parent, guardian, or other person supervising the welfare of a child under 18 commits a misdemeanor if he knowingly endangers the child's welfare by violating a duty of care, protection or support.

§ 230.5. Persistent Non-Support.

A person commits a misdemeanor if he persistently fails to provide support which he can provide and which he knows he is legally obliged to provide to a spouse, child or other dependent.

OFFENSES AGAINST PUBLIC ADMINISTRATION

ARTICLE 240. BRIBERY AND CORRUPT INFLUENCE

§ 240.0. Definitions

In Articles 240-243, unless a different meaning plainly is required:

(1) "benefit" means gain or advantage, or anything regarded by the beneficiary as gain or advantage, including benefit to any other person or entity in whose welfare he is

interested, but not an advantage promised generally to a group or class of voters as a consequence of public measures which a candidate engages to support or oppose;

(2) "government" includes any branch, subdivision or agency of the government of the State or any locality within it;

(3) "harm" means loss, disadvantage or injury, or anything so regarded by the person affected, including loss, disadvantage or injury to any other person or entity in whose welfare he is interested;

(4) "official proceeding" means a proceeding heard or which may be heard before any legislative, judicial, administrative or other governmental agency or official authorized to take evidence under oath, including any referee, hearing examiner, commissioner, notary or other person taking testimony or deposition in connection with any such proceeding;

(5) "party official" means a person who holds an elective or appointive post in a political party in the United States by virtue of which he directs or conducts, or participates in directing or conducting party affairs at any level of responsibility;

(6) "pecuniary benefit" is benefit in the form of money, property, commercial interests or anything else the primary significance of which is economic gain;

(7) "public servant" means any officer or employee of government, including legislators and judges, and any person participating as juror, advisor, consultant or otherwise, in performing a governmental function; but the term does not include witnesses;

(8) "administrative proceeding" means any proceeding, other than a judicial proceeding, the outcome of which is required to be based on a record or documentation prescribed by law, or in which law or regulation is particularized in application to individuals.

§ 240.1. Bribery in Official and Political Matters.

A person is guilty of bribery, a felony of the third degree, if he offers, confers or agrees to confer upon another, or solicits, accepts or agrees to accept from another:

(1) any pecuniary benefit as consideration for the recipient's decision, opinion, recommendation, vote or other exercise of discretion as a public servant, party official or voter; or

(2) any benefit as consideration for the recipient's decision, vote, recommendation or other exercise of official discretion in a judicial or administrative proceeding; or

(3) any benefit as consideration for a violation of a known legal duty as public servant or party official.

It is no defense to prosecution under this section that a person whom the actor sought to influence was not qualified to act in the desired way whether because he had not yet assumed office, or lacked jurisdiction, or for any other reason.

§ 240.2. Threats and Other Improper Influence in Official and Political Matters.

(1) *Offenses Defined.* A person commits an offense if he:
  (a) threatens unlawful harm to any person with purpose to influence his decision, opinion, recommendation, vote or other exercise of discretion as a public servant, party official or voter; or
  (b) threatens harm to any public servant with purpose to influence his decision, opinion, recommendation, vote or pecuniary benefit as consideration for exerting

special influence upon a public servant or procuring another to do so. "Special influence" means power to influence through kinship, friendship or other relationship, apart from the merits of the transaction.

. . .

(3) *Paying for Endorsement or Special Influence.* A person commits a misdemeanor if he offers, confers or agrees to confer any pecuniary benefit receipt of which is prohibited by this Section.

ARTICLE 241. PERJURY AND OTHER FALSIFICATION IN OFFICIAL MATTERS

§ 241.0. Definitions.

In this Article, unless a different meaning plainly is required:

(1) the definitions given in Section 240.0 apply; and

(2) "statement" means any representation, but includes a representation of opinion, belief or other state of mind only if the representation clearly relates to state of mind apart from or in addition to any facts which are the subject of the representation.

§ 241.1. Perjury.

(1) *Offense Defined.* A person is guilty of perjury, a felony of the third degree, if in any official proceeding he makes a false statement under oath or equivalent affirmation, or swears or affirms the truth of a statement previously made, when the statement is material and he does not believe it to be true.

(2) *Materiality.* Falsification is material, regardless of the admissibility of the statement under rules of evidence, if it could have affected the course or outcome of the proceeding. It is no defense that the declarant mistakenly believed the falsification to be immaterial. Whether a falsification is material in a given factual situation is a question of law.

(3) *Irregularities No Defense.* It is not a defense to prosecution under this Section that the oath or affirmation was administered or taken in an irregular manner or that the declarant was not competent to make the statement. A document purporting to be made upon oath or affirmation at any time when the actor presents it as being so verified shall be deemed to have been duly sworn or affirmed.

(4) *Retraction.* No person shall be guilty of an offense under this Section if he retracted the falsification in the course of the proceeding in which it was made before it became manifest that the falsification substantially affected the proceeding.

(5) *Inconsistent Statements.* Where the defendant made inconsistent statements under oath or equivalent affirmation, both having been made within the period of the statute of limitations, the prosecution may proceed by setting forth the inconsistent statements in a single count alleging in the alternative that one or the other was false and not believed by the defendant. In such case it shall not be necessary for the prosecution to prove which statement was false but only that one or the other was false and not believed by the defendant to be true.

(6) *Corroboration.* No person shall be convicted of an offense under the Section where proof of falsity rests solely upon contradiction by testimony of a single person other than the defendant.

§ 241.2. False Swearing.

(1) *False Swearing in Official Matters.* A person who makes a false statement under oath or equivalent affirmation, or swears or affirms the truth of such a statement previously made, when he does not believe the statement to be true, is guilty of a misdemeanor if:

    (a) the falsification occurs in an official proceeding; or

    (b) the falsification is intended to mislead a public servant in performing his official function.

OFFENSES AGAINST PUBLIC ORDER AND DECENCY

ARTICLE 250. RIOT, DISORDERLY CONDUCT, AND RELATED OFFENSES.

§ 250.1. Riot; Failure to Disperse.

(1) *Riot.* A person is guilty of riot, a felony of the third degree, if he participates with [two] or more others in a course of disorderly conduct:

    (a) with purpose to commit or facilitate the commission of a felony or misdemeanor;

    (b) with purpose to prevent or coerce official action; or

    (c) when the actor or any other participant to the knowledge of the actor uses or plans to use a firearm or other deadly weapon.

(2) *Failure of Disorderly Persons to Disperse Upon Official Order.* Where [three] or more persons are participating in a course of disorderly conduct likely to cause substantial harm or serious inconvenience, annoyance or alarm, a peace officer or other public servant engaged in executing or enforcing the law may order the participants and others in the immediate vicinity to disperse. A person who refuses or knowingly fails to obey such an order commits a misdemeanor.

§ 250.2. Disorderly Conduct.

(1) *Offense Defined.* A person is guilty of disorderly conduct if, with purpose to cause public inconvenience, annoyance or alarm, or recklessly creating a risk thereof, he:

    (a) engages in fighting or threatening, or in violent or tumultuous behavior; or

    (b) makes unreasonable noise or offensively coarse utterance, gesture or display, or addresses abusive language to any person present; or

    (c) creates a hazardous or physically offensive condition by any act which serves no legitimate purpose of the actor.

"Public" means affecting or likely to affect persons in a place to which the public or a substantial group has access; among the places included are highways, transport facilities, schools, prisons, apartment houses, places of business or amusement, or any neighborhood.

(2) *Grading.* An offense under this section is a petty misdemeanor if the actor's purpose is to cause substantial harm or serious inconvenience, or if he persists in disorderly conduct after reasonable warning or request to desist. Otherwise disorderly conduct is a violation.

§ 250.4. Harassment.

A person commits a petty misdemeanor if, with purpose to harass another, he:

(1) makes a telephone call without purpose of legitimate communication; or

(2) insults, taunts or challenges another in a manner likely to provoke violent or disorderly response; or

(3) makes repeated communications anonymously or at extremely inconvenient hours, or in offensively coarse language; or

(4) subjects another to an offensive touching; or

(5) engages in any other course of alarming conduct serving no legitimate purpose of the actor.

§ 250.5. Public Drunkenness; Drug Incapacitation.

A person is guilty of an offense if he appears in any public place manifestly under the influence of alcohol, narcotics or other drugs, not therapeutically administered, to the degree that he may endanger himself or other persons or property, or annoy persons in his vicinity. An offense under this Section constitutes a petty misdemeanor if the actor has been convicted hereunder twice before within a period of one year. Otherwise the offense constitutes a violation.

§ 250.6. Loitering or Prowling.

A person commits a violation if he loiters or prowls in a place, at a time, or in a manner not usual for law-abiding individuals under circumstances that warrant alarm for the safety of persons or property in the vicinity. Among the circumstances which may be considered in determining whether such alarm is warranted is the fact that the actor takes flight upon appearance of a peace officer, refuses to identify himself, or manifestly endeavors to conceal himself or any object. Unless flight by the actor or other circumstances makes it impracticable, a peace officer shall prior to any arrest for an offense under this Section afford the actor an opportunity to dispel any alarm which would otherwise be warranted, by requesting him to identify himself and explain his presence and conduct. No person shall be convicted of an offense under this Section if the peace officer did not comply with the preceding sentence, or if it appears at trial that the explanation given by the actor was true and, if believed by the peace officer at the time, would have dispelled the alarm.

ARTICLE 251. PUBLIC INDECENCY

§ 251.1. Open Lewdness.

A person commits a petty misdemeanor if he does any lewd act which he knows is likely to be observed by others who would be affronted or alarmed.

(1) *Prostitution.* A person is guilty of prostitution, a petty misdemeanor, if he or she:

(a) is an inmate of a house of prostitution or otherwise engages in sexual activity as a business; or

(b) loiters in or within view of any public place for the purpose of being hired to engage in sexual activity.

"Sexual activity" includes homosexual and other deviate sexual relations. A "house of prostitution" is any place where prostitution or promotion of prostitution is regularly carried on by one person under the control, management or supervision of another. An "inmate" is a person who engages in prostitution in or through the agency of a house of prostitution. "Public place" means any place to which the public or any substantial group thereof has access.

(2) *Promoting Prostitution.* A person who knowingly promotes prostitution of another commits a misdemeanor or felony as provided in Subsection (3). The following acts shall, without limitation of the foregoing, constitute promoting prostitution:

(a) owning, controlling, managing, supervising or otherwise keeping, alone or in association with others, a house of prostitution or a prostitution business; or

(b) procuring an inmate for a house of prostitution or a place in a house of prostitution for one who would be an inmate; or

(c) encouraging, inducing, or otherwise purposely causing another to become or remain a prostitute; or

(d) soliciting a person to patronize a prostitute; or

(e) procuring a prostitute for a patron; or

(f) transporting a person into or within this state with purpose to promote that person's engaging in prostitution, or procuring or paying for transportation with that purpose; or

(g) leasing or otherwise permitting a place controlled by the actor, alone or in association with others, to be regularly used for prostitution or the promotion of prostitution, or failure to make reasonable effort to abate such use by ejecting the tenant, notifying law enforcement authorities, or other legally available means; or

(h) soliciting, receiving, or agreeing to receive any benefit for doing or agreeing to do anything forbidden by this Subsection.

(3) *Grading of Offenses Under Subsection (2).* An offense under Subsection (2) constitutes a felony of the third degree if:

(a) the offense falls within paragraph (a), (b) or (c) of Subsection (2); or

(b) the actor compels another to engage in or promote prostitution; or

(c) the actor promotes prostitution of a child under 16, whether or not he is aware of the child's age; or

(d) the actor promotes prostitution of his wife, child, ward or any person for whose care, protection or support he is responsible.

Otherwise the offense is a misdemeanor.

(4) *Presumption from Living off Prostitutes.* A person, other than the prostitute or the prostitute's minor child or other legal dependent incapable of self-support, who is supported in whole or substantial part by the proceeds of prostitution is presumed to be knowingly promoting prostitution in violation of Subsection (2).

(5) *Patronizing Prostitutes.* A person commits a violation if he hires a prostitute to engage in sexual activity with him, or if he enters or rcmains in a house of prostitution for the purpose of engaging in sexual activity.

(6) *Evidence.* On the issue whether a place is a house of prostitution the following shall be admissible evidence; its general repute; the repute of the persons who reside in or frequent the place; the frequency, timing and duration of visits by non-residents. Testimony of a person against his spouse shall be admissible to prove offenses under this Section.

§ 251.3. Loitering to Solicit Deviate Sexual Relations.

A person is guilty of a petty misdemeanor if he loiters in or near any public place for the purpose of soliciting or being solicited to engage in deviate sexual relations.

§ 251.4. Obscenity.

(1) *Obscene Defined.* Material is obscene if, considered as a whole, its predominant appeal is to prurient interest, that is, a shameful or morbid interest, in nudity, sex or excretion, and if in addition it goes substantially beyond customary limits of candor in describing or representing such matters. Predominant appeal shall be judged with reference to ordinary adults unless it appears from the character of the material or the circumstances of its dissemination to be designed for children or other specially susceptible audience. Undeveloped photographs, molds, printing plates, and the like, shall be deemed obscene notwithstanding that processing or other acts may be required to make the obscenity patent or to disseminate it.

(2) *Offenses.* Subject to the affirmative defense provided in Subsection (3), a person commits a misdemeanor if he knowingly or recklessly:

   (a) sells, delivers or provides, or offers or agrees to sell, deliver or provide, any obscene writing, picture, record or other representation or embodiment of the obscene; or

   (b) presents or directs an obscene play, dance or performance, or participates in that portion thereof which makes it obscene; or

   (c) publishes, exhibits or otherwise makes available any obscene material; or

   (d) possesses any obscene material for purposes of sale or other commercial dissemination; or

   (e) sells, advertises or otherwise commercially disseminates material, whether or not obscene, by representing or suggesting that it is obscene.

A person who disseminates or possesses obscene material in the course of his business is presumed to do so knowingly or recklessly.

(3) *Justifiable and Non-Commercial Private Dissemination.* It is an affirmative defense to prosecution under this Section that dissemination was restricted to:

   (a) institutions or persons having scientific, educational, governmental or other similar justification for possessing obscene material; or

   (b) non-commercial dissemination to personal associates of the actor.

(4) *Evidence; Adjudication of Obscenity.* In any prosecution under this Section, evidence shall be admissible to show:

   (a) the character of the audience for which the material was designed or to which it was directed;

   (b) what the predominant appeal of the material would be for ordinary adults or any special audience to which it was directed, and what effect, if any, it would probably have on conduct of such people;

   (c) artistic, literary, scientific, educational or other merits or the material;

   (d) the degree of public acceptance of the material in the United States;

   (e) appeal to prurient interest, or absence thereof, in advertising or other promotion of the material; and

   (f) the good repute of the author, creator, publisher or other person from whom the material originated.

Expert testimony and testimony of the author, creator, publisher or other person from whom the material originated, relating to factors entering into the determination of the issue of obscenity, shall be admissible. The Court shall dismiss a prosecution for obscenity if it is satisfied that the material is not obscene.

GLOSSARY

Abandoned property: Once an item is discarded, an owner loses a reasonable expectation of privacy in that item and it can be searched and seized without a warrant

Absolute decision: Forcing an eyewitness to confirm or deny a suspect is the perpetrator by showing one photograph at a time rather than six photographs simultaneously in a photo array

Absolute immunity: Judges, prosecutors, and defense counsel are protected from civil lawsuits for harm flowing from the performance of their professional duties.

Accessory after the fact: One who helped a principal party after the commission of the crime

Accessory before the fact: One who helped a principal party plan to commit a crime but who was not present during its commission

Acquit: To be found not guilty after a jury trial

Actual innocence: A defendant's claim that to he is "innocent" of a crime for which he has been convicted

Actual possession: Exercising dominion and control over contraband

Actus reus: A wrongful act; criminal responsibility attaches upon concurrence of *actus reus* with *mens rea* (a guilty mind)

Administrative regulations: Rules and guidelines enacted to fulfill the legislature's broad grant of authority to meet the administrative agency's public mission

Admissible evidence: Evidence that the judge has decided may be told or shown to the jury

Admission: Acknowledgment by the suspect or defendant that he committed one or more elements of the crime

Adversarial system: American justice is based on the prosecutor and defense acting as opponents as a way to learn the truth

Advice and consent: Legislative check on the executive branch to prevent the president from appointing a mere figurehead to a position of federal power

Affidavit: Written and sworn document signed under the pains and penalties of perjury

Affirm: An appellate court's decision to uphold a lower court's decision

Affirmative defense: A defense raised that, if successfully presented, may lead to a reduction or complete negation of criminal liability

Aggravated assault and battery: Assault that an offender commits while in the commission of another crime or against a victim who is a member of a protected class, such as a child, a law enforcement officer, or a prison employee

Aggravating circumstances: Those factors making the crime unusually heinous and perhaps warranting a more severe punishment; makes offenders death eligible in capital punishment trials

ALI substantial capacity test: Defendant may be found legally insane if at the time of the crime he lacked "substantial capacity either to appreciate the criminality of his conduct or to conform his conduct to the requirements of the law."

Alibi: A complete defense that states that the defendant could not have committed the crime because he was at a location other than the crime scene when the crime was committed

Alford plea: A plea in which the defendant does not admit that he or she is guilty of the crime charged but admits that the government has sufficient evidence to sustain a conviction if the defendant chooses to go to trial

Allocution: The defendant's right to address the court before sentence is imposed

AMBER alert system: Nationwide system using media outlets to alert the public that a child has been abducted and to be on the lookout

Anonymous tip: Information about a crime that has occurred or may soon occur, delivered to law enforcement by a person who does not reveal his or her identity. Standing alone, an anonymous tip is insufficient to establish probable cause; if the anonymous information is corroborated with independent evidence, the tip may be considered part of the probable cause determination.

Antiterrorism and Effective Death Penalty Act of 1996 (AEDPA): Shortened the time for, and the number of, *habeas corpus* petitions filed on behalf of prisoners

Appellant: The one seeking the appeal

Appellate court: A higher court that reviews a lower court's proceedings

Appellee: The one trying to maintain the case outcome

Appreciate the criminality of his conduct: *Mens rea* standard that applies to the defenses of infancy and insanity to assign the appropriate level of criminal culpability

Arraignment: Court hearing where the defendant enters a plea to the charges

Arrest: Deprivation of liberty

Arrest warrant: Required to seize someone not in public

Arson: The malicious and unlawful burning of structures and/or property

Article I of the Constitution: Grants Congress (House of Representatives and Senate) the power to make laws

Article II of the Constitution: Grants the executive branch (president and federal agencies) the power to enforce the laws

Article III of the Constitution: Creates one U.S. Supreme Court and grants federal courts the power to hear cases

Assault: An aggressive action that places the victim in fear of an imminent battery; certain specific physical attacks are also defined as assaults

Assumption of the duty: Voluntary undertaking of a course of action on behalf of someone else, such as a bystander helping an accident victim

Attempt: An intent to commit a crime, or an act taken to commit the crime, without the crime having been completed

Attendant circumstances: Those fact-specific situations that surround a crime (e.g., time of day, age of victim) that may help define the crime and its punishment

Attorney–client privilege: Protects as confidential the communication between the attorney and client

Automobile exception: Warrantless search of a private vehicle for contraband based on probable cause

Bail: Collateral (cash, property, assets) pledged before trial, usually by a suspect, his family, or friends, to secure his release and ensure attendance at trial

Battered woman syndrome: A subset of self-defense defined by a repeated cycle of physical abuse that causes the victim to live in constant fear of being beaten, maimed, or killed; today the phrase used more often is "battering and its effects"

Battery: Intentional and unconsented touching that is harmful or offensive

Beyond a reasonable doubt: The legal standard at a criminal trial by which the prosecution has to prove each and every element of the crime to establish the defendant's guilt

Bifurcated trial: In death penalty cases, first minitrial determines whether the defendant is innocent of first-degree murder; if not, case proceeds to second minitrial, where the jury decides whether to impose a life without parole or death sentence

Bill of Rights: The first ten amendments to the U.S. Constitution guaranteeing civil liberties

Bitcoin: A type of cryptocurrency, money represented by computer transactions

Booking: The taking of personal information of a suspect after arrest

Body cavity search: An invasive search of the mouth, anus, or vagina

Border searches: A type of warrantless search; people crossing the border have a lesser expectation of privacy because no one has an absolute right to enter the country

Breach of the peace: A type of disorderly conduct

Breaking and entering: Changing a structure (four walls and a roof) to enter unlawfully

Bribery: The offering, receiving, or soliciting of anything of value to influence official action or the discharge of a legal or public duty

Burden of persuasion: The burden of convincing the trier of fact (judge or jury) that the legal claim or defense is valid

Burden of production: The burden of introducing a legally sufficient quantum of evidence to permit the trier of fact (judge or jury) to consider the issue or defense during their deliberations

Burden of proof: The prosecution's obligation to introduce enough evidence to overcome the presumption (belief) that the defendant is innocent

Burglary: Breaking and entering into a structure with the intent to commit a felony once inside; the breaking may be achieved through fraud and deceit rather than by physical force

Capital punishment: Government-sanctioned homicide as a punishment for the crime of first-degree murder

Case brief: Process of organizing information from reading case law

Case law: Judicial opinions written by judges deciding cases before them

Catfishing: Posing as someone else online

Causation: Three-part test: (1) factual cause (but for?); (2) proximate cause (was the harm foreseeable?); (3) intervening cause (is there something external to the offender breaking the causal chain from the offender's conduct to the ultimate harm?)

Chain of custody: Tracks the physical evidence from its initial discovery to its presentation at trial

Challenge for cause: During jury selection, an argument made to the judge that a potential juror cannot be fair and impartial in deciding the case

Charge bargaining: The practice of dropping the more serious charges against a defendant in exchange for a defendant's guilty plea to a lesser charge

Charge conference: A meeting during which the lawyers for both sides submit proposed jury instructions to the judge on the basis of the evidence introduced at trial

Child sex abuse: Children cannot consent to sexual activity; any such activity is deemed sex abuse

Chilling effect: The impact of vague laws that repress free speech rights by making people fear criminal reprisal for the content of their speech

Circumstantial evidence: Indirect evidence from which the jury must infer (conclude) that the defendant is guilty as charged

Clean Air Act (CAA): Legislation that sets goals and standards for the quality and purity of U.S. air

Clean Water Act (CWA): Legislation that set goals and standards for the quality and purity of U.S. water

Clear and present danger: A risk posed to public safety by certain speech or conduct that incites immediate lawlessness; the government has the legal authority to suppress such speech and conduct

Closed containers: Any bags, luggage, Tupperware containers, purses, briefcases, or other items that are closed and may be searched for contraband and evidence

Closing argument: The prosecutor and defense counsels' final arguments to the jury to persuade the jury to find in their favor; arguments by counsel are not evidence

Collateral order doctrine: An exception that allows appeals before a final judgment

Collective knowledge: At the time of a search or seizure, all information known to all law enforcement and shared with officers on the scene

Color of law: Government action that occurs under the cloak of legal authority. A "color of law" claim alleges that a government official misused his or her power while acting in an official capacity

Commerce Clause: Article I, Section 8, Clause 3 of the Constitution, conferring jurisdiction on the federal government to prosecute crimes when the alleged criminal activity substantially affects interstate commerce

Common enterprise: The legal doctrine holding all occupants in a vehicle liable for all contraband found and seized inside

Common law: Judge-made law based on societal custom and tradition

Compelling state interest: Minimum legal justification for public health, safety, and welfare required for the government to interfere with personal liberties

Competency: The ability to understand the nature of the trial proceedings and to assist defense counsel required of defendants at all stages of the criminal proceeding, from arrest to execution

Computer crime: Using a computer to perpetrate fraud or infect other computers

Concurrence: The simultaneous presence of two or more conditions; the concurrence of *mens rea* and *actus reus* generates criminal liability for an offense

Concurrent jurisdiction: Simultaneous federal and state power to hear a case, even though only one sovereign (government) typically prosecutes the case

Concurrent sentences: Sentences imposed on one offender on conviction of many crimes that run at the same time

Conditional plea: A guilty plea entered on the "condition" that the defendant preserves certain issues on appeal, such as the legality of the judge's ruling on the suppression of evidence

Confession: A statement by which the suspect or defendant accepts full responsibility for the crime charged

Conflict theory: Crime theory that posits the powerful in society use criminal justice agencies against the weak

Confrontation Clause: The Sixth Amendment of the Constitution, which gives defendants the right to see, hear, and confront (cross-examine) all witnesses against them in open court

Consecutive sentences: Sentences imposed on one offender on conviction of many crimes that run one after the other (e.g., sentence A runs for 5 years, then sentence B starts to run)

Consent: An individual's voluntary grant of authority; a defense based on the victim's willing participation in the crime

Consolidated theft statute: Combining common law theft crimes into one, catch-all statute

Conspiracy: An agreement by two or more people, often accompanied by an overt act, to commit a crime

Constructive possession: A set of circumstances from which a jury could infer that an offender had dominion and control over contraband, even if it was not in his physical possession

Content-based regulations: Unlawful for the government to suppress speech based on its content, though the government can suppress unprotected speech

Conversion: Illegally making another person's property one's own

Copyright: A right granted by statute to the creator of a literary or artistic work for a limited period to publish or copy the work

Corpus delicti: The body of the crime

Counterfeit: An item of value that purports to be real, but is not

Crimes against the public: Crimes that offend society's collective sense of ethical behavior, such as prostitution, gambling, and drug and alcohol offenses

Criminal law: Government defined acts worthy of punishment

Criminal mischief: Defacing property, including damaging the integrity of the property

Criminal procedure: Laws that guide the criminal trial and appeal process

Cross-examination: Close-ended leading questions that can be answered yes or no

Cruel and unusual: Punishment prohibited by the Eighth Amendment

Cryptocurrency: Money represented by computer transactions

Curtilage: The area immediately surrounding a structure in which a resident retains an expectation of privacy

Custodial interrogation: A session during which a suspect is not free to leave the police presence and is subject to questioning designed to elicit incriminating information. Police are required to give *Miranda* warnings prior to beginning custodial interrogation

Custody: A situation in which a suspect perceives that he or she is not free to leave, even if not formally under arrest

Cyberbullying: Using electronic devices to continually harass victims to cause emotional harm

Cyberstalking: Using electronic devices to continually contact, monitor, and surveil victims

Cycle of violence: An early way to describe battering and its effects

Dark Web: Encrypted Internet service provider that hides users' true identity to buy and sell illicit goods

Daubert test: Five-part analysis determining the admissibility of expert testimony in federal court

Deadly weapon: An item used in any manner to cause serious bodily injury or death

Deadly weapon doctrine: A standard that allows a jury to infer that the defendant had the specific intent to kill if he used a deadly weapon during the commission of a crime

Death qualification: Sitting a jury in a capital murder case where potential jurors must commit to seriously considering life without parole and the death penalty as punishment

Defense of others: A defense that a defendant may claim if he came to the aid of another in peril and if self-defense would be justified on the part of the person in peril

Defense of property: May not use deadly force to protect property with no threat to human life

Deliberate elicitation: Unlawful when the government places an informant near a suspect represented by counsel to "deliberately elicit" incriminating statements, such as asking "Why did you do it?"

Deliberations: The decision-making process in which the jury engages to determine whether or not the accused is innocent

Delusion: A false fixed belief; commonly held by mentally ill offenders

Demonstrative evidence: Illustrative evidence, such as a map, diagram, photograph, or model, used to help the jury understand the witness's testimony

Derivative evidence: Fruit from a tree that has been poisoned by an initial illegal act in securing evidence that triggers the exclusionary rule

Determinate sentencing: A sentence imposed for a fixed period of time

Deterrence: Punishing offenders, or passing laws that guarantee certain penalties for crimes, as a warning to would-be criminals that crime does not pay

Deviate sexual intercourse: Unlawful sexual activity often involving minor children

Diminished capacity: A defense maintaining that the functioning of an offender's brain at the time he or she committed an offense was impaired

Direct evidence: Tangible items and witness testimony tending to prove a fact in the case

Direct examination: Open-ended questions that invite the witness to do all of the talking

Dirtbox: A cell site simulator that mimics cell phone tower signals to intercept information from nearby cell phones

Discovery: The pretrial exchange of evidence between the prosecution and defense

Disorderly conduct: Conduct that disturbs the public order

Disturbing the peace: Conduct that tends to disrupt the community by its noise

DNA collection: Government search and seizure; may happen on conviction without a warrant

Dog sniff: A procedure involving dogs trained to seek out drugs, bombs, or other contraband by smell and alert their handlers to the presence of these items. A dog sniff does not count as a search, but may establish probable cause.

Driving checkpoint: Brief, investigatory stop to check for driver impairment, not to search the vehicle for drugs

Driving under the influence: The crime of impaired driving established by a specific level of blood alcohol content

Drug and alcohol offenses: Crimes related to the legal or illegal use or abuse of substances

Drug testing: Warrantless searches of people whose special status means that they have fewer rights to privacy than other people

Dual court system: Trial and appellate courts at both state and federal levels

Due process: Clause found in the Fifth and Fourteenth amendments that guarantees fair treatment by the government

Duress: A defense claiming that a person committed a crime because of force or a threat of force. Duress is never a defense to murder.

Duty by contract: A relationship created by contract that defines legal obligations between two or more parties, such as landlord/lessee or employer/employee

Duty by relationship: A legal obligation created by family relationships defined by marriage, birth, or adoption

Duty by statute: A legal obligation imposed by law (e.g., remain at the scene of an automobile accident)

Eighth Amendment: Prohibits cruel and unusual punishments, excessive bails and fines

Element: Each part of a crime—the prohibited act(s) and the required mental state (except for strict liability crimes)—that must be proven to the jury for a finding of guilt

Embezzlement: Lawfully acquiring another's property and converting it for personal use

Entrapment: A defense based on government inducement to commit a crime that the defendant was not otherwise predisposed to commit

Environmental crimes: Crimes that punish polluters for tainting the country's air and water supply and land resources

Environmental Protection Agency (EPA): Executive branch agency of the federal government responsible for enforcing environmental laws

Espionage: The surreptitious gathering and transmitting of U.S. national security information on behalf of a foreign power

Establishment Clause: The government cannot interfere with the establishment of religion pursuant to the First Amendment. The *Lemon* test is used to ensure laws remain secular and do not foster an excessive entanglement with religion.

Equal protection: The Fourteenth Amendment clause that mandates equal treatment for all under the law

Evolving standards of decency: The legal standard by which the U.S. Supreme Court removes certain defendants (e.g., juveniles who kill, and intellectually disabled offenders) from eligibility for the death penalty

Excessive force: All force used to seize people (arrest) is guided by the Fourth Amendment's reasonableness clause

Exclusionary rule: A judge-made rule that excludes from trial evidence seized in violation of the Constitution (e.g., evidence taken in violation of the Fourth Amendment ban on unreasonable search and seizure, the Fifth Amendment prohibition against compelled self-incrimination, or the Sixth Amendment right to counsel)

Exculpatory evidence: Evidence tending to exonerate (prove the innocence of) the accused

Exercise Clause: The government cannot prohibit the free exercise of religion pursuant to the First Amendment, although people may not harm and kill others and claim religious freedom.

Exhaustion of remedies: The process a convicted defendant must go through to finish all available levels of legal review before a higher court entertains an appeal

Exigent circumstances: Emergencies that require fast action on the part of law enforcement to prevent the dissipation or disappearance of evidence or to help those in need

Expert witness: A witness, usually with particular expertise, who can testify about his opinion on an ultimate issue at trial on the basis of his knowledge, training, and experience; different rules apply when insanity is raised as a defense

Expungement: The sealing or destroying of a defendant's criminal record

Expressive conduct: Meant to communicate ideas such as burning the flag or a cross; protected free speech

Extortion: Blackmail; threatening to ruin the victim's reputation or business unless the victim gives the offender something of value

Eyewitness identification: Eyewitness identifies the defendant as the perpetrator. Such identifications hold great influence over juries, but may be unreliable.

Facially deficient: If by looking at the face of a warrant a reasonable officer can tell the warrant is legally deficient, she may be personally liable if she executes the defective warrant.

Facially valid: A law or warrant that appears legal "on its face"

Factual cause: The underlying reason for the ultimate harm; "but for" (if not for) this initial act, the harm would not have occurred

Factual impossibility: A defense based on the physical impossibility of completing the crime (e.g., it is impossible to pick an empty pocket)

Fair Sentencing Act: Reduced the 100:1 powder cocaine to crack disparity in federal guideline sentencing

False imprisonment: Restraining someone's liberty or freedom of movement by force or threat of force

False pretenses: Lies intended to induce the owner of property to surrender title or possession of the property

False statements: Lies that a person knowingly makes to the federal government with the purpose to mislead or deceive

Federal preemption: Federal law will supersede a state law that is not aligned with a federal objective.

Federal Sentencing Guidelines: Enacted in 1987 to reduce sentencing disparities in federal courts; made federal sentencing a mathematical equation; once mandatory, now advisory

Federalism: Dual sovereignty of the federal and state governments

Felony murder: A crime in which a death results from the commission, or attempted commission, of a felony (rape, robbery, kidnapping, arson, mayhem, felonious escape, burglary); all co-felons may be responsible for the death

Fifth Amendment: Protects against compelled self-incrimination, requires an indictment for "infamous" crimes, prevents double jeopardy

Fighting words: Statements that, by their very utterance, inflict injury

Final judgment rule: A rule that allows appeals only from decisions that definitively resolve an issue in the case

Financial cybercrime: The use of computers to steal things of value

Firearm offenses: Crimes that run afoul of state and federal firearm regulations

First Amendment: Protects five freedoms: to establish and practice religion, practice free speech (which includes expressive conduct), maintain a free press, to peaceably assemble, and to petition the government for redress of grievances

First appeal of right: All convicted offenders have a right to one appeal under state or federal law; counsel appointed for mandatory appeals

First-degree murder: Willful, deliberate, and premeditated murder; the highest form of specific-intent murder

Forgery: Alteration of signatures or documents for financial gain

Fourteenth Amendment: Amendment to the Constitution that was enacted to make all persons born in the country citizens; contains Equal Protection and Due Process clauses that protect all citizens from government overreach

Fourth Amendment: Protects against unreasonable searches and seizures; lists the requirements for a warrant as probable cause, supported by oath or affirmation, and particularly describing the place to be searched and the things to be seized

Fruit of the poisonous tree: Doctrine that punishes police misconduct by excluding from trial all evidence derived from an initial illegal action when police seized said evidence in violation of the Constitution

Functional equivalent: Words or actions similar to an interrogation that officers should know might lead the suspect to make incriminating statements

Gambling: The dealing of, operating, and maintaining for pay any game of chance not controlled by the government; frequently, but not always, illegal

Gang: A group of three or more people who identify themselves through unique clothing, hand signals, and nicknames; may be responsible for street violence related to the gang's criminal activities

***Garcetti* test:** Public employee speech is protected by the First Amendment if it relates to a matter of public concern and does not interfere with their boss's ability to run the agency effectively.

General intent: The taking of action, but not necessarily to bring about a specific result

General warrants: Issued by King George III to seize and arrest American colonists' publications critical of the king and his governance

Good faith: Government action with no nefarious motive

Good faith exception: An exception to the warrant requirement; officers who execute a defective warrant in good faith will not be penalized by the exclusionary rule in jurisdictions that recognize this exception

Good Samaritan laws: Laws protecting medical workers from personal injury lawsuits when they assist an injured person

Grand jury: An investigative body composed of ordinary citizens who determine whether there exists probable cause that a felony has been committed

Guilty but mentally ill: A finding that the defendant is criminally responsible for his conduct but not insane

Guilty plea: An admission of guilt by the defendant that negates the need for a trial

Habeas corpus: A writ (motion) that permits a prisoner to challenge the legality of his confinement

Harmless error: Mistake at a criminal trial that does not affect the result

Hate crime: Choosing to physically harm a victim based on the person's perceived race, religion, gender, or sexual identity

Hearsay: An out-of-court statement offered for its truth

Heat of passion: An act of provocation so severe that it would induce a reasonable person to kill; raised successfully at trial, it may reduce murder charges to manslaughter

Holding: The court's decision on a case or its answer to the legal questions presented in the case

Homicide: The killing of one human being by another. Not all homicides are crimes; some are accidents, and some are justified

Hot pursuit: Officers may continue to chase a retreating suspect who poses a danger to the public into a dwelling without first obtaining a warrant.

Human trafficking: Enslaving people for the sex trade, especially children, or for forced labor

Hunch: Legally insufficient basis for the police to forcibly engage the public

Identity theft: Acquisition of personal information about another to gain something of value

Imperfect self-defense: Legally defective claim of self-defense that involves the use of excessive force to repel an attack

Impossibility: The defense that one cannot be guilty of an attempt crime that was impossible to commit

Inbau and Reid nine steps: A systematic process whereby guilty suspects are induced to confess

Incarceration: Incapacitation of offenders by imprisonment

Incest: Sexual relations between nonspousal family members related by blood, marriage, or adoption

Inchoate crimes: Incomplete crimes; attempt, solicitation, conspiracy

Incorporation: Through the fulcrum of the 14th Amendment, the U.S. Supreme Court required states to provide the Bill of Rights' protections to its citizens

Incorporated by reference: An affidavit establishing probable cause attached to the warrant and integrated into the legal authority for the warrant

Independent source: An exception to the exclusionary rule; illegally obtained evidence may be admissible if it is discovered from a source independent of the officers' initial illegal conduct

Indeterminate sentencing: A sentence of a range of years of imprisonment, such as 7 to 15 years, with the expectation that good behavior while in prison will result in an earlier release

Indictment: Formal felony charges brought by a grand jury

Individualized suspicion: The requirement under the Fourth Amendment that there be a specific reason to stop, arrest, or convict each individual

Ineffective assistance of counsel: Under the standard announced by *Strickland v. Washington* (1984), counsel's performance must fall below that expected of a reasonable attorney and such deficient performance must have affected the outcome of the case against the defendant

Inevitable discovery: The judgment that illegally obtained evidence would eventually have been discovered by police as they proceeded in their immediate investigation, making the evidence in question admissible at trial

Infancy: Irrebutable presumption that children up to age 7 possess no *mens rea*. There is a rebuttable presumption that children aged 8 through 14 years possess no *mens rea*, but such presumption can be overcome by proof that the juvenile is able to appreciate the criminality of his conduct.

Informant: Person who works undercover on behalf of the government, often in exchange for personal benefit with the informant's own criminal case; must be proven to be reliable prior to use in a probable cause affidavit

Information: A charging document filed by a prosecutor

Initial appearance: Defendant's first appearance before a judge, typically within 72 hours of arrest

Intellectual disability: Formerly mental retardation; characterized by an IQ of 70 or lower and two or more substantive deficits in adaptive or social functioning that manifest before the age of 18

Intelligible principle: A guiding precept that restrains and limits the power Congress delegates to the executive or judicial branches to carry out government functions

Intent: The mental desire to bring about a particular result

Interlocutory appeal: An appeal filed before a final judgment is rendered in a particular case

Interrogation: Questioning by law enforcement designed to elicit incriminating information

Intervening cause: An independent event that breaks the causal chain between the initial offender's actions and the ultimate harm suffered

Intoxication: An altered state produced by the ingestion of drugs or alcohol; the condition may be voluntary or involuntary and may negate specific intent *mens rea* for some crimes

Inventory search: A warrantless search and eventual accounting of an offender's personal property in government custody

Investigatory detention: A brief seizure of an individual conducted for the sole purpose of confirming or dispelling the officer's suspicion that criminal activity is afoot

Invoking *Miranda*: Suspect informs law enforcement that he wishes to exercise either his right to remain silent or to have counsel present during questioning

Irrebutable presumption: Children age 7 and younger cannot form *mens rea*

Irresistible impulse: A mental disease or defect that prevents an offender from being able to resist the strong sudden urge to commit a criminal act

Judge: An individual who presides over the courtroom and who is either appointed or elected, hears and decides pretrial motions, rules on the admissibility of evidence both before and during trial, and instructs the jury on the particular law to apply to the facts of the case; must be neutral and detached

Judicial review: The power that the U.S. Supreme Court granted to itself to invalidate an act or law of the executive and legislative branches

Jurisdiction: Area of control for a court, state or federal government

Jury instructions: Rules and definitions of law that control the issues in the case; read to the jury by the judge before deliberations

Justifiable homicide: A murder that is legally justified by the circumstances (e.g., self-defense)

Kickback: Obtaining a portion of a contract back as an illegal payment for awarding the contract

Kidnapping: The unlawful taking away and confinement of another by force or threat of force

Knock and announce: Legal requirement for law enforcement to knock and announce police presence prior to executing a warrant; should wait 15 to 20 seconds between knocking and entering, but the exclusionary rule will not apply even if the wait is as short as 3 to 5 seconds

Knock and talk: A method to gain consent to enter a suspect's home and engage in conversation

Knowingly: *Mens rea* state in which the actor takes certain actions not necessarily to bring about the desired result but with the substantial certainty that such a result will occur

Labeling theory: Asserts criminal behavior comes from being labeled a deviant by others

Larceny: The taking away of the personal property of another without that person's consent and with the intent to permanently deprive the owner

Larceny by trick: Theft that results when a thief's lies convince the owner to turn over his property

Lay witness: An ordinary person who can testify to matters such as intoxication, speed, insanity, and distance within the normal range of adult experience

Least restrictive means: Government laws may not overburden civil liberties

Legal impossibility: Actions that do not constitute a crime under the law

Lemon test: Asks under the First Amendment's Establishment Clause whether the law under review is secular, whether it fosters an extensive entanglement with religion, and whether it either advances or inhibits religion; a way to separate church and state

Lesser included offense: A less serious offense that is included in the charge of a more serious offense (e.g., battery is subsumed under murder)

Line-up: A technique in which a witness stands behind a two-way mirror and looks at five or six similar-looking people lined up in an effort to identify the offender

Magistrate: A lower level federal judge who typically signs warrants

Mail fraud: A scheme to defraud that uses the U.S. Postal Service or a private mail carrier in its execution

Mala in se: Crimes regarded as inherently evil, such as murder, rape, and kidnapping

Mala prohibita: Crimes that are punishable because the laws define such conduct as criminal (e.g., prostitution and gambling)

Malice aforethought: The historical term for premeditation

Malware: Software deployed to infect computers

Mandatory minimum sentence: A sentence that ensures an offender will serve no less than a certain number of years of incarceration

Manifest injustice: If an offender cannot get proper redress on appeal, courts may examine the case to fix a grave mistake; for some cases, redress is to obtain executive clemency

Manslaughter: An unintentional killing (involuntary), or an intentional killing done in the heat of the passion and without premeditation (voluntary)

Mayhem: Permanent disfigurement of a victim

Megan's Laws: Laws that require sex offenders to register and possibly notify the communities in which they live of their criminal history

Mens rea: A guilty mind; purposefully, knowingly, recklessly, negligently

Mental defect: A mental disorder that impairs the way the brain processes information

Mental disease: A mental disorder recognized by the American Psychological Association and listed in the *DSM-V*

Merger: The combination of lesser offenses into a more serious crime on conviction for the more serious offense (e.g., battery merges into attempted murder)

Miller test: For obscenity, does the work appeal to the prurient interest? Is the work patently sexually offensive? Does the work taken as a whole lack serious literary, artistic, political, or scientific value?

Mistake of fact: The erroneous belief in certain facts that leads the person to act (or fail to act) accordingly

Mistake of law: An erroneous legal conclusion arrived at by a party who knows all the facts

Mistrial: Judge declares trial fatally flawed; prosecution must start a new

Mitigating circumstances: Circumstances tending to explain, but not excuse, the offender's crime; introduced by a defendant at a capital murder trial and which will be weighed against the aggravating circumstances before sentencing

M'Naghten test: The defendant is insane if, at the time he committed the crime, he suffered from a mental defect that rendered him unable to understand the difference between right and wrong or to be unable to appreciate the criminality of his conduct

Model Penal Code (MPC): The model that defines uniform concepts of criminal liability, defenses, and sentencing; the MPC is not law, but is a model on which many states have patterned their own criminal and penal codes

Money laundering: Interjecting illegally obtained money into a legal stream of commerce to disguise the money's illegal origins

Motion: An oral or written application for a court order

Motion for a new trial: Motion alleging errors committed during a trial and typically filed 7 days after the verdict with the original trial judge.

Motion *in limine*: Motion for the court to rule on the admissibility of, or to limit, specific evidence before trial

Motion to change venue: A motion to hold the trial in a different place than where the crime was committed; occurs most often because extensive pretrial publicity has compromised the defendant's ability to receive a fair and impartial trial

Motion to dismiss: Defendant asks court to eliminate charges or dismiss the case

Motion to sever: Motion to be tried separately from codefendants

Motion to suppress: Motion to exclude specific evidence at trial, typically on the grounds that the evidence was seized illegally

Motive: The reason an offender may commit a crime; not an element of the offense

Narrowly tailored: If a law will infringe on civil liberties, it must be written in the least intrusive manner

Necessary and Proper Clause: Article I, Section 18, of the Constitution, which gives Congress broad authority to make all laws that are "necessary and proper" for carrying out its government functions

Necessity: A defense created by having to choose the lesser of two evils

Negligently: Describes actions that deviate from the standard of care that a reasonable person would exercise

No contest plea: Operates as a guilty plea for a defendant who refuses to admit guilt

"No retreat" doctrine: The law assumes it is better to retreat than use deadly force; generally inapplicable to home invasions

No-knock warrant: If serving a warrant will threaten officer safety, the judge may dispense with the knock and announce requirement by making a notation on the face of the warrant.

Nondelegation doctrine: Congress may share what power it has with the executive and judicial branches, subject to an intelligible principle.

Nonfinancial cybercrime: Cybercrime that causes personal harm

Not guilty by reason of insanity: A plea entered by a defendant or a verdict decided by a jury that eliminates criminal responsibility because the defendant is insane

Notice: The government notifying a defendant of the charges

Objection: Preserving the record for appeal by formally protesting the opponent's actions or the trial court's decisions

Objectively reasonable: Everyone agrees the criminal justice professional's behavior is correct under the circumstances.

Obscenity: Patently offensive sexual material that is defined by the *Miller* test as having no artistic, political, scientific, or literary value (e.g., child pornography)

Obstruction of justice: Impeding the administrative, judicial, or legislative process

Open field: The Fourth Amendment recognizes privacy interests only in "persons, papers, houses, and effects," not open spaces

Opening statements: The prosecutor and defense counsels' opening remarks to the jury informing them what evidence they intend to introduce at trial

Opportunity to be heard: Giving a person his day in court

Ordinances: Local government restrictions

Overbroad: A doctrine that invalidates laws that criminalize both protected and unprotected speech

Panhandling: The practice of asking strangers for money in public places

Pardon: The executive branch (federal and all states) can commute an offender's conviction.

Parole: A prisoner's early release from confinement under court supervision

Particularity requirement: The place to be searched and things to be seized must be described specifically.

Party opponent: The party on the other side of the "*v*" in a case; when the opponent speaks, what they say may be used against them in court

Patent and Copyright Clause: Article I, Section 8, Clause 8, of the Constitution, which secures the exclusive right of authors and inventors to their respective works for a limited time

Pattern of racketeering activity: Two or more predicate acts committed and have the threat to continue

Pen register: Captures the numbers a phone receives and makes; no reasonable expectation of privacy

Peremptory challenge: A limited number of strikes a lawyer may use to eliminate potential jurors; the government cannot base peremptory challenges on race or gender

Perjury: A knowing and willful lie made under oath in a judicial or administrative or legislative proceeding

Personal property: Personal possessions that can be moved from one place to another

Personal status: Not a basis for criminal liability (e.g., alcoholic)

Phishing: A phony, but real-looking, Internet website that steals patrons' passwords, personal information, or money

Photo array: A series of photographs of similar-looking people shown to a witness, who attempts to identify the perpetrator among them

Plain feel: While patting down a suspect during a *Terry* stop, officers are allowed to remove obvious contraband from the suspect's person.

Plain view: A warrantless seizure of contraband out in the open by officers lawfully on the premises

Plea bargaining: A process of negotiation between the prosecutor and the defendant to avoid trial; the defendant pleads guilty to certain charges in exchange for concessions from the government

Plea colloquy: A series of questions asked of the defendant under oath by the judge in open court to ensure that the defendant is aware of the rights he is waiving by pleading guilty

Plea pursuant to a negotiated agreement: Defendant pleads guilty in exchange for government's lenient treatment either in reduced charges or a favorable sentencing recommendation.

Police power: A state's power to enact laws and regulations for the health, safety, and welfare of residents

Precedent: Prior cases that are close in facts or legal principles to the case now under consideration that controls the decision in the present case

Predicate acts: A list of state and federal crimes that form the basis of racketeering charges

Preliminary hearing: An evidentiary hearing to determine whether there is sufficient evidence to hold the defendant for trial

Preponderance of the evidence: A legal standard that makes the existence of the disputed fact in question more likely than not; 51% of the evidence

Presentence investigation: An investigation by the court of the defendant's life and crime conducted to assist the judge in imposing an appropriate sentence

Presentence report: The written result of the presentence investigation

Presumption of innocence: The assumption that, under the law, a defendant is innocent until the prosecutor proves each and every element of the crime beyond a reasonable doubt

Pretrial identification: Before trial, the identification of the suspect by a witness

Pretrial motions: A series of motions brought to resolve issues before trial begins (e.g., venue and admission or exclusion of specific evidence and testimony)

Principal to the crime: The primary criminal actor who orchestrated and committed the crime

Principle of legality: Government notice of what conduct is criminal by enacting criminal laws

Probable cause: A determination made by examining all the facts and circumstances tending to establish that a crime has been, is being, or will be committed; more than a suspicion

Probation: A sentence releasing the defendant into the community under court supervision without the defendant having served any time in prison

Procedural justice: When litigants feel they were treated fairly by the judicial system, despite the case outcome

Procedural due process: Notice from the government to citizens that there is a complaint against them and that the citizens will have the opportunity to in court to defend against the complaint

Proportionality review: Process by which a court compares sentences imposed on similarly situated defendants to ensure that they have been sentenced fairly

Prosecutorial discretion: The sole decision-making authority of the prosecutor to decide who to charge and what to charge

Prostitution: The performance of sex favors in exchange for a thing of value

Protected speech: The First Amendment protects speech and expressive conduct that communicates ideas, even if such speech is offensive.

Protective sweep: A cursory examination by police to eliminate a possible threat to officer safety, following specific information that armed people are on the premises

Provoking act: Must be so severe that a reasonable person would react with deadly violence; a precursor for "heat of passion" voluntary manslaughter

Proximate cause: An act from which the harm suffered was a reasonably foreseeable consequence

Prurient interest: A lustful, morbid, or shameful interest in nudity, sex, and/or excretion

Psychosis: A break from reality suffered by some mentally ill offenders

Public corruption: Unlawful acts that degrade the public trust in the body politic

Public forum: Protected under the First Amendment as a marketplace for the exchange of ideas, the hallmark of democracy

Purposely: Having a specific intent or a desire to cause a specific result

Qualified immunity: Limited protection for criminal justice professionals, typically law enforcement and correctional officers, from civil lawsuits brought by the public for a deprivation of their civil rights

Quid pro quo: An exchange of benefits common in public corruption cases

Racketeer Influenced and Corrupt Organizations (RICO) Act: Comprehensive law enacted in the 1970s to combat organized crime. Elements include a pattern of racketeering activity and investment of criminal proceeds in a business that affects interstate commerce.

Rape: Sex against the victim's will, without consent, by force or threat of force

Rape shield laws: Laws that prevent the defendant from introducing evidence about the victim's sexual reputation or previous sexual activity with people other than the defendant to discredit their report of rape, except where such exclusion would violate the Confrontation Clause

Real property: Land and its permanent structures, such as houses, barns, and other buildings

Reasonable belief: More than reasonable suspicion but less than probable cause; standard to conduct a pat down for weapons during a Terry stop

Reasonable expectation of privacy: An individual's confidence that certain places and things will not be examined by others. When an expectation of privacy exists, officers typically need a warrant to search and seize

Reasonable force: The government must use only as much force is necessary to effectuate an arrest.

Reasonable man: Fictional person used as a measuring stick to gauge the legal appropriateness of other's behavior

Reasonable suspicion: Legal standard based on specific and articulable facts (more than a hunch) that criminal activity is afoot, which means that a crime has been, is being, or will be committed

Rebuttable presumption: Can overcome conclusion children ages 8–14 have no *mens rea*

Receiving stolen property: Must have scienter (knowledge) that the property is stolen to be criminally responsible for its receipt

Recidivism: To recommit crime after punishment

Recklessly: Manner whereby an actor consciously disregards a substantial and unjustifiable risk of harm that his behavior creates; the actor knows of the risk of harm and ignores it

Rehabilitation: Providing educational and employment training to help an offender successfully reintegrate into society

Relative judgment: Asking an eyewitness to identify an offender from six similar-looking people in a photo array. The witness tends to choose the person who looks most like the offender "relative" to the other five people in the array, but who may not actually be the culprit

Relevant conduct: Acts surrounding the commission of a crime that the judge may consider in fashioning an appropriate sentence without increasing the sentence in violation of *Apprendi v. New Jersey* (1999)

Restitution: An offender's repayment to society and the victim for the harm caused by his crime

Restorative justice: Basis for juvenile justice; offender makes the victim whole to restore the victim for what the crime took from the victim

Retribution: Paying society back for the harm the offender caused

"Revenge porn": A partner who posts to social media their former partner's intimate photos shared during the course of the relationship

Reverse and remand: Actions taken by an appellate court if it finds error in a lower court's proceedings; the appellate court will reverse (overturn) the lower court's decision and remand the case (send the case back to the lower court) for further proceedings consistent with the appellate court's decision

Reversible error: A fatal flaw at trial that invalidates the defendant's conviction

Right to self-representation: Recognized, although not explicitly stated, in the Sixth Amendment to the U.S. Constitution

Riot: Public disturbance usually by three or more people involving threats or actual acts of violence

Risk assessment: A method of calculating the odds an offender will commit more crime

Robbery: The taking of personal property by force or threat of force

Rule of lenity: Courts will interpret criminal statutes to benefit the defendant and not the government

Scienter: Knowledge that an offender must possess to be held criminally responsible for some crimes

Scientific evidence: A type of evidence usually introduced by experts, such as DNA

Scrupulously honor: Do without fail. During interrogation, if a suspect expresses a desire to stop talking or to speak to an attorney, officers must stop questioning immediately.

Search: A government invasion to look for contraband or other evidence of an area in which a person has a reasonable expectation of privacy

Search incident to an arrest: A warrantless search of an arrestee's person and the area within his immediate control

Second Amendment: Recognizes the right to bear arms

Second-degree murder: A death that results from an offender's intent to cause serious bodily harm or a murder that lacks one element of first-degree murder

Sedition: Communication or agreement to commit treason or lesser similar offenses against the United States

Seizure: The government's acquisition of certain personal property, either contraband or potential evidence of a crime, or the deprivation of a person's liberty due to the person's arrest

Selective prosecution: The government's use of an impermissible motive to choose certain defendants for prosecution

Self-defense: A complete defense based on the use of reasonable force to repel a physical attack

Sentencing hearing: After conviction, a hearing to help the judge determine an appropriate sentence

Separation of powers: A system of checks and balances the three branches of government operate on each other

Sex offenses: Crimes of violence that use sex as a weapon

Sexting: A crime typically engaged in by juveniles who text intimate photos of themselves to one another

Show-up: Type of pretrial identification in which the suspect, alone, is brought before the witness for identification; the most suggestive type of pretrial identification

Sixth Amendment: Provides for the assistance of counsel, the right to confront witnesses, a public and speedy trial that will be held in the venue where the crime was committed, and provides for compulsory process (subpoenas) for obtaining witnesses in the defendant's favor

Social control theory: Criminal theory that posits people who share common bonds are less likely to commit crimes

Social learning theory: Criminal theory that posits people learn from others how to commit crime

Sodomy: Oral/genital contact or anal intercourse

Solicitation: The procurement of others to commit a crime. The crime of solicitation is complete when one person entices another to commit a crime, regardless of whether the crime is completed.

Special needs searches: Warrantless searches justified by public safety concerns

Specific and articulable facts: Facts that a police officer can cite that support the legality of his actions

Specific intent: The intent to bring about a desired result

Speech: What people communicate, includes expressive conduct

Stalking: Repeated acts of communication or physical harassment by a compulsive offender toward a victim

Stand your ground: Some jurisdictions allow a person to use deadly force if threatened in a place where they have a legal right to be.

Standard of review: The legal standard by which courts review and decide appeals

Standing: The legal right to challenge the government's actions

Stare decisis: Let the decision stand; a judgment that precedent should be followed

Statute of limitations: A defense alleging that the time in which to prosecute certain crimes has elapsed. There is no statute of limitations for the crime of murder.

Statutory law: Laws written and passed by federal and state legislatures and then codified and compiled in code books

Statutory rape: Typically nonforcible sexual relations involving a teenager and a partner older by 4 years or more

StingRay: Cell site simulator that can intercept and track nearby cell phone signals

Strain theory: People turn to crime when they cannot achieve their goals by legitimate means

Strict liability: No *mens rea* required to be punished; guilt attaches when the act is committed

Strict scrutiny: The highest level of review that courts use to examine government regulation of fundamental freedoms

Subjective: Personal perspective

Submission to authority: Pretending that a warrant is on the way to coerce consent to search

Subornation of perjury: Inducing another to lie under oath for the benefit of the offender

Supremacy Clause: Article VI of the Constitution that operates to make federal law superior to state law and when the U.S. Supreme Court speaks, it is the final word in the land

Suspended sentence: Imposition of a sentence in which the amount of time to be served is nullified

Swatting: A fraudulent call for an armed response by a tactical SWAT (Special Weapons And Tactics) team to an unsuspecting location

Tenth Amendment: Provides that all powers that the Constitution does not grant the federal government, if not prohibited by the Constitution, are left to the states

Terrorism: Using threats, murder, and mayhem to achieve illegitimate political goals

Terroristic threats: Threatening violence to a specific person or to cause public pandemonium

Terry stop: The brief detainment and questioning of a person by police to either confirm or dispel their reasonable suspicion that criminal activity is afoot. If officers have a reasonable belief that the person is armed, officers can pat down the outer clothing for weapons only.

Testimonial evidence: Evidence generated by a witness answering questions in a legal proceeding

The §1983 claim: Title 42 U.S.C. §1983, the legal gateway to sue the government for any official acting "under the color of law" to deprive a citizen of a federally protected right

Theft of honest services: Prosecuted as wire fraud; assigns criminal liability to elected officials who personally benefit by committing crimes at the public's expense

Third degree: Torturous interrogation tactics that induce the defendant to confess to the crime

Third-party doctrine: No reasonable expectation of privacy in information one shares with third parties such as banks or telephone companies

"Three-strikes" laws: Punitive laws imposing mandatory life sentence in prison on conviction of a third felony

Time, manner, and place restriction: Permissible restriction on speech to accommodate civilized living (e.g., no speeches by bullhorn at 2:00 a.m.)

Title IX: Federal law guaranteeing the equal treatment of the sexes in educational institutions that receive federal aid; used to prosecute sex-related acts at a college tribunal

Totality of the circumstances: When judged as a whole, all the facts and circumstances used to determine the legality of government action

Trademark: A distinctive mark of authenticity and ownership

Transferred intent: The intent to harm one person transfers when the offender instead harms someone else.

Treason: The offense of attempting by overt acts to overthrow the government or of betraying the country for the benefit of a foreign power

Trickery and deceit: A legal interrogation technique where investigators lie to the suspect to induce a confession

True bill: Indictment returned by a grand jury

True threats: The unlawful communication of a threat of violence to identifiable people; the speaker need not actually intend to carry out the threat; unprotected speech

Unlawful assembly: The gathering of no fewer than five people for the purpose of engaging in disorderly conduct

Unprotected speech: Speech and expression not protected by the First Amendment, such as fighting words, statements posing a clear and present danger, and obscene material

U.S. Supreme Court: Highest appellate court in the country where nine justices sit in judgment; decides to hear a limited number of appeals by granting *writs of certiorari*

USA PATRIOT Act: Post–9/11 legislation that consolidates law enforcement efforts to combat terrorism against the United States of America

Uttering: Passing fraudulent checks

Vagrancy: The crime of being a person who, with no visible means of support, travels from place to place and depends on the kindness of strangers for food, clothing, and shelter

Vague: A statute is void-for-vagueness and unconstitutional when people of ordinary intelligence must guess at the words' meaning

Venire: Panel of potential jurors

Venireman: Potential juror

Venue: The place where a trial is held, usually in the same district that the crime was committed

Verdict form: The form on which the jury enters their verdict

Victim impact statement: At the defendant's sentencing hearing, the statements by victims during which they inform the court of the harm caused by the defendant's crime

Viewpoint discrimination: The government cannot suppress speech because it disagrees with the speech's content or message; the government can suppress unprotected speech.

Voir dire: French "to speak the truth"; the questioning of potential jurors to determine if the venireperson can listen to the evidence and fairly and impartially decide the case

Voluntary, intelligent, and knowing waiver: To waive one's rights pursuant to *Miranda*, it must be voluntary (no coercion), intelligent (know the consequences of the rights given up), and knowing (understand the function of *Miranda* protections).

Warrant: A legal order to seize specific property connected to crimes or to arrest a specific person suspected of criminal activity

Whaling: Phishing for corporate targets

Wharton's Rule: One person cannot be held criminally responsible for conspiracy to commit a crime that, under the law, takes two to commit (e.g., gambling or prostitution)

White-collar crimes: Crimes committed by people who hold positions of trust

Wire fraud: A scheme to defraud and the use of wires (telephones, bank transfers, computers) to execute the scheme

Writ of certiorari: An order from the U.S. Supreme Court ordering a lower court to forward the case record

Writ of mandamus: An application to the court to order a public official to perform a duty imposed by law

Writs of assistance: Papers authorizing the seizure of property from American colonists to help pay King George III's debtors

Year-and-a-day rule: Doctrine that if victim died within one year and one day of harm caused by offender, offender would be liable for the death; advances in medical science have rendered such laws obsolete

Zealous advocate: An attorney who passionately advances his client's interests

NOTES

CHAPTER 1

1. Learned Hand (1959). *The Spirit of Liberty: Papers and Addresses.*
2. "Last Sunday, at 11:30 in the evening, Vincent Vaugogh [sic], a painter of Dutch origin, called at the Brothel No. 1, asked for a woman called Rachel and handed her . . . his ear, saying, 'Guard this object with your life' . . . The police went the next day to his house and discovered him lying on his bed apparently at the point of death. The unfortunate man has been rushed to hospital." *Le Forum Républicain*, December 30, 1888.
3. Alice Hines (2018, May 12). "Magnetic Implants? Welcome to the World of Medical Punk." *New York Times.*
4. The Formation of the Union (National Archives Publication No. 70-13).
5. Article I, Section 8, Clause 18 to "make all laws which shall be necessary and proper for carrying into execution the foregoing powers."
6. *Touby v. United States*, 500 U.S. 160 (1991).
7. *Marbury v. Madison*, 5 U.S. (1 Cranch) 137 (1803).
8. *Roe v. Wade*, 410 U.S. 113 (1973).
9. Some rights have not been incorporated to the states, most notably the Fifth Amendment's right to be charged by a grand jury; the prosecution may charge by an information, discussed in Chapter 2.
10. *Brown v. Board of Education*, 347 U.S. 483 (1954); *Loving v. Virginia*, 388 U.S. 1 (1967); *Obergefell v. Hodges*, 135 S.Ct. 2584 (2015).
11. Randy E. Barnett (2004). "The Proper Scope of the Police Power." *Notre Dame Law Review*, Vol. 79, pp. 429–495.
12. *Keeler v. Superior Court*, 470 P.2d 617 (1970). California later amended its statute to be more specific to define causing the death of a fetus as murder.
13. If there is a blank space in a citation, for example, 573 U.S. ___ (2014), it means the page number has yet to be assigned in the Official Reporter.
14. *Black's Law Dictionary*, 5th ed. (St. Paul, MN: West, 1979).
15. DNA = deoxyribonucleic acid, molecules that carry our genetic code.
16. *United States v. Whiteside*, 2015 U.S. Dist. LEXIS 84369.
17. *Birchfield v. North Dakota*, 136 S.Ct. 2160 (2016).
18. *In re Oliver*, 333 U.S. 257 (1948).
19. See, generally, Mayo Moran (2010). "Who Is the Reasonable Person? The Reasonable Person: A Conceptual Biography in Comparative Perspective." *Lewis & Clark Law Review*, Vol. 14, pp. 1233–1283.
20. Ibid.
21. *Moran v. Burbine*, 475 U.S. 412 (1986).
22. *Illinois v. Rodriguez*, 497 U.S. 177 (1990).
23. The 80-yard beyond a reasonable doubt analogy may be insufficient to use in a court of law.
24. Tom R. Tyler (2006). *Why People Obey the Law* (Princeton, NJ: Princeton University Press).
25. Jill Lepore (2018, May 21). "The Rise of the Victims'-Rights Movement: How a Conservative Agenda and a Feminist Cause Came Together to Transform Criminal Justice." *New Yorker.*
26. *Carey v. Musladin*, 549 U.S. 70 (2006).
27. *Payne v. Tennessee*, 501 U.S. 808 (1991). A factfinder in a guilty plea is the judge and, in a trial, the factfinder is the jury.
28. *Roberts v. Louisiana*, 428 U.S. 325 (1976) (mandatory death penalty on first-degree murder conviction held to violate the Eighth Amendment because criminal sentencing is not one-size-fits-all).
29. Edward W. Seih (2006). *Community Corrections and Human Dignity* (Boston: Jones & Bartlett).
30. Paul Bator (1963). "Finality in Criminal Law and Federal *Habeas Corpus* for State Prisoners." *Harvard Law Review*, Vol. 76, No. 3, pp. 441–528.
31. *Roper v. Simmons*, 543 U.S. 551 (2005).
32. *McKeiver v. Pennsylvania*, 403 U.S. 528 (1971).
33. *In re Gault*, 387 U.S. 1 (1967). *In re* means "in regard to," "in the case of."
34. Office of Justice Programs, National Institute of Justice, Drug Courts.
35. *Upjohn Company v. United States*, 449 U.S. 383 (1981).
36. *New York v. Belge*, 372 N.Y.S.2d 798 (1975).
37. Model Code of Professional Conduct Rule 1.6 (2003). The rule states as follows: (a) A lawyer *shall not* reveal information relating to representation of a client unless the client gives informed consent, the disclosure is impliedly authorized in order to carry out the representation, or the disclosure is permitted by paragraph (b). (b) A lawyer *may* reveal information relating to the representation of a client to the extent the lawyer reasonably believes necessary: (1) to prevent reasonably certain death or substantial bodily harm . . . (italics added).
38. *Lo-Ji Sales, Inc. v. New York*, 442 U.S. 319 (1979).
39. *Williams v. Pennsylvania*, 136 S.Ct. 1899 (2016).
40. Ronald F. Wright, Kay L. Levine, and Marc L. Miller (2014). "The Many Faces of Prosecution." *Stanford Journal of Criminal Law & Policy*, Vol. 1, pp. 27–47.
41. *Berger v. United States*, 295 U.S. 78 (1935).
42. Robert H. Jackson (1940). "The Federal Prosecutor." *Journal of the American Judicature Society*, Vol. 24, pp. 18–20.
43. Adapted from the *United States Attorneys' Manual*. https://www.justice.gov/usam/united-states-attorneys-manual.
44. *Monroe v. Pope*, 365 U.S. 167 (1961), overruled in part *Monell v. Department of Social Services*, 436 U.S. 658 (1978).
45. Information for this section derived from Alan K. Chen (2006). "The Facts About Qualified Immunity." *Emory Law Review*, Vol. 55, pp. 229–277.
46. *Saucier v. Katz*, 533 U.S. 194 (2001).
47. *Pearson v. Callahan*, 555 U.S. 223 (2009).

48. Peter Kwan (1997). "Jeffrey Dahmer and the Cosynthesis of Categories." *Hastings Law Journal*, Vol. 48, pp. 1257–1292 (citing approximately 38 newspaper articles reporting on the incidents described herein).

49. Officers Balcerzak and Gabrish were later found to have violated their duty to protect Sinthasomphone and were fired in September 1991. In 1994, the officers were reinstated and honored by the police union as officers of the year for fighting for their jobs. Balcerzak was later elected president of the police union, and Gabrish became a police lieutenant in an adjacent town.

50. *Estate of Konerak Sinthasomphone v. City of Milwaukee*, 785 F.Supp. 1343 (1992).

51. *Arizona v. United States*, 132 S.Ct. 2492 (2012).

52. Kera Wanielista (2017, April 2). "Local Police: Immigration Enforcement Issue of Law, Not Politics." www.Goskagit.com.

53. *City of Chicago v. Sessions*, No. 17-2991 (7th Cir. 2018).

54. *Trump v. Hawaii*, 535 U.S. ___ (2018).

55. *The Federalist Papers* (No. 9).

56. Randy E. Barnett (2004). "The Proper Scope of the Police Power." *Notre Dame Law Review*, Vol. 79, pp. 429–495.

57. Brady Handgun Violence Prevention Act, Pub. L. No. 103-159 (1993).

58. *Printz v. United States*, 521 U.S. 898 (1997).

59. 28 U.S.C. §3702, Unlawful Sports Gambling.

60. *Boyd v. United States*, 116 U.S. 616 (1886).

61. Article I, Section 8, Clause 3, Commerce Clause.

62. No Commerce Clause nexus is required for a uniquely federal crime such as treason, counterfeiting, or crimes that occur on federal property.

63. *Heart of Atlanta Motel v. U.S.*, 379 U.S. 241 (1964); *Katzenbach v. McClung*, 379 U.S. 294 (1964) (restaurants); *Hodel v. Indiana*, 452 U.S. 314 (1981) (coal); and *Wickard v. Filburn*, 317 U.S. 111 (1942) (wheat), case excerpt in this chapter *Gonzales v. Raich*, 545 U.S. 1 (2005).

64. *United States v. Lopez*, 514 U.S. 549 (1995). After the *Lopez* ruling, Congress rewrote the law to require prosecutors to prove the gun found in the prohibited school zone "has moved in or otherwise affects interstate commerce." Gun Free School Zones Act, Pub. L. No. 101-647 (1990).

65. *United States v. Morrison*, 529 U.S. 598 (2000).

CHAPTER 2

1. Janet Reitman (2013, July 17). "Jahar's World." *Rolling Stone*.

2. Felice J. Levine & June Lovin Tapp (1973). "The Psychology of Criminal Identification: The Gap From *Wade* to *Kirby*." *University of Pennsylvania Law Review*, Vol. 121, pp. 1079–1131.

3. Nina Golgowski (2013, June 6). "Boston Marathon Bombing 'Bag Men' Suing *New York Post* for Falsely Portraying Them as Suspects." *New York Daily News*.

4. Gary L. Wells, Mark Small, Steven Penrod, Roy S. Malpass, Solomon M. Fulero, & C. A. E. Brimacombe (1998). "Eyewitness Identification Procedures: Recommendations for Lineups and Photospreads." *Law and Human Behavior*, Vol. 22, No. 6, pp. 603–647.

5. *Neil v. Biggers*, 409 U.S. 188 (1972); *Manson v. Brathwaite*, 432 U.S. 98 (1977).

6. *Foster v. California*, 394 U.S. 440 (1969).

7. See also *Stovall v. Denno*, 388 U.S. 293 (1967).

8. Nancy M. Steblay, Jennifer E. Dysert, Solomon Fulero, & Roderick C. L. Lindsay (2001). "Eyewitness Accuracy Rates in Sequential and Simultaneous Line-Up Presentations: A Meta-Analytic Comparison." *Law & Human Behavior*, Vol. 25, pp. 459–473.

9. *Perry v. New Hampshire*, 132 S.Ct. 716 (2012).

10. *United States v. Wade*, 388 U.S. 218 (1967).

11. Adapted from Edith Greene, Kirk Heilbrun, William H. Fortune, & Michael T. Nietzel (2007). *Wrightsman's Psychology and the Legal System*, 6th ed. (Belmont, CA: Thomson Wadsworth).

12. Kenneth J. Melilli (1992). "Prosecutorial Discretion in an Adversary System." *Brigham Young University Law Review*, Vol. 3, No. 4, pp. 669–707.

13. See Claudia L. Cowan, William C. Thompson, & Phoebe C. Ellsworth (1984). "The Effects of Death Qualification on Jurors' Predisposition to Convict and on the Quality of Deliberation." *Law and Human Behavior*, Vol. 8, No. 1–2, pp. 53–79.

14. Vincent Bugliosi (1996). *Outrage: The Five Reasons Why O. J. Simpson Got Away With Murder* (New York: Norton).

15. Neither the government nor the defense is required to turn over internal memoranda made in preparing the case for trial, often called "work product."

16. *Brady v. Maryland*, 373 U.S. 83 (1963).

17. See *Youngblood v. West Virginia*, 547 U.S. 867 (2006) (*Brady* obligations apply to the government when evidence is known only to the police and not the prosecutor).

18. Ira Mickenberg (2008). "A Practical Guide to *Brady* Motions" (Chapel Hill, NC: New Felony Defender Program); *Kyles v. Whitley*, 514 U.S. 419 (1995).

19. *United States v. Bagley*, 473 U.S. 667 (1985); *Giglio v. United States*, 405 U.S. 150 (1972).

20. John Thompson sued the New Orleans district attorney (DA), Harry Connick, Sr., in civil court and won a $14 million jury trial against the city. The verdict was overturned on appeal by the U.S. Supreme Court, which held a DA could not be held legally responsible for a one-time *Brady* violation (*Connick v. Thompson*, 131 S.Ct. 1350, 2011).

21. See, e.g., The shooting of Michael Brown, St Louis County, MO, November 2014 (No Bill Issued); the shooting of Jordan Edwards, Dallas County, TX, April 2017 (Indictment Returned).

22. Federal Rule of Criminal Procedure 7(c)(1). *In General*. The indictment or information must be a plain, concise, and definite written statement of the essential facts constituting the offense charged and must be signed by an attorney for the government.

23. *Stack v. Boyle*, 342 U.S. 1 (1951).

24. See, e.g., The Bail Reform Act of 1984, 18 U.S.C. §3142. A full description of the law's provisions, published by the Federal Judicial Center, can be found at https://www.fjc.gov/sites/default/files/2012/BailAct3.pdf.

25. See Alysia Santo (2015, November 12). "Kentucky's Protracted Struggle to Get Rid of Bail: 'Is There Any Better Way Than Money?'" https://www.themarshallproject.org/2015/11/12/kentucky-s-protracted-struggle-to-get-rid-of-bail; Ginia Bellafante (2017, June 1). "Getting Rid of Bail Is Only the Start." https://www.nytimes.com/2017/06/01/nyregion/getting-rid-of-bail-is-only-the-start.html.

26. 18 U.S.C. §3161-3171 (1974).

27. *Barker v. Wingo*, 407 U.S. 514 (1972).

28. *Santobello v. New York*, 404 U.S. 257 (1971).

29. *North Carolina v. Alford*, 400 U.S. 25 (1970).

30. Saul M. Kassin (2008). "Confession Evidence: Commonsense Myths and Misconceptions." *Criminal Justice & Behavior*, Vol. 35, No. 1, pp. 1309–1322.

31. Docket entry #028698; *California v. Wozniak*, Amended Notice of Motion to Preserve Evidence, filed May 10, 2017, Elias letter on p. 54.

32. Ibid.

33. The terms of a typical plea bargain state, "in exchange for truthful testimony" at the target defendant's trial, the government will recommend the testifying witness will get a reduced sentence. The fallacy is that *only* the government determines what the "truth" is in any given case, which is, typically, the story the government wants to hear at trial, that is, that the target defendant is guilty. On June 7, 2017, a petition was filed at the U.S. Supreme Court by Mickey Davis, who was convicted as part of a criminal conspiracy involving loans and a car dealership. Two brothers, John and Gigi Rovito, were witnesses at Davis's trial. John said Davis was guilty, whereas Gigi said Davis was not guilty. The prosecutor granted immunity (protection from prosecution for crimes committed) to John but refused to grant immunity to Gigi because the prosecutor did not "believe" his story. Davis was convicted and is appealing to the U.S. Supreme Court on the basis that the government's refusal to grant immunity based on who prosecutors believe is "telling the truth" violates his due process rights. See *United States v. Michael "Mickey" Davis*, 845 F.3d 282 (7th Cir. 2016).

34. *In re Winship*, 397 U.S. 358 (1970).

35. Ibid.

36. Typically, the defense makes a motion to dismiss the case on the basis that the prosecution has failed to meet their burden of proof; most often, the motion is denied and the case continues.

37. *Batson v. Kentucky*, 476 U.S. 79 (1986).

38. *Holland v. Illinois*, 493 U.S. 474 (1990).

39. *Snyder v. Louisiana*, 552 U.S. 472 (2008).

40. The precedent of *Batson* also applies to prevent gender discrimination in jury selection as well. *J.E.B. v. Alabama ex rel. T.B.*, 511 U.S. 127 (1994).

41. *J.E.B. v. Alabama ex rel. T.B.*, 511 U.S. 127 (1994).

42. See Equal Justice Initiative (2010, June). "Illegal Racial Discrimination in Jury Selection: A Continuing Legacy" (EJI report). https://eji.org/sites/default/files/illegal-racial-discrimination-in-jury-selection.pdf

43. *Foster v. Chatman*, 136 S.Ct. 1737 (2016).

44. Ann O'Neill & Mariano Castillo (2015, March 4). "Tsarnaev Attorney: 'It Was Him.'" https://www.cnn.com/2015/03/04/us/boston-marathon-bombing-trial/index.html

45. John H. Wigmore (1904). *A Treatise on the System of Evidence in Trials at Common Law*, Vols. 1–4 (Boston, MA: Little, Brown).

46. New Jersey Superior Court, Jury Instructions (1993).

47. For an example, see Federal Rule of Evidence 702: Testimony by Expert Witnesses.

48. *Frye v. United States*, 293 F. 1013 (D.C. Cir. 1923).

49. See *United States v. Scheffer*, 523 U.S. 303 (1998).

50. *Daubert v. Merrill Dow Pharmaceuticals*, 509 U.S. 579 (1993).

51. *Kumho Tire Co., Ltd. v. Carmichael*, 119 S.Ct. 1167 (1999).

52. *United States v. Tsarnaev*, Trial Transcript, March 23, 2015, pp. 157–160.

53. Note, in general, Oklahoma City Police Department forensic examiner Joyce Gilchrist, who submitted false evidence reports and was fired in 2001, and Annie Dookhan, a Massachusetts state lab scientist arrested in 2012 for submitting lab reports on evidence never tested.

54. FBI (2015, April 20). "FBI Testimony on Microscopic Hair Analysis Contained Errors in at Least 90 Percent of Cases in Ongoing Review" (Press release). https://www.fbi.gov/news/pressrel/press-releases/fbi-testimony-on-microscopic-hair-analysis-contained-errors-in-at-least-90-percent-of-cases-in-ongoing-review

55. *Chambers v. Mississippi*, 410 U.S. 284 (1973).

56. This passage comes from the Book of Genesis. "Whoso sheddeth man's blood, by man shall his blood be shed: for in the image of God made he man." Genesis 9:6 (King James Version).

57. *Carruthers v. State*, 528 S.E.2d 217 (Ga. 2000).

58. Michael McLaughlin (2015, April 16). "In Closing Arguments, Prosecution Says Tsarnaev 'Wanted to Punish America.'" https://www.huffingtonpost.com/2015/04/06/closing-arguments-boston-marathon-trial_n_7012360.html

59. *Pena-Rodriguez v. Colorado*, 580 U.S. ___ (2017).

60. *Allen v. United States*, 164 U.S. 492 (1896) (permits jury instructions to prevent a deadlocked jury).

CHAPTER 3

1. Harold J. Berman (1983). *Law and Revolution: The Formation of the Western Legal Tradition* (Cambridge, MA: Harvard University).

2. Geraldine Szott Moohr (2010). "Playing With the Rules: An Effort to Strengthen the *Mens Rea* Standards of Federal Criminal Laws." *Journal of Law, Economics & Policy*, Vol. 7, pp. 685–710.

3. Ohio Revised Code Annotated §2901.21 (2015).

4. See *United States v. Santos*, 553 U.S. 507 (2008) (in which the high Court said "under a long line of our decisions, the tie must go to the defendant").

5. *State v. Morris*, 2016-Ohio-5490.

6. 18 United States Code §922(g)(9).

7. Maine Revised Statute Annotated Title 17–A, §207(1)(A).

8. *Voisine v. United States*, 136 S.Ct. 2272 (2016).

9. *Myers v. State*, 422 N.E.2d 745 (1981).

10. *Linehan v. Florida*, 442 So.2d 244 (1983).

11. 18 U.S.C.A. §111.

12. *United States v. Feola*, 420 U.S. 671 (1975).

13. *Morissette v. United States*, 342 U.S. 246 (1952).

14. *Commonwealth v. Twitchell*, 617 N.E.2d 609 (1993).

15. *Johnson v. United States*, 135 S.Ct. 2551 (2015).

16. *Doe v. City of Lafayette*, 377 F.3d 757 (7th Cir. 2004) (previously convicted pedophile sex offender was legally banned from going to a city park after he disclosed that he went to the park and had thoughts of molesting children).

17. *Morissette v. United States*, 342 U.S. 246 (1952).

18. *Palsgraf v. Long Island Railroad*, 162 N.E. 99 (N.Y. 1928).

19. Damien Schiff (2005). "Samaritans: Good, Bad and Ugly: A Comparative Law Analysis." *Roger Williams University Law Review*, Vol. 11, pp. 77–141.

20. *Robinson v. California*, 370 U.S. 660 (1962).
21. *People v. Tocco*, 525 N.Y.S.2d 137 (N.Y. 1988).
22. The "but for" formulation is counterintuitive. If the answer to the question "but for the offender's actions, would the harm have occurred?" is *no*, then the offender *is* the factual cause.
23. *Delawder v. Commonwealth*, 196 S.E.2d 913 (1973); *Baxley v. Fischer*, 134 S.E.2d 291 (1964).
24. Michigan Compiled Laws §767.39 (2015).
25. *Salinas v. United States*, 522 U.S. 52 (1997).
26. 18 Pa. Code §903(F).
27. *Peters v. Sec'y, Dep't of Corr.*, 2016 U.S. Dist. LEXIS 165013 (M.D. Fla. Nov. 30, 2016).
28. *State v. Damms*, 9 Wis.2d 183 (Wis. 1960).

CHAPTER 4

1. See *Allen v. Hannaford*, 138 Wash. 423 (1926).
2. Stephanie A. Jirard (2010). "The Missing White Women Syndrome: Why Missing Women of Color Are Easy for the Media to Ignore," in *Race, Crime, and the Media*, ed. Robert L. Bing, III (New York: McGraw-Hill), pp. 85–99.
3. For example, Mississippi Code Annotated §97-3-53 (2011), defines the punishment for kidnapping any child under the age of 16: "If the jury fails to agree on fixing the penalty at imprisonment for life, the court shall fix the penalty at not less than one (1) year nor more than thirty (30) years in the custody of the Department of Corrections."
4. *People v. Delacerda*, 236 Cal.App.4th 282 (2015) (boyfriend tackled girlfriend to keep her in apartment and shoved her in a closet to prevent escape; boyfriend convicted of kidnapping; movement of girlfriend not incidental to boyfriend's domestic violence assault).
5. *People v. Apo*, 25 Cal.App.3d 790 (1972).
6. 28 U.S.C. §1738A (2002).
7. The U.S. Department of Justice has published recommended criteria for states to follow for the issuing of an AMBER alert:

   1. Law enforcement has a reasonable belief that an abduction has occurred.
   2. The child is under 17 years old.
   3. Law enforcement believes the child is in imminent danger of serious bodily injury or death.
   4. There is enough descriptive information about the abduction and the child to assist in the recovery of the child.

8. Lucas I. Alpert (2010, April 2). "Ivanka's Stalker Ordeal Featured Crazed Talk, Threats and Blood Pix." *New York Post*, http://nypost.com/2010/04/02/ivankas-stalker-ordeal-featured-crazed-talk-threats-and-bloody-pix
9. J. Reid Meloy (2007). "Stalking: The State of the Science." *Criminal Behavior & Mental Health*, Vol. 17, No. 1, pp. 1–7.
10. Sameer Hinduja & Justin W. Patchin (2009). "Cyberbullying Fact Sheet: What You Need to Know About Online Aggression" (Orlando, FL: Cyberbullyng Research Center). http://cyberbullying.org/cyberbullying_fact_sheet.pdf
11. Kenneth France, Azim Danesh, & Stephanie Jirard (2013). "Informing Aggression-Prevention Efforts by Comparing Perpetrators of Brief vs. Extended Cyber Aggression." *Computers in Human Behavior*, Vol. 29, pp. 2143–2149.
12. Stephanie Jirard, Azim Danesh, & Kenneth France (2015). "Reporting Cyberbullying: An Examination of Victims Who Did Not Seek Formal Sanctions." *Journal of Scholastic Inquiry: Behavioral Sciences*, Vol. 4, No. 1, pp. 8–24.
13. *State v. Van Buren*, Vermont Superior Court, 2016, Docket No. 1144-12-15Bncr.
14. On June 1, 2018, right before he resigned from office, Missouri Governor Eric Greitens signed a law criminalizing "revenge porn," the very crime that drove him from office. https://www.msn.com/en-us/news/us/outgoing-gov-eric-greitens-accused-of-revenge-porn-signs-law-criminalizing-it/
15. *Wisconsin v. Mitchell*, 113 S.Ct. 2194 (1993).
16. Brian Levin & Jack McDevitt (2009, June 29). "Why Hate Crimes Are Different." www.CNN.com
17. See, in general, U.S. Department of Justice, Bureau of Justice Statistics (2014, January 23). "Sexual Victimization Reported by Adult Correctional Authorities, 2009–2011."
18. Matthew Hale, *History of the Pleas of the Crown* (1847).
19. George E. Dix & Michael M. Sharlot (1999). *Criminal Law*, 4th ed. (Belmont, CA: Wadsworth).
20. *Griswold v. Connecticut*, 381 U.S. 479 (1965); *Roe v. Wade*, 410 U.S. 113 (1973).
21. Susan Brownmiller (1975). *Against Our Will* (New York: Simon & Schuster).
22. Douglas N. Husak & George C. Thomas III (1992). "Date Rape, Social Convention, and Reasonable Mistakes." *Law & Philosophy*, Vol. 11, No. 1, pp. 95–126.
23. Title IX, enacted as part of the Education Amendments of 1972, Pub. L. No. 92-318, 20 U.S.C. §§1681-1688, renamed in 2002 "The Patsy Mink Equal Opportunity in Education Act" for its author and co-sponsor, the late congresswoman from Hawaii.
24. *Doe v. Brown University*, 166 F.Supp.3d 177 (2016).
25. See Jennifer Steinhauer (2013, September 21). "Navy Hearing in Rape Case Raises Alarm." *New York Times*, p. A1; Melinda Henneberger & Annys Shin (2013, September 1). "Aggressive Tactics Highlight the Rigors of Military Rape Cases." *Baltimore Sun*.
26. *Michael M. v. Sonoma County Superior Court*, 450 U.S. 464 (1981).
27. Rigel Oliveri (2000). "Statutory Rape Law and Enforcement in the Wake of Welfare Reform." *Stanford Law Review*, Vol. 52, pp. 463–508.
28. North Dakota Century Code §12.1-20-01(2) (2007).
29. New Jersey Statutes §2C:14-5 (1978).
30. *State v. Guest*, 583 P.2d 836 (Alaska 1978).
31. Kenneth V. Lanning (2010). *Child Molesters: A Behavioral Analysis for Professionals Investigating the Sexual Exploitation of Children*, 5th ed. (Alexandria, VA: National Center for Missing and Exploited Children). https://www.icmec.org/wp-content/uploads/2015/10/US-NCMEC-Child-Molesters-A-Behavioral-Analysis-Lanning-2010.pdf
32. Kenneth V. Lanning (2010). *Child Molesters: A Behavioral Analysis for Law Enforcement Officers*, 5th ed. (Washington, DC: National Center for Missing and Exploited Children).
33. *Douglas v. State*, 327 P.3d 492 (Nev. 2014).
34. Leigh B. Bienen (1998). "Defining Incest." *Northwestern University Law Review*, Vol. 92, pp. 1501–1580.

35. *In re L. Z.*, 61 N.E.3d 776 (2016).
36. Report of the Royal Commission on Capital Punishment, 1949–1953, pp. 25–28.
37. University of California, Davis School of Law (2012, October 2). "Is Homicide a Gendered Crime?" (Feminist Legal Theory blog). http://femlegaltheory.blogspot.com/2012/10/is-homicide-gendered-crime.html
38. *Auman v. People*, 109 P.3d 647 (2005).
39. *Enmund v. Florida*, 458 U.S.782 (1982).
40. *Tison v. Arizona*, 481 U.S. 137 (1987).
41. *Elonis v. United States*, 135 S.Ct. 2001 (2015).

CHAPTER 5

1. *Harrison v. People*, 50 N.Y. 518 (1872).
2. *People v. Drake*, 462 N.E.2d 376 (1984).
3. See Wayne R. LaFave (2003). *Criminal Law*, 4th ed. (St. Paul, MN: Thomson West).
4. Facts based on *People v. Sattlekau*, 104 N.Y.S. 805 (1907).
5. *State v. Parris*, 363 S.C. 477 (2005).
6. Donald Cressy (1953). *Other People's Money: A Study in the Social Psychology of Embezzlement* (Glenco, IL: Free Press).
7. See, generally, Cliff Roberson (1986). *Preventing Employee Misconduct: A Self-Defense Manual for Businesses* (Lexington, MA: Lexington Books).
8. Ibid.
9. Jeremy M. Wilson, Brandon A. Sullivan, Johnson Roy Fenoff, & Kari Kammel (2016). "Product Counterfeiting Legislation in the United States: A Review and Assessment of Characteristics, Remedies, and Penalties." *Journal of Criminal Law & Criminology*, Vol. 106, pp. 521–564.
10. *Illinois v. Downey*, 458 N.E.2d 160 (1983).
11. James Verini (2010, November 10). "The Great Cyberheist." *New York Times Magazine*.
12. Ibid.
13. In his *pro se* (representing himself) petition for a writ of *habeas corpus*, Albert claimed his work as a government informant gave him license to commit certain crimes to help the government. The court rejected his arguments, *Gonzalez v. United States*, 2012 U.S. Dist. LEXIS 160230.
14. "Bitcoin Forensics: A Journey Into the Dark Web." (2013, November 1). https://www.magnetforensics.com/computer-forensics/bitcoin-forensics-a-journey-into-the-dark-web/
15. "Criminal Underworld Is Dropping Bitcoin for Another Currency." (2018, January 3). www.Bloomberg.com
16. Jennifer Lynch (2005). "Identity Theft in Cyberspace: Crime Control Methods and Their Effectiveness in Combating Phishing Attacks." *Berkeley Technology Law Journal*, Vol. 20, No. 1, pp. 259–300.
17. Gallup Poll, "Hacking Tops List of Things Americans Worry About" (2014, October 14). http://news.gallup.com/poll/178856/hacking-tops-list-crimes-americans-worry
18. Gramm–Leach–Bliley Act, 113 Stat. 1338, 106 Pub. L. No. 102 (1999).
19. *United States v. Scott*, 270 F.3d 30 (1st Cir. 2001).
20. Adapted from facts of *A.B. v. Indiana*, 863 N.E.2d 1212 (2007).
21. The following states have consolidated theft statutes: Alabama, Alaska, Arizona, Arkansas, California, Colorado, Connecticut, Delaware, Florida, Georgia, Hawaii, Illinois, Indiana, Iowa, Kansas, Kentucky, Louisiana, Maine, Maryland, Minnesota, Missouri, Montana, Nebraska, Nevada, New Hampshire, New Jersey, New York, North Dakota, Ohio, Oregon, Pennsylvania, South Dakota, Texas, Utah, Washington, Wisconsin, and Wyoming.
22. In 2002, Congress passed the Sarbanes–Oxley Act that increased punishment for executives who commit public and private company crimes from 5 to 20 years in prison.
23. *United States v. Maze*, 414 U.S. 395 (1973).
24. Information for this section derived from S. L. Perryman (2006). "Mail and Wire Fraud." *American Criminal Law Review*, Vol. 43, pp. 715–738.
25. See *Neder v. United States*, 527 U.S. 1 (1999).
26. *Pereira v. United States*, 347 U.S. 1 (1954).
27. *United States v. C. Ray Nagin*, No. 14-30841 (5th Cir., Jan. 7, 2016).
28. The parallel laundering provision is found in 18 U.S.C. §1957 titled "Engaging in monetary transactions in property derived from specified unlawful activity," and provides, in part: "(a) Whoever, in any of the circumstances set forth in subsection (d), knowingly engages or attempts to engage in a monetary transaction in criminally derived property that is of a value greater than $10,000 and is derived from specified unlawful activity, shall be punished as provided in subsection (b)."
29. *National Organization of Women (NOW) v. Scheidler*, 510 U.S. 249 (1994).
30. A parallel law to RICO is the Violent Crimes in Aid of Racketeering Activity (VICAR), 18 U.S.C. §1959, which takes the crime of violence acts out of RICO and has only one predicate act for conviction, such as kidnapping, murder, arson, or robbery.
31. *H. J. Inc. v. Northwestern Bell Telegram Co.*, 492 U.S. 229 (1989) (customer class action suit against rate setters for phone company).
32. U.S. Attorney's Office, Southern District of New York (2018, January 5). "Scott Tucker Sentenced to More than 16 Years in Prison for Running $3.5 Billion Unlawful Internet Payday Lending Enterprise" (Press release). https://www.justice.gov/usao-sdny/pr/scott-tucker-sentenced-more-16-years-prison-running-35-billion-unlawful-internet-payday
33. *Davis v. State*, 737 So.2d 480 (1990).
34. *Lyons v. Oklahoma*, 516 P.2d 283 (1973).
35. 18 U.S.C. §844(i).

CHAPTER 6

1. 31 U.S.C. §§5361-5367 (2006).
2. Ronald J. Rychlak (2005). "Legal Problems With On-Line Gambling." *Engage*, Vol 6, No. 1, pp. 36–41.
3. 28 U.S.C. §3701-3704 (2006), known as the "Bradley Act."
4. *Murphy v. National Collegiate Athletic Association*, 584 U.S. ___ (2018).
5. Tim Fiorvanti (2018, May 16). "Does the SCOTUS Sports Betting Ruling Help in the Legalization Efforts of Online Poker?" ESPN.com. http://www.espn.com/chalk/story/_/id/23513317/online-poker-potential-supreme-court-paspa-ruling
6. Beverly Balos & Mary Louise Fellows (1999). "A Matter of Prostitution: Becoming Respectable." *New York University Law Review*, Vol. 74, pp. 1220–1303.

7. Robert F. Meier & Gilbert Geis (1997). *Victimless Crime? Prostitution, Drugs, Homosexuality, Abortion* (Los Angeles: Roxbury).

8. Ine Vanwesenbeeck (1994). *Prostitutes' Well Being and Risk* (Amsterdam: VU Uitguerij).

9. "Protocol to Prevent, Suppress, and Punish Trafficking in Persons, Especially Women and Children." United Nations Resolution 55/25, Article 3 (November 15, 2000).

10. Pub. L. No. 106-386, 114 Stat. 1464.

11. Erin N. Kauffman (2014). "The Uniform Act of and Remedies for Human Trafficking: State Law and the National Response to Labor Trafficking." *Journal of Legislation*, Vol. 41, pp. 291–328.

12. Pub. L. No. 59-384, 59th Congress, Session I, June 30, 1906.

13. Steven R. Belenko, ed. (2000). *Drugs and Drug Policy in America: A Documentary History* (Westport, CT: Greenwood Press).

14. Nathaniel Popper (2017, June 11). "Dark Trade Rises in Dark Corners of the Internet." *New York Times*, p. 20.

15. The seven crimes of conviction were (1) distribution and aiding and abetting distribution of narcotics, 21 U.S.C. §812, §841(a)(1), §841(b)(1)(A) and 18 U.S.C. §2; (2) using the Internet to distribute narcotics, 21 U.S.C. §812, 841(h), §841(b)(1)(A); (3) conspiracy to distribute narcotics, 21 U.S.C. §846; (4) engaging in a continuing criminal enterprise, 21 U.S.C. §848(a); (5) conspiring to obtain unauthorized access to a computer for purposes of commercial advantage and private financial gain and in furtherance of other criminal and tortious acts, 18 U.S.C. §1030(a)(2) and §1030(b); (6) conspiring to traffic in fraudulent identification documents, 18 U.S.C. §1028(f); and (7) conspiring to launder money, 18 U.S.C. §1956(h).

16. Massachusetts General Laws Ch. 138, §34 (2004).

17. See William J. Bernat (2006). "Party on? The Excellent Adventures of Social Host Liability in Massachusetts." *Suffolk University Law Review*, Vol. 39, pp. 981–1000.

18. Pub. L. No. 98-363, 6(a), 98 Stat. 435, 437 (1984) (codified as amended at 23 U.S.C. §158, 2000).

19. Pub. L. No. 90-618, 82 Stat. 1213, now codified in Chapter 44 of Title 18, United States Code.

20. Pub. L. No. 103-159, 107 Stat. 1536 (Nov. 30, 1993).

21. The NICS Improvement Amendments Act of 2007 was designed to close the loophole that allowed Virginia Tech student Seung-Hui Cho to purchase handguns despite being adjudicated by a Virginia court to be a danger to himself or others. Before he left office, President Obama finalized an executive branch rule on December 19, 2016, designed to implement the NICS Improvement Act by requiring the Social Security Administration (SSA) to report those who had been adjudicated (found by a court) to be a "mental defective" and had applied for social security benefits. But under the Congressional Review Act of 1996, 5 U.S.C. §§801-806, a new administration can rescind any order of its predecessor within 60 days, and on February 28, 2017, President Trump rescinded the SSA's mandatory reporting requirement.

22. Firearm Control Regulations Act of 1975: D.C. Code §§7-2501.01(12); 7-2502.01(a); 7-2502.02(a)(4) (total ban on handguns); D.C. Code §7-2507.02 (firearms in the home must be nonfunctional).

23. *District of Columbia v. Heller*, 554 U.S. 570 (2008).

24. *McDonald v. City of Chicago*, 561 U.S. 742 (2010)

25. *Caetano v. Massachusetts*, 136 S.Ct. 1027 (2016).

26. *Gillespie v. City of Indianapolis*, 185 F.3d 693 (7th Cir. 1999).

27. *Loper v. New York City Police Department*, 999 F.2d 699 (2d Cir. 1993).

28. *Feinstein v. City of New York*, 283 N.Y.S. 335 (1935).

29. *State v. Moseley*, 251 N.C. 285 (1959).

30. Albert Cohen (1955). *Delinquent Boys: The Culture of the Gang* (New York: Free Press).

31. Pub. L. No. 90-445, enacted "to assist the courts, correctional systems, community agencies, and primary and secondary public school systems to prevent, treat, and control juvenile delinquency; to support research and training efforts in the prevention, treatment, and control of juvenile delinquency; and for other purposes."

32. Donna Ladd (2018, April 5). "Dangerous, Growing, Yet Unnoticed: The Rise of America's White Gangs." *The Guardian*. https://www.theguardian.com/society/2018/apr/05/white-gangs-rise-simon-city-royals-mississippi-chicago

33. *City of Chicago v. Morales*, 527 U.S. 41 (1999).

34. National Gang Center (n.d.). "Gang Prosecution." http://www.nationalgangcenter.gov/Legislation/Prosecution

35. *Dixson v. United States*, 465 U.S. 482 (1984).

36. *Skilling v. United States*, 561 U.S. 358 (2010).

37. Bruce Weyhrauch, convicted of a failure to disclose a conflict of interest as a member of the Alaska legislature, and Conrad Black, a newspaper magnate from Canada convicted in a private sector fraud case, had their convictions overturned based on the high Court's decision in *Skilling*.

38. *McDonnell v. United States*, 136 S.Ct. 2355 (2016).

39. As a result of Governor McDonnell's successful appeal, former representative William Jefferson from New Orleans, convicted on public corruption and bribery charges in 2012 and sentenced to 13 years in prison, was resentenced to time served and ordered released from prison on October 5, 2017.

40. *United States v. Blagojevich*, 794 F.3d 729 (7th Cir. 2015). Governor Blagojevich was convicted of bribery for promises to take official acts, such as promising to sign laws to benefit specific parties in exchange for payment.

41. Utah Code Annotated §76-8-306 (2017).

42. Nebraska Revised Statutes Annotated §28-915 (2017).

43. The statement of the offense, plea agreement, and statement by General Flynn regarding his conviction can be found at the lawfare link https://www.lawfareblog.com/michael-flynn-plea-agreement-documents.

44. Clean Air Act, 42 U.S.C. §§7401 et seq.; *Whitman v. American Trucking Assn's, Inc.*, 531 U.S. 457 (2001).

45. Clean Water Act, 33 U.S.C. §§1251 et seq.

46. Elisha Anderson (2017, October 9). "Manslaughter Charges Sought Against Top Michigan Medical Executives in Flint Water Crisis." *Detroit Free Press*. https://www.freep.com/story/news/local/michigan/flint-water-crisis/2017/10/09/eden-wells-flint-water-crisis-charges/745571001/

47. *Mays v. City of Flint*, 871 F.3d 437 (2017).

48. Department of Justice (2015). "Prosecuting Computer Crimes." https://www.justice.gov/sites/default/files/criminal-ccips/legacy/2015/01/14/ccmanual.pdf

49. Orin S. Kerr (2018). *Computer Crime Law*, 4th ed. (St. Paul, MN: West Academic).

50. *United States v. Kramer*, 631 F.3d 900 (8th Cir. 2011).

51. Presidential Policy Directive (PPD-41). *United States Cyber Incident Coordination* (July 26, 2016).

52. FBI (n.d.). "What We Investigate: Cyber Crime." https://www.fbi.gov/investigate/cyber

53. For example, the Secret Service Electronic Crimes Task Force, the Department of Justice Computer Crime and Intellectual Property Section, and the Department of Homeland Security's CyberSecurity Division.

54. Matthew Ashton (2017). "Debugging the Real World: Robust Criminal Prosecution in the Internet of Things." *Arizona Law Review*, Vol. 59, pp. 805–835.

55. See *United States v. Sayer*, 748 F.3d 425 (1st Cir. 2014).

56. Thaddeus Hoffmeister (2014). "The Challenges of Preventing and Prosecuting Social Media Crimes." *Pace Law Review*, Vol. 35, pp. 115–134.

57. 18 U.S.C. §2261(A).

58. Justin Wm. Moyer (2016, February 18). "After Computer Hack, L.A. Hospital Pays $17,000 in Bitcoin Ransom to Get Back Medical Records." *Washington Post*.

59. See Arie W. Kruglanski, Michele J. Gelfand, Jocelyn J. Belanger, Anna Sheveland, Melkanthi Hetiarachchi, & Rohan Gunarayna (2014). "The Psychology of Radicalization and Deradicalization: How Significance Quest Impacts Violent Extremism." *Political Psychology*, Vol. 35, pp. 69–93.

60. Chris Mooney (2014, August 29). "Here Are the Psychological Reasons Why an American Might Join ISIS." *Mother Jones*. https://www.motherjones.com/politics/2014/08/inquiring-minds-arie-kruglanski-psychology-extremism-isis/

61. Pub. L. No. 107-56, 115 Stat. 272.

62. *United States v. U.S. District Court*, 407 U.S. 297 (1972).

63. As amended, 50 U.S.C. §§1801-1862 (2000 & Supp. II 2002).

64. Pub. L. No. 107-56, 208, 115 Stat. 272 (2001).

65. Jonathan Witmer-Rich (2014). "The Fatal Flaws of the 'Sneak and Peek' Statute and How to Fix It." *Case Western Reserve Law Review*, Vol. 65, pp. 121–179, citing USA PATRIOT Act §213. See 147 CONG. REC. S20, 683 (statement of Senator Leahy referring to seizure provision as "sneak and steal").

66. USA PATRIOT Act Improvement and Reauthorization Act of 2005, House Resolution 3199.

67. Pub. L. No. 65-24.

68. *Rasul v. Bush*, 542 U.S. 466 (2004); *Hamdi v. Rumsfeld*, 542 U.S. 507 (2004).

69. See, generally, J. A. Bauer (2006). "Detainees Under Review: Striking the Right Constitutional Balance Between the Executive's War Powers and Judicial Review." *Alabama Law Review*, Vol. 57, pp. 1081–1103.

70. Pub. L. No. 109-148 §1005(e), 119 Stat. 2680, 2742-44.

71. *Hamdan v. Rumsfeld*, 126 S.Ct. 2749 (2006).

72. Sheryl Gay Stolberg (2006, October 18). "President Signs New Rules to Prosecute Terror Suspects." *New York Times*, p. A14.

73. Gene Atherton & Andjela Jurisic (2017, November 14). "5 Principles of Managing Terrorists in Prison." *CorrectionsOne*. https://www.correctionsone.com/gang-and-terrorist-recruitment/articles/8694916-5-principles-of-managing-terrorists-in-prison/

74. Eric Lichtblau (2006, October 12). "American in Qaeda Tapes Accused of Treason." *New York Times*.

75. 18 U.S.C. §953.

76. 18 U.S.C. §2384 (seditious conspiracy).

CHAPTER 7

1. Nelson B. Lasson (1937). *The History and Development of the Fourth Amendment to the United States Constitution* (Baltimore: Johns Hopkins).

2. William W. Greenhalgh (2003). *The Fourth Amendment Handbook: A Chronological Survey of Supreme Court Decisions*, 2nd ed. (Chicago: American Bar Association).

3. *Beck v. Ohio*, 379 U.S. 89 (1964).

4. *Illinois v. Gates*, 462 U.S. 213 (1983) (overruling the two-part *Aguilar-Spinelli* test requiring information about the reliability of an informant or anonymous tip as too narrow in making probable cause determinations, citing *Aguilar v. Texas*, 378 U.S. 108 [1964] and *Spinelli v. United States*, 393 U.S. 410 [1969]).

5. 18 U.S.C. §1084. That statute provides in pertinent part: "(a) Whoever being engaged in the business of betting or wagering, knowingly uses a wire communication facility for the transmission in interstate or foreign commerce of bets or wagers . . . shall be fined not more than $10,000, or imprisoned not more than two years, or both."

6. "It is true that this Court has occasionally described its conclusions in terms of "constitutionally protected areas," (citations omitted) but we have never suggested that this concept can serve as a talismanic solution to every Fourth Amendment problem."

7. *Minnesota v. Olson*, 495 U.S. 91 (1990).

8. *Minnesota v. Carter*, 119 S.Ct. 469 (1998).

9. *Byrd v. United States*, 584 U.S. ___ (2018).

10. *Vernonia School Dist. 47J v. Acton*, 515 U. S. 646 (1995).

11. *Smith v. Maryland*, 442 U.S. 735 (1979).

12. See *United States v. Miller*, 425 U.S. 435 (1976).

13. *United States v. Knotts*, 460 U.S. 276 (1983).

14. *United States v. Karo*, 468 U.S. 705 (1984).

15. *Kyllo v. United States*, 533 U.S. 27 (2001).

16. *Florida v. Worsham*, No. 4D15-2733 (Fla. Dist. Ct. App. Mar. 29, 2017).

17. *United States v. Jones*, 132 S.Ct. 945 (2012).

18. Federal government guidance requires a warrant for international mobile subscriber identity (IMSI) catchers absent exigent circumstances. *See* Department of Justice Policy Guidance: Use of Cell-Site Simulator Technology (2015). https://www.justice.gov/opa/file/767321/download

19. See Jennifer Valentino-Devries (2011, September 21). "How 'Stingray' Devices Work." *Wall Street Journal*. http://blogs.wsj.com/digits/2011/09/21/how-stingray-devices-work/

20. Devlin Barrett (2015, May 3). "U.S. Will Change Stance on Secret Phone Tracking." *Wall Street Journal*, p. A1; Devlin Barrett (2014, November 13). "Americans' Cellphones Targeted in Secret U.S. Spy Program." *Wall Street Journal*.

21. *Carpenter v. United States*, 585 U.S. ___ (2018).

22. Written by Francis Scott Key on September 14, 1814, originally titled the "Defence of Fort McHenry" as Key witnessed British ships bombard the Fort from Baltimore Harbor.

23. *Terry v. Ohio*, 392 U.S. 1 (1968).

24. *United States v. Sokolow*, 490 U.S. 1 (1989) (internal citations omitted).

25. Douglas R. Mitchell & Gregory J. Connor (2018). *Stop and Frisk: Legal Perspectives, Strategic Thinking, and Tactical Procedures*, 3rd ed. (New York: Routledge).

26. Both women were born in the United States and recorded the encounter on a cell phone. https://www.nbcnews.com/news/latino/border-patrol-agent-detains-women-speaking-spanish-montana-gas-station-n876096

27. *Hayes v. Florida*, 470 U.S. 811 (1985).

28. *United States v. Sharpe*, 470 U.S. 675 (1985).

29. *Rodriguez v. United States*, 135 S.Ct. 1609 (2015).

30. *Hiibel v. Nevada*, 124 S.Ct. 2451 (2004).

31. *Delaware v. Prouse*, 440 U.S. 648 (1979).

32. *Brendlin v. California*, 127 S.Ct. 2400 (2007).

33. *Pennsylvania v. Mimms*, 434 U.S. 106 (1977); *Maryland v. Wilson*, 519 U.S. 408 (1997).

34. *Arizona v. Johnson*, 555 U.S. 323 (2009).

35. *Whren v. United States*, 517 U.S. 806 (1996).

36. Paul G. Cassell and Richard Fowles have published preliminary research that indicates a lack of aggressive *Terry* stop enforcement in Chicago may have led to that city's dramatic spike in homicides in 2016.

37. Class action suit against the New York Police Department brought in *Floyd v. City of New York* (2008), Final Report, New York City Joint Remedial Process on New York Police Department's Stop, Question, and Frisk and Trespass Enforcement Policies, https://ccrjustice.org/ released May 15, 2018; "Driving While Black," *United States v. Leviner*, 31 F.Supp.2d 23 (D. Mass. 1998).

38. *Utah v. Strieff*, 136 S.Ct. 2056 (2016). Justice Sotomayor's dissent was written after Officer Michael Slager killed Black motorist Walter Scott by shooting Scott in the back as he ran away from a *Terry* stop when Slager pulled Scott over for a license plate violation. On December 7, 2017, Slager was sentenced to 20 years in prison. http://www.foxnews.com/us/2017/12/07/ex-cop-michael-slager-sentenced-to-prison-for-killing-unarmed-black-man.html

39. *Illinois v. Wardlow*, 528 U.S. 119 (2000).

40. *Commonwealth v. Warren*, 58 N.E.3d 333 (2016).

41. *Florida v. Royer*, 460 U.S. 491 (1983).

42. *United States* v. *Mendenhall, 446 U.S. 544 (1980)*.

43. *United States v. Drayton*, 536 U.S. 194 (2002).

44. The information for this section was derived from Larry E. Holtz (2004). *Contemporary Criminal Procedure: Court Decisions for Law Enforcement* (Longwood, FL: Gould).

45. *California v. Hodari D.*, 499 U.S. 621 (1991).

46. *Tennessee v. Garner*, 471 U.S. 1 (1985).

47. *Graham v. Connor*, 490 U.S. 386 (1989).

48. Chad Flanders and Joseph C. Welling (2016, January 15). "Police Use of Deadly Force: State Statutes 30 Years After *Garner*." www.SLULawJournal.

49. *Scott v. Harris*, 550 U.S. 372 (2007); The video of the chase and interview with the driver Victor Harris, titled "Why I Ran," is available on YouTube https://www.youtube.com/watch?v=JATVLUOjzvM

50. *Payton v. New York*, 445 U.S. 573 (1980).

51. *Steagald v. United States*, 451 U.S. 204 (1981).

52. See, generally, *State v. Kerr*, 511 N.W.2d 586 (1994).

53. *United States v. Green*, 670 F.2d 1148 (D.C. Cir. 1981).

54. *United States v. Lima*, 819 F.2d 687 (7th Cir. 1987).

55. *Alabama v. White*, 496 U.S. 325 (1990).

56. *Florida v. J. L.*, 529 U.S. 266 (2000).

57. *Navarette v. California*, 134 S.Ct. 1683 (2014).

58. *United States v. Espinoza-Valdez*, 2018 16-10395 (9th Cir., May 6, 2018).

59. *Davis v. United States*, 564 U.S. 229 (2011).

60. *Franks v. Delaware*, 438 U.S. 154 (1978)

61. *Coolidge v. New Hampshire*, 403 U.S. 443 (1971).

62. See also *Lo-Ji Sales, Inc. v. New York*, 442 U.S. 319 (1979) (town justice who signed warrant could not then participate in search of adult bookstore for obscene materials).

63. *Andresen v. Maryland*, 427 U.S. 463 (1976).

64. *United States v. Bonner*, 808 F.2d 864 (1st Cir. 1986).

65. The full 61-page affidavit can be found on the World Wide Web.

66. *Groh v. Ramirez*, 540 U.S. 551 (2004).

67. *Messerschmidt v. Millender*, 565 U.S. 535 (2012).

68. 18 U.S.C. §3109 (2000).

69. *United States v. Banks*, 124 S.Ct. 521 (2003).

70. *Hudson v. Michigan*, 126 S.Ct. 2159 (2006).

71. *Michigan v. Summers*, 452 U.S. 692 (1981).

72. See *Muehler v. Mena*, 544 U.S. 93 (2005). In an ancillary issue, the high Court dismissed Mena's claim that the officers' questions about Mena's immigration status violated her Fourth Amendment right against unreasonable searches. The Court said questioning by law enforcement is not a search.

73. *Los Angeles v. Rettele*, 127 S.Ct. 1989 (2007).

74. *Bailey v. United States*, 133 S.Ct. 1031 (2013).

75. Wayne LaFave, *Search and Seizure: A Treatise on the Fourth Amendment*, 3rd ed. (St. Paul, MN: West, 1996).

76. *Mincey v. Arizona*, 437 U.S. 385 (1978).

CHAPTER 8

1. *Florida v. Royer*, 460 U.S. 491 (1983).

2. *Schneckloth v. Bustamonte*, 412 U.S. 218 (1973).

3. Although one might expect that a person with a low level of intellectual functioning, a person under the influence of alcohol or drugs, or a person suffering extreme emotional distress would not be capable of giving voluntary consent, they can.

4. *State v. Smith*, 488 S.E.2d 210 (1997).

5. *Bumper v. North Carolina*, 391 U.S. 543 (1968).

6. See, generally, *United States v. Dichiarinte*, 445 F.2d 126 (7th Cir. 1971).

7. *United States v. Warner*, 843 F.2d 401 (9th Cir. 1988).

8. *Illinois v. Rodriguez*, 497 U.S. 177 (1990); see, e.g., *United States v. Carrasco*, 540 F.3d 43 (1st Cir. 2008) (boat owner's consent valid because officers reasonably believed he had apparent authority to consent to search of containers as they were located on boat, unlocked, and not identified as defendant's personal property).

9. *Georgia v. Randolph*, 126 S.Ct. 1515 (2006).

10. *Fernandez v. California*, 134 S.Ct. 1126 (2014).

11. *United States v. Knights*, 534 U.S. 112 (2001).

12. *Samson v. California*, 126 S.Ct. 2193 (2006) (methamphetamine possession conviction based on a warrantless search of a parolee upheld).

13. *Chimel v. California*, 395 U.S. 752 (1969).

14. *Rawlings v. Kentucky*, 448 U.S. 98 (1980).

15. *Vale v. Louisiana*, 399 U.S. 30 (1970).

16. *South Dakota v. Opperman*, 428 U.S. 364 (1976).

17. *Carroll v. United States*, 267 U.S. 132 (1925).

18. Motorhomes also fall within the automobile exception because of their ability to drive away and escape, *California v. Carney*, 471 U.S. 386 (1985), but trailer homes typically have no

wheels and are often granted the same Fourth Amendment protection homes enjoy.

19. *Collins v. Virginia*, 584 U.S. ___ (2018).

20. *New York v. Belton*, 453 U.S. 454 (1981).

21. See, generally, Leslie A. Shoebotham (2004). "The Inevitably Arbitrary Placement of Bright Lines: *Belton* and Its Progeny." *Tulane Law Review*, Vol. 79, pp. 365–400.

22. See *United States v. Milton*, 52 F.3d 78 (4th Cir. 1995).

23. *Thornton v. United States*, 124 S.Ct. 795 (2004).

24. *Arizona v. Gant*, 556 U.S. 332 (2009).

25. *South Dakota v. Opperman*, 428 U.S. 364 (1976).

26. *Florida v. Wells*, 495 U.S. 1 (1990); *Colorado v. Bertine*, 479 U.S. 367 (1987) (lawful during an inventory search to open closed containers).

27. *Florida v. Meyers*, 466 U.S. 380 (1984).

28. *United States v. Stegall*, 850 F.3d 981 (8th Cir. 2017).

29. *United States v. Ross*, 456 U.S. 798 (1982).

30. *Florida v. Jimeno*, 500 U.S. 248 (1991).

31. *New York v. Belton*, 453 U.S. 454 (1981).

32. *Florida v. Wells*, 495 U.S. 1 (1990).

33. *Illinois v. Caballes*, 125 S.Ct. 834 (2005).

34. *Florida v. Harris*, 133 S.Ct. 1050 (2013).

35. *Florida v. Jardines*, 569 U.S. 1 (2013).

36. *United States v. Whitaker*, 820 F.3d 849 (7th Cir. 2016).

37. *Ybarra v. Illinois*, 444 U.S. 85 (1979).

38. *Maryland v. Pringle*, 540 U.S. 366 (2003).

39. *Michigan Dept. of State Police v. Sitz*, 496 U.S. 444 (1990); *United States v. Martinez-Fuerte*, 428 U.S. 543 (1976).

40. *Illinois v. Lidster* 124 S.Ct. 885 (2004).

41. *City of Indianapolis v. Edmond*, 531 U.S. 32 (2000).

42. *Arizona v. Hicks*, 480 U.S. 321 (1987).

43. *Oliver v. United States*, 466 U.S. 170 (1984).

44. *United States v. Desir*, 257 F.3d 1233 (11th Cir. 2001).

45. *United States v. Dunn*, 480 U.S. 294 (1987).

46. *California v. Greenwood*, 486 U.S. 35 (1988).

47. See *Johnson v. United States*, 333 U.S. 10 (1948) (plain smell); *United States v. Jackson*, 588 F.2d 1046 (5th Cir. 1979) (plain hearing).

48. *Ybarra v. Illinois*, 444 U.S. 85 (1979).

49. *Warden v. Hayden*, 387 U.S. 294 (1967).

50. Information derived from John L. Worrall (2004). *Criminal Procedure: From First Contact to Appeal* (Upper Saddle River, NJ: Pearson).

51. *United States v. Al-Azzawy*, 784 F.2d 890 (9th Cir. 1985).

52. *Brigham City v. Stuart*, 547 U.S. 398 (2006).

53. *Michigan v. Fisher*, 130 S.Ct. 546 (2009).

54. There is no "general crime scene" exception to the warrant requirement. If police respond to a crime scene, they cannot simply walk in and start searching. Police may secure the scene, get help for survivors, and call in for a warrant attesting to the probable cause giving rise to the need for a search warrant.

55. *Kentucky v. King*, 563 U.S. 452 (2011).

56. *Missouri v. McNeely*, 133 S.Ct. 1552 (2013).

57. *Birchfield v. North Dakota*, 136 S.Ct. 2160 (2016).

58. *United States v. Montoya de Hernandez*, 473 U.S. 531 (1985).

59. *Florence v. Board of Chosen Freeholders of the County of Burlington*, 566 U.S. 318 (2012).

60. *Maryland v. King*, 133 S.Ct. 1958 (2013).

61. Maryland Code Annotated, Public Safety §2-501, et seq. (West 2009). The safeguards are (1) A DNA sample collected from an individual charged with a crime under subsection (a)(3) of this section may not be tested or placed in the statewide DNA data base system prior to the first scheduled arraignment date unless requested or consented to by the individual as provided in paragraph (3) of this subsection.

(2) If all qualifying criminal charges are determined to be unsupported by probable cause:

   (i) the DNA sample shall be immediately destroyed; and

   (ii) notice shall be sent to the defendant and counsel of record for the defendant that the sample was destroyed.

(3) An individual may request or consent to have the individual's DNA sample processed prior to arraignment for the sole purpose of having the sample checked against a sample that:

   (i) has been processed from the crime scene or the hospital; and

   (ii) is related to the charges against the individual.

62. Facts adapted from *Brown v. Conrado*, 2014 U.S. Dist., LEXIS 22488.

63. *Tinker et al. v. Des Moines Independent Community School District et al.*, 393 U.S. 503 (1968).

64. *Vernonia School District 47J v. Acton*, 515 U.S. 646 (1995).

65. *Safford Unified School District #1 v. Redding*, 557 U.S. 364 (2009).

66. *National Treasury Employees Union et al. v. Von Raab*, 489 U.S. 656 (1989).

67. *City of Ontario v. Quon*, 130 S.Ct. 2619 (2010).

68. *MacWade v. Kelly*, 460 F.3d 260 (2d Cir. 2006).

69. *United States v. Aukai*, 497 F.3d 955 (9th Cir. 2007).

70. See *Michigan v. Chesternut*, 486 U.S. 567 (1988) (if person feels free to terminate police encounter, she is not seized).

71. *Florida v. Bostick*, 501 U.S. 429 (1991); *United States v. Drayton*, 536 U.S. 194 (2002).

72. *Schneckloth v. Bustamonte*, 412 U.S. 218 (1973) (knowing of your right to refuse consent is not determinative to finding valid consent).

73. Ric Simmons (2005). "Not Voluntary but Still Reasonable: A New Paradigm for Understanding the Consent Searches Doctrine." *Indiana Law Journal*, Vol. 80, pp. 773–824.

74. *United States v. Cortez-Rocha*, 394 F.3e 1115 (9th Cir. 2005); *United States v. Flores-Montano*, 541 U.S. 149 (2004).

75. *United States v. Leon*, 468 U.S. 897 (1984).

76. *Davis v. United States*, 564 U.S. 229 (2011).

77. *Virginia v. Moore*, 533 U.S. 164 (2008).

78. *Heien v. North Carolina*, 135 S.Ct. 530 (2014).

79. *Utah v. Strieff*, 136 S.Ct. 2056 (2016).

80. *Herring v. United States*, 555 U.S. 135 (2009).

81. *Arizona v. Evans*, 514 U.S. 1 (1995).

82. Manny Fernandez & David Montgomery (2016, May 18). "Year After Shootout, Waco's Bikers Try to Move Forward." *New York Times*, p. A10.

CHAPTER 9

1. Facts modified from *United States v. LeBrun*, 363 F.3d 715 (8th Cir. 2004).

2. The privilege against self-incrimination was deemed applicable to the states via the Fourteenth Amendment's Due Process Clause (*Malloy v. Hogan*, 378 U.S. 1, 1964).

3. Lawrence S. Wrightsman & Saul M. Kassin (1993). *Confessions in the Courtroom* (Newbury Park, CA: Sage).

4. *Smith v. United States*, 348 U.S. 147 (1954).

5. *Nix v. Williams*, 467 U.S. 431 (1984).

6. Richard A. Leo (1992). "From Coercion to Deception: The Changing Nature of Police Interrogation in America." *Crime, Law and Social Change*, Vol. 18, pp. 35–59.

7. *Malinski v. New York*, 324 U.S. 401 (1945) (confession was coerced from a defendant who after arrest was taken to a hotel, stripped, and kept naked, whereupon, after being held from 8 a.m. to 6 p.m., he confessed).

8. *Leyra v. Denno*, 347 U.S. 556 (1954) (confession was coerced from a murder suspect who had been subjected to many hours of day-and-night questioning; a state psychiatrist was then introduced to him as a "doctor," who questioned the defendant).

9. *Payne v. Arkansas*, 356 U.S. 560 (1958) (confession was coerced from a "mentally dull 19-year-old Negro" when the police chief threatened him with mob violence).

10. *Lynumn v. Illinois*, 372 U.S. 528 (1963) (confession was coerced from a defendant who was told by police that welfare aid to her children would be cut off and that she would lose custody if she did not "cooperate").

11. *Chambers v. Florida*, 309 U.S. 227 (1940). ("Confessions of the commission of a robbery and murder must be deemed involuntary, so as to render their use in obtaining convictions a violation of the due process clause of the Fourteenth Amendment, where obtained from young negroes arrested without warrant, held in jail without formal charges, and without being permitted to see or confer with counsel or friends, believing that they were in danger of mob violence, made at the end of an all-night session following five days of fruitless questioning, each by himself, by state officers and other white citizens, in the presence of from four to ten white men, and after a previous confession had been pronounced 'unsatisfactory' by the prosecuting attorney").

12. *Gideon v. Wainwright*, 372 U.S. 335 (1963).

13. *Malloy v. Hogan*, 378 U.S. 1 (1964).

14. *Mapp v. Ohio*, 367 U.S. 643 (1961).

15. *Escobedo v. Illinois*, 378 U.S. 478 (1964).

16. See, generally, *Johnson v. Trigg*, 28 F.3d 639 (7th Cir. 1994) (confession was ruled voluntary, although the 14-year-old defendant of below-average intelligence saw police arrest his terminally ill mother before confessing); *Cooks v. Ward*, 165 F.3d 1283 (10th Cir. 1998) (confession was ruled voluntary despite the police threat that the defendant would "get the needle" unless he talked, because defendant later requested to speak to police); *Thompson v. Haley*, 255 F.3d 1292 (11th Cir. 2001) (confession was ruled voluntary, although police told defendant his girlfriend might go to the electric chair if he did not confess because police had probable cause to arrest his girlfriend for murder).

17. *Colorado v. Connelly*, 479 U.S. 157 (1986).

18. Fred E. Inbau, John E. Reid, Joseph P. Buckley, & Brian C. Jayne (2013). *Criminal Interrogation and Confessions*, 5th ed. (Sudbury, MA: Jones & Bartlett).

19. Salazar's case was eventually dismissed because of the state improperly withholding evidence, but when the state found a DNA expert who confirmed Salazar could not be excluded as a suspect, he was reindicted. Grand Jury Indictment of Martin Salazar for First Degree (Palm Beach County Ct., Oct. 7, 1997) (No. 97-11428CFA02).

20. *Escobedo v. Illinois*, 378 U.S. 478 (1964).

21. *Cohens v. Virginia*, 6 Wheat. 264 (1821).

22. *Dickerson v. United States*, 530 U.S. 428 (2000).

23. *Duckworth v. Eagan*, 492 U.S. 195 (1989).

24. *Thompson v. Keohane*, 516 U.S. 99 (1995).

25. See, generally, *United States v. Booth*, 669 F.2d 1231 (9th Cir. 1981); *California v. Beheler*, 463 U.S. 1121 (1983).

26. *Maryland v. Shatzer*, 559 U.S. 98 (2010).

27. *Illinois v. Perkins*, 496 U.S. 292 (1990).

28. *Oregon v. Mathiason*, 97 S.Ct. 711 (1977) (declining to find that *Miranda* warnings are required "simply because the questioning takes place in the station house, or because the questioned person is one whom the police suspect").

29. *Stansbury v. California*, 511 U.S. 318 (1994) (a "reasonable person [would] have felt he or she was not at liberty to terminate the interrogation and leave"); *Thompson v. Keohane* (1995).

30. *Brewer v. Williams*, 430 U.S. 387 (1977).

31. *Rhode Island v. Innis*, 446 U.S. 291 (1980).

32. *Yarborough v. Alvarado*, 541 U.S. 652 (2004).

33. *J.D.B. v. North Carolina*, 564 U.S. 261 (2011).

34. *Illinois v. Perkins*, 496 U.S. 292 (1990).

35. There is a split of lower court opinions on whether fabricating evidence to use during a confession is permissible, for example creating fake DNA or laboratory reports. Some courts hold the government fabricating evidence is a step too far because the fake evidence may be introduced in court, while other courts find the act of fabrication legal. See Laurie Magid (2001). "Deceptive Police Interrogation Practices: How Far Is Too Far?" *Michigan Law Review*, Vol. 99, pp. 1168–1210.

36. See *Kyger v. Carlton*, 146 F.3d 374 (6th Cir. 1998).

37. *Michigan v. Mosley*, 423 U.S. 96 (1975).

38. *Minnick v. Mississippi*, 498 U.S. 146 (1990).

39. *Edwards v. Arizona*, 451 U.S. 477 (1981).

40. *Montejo v. Louisiana*, 129 S.Ct. 2079 (2009).

41. *Maryland v. Shatzer*, 559 U.S. 98 (2010).

42. *Moran v. Burbine*, 475 U.S. 412 (1986).

43. *Kirby v. Illinois*, 406 U.S. 682 (1972).

44. The prosecution bears the burden of proving at least by a preponderance of the evidence the *Miranda* waiver and the voluntariness of the confession and some states require proof of waiver be made beyond a reasonable doubt. See, e.g., *State v. Galloway*, 133 N.J. 631 (1993) (prosecution must prove *Miranda* waiver beyond a reasonable doubt).

45. Saul M. Kassin & G. H. Gudjonsson (1981), quoting T. Grisso. *Juveniles' Waiver of Rights: Legal and Psychological Competence* (New York: Plenum).

46. Burbine's sister had hired an attorney, who was trying to contact him in police custody, but police did not tell Burbine about the attorney. When officers spoke to the attorney, they lied and said that Burbine would not be questioned that day. The Court held Burbine's confession admissible because police conduct outside the interrogation room had no bearing on Burbine receiving *Miranda* warnings and waiving his rights (*Moran v. Burbine*, 475 U.S. 412, 1986).

47. *North Carolina v. Butler*, 441 U.S. 369 (1979).

48. Berghuis *v. Thompkins*, 560 U.S. 370 (2010).
49. See *Hart v. Attorney General of the State of Florida*, 323 F.3d 884 (2003).
50. *Salinas v. Texas*, 133 S.Ct. 2174 (2013).
51. *Griffin v. California*, 380 U.S. 609 (1965).
52. *New York v. Quarles*, 467 U.S. 649 (1984).
53. *Pennsylvania v. Muniz*, 496 U.S. 582 (1990).
54. Originally reported as *Brewer v. Williams*, 430 U.S. 387 (1977).
55. *Silverthorne Lumber Company v. United States*, 251 U.S. 385 (1920).
56. *Murray v. United States*, 487 U.S. 533 (1988).
57. *United States v. Ruhe*, 191 F.3d 376 (4th Cir. 1999).
58. *Nix v. Williams*, 467 U.S. 431 (1984).
59. *Harris v. New York*, 401 U.S. 222 (1971).
60. See *United States v. Kimball*, 884 F.2d 1274 (9th Cir. 1989).

CHAPTER 10

1. Erwin Chemerinsky & Laurie Levenson (2009). *Criminal Procedure* (New York: Aspen Publishers).
2. Michael J. Klarman (2000). "The Racial Origins of Modern Criminal Procedure." *Michigan Law Review*, Vol. 99, pp. 48–97, citing at p. 50 *Moore v. Dempsey*, 261 U.S. 86 (1923); *Powell v. Alabama*, 287 U.S. 45 (1932); *Norris v. Alabama*, 294 U.S. 587 (1935); *Brown v. Mississippi*, 297 U.S. 278 (1936).
3. Today, a few rights remain unincorporated, such as the Third Amendment's quartering of soldiers, the Seventh Amendment's money threshold for civil suits, the Fifth Amendment's right to grand jury indictment, for the prosecutor can file an information as a charging document.
4. Douglas Linder (n.d.). *Famous Trials*. http://www.famous-trials.com/scottsboroboys/1531-home
5. Ida B. Wells (1892). *Southern Horrors: Lynching Law in All Its Phases* (New York: New York Age Press).
6. *New York Times*, full Dylann Roof confession. https://www.nytimes.com/video/us/100000004815369/full-dylann-roof-confession.html
7. *Betts v. Brady*, 316 U.S. 455 (1942).
8. *Gideon v. Wainwright*, 372 U.S. 335 (1963).
9. See, generally, Charles Ogletree (1993). "Beyond Justification: Seeking Motivations to Sustain Public Defenders." *Harvard Law Review*, Vol. 106, pp. 1239–1294.
10. *State v. Peart*, 621 So.2d 780 (La. 1993).
11. *Louisiana v. Boyer*, No. 10-693 (Court of Appeal for Louisiana, Third Cir. 2011). On appeal, the U.S. Supreme Court decided they had improvidently granted Boyer's *writ of certiorari* and declined to decide the case.
12. *Ake v. Oklahoma*, 470 U.S. 68 (1985).
13. *Kirby v. Illinois*, 406 U.S. 682 (1972).
14. *Massiah v. United States*, 377 U.S. 201 (1964).
15. See *Kuhlmann v. Wilson*, 477 U.S. 436 (1986).
16. The case was litigated for over 10 years as *Brewer v. Williams*, 430 U.S. 387 (1977) and *Nix v. Williams*, 467 U.S. 431 (1984), until the victim's body was allowed at trial under the inevitable discovery exception to the exclusionary rule.
17. James J. Tomkovicz (2007). "Saving *Massiah* From *Elstad*: The Admissibility of Successive Confessions Following a Deprivation of Counsel." *William & Mary Bill of Rights Journal*, Vol. 15, pp. 711–764.
18. *Texas v. Cobb*, 532 U.S. 162 (2001).
19. *Blockburger v. United States*, 284 U.S. 299 (1932).
20. *Michigan v. Jackson*, 475 U.S. 625 (1986).
21. *Miranda v. Arizona*, 384 U.S. 436 (1966).
22. Jacob E. Warren (2009). "*Montejo v. Louisiana*: Affirmative Requests and the Sixth Amendment Right to Counsel." *Duke Law Journal of Constitutional Law & Public Policy*, Vol. 4, pp. 293–304.
23. *United States v. Gonzalez-Lopez*, 548 U.S. 140 (2006).
24. *United States v. Wade*, 388 U.S. 218 (1967); *Massiah v. United States*, 377 U.S. 201 (1964); *United States v. Henry*, 447 U.S. 264 (1980).
25. *Patterson v. Illinois*, 487 U.S. 285 (1988).
26. *United States v. Leon*, 468 U.S. 897 (1984) (Court holds the good faith exception applies to the exclusionary rule because the rule extracts a "high cost" to society by letting the guilty go free when evidence is suppressed due to police misconduct. The exclusionary rule must "pay its way" in punishing the police for egregious misconduct, not mere negligence.)
27. *Maryland v. Shatzer*, 559 U.S. 98 (2010).
28. *Patterson v. Illinois*, 432 U.S. 197 (1997).
29. Andrew D. Leipold (2005). "How the Pretrial Process Contributes to Wrongful Convictions." *American Criminal Law Review*, Vol. 42, pp. 1123–1165.
30. Ibid. at p. 1133.
31. Even when the defendant's guilt seems obvious to all, the law still requires that the defendant is presumed innocent until the state proves him guilty beyond a reasonable doubt. If jurors come to the trial with their minds made up about the defendant's innocence or guilt, they are legally ineligible to sit on the jury because they will not listen to the evidence. Usually in a death-penalty case, defendants are forced to go to trial to convince a jury to sentence them to life without parole. If the state removed the death penalty as a sentencing option, many more "obviously guilty" defendants would plead guilty in exchange for a sentence of life without parole.
32. *Irvin v. Dowd*, 366 U.S. 717 (1961).
33. *Sheppard v. Maxwell*, 384 U.S. 333 (1966).
34. *Faretta v. California*, 422 U.S. 806 (1975).
35. January 2, 2017, hearing, transcript pp. 197–216, case 2:15-cr-00472-RMG.
36. *Florida v. Nixon*, 543 U.S. 175 (2004).
37. *Strickland v. Washington*, 466 U.S. 668 (1984).
38. *Burdine v. Johnson*, 231 F.3d 950 (5th Cir. 2001).
39. *United States v. Cronic*, 466 U.S. 648 (1984).
40. *Padilla v. Kentucky*, 559 U.S. 356 (2010).
41. *Crawford v. Washington*, 541 U.S. 36 (2004).
42. After the *Crawford* decision, "testimonial statements are only admitted against a criminal defendant when the declarant is unavailable, and the defendant had a previous opportunity to cross examine."
43. *Coy v. Iowa*, 487 U.S. 1012 (1988).
44. *Maryland v. Craig*, 497 U.S. 836 (1990).

CHAPTER 11

1. "Texas Teacher Fired After Racist Facebook Post" (2015, June 13). http://thegrio.com/2015/06/13/texas-teacher-fired-after-racist-mckinney-facebook-post/
2. *Tinker v. Des Moines Independent Community School District*, 393 U.S. 503 (1969).

3. *Whitney v. California*, 274 U.S. 357 (1927).

4. *Elli v. City of Ellisville*, 997 F.Supp.2d 980 (E.D. Mo. 2014).

5. *McCullen v. Coakley*, 134 S.Ct. 2518 (2014).

6. *Snyder v. Phelps*, 131 S.Ct. 1207 (2011).

7. *Hague v. CIO*, 307 U.S. 496 (1939).

8. *Terminiello v. Chicago*, 337 U.S. 1 (1949).

9. See *Grayned v. City of Rockford*, 408 U.S. 104 (1972) (government can regulate time, manner, and place of speech that might disrupt school located nearby).

10. See *Clark v. Community for Creative Non-Violence*, 468 U.S. 288 (1984); *Metromedia, Inc. v. San Diego*, 453 U.S. 490 (1981); *Cox v. Louisiana*, 379 U.S. 559 (1965).

11. North Carolina General Statutes Annotated §§14–202.5(a), (e).

12. *Packingham v. North Carolina*, 137 S.Ct. 1730 (2017).

13. Citing *Reno v. American Civil Liberties Union*, 521 U. S. 844 (1997).

14. *Connally v. General Construction Co.*, 269 U.S. 385 (1926).

15. See *Kolender v. Lawson*, 461 U.S. 352 (1983).

16. *United States v. O'Brien*, 391 U.S. 367 (1968).

17. *Texas v. Johnson*, 491 U.S. 397 (1989).

18. *United States v. Eichman*, 496 U.S. 310 (1990).

19. Citation from case: See M. Newton and J. Newton (1991). *The Ku Klux Klan: An Encyclopedia*, p. 145.

20. Citation from case: See W. Scott, "The Lady of The Lake," canto third.

21. Citation from case: S. Kennedy, *Southern Exposure* 31 (1991).

22. Citation from case: W. Wade (1987). *The Fiery Cross: The Ku Klux Klan in America*, pp. 48–49.

23. Citation from case: D. Chalmers (1980). *Hooded Americanism: The History of the Ku Klux Klan*, p. 333.

24. *Chaplinsky v. New Hampshire*, 315 U.S. 568 (1942).

25. *Cohen v. California*, 403 U.S. 15 (1971).

26. *In re John M.* (JV-145099), Arizona Court of Appeals (2001). The court cited *Webster's Dictionary* for the harmful racist context of what we euphemistically call the "N word" in defining John M's speech. Today *Webster's* states in commentary about the word "n****r," that "The word now ranks as almost certainly the most offensive and inflammatory racial slur in English, a term expressive of hatred and bigotry. Its self-referential uses by and among black people are not always intended or taken as offensive (although many object to those uses as well), but its use by a person who is not black to refer to a black person can only be regarded as a deliberate expression of contemptuous racism." https://www.merriam-webster.com/dictionary/

27. *Wisconsin v. Ovadal*, Appeal No. 03-0377, Court of Appeals (2003).

28. See also *Houston v. Hill*, 482 U.S. 451 (1987) (municipal ordinance that makes it unlawful to interrupt a police officer in the performance of his duty is substantially overbroad and, therefore, invalid under the First Amendment).

29. *Lewis v. City of New Orleans*, 415 U.S. 130 (1974).

30. *Schenck v. United States*, 249 U.S. 47 (1919).

31. *Brandenburg v. Ohio*, 395 U.S. 444 (1969).

32. Ibid.

33. *Watts v. United States*, 394 U.S. 705 (1969).

34. David L. Hudson (2008, May 12). "True Threats." http://www.firstamendmentcenter.org/true-threats

35. *Roth v. United States*, 354 U.S. 476 (1957).

36. *Jacobellis v. Ohio*, 378 U.S. 184 (1964).

37. *Miller v. California*, 413 U.S. 15 (1973).

38. *Attorney General v. Book Named "John Cleland's Memoirs of a Woman of Pleasure,"* 349 Mass. 69 (1965).

39. Official Code of Georgia Annotated, §16-12-80, Obscenity Defined.

40. *New York v. Ferber*, 458 U.S. 747 (1982).

41. *Osborne v. Ohio*, 495 U.S. 103 (1990).

42. Monique M. Ferraro & Eoghan Casey (2005). *Investigating Child Exploitation and Pornography: The Internet, the Law and Forensic Science.* (Burlington, MA: Elsevier Academic Press).

43. Ibid.

44. *R.A.V. v. City of St. Paul*, 505 U.S. 377 (1992).

45. 18 U.S.C. §2251 et seq.

46. *Miller v. California*, 413 U.S. 15 (1973).

47. Citation in case: See "Predictable and Less So, the Academy Award Contenders," *The New York Times*, February 14, 2001, p. E11.

48. Citation in case: See "'American Beauty' Tops the Oscars," *The New York Times*, March 27, 2000, p. E1.

49. *United States v. Stephens*, 559 U.S. 460 (2010).

50. Pub. L. No. 108-21, 117 Stat. 650, S. 151, enacted April 30, 2003; other statutes enacted for child safety are Protection of Children from Sexual Predators Act of 1998, Pub. L. No. 105-314, §102(2) (1998); Adam Walsh Child Protection and Safety Act, Pub. L. No. 109-248 (2006).

51. *United States v. Handley*, 564 F.Supp.2d 996 (S.D. Iowa, 2008).

52. *West Virginia State Board of Education v. Barnette*, 319 U.S. 624 (1943).

53. *Tinker v. Des Moines Independent Community School District*, 393 U.S. 503 (1969).

54. *Bethel School District No. 403 v. Fraser*, 478 U.S. 675 (1986).

55. *Morse v. Frederick*, 127 S.Ct. 2618 (2007).

56. *Ponce v. Socorro Independent School District*, 508 F.3d 765 (5th Cir. 2007); see also *Wynar v. Douglas County School District*, 728 F.3d 1062 (9th Cir. 2013) (upholding student's suspension for sitting at home and transmitting via instant message threats to shoot fellow students).

57. In contrast, when students threaten violence to specific teachers or adults, such threats do not rise to the level of public threat safety and the *Tinker* substantial disruption test is not met. *Boim v. Fulton County School District*, 494 F.3d 978 (11th Cir. 2007); *Wisniewski v. Board of Education of the Weedsport Central School District*, 494 F.3d 34 (2d Cir. 2007). Student speech is also protected to parody school administrators, for example, using social media to create a fake profile of a principal, insufficient to establish a connection to a disruptive school environment. *Layshock v. Hermitage School District*, 650 F.3d 205 (3d Cir. 2011); *J. S. v. Blue Mountain School District*, 650 F.3d 915 (3d Cir. 2011) (off-school creation of fake MySpace account parodying principal did not justify 10-day suspension because the exception to *Tinker*-protected speech that allows suppression of vulgar and lewd speech under *Bethel* was not present).

58. *Bell v. Itawamba County School Board*, 799 F.3d 379 (5th Cir. 2015).

59. "Bob Jones University Drops Interracial Dating Ban" (2000, March 1). http://www.christianitytoday.com/ct/2000/marchweb-only/53.0.html

60. *McCauley v. University of the Virgin Islands*, 618 F.3d 232 (3d Cir. 2010).

61. *Bair v. Shippensburg University*, 280 F. Supp. 2d 357 (M.D. Pa. 2003).

62. *Corlett v. Oakland University Bd. of Trustees*, 958 F. Supp. 2d 795 (E.D. Mich. 2013).

63. *Beard v. Banks*, 542 U.S. 406 (2006).

64. *Holt v. Hobbs*, 135 S.Ct. 853 (2015).

65. *Johnson v. California*, 543 U.S. 499 (2005).

66. *Overton v. Bazzetta*, 539 U.S. 126 (2003).

67. *McAuliffe v. Mayor of New Bedford*, 29 N.E. 517 (1892).

68. *Garcetti v. Ceballos*, 547 U.S. 410 (2006).

69. *Pickering v. Board of Education*, 391 U.S. 563 (1968).

70. See Steve Miletich (2016, February 26). "Seattle Police Officer Suspended After Racial Slur Was Caught on Dash-Cam Video." *Seattle Times*. https://www.seattletimes.com/seattle-news/crime/spd-officer-suspended-over-description-of-black-suspect/

71. *City of Chicago v. Morales*, 527 U.S. 41 (1999).

72. *Lemon v. Kurtzman*, 403 U.S. 602 (1971).

73. *Van Orden v. Perry*, 125 S.Ct. 2854 (2005); *McCreary County v. ACLU of Kentucky*, 545 U.S. 844 (2005).

74. *Greece v. Galloway*, 134 S.Ct. 1811 (2014).

75. See *Reynolds v. United States*, 98 U.S. 145 (1878).

76. See *Dep't of Human Resources v. Smith*, 494 U.S. 872 (1990) (allowing the denial of worker's compensation benefits to Native Americans who were fired from a private drug rehabilitation center for ingesting peyote as part of a religious ritual); *Sherbert v. Verner*, 374 U.S. 398 (1963) (overturning dismissal of a Seventh-Day Adventist for refusing to work on Saturdays because law benefited Sunday Sabbath observers; outcome would have been different if the Saturday Sabbath observer refused to work at all).

77. *Employment Division, Dept. of Human Resources of Oregon v. Smith*, 494 U.S. 872 (1990).

78. Citation in case: See J. Story, *Commentaries on the Constitution of the United States* §§991–992 (abridged ed. 1833) (reprint 1987).

79. See *State v. Hodges*, 695 S.W.2d 171 (1985) (defendant dressed as chicken to attend court; judge was wrong to not investigate whether or not Hodges had a sincerely held belief legitimizing his religious practices).

CHAPTER 12

1. *Hall v. Florida*, 134 S.Ct. 1986 (2014).

2. George P. Fletcher (1978). *Rethinking Criminal Law* (Baltimore: Johns Hopkins University).

3. *Patterson v. New York*, 432 U.S. 197 (1977) (quoting W. Blackstone, Commentaries 201).

4. *Kansas v. Cheever*, 134 S.Ct. 596 (2013).

5. Lawrence K. Furbish (1999, October). Office of Legislative Research Report, Connecticut. https://www.cga.ct.gov/ps99/rpt/olr/htm/99-r-0984.htm

6. See *In re Winship*, 397 U.S. 358 (1970); *Mullaney v. Wilbur*, 421 U.S. 684 (1975). The discussion whether some defenses negate element offenses is beyond the scope of this text. See, generally, *Smith v. United States*, 133 S.Ct. 714 (2013) (a defendant bears the burden of proving the defense that he withdrew from a conspiracy before the criminal objective was met).

7. *Stogner v. California*, 539 U.S. 607 (2003).

8. 18 U.S.C. §4241.

9. *Drope v. Missouri*, 420 U.S. 162 (1975).

10. *Washington v. Harper*, 494 U.S. 210 (1990).

11. *Riggins v. Nevada*, 504 U.S. 127 (1992).

12. Ana Swanson (2015, April 30). "A Shocking Number of Mentally Ill Americans End Up in Prison Instead of Treatment." *Washington Post* (referencing a Treatment Advocacy Center Report [2014, April]. *The Treatment of Persons With Mental Illness in Prisons and Jails: A State Survey*).

13. Also remember Chapter 3's discussion on strict liability crimes, which do not require *mens rea* to be found guilty of the act (e.g., speeding) and for which no mistake will lie as a defense.

14. See George Fletcher, *Rethinking Criminal Law*, §9.3.4 (1978).

15. *People v. Snyder*, 32 Cal.3d 590 (1982).

16. *In re Gault*, 387 U.S. 1 (1967).

17. *Gammons v. Berlat*, 144 Ariz. 148 (1985).

18. Arkansas law has since changed and now allows juveniles to be tried as adults.

19. Meghan Keneally (2016, February 17). "The Only Two Living U.S. Mass School Shooters Who Are Not Incarcerated." http://abcnews.go.com/US/living-us-mass-school-shooters-incarcerated/story?id=36986507

20. *Roper v. Simmons*, 543 U.S. 551 (2005).

21. *United States v. Solano*, 10 F.3d 682 (9th Cir. 1993).

22. In *Dixon v. United States*, 126 S.Ct. 2437 (2006).

23. Further investigation revealed a conspiracy between Wells and two other friends to rob the bank, but Wells believed the bomb would not be armed. When Wells discovered the bomb would be live, he tried to withdraw from the conspiracy but was forced into the bomb collar and forced to rob the bank. John Canglia (2007, July 11). "Erie Bombing 'Victim' Was in on Bank Robbery." www.cleveland.com

24. Nina Bernstein (2016, May 16). "Unearthing the Secrets of New York's Mass Graves." *New York Times*, p. A16.

25. For example, see Missouri jury instructions MAI-CR3d 306.02, 306.03, and Missouri Revised Statutes §552.010.

26. See Edith Greene, Kirk Heilbrun, William H. Fortune, & Michael T. Nietzel (2007). *Wrightsman's Psychology and the Legal System*, 6th ed. (Belmont, CA: Thomson Wadsworth).

27. *Durham v. United States*, 214 F.2d 862 (D.C. Cir. 1954).

28. *United States v. Brawner*, 471 F.2d 969 (1972).

29. *State v. Thompson*, 28 Ohio Rep. 617 (1854).

30. *United States v. Kunak*, 5 U.S.C.M.A. 346 (1954).

31. *Hall v. Florida*, 134 S.Ct. 1986 (2014).

32. *Ex parte Briseno*, 135 S.W.3d 1 (2004).

33. *E.g.*, American Association on Intellectual and Developmental Disabilities clinical manual (11th ed.).

34. American Psychiatric Association (2013). *Diagnostic and Statistical Manual of Mental Disorders*, 5th ed. (Washington, DC: Author).

35. See 19 Texas Administrative Code §89.1040(c)(5) (2015).

36. 37 Texas Administrative Code §380.8751(e)(3) (2016).

37. Margaret E. Noonan (2012, December). "Mortality in Local Jails and State Prisons, 2000-2010—Statistical Tables" (NCJ 239911). (Washington, DC: Bureau of Justice Statistics).

38. Anna Guv (2016, September 8). "Locked Up and Locked Down: Segregation of Inmates With Mental Illness." http://avidprisonproject.org/

39. *Jones v. United States*, 463 U.S. 354 (1983).

40. Spencer S. Hsu & Ann E. Marimow (2016, July 27). "Would-Be Reagan Assassin John Hinckley Jr. to Be Freed After 35 Years." *Washington Post*. https://www.washingtonpost.com/local/public-safety/

41. *Regina v. Dudley and Stephens*, 14 Q.B.D. 273 (1884).

42. (a) *United States v. Newcomb*, 6 F.3d 1129 (6th Cir. 1993); (b) *United States v. Burton*, 894 F.2d 188 (6th Cir. 1990); (c) *United States v. Aguilar*, 883 F.2d 693 (9th Cir. 1989); (d) *United States v. Montgomery*, 772 F.2d 733 (11th Cir. 1985); (e) *United States v. Richardson*, 588 F.2d 1235 (9th Cir. 1978).

43. Sir Edward Coke, Third Institute.

44. *People v. Tomlins*, 107 N.E. 496 (N.Y. 1914) ("It is not now and never has been the law that a man assailed in his own dwelling is bound to retreat").

45. *People v. Ceballos*, 526 P.2d 241 (1974).

46. See Cynthia V. Ward (2015, Spring). "Stand Your Ground and Self Defense." *American Journal of Criminal Law*, Vol. 42, pp. 89–138.

47. Chandler B. McClelland & Erdal Tekin (2012). *Stand Your Ground Laws, Homicides, and Injuries* (Working Paper No. 18187). Cambridge, MA: National Bureau of Economic Research.

48. *People v. Young*, 12 A.D.2d 262 (1st Dept. 1961), rev'd 11 N.Y.2d 274 (1962).

49. *United States v. Peterson*, 483 F.2d 1222 (1973).

50. See, generally, *State v. Borrelli*, 629 A.2d 1105 (1993).

51. For clarity, the word "Appellant" in the opinion has been replaced by "Stonehouse."

52. *Commonwealth v. Watson*, 431 A.2d 949 (1981).

53. The court's footnote reads: See *State v. Hundley*, 236 Kan. 461 (1985), where the court stated: The abuse is so severe, for so long a time, and the threat of great bodily harm so constant, it creates a standard mental attitude in its victims. Battered women are terror-stricken people whose mental state is distorted and bears a marked resemblance to that of a hostage or a prisoner of war. The horrible beatings they are subjected to brainwash them into believing there is nothing they can do. They live in constant fear of another eruption of violence. They become disturbed persons from the torture. See also Crocker, "The Meaning of Equality for Battered Women Who Kill Men in Self-Defense," *Harvard Women's Law Journal*, Vol. 8, No. 30 (1985), pp. 121–128. Researchers have suggested that the psychological effects of the battered woman syndrome can be compared to classic brainwashing. Comment, "The Battered Spouse Syndrome as a Defense to a Homicide Charge Under the Pennsylvania Crimes Code," *Villanova Law Review*, Vol. 26 (1981), pp. 105–112. These effects include fear, hyper-suggestibility, isolation, guilt, and emotional dependency, which culminate in a woman's belief that "she should not and cannot escape."

54. National Registry of Exonerations run by University of California, Irvine, University of Michigan Law School, and Michigan State University College of Law, http://www.law.umich.edu/special/exoneration/Pages/about.aspx

55. David B. Wexler (1999). "The Broken Mirror: A Self-Psychological Treatment Perspective for Relationship Violence." *Journal of Psychotherapy Practice and Research*, Vol. 8, No. 2, pp. 129–141.

56. *Sorrells v. United States*, 287 U.S. 435 (1932).

CHAPTER 13

1. Kent Greenawalt (1983). "Moral Justifications and Legal Punishment," in *Encyclopedia of Crime and Justice*, ed. Stanford H. Kadish (Upper Saddle River, NJ: Prentice Hall).

2. 18 U.S.C. §3577.

3. U.S. Sentencing Guidelines, §1B1.3.

4. *United States v. Figueroa-Labrada*, 720 F.3d 1258 (2013).

5. *United States v. Tucker*, 404 U.S. 443 (1972).

6. *Payne v. Tennessee*, 501 U.S. 808 (1991).

7. See *Setser v. United States*, 132 S.Ct. 1463 (2012).

8. *Mistretta v. United States*, 488 U.S. 361 (1989).

9. The Comprehensive Crime Control Act of 1984, Pub. L. No. 98-473; The Sentencing Reform Act of 1984, 18 U.S.C. §§3551-3626.

10. *Apprendi v. New Jersey*, 530 U.S. 466 (2000).

11. *Blakely v. Washington*, 542 U.S. 296 (2004).

12. *United States v. Booker*, 543 U.S. 220 (2005) (and a companion case, *United States v. Fanfan*).

13. *Ring v. Arizona*, 536 U.S. 584 (2002).

14. Judges, not juries, sentenced defendants to death in Nebraska, Montana, Arizona, and Idaho.

15. *Schriro v. Summerlin*, 542 U.S. 348 (2004).

16. For further examination about watershed rules, see *Teague v. Lane*, 489 U.S. 288 (1989).

17. Robert Barnes (2012, April 17). "Supreme Court Weighs Whether Law Reducing Crack Cocaine Sentences Is Retroactive." *Washington Post*. https://www.washingtonpost.com/politics/supreme-court-weighs-whether-law-reducing-crack-cocaine-sentences-is-retroactive/2012/04/17/gIQAjRf2OT_story.html?utm_term=.4862a442524e

18. *Dorsey v. United States*, 132 S.Ct. 2321 (2012).

19. *People v. Broadie*, 371 N.Y.S.2d 471 (1975).

20. See Chapter 2 discussion about plea bargains.

21. United States Sentencing Commission. 2011 Report to the Congress: Mandatory Minimum Penalties in the Federal Criminal Justice System.

22. See Jon Schuppe (2017, November 25). "Louisiana Is Shedding Its Reputation as U.S. Biggest Jailer." *NBCNews.com*. https://www.nbcnews.com/news/us-news/louisiana-shedding-its-reputation-u-s-s-biggest-jailer-n822981

23. Department of Justice, Bureau of Justice Statistics (2016, December, Summary). National Criminal Justice Reference Service #250230.

24. States that have abolished parole are Arizona, Delaware, Illinois, Indiana, Kansas, Maine, Minnesota, Mississippi, New Mexico, North Carolina, Ohio, Oregon, Virginia, and Washington.

25. Facts taken from the case of entertainer "Foxy Brown," whose real name is Inga Marchand, who was sentenced to jail on September 7, 2007, for violating conditions of probation. Retrieved from http://www.muchmusic.com

26. *Lockyer v. Andrade*, 123 S.Ct. 1166 (2003).

27. Michael Tonry (1996). *Sentencing Matters* (New York: Oxford University Press).

28. Specifics of Megan's Law derived from R. Corrigan (2006). "Making Meaning of Megan's Law." *Law & Social Inquiry*, Vol. 31, pp. 267–308.

29. In the Matter of Registrant R.F., 317 N.J. Super. 379 (1998).

30. See *Connecticut Department of Public Safety v. Doe* (2003); *Smith v. Doe* (2003).

31. *Kansas v. Hendricks*, 521 U.S. 346 (1997).

32. 42 U.S.C. §§16901-16991 (2006).

33. According to the U.S. Department of Justice, "Section 111 of the Adam Walsh Act, codified at 34 U.S.C. §20911, governs the applicability of SORNA's sex offender registration requirements to juvenile offenders who are adjudicated delinquent of a sex offense. 34 U.S.C. §20911(8) provides that:

    The term 'convicted' or a variant thereof, used with respect to a sex offense, includes adjudicated delinquent as a juvenile for that offense, but only if the offender is 14 years of age or older at the time of the offense and the offense adjudicated was comparable to or more severe than aggravated sexual abuse . . . or was an attempt or conspiracy to commit such an offense."

34. Rodney K. Hopson and Jennifer E. Obidah (2002). "When Getting Tough Means Getting Tougher: Historical and Conceptual Understandings of Juveniles of Color Sentenced as Adults in the United States." *Journal of Negro Education*, Vol. 71, No. 3, pp. 158–174.

35. Pricilla F. Clement and Albert G. Hess, eds. (1990). *History of Juvenile Delinquency: A Collection of Essays on Crime Committed by Young Offenders*, Vol. 1 (Germany: Scientia Verlag, 1990).

36. David S. Tanenhaus (2004). *Juvenile Justice in the Making* (New York: Oxford University Press).

37. George Lipsitz (1982). *Class and Culture in Cold War America: A Rainbow at Midnight* (South Hadley, MA: Bergin & Garvey).

38. Jason Barnosky (2006). "The Violent Years: Responses to Juvenile Crime in the 1950s." *Polity*, Vol. 38, No. 3, pp. 314–344.

39. James Gilbert (1988). *A Cycle of Outrage: America's Reaction to the juvenile Delinquent in the 1950s* (New York: Oxford University Press).

40. Edmund F. McGarrell (1988). *Juvenile Correctional Reform: Two Decades of Policy and Procedural Change* (Albany: State University of New York Press).

41. *Graham v. Florida*, 560 U.S. 48 (2010).

42. *Kennedy v. Louisiana*, 544 U.S. 407 (2008); *Atkins v. Virginia*, 536 U.S. 304 (2002).

43. *Montgomery v. Louisiana*, 136 S.Ct. 718 (2016).

44. Pub. L. No. 108-79; 117 Stat. 972.

45. Bryan Denson (2014, June 23). "Oregon's Corrections Officers: Study Finds They're Stalked by Fear, Stress, and Exhaustion." *The Oregonian*. http://www.oregonlive.com/politics/

46. *Dickerson v. New Banner Institute, Inc.*, 103 S.Ct. 986 (1983).

47. Samuel T. Morison (2005). "The Politics of Grace: On the Moral Justification of Executive Clemency." *Buffalo Criminal Law Review*, Vol. 9, pp. 1–37.

48. *Furman v. Georgia*, 408 U.S. 238 (1972).

49. *Gregg v. Georgia*, 428 U.S. 153 (1976).

50. Dan Elliott (2015). "Colorado Theater Shooting Case Costs $2.2 Million Before Trial." CBS Denver. http://denver.cbslocal.com/2015/04/01/colorado-theater-shooting-case-costs-2-2-million-before-trial/

51. *Witherspoon v. Illinois*, 391 U.S. 510 (1968); *Wainwright v. Witt*, 469 U.S. 412 (1985).

52. *See* Claudia L. Cowan, William C. Thompson, and Phoebe C. Ellsworth (1984). "The Effects of Death Qualification on Jurors' Predisposition to Convict and on the Quality of Deliberation." *Law and Human Behavior*, Vol. 8, pp. 53–80. (Study results provide strong support for the hypothesis that death-qualified jurors are more likely to convict than are jurors excludable under the *Witherspoon* criteria.)

53. *Uttecht v. Brown*, 127 S.Ct. 2218 (2007).

54. Theodore Eisenberg, Stephen P. Garvey, and Martin T. Wells (2001). "The Deadly Paradox of Capital Jurors." *Cornell Law Faculty Publications*, Paper No. 284, pp. 371–397.

55. *Kansas v. Marsh*, 126 S.Ct. 2516 (2006).

56. *House v. Bell*, 126 S.Ct. 2064 (2006).

57. Richard C. Dieter (2005, October). *Blind Justice: Juries Deciding Life and Death With Only Half the Truth* (Washington, DC: Death Penalty Information Center). http://www.deathpenaltyinfo.org/BlindJusticeReport.pdf

58. *Oregon v. Guzek*, 126 S.Ct. 1226 (2006).

59. *Coker v. Georgia*, 433 U.S. 584 (1977).

60. As discussed in Chapter 12, the American Association of Intellectual Disability (formerly Mental Retardation) defines the condition as suffering from "substantial limitations in present functioning, existing concurrently with related limitations in two or more of the following applicable adaptive skill areas: communication, self-care, home living, social skills, community use, self-direction, health and safety, functional academics, leisure, and work. Mental retardation manifests before age 18."

61. *Penry v. Lynaugh*, 492 U.S. 302 (1989).

62. *Roper v. Simmons*, 543 U.S. 551 (2005).

63. *Ford v. Wainwright*, 477 U.S. 399 (1986).

64. Emily Bazelon (2012, May 11). "Texas Wants to Drug a Prisoner So That They Can Kill Him." *Slate Magazine*. http://www.slate.com/articles/news_and_politics/crime/2012/05/the_execution_of_steven_staley_forcible_medication_on_death_row_in_texas_.html

65. *Panetti v. Quarterman*, 127 S.Ct. 2842 (2007).

66. Ralph Blumenthal (2007, June 29). "Justices Block Execution of Delusional Texas Killer." *New York Times*, p. A21.

67. *Panetti v. Davis*, 863 F.3d 366 (2017).

68. These facts are adapted from *Singleton v. Norris*, 319 F.3d 1018 (8th Cir. 2003). In 2003, the federal court of appeals held that forcing Singleton to take medication to treat his schizophrenia to make him "sane" enough to be executed was legal. The U.S. Supreme Court refused to hear his case. Toward the end of the legal battle, Singleton abandoned his appeals, willingly took his medication, was restored to competency, and was executed by the state of Arkansas on January 6, 2004.

69. *Baze v. Rees*, 553 U.S. 35 (2008).

70. *Glossip v. Gross*, 135 S.Ct. 2726 (2015).

71. Paulina Deda (2018, August 19). "Nebraska Uses Fentanyl for First Time in Execution." www.foxnews.com

72. See Georgia Code §42-4-36 (2013) classifies as state secrets the identities of those who participate in executions and suppliers of the drugs.

73. Federal Rule of Criminal Procedure 33.

74. *Douglas v. California*, 372 U.S. 353 (1963).

75. *Cohen v. Beneficial Industrial Loan Corp.*, 337 U.S. 541 (1949).

76. See, generally, *United States v. Filippi*, 211 F.3d 649 (2000); *United States v. Gomes*, 289 F.3d 71 (2002).

77. "Annual Review of Criminal Procedure (Federal)." *Georgetown Law Journal* (2003).

78. *Carroll v. United States*, 354 U.S. 394 (1957).

79. *Anderson v. Harless*, 459 U.S. 4 (1982).

80. *Picard v. Connor*, 404 U.S. 270 (1971).

81. "Annual Review of Criminal Procedure (Federal)." *Georgetown Law Journal* (2003).

82. *Brown v. Allen*, 344 U.S. 443 (1953).

83. Title 28 U.S.C §2244(d)(1)

84. *Cullen v. Pinholster*, 131 S.Ct. 1388 (2011).

85. *Herrera v. Collins*, 506 U.S. 390 (1993).

86. *McQuiggen v. Perkins*, 133 S.Ct. 1924 (2013).

87. Hurst wins. The Sixth Amendment requires a jury, not the judge, to weigh the mitigating and aggravating circumstances and impose the death sentence. *Hurst v. Florida*, 136 S.Ct. 616 (2016).

CASE INDEX

SUBJECT INDEX

Common enterprise, 226
Common law, 7
Community caretaking function of police officers, 224
COMPAS (Correctional Offender Management Profiling for
    Alternative Sanctions) report, 361
Compelling state interest (CSI), 307
Competency, 334–335, 417–418
    to be executed, 379–380
    forcible medication to restore, 334–335, 380
Comprehensive Crime Control Act and the Sentencing Reform
    Act of 1984, 364
Comprehensive Drug Abuse and Controlled Substances Act,
    157–158
Computer crimes, 154, 167–172
    computer fraud crimes, 167–169
    malware and disruption of public services, 172
    nonfinancial cybercrime, 170–171
    social media and personal victimization, 171
Computer databases, mistakes in leading to arrest, 242–243
Concurrence, 11, 79
Concurrent sentences, 364
Conditional plea, 50
Confessions and admissions, 58, 247
    exclusionary rule and, 248
    false confessions, 250, 259
    Miranda warnings required, 247
    physical fruits of, 269
    right to counsel and, 271
    voluntariness of, 249
Conflict theory, 18
Confrontation Clause, 41, 275, 298–300. *See also*
    Sixth Amendment
    child sex abuse victims, 298–300
    testimonial evidence, 298
Consecutive sentences, 364
Consent, 219–221, 409. *See also* Warrantless searches
    and seizures
    as a defense, 335
    lying to obtain, 220
    no consent required to search those on probation or
        parole, 221
    to search given by co-occupant, 220–221
    submission to authority is not, 220
    vehicles and, 225
    voluntariness requirement, 219
Consolidated theft statutes, 139–140
Conspiracy, 87–88, 421–422
    defined, 87
    limitations to parties to, 88
    Wharton rule and, 88
Constitution. *See* U.S. Constitution
Constructive possession, 81
Containers, search of, 224–225
Content-based regulation of speech, 307
Conversion (theft), 126
Co-occupants, consent to search given by, 220–221
Copyright, 133
Corpus delicti, 247
Correctional officers
    mentally ill inmates and, 345
    warrantless searches in jail or prison, 233

Counsel. *See also* Right to counsel
    constitutional requirements to assistance of, at trial, 276–281
    government appointment of, 279–281
    ineffective assistance of, 275, 297–298
Counterfeiting, 133
Courts
    jurisdiction, 7
    specialty, 20–21
    structure of, 8
Crime. *See also* Theft crimes; White-collar crime
    classes of, 401
    computer, 167–172
    environmental, 167
    hate, 97, 107–108, 305, 316
    inchoate, 86–92, 419–423
    parties to, 85–86
    that interfere with government services, 165–167
Crimes against morality, 180
Crimes against the person, 98–108
    assault and battery, 98–99
    cyberstalking and cyberbullying, 105–107
    felony murder, 119–120
    first- and second-degree murder, 115–116
    hate crimes, 107–108
    homicide, 114–120
    kidnapping and false imprisonment, 100–103
    manslaughter, 116–119
    rape, 108–114
    robbery, 120–121
    sex offenses, 108–114
    stalking, 103–105
    terroristic threats, 99–100
Crimes against the public, 155–165
    breach of the peace, 163–165
    computer fraud, 167–169
    drug and alcohol offenses, 157–161
    environmental crimes, 167
    firearm offenses, 161–162
    gambling, 155–156
    human trafficking, 157
    panhandling, 163
    prostitution, 156–157
    social media, 171
    terrorism, 172–179
    treason, 179
    vagrancy, 163
Crime scene investigation questions, 268
Criminal case, 286–300
    ineffective assistance of counsel, 297–298
    right to appointed counsel on appeal, 300
    right to assert innocence at trial, 295
    right to control the, 288–298
    right to self-represent at trial, 288–295
    Sixth Amendment's Confrontation Clause and, 298–300
    venue, 286
Criminal justice system
    actors in, 16–25
    specialty courts, 20–21
Criminal law
    American legal history and, 4–5
    Bill of Rights and, 6

Double interviewing, prohibition against, 266
Double jeopardy, 52, 382
Doubt. *See* Beyond a reasonable doubt
Driving checkpoints, 226
Driving under the influence (DUI), 161
    roadblocks and, 226
Drug courts, 20–21
Drug Enforcement Administration (DEA), 158
Drugs
    dog sniffs, 225–226
    drug courier profile, 205
    offenses, 157–160
    warrantless searches for, in schools, 235–236
Drug testing
    of government employees, 236–237
    in schools, 235–236
Dual court system, 60
Due process, 6, 12–13
    Sixth Amendment and, 275–281
Due Process Clause, Fourteenth Amendment, 248, 276
Duress, 338, 409
Durham rule, 340
Duty by contract, 80
Duty by relationship, 80
Duty by statute, 80
Duty to act, 80–81
Duty to retreat and defense of property, 346–347

Eighth Amendment, 6, 395
    on bail, 43
    ban on cruel and unusual punishment, 361, 362
    death penalty and, 376, 379
    individualized sentencing and, 362
    judicial review of death-penalty cases and, 60
Electronic devices
    search and seizing output of, 190–191
    searching and seizing, 190–191
    searching and seizing output of to pinpoint location, 192–193
    warrantless searches and, 224–225
Electronic surveillance, 192–193
Element analysis, 77–79
Embezzlement, 125, 130–131
Entrapment, 330, 354, 410
Environmental crimes, 167
Environmental Protection Agency (EPA), 167
Equal Protection Clause, 7, 276
Error
    harmless, 13, 15
    reversible, 13, 15
Espionage, 180
Espionage Act of 1917, 174
Establishment Clause. *See* First Amendment
Ethics
    of defense counsel, 21–22
    of law enforcement, 24
    of prosecutor, 23
Evidence
    circumstantial, 56
    collection of, 56
    demonstrative, 58
    direct, 56

excluded, 271
exclusion or admission of, 188
exculpatory, 41
physical, 56, 268–269
presentation of, 55–56
quantum of, 15–16
scientific, 56–58
testimonial, 56–58
Evidentiary hearings, 286
Evolving standards of decency, 379
Excessive force, 200
Excluded evidence, collateral uses of, 271
Exclusionary rule
    defined, 188
    fruit of the poisonous tree and, 188, 270
    good faith exception, 188, 240–243
    under *Massiah*, 282
    under *Miranda*, 282
Exculpatory evidence, 41
Excuse, defenses based on, 332, 335–345
Execution, 361. *See also* Death penalty
Execution process, 380
Executive branch of government, 4
Executive clemency, 376
Exercise Clause. *See* First Amendment
Exhaustion of remedies, 381
Exigent circumstances, 218, 232–235. *See also* Warrantless searches and seizures
Exonerations, 378–379
Expert witnesses, 56–58
    on intimate partner violence, 353
Ex post facto, 334
Expressive conduct, 306–307, 310–311
Expungement of sentences, 376
Extortion, 126, 134
    theft by, 437
Eyewitness identification, 37–38
    absolute decision, 39
    guidelines for, 39
    line-up, 39–40
    photograph array, 39
    problems with, 39
    relative decision, 39
    show-up, 39
    suggestive, 38

Facially deficient warrant, 207
Facially valid warrant, 324
Facial recognition technology, 39
Facts, of case, 9
Factual cause, 82, 84, 120
Factual impossibility, 87, 92
Failure to disperse, 443
Fair and impartial trial, 287, 288
Fair Sentencing Act of 2010, 158, 368
False imprisonment, 97, 100–102, 428
False pretenses, 129–130
False statements, 167
False swearing, 443
Family, offenses against the, 440
Federal constitutional issues, Supreme Court cases and, 60–61

Government services, crimes that interfere with, 165–167
Government surveillance, 192–193
Gramm–Leach–Bliley Act of 1999, 137
Grand (felony) larceny, 127
Grand jury
    secrecy to, 43
    selection of, 42–43
Guantánamo Bay, detention of terror suspects at, 178
Guests, expectation of privacy and, 189
Guidelines, sentencing. *See* Federal Sentencing Guidelines
Guilt, silence as admission of, 265
Guilty but mentally ill (GBMI), 341
Guilty plea, 50. *See also* Pleas
Gun Control Act of 1968, 161
Gun Free School Zones Act of 1990, 30
Guns. *See* Firearms

Habeas corpus, 178
    actual innocence and, 383
    writ of, 382–384
Hackers, 168, 170
    motivations for, 170
Harassment, 444
Harmless error, 13, 15
Harrison Act of 1914, 157
Hate crime, 97, 107–108, 305, 316
Hate crime enhancement, 366
Hate speech, 305, 316
Hearsay, 58
Heat of passion, 117
Holding, 9
Homicide, 114–120, 423–426
    felony murder, 119–120, 424
    first- and second-degree murder, 115–116
    manslaughter, 116–119, 424
    negligent, 424
Honest services fraud, 144
Hot pursuit, 219, 231–232. *See also* Warrantless searches
        and seizures
Houses
    searches in, 189
    warrants to arrest third parties in, 201
Human trafficking, 157
Hunch, 188
Hung jury, 54

Identification
    pretrial, 37–40
    requests for, 196–197
Identity theft, 126, 136–138
Illegal aliens
    boarding buses to find, 217
    roadblocks to check for, 226
Immigration, 28
Immigration and Customs Enforcement (ICE), 28
Immunity
    absolute, 25
    for criminal justice professionals in section 1983
        claims, 25–27
    qualified, 25
Imperfect self-defense, 348

Impossibility defense, 66, 92
    factual, 87, 92
    legal, 92
Inbau and Reid nine steps of interrogation, 246, 249–252
Incarceration, 17
Incest, 113, 440
Inchoate crimes, 86–92, 419–423
    attempt, 88–92
    conspiracy, 87–88
    defense of impossibility, 92
    solicitation, 86–87
Incorporated by reference on the face of the warrant, 205
Incorporation doctrine, 6
Indecent exposure, 431
Independent source exception, 270–271
Indeterminate sentence, 364
Indictment, 42, 43
Ineffective assistance of counsel, 275, 297–298
Inevitable discovery exception, 270
Infancy defense, 336–337
Informants, 185, 204
    anonymous tips *vs.*, 204
    Miranda warnings and, 268
    probable cause and, 204
    test for reliability of, 204
Information, 42
Initial appearance, 43
Innocence
    habeas corpus and actual, 383
    new evidence of, 378–379
    presumption of, 52–53
    right to assert at trial, 295
Insanity. *See also* Diminished capacity
    death penalty and, 379
Insanity Defense Reform Act of 1984, 341
Instructions, to jury, 54, 60
Intellectual disability
    definitions of, 342
    exemption from death penalty and, 342–345
    graph of intellectual functioning skills, 343
Intelligent, waiver of *Miranda* rights, 262
Intelligible principle, 5
Intent, 70–77. *See also* Mens rea
    to defraud, 141–142
    to inflict serious bodily injury, 77, 99
    scienter requirement, 76
    specific and general, 70–76
    strict liability, 76
    transferred, 77
Interlocutory appeal, 382
International mobile subscriber identity (IMSI) catcher, 193
Internet
    gambling on, 155
    as public forum, 310 (*See also* First Amendment)
Internet threats, specific intent required for criminal responsibility
        for, 72, 74–75
Interrogation, 259. *See also* Questioning; Reinterrogation
    custodial, 255–258
    Inbau and Reid technique, 246, 248–252
    prohibition against double interviewing, 266
    trickery and deceit, 260–261

Sexual offenses, 429–432
  deviate sexual conduct, 113
  incest, 113
  juveniles and sexting offenses, 113–114
Show-ups
  defined, 39
  due process rights and, 39
Silence
  as admission of guilt, 265
  Miranda rights and *Miranda* warning and, 247, 263, 265
Sixth Amendment, 6, 275, 395
  Confrontation Clause, 41, 298–300
  as due process protection, 275–281
  fair and impartial jury, 54
  jury selection and, 54
  right to counsel under, 262, 271, 275, 284–286
  speedy trial and, 45
  venue and, 49
Social control theory, 18
Social learning theory, 18
Social media
  free speech rights and, 321
  personal victimization and, 171
Sodomy, 113
Solicitation, 86–87
Spamming, 139
Special needs searches, 235–237. *See also* Warrantless searches
  and seizures
Specialty courts, 20–21
Specific and articulable facts, 195, 218
Specific intent, 70–76
  illustrated in *Linehan* case, 71–72, 73
  required for criminal responsibility for Internet threats, 72, 74–75
Speech, 306. *See also* First Amendment
  content-based regulation of, 306–309
  protected, 306–313
  unprotected, 313–320
Speedy Trial Act of 1974, 45
Spoofing, 139
Sports gambling, 155–156
Stalking, 103–105
Standard of care, negligence and deviation from, 69
Standing, 9
Stand your ground laws, 347
Stare decisis, 10
State courts, 61
States. *See also* Tenth Amendment
  constitutions, 4
  federal deference to, 4
  requirement to pay for indigent defense, 280–281
States' rights, 27–32
  federal jurisdiction and Commerce Clause, 30–32
  federal preemption of state law, 27–28
  Tenth Amendment and, 28–29
State trial judges, 22
Status as an act, 81–82
Statute of limitations, 334
Statutes, how to read, 9–12
Statutory law, 8
Statutory rape, 111, 430–431
StingRay, 193

Stolen property, receiving, 133, 437–438
Stolen Valor Act, 308
Stored Communications Act, 194
Strain theory, 18
Strict liability crimes, 66, 76
  no *mens rea* and, 76
Strict scrutiny, 307
Students. *See also* Schools
  codes of conduct and free speech, 321
  free speech rights, 305, 321
  school lockers and right of privacy, 190
Subjective test
  entrapment and, 354
  reasonable expectation of privacy and, 187, 188
  specific and general intent, 72
Submission to authority, 220
Subornation of perjury, 167
Subways, warrantless searches and, 237–238
Suicide, causing or aiding, 424
Supremacy Clause, 6, 27, 61
Supreme Court. *See* U.S. Supreme Court
Suspended sentences, 370
Swatting, 171
"Sword of Damocles," 52

Tenth Amendment, 6, 395
  states' rights and, 28–29
Terrorism, 155, 172–179
  aiding and abetting ISIL, 174–178
  detention of terror suspects, 178–179
  providing material support for, 174
  USA Patriot Act, 172–173
Terroristic threats, 99–100, 427
Terry patdown, 195
Terry stop, 16, 185, 195–199
  of automobiles, 197
  duration of, 196
  intersection of suspect's race and, 197–199
  questioning during, 268
  requests for identification, 196–197
Testimonial evidence, 56–58
Theft crimes, 126–140, 435–438
  consolidated theft statutes, 139–140
  embezzlement, 130–131
  extortion, 134
  false pretenses, 129–130
  financial cybercrime, 135–139
  forgery and passing bad checks, 132–133
  of honest services, 144, 165
  larceny, 126–128
  receiving stolen property, 133
Third-party doctrine, 191, 194
  precedent hierarchy from, 194
  right to search and, 191
Threats
  Internet, 72, 74–75
  terroristic, 99–100, 427
  true, 314
Three-strikes laws, 361, 371
Time, manner, and place (TMP) restrictions, 309–310. *See also*
  First Amendment